LEARNING TEXT

TAX LAW

John Snape MA (Oxon)
Solicitor and Senior Lecturer, Nottingham Law School

BLACKSTONE PRESS LIMITED

First published in Great Britain 1999 by Blackstone Press Limited,
Aldine Place, London W12 8AA.   Telephone 0181–740 2277

© Nottingham Law School, Nottingham Trent University, 1999

ISBN: 1 85431 739 3

British Library Cataloguing in Publication Data
A CIP catalogue record for this book is available from the British Library.

Typeset by Style Photosetting Limited, Mayfield, East Sussex
Printed by Livesey Limited, Shrewsbury, Shropshire

LEARNING TEXT

TAX LAW

FOREWORD

The books in the LLB series have been written for students studying law at undergraduate level. There are two books for each subject. The first is the *Learning Text* which is designed to teach you about the particular subject in question. However, it does much more than that. By means of Activities, Self Assessment, and End of Chapter Questions, the *Learning Text* allows you to test your knowledge and understanding as you work. Each chapter starts with 'Objectives' which indicate what you should be able to do by the end of it. You should use these Objectives in your learning — check them frequently and ask yourself whether you have attained them.

The second book is a volume of *Cases and Materials*. This is cross-referenced from the *Learning Text*. It contains the primary sources of law such as statutes and cases plus subsidiary sources such as extracts from journals, law reform papers and textbooks. This is your portable library. Although each volume can stand alone, they are designed to be complementary.

The two-volume combination aims to support your learning by challenging you to demonstrate your mastery of the principles and application of the law. They are appropriate whatever your mode of study — full-time or part-time.

CONTENTS

PREFACE

The aim of this book is understanding. It attempts to give you a clear and full explanation of tax law. The text was designed for the tax law elective of the LLB (Distance Learning) degree at Nottingham Law School, The Nottingham Trent University. As such, it had to be a user-friendly book for students working largely on their own, sometimes in circumstances which might not traditionally be regarded as conducive to study. The general format of the series of books as a whole was well-established. In the context of tax law, a number of specific criteria had to be adopted also.

First of all, the text had to be as concise as possible. On picking up the text for the first time, the student had to be convinced of being able to get to the end of it! Secondly, it had to explain law which is unfamiliar and arcane, by reference to everyday matters. It was therefore important for a basic outline of value added tax and national insurance contributions, both of which are a reality of everyday life, to be fully integrated into a text which also explored some of the more recondite areas of tax law. Thirdly, it had to present the student with an in-depth analysis of the subject matter. This is crucial to encouraging the student to develop the ability to solve tax law problems. In the light of the second criterion, this encouragement involved placing a constant emphasis on the way in which the various taxes interact with each other. With other areas of law, such as contract or tort, students approach the law in terms of phenomena encountered every day, negligence in relation to a car accident, for instance. In an attempt to complement this approach in tax law, the text relates the detail of the law to everyday transactions, such as receiving wages from a job, selling investments, or giving property away. The text is therefore divided into three parts: income taxation (Chapters 1 to 19), investment taxation (Chapters 20 to 25), and the taxation of gratuitous transfers (Chapters 26 to 33). This transactional approach enables the interaction of the taxes to be fully explained. It also promotes a greater level of understanding in areas which, as experience shows, students find difficult, e.g. the interaction of capital gains tax and inheritance tax in the taxation of gratuitous transfers. Equally, it is not an approach so different that it cannot usefully be related to the one you are yourself adopting. You should be able to use it, however your course is structured.

The fourth criterion was that the traditional areas of difficulty should be uncompromisingly confronted from the outset. Companies, partnerships, trustees and personal representatives of deceased individuals were thus made part of the discussion, right from the beginning of the book. These persons, or bodies of persons, are just as likely to be encountered in practice as is the individual, and a text which did not recognise this likelihood would surely be incomplete. Fifthly, prudent use had to be made of calculations. Prudent because the subject ought not to be naively presented as just another use for arithmetical exercises. It has been well said that the ability to carry out tax calculations is not a prerequisite for a tax lawyer. Even so, it can be convincingly argued that the prudent inclusion of calculation exercises is, at the very least, a convenient way of illustrating the practical application of tax law rules. In this respect, the format chosen for this series of books as a whole, with its use of Self-Assessment Questions ('SAQs'), Activities and End of Chapter Assessment Questions proved to be virtually ideal. It enabled many examples to be given, together with their answers. Finally, the text had to be up-to-date. These are changing times for tax law, but the attempt has been made to state the law at 1 July 1998, incorporating the data relevant to the 1998/99 tax year. Where changes of the law have been announced, or enacted, to take effect in 1999, these changes have been discussed in as much detail as possible.

It was Lord Reid who once attempted to excuse the drafter of a particularly intractable piece of legislation with the words 'Draftsmen as well as Homer can nod. . .'. As draftsmen, so also textbook writers. Enormous care has been taken to ensure the accuracy of the text. That said, this is not a reference work, and should not be used as such. It is not intended to contain legal advice on any particular matter and you must not therefore regard it as providing legal advice on which you may place reliance. You must always obtain professional advice before any action is taken as discussed. Certain conventions have been adopted: the All England Reports reference of cases has been given, wherever possible; the pronoun 'it' is sometimes used in reference to persons.

J.S.,
Nottingham
A.M.D.G.

ACKNOWLEDGEMENTS

I would like to thank Patrick Leahy, who read an early draft of the book, and made a number of useful suggestions, and also Jeremy de Souza, consultant to Farrer & Co., who read the final version, and who also provided me with useful suggestions. Also to Sheila Parrington who read the proofs. Any errors and omissions are, of course, the responsibility of the author. I would also like to thank Roger Summerton, who kindly invited me to KPMG's Budget seminars in Nottingham; Terry Hanstock, of the Library and Information Services, The Nottingham Trent University; Chris Garratt, formerly of the Library and Information Services, The Nottingham Trent University, and now of Hammond Suddards in Manchester; and Phil Huxley, Principal Lecturer in Law, Nottingham Law School, The Nottingham Trent University.

ABBREVIATIONS

ACT	advance corporation tax
AEA	Administration of Estates Act 1925
APA	additional personal allowance
APR	agricultural property relief
BPR	business property relief
CA 1985	Companies Act 1985
CA(s)	capital allowance(s)
CAA 1990	Capital Allowances Act 1990
CGT	capital gains tax
CIC	close investment-holding company
CTT	capital transfer tax
CYB	current year basis, i.e. the tax period is the accounting period ending in the tax period under consideration
DSS	Department of Social Security
EIS	enterprise investment scheme
ESC	extra statutory concession
EU	European Union
FA	Finance Act, e.g. FA 1998, Finance Act 1998
FII	franked investment income, i.e. of a company
F (No. 2) A 1997	Finance (No. 2) Act 1997
FA 1998	Finance Act 1998
FRS	financial reporting standard
FSA 1986	Financial Services Act 1986
FYA(s)	first year allowance(s)
GAAP	generally accepted accounting principles
IA	indexation allowance
IBS(s)	industrial building or structure(s)
ICR	Industrial Cases Reports
ICTA 1988	Income and Corporation Taxes Act 1988
IHT	inheritance tax
IHTA 1984	Inheritance Tax Act 1984
IPT	insurance premium tax
ISA	Individual Savings Account
LCA 1972	Land Charges Act 1972
LEL	lower earnings limit (national insurance contributions)
LPA 1925	Law of Property Act 1925
Ltd	limited (as in limited company)
MCA	married couples' allowance
MIRAS	mortgage interest relief at source
NAA 1948	National Assistance Act 1948
NICs	national insurance contributions
NSB	National Savings Bank
NVQ	National Vocational Qualification
QCB	qualifying corporate bond

PAYE	pay as you earn
PEP	Personal Equity Plan
PET	potentially exempt transfer
PRR	private residence relief
plc	public limited company
PR	personal representative of a deceased individual
RPI	Retail Prices Index
SA	Société Anonyme (French limited company)
SA 1891	Stamp Act 1891
SERPS	State Earnings-Related Pension Scheme
SP	Inland Revenue Statement of Practice
SpA	Italian public company
SSAA 1992	Social Security Administration Act 1992
SSAP	statement of standard accountancy practice
SSCR 1979	Social Security (Contributions) Regulations 1979
SSCBA 1992	Social Security Contributions and Benefits Act 1992
STC	Simon's Tax Cases
STC(SCD)	Simon's Tax Cases (Special Commissioners' Decisions)
SVQ	Scottish Vocational Qualification
TA 1925	Trustee Act 1925
TC	Tax Cases
TCGA 1992	Taxation of Chargeable Gains Act 1992
TESSA	Tax-Exempt Special Savings Account
TLA 1996	Trusts of Land and Appointment of Trustees Act 1996
TMA 1970	Taxes Management Act 1970
UEL	upper earnings limit (national insurance contributions)
VAT	value added tax
VATA 1994	Value Added Tax Act 1994
VATR 1995	Value Added Tax Regulations 1995
VCT	venture capital trust
WBA	widow's bereavement allowance
WDA(s)	writing-down allowance(s)

TABLE OF CASES

TABLE OF STATUTES

TABLE OF STATUTORY INSTRUMENTS

CHAPTER ONE

INCOME TAXATION: CONTEXTS AND HISTORY

1.1 Objectives

By the end of this chapter, you should be able to:

■ describe the main features of a *tax*;

■ distinguish the term *tax* from *taxation*;

■ define the scope of the expression *income taxation*;

■ relate your study of tax law to the *contexts* in which it is encountered;

■ outline the *history* of income taxation in the UK;

■ describe the timing and purpose of the annual *Budget*.

1.2 Introduction

Tax law is part of everyday life. You will even understand something as mundane as a gas bill better, if you know something about VAT: see *Cases and Materials* (**1.1**). This chapter is about the contexts and history of tax law. Tax law could easily be presented to you as a series of unrelated abstractions. The aim of this chapter is to establish contexts for your study, and to provide an historical background to the subject.

1.3 Tax and Taxation

A tax can be defined as a compulsory charge, imposed by central or local government, in order to raise revenue, i.e. government income, to be used for general public purposes. On this definition, not every payment a person might make to a public authority is a tax. Water rates, for instance, are charged for the *particular* public purpose of supplying water to homes, businesses, etc. In addition, water rates are charged, not by central or local government, but by public authorities in private ownership. Severn Trent Water plc is an example of such an authority. It is a privately-owned trading company, with statutory powers to charge customers for the water which it has a duty to supply. Water rates are not therefore taxes.

Another example. National insurance contributions ('NICs') are charged by central government for public purposes. These purposes are partly to raise money for the national insurance fund and partly to fund the National Health Service: SSCBA 1992, s. 1(1): see *Cases and Materials* (**1.2**).

According to the above test, are NICs taxes?

No.

You own a company, which I am buying from you. The principle of *caveat emptor* ('let the buyer beware') applies. To ensure that the company is worth what I believe it to be, an indemnity is included in the sale agreement, in my favour. You agree to indemnify me for any *tax* the company has failed to pay, from the time you acquired the company, until the date of its sale to me. The word *tax* is not defined in the agreement.

Will this wording, by itself, cover water rates and NICs which the company has failed to pay?

No.

We shall not be discussing water rates any further. However, since NICs raise twice as much revenue for central government as the main tax on company profits, i.e. corporation tax, NICs are pragmatically considered to be a tax, and we shall be treating them as such. The word *taxation* denotes the act of taxing, i.e. by the government, or the fact of being taxed.

1.4   Income Taxation

In **Chapters 1** to **19**, we shall be discussing three main forms of income taxation:

■   income tax;

■   corporation tax; and

■   NICs.

In **Chapter 3**, I suggest that VAT is a fourth form of income taxation. That controversial point, however, must keep until then. *Income tax* is typically paid by individuals. *Corporation tax* is paid by companies, although they may *exceptionally* pay income tax instead. *NICs* may be paid by individuals or companies. All three of these tax a person's income profits, although NICs do so differently from the other two. The expression *income taxation* is therefore a useful collective term for these three forms of taxation.

For the moment, let us think about the expression *income taxation* in a little more detail. When income tax was being devised, late in the eighteenth century, there was thought to be an economic distinction between income and capital. It was a distinction propounded by the political economist Adam Smith (1723–1790). Capital was something a person used to generate income: see *Cases and Materials* (**1.3**). Later tax legislators have been less enamoured of the distinction and it is not made in relation, e.g. to VAT. Income tax and corporation tax are saddled with it, however, and we shall be referring to the distinction often. Although there are mountains of tax legislation, nowhere is *income* given a general definition. However, a good way of thinking of income, for the moment, is of money received on a regular basis from some source or other. We shall improve on that short definition later in the book.

Which of the following is an income receipt and which is a capital receipt:

    (a)   **the proceeds of sale of a valuable painting you bought as an investment?**

    (b)   **the salary from your job? and**

    (c)   **a £1,000,000 lottery prize?**

See above: (a) is a capital receipt; (b) is an income receipt; and (c) is a capital receipt.

The counterpart of income is therefore *capital*. We shall be considering the meaning of capital in more detail in **Chapter 3**. A good shorthand way of thinking of a capital receipt for the present, however, is as money received on a one-off basis from the disposal of an asset. Another word for *income* is *revenue*. The meaning of revenue changes, depending on its context. We shall restrict its use to the income of the government. This is why tax law is sometimes referred to as *revenue law*. *The Revenue* is short for the Inland Revenue, i.e. the tax authority responsible for income tax and corporation tax.

1.5   Contexts

In this section, I would like to consider the contexts in which you might encounter tax law.

1.5.1 THE PERSONAL CONTEXT

In an imprecise but fundamental sense, tax means *money*. We live in a society which does not allow us to avoid the ramifications of tax law, any more than those of tort, contract or crime. However, the implications of the statement are striking and, in the course of this book, you should begin to recognise its truth in senses far more profound than you can perhaps at this stage imagine. For instance, I am employed as a lecturer, and I am paid a salary for doing the job. A number of persons will take an interest in the salary paid to me. They will do so for a variety of reasons. The most important of those interested persons, besides myself, are my employer and the taxation authority, i.e. the Inland Revenue. However:

■   as an individual taxpayer, I need to ensure that I am not paying more tax than I am
    obliged to do;

■   the university, my employer, needs to be sure that it is discharging any obligations
    it may have to the Inland Revenue in paying my salary to me; and

■   the Inland Revenue needs to be sure that the university and I are complying with
    the obligations imposed on us by tax legislation.

The personal context is probably the most obvious one in which you will encounter tax
law. However, you may also have to consider it if you are, e.g. selling investments or
making a will. These are matters we examine later on in the book. Remember Alexander
Pope's aphorism, however: see *Cases and Materials* (**1.4.1**). You might be tempted to
relate the tax law you learn too hastily to your own personal situation. I cannot
overemphasise the fact that you are not at this stage equipped even to begin to advise
either yourself, or other people, on their tax affairs. If you attempt to do so, you will
certainly miss some vital point.

1.5.2   THE PROFESSIONAL LEGAL CONTEXT

You will find it helpful to imagine the material in this book as though you were a solicitor
or a barrister acting for a client on a transaction or in litigation, e.g. the purchase of
property as an investment, or a claim for damages in tort. In each of these situations, you
would need to know the tax effect of the transaction or claim. If you did not know this,
you could be held to have given your client negligent advice, because your ignorance
may have produced a cost to your client, in the form of a tax charge: see *Cases and
Materials* (**1.4.2**).

It would be impossible to define exactly the issues which lawyers may encounter in
relation to tax. Typical ones are:

■   if a money payment is being made by one party to another, lawyers need to consider
    whether the payment has taxation implications and for whom;

■   lawyers need to beware of rushing to conclusions about the tax implications of a
    transaction or a claim, either of which may involve more than one tax;

■   lawyers need to ensure that they consider the implications of a payment from the
    perspective of the client whose interests they represent.

It is often difficult to understand fully where tax law fits into the areas of law studied
previously. However, if you think for a moment about the few issues listed, you will
realise the importance of tax law to the lawyer.

1.5.3   THE ACCOUNTING CONTEXT

As a lawyer, you will need to discuss tax law with accountants and bankers. The problem
here is that we do not all speak the same language. For instance, in producing the two
documents which show the financial position of a business, namely, the *balance sheet* and
the *profit and loss account* (see *Cases and Materials* (**1.4.3**)), accountants do not always use
the same principles and rules as are used in tax legislation. There are a number of
examples of this divergence of approach in this book. Suffice it to say that treatises have
been written about the difference, in the context of a trading company, between *profit per
accounts* (accountants' language) and *taxable profits* (tax law language). There has even
been litigation over the difference: *Gallagher* v *Jones* [1993] STC 537, see *Cases and
Materials* (**15.1.1**).

SAQ 4

Are similar linguistic problems apparent in other areas of law, do you think?

Yes, e.g. a criminal lawyer would have to understand accounting principles, to defend a client accused of a complex commercial fraud.

Here is a very simple example of the divergence of approach. Suppose I am in business by myself as a car mechanic. On a given day, I might need to know whether my business ran at a profit or a loss, over the year ending on that day. This is the date up to which I produce my accounts, i.e. my accounting date. I therefore add up all my income during that period. It is money coming in from the goods and services I supply to my customers. To find out whether my business is running at a profit or at a loss, I subtract from the total of the income from the business the money I have spent during the year. In other words, I prepare a *profit and loss account*. As I go through my heap of receipts from my suppliers, I find a receipt for a restaurant meal to which I treated a customer of the business during the year. For the purposes of preparing my profit and loss account, I need to subtract the receipt for the meal from my income during the year, to ascertain how much money I am actually left with at the end of the year. If that leaves me with a profit, I will be happy. However, for the purpose of calculating my trading profits for income tax purposes, I cannot deduct the receipt for the meal. This is because s. 577, ICTA 1988, generally makes such a deduction illegal for tax purposes, except in limited circumstances: see *Cases and Materials* (1.4.3). My income profit for tax purposes will exceed by the cost of the meal the amount of money I actually have in my bank account, on the date I prepare the profit and loss account.

The discussion demonstrates a basic difference in the rules between tax law and accountancy as to allowable deductions. On a more complex level, differences will be created by the *time* at which I can make such deductions. For example, generally accepted accounting principles ('GAAP') may tell me that I can make a deduction on one date and the rules of tax law may tell me that I can only make the equivalent tax law deduction, in calculating my income profits, on another date. This more complex type of difference – referred to as a *timing difference* – commonly occurs in matters involving tax. Recent reforms to tax law are beginning to tackle the differences between tax law and GAAP, to remove the sometimes absurd results created by those differences.

SAQ 5

Who would you guess produced the differences of approach?

Parliament and the judges, mainly in Victorian times, by not developing the law in accordance with accounting principles (or *vice versa*).

One explanation is that the number of accountants in the nineteenth century was comparatively small, so that their influence was fairly insignificant. How times change!

1.5.4 THE POLITICAL CONTEXT

Leading up to the annual Budget (see 1.7), or a General Election, arguments about taxation policy figure prominently. The popular perception, which may not yet match the reality, is that the Labour Party is the party of high taxation, and that the Conservative Party is the party of low taxation: see *Cases and Materials* (**1.4.4**). This is because the purpose of taxation is to fund government expenditure and, in the modern conditions of Western Europe, revenue is expended largely on social welfare. Traditionally, the Labour Party has favoured more government expenditure on social welfare than the Conservative Party. Although, in the two Budgets which have followed the General Election of May 1997, there have been signs that this divergence may be narrowing, the perceived difference of ideology between Labour and Conservative in terms of taxation can be illustrated by a typical debate conducted prior to the 1995 Budget. *The Times* of 15 November 1995 carried a report that it was still the long-term objective of the Conservative Government to abolish, not income taxation, but the taxation of *capital* profits: **Chapters 21** to **25**. This became part of the Conservative manifesto at the General Election in May 1997.

The then *Shadow* Chancellor of the Exchequer, Gordon Brown, said that the effect of such an abolition would be to '. . . bring about the biggest shift of wealth to the elite this century'. However, the then Financial Secretary to the Treasury, Michael Jack, was reported as having replied by saying that: 'By opposing our policy to abolish tax on [investment profits], Gordon Brown has shown once again that Labour is against enterprise and against the creation of wealth'.

Why would each have said these things?

There is a perception that a proliferation of taxes and high rates of tax discourage private enterprise, i.e. wealth-creation. By contrast, low taxation is said to be an abdication of responsibility to less well-off people.

As a lawyer reading the newspapers and the professional press, you will certainly be interested in the taxation policies of both the Government and Opposition, because these could affect the taxation position of your clients. You may even wish to advise them of steps designed to avoid the adverse effects of proposed legislation. How far you can go in this is another major strand of the book.

Whatever the political ideology of the Government currently in office, prevailing economic conditions may make the implementation of a particular taxation policy impossible in practice.

Can you think of any recent well-known examples of practical reality allegedly making tax-cuts impossible?

One recent example of the gap between aspirations and reality concerns VAT: see **3.4.2**. This story requires no prior knowledge. You simply need to appreciate that VAT raises a vast amount of money for the Government and for the EU, of which the UK is a Member State. In February 1996, it seemed that the UK public sector borrowing requirement (the difference between what the Government receives in revenue, and what it actually spends) would remain at about £30 billion for the two following years. This was because the Treasury was then unable to ascertain why the revenue which it originally estimated would be raised by VAT had *in fact* fallen short of those estimates! Think also about the crisis caused by the much-disputed link between Creutzfeld-Jakob Disease ('CJD') and Bovine Spongiform Encephalopathy ('BSE'), which forced the last Conservative Government to formulate a plan for paying compensation to beef and dairy farmers for a cattle-cull. This led to suggestions, then fiercely denied by the Government, that its opposition to the European Commission's ban on UK beef exports had been motivated by a desire to avoid the payment of compensation to farmers. In either case, a VAT shortfall and large compensation payments, so the Government argued, made tax cuts impossible in practice.

1.5.5 THE ECONOMIC CONTEXT

It is often difficult to recognise where the political context shades into the economic one. However, if a new tax is being proposed, or an existing tax is being reformed, some objective criteria are required to validate any conclusion. Some economists evaluate taxes in terms of five principles, or *maxims*, four of which were originally propounded by Adam Smith. The five principles are fairness, certainty, convenience, economy and efficiency; see *Cases and Materials* (**1.4.5**).

Read *Cases and Materials* (**1.4.5**), and match up the five principles to the points made in the extract from Adam Smith.

Whether you agree with Adam Smith depends to a large extent on your own political sympathies. Adam Smith believed in a free market economy.

A tax law of 1696 provided that each window in houses above a certain size would attract a tax charge. House owners therefore bricked up their windows, to avoid paying the tax. How many of the five principles did the window tax breach?

Two, economy and efficiency: see also *Cases and Materials* (**1.4.5**).

Adam Smith's maxims may help you to evaluate the nature of the taxes with which you have to contend.

1.6   History

1.6.1   THE INCOME TAX OF PITT AND ADDINGTON

You should know something about the historical background of income taxation. Income tax was originally introduced by the Finance Bill of January 1798. Its purpose was to raise revenue to meet the cost of the war with Revolutionary France. Its inspiration was the Tory Prime Minister, William Pitt, who wanted to raise revenue without massive government borrowing. For this insight, as in other ways, Pitt was a remarkable individual. He had first been Prime Minister at the age of 22 and was still only 39 when, again as Prime Minister, he introduced 'the income tax'. Giving the reason for the tax in the House of Commons, on 24 November 1798, he said:

> We ought to consider how far the efforts we shall exert to preserve the blessings we enjoy will enable us to transmit the inheritance to posterity unencumbered with those burdens which would cripple their vigour and prevent them from asserting that rank in the scale of nations which their ancestors so long and so gloriously maintained.

What did he mean in modern English?

He meant that, if the Government was saddled with debt caused by borrowing to pay for the war effort, Britain would lose its influence overseas.

The introduction of the tax was a bold move, since war had historically been financed by borrowing and donations, together with a collection of taxes already imposed on features of privileged living, e.g. the window tax (see above and *Cases and Materials* (**1.5.1**)); a tax on hair powder (1795); a tax on dogs (1796); and a tax on watches and clocks (1797). Income tax was discontinued in 1802 by Pitt's successor as Prime Minister, Henry

Addington (1757–1844), although Addington was forced by circumstances to reintroduce it in 1803.

SAQ 10

Why **would political, military and naval circumstances force him to do this in 1803?**

The need to raise revenue to pay for the war.

So much less of a statesman did Addington appear to be than Pitt, that a contemporary invented the doggerel:

> Pitt is to Addington
> As London is to Paddington.

Addington and not Pitt, however, invented income tax in its modern form. In structuring it, so as to ensure that it could be collected effectively, Addington gave it two features which remain features of the income tax system today:

■ Wherever possible, if income tax was chargeable on a sum of money, the tax would be deducted by the payer from that sum when making the payment. The payer then sent the tax to the tax authority. As Addington said, this meant that taxpayers no longer had to 'decide between their interest [i.e. selfishness] and their duty'.

■ Taxpayers had underdeclared their income profits under Pitt's system, since they did not want other people to know how much income they had, nor the business activities from which it came. Addington therefore categorised all income according to its source, under five so-called Schedules, requiring the taxpayer to make a separate declaration to a different tax collector of the income from each source.

This Schedular System is still with us today, although legislative changes mean that there are now only four income tax Schedules. You no longer make separate declarations to different collectors of your income profits from each source. However, the calculation of these amounts makes up your statutory income, which is Stage One of your income tax calculation: see **7.3.**

SAQ 11

'Income tax is more efficiently collected at source than direct from the taxpayer'. True or false?

True.

With these two features, Addington's income tax raised far more revenue than Pitt's had done: see *Cases and Materials* (**1.5.1**). Income tax was discontinued again, however, in 1816, after the wars with France finally came to an end. It had been understood that the tax would only last for the duration of hostilities. The Government of Lord Liverpool (1770-1828), Prime Minister in 1816, was therefore forced to repeal it.

1.6.2 SIR ROBERT PEEL AND THE LATER DEVELOPMENT OF INCOME TAX

From 1816 to 1842, there was no income tax. In 1842, however, it was reintroduced by the Conservative Government of Sir Robert Peel (1788-1850). The reasons for its reintroduction were complex but they included the need to make up the shortfall in revenue which would be caused by the projected repeal of the so-called 'Corn Laws', which had for centuries been a form of indirect taxation (see **3.4.1**) on the import and export of cereal produce. Peel seems to have been a fairly humourless character, which you may think of as being rather appropriate. The son of a rich calico printer from Bury, in Lancashire, he was described by Daniel O'Connell (1775–1847), Irish barrister and nationalist politician, as having a smile like '. . . moonlight falling upon the silver plate of a child's coffin'. Taking Addington's basic model for the tax, Peel's income tax has been a major component of the system of income tax ever since. The interesting thing is that, at the time, people thought it would be merely a temporary measure – Peel's tax was intended to last for three years! Lord Ashburton – a famous banker of the day – opined that 'It would be next to insupportable to live in a country where such a tax were permanent'!

In his biography of Peel, Professor Norman Gash says: 'Ever since the House of Commons had forced Liverpool's ministry to abandon [income tax] in 1816, it had lain unused in the armoury of theoretical policies, unused, repugnant, but not forgotten'. Why?

Although unpopular, it could raise much revenue: see *Cases and Materials* (**1.5.1**).

In his Budget Speech of 1853, the coalition Chancellor of the Exchequer, William Ewart Gladstone (1809–1898), referred to income tax as: '. . . an engine of gigantic power for great national purposes', proposing that the tax only be continued for seven years, at reducing rates, until 1860. 138 years on from 1860, it is still with us, although it is renewed annually by Parliament.

The significance of the tax during the century after 1860 and beyond increased dramatically. Greater rates of tax, among other factors, meant that the amount of revenue raised by income tax increased seventeen times over, to meet the financial cost of the First World War (1914–18) and, by the end of the Second World War (1939–45), the revenue raised by the tax was three times greater than it had been in 1938.

1.6.3   NATIONAL INSURANCE CONTRIBUTIONS AND CORPORATION TAX

NICs were introduced in 1948. They were a result of the so-called 'Beveridge Report'. Today, NICs are more important than ever as a means of raising revenue. Statistics now show that they raise twenty-five times the amount raised by the main tax on investment profits, namely capital gains tax (CGT).

This, then, is the historical background to income tax and NICs. What about the history of the income taxation of companies, however? Modern company law only dates from the Joint Stock Companies Act 1844. Until 1965, when corporation tax was introduced, companies paid income tax, although the system under which corporation tax operated was not the same as the one under which it has operated until quite recently: see **8.3**.

Compared with income tax, corporation tax and NICs, VAT is a newcomer to the tax system in this country. I must emphasise that VAT is not, on a conventional analysis, a form of income taxation. However, after having studied **Chapter 3**, you may decide that the conventional analysis needs further thought. VAT was introduced into the UK in 1973 as a result of the UK's entry to the European Economic Community.

Parallel systems of VAT operate in the other 14 Member States of the EU and there is a special system of VAT for trade in goods between Member States. However, as you may know, there are still considerable divergences, both in terms of VAT rates and in terms of those items which carry a VAT charge.

1.7 The Annual Budget

I must mention finally another historical feature of the tax system. Annual Budgets are speeches delivered by the Chancellor of the Exchequer in the House of Commons, setting out the Government's spending plans and the taxation measures necessary to pay for them. Because of its economic importance, the contents of the Budget speech are secret before it is made. The measures contained in the Budget are given immediate force, where appropriate, by Budget Resolutions, but they take formal shape in the annual Finance Bill, which becomes the annual Finance Act. As a result of reforms by Chancellor Norman Lamont in 1992, annual Budgets occurred during the autumn of each year, in the later stages of the last Government. However, following the General Election in May 1997, from 1998 they occur in the spring, with a 'pre-Budget statement' each autumn. In 1997, because of the General Election, there were two Finance Acts, reflecting the measures taken in the autumn 1996 Budget (by Chancellor Kenneth Clarke) and in the July 1997 Budget (by Chancellor Gordon Brown). The 1998 Budget speech was made by Chancellor Gordon Brown on 17 March 1998: see *Cases and Materials* (**1.6**).

1.8 Summary

The idea of taxing a person's income profits has been around for a long time. It was largely the work of Pitt, Addington and Peel, inspired by Adam Smith. Modern income taxation takes the form of income tax, corporation tax, NICs and possibly VAT. Taxation, not just income taxation, presents issues for the lawyer in a variety of contexts: the personal, the professional legal, the accounting, the political and the economic. In the next chapter, we emphasise the fact that income tax and corporation tax both tax income profits, and we examine the nature of that concept, as well as the concept of the *income loss*. We also consider the types of persons liable to pay income taxation and the capacities in which their liability could arise.

CHAPTER TWO

INCOME TAXATION: INCOME PROFITS, PERSONS AND CAPACITIES

2.1 Objectives

By the end of this chapter, you should be able to:

■ explain the scope of the term *income profits*;

■ explain the scope of the term *income losses*;

■ identify the two main types of *persons* liable to pay income taxation, i.e. the individual and the company;

■ identify the *capacities* in which an individual may be liable to pay income taxation;

■ relate *income tax*, *corporation tax* and *NICs* to the persons identified above and the capacities in which an individual may be liable to pay them.

2.2 Introduction

In this chapter, we shall be discussing two fundamentals. First the point that, if a person makes an income profit from a particular source, that person is generally liable to pay income tax or corporation tax on it, as the case may be. Likewise, if a person makes an income loss, that person pays *no* income tax or corporation tax on it. Instead, the loss may be a valuable tax relief, capable of being used in the ways described in **Chapter 13**. Secondly, a person may make such income profits or income losses as one of two types of person, i.e. an individual or a company. As an individual, you may be liable to pay income tax in one or more of a number of different *capacities*: your personal capacity, the capacity of a partner, the capacity of a trustee, or the capacity of a personal representative (PR): see *Cases and Materials* (**2.1**).

2.3 *Income Profits* and *Income Losses*

Income tax and corporation tax are charged on income profits: ICTA 1988, ss. 15, 18, 19 and 20: see *Cases and Materials* (**2.2**). NICs are almost always charged, as we shall discover, not on income profits but on *earnings*: SSCBA 1992, ss. 6, 11 and 15 and see **6.4**.

2.3.1 INCOME PROFITS

Income profits could come from any one or more of a number of sources, e.g. from:

- letting land; and/or

- carrying on a trade; and/or

- carrying on a profession or vocation; and/or

- an employment; and/or

- holding investments.

'Income tax' is a misnomer. Income tax is calculated, not on your income as such, but on your *income profits*. Thus, I may have income from a trade, carried on by myself as a sole trader. I may also have expenditure in carrying on that trade, namely the cost to me of trading, e.g. acquiring trading stock. Income tax law provides, in essence, that I will be taxed on the difference between these two amounts, income and expenditure, provided that the difference between them represents a profit, i.e. is a positive figure.

I carry on the trade of selling antiques. My income from the trade is £1,000 during a certain period. My expenditure on trading stock is £600 in that period. My *income profit* is therefore £400, i.e. the positive difference between the two.

On which amount will income tax be calculated?

£400, i.e. *not £1,000*.

This conclusion is, however, subject to two *major* qualifications:

- Precise income tax rules tell me exactly how to calculate the figures for my income and expenditure. A discussion of these rules forms a large part of this book. As we shall discover, the legislation will not allow me to take certain items of expenditure into account. Equally, some income will have to be taken into account, even though I may not actually have received it from my customers in the period under consideration.

- Unless the expenditure falls into certain categories of expenditure covered by so-called *capital allowances*, I cannot include the cost of any capital item in my expenditure: see **12.2**.

The term *income profits* is therefore used in tax law in the sense of the income, *less* the deductions which I am allowed to make from that income, under the relevant statutory rules. What those statutory rules are, as we shall discover, depends on the *source* from which the income comes. The deductions are referred to as *allowable deductions*. Income profits are not, therefore, the same as income. Instead, income corresponds to the expressions *income receipts* or *turnover*: see **Cases and Materials (2.2.1)**.

This should be fairly straightforward, but I want to draw your attention to a number of related points also. This use of the term income profits, although essential to an understanding of income taxation, means that, in certain contexts, its use may seem slightly odd.

SAQ 14

Would you normally talk about the *income profits* from your employment?

No, you would normally refer to your *salary* or *wages*.

None the less, the relevant legislation refers to income profits (i.e. *'emoluments'*)! The reality for income tax purposes is that, in receiving wages or a salary or even *fringe benefits*, an employee is receiving a form of income profit. However, the rules governing the deductions from your salary which you are allowed to make for income tax purposes are very restrictive.

Take another point. Say I have savings in a deposit account at a bank. My income from those savings will be in the form of interest. This interest is *pure income profit* for me. Unlike for several other types of profit, e.g. trading profits, income tax and corporation tax rules provide no allowable deductions from interest. It is still necessary to talk about income profits in the form of interest, however, since we need to concentrate on the fact that it is *pure income profit*. Two final points:

- The term *income profits* is to be contrasted with the term *capital profits*: see **Chapter 3**. This contrast exists because, generally speaking, income tax is charged only on income profits. Corporation tax is charged both on income profits and capital profits. However, as we shall discover in **Chapter 21**, the rules for calculating corporation tax on income profits are different from those for calculating corporation tax on capital profits.

- The result of a person making an income profit in a particular period is for that profit to be included at Stage One of its income tax or corporation tax calculation for that period: **7.3** and **7.4**.

2.3.2   INCOME LOSSES

Income losses could come from any one or more of the sources listed in **2.3.1**. In relation to income losses, both income tax law and corporation tax law provide that, if the difference between the income and expenditure figures in the period under consideration is a negative figure, i.e. a loss, then I am *not liable* to pay any income tax for that period on my income from that source.

SAQ 15

I carry on the trade of selling antiques. My income from the trade is £400 during a certain period. My expenditure in the trade is £1,000 in that period. My *income loss* is therefore £(600), i.e. the negative difference between the two.

What amount will be included in my income tax calculation for that period?

Zero.

This conclusion is, however, subject to one *major* qualification. Precise rules of income tax law tell me exactly how to calculate the figures for my income and expenditure, as above. Therefore, I cannot 'create' income losses without satisfying these rules. The term *income loss* is therefore used in tax law to denote any negative figure resulting from making allowable deductions from income in a certain period. Again, this is fairly straightforward. Note the following related points:

■ Income losses are more likely from some sources than others. It is time to pack up and go home if you make an income loss on your employment income, although the situation is provided for in ICTA 1988, s. 380(1): see **13.5**!

■ Savings accounts at a bank cannot produce an income loss, although they might produce a *capital* loss: see **20.5.2**.

Again, two final points need to be made here. First, the term income loss is to be contrasted with the term *capital loss*. We shall mention the difference between these two forms of loss in **Chapter 3**. Secondly, an income loss in a particular period has two consequences:

■ no figure for income from that source is included in the income tax or corporation tax calculation for that period in Stage One of that calculation; and

■ the amount of the negative figure, the income loss, *may* be available – subject to strict rules – for use as a deduction in the same or another period, either from income from the same, or a different source, or a number of different sources: **Chapter 13**.

2.4   Persons and Capacities

2.4.1   PERSONS

You and I are each a person in law, i.e. a natural person, a human being. This is by contrast with an artificial person, e.g. a limited company. We are *individuals*. Provided we are not under any legal disability, we are subject to *obligations* and have *rights*.

2.4.1.1   Individuals

General obligations are imposed on us by the criminal law. In addition, specific obligations may be imposed on us by the civil law, e.g. under a contract of employment. An example of a *right* conferred by a contract of employment would be the employee's right to be paid for work done under it. An example of an *obligation* imposed by the contract would be the employee's obligation to work a certain number of hours in return.

A contract of employment is obviously not the only type of contract under which we have rights and are subject to obligations. However, for tax law purposes, a contract of employment is a very important way in which rights are conferred on individuals, since it provides them with a source of employment income. An individual might have rights or be subject to obligations imposed by types of contractual relationship other than employment contracts: e.g. you own a house which you let to a tenant. This gives you the right to another source of income, rental income.

You own a cottage in the country, which you let to tenants at a rent. You insure it and repair it regularly. What allowable deductions would you expect to be entitled to make in calculating your rental profits?

The cost of insurance and repairs.

Again, you might own shares in a company. You would therefore have a source of dividend income, if any dividends were declared and paid on those shares: see **2.4.1.2**.

Again, you might be a sole trader. If so, any trading profits will be in the form of profits made on the contracts entered into with the customers to whom you supply goods or services.

Yet again, you might lend money out in return for interest payments by the debtor to you, the creditor. In that case, you would have a source of investment income, i.e. interest.

SAQ 17

I pay cash into a *deposit* account at a bank. What form will the income profit from the deposit account take?

Interest payments to me by the bank.

As an individual, you are liable to pay income tax on your income profits from all sources in the tax year under consideration, if you are resident in the UK in that tax year. It is irrelevant whether those sources are located in the UK or overseas: ICTA 1988, s. 1(1): *Cases and Materials* (**2.3.1.1**). You may also be liable to pay NICs on your earnings, if you are *present* in the UK.

2.4.1.2 Companies

The second type of person for our purposes is a *company* or, to be more precise, a company limited by shares. Such companies are persons in their own right, but they are *artificial* persons. They are recognisable by the fact that their names end with the abbreviation 'Ltd' or 'plc'. A company can be owned by individuals, but the rights conferred on the company, and the obligations to which it is subject, are different from the rights and obligations of each of the individuals who own the company, i.e. the *shareholders* in, or *members* of, the company: see *Cases and Materials* (**2.3.1.2**).

When individuals get together to carry out the formalities of forming a company, they are said to *incorporate* it. Shares are *issued* by the company, and *allotted* to the shareholders. Although they are issued and allotted at a *nominal* amount, e.g. £1 per share, the real value of the shares to the shareholders is determined, not by this nominal amount *subscribed* by them, but by a combination of the performance of the company in carrying out its business activities, and the contractual rights conferred on the shareholder by the shares. If the worst happens, and the company becomes insolvent, the shareholders' liability is limited to the nominal value of their shareholdings. The contractual rights conferred on the shareholder by the shares are determined partly by the *articles of association* (a multipartite contract made between the shareholders), and partly by general company law. For tax purposes, the most important of these contractual rights is the right to receive a *dividend* declared on the shares. This may be a right to receive only a fixed amount, in the case of *fixed rate preference shares*, or to receive any amount declared on them by the directors, in the case of *ordinary shares*. The right to vote at *general meetings* of the company is another important contractual right conferred on the shareholder. Some decisions require the consent of 75% or more of the shareholders voting at such a meeting, whilst others require only 51%. Subject to any restrictions in the articles of association, shareholders may sell or otherwise transfer some or all of their shares. If, either alone or with other shareholders, you own all the issued shares in a company, and you sell all those shares, then you sell the company: see **SAQ 2**.

Dividends must be either declared or (in the case of a final dividend) recommended by the company's *board of directors*, depending on whether the company has sufficient *distributable reserves* for the dividend to be paid. The directors are the 'brain' of the company. Some or all of the directors may at the same time be shareholders in the company.

Alexander Ltd has four *equal* ordinary shareholders: Ben, Catherine, Diana and Egbert. Ben and Catherine are also directors of the company. How many *persons* are there here?

Five. Alexander Ltd, plus each of its four shareholders.

A company is a vehicle for generating income. Just like an individual, a company can have one or more sources of income. However, it is the *company*, *not* its shareholders, which carries on the business which gives the company its sources of income.

Alexander Ltd lets houses to students in order to make rental profits. The names of individual students will appear in the tenancy agreements as tenants. Whose name will appear as landlord?

Alexander Ltd's.

The idea of a company is therefore for the company to generate an income profit from its business activities, which is then paid out to its shareholders as dividends.

Refer to Alexander Ltd in SAQ 19 above. The company makes rental profits of £2,000. Ben, Catherine, Diana and Egbert wish to extract this money from the company. How will it be extracted, and what amount will each of them receive?

Declaration and payment of a dividend, subject to the £2,000 being available for distribution. Each will be entitled to £500 (i.e. £2,000/4).

You might imagine that this might mean that tax would be charged *twice* on those income profits, i.e. once in the company, and again when the shareholders receive them as dividends. We shall be considering how income taxation has sought to avoid this problem in **Chapters 8** and **16**. The problem of the same profits being taxed twice is referred to as *double taxation*, and it is something which can occur in a number of different contexts.

Companies resident in the UK in the accounting period under consideration are liable to pay corporation tax on their income profits in that accounting period, and it is irrelevant whether these income profits have a source in the UK or overseas: ICTA 1988, ss. 6(1), 8(1) and 8(3): see *Cases and Materials* (**2.3.1.2**). If a company has employees, it is also liable to pay NICs in relation to them.

Read the extracts from Lord Macnaghten's speech in *Salomon* v *Salomon & Co. Ltd* [1895–99] All ER Rep 33, 46–49 (*Cases and Materials* (**2.3.1.2**)). Briefly summarise the principle stated by Lord Macnaghten.

2.4.2   CAPACITIES

As an individual, I could receive income from any one or more of the sources mentioned above, either in my own personal capacity or in one or more of a number of other capacities.

2.4.2.1   Partners

This capacity is that of the partner in a partnership or firm: see *Cases and Materials* (**2.3.2.1**). In English law, a partnership is not a separate person from its partners, unlike in Scots law. Being a partner is simply a *capacity* in which an individual may act, in order to generate income from some business activity. It is only one of a number of capacities in which an individual may act. Say you are employed as a shop assistant and, after work and at weekends, you carry on a trade in partnership with another, or several other, individuals. In addition, you own shares in Frank plc. In this situation, you have two capacities (your personal capacity and your capacity as a partner), and three sources of income: employment income, dividend income and a share of the trading income from the trade carried on by the partnership.

As an individual, you merely have a capacity in which you act as a partner in the partnership. However, your income profits from the partnership, for income tax purposes, would be calculated separately from your other income profits. Your share of the income profits of the partnership as a whole would be included in Stage One of your income tax calculation: see **7.5**. This illustrates that the concept of partnership has what is known as *tax transparency* or *fiscal transparency*: see *Cases and Materials* (**2.3.2.1**).

ACTIVITY3

On a separate piece of paper, note down as you read this and the following chapters, as many *similarities* and *differences* between partnerships and companies as you can.

2.4.2.2 Trustees and personal representatives

Being a trustee or PR is a *capacity* in which you might be liable to pay income tax. At the same time, a trust or estate is *proprietary*, since it is not available to pay the personal debts of the trustee or PR.

PRs include both *executors*, if the deceased left a will under which they have been validly appointed, and *administrators*, if the intestacy legislation applies to their appointment. The income tax liability of the trust or estate on its income profits must be treated separately from the personal income tax position of the individuals who act as trustees or PRs. This is because both trustees and PRs hold any income profits generated by the trust or estate property for the benefit of someone else, i.e. the beneficiaries of the trust or estate. However, there are a number of crucial respects in which trustees and PRs are different from each other: see *Corbett* v *IRC* [1938] 1 KB 567, *Stamp Duties Commissioner (Queensland)* v *Livingston* [1964] 3 All ER 692, 696 (*Cases and Materials* (2.3.2.2)). Both are *fiduciaries* and, for the present at least, we can assume they are analytically similar to each other.

Suppose, in addition to acting in my personal capacity, I am a trustee, holding property for beneficiaries, or a PR, holding the deceased's property for the benefit of beneficiaries. As a trustee, I may hold trust property which generates an income. As a PR, I may hold estate property which continues to generate an income after the deceased's death. For instance, shares in Gordon plc might be registered in my name in the company's *share register*, as trustee for the beneficiaries of the trust; or a dividend might be declared and paid on shares after the deceased's death. Again, the deceased might have rented properties out to tenants, which properties I now hold as the deceased's PR, and which continue to generate rental income. My income tax liability as a PR will have to be calculated separately from my personal income tax liability.

A further point needs to be made in relation to trustees, since the fundamental question is whether they, or the beneficiaries, are liable to pay income tax on the taxable income of the trust. This depends on two factors:

(a) whether the beneficiaries have an immediate entitlement to the income of the trust property or not; and

(b) whether the trustees are resident in the UK: see **4.5.4.1**.

Saying that the beneficiaries have an immediate entitlement to the income is another way of saying that the *income accrues directly to the beneficiaries*. This will rarely happen, because trust income accrues initially to the trustees in whose name the income-generating property (e.g. loan stock, shares, land, etc. is registered or vested). One case where it does accrue directly to the beneficiary, however, is where the trustees *mandate* the trust income direct to the beneficiaries: *Williams* v *Singer* [1921] 1 AC 65 (*Cases and Materials* (2.3.2.2); also *Reid's Trustees* v *IRC* (1929) 14 TC 512 (*Cases and Materials* (2.3.2.2)).

SAQ 21

Louis and Michel, trustees of a trust of which Nigel is the life tenant, execute a mandate of all the interest from the trust's deposit account to Nigel. Who is liable for the income tax?

Nigel.

So the rule is that, if *trustees* have the immediate entitlement to the trust income, they are liable to pay income tax on the taxable income of the trust. Both *life interest trusts* and *accumulation and maintenance settlements* are examples of trusts where the income does *not* accrue directly to the beneficiaries: see **16.3.1** and **27.4.2.3**. In both cases, the trustees will be liable for the income tax unless, in the case of the former, the *Williams* v *Singer* exception applies. For present purposes, think of an *accumulation and maintenance settlements* as a trust for the maintenance of individuals under 25 years of age.

SAQ 22

Henrietta and Ivan, trustees of The Jake 1998 Discretionary Trust, hold shares worth £10,000 in Kenneth plc, on trust to pay the income (i.e. any dividends) to 'such of the settlor's children as they shall in their absolute discretion think fit'. Are Henrietta and Ivan liable to pay income tax on the dividends?

Yes.

2.5 Summary

The concepts of *income profits* and *income losses* are crucial for income tax and corporation tax purposes. Turnover or income, by itself, is not the important thing. Income tax is therefore a mis-named tax! As we shall discover in **Chapter 3**, however, income tax and corporation tax contrast with VAT in this respect, as in many others, since VAT depends on the concept of *turnover* rather than upon profit. It is essential to understand clearly the distinction between the two types of person, and to appreciate the significance of the different capacities in which an individual may receive income from an income source. It is particularly important to note that only when a *beneficiary* has an immediate entitlement to the income of the trust property is the *trustee* not liable to pay income tax on the income profits of the trust.

2.6   End of Chapter Assessment Question

Amber Ltd manufactures metal fastenings at its factory in Grimetown. It sells the metal fastenings to wholesalers. On 6 April 1998, it has four shareholders, Alan, Bertram, Charlie and Deborah, each of whom owns 25% of the issued ordinary share capital of the company. Alan and Bertram are brothers, Deborah is their sister, and Charlie is the father of all three of them. They are all directors of the company, including even Charlie, who is exactly 85 years old on 6 April 1998, and in failing health. All four are employed under service contracts with the company, and all receive a relatively small salary.

On 28 September 1998, Charlie dies. Bertram is his sole executor, although he did not witness the execution of the will, which took place in 1988. Under Charlie's will, cash gifts of £2,000 each are made to Alan, Bertram and Deborah. The will provides for them to receive interest on their cash gifts, from the date of Charlie's death, to the date of the receipt of the cheques by them. They are likely to receive the separate cheques for the gifts and the interest sometime in March 1999.

Besides being a director of, and shareholder in, Amber Ltd, Deborah is a partner in Brown & Co., a firm of solicitors in Grimetown. Brown & Co. has three partners, including Deborah. Deborah is single, and lets a room in her house to her cousin, Edwina, for £150 per month. She also receives interest on securities held for her by Georgina and Harry, who are the trustees of Deborah's uncle Frederick's will trust. Frederick died in 1993, and she has a life interest in possession under the will trust.

On 30 November 1998, Alan, Bertram and Deborah declared, and Amber Ltd paid, a dividend, which is divided equally between the four shareholders.

Identify the persons involved in these facts, the capacities which they have, and the sources of income which they possess.

(Word limit: 350 (100 marks).)

See *Cases and Materials* (2.5), for a specimen answer.

CHAPTER THREE

INCOME TAXATION: CAPITAL PROFITS, DIRECT AND INDIRECT TAXATION AND VAT

3.1 Objectives

By the end of this chapter, you should be able to:

■ distinguish *income profits* from *capital profits*;

■ assess the *importance* of distinguishing between income profits and capital profits;

■ explain the differences between *direct* and *indirect taxation*;

■ place income tax, corporation tax, NICs and VAT in the appropriate category;

■ outline how VAT works;

■ decide whether VAT is a possible fourth form of income taxation.

3.2 Introduction

In this chapter, we shall be exploring the differences between income profits and capital profits, and assessing why these differences might be important. We shall then be considering the problematic distinction drawn between direct and indirect taxation: see *Cases and Materials* (3.1). Our discussion of indirect taxation will involve a description of VAT, a crucially important tax which we have so far mentioned only briefly.

3.3 Income Profits and Capital Profits

3.3.1 INTRODUCTION

The taxation of income profits has long been part of UK tax law. However, income profits are not the only type of profit which are taxed. Capital profits, sometimes referred to as *investment profits*, are also taxed.

What would you imagine the expression *capital profits* to mean?

Profits generated by the disposal of investments.

To be precise, there must be a *chargeable gain*, which is produced by the *chargeable disposal*, by a *chargeable person* of a *chargeable asset*. If all of these elements are present, there will be a CGT charge on the disposal of an investment (disregarding any available exemptions and reliefs). As with income profits, there are precise tax law rules, stating *exactly how* a profit on the disposal of an investment is to be calculated. We mention these briefly below and develop this analysis in **Chapters 20** to **25**.

For well over a century after the introduction of income tax, profits on the disposal of investments had not been taxed at all, except in a very small number of situations, or in wartime. It was not until Chancellor James Callaghan's Budget Speech of 6 April 1965, which followed a number of legislative experiments in the early 1960s, that the capital profits of individuals were made liable to CGT and a tax called *profits tax*, long-since abolished, was introduced to tax the capital profits of companies: see *Cases and Materials* (3.2.1).

The two obvious questions, therefore, whichever type of person is being considered, and whatever the capacity in which that person is acting, are:

■   is it important to classify a particular profit as an income or a capital one? *And*

■   how do we know whether the profit under consideration is an income profit or a capital one?

The answer to the first question is Yes although, as we shall discover, the likelihood of the question being asked will be greater in relation to profits from some sources than from others. The simple answer to the second question is that, once the relevant criteria are known, it is usually very easy to classify a profit, although there are cases in which the classification is difficult.

3.3.2   IS THE CLASSIFICATION IMPORTANT?

The answer to this question is Yes. The reason is that, in principle, only income profits are liable to income tax or corporation tax on income. Capital profits may, however, be subject to CGT or corporation tax on chargeable gains. A good way of characterising income and capital profits is to think of capital profits as being *one-off* in nature and income profits as being *recurrent*. You will generally be able to recognise an income profit when you encounter it, however, not least because the type of profit you are considering will fall within the wording of one of the Schedules mentioned in **Chapter 1**, and which we shall be discussing in detail in **Chapter 5**. Because of the antiquity of the original legislation, the words *income profits* are not used in ICTA 1988. Instead, e.g. in relation to trading profits, the term '*annual profits or gains*' from a trade is used.

SAQ 24

In the context of the phrase 'the annual profits or gains', what do you think the word 'annual' means?

'Income'.

Thus the Schedule which taxes the annual profits or gains of a trade is intended to tax the income profits of a trade carried on by a person. It is not intended to bring capital profits into the scope of income tax. In general, the question of whether a profit is an income one or a capital one is likely to be more relevant to companies than to individuals. In relation to individuals, it is likely to be of most relevance to trading profits. For companies, the answer to the question of whether a profit is an income one or a capital one will be important because, as we have said, corporation tax as a whole embodies two sets of rules. It taxes the profits chargeable to corporation tax of a company, with the result that it taxes both income profits and capital profits. The directors of a company and its advisers will need to know into which of the categories of income or capital profit a particular profit falls, so that they know whether to use the rules on the taxation of income profits or those on the taxation of capital profits, in order to decide how much tax is chargeable on a particular sum received by them. By contrast, as an individual, it is virtually impossible, so long as you continue to have a source of employment income – i.e. a job – to receive a sum of money from your employer which you can characterise as a capital sum instead of an income one. This is because of the cunning wording of the legislation, which deems even capital sums to be income ones: see **Chapter 14**.

It would be easy to exaggerate the practical effect of the distinction between income profits and capital profits, however. A company pays the same rate of tax on its income profits as on its capital profits. Until 1 April 1999, this will be 31%, tapering down to 21%, depending on the level of the company's profits in both categories. The distinction used to be much more important when there was no taxation of capital profits or, as was the case for many years, the rate of tax on capital profits was less than the rate of tax on income profits.

SAQ 25

What effect would you expect a difference in income tax and CGT rates to have had?

Efforts being made to disguise profits as capital ones, to avoid them being classified as income.

In 1978, the Meade Committee's report *The Structure and Reform of Direct Taxation* identified the exploitation of the distinction between income and capital as being one of the most frequently-used devices by which people sought to avoid paying income tax. This was against a background of differing CGT and income tax rates: see *Cases and Materials* (**3.2.2**). Accordingly, as a way of preventing a person deriving taxation advantages from being able to disguise an income profit as a capital one, some profits which may at first appear to be capital ones, are deemed to be income profits instead.

One example is the legislation on the taxation of *offshore roll-up funds*. Before considering this in detail, however, we need briefly to mention the way in which capital profits are taxed. (We are assuming here that there has been a chargeable disposal by a chargeable person of a chargeable asset.) You first apply the CGT rules, in order to find out how much the property disposed-of cost you in total. You then subtract that amount from the sum you have received on its sale. You pay CGT on a percentage of the difference between the two, provided it is a positive figure, i.e. a chargeable gain, and the chargeable gain may in certain cases be reduced by *taper relief*.

SAQ 26

Bearing in mind what you know about income losses (see Chapter 2), what would be the result of getting a negative figure from this process?

A capital loss.

Applying the CGT rules in this way to a sum you have received on the sale of property (say as a sole trader) may mean that you pay less tax than if the income taxation rules were applied. There are two reasons for this. One is that, with the CGT rules, an allowance can be made for the effect of inflation on the cost of the property. The other is the availability of tapering relief. This inflation allowance is called the *indexation allowance*.

ACTIVITY4

Find a good dictionary and look up the meaning of the word 'inflation'.

Inflation is an economic effect which causes the real value of money to fall. This means that the cost of property decreases in real terms with the passage of time: see *Cases and Materials* (**3.2.2**).

The indexation allowance does not apply in relation to income tax and corporation tax on income. It does apply to the taxation of capital profits, however, and its effect is to increase the cost of the property, in order to reflect the effect of inflation. This, in turn, has the effect of reducing the profit, which is, of course, the sum on a percentage of which you pay CGT. Its importance has, however, been reduced by FA 1998, which disapplies indexation to costs incurred after April 1998 by individuals.

The *offshore roll-up fund legislation* is only one example of a situation in which tax law deems a profit to be an income profit when it looks like a capital profit. (We shall be considering other examples in **Chapter 19**.) The 'deeming' provisions for investments in offshore roll-up funds are in ICTA 1988, ss. 757 to 764: see *Cases and Materials* (**3.2.2**). The provisions apply to collective investment schemes under FSA 1986.

They proceed on the basis that if, for instance, you are a shareholder in a non-resident company, and you do not receive any money from it – you let the dividends 'roll-up' – the eventual sale of your shares would otherwise be taxed as capital profits. This is because the profit would not be income, for the reasons discussed below, and the effect of allowing money to roll-up in the offshore company is to increase the value of your shares in that company. Provided the conditions of ss. 757 to 764 are fulfilled, however, the increase in value of the shares, the profit, is deemed to be an income profit.

The offshore roll-up fund legislation has been in force since FA 1984. Can you think why its importance may have become less since 1988?

Since 1988, the rates of tax paid by an individual on capital profits and income profits have been the same, which has meant that such schemes have lost much of their appeal.

3.3.3   INCOME PROFIT OR CAPITAL PROFIT?

There are two basic tests:

■   If an item forms part of the *permanent structure* of a business, then a profit on its sale will be a capital one (the *'permanent structure'* test).

■   If an item is *retained in a business* with the object of making profits, a profit on its disposal will be a capital profit, since the item counts as fixed capital (*the 'fixed capital' test*). However, goods acquired in order to be used or sold are known as circulating capital and a profit on the sale of these would be an income profit.

Note the application of the 'fixed capital' test in *Davis* v *Shell Company of China Ltd* (1951) 32 TC 133: see *Cases and Materials* (**3.2.3**).

In *Davis* v *Shell Company of China Ltd*, would any other tax have been payable on this one-off amount in 1951?

No. The facts took place before the introduction of CGT.

You win a National Lottery jackpot of £1,000,000. This gives you a windfall of 100% pure profit. Will you be liable to pay income tax on it?

No. It is a capital profit (also exempted from CGT under TCGA 1992, s. 51). Your subsequent dealings with it will have implications for taxes other than income tax, however, which may be every bit as nasty or even worse for you: see **27.3.1**.

3.4 Income Taxation and Indirect Taxation

Another distinction, that between direct and indirect taxation, is conventionally drawn in analyses of tax law: see *Cases and Materials* (**3.1**). We therefore need to consider briefly the relationship between indirect taxation and income taxation, especially VAT. VAT may of course be payable by a person in addition to any or all of income tax, corporation tax and NICs.

In principle, all taxes are either direct or indirect. All three forms of income taxation we have discussed so far, income tax, corporation tax and NICs, are direct taxes. A so-called direct tax is one which is charged directly on the person upon whom the burden of it ultimately falls.

3.4.1 INDIRECT TAXES GENERALLY

Income taxation, whether as income tax, corporation tax or NICs, is a form of direct taxation. Income tax and NICs on an individual's salary are charged directly on that individual. NICs are particularly burdensome since, being a form of income taxation in themselves, they are not tax-deductible: see **Chapter 6**. They are a form of direct taxation since, like income tax, you cannot generally shift the burden of them to someone else!

By contrast, the theory of *indirect taxation* is that it is not charged on the person on whom the burden of it ultimately falls. Instead, it is a charge incorporated into the price of goods or services. Although an indirect tax is actually charged on the supplier of the product (e.g. a sole trader), it is the customer who ultimately bears the burden of the tax, since the price of the product is higher than it would have been without the tax: see *Cases and Materials* (**3.3.1**). Examples of indirect taxation are customs duties and excise duties (e.g. wine, beer and tobacco duties), insurance premium tax (IPT) and landfill tax.

Customs duties do not apply for trade between Member States of the EU, since the EU is based on a customs union. However, excise duties do apply to trade in exciseable goods within the EU as with the rest of the world. IPT is an indirect tax which has been incorporated into the price of most everyday insurance premiums since 1 October 1994 (e.g. motor insurance and buildings and contents insurance). We only mention IPT in passing.

How could it be argued that corporation tax is an *indirect tax* on companies?

The burden of corporation tax is passed on to the company's customers through increases in the prices of the goods and services supplied by it.

3.4.2 VAT: A SPECIAL TYPE OF INDIRECT TAX

There is a more obvious example still of an indirect tax, i.e. VAT. This relatively recent tax is a direct consequence of the UK's status as an EU Member State. It relates to income taxation in a very interesting way, and it is worth taking some time to consider this relationship.

VAT is a tax on economic (i.e. business) activities. It is charged on supplies of goods or services made in the UK, by a taxable person, in the course or furtherance of a business, which are not exempt or zero-rated: VATA 1994, s. 4; see *Cases and Materials* (3.3.2). It is therefore relevant to anyone carrying on a business, individuals and companies alike, including individuals acting in the capacities of partners, trustees or PRs. It is not directly relevant to employment income or dividends, since neither are subject to VAT. However, it is directly relevant to trading income and rental income, especially rental income from commercial properties. In both cases, the income receipt may count, for VAT purposes, as the consideration for a supply. VATA 1994, s. 5(2)(a) states that a supply is anything done by the supplier for a consideration: see *Cases and Materials* (3.3.2).

A person carrying on a trade, in whatever capacity, may be liable to income or corporation tax, as we have said, on the profits of the trade. However, that person may *in addition* be liable for VAT on the prices of the goods or services supplied in the course of the trade, depending on a number of factors, including the level of its turnover in certain periods. Likewise, a landlord of commercial property, surprising as it may seem, may be liable not only to income or corporation tax on the rental profits, but also to VAT on the rents charged.

Sales of new commercial buildings count as taxable supplies: see *Cases and Materials* (17.2.1). Assume that Vatco Ltd, a taxable person, has agreed to sell an office block to Bert. What must Vatco Ltd ensure, in agreeing a price with Bert?

That the price incorporates a sum representing VAT for which Vatco must account to the tax authority: see **8.7**.

Note, however, that the term *taxable supplies* covers both supplies on which VAT must be charged at the standard rate – so called standard-rated supplies – and zero-rated supplies. This is important because, although a taxable person must not charge VAT on a zero-rated supply, zero-rated supplies are treated in all other respects as though they were taxable supplies. This makes zero-rated supplies the most favourably-treated supplies in VAT terms.

Why might it be argued that VAT is *not* a form of income taxation?

VAT is not charged by a taxable person on the profit element of the price of goods or services, but on the value of the supply, i.e. the whole price charged by the taxable person.

If a person makes standard-rated supplies exceeding certain levels (see **19.5**), it must account to the tax authority for VAT on those supplies, as a *taxable person*. This is called *output VAT* or *output tax* and is charged to customers on the prices of the goods and services supplied to them. By the same token, VAT charged on supplies made to a taxable person, by other taxable persons, is called its *input VAT* or *input tax*. We consider how much VAT a taxable person must charge in **Chapter 8**. The crucial point for the taxable person is that, if it makes only standard-rated or zero-rated supplies, it can deduct its input VAT *in full* from its output VAT. Usually every quarter, the taxable person accounts to the tax authority for the excess of output VAT over input VAT in that quarter. If its input VAT exceeds its output VAT in that quarter, however, the difference can be reclaimed from the tax authority. All this depends, however, on the taxable person being a *fully-taxable person*, i.e. one who makes only taxable supplies. If it is not a fully-taxable person, then it may not be able to reclaim all or part of its input VAT. Either individuals or companies may be taxable persons if they are, or are required to be, registered for VAT. A person is required to be registered for VAT if it makes taxable supplies in excess of certain limits.

As a trader and a taxable person, will your input VAT be a form of income taxation if you only make taxable supplies? What if you are a trader and you only make exempt supplies? What if you are an ordinary individual who is not a taxable person?

If you are a taxable person making only taxable supplies, your input VAT will not be a form of income taxation, since you will be entitled to deduct it all. As a trader making only exempt supplies, however, your input VAT will be a form of income taxation, since you will not be entitled to deduct any of it.

Educational institutions, who make predominantly exempt supplies (see VATA 1994, sch 9, Group 6) often have a huge burden of input VAT which cannot be reclaimed by them. The position is the same for the ordinary individual, being someone who does not make supplies at all, as for the person who makes only exempt supplies. Other charities, ones which do not make taxable supplies at all, also carry large burdens of input VAT which cannot be reclaimed by them: see *Cases and Materials* (**3.3.2**).

On the basis of the above points, is VAT a form of income taxation?

VAT is only a form of income taxation for the person who cannot deduct input VAT, and who obtains no income tax or corporation tax deduction for irrecoverable VAT. These are basically persons who are not taxable persons and who are not traders or landlords. The fact that VAT is paid by them out of their taxed income means that for you, as an individual who is not a taxable person, VAT can properly be described as a form of income taxation, even though it is an indirect tax.

Why is it so important that VAT has a neutral effect so far as the trader who makes only taxable supplies, is concerned?

VAT does not discourage specialisation. No matter how many stages a product may go through, in the manufacture and distribution process, VAT is charged only on the value added by each stage in the process, not on any VAT charged by anyone else in that chain of manufacture and distribution. This, together with a taxable person's right to deduct all their input VAT, makes the effect of VAT neutral, except in relation to exempt supplies. VAT therefore satisfies the efficiency principle: see **1.5.5**.

3.5 Summary

The fact that VAT may be seen as a form of income taxation does not exclude it from being a form of capital taxation, too. As we mentioned much earlier, VAT does not rely on the distinction between income and capital. Corporation tax and income tax, however, do rely on the distinction. This is because the thinking of the eighteenth-century political economist, Adam Smith, closely informed the drafters of the original income tax legislation. Traces of the original legislation can still be found in the most recent income tax legislation. The distinction was carried over into corporation tax, since corporation tax is an amalgam of income tax and CGT. We now need to consider a few more introductory concepts, before moving on to looking at what makes a person liable to tax on their income profits, and the profits on which that tax is payable.

3.6   End of Chapter Assessment Question

Amber Ltd (see **2.6**) is registered for VAT. It makes only supplies taxable at the standard rate. Comment on the implications of these facts, paying particular attention to the question of whether, in your opinion, VAT is a form of income taxation for Amber Ltd.

(Word limit: 200 (100 marks).)

See *Cases and Materials* (**3.5**), for a specimen answer.

CHAPTER FOUR

INCOME TAXATION: TAX PERIODS, TAX AVOIDANCE AND RESIDENCE

4.1 Objectives

By the end of this chapter, you should be able to:

■ explain the significance of the expression *tax period*;

■ differentiate between *tax avoidance* and *tax evasion*;

■ write down the *Ramsay* principle;

■ give the meaning of *residence, ordinary residence, presence* and *domicile*;

■ begin to develop an *approach to reading* tax law;

■ explain the significance of *Pepper* v *Hart* [1993] 1 All ER 42;

■ state briefly the functions of the main *income taxation authorities*.

4.2 Introduction

In this chapter, we conclude our introduction to income taxation. The points discussed are connected in only the most general way. None the less, they are crucial to a proper understanding of later chapters. To start with, we identify the tax periods for each type of income taxation, including VAT. Then we examine how the courts have tried to counter tax avoidance, using the *Ramsay* principle. We shall be referring to the *Ramsay* principle at various stages of the book, so it is important to understand it now. Also important is an understanding of the important concepts of *residence, ordinary residence, presence* and *domicile*, also to be examined in this chapter. Towards the end, we identify the main tax authorities in the UK, and try to draw some conclusions about the way in which reading tax law should be approached. In this context, we discuss the implications of the judgment of the House of Lords in *Pepper* v *Hart* [1993] 1 All ER 42 (*Cases and Materials* (4.1)).

4.3 Tax Periods

In deciding when a person is liable to income taxation and, if so, the amount taxable, it is necessary to consider a particular *tax period*. *Tax period* is a general term for the period of time by reference to which the particular form of income taxation under consideration is calculated. Tax periods are different for each type of income taxation.

4.3.1   INCOME TAX

The tax year begins on 6 April in one calendar year and ends on 5 April in the following calendar year. This comes from ICTA 1988, s. 2(2) and the reason for it is historical: see *Cases and Materials* (**4.2.1**). It applies whatever the capacity in which you are liable to pay income tax. In **7.3**, we shall consider how Stage One of your income tax calculation involves gathering together the various sources of your income in the tax year under consideration. Each source of income falls under one of four Schedules: A, D, E and F: see **5.4**. The tax period for A, E, F and the Cases of Schedule D, other than Cases I and II, is the tax year under consideration (e.g. 1998/99). However, for Schedule D, Cases I and II only, the tax period is generally the *accounting period* which ends in the tax year under consideration. There are three exceptions to this, however, which apply to:

(a)   the *opening years* of a trade, profession or vocation;

(b)   the *closing years* of a trade, profession or vocation; and

(c)   a change in the partners of a firm.

4.3.1.1   *Opening year* rules

These rules apply to sole traders and partners:

- for the *first tax year*, the profits from commencement of the trade or profession, to the following 5 April are included in Stage One of your income tax calculation;

- for the *second tax year*, the income profits of the accounting period ending in that second tax year are included in Stage One of your income tax calculation; *and*

- for the *third tax year and later tax years*, the income profits of the accounting period ending in that third or later tax year, as appropriate, are included in Stage One of your income tax calculation.

The effect of these rules is to produce *double taxation* of some of the first year's profit, where your accounting period ends on some date other than 5 April. *Overlap relief*, which is beyond the scope of this book, is available to minimise the unfairness of this double taxation.

4.3.1.2   *Closing-year* rules

As a sole trader or partner, the income profits which go in Stage One of your income tax calculation for the tax year in which your business ceases are the income profits for the period from the end of the previous accounting period to the date of discontinuance. Say the partners of Briggs & Co. make up their accounts to 30 June in each calendar year. On 31 January 1999, the partnership is discontinued. Say that each partner's income profits for the accounting period ending on 30 June 1998 are £800,000. From 1 July 1998 to 31 January 1999, the income profits of each partner are £400,000. The income profits of each partner for the accounting period ending on 30 June 1997 (tax year 1997/98) are £777,000. The tax periods of each partner for the tax years 1997/98, 1998/99 and 1999/2000 are:

1997/98   Accounting period to 30 June 1997 – £777,000;
1998/99   Accounting period to 30 June 1998 – £800,000; and
            Period from 1 July 1998 to 31 January 1999 – £400,000.

If, having begun to carry on your business in one tax year, you cease trading in the next tax year, the position is as follows. The figure for your Schedule D, Case I income profits is your income profits from the end of the first tax year, until discontinuance. If, for some reason, you not only begin, but also end your trade in one and the same tax year, the figure which goes in Stage One of your income tax calculation for that tax year would be the *actual income profit*, if any, earned in the trade.

4.3.1.3   Changes in a firm

If a partner in a firm leaves the partnership in the tax year under consideration, there will be no effect on the tax periods operating for the continuing partners, provided at least one partner is a partner in the firm both before and after the change in partners: ICTA 1988, s. 113(2). So far as the partner who leaves is concerned, that person's trade or profession will have ceased in the tax year, so the rule in **4.3.1.2** applies to the income profits made by the partner in the partnership he or she has left. If no partner is a partner in the firm both before and after the change in partners, then all the partners will be treated as having discontinued their trade or profession and the income profits included in Stage One of their individual income tax calculations for the tax year under consideration will be determined as above.

Suppose that, instead of Briggs & Co. being discontinued on 31 January 1999, Annette Briggs, one of its 12 partners, leaves Briggs & Co. to join another firm on that date. Say that her share of the income profits of the period from 1 July 1998 to 31 January 1999 is £400,000/12, i.e. £33,333. The figure for inclusion in Stage One of her individual income tax calculation for 1998/99 will be determined as follows:

Tax year 1997/98   Accounting period to 30 June 1997, £777,000/12 = £64,750;
Tax year 1998/99   Accounting period to 30 June 1998, £800,000/12 = £66,666; *and*
                     Period from 1 July 1998 to 31 January 1999, £33,333.

So far as Annette's joining her new firm is concerned, the opening year rules will apply to the calculation of her income profits as a partner in the new firm for 1998/99: see **4.3.1.1**.

4.3.2   CORPORATION TAX

The tax period is different for the taxation of companies. Corporation tax is charged on both income profits and capital profits of companies, although according to different rules for each type of profit.

Tax on both the income and capital profits of companies is charged by reference to a financial year, which begins on 1 April in one calendar year and ends on 31 March in the following calendar year: ICTA 1988, s. 834(1): see *Cases and Materials* (4.2.2). The financial year 1998 is thus the period from 1 April 1998 to 31 March 1999.

However, corporation tax is calculated on a company's *profits chargeable to corporation tax*, not for each financial year, but for each of the company's *accounting periods*: see **7.4**. The expression *accounting period*, as used in relation to companies, is not to be confused with the use of the same expression in relation to partners and sole traders. Unfortunately, the same term is used to describe the tax period of a company as is used to describe the period by reference to which income profits are calculated for the tax year under consideration of a partner or sole trader.

For a company, an accounting period begins either at the end of the previous one or, when a new business of the company begins, as soon as the company becomes liable to pay corporation tax on the income profits of the business. It ends 12 months later unless the company ceases in the meantime to be liable to corporation tax. If, therefore, an accounting period of a particular company runs across two financial years in which corporation tax rates are different, then the *profits chargeable to corporation tax* of the accounting period must be apportioned and the rate for each financial year applied to each part so apportioned. For instance, corporation tax rates will differ as between the 1998 financial year and the 1999 financial year, since the rates of corporation tax will reduce by 1% in the 1999 financial year.

In the case of companies, therefore, the tax year under consideration for our purposes must be read as the *accounting period under consideration*.

4.3.3   NATIONAL INSURANCE CONTRIBUTIONS

NICs fall into a number of different Classes: see **Chapter 6**. For the present, note that Class 1 contributions (which apply to employed earners and employers) and Class 2 contributions (which apply to self-employed earners) are recorded on the basis of years ending on 5 April in each calendar year.

Liability to pay these Classes of contributions arises on the basis of *contribution weeks* (Class 2) and *earnings periods* (Class 1), rather than on an annual basis. These are referred to together as *contributions periods*. However, *Class 1A* contributions (payable by employers in relation to company cars) do arise on an annual basis, as also do Class 4 contributions. Earnings periods are generally the same as the intervals between payments of earnings, provided they exceed one week. There is an exception for directors, whose earnings period is one year, irrespective of the intervals between the payments of their earnings: see SSCR 1979 (SI 1979 No. 591), reg. 6A(3).

4.3.4   VALUE ADDED TAX

A taxable person accounts for the excess of *output VAT* over input VAT, or reclaims all or part of any excess of *input VAT* over output VAT, usually every quarter of a calendar year, i.e. for every VAT return period.

■   For each return period, the output VAT for which the taxable person is liable to account, or the input VAT which that person is entitled to reclaim, is calculated on a provisional basis.

■   Any adjustments are then made at the end of the VAT prescribed accounting period, namely a period of a year ending on 31 March, 30 April or 31 May in any calendar year: see VATR 1995 (SI 1995 No. 2518), reg. 99.

Basford Ltd started to trade on 1 October 1997. It registered for VAT immediately: see 8.5. It has employees in respect of which it must pay secondary Class 1 NICs. What are the tax periods relevant to Basford Ltd, in relation to:

(a)   **corporation tax;**

(b)   **VAT; and**

(c)   **NICs?**

See the discussion above.

4.4   Tax Avoidance

Unlike *tax evasion*, which is illegal, *tax avoidance* is not illegal. A famous case from the 1930s, *IRC* v *Duke of Westminster* [1935] All ER Rep 259, the tax avoidance scheme in which is long outdated, established the principle that persons are entitled to order their affairs in the most tax advantageous way: see *Cases and Materials* (**4.3**).

However, a subsequent line of cases, beginning with *WT Ramsay Ltd* v *IRC* [1982] AC 300 and *Furniss* v *Dawson* [1984] 1 All ER 530 has established that:

■ the courts may nullify a tax advantage sought to be obtained where there is a *pre-ordained series of transactions* or a *single composite transaction*, having steps inserted which have no commercial purpose other than the avoidance of tax.

This is called the *Ramsay* principle.

We shall return to a detailed survey of these cases in **Chapter 25**. For the moment, however, note the existence of the *Ramsay* principle, and be able to write it down from memory. Unlike *IRC* v *Duke of Westminster*, which says in effect that it is the *form* of a transaction which matters, *Ramsay* v *IRC* and *Furniss* v *Dawson* insist that there are circumstances where the courts can look at the *substance* of a series of transactions in their entirety to strike down the tax advantage sought to be obtained by a tax avoidance scheme.

Craven v *White* [1988] 3 All ER 495 and *IRC* v *Fitzwilliam* [1993] 3 All ER 184 indicated a desire to limit the *Ramsay* principle, by reference to the concept that it was a rule of statutory construction. More recently, *IRC* v *McGuckian* [1997] 3 All ER 817 (see *Cases and Materials* (**4.3**)) has extended the scope of the *Ramsay* principle, by adopting a *purposive*, rather than a *literal* principle of construction.

In addition to this case law, taxation statutes often contain anti-avoidance provisions. The Government has recently announced its intention to introduce a *statutory anti-avoidance measure*.

ACTIVITY 5

Read the extracts from *IRC* v *McGuckian* in *Cases and Materials* (4.3). Take a separate sheet of paper, and keep it with you throughout your reading of the book. On it, list as many anti-avoidance provisions as you can, noting exactly how each one operates.

It is fair to say that tax avoidance, in relation to income taxation, usually seems to involve manipulating the rules as to the availability of deductions and reliefs: see **Chapters 9** to **13**.

4.5   Residence and Domicile

These two concepts are fundamental to a person's liability for direct taxation, including income tax, corporation tax and NICs.

■ *Residence* is mainly important to the taxation of income profits and investment profits.

■ *Domicile* is mainly important to the taxation of gratuitous transfers (see **Chapters 26 to 33**). However, it also has a part to play in determining individuals' liability to pay income tax on emoluments from their employment, and the residence of trustees and PRs.

The exact significance of each concept depends on the provision of the tax legislation under consideration. It is possible for a person to be resident in more than one country at the same time.

The *direct* tax system operates on the basic principle that, provided a person's connection with the UK is close enough, that person will be taxed on income profits wherever in the world they come from. According to the same principle, if a person's connection is only a tenuous one, then that person will be taxed on income arising only in the UK. The required degree of connection is determined primarily by the terms *residence* and *domicile*. The principle is called *the territoriality principle*.

The territoriality principle was justified by Lord Wrenbury in *Whitney* v *IRC* (1926) 10 TC 88, 112, thus:

> The [UK resident] . . . is taxed because (whether he be a British subject or not) he enjoys the benefit of our laws for the protection of his person and his property. The [non-UK resident] . . . is taxed because in respect of his property in the UK he enjoys the benefit of our laws for the protection of that property.

The *indirect* tax system operates on a different principle. For instance, for VAT purposes, the crucial question is the *place of supply* or *place of importation or acquisition* of goods or services. Special rules exist to answer these questions, which are outside the scope of this book.

4.5.1   RESIDENCE OF INDIVIDUALS

Residence means '[t]o dwell permanently or for a considerable time, to have one's settled or usual abode, to live in or at a particular place': *Levene* v *IRC* [1928] AC 217, 222, per Lord Cave LC.

To be resident in the UK in the tax year under consideration, you must be *physically present in the UK during some part of that tax year*. In practice, the following factors are taken into account:

■ *The six-month rule*: you will be resident in the UK in the tax year under consideration if you spend six months or longer in this country in that tax year in question: ICTA 1988, s. 336.

■ *Established ordinary residence*: you will remain resident in the UK in the tax year under consideration, even if you go abroad for an occasional residence, where you have been ordinarily resident in the UK during the previous tax year. *Ordinary residence* is explained below.

■ *Temporary residence*: depending on whether your visits to the UK are *frequent* or *substantial*, you may be UK-resident even if you spend less than six months in the UK during the tax year under consideration.

ACTIVITY 6

Read the extracts from IR20 in *Cases and Materials* (4.4.1). Consider the circumstances in which a visitor to the UK could be resident here in a tax year.

4.5.2   RESIDENCE OF COMPANIES

With effect from 15 March 1988, a company is resident in the UK for corporation tax purposes if:

■   it was incorporated in the UK; or

■   even if it was not incorporated in the UK, if its central management and control is located in the UK: FA 1988, s. 66, sch 7, SP 1/90.

(See *Cases and Materials* (4.4.2).)

4.5.3   RESIDENCE OF PARTNERS

If, as a partner, you are resident in the UK, you will be liable to pay income tax on your share of the trading profits of the partnership, wherever in the world they have been made.

4.5.4   RESIDENCE OF TRUSTEES AND PRs

4.5.4.1   Trustees

If you are one of a number of trustees and your number includes one UK-resident and one non-UK-resident trustee in any part of the tax year under consideration, all of you will be resident in the UK in that tax year unless, at the point the trust was set up, or funds were paid into it, the settlor was *not* resident, *not* ordinarily resident and *not* domiciled in the UK: FA 1989, ss. 110, 111 and 151.

The residence of the trustees is not always the crucial factor in determining whether income generated by trust property is subject to income tax. If the beneficiaries have an *immediate entitlement to the income*, it is the *beneficiaries' residence as individuals* which is the crucial factor in determining the liability to income tax of the income of the trust property: see **2.4.2.2**.

4.5.4.2   Personal representatives

A very similar rule applies for determining the residence of PRs to the rule for determining the residence of trustees. Imagine you are a PR of a deceased individual and resident in the UK. Finance Act 1989, s. 111 states that a deceased individual's PRs are deemed to include any PRs appointed under a foreign will: FA 1989, s. 111(3)(d). If therefore, at the date of the deceased's death, there were UK and foreign PRs then, unless at that date the deceased was *not* resident, *not* ordinarily resident *and* not domiciled in the UK (FA 1989, ss. 110, 111 and 151), both of you, the UK PR, and the foreign PRs, will be deemed to be resident in the UK.

Prior to his death on 1 September 1998, Gunter was *domiciled* in Germany (see 4.5.5), but *resident* in the UK. He had made a UK will, appointing UK-resident executors, to administer property owned by him in the UK. Before coming to the UK, he had also made a German will, appointing German executors, to administer his German property.

Who will be his executors for the purposes of UK income taxation? (Assume that the two wills are perfectly consistent with each other.)

Both the UK and German executors appointed under each will.

4.5.5   DOMICILE

The connection with the UK necessary for the taxation of income is mainly founded on *residence*. Domicile is only occasionally important. We return to the concept when we consider the taxation of gratuitous transfers. Suffice it to say for the present that you must have a domicile and that you can only be domiciled in one place at a time: *Re Clore (No. 2)* [1984] STC 609.

4.5.6   ORDINARY RESIDENCE

This means habitual residence. In the tax year under consideration, therefore, you could be *ordinarily resident* in the UK but not *resident*, and *vice versa*.

4.5.7   PRESENCE

Presence is a term of relevance in relation to NICs. It seems to mean what it suggests.

4.6   Reading Tax Law

Nowhere is the precise meaning of words more important than in tax law. It is therefore necessary to develop a way of reading a provision of a tax statute which enables you to ascertain quickly the essence of that provision, whilst giving due attention to its detail: see *Cases and Materials* (4.5). Always begin by asking what a particular section is trying to achieve.

Words are to be given their ordinary meaning:

> One has to look merely at what is clearly said. There is no room for any intendment. There is no equity about a tax. There is no presumption as to a tax. Nothing is to be read in, nothing is to be implied. One can only look fairly at the language used.

(*Cape Brandy Syndicate* v *IRC* [1921] 1 KB 64, 71, per Rowlatt J.)

Cases on tax law are almost always concerned with statutory interpretation. However, other materials may be relied on by the relevant taxation authority, namely Inland Revenue Statements of Practice (SPs) and Extra-Statutory Concessions (ESCs). An ESC may not be used for tax avoidance. Judicial attitudes to ESCs vary. In *Vestey (No. 2) v IRC* [1979] 2 All ER 225, 233, Walton J asked:

> If this kind of concession can be made, where does it stop: and why are some groups favoured against others? . . . This is not a simple matter of tax law. What is happening is that, in effect, despite the words of Maitland, commenting on the Bill of Rights, 'this is the last of the dispensing power', the Crown is now claiming just such a power . . .

Contrast McNeill J in *R v IRC, ex parte Fulford-Dobson* [1987] STC 344: see **Cases and Materials (4.5)**.

Note also the effect of the decision in *Pepper v Hart* [1993] 1 All ER 42. We consider the exact issue involved in the case in **14.3.4**, but it is also summarised in **Cases and Materials (4.1)**. *Pepper v Hart* was of relevance in all areas of law, since it established the circumstances in which Parliamentary material could be used to ascertain the intention of Parliament in passing legislation.

Under *Pepper v Hart*, Parliamentary material may be consulted when:

■ legislation is ambiguous, obscure or leads to absurdity;

■ the statements on which it is sought to rely are clear; and

■ it consists of ministerial statements or statements by the promoter of a Bill and other material needed to understand the effect of the statement.

Do you think *Pepper v Hart* will often be of use in interpreting a tax statute?

Not very often – the circumstances in which Parliamentary materials can be consulted under the principle of *Pepper v Hart* are very restrictive.

Cases and Materials (**4.5**) contains extracts from Lord Browne-Wilkinson's speech in the case, together with an article highly critical of the decision.

A so-called *tax law rewrite* was instigated by the last Government in 1995, intending to simplify the language of tax legislation, generally without disturbing the substance of it. Sections of the rewritten legislation were published in 1996, and FA 1998 contains, e.g., a new ICTA 1988, s. 148, drafted on this basis (see **14.3.3**: termination payments to employees).

4.7 UK Tax Authorities

For direct taxation, the relevant tax authority is generally the Inland Revenue, although NICs are presently administered by the DSS's Contributions Agency. Chancellor Gordon Brown announced on 17 March 1998 that the Contributions Agency will be transferred from the DSS to the Inland Revenue in April 1999. The relevant tax authority for VAT and duties of customs and excise is Customs, which is also the relevant taxation authority for insurance premium tax (IPT) and landfill tax: see **17.8.3**. Appeal procedures apply for both direct and indirect taxes (**Chapter 19**), although they are currently very limited for NICs.

4.8   Summary

In this chapter, we have noted that tax periods do not necessarily coincide with the accounting periods of an individual who has a source of income under Schedule D, Cases I or II. We have also noted that the expression 'accounting period' is used in a different sense for sole traders and partners from the sense in which it is used for companies.

The *Ramsay* principle has been introduced in outline, and we are now alert for legislative examples of rules designed to prevent tax avoidance in specific cases. We are also aware of the principles emerging from *Pepper* v *Hart*.

The Inland Revenue, together with the Contributions Agency, are the main income taxation authorities in the UK. VAT and other indirect taxes are administered by HM Customs and Excise. In **Chapter 5**, we begin to analyse the *scheme* of income taxation, and conclude this analysis in **Chapter 8**.

4.9   End of Chapter Assessment Questions

(a) 'Every tax avoidance scheme involves a trick and a pretence. It is the task of the Revenue to unravel the trick and the duty of the court to ignore the pretence.'

(*Matrix-Securities Ltd* v *IRC* [1994] 1 All ER 769, 780, per Lord Templeman.)

Briefly discuss the issues raised by this quotation.

(Word limit: 250 (50 marks).)

(b) Refer to **2.6**, and note the following additional facts. Amber Ltd makes its accounts up to 31 December in each calendar year. Amber Ltd was incorporated in the UK on 20 April 1990.

The firm of solicitors in which Deborah is a partner, Brown & Co., makes its accounts up to 30 November in each calendar year. The same firm has been in business for many years, although one of the partners retired from the firm on 30 November 1997.

Comment on the significance of these facts, in terms of income tax and corporation tax.

(Word limit: 40 (50 marks).)

See *Cases and Materials* (**4.7**), for specimen answers.

CHAPTER FIVE

INCOME TAX AND CORPORATION TAX: LIABILITY AND INCOME SOURCES

5.1 Objectives

By the end of this chapter, you should be able to:

■ explain *how* liability to pay income tax or corporation tax arises in the tax period under consideration;

■ identify *which* income profits are included in a person's income tax or corporation tax calculation;

■ relate these points to an individual liable to pay income tax in the capacity of a partner, a trustee or a PR;

■ describe *the Schedular System*.

5.2 Introduction

In this chapter, we seek to answer two questions, for both income tax and corporation tax. We ask the same two questions in **Chapter 6**, in relation to NICs. The first question is that of *how* a person is liable to pay income tax or corporation tax, as the case may be, in the tax period under consideration. The second question is that of *which* of a person's income profits must be included in that person's income tax or corporation tax calculation for that tax period.

In *Cases and Materials* (5.1), there is a discussion of the political and economic context of these questions.

5.3 Persons Liable to Pay Income Tax or Corporation Tax

In answering the first of the questions, the concept of *residence* (see **4.5**) is fundamental, whether an individual or a company is involved, and whatever the capacity in which an individual is liable to pay income tax. The concept of *ordinary residence* (see **4.5.6**) may be important, in addition to that of residence, if employment income is under consideration, or if individuals are liable to pay income tax as trustees or PRs. It may be helpful to refer to **4.5**, before reading further.

Note that all references to income taxation in this book are to UK income taxation only. This is important for two reasons. First, even if a person is not liable to income taxation, that person may still be liable to comparable taxation in another jurisdiction. Secondly, a person could be liable to pay some form of income taxation in the other jurisdiction, as well as being liable to pay income taxation in the UK. In the second situation, the person in question needs to obtain some form of *double taxation relief*: see **Cases and Materials (5.2)**.

SAQ 39

In the 1998/99 tax year, Arthur is resident in the Isle of Man, having sold up his UK business in 1992. Although he is not resident in the UK, he continues to receive dividends from a number of UK-resident companies. What is his tax problem here?

He is liable to pay both Isle of Man and UK income tax on the dividends.

5.3.1 INDIVIDUALS

Whether you, the individual, are liable to income taxation, depends on whether you are resident in the UK in the tax year under consideration. The relevant rules are detailed. However, their effect can be summarised thus. Where you are resident in the UK in the tax year under consideration, you are liable to pay income tax on the whole of your income profits in that tax year, whatever their source and wherever that source is located. It does not matter that the source of any of your income profits is located outside the UK.

Income profits coming from a source outside the UK are referred to as *foreign income*. If you are resident in the UK in the tax year under consideration, you are referred to as a *UK taxpayer*.

By contrast, where you are not resident in the UK in the tax year under consideration, the rule is that you are liable to pay income tax only on income profits arising in the UK in that tax year. If you are not resident in the UK in the tax year, you are referred to as a *foreign taxpayer*.

5.3.1.1 UK taxpayers

The detailed rules for identifying the income profits on which you are liable to pay income tax, as a UK taxpayer, on income profits from various sources are as follows.

Employment income ('emoluments')
A distinction is made between foreign emoluments and UK emoluments. Foreign emoluments are emoluments paid to an employee who is not domiciled in the UK, and who is employed by a non-UK-resident employer: ICTA 1988, s. 192: see **Cases and Materials (5.2.1.1)**. *UK emoluments* are all emoluments which are not within this definition of foreign emoluments. Accordingly, the position in relation to employees is as follows:

Where you are resident *and* ordinarily resident in the UK in the tax year under consideration, you are liable to pay income tax on both your UK emoluments *and* on your foreign emoluments. The fact that any foreign emoluments have not been sent back to the UK, i.e. *remitted to the UK*, does not affect your liability to income tax on those foreign emoluments – you are still liable to income tax on them: Schedule E, Case I, s. 19(1).

There is, however, an important exception to this rule. This is where you are resident and ordinarily resident in the UK in the tax year under consideration, but you are required by your employment to perform your duties as an employee *wholly outside* the UK. In this situation, you should only be liable to pay income tax on foreign emoluments which have been remitted to the UK: ICTA 1988, s. 192(2).

SAQ 40

Consider these situations:

(a) **I am employed by Boris GmbH, a German-resident company, and I am resident and ordinarily resident in the UK in the tax year 1998/99. Will I be liable to pay UK income tax on my salary in 1998/99? Is my salary a UK emolument?**

(b) **I am employed by Charles Ltd, a UK-resident company. I am resident and ordinarily resident in the UK in the tax year 1998/99. I am given the duty of seeking investment opportunities in the Czech Republic, and it is necessary for me to go and live there. Whilst abroad, my salary will continue to be paid from Nottingham. Will I be liable to pay UK income tax on my salary in the tax year 1998/99? Is my salary a UK emolument?**

As to (a), Yes – my emoluments are UK emoluments. As to (b), Yes – my emoluments are UK emoluments.

Where you are resident, but not ordinarily resident, in the UK in the tax year under consideration, you are only liable to pay income tax on your emoluments for work performed in the UK as an employee: Schedule E, Case II, ICTA 1988, s. 19(1).

Where you are not resident, *nor* ordinarily resident in the UK in the tax year under consideration, you are only liable to pay income tax on your emoluments for that tax year, for work performed in the UK as an employee: Schedule E, Case II, ICTA 1988, s. 19(1).

SAQ 41

Diane is a columnist for a Paris magazine. She is domiciled in France and, in the tax year 1998/99, is resident in the UK. She is paid direct by her employer, the publishing company, which is resident in France. Is Diane liable to pay income tax on her salary in the tax year 1998/99? Is her salary a foreign emolument?

Yes, she is liable – her salary is a *foreign* emolument.

Where you are resident, whether or not you are ordinarily resident, in the UK in the tax year under consideration, and:

(a) your emoluments are foreign emoluments; and

(b) you performed your duties as an employee wholly outside the UK;

then you are only liable to pay income tax on these foreign emoluments for that tax year if they have been remitted to the UK: Schedule E, Case III, ICTA 1988, ss. 19(1) and 192(2).

Where you are resident, but not ordinarily resident, in the UK in the tax year under consideration, and you performed your duties as employee *outside* the UK, you are liable to pay income tax on your emoluments for the tax year only if they have been remitted to the UK: Schedule E, Case III, ICTA 1988, s. 19(1).

Eduardo, domiciled in Spain, is a waiter who is resident in the UK in the tax year 1998/99 and who is employed by an hotel company resident in Spain. In the tax year 1998/99, he is seconded by his employer on a daily basis to a restaurant in Guernsey but returns to the UK every evening. His salary is paid direct by his Spanish employers. Is he liable to pay income tax on his salary? Is his salary a foreign emolument? On what part of his salary is he liable to pay income tax?

Yes. The salary is a foreign emolument. If he can demonstrate that he performed his duties wholly outside the UK, i.e. in Guernsey, he will only have to pay income tax on so much of his salary as is remitted to the UK by his employers. He might also be liable to Guernsey income tax.

Where emoluments are taxed only if they are sent back to the UK, they are described as being taxed on the *remittance basis*. This contrasts with the so-called *arising basis*, where you would be taxed whether or not the income profits were remitted to the UK.

Rental income
If you are resident in the UK in the tax year under consideration, you are liable to pay income tax on the rental profits from letting property in that tax year, wherever the property is situated: Schedule A, ICTA 1988, s. 15(1) (UK lettings); Schedule D, Case V, ICTA 1988, s. 18(3) (non-UK lettings).

In the 1998/99 tax year, you are resident in the UK and own a house in Brittany, which you let out to tenants. Are you liable to pay income tax on the rental profits?

Yes. You may also be liable to pay French income tax.

Dividend income
As a shareholder, if you are resident in the UK in the tax year under consideration, you are liable to pay income tax on any dividend income from your shares in that tax year, wherever the company in which the shares are owned by you is resident: Schedule F, ICTA 1988, s. 20(1) (UK companies); Schedule D, Case V, ICTA 1988, s. 18(3) (overseas companies).

SAQ 44

You are resident in the UK, and you are a shareholder in a French-resident company, François SA. Are you liable to pay income tax on any dividends you receive?

Yes.

Trading income
Where you are resident in the UK in the tax year under consideration, unless the *whole* of your trade is carried on overseas, you are liable to income tax on the whole of the income profits of your accounting period ending in that tax year: ICTA 1988, s. 18(3), Schedule D, Case I.

Interest
Where you are resident in the UK in the tax year under consideration, you are liable to pay income tax on the whole of any interest on the loan arising in the tax year, irrespective of where the source of the interest payments is located: ICTA 1988, s. 18(3), Schedule D, Case III.

Note, however, that if you are a lender domiciled outside the UK, you are liable to pay income tax on interest arising in the tax year from foreign securities *only* if the interest is remitted to the UK: ICTA 1988, s. 65(5), Schedule D, Case IV.

UK taxpayers: a summary
That covers *UK taxpayers*. Your income profits from any one or more of these sources on which you are liable to income tax are gathered together in Stage One of your income tax calculation for the tax year: see **Chapter 7**.

5.3.1.2   Foreign taxpayers

The rules for determining whether you are liable to pay income tax, as a foreign taxpayer, on any of the sources of income discussed in **5.3.1.1** are as follows:

■ *Employment income*: the position is as discussed in **5.3.1.1**: Schedule E, Case II, ICTA 1988, s. 19(1).

■ *Rental income*: even if you are not resident in the UK in the tax year under consideration, you are liable to pay income tax on the income profit from the letting in that tax year: ICTA 1988, s. 42A; Taxation of Income from Land (Non-Residents) Regulations 1995 (SI 1995 No. 2902) – this contains provisions on the mechanics of tax collection here: see *Cases and Materials* (**5.2.1.2**).

SAQ 45

Femi, resident in Nigeria in the 1998/99 tax year, owns a flat in London, which he lets out. Is he liable to pay UK income tax on the rental profits?

Yes.

■ *Dividend income*: if you are not resident in the UK in the tax year under consideration, you are liable to pay income tax on your UK dividend income in that tax year. Dividends are, however, subject to special rules: ICTA 1988, s. 231(1).

- *Trading income*: if you are not resident in the UK in the tax year under consideration, you are liable to pay income tax on your income profits in that tax year if the trade is conducted within the UK, i.e. not *wholly* outside it.

- *Interest*: if you are not resident in the UK in the tax year under consideration, your income tax liability is limited to tax deducted at source by the payer: FA 1995, s. 128.

These are the circumstances in which you are liable to pay income tax *even though* you are a *foreign taxpayer*.

5.3.2   COMPANIES

Whether a company is liable to pay corporation tax on its income profits depends on whether it is resident in the UK or not. Unlike with individuals, however, there is no distinction between residence and ordinary residence. If the company is resident in the UK, it is liable to pay corporation tax on the whole of its income profits of an accounting period, wherever they arise: ICTA 1988, s. 8(1): see *Cases and Materials* (**5.2.2.1**).

It does not matter that the source of these income profits is located outside the UK – the company is still liable to corporation tax on those profits. Any income profits coming from a source located outside the UK are referred to as *foreign income*. If a company is resident in the UK, it is referred to as being a *UK company*.

By contrast, if the company is not resident in the UK, it is liable to pay corporation tax on any income profits from a trade carried on in the UK through a branch or agency (ICTA 1988, s. 11(1)) and *income tax* on any other income profits arising from a source located in the UK: ICTA 1988, s. 6(2).

A branch or agency is defined as any factorship, agency, receivership, branch or management: ICTA 1988, s. 834. If the company is not resident in the UK, it is referred to as an *overseas company*. If there were no branch or agency, any trading profits would automatically be subject to *income tax*, although it would be arguable as to which tax authority should seek to collect it!

5.3.2.1   UK companies

A company may have a number of sources of income (the term sole trader is not used to describe a *trading company*).

The rule for determining on which income profits a UK company pays corporation tax is a very simple one. A UK company is liable to pay corporation tax on its income profits wherever they are made.

A UK company can normally avoid foreign taxation, however, by merely trading *with* another country, using a *representative office* only, in the foreign jurisdiction. Whether it can so avoid foreign taxation depends on the definition of 'permanent establishment' in the relevant double tax treaty.

SAQ 46

Georgina Ltd is a UK company which manufactures bicycles for export to Malaysia, where it has a representative office. Will it be liable to corporation tax on the trading profits?

Yes. It could also be liable to pay Malaysian income taxation.

5.3.2.2 Overseas companies

Overseas companies are subject to corporation tax profits from a trade carried on *within* the UK through a *branch or agency*. However, if the trade is with, rather than *within* the UK, there should be no corporation tax liability. Other income profits, such as letting income, are subject to income tax: ICTA 1988, s. 6(2): see *Cases and Materials* (**5.2.2.2**).

Henri SA, a company resident in France, owns an office block in the City, the various floors of which it leases to firms of stockbrokers, solicitors, accountants, etc. Will it be subject to corporation tax on the rental profits?

No. It will be liable to *income tax* on them: see *Cases and Materials* (**5.2.2.2**).

Imagine you are advising a US company, wishing to sell its products in the UK. Prepare a short note setting out the income tax and/or corporation tax consequences of so doing.

5.3.3 PARTNERS

The question is whether the partners, *as individuals*, are resident in the UK in the tax year under consideration.

If you are a partner resident in the UK in the tax year under consideration, the rule is that you are liable to pay income tax on the whole of your share of the partnership's income profits in that tax year, wherever they arise. It does not matter that the source of any of your income profits is located outside the UK – you are still liable to income tax on that share of profit.

By contrast, if you are a non-UK resident partner, the rule is that you are liable to pay income tax only on your share of the partnership's income profits arising in the UK in that year.

SAQ 48

Irena is an Italian resident and is a partner in an international firm of accountants, in their Milan office. The partnership comprises partners resident in countries all over the world. Its only office in the UK is in London. On what will she be liable to pay income tax (i.e. UK income tax)?

On her share of the partnership's income profits arising from the London office.

5.3.4   TRUSTEES AND PERSONAL REPRESENTATIVES

5.3.4.1   Trustees

The question of liability to pay income tax depends partly on whether the trustees are resident in the UK, and partly on whether the beneficiaries have an *immediate entitlement* to the income of the trust or not, in the tax year under consideration: see **2.4.2.2**. Such an immediate entitlement, remember, means that the income accrues directly to the beneficiaries.

If the trustees are resident in the UK in the tax year, and the beneficiaries do *not* have an immediate entitlement to the income, the rule is that the trustees are liable to pay income tax on the *whole* of the trust's taxable income in the tax year, wherever they arise. The trustees are still liable to pay income tax on the taxable income if any of the trust's income is located *outside* the UK.

However, if the trustees are resident in the UK, and the beneficiaries *do* have an immediate entitlement to the income, the rule is that, *if the beneficiaries are resident in the UK*, they are liable to pay income tax on the whole of the trust's taxable income in the tax year, wherever they arise. Again, it does not matter that the source of any of the trust's income is located outside the UK.

If the trustees are not resident in the UK in the tax year, and the beneficiaries do *not* have an immediate entitlement to the income, the general rule is that the non-resident trustees are liable to pay income tax only on taxable income *arising in the UK*.

That said, if the trustees are not resident in the UK, and the beneficiaries *do* have an immediate entitlement to the income, the rule is that, if the beneficiaries are resident in the UK, the *beneficiaries* are liable to pay income tax on the whole of the trust's taxable income in the tax year, wherever they arise. Again, it does not matter that the source of any of the trust's income is located *outside* the UK.

5.3.4.2   Personal representatives

The question whether PRs are liable to pay income tax on the income profits of the estate is much simpler to answer than the same question for trustees, although the rules for determining their residence is the same as for trustees, a point which has been much criticised, since it creates the possibility of double taxation: see **4.5.4.2**.

The basic rule is that, if the PRs are resident in the UK in the tax year under consideration *and the deceased was at his or her death resident, ordinarily resident or domiciled in the UK*, the PRs are liable to pay income tax on all the income profits of the deceased's estate wherever they come from.

If the deceased was not resident, etc. in the UK as above, any UK-resident PRs are liable to pay income tax on income profits arising in the UK only.

Are these reasonably sensible rules?

Yes: see **4.5**.

5.4   The Schedular System

The Schedular System, part of Addington's income tax (see **1.6.1**), is still with us today, although there are now only four Schedules instead of five. The 'tax law rewrite' may mean that its days are numbered, however: see **4.6**. It is fair to say that all the Schedules have undergone considerable legislative changes in their long history.

The significance of the Schedular System is that it applies for both income tax and corporation tax purposes, some necessary adjustments being made. The calculation of a person's income profits under each Schedule is Stage One of an income tax or corporation tax calculation, as the case may be. (The Schedular System does not apply for the purposes of NICs or VAT, obviously.)

Jake Ltd has trading profits of £10,000 in its accounting period ending on 30 November 1998. Will these profits fall under the same Schedule for corporation tax purposes as they would have done for income tax purposes?

Yes.

The Schedular System therefore applies whichever type of person is under consideration, and whatever the capacity in which the individual is liable to pay income tax. We next need to be clear about how the Schedular System determines *which* income profits are liable to income tax or corporation tax in the tax period under consideration.

To this end, the table set out below is intended to show:

■   the Schedule, and Case within each Schedule (abbreviated in the table to 'Sch.'), under which a particular income profit falls (first column);

■   what type of income profit (abbreviated in the table to 'profit') is taxed under which Schedule and Case (second column); *and*

■   how to ascertain which income profit is taxed in the tax year under consideration.

A full commentary is given in the text below.

TABLE: SUMMARY OF THE SCHEDULAR SYSTEM		
Sch. A	Profits of letting land in the UK	Profits of tax year under consideration
Sch. D Case I	Profits of a trade	Profits of the accounting period ending in the tax year under consideration
Case II	Profits of a profession or vocation	
Case III	Interest, annuities and other annual payments	Profits of tax year under consideration
Case IV	Profits from foreign securities	
Case V	Profits from foreign possessions	
Case VI	Profits not charged under any other Sch. or Case; certain other profits specifically charged under this Case	Profits of tax year under consideration
Sch. E Case I Case II Case III	Profits from offices, employments and pensions; also taxable DSS benefits	Profits of tax year under consideration
Sch. F	Dividends and certain other distributions by UK-resident companies	Profits of tax year under consideration

If the income profits of a company are under consideration, the expression *tax year under consideration* in the table obviously becomes *accounting period under consideration*: see **4.3.2**. However, for Schedule D, Cases I and II, the third column must be read as referring to the *profits of the accounting period under consideration* for corporation tax purposes.

The first point to recognise is that the sources of income which persons may have are all reflected here. However, Cases IV and V of Schedule D are not discussed further in this book.

SAQ 51

Consider the following situations:

(a)   **Keith is an assistant solicitor employed by a firm of solicitors;**

(b)   **Lorna lets property to students;**

(c)   **Mike owns shares in Noxious Ltd;**

(d)   **Oliver is a partner in a firm of accountants; and**

(e)   **Penny has her own business selling mobile phones.**

Under which Schedule does the income profit made by each one of these fall? (Assume each one has no other source of income.)

Keith – Schedule E; Lorna – Schedule A; Mike – Schedule F; Oliver – Schedule D, Case II; and Penny – Schedule D, Case I.

The second point to recognise is that, although we refer to *income profits* falling under each of the Schedules, the reason why we use this expression is that this figure is the *income* falling under the relevant Schedule, less any *allowable deductions*. Schedule D, Case III income and Schedule D, Case IV income does not have any allowable deductions and, although referred to as income profit, is *100% pure income profit*.

Why do income profits under Schedule D, Cases III and IV, and Schedule F not have any allowable deductions, i.e. why are they 100% income profit?

See **2.3.1** for the answer.

The third point to recognise is that an individual could have income profits falling under any one or more of the Schedules.

What would you imagine to be the difference between a trading partnership and a professional partnership?

A trading partnership will carry on a business in common which could consist of supplying either or both of *goods* and *services*. A professional partnership will carry on a business in common which consists of supplying services (e.g. a solicitors' firm, an accountancy firm, etc.), and may be regulated by professional rules of conduct. As a partner, you might also have a source of income profits under any of the other Schedules, depending on what types of business activities are carried on by the partnership.

Likewise, where the beneficiaries do *not* have an immediate entitlement to the income, you might as a *trustee* receive income under any of the Schedules, except Schedule E, for their benefit. Again, as a PR, you might receive income under any one or more of the Schedules, on behalf of the estate of the deceased individual.

SAQ 54

It is 1 September 1998. You are the executor of the will of Quentin, deceased. Quentin died two months ago. Quentin was the managing director of Russell plc, and had employment income from that source. He also had a source of rental income.

Under which Schedules will these income profits fall?

E and A.

The fourth point to recognise is that the table assumes that the relevant income profits are those of the tax year under consideration. This is called the *current year basis of assessment* and has applied from the tax year 1997/98 onwards.

The fifth point is simply to note that the method of taxing dividends under Schedule F is special: see **Chapter 8**.

Sixthly, you should note the existence of the *mutually exclusive rule*, which applies for both income tax and corporation tax purposes. Income profits are any positive figure left after making allowable deductions from income. The rules under which the allowable deductions are made may differ, according to the Schedule under which the income profits fall. The mutually exclusive rule says this. For assessment purposes, the Revenue must place income profits under the correct Schedule and Case but, equally, a person is only entitled to make those allowable deductions applicable to that particular Schedule and Case: *Fry* v *Salisbury House Estate Ltd* [1930] All ER Rep 538, see *Cases and Materials* (**5.3**). The rules governing those allowable deductions are the subject matter of **Chapter 11**.

SAQ 55

In the tax year 1998/99, Edward has income profits falling under both Schedule D and Schedule E. In calculating his income profit under Schedule D, he is allowed to deduct from his trading income expenditure *wholly and exclusively* incurred for the purpose of the trade.

However, he is only allowed to deduct from his salary expenditure (other than travelling expenditure) wholly, exclusively and *necessarily* incurred in the perform-ance of the duties of his office or employment.

In the performance of the duties of employment, he incurs an *un*necessary expense wholly and exclusively for the purposes of his employment. Can he deduct it from his trading income instead?

No.

In general, income falls under a particular Schedule and Case only so long as the source of the income exists. There are special provisions designed to prevent this rule being used for tax avoidance.

Imagine you are a sole trader. You plan to cease trading and to sell your trading stock after the cessation. Your reasoning is that the source of income, the trade, will have ceased when you sell the stock, so that those profits will not fall under Schedule D, Case I. However, the plan will fail, because of ICTA 1988, s. 100. Under ICTA 1988, s. 100, the value of the stock unsold at the date of the cessation of the trade will be added to your trading profits, if any, for the tax year in which the trade ceases.

By contrast, you may have guessed that the interaction of the residence issues discussed above and the Schedular System means that income sources might sometimes be manipulated successfully. In the absence of a provision similar to ICTA 1988, s. 100, income profits escape income tax or corporation tax if they do not fall anywhere within the Schedules.

Paul emigrated from the UK in 1995. In the 1998/99 tax year, he is resident, ordinarily resident and domiciled in France. His employer is a company resident in France. Paul performs all the duties of his employment in France. Does his 1998/99 salary fall under any of the Schedules?

No. He will almost certainly be liable to pay French income taxation, however.

5.5 Summary

In this chapter, we have sought to answer two questions, for both income tax and corporation tax purposes: *how* a person is liable to pay income tax or corporation tax, in the tax period under consideration, and *which* of that person's income profits must be included in its income tax or corporation tax calculation. In summary, the rule is that, if a person is resident in the UK, it is liable to pay income tax or corporation tax on its income profits in the tax year/accounting period under consideration, wherever that source is located. However, if that person is not so resident, it is liable to pay income tax or corporation tax only on income profits arising in the UK. Those profits fall under specific Schedules and Cases. With the exception of Cases IV and V of Schedule D, we shall be examining the detail of the Schedules and Cases in **Chapters 11**, and **14 to 18**.

5.6   End of Chapter Assessment Question

Reflect on the facts relating to Amber Ltd and its shareholders: see **2.6**, **3.6** and **4.9**. Note the following additional facts. Charlie was a shareholder in Megabucks plc. Amber Ltd exports metal fastenings to Malaysia.

Answer, with reference to the appropriate authority, the following questions:

(a)   Which of the eight persons involved is liable to income tax or corporation tax on their income profits?

(b)   In what capacity are each of the eight liable to income tax or corporation tax on their income profits?

(c)   On which of their income profits are they liable to income tax?

(d)   Under which of the Schedules and Cases do their income profits fall?

(Word limit: 550 (100 marks).)

See *Cases and Materials* (**5.5**), for a specimen answer.

CHAPTER SIX

NATIONAL INSURANCE CONTRIBUTIONS: LIABILITY AND EARNINGS

6.1 Objectives

By the end of this chapter, you should be able to:

■ explain *how* liability to pay NICs arises in the tax period under consideration;

■ identify the *earnings* on which an individual will be liable to pay NICs in the tax period under consideration.

6.2 Introduction

In **1.4**, subject to qualification, we described NICs as the third main form of income taxation. We now ask, in the context of NICs, two questions similar to those asked in relation to income tax and corporation tax in **Chapter 5**. The first question is that of *how* a person is liable to pay NICs in the tax period under consideration. The second question is that of which *earnings* or, exceptionally, income profits, are ones on which a person is liable to pay NICs in the tax period under consideration.

Liability to pay NICs is generally independent of liability to pay income tax. NICs are divided into five classes: 1, 1A, 2, 3 and 4, details of which are given in **6.4**.

6.3 Persons Liable to Pay National Insurance Contributions

NICs are relevant to individuals with sources of income falling, for income tax purposes, under Schedule E. They are also relevant to individuals, whether sole traders or partners, who have sources of income falling under Schedule D, Cases I or II for income tax purposes. The former are redesignated as *employed earners*, for NIC purposes, and the latter as *self-employed earners*. Finally, NICs are relevant to the employers, whether individuals or companies, which employ employed earners.

Thus, if you are an *employed earner*, you may be liable to pay primary Class 1 NICs: SSCBA 1992, s. 1(2)(a)(i).

SAQ 57

Anne is a director of Bertha Ltd. Charlotte is a sole trader. Which of the three may be liable to pay Class 1 *primary* NICs?

Anne.

If you are a *self-employed earner*, as opposed to an employed earner, you may be liable to pay both Class 2 and Class 4 NICs: SSCBA 1992, s. 1(2)(c) and (e).

SAQ 58

Could Class 2 and Class 4 NICs be payable by Charlotte?

Yes.

Obviously, if you are a self-employed earner, you might also be an employer. If so, you may be liable to pay *secondary Class 1 NICs* and Class 1A NICs. Thus, secondary Class 1 NICs and Class 1A NICs may be payable by any person acting in a capacity which involves the employment of individuals, e.g. trustees and partners. Equally companies, as employers, may be liable to pay secondary Class 1 NICs and Class 1A NICs.

The answer to the question of *how* employed earners, self-employed earners and employers are liable to pay NICs depends on the concepts of *residence* and *ordinary residence*. In this respect, NICs are similar to income tax. The definition of an employed earner is:

> . . . a person who is gainfully employed in Great Britain either under a contract of service, or in an office (including elective office) with emoluments chargeable to income tax under Schedule E.

> (SSCBA 1992, s. 2(1)(a).)

However s. 1(6), SSCBA 1992 and SSCR 1979 (SI 1979 No. 591), reg. 119 together state that your *ordinary residence*, as an employee, or even *presence* in Great Britain at the time of the employment, is sufficient to make you liable to pay NICs.

Ordinary residence and *presence* are discussed at **4.5.6** and **4.5.7**.

SAQ 59

Douglas is an employed earner, with earnings of £34,000 per annum. In the 1998/99 tax year, he is resident and ordinarily resident in the UK. Could he be liable to pay Class 1 primary NICs?

Yes.

As with an employed earner, the definition of a self-employed earner incorporates the residence requirement. It states that a self-employed earner is: '. . . a person who is gainfully employed in Great Britain otherwise than in employed earner's employment . . .' (SSCBA 1992, s. 2(1)(b)). Again, s. 1(6), SSCBA 1992 and SSCR 1979, reg. 119(1)(d) together state that your ordinary residence in Great Britain or, if you are not ordinarily resident here, residence here for 26 out of the previous 52 *contribution weeks*, is sufficient to make you liable to pay NICs.

Contribution weeks are discussed at **4.3.3**.

Elvira, ordinarily resident in Milan, is a self-employed art dealer. It is 10 October 1998. She has been resident in London since 1 April 1998. Is she liable to pay Class 2 NICs?

Yes.

Unlike with an employed or self-employed earner, the definition of an *employer* does not incorporate the residence requirement. It says that an employer is: '. . . the person who . . . is resident or present in Great Britain when such contributions become payable or then has a place of business in Great Britain . . .' (SSCR 1979, reg. 119(1)(b)).

Federico SpA has a registered place of business in the UK under CA 1985. It employs Georgina, a UK-resident and domiciled individual, as a receptionist. Is it liable to pay secondary Class 1 NICs on her salary?

Yes.

6.4   Earnings

By a parallel process of reasoning to that employed for income tax and corporation tax, we now need to clarify *which* of the earnings of employed earners and self-employed earners are liable to NICs in any *earnings period*, in the case of employees, and *contribution weeks*, in the case of the self-employed. The rules as to which earnings of employed earners and self-employed earners are liable for NICs are different from the rules determining which income profits are liable for income tax.

Except in relation to Class 4 NICs, they are not based on the Schedular System, nor on the concept of income profits. Instead, they are based on your earnings from your employment. Class 4 NICs are the exception, and they are calculated as a percentage of your income profits: see **8.5.3**.

Earnings are defined as including: '. . . any *remuneration or profit* derived from an employment' (SSCBA 1992, s. 3(1)(a) [*emphasis added*]).

The term 'employment' has a much wider meaning than for income tax. By s. 122(1), SSCBA 1992, it includes: ' . . . any trade, business, profession, office or vocation'.

SAQ 62

Would you expect 'employment' to include trade here, on the basis of what you know about income tax?

No.

Whereas the term 'emoluments' is endlessly discussed in the context of Schedule E (**Chapter 14**), *remuneration* and *profit*, in the context of NICs, have been discussed only rarely. This is because NIC law does not *at present* provide for a proper appeals procedure, permitting appeals to a High Court judge only: SSCBA 1992, s. 18. This is set to change, the Social Security Bill before the House of Lords for its third reading, at the time of writing. For the present, however, there is therefore no direct authority for the correct meaning of the term *remuneration* in the context of SSCBA 1992, s. 3(1)(a). However, a non-tax case called *S & U Stores Ltd* v *Wilkes* [1974] ICR 645 is believed to contain some strongly persuasive *dicta*.

ACTIVITY 8

Read the extract from Sir John Donaldson P's judgment in *S & U Stores* v *Wilkes* at *Cases and Materials* (6.1).

S & U Stores v *Wilkes* suggests that the term remuneration *excludes* benefits in kind and payments to an employee by someone other than the employer. As we shall discover in **14.3.2**, such benefits and payments are *emoluments* for income tax purposes. However, remuneration obviously includes any salary, wages or repayment of employees' expenses which is more than reimbursement of those expenses.

SAQ 63

Would you imagine that the DSS are happy to agree to this interpretation of 'remuneration'?

No – they reject the relevance of *S & U Stores* v *Wilkes*.

Instead, the DSS read 'remuneration' as meaning *gross pay*, subject to the payments directed to be disregarded in SSCR 1979, reg. 19. Gross pay is cash, or anything convertible into cash not by sale, but by *surrender*.

ACTIVITY 9

Read the extracts from Booklet CWG2 (1997), *Employer's Further Guide To PAYE and NICs*, at *Cases and Materials* (6.1), referring to the column headed 'NICs?'. Consider whether the interpretation of remuneration here is *entirely* inconsistent with *S & U Stores* v *Wilkes*.

As an *employed* earner over 16, you are liable to pay primary Class 1 NICs where the earnings paid to you, or for your benefit, in any earnings period are equal to or exceed the current *lower earnings limit*: see **8.5.1**. As a *self-employed* earner over 16 and under 60 for women or 65 for men, you are liable to pay Class 2 NICs for any week in which you are such an earner. They are payable at a flat rate per week: see **8.5**. Class 4 NICs are payable by you, as a self-employed earner, *in addition to* your liability to pay Class 2 NICs, in relation to *tax years*.

For secondary Class 1 and Class 1A NICs, the position is as follows. As you will recall, these are payable by employers. Secondary Class 1 NICs are payable by you in respect of employed earners over 16, where the earnings paid to the employed earner or for the employed earner's benefit, in any earnings period, are equal to or exceed the *current lower earnings limit*: see **8.5**.

The term *earnings period* was considered in **4.3.3**.

Class 1A NICs are payable by employers in respect of employees (i.e. employed earners) who have the private use of a car: SSCBA 1992, ss. 1(2)(a)(ii) and 1(2)(b). They are payable once annually, in relation to the tax year under consideration: see **19.6**. Class 3 NICs are voluntary and we do not consider them further in this book. According to SSCBA 1992, s. 1(2)(d), Class 3 NICs are '. . . payable . . . by earners and others voluntarily with a view to providing entitlement to benefit, or making up entitlement . . .'.

6.5   Summary

It is no doubt strange how NICs have developed alongside income tax law, without reference to it and without a detailed jurisprudence. The most obvious disparity is between the concept of Schedule E *income profits* or emoluments, applied for the purposes of income tax, and *earnings*, applied for NIC purposes. Earnings are *deemed* to be the profit. In other words, earnings are not arrived at having made allowable deductions. They are simply taken to be synonymous with the concept of gross pay. Little wonder that there is an ongoing governmental discussion of the possibility of merging NICs with Schedule D, Cases I and II and Schedule E.

6.6   End of Chapter Assessment Question

Refer to the facts concerning Amber Ltd and its shareholders at **2.6**, **3.6**, **4.9** and **5.6**. Note the following additional facts. The salaries of Alan, Bertram, Charlie and Deborah, as directors of Amber Ltd, are £8,000 each, before income tax and NICs. Up to his death on 28 September 1998, Charlie has lived in a house in Knightsbridge, owned by the company, at a very subsidised rent, Amber Ltd paying the council tax on the property. Deborah had a car provided for her general use by Amber Ltd on 6 April 1998.

On the basis of the information in this chapter, comment on the NIC implications of these facts for the persons involved.

(Word limit: 200 (100 marks).)

See *Cases and Materials* (**6.3**), for a specimen answer.

CHAPTER SEVEN

INCOME TAXATION: CALCULATION (1)

7.1 Objectives

By the end of this chapter, you should be able to:

- compare and contrast the *income tax* and *corporation tax* calculations;

- describe the *differences* between your income tax calculation in your personal capacity, and in the capacity of a trustee or PR;

- write down from memory the *Stages* of an *income tax* calculation;

- write down from memory the *Stages* of a *corporation tax* calculation;

- *attempt* an income tax or corporation tax calculation;

- outline the *separate treatment of spouses* for income tax purposes.

7.2 Introduction

The main objective of this chapter is to enable you to attempt an income tax or corporation tax calculation. It therefore shows you how to calculate your *total income tax due* for a tax year, whatever the capacity in which you are making the calculation. It then demonstrates how to calculate the *mainstream corporation tax liability* of a company for an accounting period. The Stages in which these calculations take place is crucial. It is true to say that an accurate understanding of everything on income tax and corporation tax in **Chapters 8** to **19** depends on your being able to write these Stages down from memory.

No distinction is made in this book between *earned* and *unearned* income: see **Cases and Materials (7.1)**. The distinction is mainly relevant for calculating an individual's *pensionable earnings*, although pensions are outside the scope of the book.

7.3 Calculating the *Total Income Tax Due* from an Individual

Here you perform the calculation in your own personal capacity. The calculation has seven Stages, and it is done for a particular tax year, e.g. 1998/99. In what follows, X represents a number. If X appears within round brackets, the number it represents is to be deducted from the number represented by the X appearing above it.

Stage One is to calculate your income profits under each Schedule and Case. Income profits are your income, i.e. receipts, *less* your allowable deductions in the tax period under consideration: see **2.3.1**, **4.3.1**. If, under Schedules A, D (Case I or II) or E, allowable deductions *exceed* your income, the income profits under that Schedule are Nil (see **2.3.2**), and this negative figure is dealt with as described in **Chapter 13**. The figures used for any dividends (Schedule F) or interest (Schedule D, Case III) must be the *gross* figures, although the full significance of this will not become clear until you have read **Chapter 8**.

Chapter 11 contains the detailed rules for making allowable deductions under Schedules A, D (Cases I and II) and E. Totalling up your income profits under each Schedule and Case gives your *statutory income*. Stage One of your calculation is thus:

Profit from employment (Sch. E)	X
Plus Profit from sole trade (Sch. D, Case I)	X
Plus Profit from lettings (Sch. A)	X
Plus Dividends (Sch. F) (gross)	X
Plus Interest (Sch. D, Case III) (gross)	X
Statutory income	X

Angela, who is single, earns a gross salary in the tax year 1998/99 of £22,000 from her employment. Also, in that tax year, she has rental income of £11,000 and gross dividend income of £2,000. She has incurred allowable deductions, in relation to the cottage, of £2,000. What is her statutory income in 1998/99?

£33,000, i.e. £22,000 + £9,000 + £2,000.

Stage Two is to total up, in a separate calculation, your *charges on income* (gross). These are explained in **Chapter 9**. Your total charges on income are then deducted from your statutory income, in order to give your *total income*: ICTA 1988, s. 835, see *Cases and Materials* (**7.2**). Thus:

Statutory income	X
Less Charges on income (gross)	(X)
Total income	X

Imagine that Angela (see SAQ 64) pays a charge on income of £1,000 (gross) in 1998/99, i.e. a charitable covenant in favour of the RSPCA: see 9.3.1.1. What is her *total income*?

£32,000, i.e. £33,000 − £1,000.

Stage Three is to deduct certain personal reliefs, as applicable, from your total income, in order to give your *taxable income*. Personal reliefs are discussed in **Chapter 10**, and it is not every personal relief which can be deducted at Stage Three. When you read **Chapter 10**, note which ones *are* and which ones *are not* deducted at Stage Three. A relief which is so deducted is the *personal allowance*, to which every individual resident in the UK in the tax year under consideration is entitled, including minors: ICTA 1988, ss. 257(1), 278(1). Thus:

Total income	X
Less Personal allowance	(X)
Taxable income	X

Angela (see SAQ 64) is entitled to the personal allowance of £4,195 in 1998/99. What is her *taxable income*?

£27,805, i.e. £32,000 − £4,195.

Stage Four is to apply whichever of the three income tax rates are relevant to the relevant band of taxable income. For the tax year 1998/99, these are:

First £4,300 at 20% (lower rate) – £1 to £4,300;

Next £22,800 at 23% (basic rate) – £4,301 to £27,100; and

Remainder at 40% (higher rate) – amount exceeding £27,100.

If your taxable income is £4,300 or less, you only pay 20% tax. If it is over £4,300 but less than £27,100, you pay 23% tax *on the amount above £4,300*. However, if your taxable income exceeds £27,100, you pay 40% tax on that excess. Thus:

Taxable income	X
£4,300 at 20%	X
Next £22,800 at 23%	X
Excess over £27,100 at 40%	X
Total tax	X

If your taxable income does not exceed £4,300, you are referred to as a *lower rate taxpayer*; if it does not exceed £27,100, you are referred to as a *basic rate taxpayer*; and if it *does* exceed £27,100, you are referred to as a *higher rate taxpayer*.

What is the *total tax* chargeable on Angela?

The first £4,300 at 20% will give £860. The next £22,800 at 23% will give £5,244 and the balance of her taxable income, £705, at 40% will give £282. Her total tax is therefore £6,386, i.e. £860 + £5,244 + £282.

(*Note*: In the tax year 1998/99, where an individual's taxable income equals or exceeds £27,100, the figures of £860 and £5,244 will be constant.)

Stage Five is to deduct the other applicable *personal reliefs* (also known as *income tax reductions* or *tax credits*) from your total tax, to find your *tax liability*. Only certain reliefs are deducted at this Stage and they may be deductible at only a percentage of their stated value, e.g. you can only deduct 15% of the married couple's allowance of £1,900, *not* the full £1,900: see **10.3.2**.

If you are entitled to two or more of these personal reliefs, you should strictly deduct them in a particular order: see **10.3.3**. Thus:

Total tax	X
Less income tax reductions	(X)
Tax liability	X

SAQ 68

What do these income tax reductions represent? How are they different from the personal reliefs deductible from *total income* in Stage Three above?

They represent an amount of tax which you are exempted from paying. They differ from the reliefs shown in Stage Three because the ones deducted in Stage Three are amounts of income profit on which you are exempted from tax.

Stage Six is to deduct from your tax liability any tax deducted at source or credited as paid, e.g. income tax deducted at source by the payer of interest to you, ACT on net dividends paid to you: see **8.3**, **8.4**. Thus:

Tax liability	X
Less tax deducted at source/credited as paid	(X)
Sub-total tax due	X

SAQ 69

Refer to SAQ 64. Imagine that Angela is claiming the married couple's allowance (MCA) (see 10.3.2), to which she is entitled at 15% of £1,900 (£285) and that she is credited as having paid income tax of *£400* on the dividends: see 8.3. What will be the *sub-total tax due* from her?

	£
Total tax	6,386
Less MCA	(285)
Tax liability	6,101
Less tax deducted at source/credited as paid	(400)
Sub-total tax due	5,701

Stage Seven is to add back basic rate income tax on any charges on income from which you will have deducted basic rate income tax in making the payment. Full details of this are given at **9.3.1.1**. Thus:

Sub-total tax due	X
Plus tax on charges paid	X
Total income tax due	X

Angela will have deducted income tax at the basic rate (i.e. £230) from the gross payment of £1,000. What is the *total tax due* from Angela for 1998/99?

£5,931, i.e. £5,701 + £230.

Joining all these parts together, the layout of your specimen income tax calculation is therefore:

YOUR INCOME TAX CALCULATION FOR THE TAX YEAR 1998/99

Profit from employment (Sch. E)	X
Plus Profit from sole trade (Sch. D, Case I)	X
Plus Profit from lettings (Sch. A)	X
Plus Dividends (Sch. F) (gross)	X
Plus Interest (Sch. D, Case III) (gross)	X
Statutory income	X
Less Charges on income (gross)	(X)
Total income	X
Less Personal allowance	(X)
Taxable income	X
£4,300 at 20%	X
Next £22,800 at 23%	X
Excess over £27,100	X
Total tax	X
Less income tax reductions	(X)
Tax liability	X
Less tax collected at source/credited as paid	(X)
Sub-total tax due	X
Plus tax on charges paid	X
Total income tax due	X

ACTIVITY 10

Take a blank sheet of paper. Try to memorise the whole of the specimen income tax calculation, as above, and then write it down.

An easy way to remember the structure is to divide it into four parts: (1) calculation of *statutory income*; (2) calculation of *total income*; (3) calculation of *taxable income*; and (4) calculation of *total income tax due*.

Note also that full details of charges on income – including the mechanics of their payment – personal reliefs and income tax reductions, will be given in **Chapters 9** and **10**. If you are an employee calculating the total income tax due from you at the end of the tax year under consideration, you should *have already paid a large part of it through PAYE:* see **19.3.7**.

7.4   Calculating the *Mainstream Corporation Tax Liability* of a Company

The calculation of the mainstream corporation tax liability of a company for an accounting period has *six* Stages.

Here we are calculating the corporation tax liability of a company on its *income profits*, and we therefore assume that it has made *no* capital profits in the accounting period under consideration. The total profits of a company can, in an appropriate case, consist of both income profits and capital profits: see **21.5**.

Stage One is to calculate the company's income profits under each Schedule and Case. This is the same process as for an individual, except that it is for an accounting period rather than for a tax year: see **4.3.2**. Otherwise, the same comments apply to Stage One as to the income tax calculation. Thus:

Profit from lettings (Sch. A)	X
Plus	
Trading profit (Sch. D, Case I)	X
Plus	
Interest (Sch. D, Case III) (gross)	X̲
Statutory income	X̲

Note that Schedule F (dividend) income (*franked investment income*: below) is not included: ICTA 1988, s. 208: see *Cases and Materials* (**7.3**).

SAQ 71

Consider Alexander Ltd: see SAQs 18 to 20. Instead of imagining Alexander Ltd to have income profits of £2,000, imagine the following.

Alexander Ltd makes its accounts up to 31 August in each calendar year. In the accounting period ending on 31 August 1998, the company has income from its business of letting properties of £100,000. In relation to that business, it has incurred allowable deductions of £20,000 and has other income, i.e. interest on loans of £75,000 (gross) and a dividend from a company in which it owns shares of £36,000 (gross).

What is the company's *statutory income* for the accounting period ending on 31 August 1998?

£155,000, i.e. £100,000 − £20,000 + £75,000.

(*Note*: (1) If, instead of the gross figure for the interest, the figure had been given net, it would have been necessary to *gross-up* the net figure for inclusion in the calculation: see **8.4** (this point would apply to Stage One of the income tax calculation also); and (2) dividend income has *no place* in the calculation of the statutory income of a company: ICTA 1988, s. 208: see *Cases and Materials* (7.3).)

Stage Two, unlike for income tax, is to add to the statutory income any capital profits in the accounting period, to give the company's *total profits*. We are assuming until **Chapter 21** that the company's profits are all income ones, so this Stage is not applicable here.

SAQ 72

Why is the concept of the charge on income, deducted at Stage Three below, such a powerful concept?

Charges on income are deducted from *both* the income profits and any capital profits.

Stage Three is to total up, in a separate calculation, the company's *charges on income*. A different list of payments qualify as charges on income for a company than for an individual: see **9.3.2**. The company's total charges on income are then deducted from its total profits, in order to give the company's *profits chargeable to corporation tax*: ICTA 1988, s. 338(1). Thus:

Total profits	X
Less Charges on income	(X)
Profits chargeable to corporation tax	X

Although these are not discussed until **11.3**, Stage Three is also the stage at which the management expenses of an *investment company* are deducted, as well as any deficits on a company's *non-trading loan relationships*: see **11.7** (FA 1996, s. 82).

SAQ 73

Imagine that Alexander Ltd (see SAQ 71) makes a covenanted payment of £2,000 (gross) to the Haydn House Trust (a registered charity) in the accounting period ending on 31 August 1998. What are the *total profits* of Alexander Ltd, and what are its *profits chargeable to corporation tax*?

Total profits are the same as statutory income, i.e. £155,000 (no capital profits). Profits chargeable to corporation tax are £153,000, i.e. £155,000 − £2,000.

Personal reliefs are *not* relevant in a *corporation tax* calculation. Instead, we go to Stage Four, and apply whichever corporation tax rates are relevant to the *profits chargeable to corporation tax*.

For the financial year 1998, there are three rates of corporation tax. Which rate, or combination of rates, applies depends on the level of the company's profits chargeable to corporation tax:

First £300,000 at 21% − £1 to £300,000;

Next £1,200,000 at tapering (or *marginal*) rate − £300,001 to £1,500,000; and

Remainder at 31% − amount exceeding £1,500,000.

The tapering rate works in a rather surprising way. To avoid a jump in the rate of tax on chargeable profits, between £300,000 and £1,500,000, the tapering rate on the band to which it applies is 33.5%.

SAQ 74

In what circumstances does a company have an advantage over an individual in relation to tax rates on its income profits?

Where the company's profits chargeable to corporation tax are less than £300,000 (an individual pays 40% on taxable income over £27,100, although a company pays 21% up to £300,000).

The 21% tax rate is known as the *small companies rate*; the maximum rate is referred to as the *full rate of corporation tax*. Thus:

Profits chargeable to corporation tax   X
Corporation tax on profits at relevant rate(s)   X
Total tax   X

Alexander Ltd's profits chargeable to corporation tax are £153,000: see SAQ 73. What will be the company's total tax?

£32,130, i.e. £153,000 × 21%.

Stage Five is to deduct from the company's total tax any tax deducted at source or credited as paid, e.g. income tax deducted at source by the payer of interest, and *advance corporation tax* (ACT): see **8.3**. Thus:

Total tax   X
Less tax deducted at source/credited as paid   (X)
Sub-total tax due   X

Suppose Alexander Ltd (see SAQ 73) had paid out a net dividend to its shareholders of £10,000 and had paid ACT on that dividend to the Revenue: see 8.3. The ACT was £2,500. What is the sub-total tax due?

£14,630, i.e. £32,130 − £2,500 − £15,000 (i.e. income tax on gross interest of £75,000: see **8.4**).

Stage Six is to add back *basic* rate income tax on any charges on income and *lower* rate income tax on payments of yearly interest under the company's loan relationships, in order to find the company's *mainstream corporation tax liability*: see **11.4.2** and **11.6**. Thus:

Sub-total tax due   X
Plus tax on charges and yearly interest   X
Mainstream corporation tax liability   X

What is Alexander Ltd's mainstream corporation tax liability?

	£
Sub-total tax due	14,630
Plus tax on charges and yearly interest	460
Mainstream corporation tax liability	15,090

Joining the parts together, as we did for income tax, we get:

CORPORATION TAX CALCULATION OF ALEXANDER LTD FOR THE ACCOUNTING PERIOD OF TWELVE MONTHS ENDED 31 AUGUST 1998

Profit from lettings (Sch. A)	X
Plus	
Trading profit (Sch. D, Case I)	X
Plus	
Interest (Sch. D, Case III)	X
Statutory income	X
[*Plus* capital profits	X]
Total profits	X
Less Charges on income (gross)	(X)
Profits chargeable to corporation tax	X
Corporation tax on profits at relevant rate(s)	X
Total tax	X
Less tax deducted at source/credited as paid	(X)
Sub-total tax due	X
Plus tax on charges and yearly interest	X
Mainstream corporation tax liability	X

ACTIVITY 11

Take a blank sheet of paper. Try to memorise the whole of the specimen corporation tax calculation, as set out above, and then write it down.

7.5 Calculating the *Total Income Tax Due* from a Partner

If you are a partner, the calculation of the total income tax due from you is exactly the same as in **7.3**. The only difference is that any income profits entered in Stage One under Schedule D, Case I or II, will be your share of the profits of the partnership. Special rules apply to the early years of the business: see **4.3.1**.

Imagine for a moment that, on 1 June 1998, Alan and Bert begin to carry on a trade in partnership. Under their partnership agreement, they agree to share all profits, and bear all losses, equally. They decide to produce accounts to 31 May in each calendar year. They have no other income from any source. They are very successful and, they each have the following trading profits, i.e. their half shares under the partnership agreement are:

	£
Accounting period ended 31 May 1999	217,500
Accounting period ended 31 May 2000	475,000
Accounting period ended 31 May 2001	625,000

In the first tax year of the partnership (1998/99), the Schedule D, Case I profit to be included in Stage One of their individual income tax calculations is the profit for the period from 1 June 1998, when the partnership commenced, to 5 April 1999. This is a period of ten months, so the trading profit to be included is ten-twelfths of £217,500, i.e. £181,250.

In the second tax year of the partnership (1999/2000), the Schedule D, Case I profit to be included in Stage One of their individual income tax calculations is the profit for the first 12 months of trading, i.e. £217,500 (accounting period ending 31 May 1999).

In the third tax year of the partnership (2000/2001), the Schedule D, Case I profit to be included in Stage One of their individual income tax calculations is the profit of the accounting period ending in the 2000/2001 tax year, i.e. £475,000 (accounting period ending 31 May 2000).

On these figures, what will be each of Alan and Bert's total income in their individual tax calculations for 1998/99, 1999/2000 and 2000/2001?

£181,250 (1998/99), £217,500 (1999/2000) and £475,000 (2000/2001).

It is important to note that 'salaries' paid to partners under some partnership agreements are treated as part of their profit share for these purposes, unless those partners are *in reality* employees: *MacKinlay* v *Arthur Young McClelland Moores & Co.* [1990] 1 All ER 45, per Lord Oliver.

7.6   Calculating the *Total Income Tax Due* from Trustees and PRs

7.6.1   TRUSTEES

Here you perform the income tax calculation in your capacity as a trustee. As a trustee, you need to do this wherever the trust income does *not* accrue directly to the beneficiaries: see **5.3.4.1**.

However, as a trustee, you must keep the calculation of the total income tax due from the trust separate from the total income tax due from you in your personal capacity – you receive the income from the property you hold for the benefit of the beneficiaries. The calculation is very similar to an individual's: see **7.3**. Thus, Stages One and Two are virtually identical to an individual's income tax calculation, although a deduction is sometimes permitted, to cover *administration expenses* of the trust: see **16.6.3**. *Stage Three* of the individual's calculation is omitted, since you cannot use your personal reliefs *in your capacity as a trustee*. The taxable income of a trust is therefore *the same* as its total income.

Stage Three is to apply the appropriate rate of income tax to the taxable income, to find your *tax liability* as a trustee. This could be the basic rate (23%), or it could be the *special rate applicable to trusts*. For the 1998/99 tax year, this special rate is 34%. It is charged on the taxable income of all trusts under which trustees have a power to *accumulate* the income and those which give trustees a *discretion* as to the distribution of income to the beneficiaries: ICTA 1988, ss. 686, 686A. ICTA 1988, s. 686(2) says:

This section applies to income arising to trustees in any [tax year] so far as it—

    (a) is income which is to be accumulated or which is payable at the discretion of the trustees or any other person (whether or not the trustees have power to accumulate it); and

    (b) is not, before being distributed, either—

        (i)   the income of any person other than the trustees, or

        (ii) treated for any of the purposes of the Income Tax Acts as the income of a settlor; and

    (c) is not income arising under a trust established for charitable purposes only ...

What do trusts under which the trustees have a power to *accumulate* the income, and those under which they have a discretion as to the distribution of the income profits to the beneficiaries have in common?

Beneficiaries have no fixed interest in the income or capital of the trust fund in each case.

Stage Four of the individual's income tax calculation is omitted. *Stage Four* of the trustees' calculation is therefore to deduct from the tax liability any tax deducted at source or credited as paid, e.g. income tax deducted at source by the payer of interest to you, the trustees, or ACT on net dividends paid to you: see **8.3**, **8.4**. This is the same as Stage Six for an individual. Finally, *Stage Five* of the trust income tax calculation is the same as Stage Seven of the individual's income tax calculation.

It is very important to recognise that, subject to a point to be discussed in **16.6.3**, no deduction can be given for the administrative expenses of the trustees, in calculating the total income tax due from them. It means that, although the beneficiaries get a partial credit for the income tax paid by the trustees, they do not get full credit: *MacFarlane* v *IRC* (1929) 14 TC 532. The point will be discussed in full in **16.6.3**.

7.6.2 PERSONAL REPRESENTATIVES

Personal representatives of a deceased individual need to make at least two separate income tax calculations.

7.6.2.1 Calculating the total income tax due from the deceased

Here you are calculating, as the deceased's PR, the total income tax due from the deceased between the beginning of the tax year *in which the deceased died*, and the date of the death. The calculation may also need to be done for earlier years too, if the deceased was a bad taxpayer. Subject to the points mentioned below, the calculation is identical to that in **7.3**.

As a PR, you stand in the deceased's shoes, so you are liable to pay the deceased's unpaid income tax due up to his or her death: TMA 1970, s. 74(1). However, unlike trustees, and unlike PRs in **7.6.2.2**, you are entitled in full to the personal reliefs available to the deceased in the tax year of the death.

Certain other special points need to be made where:

  (a) the deceased was a sole trader or a partner;

(b) the deceased was a beneficiary under a trust under which the deceased received trust income when still alive; and

(c) the deceased was a shareholder.

If the deceased was a *sole trader or a partner*, the rules which apply to the discontinuance of a trade will apply: see **4.3.1.2**. This will affect the figure inserted in Stage One for Schedule D, Case I or II profits.

If the deceased was a beneficiary under a trust, as above, any income received by the deceased as a beneficiary must be included by you, the PR, in Stage One. Finally, if the deceased was a shareholder, dividends *received* before the date of the deceased's death must be included in Stage One: *IRC* v *Henderson's Executors* (1931) 16 TC 282.

7.6.2.2 Calculating the total income tax due on the estate income

Here you are calculating, as the deceased's PR, the total income tax due from the estate between the *death* and the ascertainment of the residue of the estate, ready for distribution to the beneficiaries under the will or on intestacy, as the case may be (the *administration period*). The income tax position of the *beneficiary* under the will or on intestacy is covered in **16.3.2**.

When, if at all, do PRs become *trustees*?

Where the will or intestacy rules state that the residue is to be held on trust for the beneficiaries: see **26.5.4, 26.6.3**.

When the calculations in **7.6.2.1** are done, income tax calculations for the estate income will need to be done where the estate property continues to produce income. In your capacity as a PR, you are liable for the income tax on the taxable income of the estate during the administration period. The total income tax due from you, in your capacity as a PR, must be kept separate from any liability you may have in your personal capacity. PRs, like trustees, receive any income from the estate property for the beneficiaries.

The calculation is very similar to an individual's: see **7.3**. Thus, Stages One and Two are almost identical to an individual's income tax calculation. Some additional points need to be made, however, in relation to *dividends* and *trading profits*. Dividends are paid out by a company to its shareholders in two stages. The board of the company first *declares* them, and then it *pays* them, subject to certain formalities. Thus, if dividends are *declared* before the death, and *paid* after the death, they are the income *of the deceased* in the tax year of death, *rather than* income of the estate: see **7.6.2.1**. In relation to trading profits, if the deceased was a sole trader or a partner and you, as the deceased's PR, continue to carry on the trade, in order to sell it as a going concern, the trading profits are calculated in the same way as for an individual (see **7.3**).

Since estate income is separate from your own income, you are not allowed to deduct from the total income of the estate any personal reliefs which are available to you in your personal capacity. Stage Three of the *individual's calculation* is therefore omitted. Stage Three of the estate income calculation is therefore to apply *the basic rate of income tax* (23%) to the taxable income, to find the *tax liability* of the estate. Because the basic rate applies, there is no additional liability either on dividends, or on other savings income: see **Chapter 16**.

Stage Four of the individual's calculation is omitted, so *Stage Four* of the estate income calculation is to deduct from the tax liability any tax deducted at source or credited as paid, e.g. income tax deducted at source, ACT, etc. This is, of course, the same as Stage Six for an individual. Finally, *Stage Five* of the estate income tax calculation is the same as Stage Seven of the individual's income tax calculation.

7.7   Calculating the Total Income Tax due from an Individual: *Separate Taxation of Spouses*

It is enough to mention that the calculation in **7.3** needs to be made for each spouse and that, until 6 April 1990, the total income of a married woman living with her husband in the tax year under consideration had been treated as part of his total income. This rule, which had originally been enacted in Addington's income tax (see **1.6.1**) last applied in the 1989/90 tax year.

7.8   Summary

The main objective of this chapter has been to enable you to attempt an income tax or corporation tax calculation. The End of Chapter Assessment Question below provides you with an opportunity to do so. You need to know how to calculate your *total income tax due* for a tax year, irrespective of the capacity in which you are calculating it. You also need to know how to calculate the *mainstream corporation tax liability* of a company for an accounting period. In both cases, the Stages in which these calculations unfold is everything. At the beginning of the chapter, it was said that an accurate understanding of everything on income tax and corporation tax depends on your being able to write these Stages down from memory. Try to make sure you can do this before moving on and, if there is the opportunity to do so, think deeply about what you have memorised.

7.9   End of Chapter Assessment Question

Alan, Bertram and Deborah (see **6.6**) have a cousin called Hugh. Hugh is a barrister in private practice, aged 28. At 6 April 1998, he has been in private practice for five years. He owns a few investments, and he supplements the income from his practice at the bar by lecturing. He makes up his accounts for his bar practice to 30 June in each calendar year.

In the tax year 1998/99, he has the following income and expenditure:

	£
Brief fees (to 30 June 1998) (Sch. D, Case II)	15,000
Allowable deductions in bar practice (to 30 June 1998)	8,000
Lecturing pay (Sch. E)	6,000
Sch. E allowable deductions	650
Rental income	10,000
Allowable deductions on rented-out properties:	
Insurance	2,500
Repairs	9,000
Dividend income (gross)	2,000

Hugh has covenanted to pay £1,500 gross per annum to a registered charity. The dividend income above includes an ACT credit of £400. The rental income and expenditure shown relates to three houses in Stepney, which he owns.

Hugh is married to Jane.

Calculate the total income tax due from Hugh in the 1998/99 tax year.

(The personal allowance for 1998/99 is £4,195 and the married couples' allowance is £1,900.)

(100 marks.)

See *Cases and Materials* (**7.5**), for a specimen answer.

CHAPTER EIGHT

INCOME TAXATION: CALCULATION (2)

8.1 Objectives

By the end of this chapter, you should be able to:

■ explain the *relationship* between income tax and corporation tax;

■ explain *when* it is necessary to gross up net income profits;

■ *gross-up* a net income profit;

■ explain *how* NICs are calculated;

■ identify supplies which are *zero-rated* or *exempt* for VAT purposes;

■ calculate the VAT on a supply taxable at the *standard rate*.

8.2 Introduction

Having discussed the shape of the income tax and corporation tax calculations, we now need to examine two specific aspects of them. The first is *ACT* which, under current law, defines the relationship between the income tax and corporation tax calculations, and has a role in both of them. The second is the concept of *grossing-up* such income profits which are received by a person *net* of income tax. Grossing-up is relevant to Stage One of both the income tax and corporation tax calculations.

Having examined these two specifics, we need to move our attention away from income tax and corporation tax, and concentrate on the calculation of NICs and VAT. Both can be regarded as forms of income taxation, and it is important to appreciate the differences between the ways in which each of them are calculated, and the calculation of income tax and corporation tax.

8.3 ACT: the Relationship between Income Tax and Corporation Tax

Until 6 April 1999, income tax and corporation tax will continue to be closely related to each other in conceptual terms. Both taxes utilise the Schedular System, subject to certain variations: see **7.3** and **7.4**. However, 6 April 1999 is the date on which FA 1998 provides for the severing of the relationship between them. That is the date on or after which no UK company is obliged to pay ACT on *qualifying distributions* of profits.

8.3.1   THE CURRENT SYSTEM

Imagine a company with trading profits for an accounting period. Its directors declare and pay a dividend to its shareholders, thus *distributing* some of the profits. Until 6 April 1999, the company must pay ACT on the dividend to the Revenue, shortly after paying the qualifying distribution, i.e. the dividend. This ACT is an 'up-front' payment of corporation tax, hence its deduction from the company's total tax, i.e. at Stage Five of its corporation tax calculation: see *Cases and Materials* (**8.1**).

Besides being an 'up-front' payment of corporation tax, the ACT paid by the company is also *imputed* to the individual shareholder, as a *tax credit*. The credit is given at Stage Six of the shareholder's income tax calculation, i.e. a deduction for ACT paid by the company is made from the shareholder's tax liability for *income* tax purposes: see **7.3**. Since ACT paid by the company is currently *imputed* to the shareholder, the corporation tax system is referred to as an *imputation system*. Note that it is inaccurate to describe the company paying the dividend as 'accounting' for ACT, since no withholding of income tax is made when the dividend is paid.

Consider the following illustration of the current system in action:

You are an ordinary shareholder in Alfred Ltd. On 1 September 1998, Alfred Ltd declares and pays to you a dividend of £750 (net). ACT is paid by Alfred Ltd at 20/80 (1/4) × net dividend. The ACT paid by Alfred Ltd is *imputed* to you as a tax credit.

Alfred Ltd pays dividend to you	750
Alfred Ltd pays ACT to Revenue (i.e. 20/80 × £750)	187.50
Alfred Ltd's total payment	937.50

The tax credit of £187.50:

(a)   forms part of the *gross* dividend received by you, making the amount of the gross dividend for insertion in Stage One of your income tax calculation £937.50; and

(b)   discharges your 20% income tax liability on the dividend (20/80 × £750 = £187.50), which means that it is deducted from your *tax liability* at Stage Six of your income tax calculation.

If you are a *basic rate taxpayer*, you will have no extra income tax to pay on the dividend. ICTA 1988, s. 1A ensures this: see *Cases and Materials* (**8.1**).

If you are a *higher rate taxpayer*, however, the tax credit does not discharge your income tax liability on the dividend in full. ICTA 1988, s. 1A and the rule that dividends are the top slice of an individual's income ensure this effect: ICTA 1988, s. 1A(5) (see *Cases and Materials* (**8.1**)). Your income tax calculation will therefore ensure that you have to pay the £187.50 difference between £187.50 and £375 (i.e. 40/80 × £750 = £375, less tax credit of £187.50).

If you are a *lower rate taxpayer*, you are unable to claim any refund of tax.

If you are a *non-taxpayer*, having no other sources of income, and an unused personal allowance, you are currently able to claim a refund of the £187.50 tax credit. Prior to 2 July 1997, pension funds and unit trusts, as well as individuals, were able to claim a refund of the tax credit. (The denial of the credit was greeted with dismay from pension funds, as you may remember from media reports.)

It is useful to note that ACT *always* equals 25% (one-quarter) of the *net* dividend and 20% (one-fifth) of the *gross* dividend, i.e. the net dividend plus the tax credit.

ACTIVITY 12

Reread the discussion above, and then study the tax voucher reproduced below. Prior to 6 April 1999, a voucher in this form will be sent to you, the individual shareholder, by the company, together with the cheque for the *net dividend*. The voucher sets out the tax treatment discussed above, and you are obliged to retain it, in order to substantiate the details of the dividend which you will give in your tax return: see 19.3.3(1).

BIGCO PLC
Ordinary shares of 25p each

TAX VOUCHER   27 September 1998

I certify that advance corporation tax of an amount equal to that shown as tax credits for the final dividend will be accounted for to the Collector of Taxes
                                      B Brown
                                      Secretary, Bigco plc

This voucher should be kept. It will be accepted by the Inland Revenue as evidence if you are entitled to claim repayment of tax.

Holding	Tax credit of	Dividment payable at the rate 46.95p per share
120	£14.08	£56.34

In studying this, identify the *net dividend* actually received by you, and calculate the gross amount to be included in Stage One of your income tax calculation.

8.3.2 THE SYSTEM ON AND AFTER 6 APRIL 1999

Further changes will take effect from 6 April 1999, which will modify the situation discussed in 8.3.1. In summary, the changes will be as follows.

In order to conform with standard double taxation treaty criteria, the tax credit will be reduced from 20% to 10%. This credit will discharge a new 10% rate on dividend income for *lower rate taxpayers*, and *basic rate taxpayers*. For *higher rate taxpayers*, a new rate of income tax on dividend income will be introduced, of 32.5%, rather than 40%, as at present: see 8.3.1. Most significantly, perhaps, *non-taxpayers*, including *charities*, will no longer be able to claim a refund of the tax credit.

The new rate of 32.5% for higher rate taxpayers is designed to compensate them for the reduction of the tax credit from 20% to 10%. In addition, the cash-flow implications for charities of the modification will be addressed by special compensation payments. These compensation payments will be a reducing percentage of the dividend income received by the charity, gradually reducing from 21%, in the 1999/2000 tax year, to 4% in the 2003/2004 tax year.

ACTIVITY 13

Read the extracts from Malcolm Gammie's article, 'The Future of ACT', in *Cases and Materials* (8.1). You may find it quite a difficult read at this stage. However, try at least to get a sense from it of the significance of the concept of *shadow ACT*.

As a postscript to this discussion, it might be appropriate to make some final comments on the *imputation system*. Legislators, both in the UK and abroad, have not always favoured the avoidance of at least some degree of double taxation by the imputation system: see **16.6.1**. Corporation tax, as originally introduced in 1965 and, as it operated till 1973, did not use the imputation system, but the *classical system*. It is my understanding that the classical system is used in Luxembourg and The Netherlands. Under the classical system, the income profits of companies are *intentionally* taxed twice, providing a tax disincentive to paying dividends out to shareholders. The classical system means that profits will tend to be retained in the company, rather than being distributed to shareholders. The political and economic aim of the classical system was expressed by Chancellor James Callaghan in 1965. It was desirable, he said, to provide ' . . . a strong incentive to all companies to plough back more of their profits for expansion'. A similar economic aim was the motive for the changes to the system of taxation of dividends introduced by Chancellor Gordon Brown in his 2 July 1997 Budget Speech.

8.4   Grossing-up

We remain with income tax and corporation tax in this section. *Grossing-up* is the calculation made by the person receiving income profits from which *either* income tax has been deducted at source, e.g. interest, *or* on which income tax has been credited as paid, e.g. dividends. The grossing-up calculation is done by the recipient in the context of Stage One of its income tax or corporation tax calculation. The object of grossing-up is to discover the *gross* amount of the receipt, where you already know the *net* amount.

To gross up, multiply the net amount received, by the *grossing-up fraction*. The grossing-up fraction is:
$$\frac{100}{100 - R},$$
where R is the rate at which tax was deducted at source, or has been credited as paid.

A common example of income received net of tax, which must therefore be grossed-up for inclusion in Stage One of the recipient's income tax calculation, is *interest*, which falls under Schedule D, Case III, paid by a bank (ICTA 1988, s. 477A), a building society (ICTA 1988, s. 480A) or, where the interest is *yearly interest*, by a company: ICTA 1988, s. 349(2): see **9.4**. In each case, 20% income tax will have been deducted from such payments by the bank or building society or company at source.

Thus, if you receive bank interest of £500 in the tax year 1998/99, from which lower rate income tax has been deducted, you must multiply it by 100/80, to discover the tax deducted. This gives a gross amount of £625, for inclusion in Stage One of your income tax calculation, with £125 being deducted from your tax liability at Stage Six: see **7.3**.

SAQ 81

Boris has a number of building society accounts, from which he receives *net* interest of £700 in the tax year 1998/99. What figure should be included as income profit from this source in Stage One of his income tax calculation?

£875, i.e. £700 × 100/80 (therefore credit of £175 at Stage Six).

The following are examples of other payments of income profits which will be received *net*, and will therefore need to be grossed-up, at the appropriate rate of tax, for insertion in Stage One of the income tax or corporation tax calculation, as the case may be:

(a) Income profits paid by trustees to you, a beneficiary: see **Chapters 16** and **17**. Here, the grossing-up fraction will either be 100/80 (savings income) or 100/77 (other income profits).

(b) Charges on income, where the payer has been obliged to deduct basic rate income tax at source, e.g. annuities and other annual payments: see **Chapter 9** and **16.5.1**.

(c) Occasionally only, income profits under Schedule E, if you do not know your gross emoluments figure. Even though wages are normally paid under PAYE (see **19.3.7.1**), you will usually know the gross amount. However, beware – PAYE is a refined system, which attempts to take into account the various reliefs to which an employee is entitled. Grossing-up a net figure paid under PAYE may not therefore produce an accurate figure for the gross amount.

(d) Dividends received by an *individual*, irrespective of the capacity in which received (*not* applicable to companies: see **7.4**). And

(e) Where the so-called *Gourley* principle applies to employment income: see **14.3.2**.

8.5   Calculation of National Insurance Contributions

We now shift our attention away from income tax and corporation tax, and return to NICs. In this chapter, it is necessary to indicate how, assuming a person is liable to pay NICs of one or another Class, those NICs are calculated. The calculation is *entirely separate from* the calculation of a person's income tax or corporation tax liability.

8.5.1   CLASS 1 NICs

For employed earners, the procedure for calculating *primary* Class 1 NICs is as follows:

(a) You calculate your *earnings* in the earnings period (see **4.3.3**).

(b) If your earnings exceed the lower earnings limits (LEL) in that period, you apply the percentage rate(s) specified by SSCBA 1992, ss. 8 and 9 to them. These rates are too detailed to set out in full. Class 1 primary contributions are currently charged at 2% up to the LEL of £64 *per week*, and at 10% between the LEL and the upper earnings limit (UEL), i.e. £485 *per week*. (Multiply these figures by four, to give the monthly equivalent, and by 52, to give the annual equivalent.)

For the *employer*, the procedure for calculating *secondary* Class 1 NICs is as follows:

(a) Calculate the employed earner's *earnings* in the *earnings period*.

(b) If they exceed the LEL in that period, you apply the percentage rate(s) specified by SSCBA 1992, ss. 8 and 9 to them. These are again too detailed to set out in full, but there is no UEL, and the rates graduate between 3% and 10% of earnings.

8.5.2   CLASS 2 NICs

These do not need to be calculated, since they are basically payable by self-employed earners at a *flat rate* of £6.35 per week (for 1998/99). There is a small earnings exception of £3,590 per annum.

8.5.3   CLASS 4 NICs

Earnings are calculated, for Class 4 purposes, in a *broadly* similar way to the calculation of trading profits under Schedule D, Case I, although there are important differences. A percentage rate of 6% is then applied to the resulting figure: SSCBA 1992, s. 15(1): see *Cases and Materials* (8.2). Note that, from the tax year 1997/98, there has no longer been a deduction in arriving at the earner's total income for *income tax* purposes, of half the self-employed earner's Class 4 NICs of the tax year. As a partner, your liability to Class 4 contributions is based on your share of the profits of the trade or profession carried on by you in partnership: SSCBA 1992, sch. 2, para. 4(1). There is a lower profits limit of £7,310 per annum, and an upper profits limit of £25,220 per annum.

8.5.4   CLASS 1A NICs

These are payable by the employer at a single (quite high) percentage rate based on the cash equivalent of the car benefit for income tax purposes and, if relevant, the fuel benefit: SSCBA 1992, s. 10(4) (see **Chapter 14**).

8.6   When a Person must Account for Value Added Tax

From NICs, we finally turn our attention to VAT. A *taxable person* must account to Customs for the VAT which it charges its customers on supplies taxable at the standard rate. A taxable person is a person which is either registered or which is *required to be* registered for VAT. That person is required to be registered for VAT if the level of its taxable supplies – including zero-rated supplies – exceeds a certain figure in a certain period (see **19.5**).

Is the level of the taxable person's *income profits*, for income or corporation tax purposes, relevant here?

No. VAT taxes the value of taxable supplies, i.e. turnover, not income profits.

The status of a supply as *taxable* or *exempt* is determined by reference to VATA 1994. Supplies of the following are *zero-rated* (VATA 1994, sch. 8):

Group 1   food
Group 2   sewerage services and water
Group 3   books, newspapers, etc.
Group 4   talking books for the blind and handicapped and wireless sets for the blind
Group 5   construction of dwellings etc.
Group 6   protected buildings
Group 7   international services
Group 8   transport
Group 9   caravans and houseboats
Group 10   gold
Group 11   bank notes
Group 12   drugs, medicines, aids for the handicapped, etc.
Group 13   imports/exports, etc.
Group 14   tax-free shops
Group 15   charities
Group 16   mainly children's clothing and footwear.

SAQ 83

What do supplies under most of these heads have in common?

Social or economic utility.

Supplies of the following are *exempt* (VATA 1994, sch. 9):

Group 1   land
Group 2   insurance
Group 3   postal services
Group 4   betting, gaming and lottery
Group 5   finance
Group 6   education
Group 7   health and welfare
Group 8   burial and cremation
Group 9   trade unions and professional bodies
Group 10   sports/sports competitions and physical education
Group 11   works of art, etc.
Group 12   fund-raising events by charities and other qualifying bodies
Group 13   · cultural services.

In order to determine the exact VAT status of a particular supply, it is necessary to look at the detailed wording of each of these Groups in the schedules to VATA 1994, e.g. sch. 8, Group 1, does *not* zero-rate supplies in the course of catering (including hot take-away food). However, sch. 9, Group 6, item 4 *exempts* some supplies of food for the direct use of students receiving educational services.

For a detailed summary of the lists given above, refer to *Cases and Materials* (8.3).

8.7 *How Much* Value Added Tax a Taxable Person must Account for

We stay with VAT in this section. A taxable person must currently account for VAT on standard-rated supplies at 17.5% of the value of the supply. A *lower rate* of 5% applies to domestic fuel supplies made on or after 1 September 1997: VATA 1994, s. 2(1A), see *Cases and Materials* (1.1). If the consideration is money, the value of the supply is generally taken to be the amount which, with the addition of the VAT chargeable, is equal to the consideration: VATA 1994, s. 19(2) (see **Chapter 18**).

This wording is serious! The supplier must always ensure that the price charged for the supply of goods and services makes provision for the VAT for which it must account on the supply. Thus, if a taxable person needs to charge £100, in order to make a profit, it must charge the customer £100 *excluding VAT* or £100 *plus VAT*. If it fails to mention VAT, the VAT for which it must account will eat into the profit: see **SAQ 31**.

If you know the figure exclusive of VAT which the taxable person needs to charge, in order to make a profit, you simply add it to the VAT-exclusive consideration. If you want to ascertain the VAT-element of a VAT-inclusive figure (i.e. one which does not refer to VAT), you simply multiply the VAT-inclusive figure by 7/47 (assuming a VAT rate of 17.5%).

What is the VAT element of £100 as a VAT-inclusive figure? (Assume a VAT rate of 17.5%.)

£14.89, i.e. 100 × 7/47. This gives a VAT-exclusive price of £85.11, i.e. £100 − £14.89.

What VAT must be charged on a VAT-exclusive figure of £100?

£17.50. This gives a VAT-*in*clusive price of £117.50.

8.8 Summary

Despite the prospective abolition of ACT, on 6 April 1999, it is important to understand its current role in both the income tax and corporation tax calculations. This is because, as discussed in **8.3.2**, it tells you much about possible theories of company taxation. It is important to understand the concept of grossing-up, since you will encounter it frequently when considering income tax or corporation tax calculations.

The important point to notice about the NIC calculations for each Class of NIC is their relative unsophistication. The crudity of NICs as a form of income taxation is their most obvious characteristic. The important point to note about the VAT calculation is the importance of the VAT-exclusive value of a standard-rated supply. Equally, the fact that VAT concentrates on *turnover*, as opposed to some form of profit, is its most striking point of contrast with the other taxes discussed.

8.9   End of Chapter Assessment Questions

Refer to the facts concerning Amber Ltd and its shareholders: see **2.6**, **3.6**, **4.9**, **5.6** and **6.6**.

(a)   On 30 November 1998, the three surviving directors declare, and the company pays, a dividend of £12,000 gross, which is divided equally between each of the four shareholders of Amber Ltd.

Calculate:

   (i)   the amount of the *net* dividend received by each of the shareholders; *and*

   (ii)   the amount of the tax credit which each receives in respect of the dividend received.

(25 marks.)

(b)   On the basis that Alan's earnings from his directorship of Amber Ltd are £8,000 in the 1998/99 tax year, what amount of NICs is he liable to pay in that tax year?

(25 marks.)

(c)   In the 1998/99 tax year, Deborah receives £800 net in interest from debentures in Megabucks plc held by the trustees of the will trust of her uncle Frederick (died 1993), under which she has a life interest in possession. What figure must be included for this interest in Stage One of her income tax calculation, and deducted by way of credit at Stage Six?

(25 marks.)

(d)   Amber Ltd makes taxable supplies of £250,000 (excluding VAT) in the three-month period ending on 31 December 1998. What will be the *output* VAT on those supplies? What would be the VAT element of VAT-*in*clusive standard-rated supplies of £293,750?

(25 marks.)

See *Cases and Materials* (8.5), for a specimen answer.

CHAPTER NINE

REDUCING INCOME TAXATION (1)

9.1   Objectives

By the end of this chapter, you should be able to:

■ explain *how* charges on income reduce a person's liability to income tax or corporation tax;

■ demonstrate the effect of a *covenanted payment to charity* on lower, basic and higher rate taxpayers;

■ list the categories of *interest payments* capable of ranking as charges on income for an individual;

■ list the *categories of payments* capable of ranking as charges on income for a company.

9.2   Introduction

This chapter begins a five-part survey of the ways in which income taxation can be reduced. In this chapter, we discuss the effect of *charges on income* ('charges') in calculating *income tax* and *corporation tax*. Payments which qualify as charges on income operate to *transfer to the recipient* the 'slice' of the payer's statutory income covered by the charge.

A wide range of payments once ranked as charges, e.g. it was once common for parents to create charges by covenanting payments in favour of their children. If the payment was within the child's personal allowance (see **7.3**), the 'slice' of the parent's statutory income represented by the charge would escape income tax. However, in 1988, the range of payments ranking as charges was curtailed. In this chapter, we investigate the small number of payments still capable of being charges. We consider individuals and companies in turn. The points made in **9.3.1** apply, irrespective of the *capacity* in which you pay the charge.

9.3   Charges on Income of Individuals

Charges on income are certain payments which, since you are legally obliged to make them, are regarded as the income of the *recipient*, rather than as your own. They are therefore deducted from your statutory income, at Stage Two of your income tax calculation.

The range of payments capable of qualifying as charges has been gradually reduced. They have tended to be used for tax avoidance, the most famous and successful attempt being made in *IRC* v *Duke of Westminster* [1935] All ER Rep 259. This success was short-lived, however, since the decision was quickly overruled by legislation, whilst the anti-avoidance principle in it was qualified, in relation to composite transactions, by the *Ramsay* principle: see **4.4**. The Duke made his gardeners a yearly payment under deeds of covenant, instead of paying them their wages. The gardeners were still entitled to claim their wages from the Duke under their employment contracts, but there was an understanding that they would not do so. The Duke claimed that he was entitled to deduct the payments under the deeds as a charge on income. The Revenue disagreed with him. They argued that he was not entitled to do so since, *in substance*, the payments made by the Duke under the deeds were payments of *wages*.

A majority of the House of Lords agreed with the Duke. The substance of the arrangement was irrelevant. All that mattered was the *form* which the transaction took. There was a principle in English law, said their Lordships, that people are entitled to order their tax affairs in the way most advantageous to them. His Grace was therefore entitled to his charge on income. Anti-avoidance legislation was quickly enacted: see **18.4.3**. Even today, however, *two* types of payment made can qualify as charges on income of an individual:

(a)   certain *annual payments* made by you (see **9.3.1**); and

(b)   payments of *interest* made by you on *certain types of loan* (see **9.3.2**).

Only three types of *annual payments* qualify as charges on income of the payer. The general rule for individuals is that annual payments *cannot* qualify as charges on income: ICTA 1988, s. 347A. The interest payments referred to here are deductible as charges on income because of ICTA 1988, s. 353(1B).

9.3.1   ANNUAL PAYMENTS

If you make covenanted payments to charity, you will be familiar with *annual payments*: see *Cases and Materials* (**9.1.1**). Annual payments are known as *income settlements*, since they settle a stream of *pure income profit* on the recipient. The recipient therefore has a source of Schedule D, Case III income: see **16.5**. Settlements of income on the gardeners were what the Duke succeeded in achieving in *IRC* v *Duke of Westminster* and, for many years, parents would make settlements of income in their children's favour. However, legislative changes mean that *a covenanted payment to charity* is now one of only *three* types of annual payments made by an individual (other than as a trustee or PR) which are capable of qualifying as annual payments. The other two are:

(a)   'alimony' payments ordered to be made *before* 16 March 1988 (not discussed further in this book); and

(b)   payments for *bona fide commercial reasons*, in connection with your trade, profession or vocation, e.g. a partnership retirement annuity, patent royalties (specifically provided for by ICTA 1988, s. 348(2)(a)).

Payments for bona fide commercial reasons are discussed in **9.3.1.2**. Note that, e.g. estate annuities paid by individuals acting as PRs *can* count as charges on income: ICTA 1988, s. 347A(3), see **16.3.2**.

9.3.1.1 Covenanted payments to charity

If payments are made by you under a covenant which:

■ is not made by you in consideration of money or money's worth;

■ is made in favour of a charity;

■ requires payments to be made for a period which may exceed three years; and

■ cannot be terminated without the consent of the charity;

the payments can be deducted as a charge on income: ICTA 1988, s. 347A(7): see *Cases and Materials* (9.1.1.1).

You are a member of the Old Mansions Trust, a registered charity. You covenant your annual subscription to it, the deed complying with ICTA 1988, s. 347A(7). As a member of the Trust, you get concessionary admission charges to the Trust's properties. Will your covenant satisfy s. 347A(7)?

Apparently not: first condition, above. (Condition relaxed in practice.)

Refer to **7.3**. In **SAQ 65**, Angela covenants to make gross payments of £1,000 per annum to the RSPCA. £1,000 is therefore the figure which is to be deducted from her statutory income in Stage Two of her income tax calculation: ICTA 1988, ss. 835 and 836. From the gross amount, Angela will have to deduct basic rate income tax for the tax year 1998/99, at 23%, on making the payment: ICTA 1988, s. 348: see *Cases and Materials* (9.1.1.1). She must keep this deducted amount, in order to pay the *total income tax due* from her for 1998/99. At Stage Seven of her income tax calculation, she must therefore add back the basic rate tax deducted by her on making the payment, to the figure for *sub-total tax due*. The 23% income tax deducted at source helps her to pay the total income tax due. The effect of the deduction of basic rate tax on the payment, and the adding back of that tax to her sub-total tax due, is to leave the RSPCA with a *net* amount of £770, and to leave her with a duty to account for £230, along with her sub-total tax due. The RSPCA, being exempt from income tax, later reclaims from the Revenue the £230 deducted at source by Angela.

So much for the position when, as above and in **SAQ 65**, Angela covenants to pay a *gross* amount of £1,000 to the charity.

Why would she *in practice* covenant a *net* amount?

The basic rate of income tax may fluctuate over the life of the deed.

If the basic rate were to rise to 29%, the charity would receive £60 less under a covenant for a gross amount of £1,000 than when the basic rate was 23%. The tax deducted by Angela would be £1,000 x 29/100 = £290, and a net amount of £710 would be paid by her to the charity. The relevant part of the deed covenanting a net amount would therefore be:

> I, Angela . . . covenant to pay the RSPCA such a sum as, after deduction of income tax at the basic rate for the time being in force, will leave in the hands of the RSPCA the net sum of £770.

In this situation, a reduction in the basic rate of income tax will not affect the fact that Angela will still pay the charity £770.

Equally, however, for the reasons below, a reduction in the basic rate of income tax will leave the charity with *less* income under the covenant than before the change in the basic rate.

We now consider the income tax position, in turn, for basic rate, higher rate, lower rate and non-taxpayers.

Basic rate taxpayers: ICTA 1988, s. 348

Say it is the 1995/96 tax year, when the basic rate of income tax was 25%. I am a basic rate taxpayer. I pay £750 under a *net* covenant worded as above. I therefore have to gross up the £750 to find the sum before deduction of tax at 25% How do I do this?

I multiply the £750 by 100/75. That gives £1,000.

Continuing SAQ 88, what will be the *net* amount paid by me to the charity?

£750. Section 348(1)(c), ICTA 1988 allows me to keep the £250, whilst giving the charity £750. I have covenanted to pay the charity such a sum as, after deduction of income tax at the basic rate for the time being in force, will leave in its hands the net sum of £750.

Continuing SAQ 89, how much income tax can the charity reclaim from the Revenue in the 1995/96 tax year, assuming that the charity is totally exempt from income tax?

£250.

Continuing SAQ 89, what is the *total* amount eventually received by the charity?

The total amount eventually received by the charity is £1,000.

Continuing SAQ 89, how much will I be allowed to deduct from my statutory income as a charge on income?

So long as the basic rate of income tax is 25%, £1,000. As stated in the deed, I am deemed to have deducted 25% tax from a gross figure of £1,000. The figure of £250 is added by me to my *sub-total tax due*, to give me my *total income tax due*, at Stage Seven of my income tax calculation. The covenant produces no tax advantages for me and no tax disadvantages either. As a basic rate taxpayer, I pay 25% income tax on a gross figure of £1,000 in 1995/96, whether I enter into the covenant or not.

Contrast this with the position in the tax year 1998/99:

I am a basic rate taxpayer in the 1998/99 tax year. I pay the £750 as above in the 1998/99 tax year and gross up the £750 to find the gross sum, before deduction of tax at 23%. What figure does this produce?

Multiplying the £750 by 100/77 gives me £974.03.

Continuing SAQ 93, what is the *net* amount paid by me to the charity?

£750, as in 1995/96.

Continuing SAQ 93, how much income tax can the charity reclaim from the Revenue, assuming it is totally exempt from income tax?

£224.03 (i.e. £974.03 x 23%, or 23/77 x £750).

Continuing SAQ 93, what is the total amount eventually received by the charity?

The total amount eventually received by the charity is £974.03. This is a drop from the total amount received by the charity in 1995/96 of £25.97.

In the same way, e.g. you might make a *net* payment of £1,000 under a covenant. In that event, the total amount eventually received by the charity in the tax year 1998/99 would be £1,298.70 (i.e. £298.70 + £1,000).

How much would eventually have been received by the charity in the tax year *1995/96* at the then basic rate of income tax of 25%, on a net covenant of £1,000?

£1,333.33 (i.e. 25/75 × £1,000 = £333.33 + £1,000 = £1,333.33). The 1998/99 basic rate of 23% gives a fall of £34.63 from the 1995/96 amount.

(The moral of all this is that charities lose out when the basic rate of income tax goes down.)

How much am I allowed to deduct in the tax year 1998/99 from my *statutory income* as a charge on income, assuming a net covenant of:

■   **£750; or**

■   **£1,000?**

Under a net covenant of £750, £974.03. If I covenant a net amount of £750, I am deemed to have deducted 23% income tax from a gross figure of £974.03. The deducted amount is added by me to my *sub-total tax due*, in order to give me my *total income tax due*, at Stage Seven of my income tax calculation. The covenant produces no income tax advantages for me and no tax disadvantages either. As a basic rate taxpayer, I pay 23% income tax on a gross figure of £974.03 irrespective of whether I enter into a covenant or not.

Equally, under a net covenant of £1,000, £1,298.70. If I covenant a net amount of £1,000, I am deemed to have deducted 23% income tax from a gross figure of £1,298.70. The deducted amount is added by me to my *sub-total tax due*, as above. Again, it produces no tax advantages for me and no tax disadvantages either. *The covenant is tax-neutral for me, a basic rate taxpayer.*

Although it is neutral for basic rate taxpayers, the process described above can produce *very beneficial* results for higher rate taxpayers, as well as very disadvantageous results for lower rate and non-taxpayers.

Higher rate taxpayers: ICTA 1988, s. 348
The process discussed above can actually produce amazing benefits to higher-rate taxpayers, as we shall discover.

I am a higher rate taxpayer. I pay the £750 under a *net* covenant worded as above. Again, I have to gross up the £750 to find the sum before deduction of tax at 23%. For revision, how do I do this?

I multiply the £750 by 100/77. That gives £974.03.

Continuing SAQ 99, what will be the *net* amount paid by me to the charity?

£750.

Continuing SAQ 99, how much income tax can the charity reclaim from the Inland Revenue in the 1998/99 tax year, assuming that the charity is totally exempt from income tax?

£224.03.

Continuing SAQ 99, what is the *total* amount eventually received by the charity?

The total amount eventually received by the charity is £974.03.

Continuing SAQ 99, how much will I be allowed to deduct from my statutory income as a charge on income?

£974.03. As above, s. 348(1)(c), ICTA 1988 allows me to keep the £224.03, whilst giving the charity £750. This is because I have covenanted to pay the charity such a sum as, after deduction of income tax at the basic rate for the time being in force, will leave in its hands the net sum of £750. My statutory income is reduced by £974.03: s. 835(6)(b), ICTA 1988: see *Cases and Materials* **(7.2)**.

Now consider s. 3, ICTA 1988. This provides that:

> Where a person is required to be assessed and charged with income tax in respect of any . . . profits . . . out of which he makes [a covenanted payment] . . . he shall, in respect of so much of the . . . profits . . . as is equal to the payment and may be deducted in computing his total income, be charged at the basic rate.

Thus, my statutory income is reduced by £974.03 and, because of ICTA 1988, s. 3, even though I am a higher-rate taxpayer, I am liable to pay only basic rate income tax on that £974.03, i.e. £224.03. I can pocket the difference between the basic rate on £974.03 (i.e. £224.03) and the higher rate on £974.03 (i.e. £389.61), namely £165.58, without paying any income tax on that £165.58.

This is how the process can actually produce very beneficial results for higher-rate taxpayers.

Consider the following example. Say I have reached the end of Stage One of my income tax calculation, and my statutory income under all Schedules is £33,000. My income tax calculation would be like the one in (A) if I make the payments under the covenant as above, and like the one in (B) if I make the payments as above not under such a covenant:

(Decimals have been rounded up/down to nearest whole number.)

	(A) £	(B) £
Statutory income	33,000	33,000
Less Charges on income	(974)	N/A
Total income	32,026	33,000
Less Personal allowance	(4,195)	(4,195)
Taxable income	27,831	28,805
£4,300 at 20%	860	860
Next £22,800 at 23%	5,244	5,244
Excess over £27,100 at 40%	292	682
Sub-total tax due	6,396	6,786
Plus tax on charges paid	224	N/A
Total income tax due	6,620	6,786

In reducing my statutory income by £974, the covenant has reduced the *sub-total tax due* from me by £390, and my *total income tax due* by £166.

In (A), the charity gets £974, at a cost to me of £584 (i.e. £750 – £166). In (B), the charity gets £750, at a cost to me of £1,250 (i.e. £750 grossed-up at the higher rate).

The reduction in my *total income tax due* of £166 in effect represents tax-free income for me.

Lower rate taxpayers: ICTA 1988, s. 348
I am a lower rate taxpayer. I pay the £750 under a *net* covenant worded as above. Again, I have to gross up the £750 to find the sum before deduction of tax at 23%, which gives me £974.03.

What will be the *net* amount paid by me to the charity?

£750, as above.

Continuing SAQ 104, how much tax can the charity reclaim from the Revenue in the 1998/99 tax year, assuming that the charity is totally exempt from income tax?

£224.03, as above.

Continuing SAQ 104, what is the *total* amount eventually received by the charity?

£974.03.

Continuing SAQ 104, how much will I be allowed to deduct from my statutory income as a charge on income?

£974.03, as above.

Consider the following example.

Say I have reached the end of Stage One of my income tax calculation, and my statutory income under all Schedules is £7,000. My income tax calculation would be like the one in (A) if I make the payments under the covenant as above, and like the one in (B) if I make the payments as above not under such a covenant:

(Decimals have been rounded up/down to nearest whole number.)

	(A) £	(B) £
Statutory income	7,000	7,000
Less Charges on income	(974)	N/A
Total income	6,026	7,000
Less Personal allowance	(4,195)	(4,195)
Taxable income	1,831	2,805
£4,300 at 20%	366	561
Sub-total tax due	366	561
Plus tax on charges paid	224	N/A
Total income tax due	590	561

In reducing my statutory income by £974, the covenant has reduced the *sub-total tax due* from me by £195, but my *total income tax due* has been *increased* by £29.

In (A), the charity gets £974, at a cost to me of £779 (£750 + £29). In (B), the charity gets £750, at a cost to me of £937.50 (i.e. £750 grossed up at the *lower* rate).

The increase in my *total income tax due* of £29 represents a *clawback* by the Revenue of the difference between the deduction made by me on payment of the charge (i.e. £224) and 20% of £974 (i.e. £195).

Non-taxpayers: ICTA 1988, s. 349
I am a non-taxpayer. I pay the £750 under a *net* covenant worded as above. Again, I must gross up the £750 to find the sum before deduction of tax at 23%, which gives me £974.03. The net amount paid by me to the charity is £750, as above.

SAQ 108

How much income tax can the charity reclaim from the Inland Revenue in the 1998/99 tax year, assuming that the charity is totally exempt from income tax?

£224.03, as above. The total amount eventually received by the charity is £974.03, as above.

There is a further problem here, however. In the previous three cases, i.e. basic rate taxpayers, higher rate taxpayers, and lower rate taxpayers, ICTA 1988, s. 348 permits me to make the basic rate deduction described above, since those payments are made *wholly out of profits or gains brought into charge to income tax*. Section 348 does *not* apply where the covenantor has insufficient statutory income to cover the amount of the annual payment.

Instead, s. 349, ICTA 1988 applies, which is *significantly different* from s. 348. The main difference is that, although the payer must deduct a sum representing basic rate tax, the deduction made by the payer is *compulsory*. Under s. 348, ICTA 1988, the deduction made by the payer is *optional* only. The relevant part of s. 349 says:

> Where —
> (a)   any annuity or other annual payment charged with tax under Case III of Schedule D, not being interest . . . is not payable or not wholly payable out of profits or gains brought into charge to income tax, the person by or through whom any payment thereof is made shall, on making the payment, deduct out of it a sum representing the amount of income tax thereon.

Say I have reached the end of Stage One of my income tax calculation, and my statutory income under all Schedules is £4,100. My income tax calculation would be like the one in (A) below if I make the payments under the covenant as above, and like the one in (B) below if I make the payments as above not under such a covenant:

(Decimals have been rounded up/down to nearest whole number.)

| | (A) | (B) |
	£	£
Statutory income	4,100	4,100
Less Charges on income	(974)	N/A
Total income	3,126	4,100
Less Personal allowance	(3,126)	(4,100)
Taxable income	Nil	Nil
Sub-total tax due	Nil	Nil
Plus tax on charges paid	224	N/A
Total income tax due	224	Nil

In reducing my statutory income by £974, the covenant has *increased* my total income tax due by £224. I am *in effect* paying the gross amount of the charge on my income. In tax terms, this is the most disadvantageous of the possibilities we have discussed so far.

In (A), the charity gets £974, at a cost to me of £974 (£750 + £224).

The increase in my *total income tax due* of £224 represents a clawback by the Inland Revenue of the difference between the deduction made by me on payment of the charge (i.e. £224) and Nil. The charge on income does not benefit me because I have no *taxable income*.

I should notify the Revenue, under ICTA 1988, s. 350(1), that I have made the payment under the covenant. I will then be *assessed* to income tax of £224: see **19.3.5**.

Conclusion on covenanted payments to charity
The following propositions should be apparent:

■   it is *advantageous* to the payer to make covenanted payments to charity as a *higher-rate* taxpayer;

■   it is *neither disadvantageous nor advantageous* to the payer to make covenanted payments to charity as a *basic rate taxpayer*; and

■   it is *disadvantageous* to the payer to make covenanted payments to charity as either a *lower-rate* taxpayer or a *non*-taxpayer.

SAQ 109

For revision, why do covenants *not* tend to take the form of covenants to pay *gross* amounts?

If the covenant is a net covenant, the advantage to you is that you will know in any tax year exactly what you will be paying to the charity over the life of the deed. The disadvantage to you will be that you will not know in any tax year exactly what you will be paying to the Revenue, and therefore the total cost to you of the deed, over the whole of its life.

If the covenant is a gross covenant, the disadvantage to you is that you will not know in any tax year exactly what you will be paying to the charity over the life of the deed. In addition, you will not know in any tax year exactly what you will be paying to the Revenue over the life of the deed, and therefore its total cost to you.

9.3.1.2 Payments for *bona fide commercial reasons*: partnership retirement annuities and patent royalties

Setting aside pre-16 March 1988 alimony payments, the only other type of annual payment capable of qualifying as a charge on your income is a payment for bona fide commercial reasons, in connection with your trade, profession or vocation: ICTA 1988, s. 347A(2)(c). In practice, this means *partnership retirement annuities* and *patent royalties* (ICTA 1988, s. 348(2)(a)). The former is where you are a partner in a firm, and an *annuity* is paid by you to a retired partner, in return for that partner having given up, on retirement from the partnership, his or her share in the assets of the partnership.

As a continuing partner, you will generally pay a proportion of this annuity. Provided the conditions listed below are satisfied, you will be able to deduct that proportion from your statutory income at Stage Two of your income tax calculation: see **7.5**.

The annuity payments in the tax year must have been made (ICTA 1988, ss. 347A(2) and 660A(9)):

■ under the terms of the partnership agreement;

■ to a former partner or his or her spouse or other dependants, provided that, where the former partner is dead, the annuity must not be payable for a period longer than 10 years; and

■ under a liability incurred for full consideration.

Such payments are made *net* of basic rate income tax: ICTA 1988, ss. 348, 349.

SAQ 110

On 1 September 1998, Harold retires from his partnership in the law firm of Sue, Grabbit & Runne. The partnership deed provides that, on retirement, partners are to be paid an annuity of £20,000 per annum (net). He retains his interest in the partnership assets. Will the annuity be a charge on income for the continuing partners?

No. (**SAQ 200** contains a modification of these facts, where it *would* be such a charge.)

9.3.2   QUALIFYING PAYMENTS OF INTEREST

In order to be able to deduct interest paid on a loan made to you as a charge on income, you will need to ensure that the loan in question falls within one of the categories discussed in this section. Unlike with the annual payments in **9.3.1**, interest on each of these types of loan will be paid by you to the lender *gross* (interest payments are excluded from the scope of ss. 348 and 349, ICTA 1988). However, the *gross amount* will be deductible from your *statutory income*, at Stage Two of your income tax calculation.

For your payments of interest to be a charge on income, you must have paid the interest on a loan falling into basically one of four categories:

- to acquire *machinery or plant*;

- to acquire an interest in a so-called *close company*;

- to acquire an interest in a *partnership*; or

- to pay IHT.

In addition, interest paid to acquire an interest in a *company controlled by its employees*, and to acquire an interest in a *co-operative* can qualify as a charge on income, under ICTA 1988, s. 361, although these are beyond the scope of this book.

You cannot inflate the amount of the charge on income, by paying more than a reasonable commercial rate of interest. If you attempt this, the amount of interest in excess of the reasonable commercial rate will not qualify as a charge on income: ICTA 1988, ss. 353(3)(b), 787.

If the loan in question does not fall within any of these categories, your interest payments might still qualify as an *allowable deduction* in calculating your income profits under Schedule A, Schedule D, Case I or II, or Schedule E.

SAQ 11

Alan is an assistant solicitor. In the tax year 1998/99, he will have paid interest on his credit card of £1,245 and on his bank overdraft of £967. Will these interest payments qualify as a charge on income?

No.

9.3.2.1 Interest paid on loan to acquire machinery or plant: ICTA 1988, s. 359

This category is relevant to you only if you are a partner in a firm, or you are an employee, being someone who has paid interest on a loan to purchase machinery or plant. 'Machinery' is a self-explanatory term, although plant does require some explanation. We shall consider its meaning in detail in **Chapter 12**. For present purposes, we simply adopt Lindley LJ's definition of 'plant' in *Yarmouth* v *France* (1887) 19 QBD 647, although the term has come to have a wider meaning than this would suggest. In *Yarmouth* v *France*, Lindley LJ (at p. 658) described 'plant' as including:

> . . . whatever apparatus is used by a businessman for carrying on his business – not his stock in trade [i.e. trading stock] but all goods and chattels, fixed or moveable . . . which he keeps for permanent employment in his business.

The *conditions* for such interest payments being a charge on income are:

- the interest is paid by you as an individual partner or an employee, as the case may be; *and*

- if you are a *partner*, the partners are entitled to claim capital allowances in relation to the plant or machinery acquired by them with the loan (see **12.4.2**); *and*

- if you are an *employee*, you are entitled to claim capital allowances in relation to the plant or machinery acquired by you with the loan (see **12.4.2**); *and*

- whether you are an employee or a partner, no more than three years has elapsed from the end of the tax year in which you incurred the debt on which the interest has been paid by you.

SAQ 112

Would you expect a sole trader to be able to claim this relief?

Yes.

However, interest on such a loan to a sole trader is an allowable deduction in calculating trading profits under Schedule D, Case I or Case II: see **11.5.1.3**.

9.3.2.2 Interest paid on a loan to acquire an interest in a close company: ICTA 1988, ss. 360 (as amended by FA 1998), 361, 363

A close company is a company which is under the control of five or fewer *participators*, or any number of *participators* who are also directors, and their associates: ICTA 1988, s. 414, see **18.5.2**. A participator is someone who has some interest in the income or capital of the company, e.g. shareholders, and some loan creditors.

The relief is therefore designed to encourage you to invest in small companies, e.g. family companies. A loan to buy an interest in a close company can be one of *three* types, i.e. one which you use:

- to buy shares in the company; *or*

- to on-lend money to the company, provided that the money is used wholly and exclusively for the business of the company; *or*

■ to pay off an earlier loan used wholly and exclusively for the business of the company.

The conditions for claiming interest payments of this type as a charge on your income are that:

■ the company is a *close company*; *and*

■ the close company is a *qualifying close company*. This means that the company must not be a close investment-holding company: see **18.5.1.3**. For the present, note that a company will be a *qualifying close company* if it exists wholly or mainly for the purpose of carrying on a trade or investment in commercial property; *and*

■ the qualifying close company is such a company when the interest is paid by you; *and*

■ you have a *material interest* in the company.

Having a *material interest in the company* means that you must *either* control more than 5% of the ordinary share capital of the company, in which case you need not work for it (ICTA 1988, s. 360(2)), or you must be a shareholder in the company and work for the greater part of your time in the management or conduct of it: ICTA 1988, s. 360(3). In determining whether you have *control* of the company, your shareholding is added to the shares owned by your relatives, partners, or trustees of a trust with which you have some connection.

You work for a qualifying close company (not as a manager of it), and you are also a member of the family that owns all its issued shares. You do not own any shares in the company, although its articles of association (see 2.4.1.2) require existing shareholders to offer their shares to you before selling them to an outsider. One of the shareholders offers to sell their shares to you for £2,500. You need to take out a bank loan for this.

Will the loan fall within these provisions?

No.

If you get back any capital which you originally put into the company by way of loan to it, or as payment for shares in it, then the amount of interest qualifying as a charge will be reduced accordingly – the repayment is taken to reduce the amount of interest paid by you on the loan.

9.3.2.3   Interest paid on a loan to acquire an interest in a partnership: ICTA 1988, s. 362

This category of charge on income is relevant to you if you are, or are about to become, a partner in a firm. A loan to acquire an interest in a partnership, i.e. to become a partner in that partnership, can be made for three purposes. It can be one which you use:

■   to buy a share in the partnership; *or*

■   to contribute capital or make a loan to a partnership, the money being used wholly for the purposes of the trade, profession or vocation which the partnership carries on; *or*

■   to pay off an earlier loan used wholly and exclusively for the purpose of the trade, etc. carried on by the partnership: ICTA 1988, s. 362(1).

The condition for claiming interest payments of this type as a charge on your income is that you are a partner of the firm from the time when the loan is applied until the date when you pay the interest on the loan.

If you get back any capital which you originally put into the partnership by way of loan to it, or as payment for a share in it, the amount of interest qualifying as a charge will be reduced accordingly, the effect of the repayment to you being to reduce the amount of interest paid by you on the loan: ICTA 1988, s. 362(2).

On 1 March 1999, Olivia becomes a partner in the law firm of Sue, Grabbit & Runne. She will have to pay £10,000 for her partnership share. She borrows £10,000 from a bank, which she pays to the other partners on acquiring her share in the firm. She makes the first repayment of capital and interest to the bank on the same day, and the second on 1 April 1999.

Will she be able to claim the interest payments made by her as a charge on her income for the tax year 1998/99?

Yes.

9.3.2.4   Interest paid on a loan to pay IHT: ICTA 1988, s. 364

This relief is relevant if you are acting in the capacity of a PR, calculating income tax on the income profits of the deceased's estate.

When someone dies, the PRs may have to deliver to the Revenue, within a year of the month of the death, an account of all the property owned by the deceased: see **33.4.1.2**. The PRs can only administer the deceased's estate if they have obtained a grant of representation, and they can only obtain a grant of representation by paying any IHT which is due: see **33.4.1.3**. They will probably need to borrow money in order to pay the IHT, therefore. If so, interest payable by you, the PR, on the loan can be deducted as a charge on income at Stage Two of the calculation discussed at **7.6.2.2**.

The conditions for claiming to deduct the interest payments as a charge on the income of the estate are that:

■   the IHT is attributable to personal property owned beneficially by the deceased and which vested in the deceased's PRs on the death (see **26.4.4**); *and*

■ the interest is payable on a loan account, not on an overdraft; *and*

■ not more than 12 months have passed since the making of the loan to you.

Ermintrude dies on 1 February 1999. On 15 February 1999, her executors, Freda and George, sign a bank loan agreement, to borrow money needed to pay IHT on Ermintrude's estate. They obtain the grant of probate and pay the IHT on 1 May 1999. Will they be able to deduct the interest paid on the loan as a charge on the income of the deceased's estate in the 1998/99 tax year?

Yes.

9.4   Charges on Income of Companies

After FA 1996, charges on income are restricted to two main types of payments by companies. These are:

■ annual payments made by a company *otherwise than* under its *loan relationships; and*

■ patent royalty payments.

The former of these includes covenanted payments to charity. The procedure for making such payments is the same as for an individual, but it is governed by ICTA 1988, s. 349, since ICTA 1988, s. 348 cannot apply to UK-resident companies, because of the reference in that section to *income tax*.

The vital point of contrast between the charges on income of companies and the charges of individuals is that, since 1 April 1996, *interest payments cannot rank* as charges of a company. Instead, they are deductible in accordance with the rules on the loan relationships of companies discussed in **Chapter 11**. Even though payments of interest under a loan relationship *cannot* rank as a charge on income, it is still necessary *in general* for a company making a payment of *yearly* interest to deduct *lower* rate income tax on making the payment: ICTA 1988, s. 349(2): see **Cases and Materials (9.2)**. *Yearly interest* is defined as interest payable on a loan capable of lasting, or expected to last, for 12 months or longer.

Read ICTA 1988, s. 349 in *Cases and Materials* (9.2). Note down the situations in which a company is *not* required to deduct lower rate income tax on making a payment of interest.

If a payment, other than an interest payment, is capable of ranking as a charge on income, it must fulfil *three conditions* before it is deductible from a company's total profits. First, the payment must be shown as an income payment in the company's accounts; secondly, the company must have no right to a reimbursement of the payment from any source; and, finally, the payment must be made for valuable and sufficient consideration, unless it is a payment to charity: ICTA 1988, s. 338(5).

9.5 Summary

Given the considerable reduction in *statutory income* or *total profits* they can provide, it is unsurprising that the sphere of operation of charges on income has become restricted. In view of the way in which corporation tax operates, it is especially unsurprising that the ambit of charges on income is even more restricted for companies than it is for individuals.

For individuals, both *annual payments* and *qualifying payments of interest* can qualify as charges. The latter are paid *gross* by individuals, but generally *not* by companies. Since the former are paid *net*, they are advantageous for the higher rate taxpayer, neutral for the basic rate taxpayer and *disadvantageous* for the lower rate or non-taxpayer.

Crucially, interest can be a charge on income for individuals, although *not* for companies. Companies pay interest under the rules applicable to their loan relationships, discussed in **Chapter 11**. Even though interest *cannot* rank as a charge for companies, where the interest is *yearly* interest, lower rate income tax must generally be deducted by the company in making the payment.

9.6 End of Chapter Assessment Question

Refer to the facts concerning Brown & Co., the firm of solicitors in which Deborah is a partner: see **2.6**. The partners make their accounts up to 30 November in each calendar year. It is 20 September 1998. The three partners in Brown & Co., Deborah, Emerald and Frances, are contemplating making a £100,000 investment in machinery and plant on which they are entitled to claim capital allowances, at some point in the period to 30 November 1999. The partners share profits and suffer losses equally. They tell you that they propose to borrow this amount, and a loan has been arranged with Dogger Bank plc. They would like you to advise them on the deductibility of the interest payments under the loan for tax purposes.

They also tell you that Gerald, who retired from the firm on 30 November 1997, is being paid a retirement annuity by them. They also ask you to advise them on the deductibility of the annuity payments.

(Word limit: 380 (100 marks).)

See *Cases and Materials* **(9.4)**, for a specimen answer.

CHAPTER TEN

REDUCING INCOME TAXATION (2)

10.1 Objectives

By the end of this chapter, you should be able to:

■ list the personal reliefs deducted *from total income* in the income tax calculation;

■ state the *main conditions* for the reliefs deducted from total income;

■ list personal reliefs deducted *from total tax* in the income tax calculation;

■ state the *main conditions* for the reliefs deducted from total tax;

■ describe how the *MIRAS system* works;

■ list the categories of *income exempt from income tax*;

■ define the terms *input VAT* and *output VAT* for VAT purposes;

■ explain, for VAT purposes, the basis on which a taxable person is entitled to *deduct* input VAT from output VAT;

■ list the available *NIC* reliefs;

■ state briefly the conditions for *NIC reliefs*.

10.2 Introduction

This chapter continues the five-part survey begun in **Chapter 9**. However, in this chapter, we shall not be considering corporation tax, discussing only income tax, VAT and NICs. In relation to income tax, the personal reliefs we shall be considering work in one of two ways, i.e. as deductions from total income at Stage Three of your income tax calculation, or as deductions from total tax at Stage Five. Note *exactly* which ones are which. Note also that, because of the order of Stages in the income tax calculation, the former mean a reduction in your total income, whilst the latter mean an income tax reduction. We also consider those deductions and reliefs which operate outside your income tax calculation, as well as certain categories of income which are exempt from income tax.

VAT is a form of income taxation for a person unable to deduct input VAT from output VAT in full, and who does not carry on a business. In this chapter, we examine the method for deducting input VAT from output VAT. We also discuss NIC reliefs in this chapter, no doubt highlighting how limited such reliefs are.

10.3 Income Tax: Personal Reliefs

10.3.1 INDIVIDUALS: PERSONAL RELIEFS DEDUCTED FROM *TOTAL INCOME*

In certain circumstances, a non-UK-resident individual, who has income source(s) in the UK, may claim the personal reliefs listed below. However, the general rule is that they are available only to UK-residents. The personal reliefs listed below are deducted from your total income, at Stage Three of your income tax calculation. Do not confuse them with the *income tax reductions* discussed in **10.3.2**! The amount of the personal allowance is related to your age and other specific circumstances. Only two reliefs are deducted at this Stage, i.e. the *personal allowance*, which varies according to your age, and the *blind person's allowance*. For the 1998/99 tax year, the reliefs are:

Personal allowance (individual under 65 years old)	£4,195
Personal allowance (individual aged 65 to 74 years old)	£5,410
Personal allowance (individual aged 75 and over)	£5,600
Blind person's allowance	£1,330

In the 1998/99 tax year, Bella is 78 and blind. How much relief does she get as above?

£6,930, i.e. £5,600 + £1,330.

Note that the two reliefs which are related to the age of the taxpayer can be reduced where the taxpayer's total income exceeds £16,200. Your age-related relief is thus reduced by £1 for every £2 by which your income exceeds £16,200, although not so as to reduce the relief below the personal allowance for those under 65, i.e. £4,195. Note also that, where your personal relief(s) exceed your total income, any balance *cannot* be carried forward to later tax years, or transferred to another person, and is therefore wasted. The need to avoid the wastage of your personal relief(s) often dictates the use of one trading loss relief rather than another: see **Chapter 13**.

Refer to SAQ 116. Bella's total income in the tax year 1998/99 is £3,000. Can she deduct the difference between £3,000 and £6,930 from her total income for 1999/2000?

No.

The conditions for claiming each of these personal reliefs are as follows:

(a) Personal relief if you are below 65: ICTA 1988, s. 257(1). You must generally be an individual resident in the UK in the tax year under consideration;

(b) Personal relief if you are 65 or over: ICTA 1988, s. 257(2):

■ you must generally be an individual resident in the UK in the tax year under consideration;

■ your relevant birthday must fall in the tax year under consideration.

Note that, even if you die before your birthday, your PRs will still be able to use the allowance in the tax year of your death.

(c) Blind person's relief: ICTA 1988, s. 265:

■ you must generally be resident in the UK in the tax year under consideration;

■ you must be registered blind, under s. 29, NAA 1948, for all or part of that tax year;

■ if you are married to someone who is also registered blind, you are both entitled to the relief.

10.3.2   INDIVIDUALS: PERSONAL RELIEFS DEDUCTED FROM *TOTAL TAX*

Like those in **10.3.1**, these are not available to companies. The personal reliefs listed below are deducted from your total tax, at Stage Five of your income tax calculation, to give your *tax liability*. The amount of each relief is related to your circumstances. The amounts shown are for the 1998/99 tax year. Crucially, relief is given *not* at the full amount shown but at 15% of that amount, i.e. the italicised figure in the right-hand column:

Married couple's allowance (under 65 years old)	£1,900	*£285*
Married couple's allowance (65 to 74 years old)	£3,305	*£495.75*
Married couple's allowance (75 years old and over)	£3,345	*£501.75*
Additional personal allowance	£1,900	*£285*
Widow's bereavement allowance	£1,900	*£285*

The age shown in brackets is the age which the *elder spouse* must have reached in the tax year under consideration. For 1999/2000, these reliefs will be given at 10%, rather than 15%.

The husband gets the married couple's allowance (MCA) initially. However, by a formal election given within a particular time period, either the wife can opt to receive one-half of the basic allowance or the husband and wife together can agree to allocate it to the wife: **SAQ 69**.

John is 35, married and living with his wife, aged 30. To which personal reliefs is he entitled and what will be the amount of each?

Personal allowance and MCA, i.e. £4,195 (Stage Three) and £285 (Stage Five).

The conditions for claiming each of these personal reliefs are:

■   MCA – ICTA 1988, s. 257A:

(a)   you must be a man married to your wife for some part of the tax year; *and*

(b)   you must be living with your wife for some part of the tax year.

(See *Cases and Materials* (**10.1.1**).)

Fred was separated from his wife on 20 March 1998. Is he entitled to claim the MCA in 1998/99?

No.

■   APA – ICTA 1988, s. 259:

(a)   you must be:

(i)   a woman who is not throughout the tax year under consideration married to and living with your husband; *or*

(ii)   a man who is either not married to or not living with his wife for any part of the tax year under consideration or the whole thereof; *or*

(iii)   a spouse who is in any part of the tax year living with a spouse totally incapacitated by physical or mental infirmity; *and*

(b)   you must have a qualifying child living with you for the whole or any part of the tax year under consideration.

A *qualifying child* is your natural, legitimate, legitimated, adopted or step-child, or any other child maintained at your own expense for the whole or part of the tax year under consideration and who is:

(i)   born in the tax year under consideration; or

(ii)   under 16 at the beginning of the tax year under consideration; or

(iii)   over 16 but undergoing a full-time educational course or course of vocational training.

(c)   you can only have one allowance, regardless of the number of children you may have;

(d)   If these conditions are fulfilled, you do not need to be living alone to claim the allowance. However, the other individual or individuals cannot also claim the allowance.

■   WBA – ICTA 1988, s. 262:

(a)   you must be the widow of a man who has died either in the tax year under consideration or the previous tax year;

(b)   you must not have remarried in the year in respect of which the claim is made.

10.3.3   INDIVIDUALS: VENTURE CAPITAL TRUST (VCT) AND ENTERPRISE INVESTMENT SCHEME (EIS) DEDUCTIONS FROM *TOTAL TAX*

EIS and VCT deductions are made for an individual's investment in an EIS company, or a VCT. Investing in a VCT or EIS company enables you to claim yet a further deduction from your total tax at Stage Five of your income tax calculation. An investment in a VCT will also enable you to receive *exempt income* (see **10.5.1**), and will in addition enable you to obtain relief from the taxation of any profit on the disposal of the investment: see **23.3.2** and **23.5.5**. The deductions operate as follows:

(a)   If you are an investor in a VCT, you will be entitled to a deduction from your total tax in the tax year of your investment of 20% of a maximum investment of £150,000: ICTA 1988, s. 290(2). You will need to make this deduction at Stage Five of your income tax calculation, before deducting the reliefs discussed in **10.3.1** and **10.3.2**, and before deducting any EIS relief to which you are entitled: ICTA 1988, sch. 15B, paras 1(5), 1(6).

(b)   If you are an investor in an EIS company, you will be entitled to a deduction from your total tax in the tax year of your investment of 20% of a maximum investment of £100,000. You must make this deduction at Stage Five of your income tax calculation, again before deducting the income tax reductions discussed above, although after deducting any VCT relief, as above, to which you are entitled. The income tax reduction must be deducted *before* the reliefs in **10.3.1** and **10.3.2**: ICTA 1988, s. 289A(5).

There are extensive conditions to be satisfied before an investment will be treated as made in an EIS company or a VCT. These have been further strengthened in FA 1998, so only a sketch is possible here. Broadly, the EIS relief applies only to subscriptions for new shares in an EIS company, i.e. one which exists for the purpose of carrying on a qualifying trade or which is the parent company of a trading group. Many trades are qualifying ones, but trades which do not include insurance, banking and other financial activities. A VCT is a company whose shares are listed on the Stock Exchange, and whose speciality is investing in unlisted, higher-risk companies. The idea is that the investor is thus able to spread the risks otherwise attendant on investing in unlisted companies.

10.4   Income Tax: Deductions and Reliefs *Outside* Your Income Tax Calculation

Some examples of these are as follows:

10.4.1   MIRAS: ICTA 1988, ss. 369-79

You can obtain MIRAS on the payments of interest made by you to the mortgagee, subject to certain conditions. You must be the owner of an estate or interest in land in the UK or Ireland, and you must pay interest on a loan made to you for the purpose of acquiring or developing that land for use as your only or main residence.

The relief has *no part* in your income tax calculation. Instead, you deduct MIRAS relief from the payments of interest you make to the mortgagee, as and when you make them. The amount which you deduct for 1998/99 is 10% of the gross interest payment made by you on a maximum of £30,000 of the loan: ICTA 1988, s. 357(1B). The mortgagee claims from the Revenue an amount equal to each deduction made by you: ICTA 1988, s. 369(6).

SAQ 120

Bob's house is subject to a mortgage throughout the 1998/99 tax year. In 1998/99, he will make monthly interest payments of £200 (gross) to the mortgagee. How much will the building society *actually receive* from Bob each month?

£180, i.e. £200 − £20.

SAQ 121

How will these payments be shown in his 1998/99 income tax calculation?

They won't!

SAQ 122

What amount will the mortgagee reclaim from the Revenue in relation to each month's net payment of interest?

£20.

SAQ 123

If mortgage interest relief were given, but *not* at source, how would it be given?

As a tax credit of 10% of the gross interest payments over the tax year, i.e. as a deduction from total tax.

The conditions for relief to be deducted at source under MIRAS are:

(a)   You must be the owner of an estate or interest in land in the UK or Ireland. PRs can claim the relief, provided that interest payments continue to be made by them out of the estate income after the death.

(b)   The interest must be paid on a loan for the purpose of acquiring or developing land for use as your only or main residence (the *qualifying purpose*). If you own two or more houses, you *cannot* choose which one is to be deemed to be your main residence, as you can for the CGT private residence relief: see **22.4.4**.

(c)   The loan on which the interest is paid must actually be used by you for the qualifying purpose when it is taken out by you, or within a reasonable time thereafter.

(d)   If the loan on which the interest is paid exceeds £30,000, you can only obtain MIRAS on the interest on the first £30,000. The £30,000 ceiling applies per residence, irrespective of whether you are a joint borrower or the sole borrower.

ACTIVITY 15

Read the extract from IR 123, *Mortgage Interest Relief – Buying Your Home*, May 1994 in *Cases and Materials* (10.2.1), noting that relief has been reduced from 15% (1997/98) to 10% (1998/99).

10.4.2   INTEREST PAID ON A LOAN TO BUY A LIFE ANNUITY

This relief is relevant if you are an individual and you are at least 65 years old: ICTA 1988, s. 365. If so, interest paid by you on loans up to £30,000 made for this purpose will be eligible for relief, not at 10%, as in the case of MIRAS, but at the basic rate of 23%. Apart from this difference, the mechanism is the same as MIRAS, so the deduction is made by you when the payment is made, not in your income tax calculation.

The conditions for claiming the relief are:

(a)   You must be at least 65 when the loan on which you pay the interest is made to you.

(b)   You, or one of the people to whom the annuity is paid, must own an estate or interest in land in the UK or Ireland.

(c)   The loan must be secured on that land.

(d)   The land must be used as your only or main residence at the time the interest is paid by you on the loan.

(e)   At least 90% of the loan must be applied by you, the borrower, in purchasing a life annuity ending either with your death or the survivor of you, the borrower, and two or more people to whom the annuity is paid.

(f)   If you do not pay the interest on the loan, it must be paid by one of the annuitants.

SAQ 124

In the tax year 1998/99, Sally pays gross interest totalling £6,000 satisfying the above requirements. If she deducts the relief from the payments at source, how will the relief be reflected in her income tax calculation?

Trick question! Not at all.

10.4.3   VOCATIONAL TRAINING RELIEF: FA 1991, SS. 32, 33

This relief was originally relevant to you if you were under 30 and paying course/exam fees leading to an NVQ/SVQ, Levels 1 to 5 in the tax year under consideration. From 1996/97, the relief has been extended to people of 30 or above, if they are paying for a full-time vocational course, not necessarily one leading to NVQs/SVQs. The relief works in the same way as MIRAS and life assurance premium relief. Like the latter, although unlike the former, a deduction of the basic rate of income tax is made by the student on making payments of the fees, i.e. 23% in 1998/99. Detailed conditions are contained in regulations.

10.4.4   CONTRIBUTIONS TO A PERSONAL PENSION SCHEME: ICTA 1988, SS. 640, 640A

This relief is relevant to you if you have a source of income from an office or employment and you make contributions to a *personal pension scheme* in the tax year under consideration. The relief works like life assurance premium relief, in that a deduction of the *basic* rate of income tax is made by you on making the contributions: ICTA 1988, s. 639(3).

10.5   Income Tax: Exempt Income

Categories of income exempt from income tax include:

10.5.1   INCOME FROM A VCT: ICTA 1988, SS. 42AA, 332A

Dividend income from a VCT, although not an EIS company, is exempt from income tax. The income produced by the VCT is not regarded as income for any income tax purposes: ICTA 1988, sch. 15B, para. 7(1).

10.5.2   SCHOLARSHIP INCOME

If you receive scholarship income, it is exempt from income tax: ICTA 1988, s. 331.

10.5.3   ONLY SOME SOCIAL SECURITY BENEFITS

Child benefit is exempt income, as also is one-parent benefit; attendance allowance; disability living allowance; family credit; maternity allowance; severe disablement allowance; guardian's allowance; war widow's pension; widow's payment; payments from the social fund; housing benefit; sickness benefit; incapacity benefit; and disability working allowance.

Others are specifically *not* exempt from income tax, e.g. state retirement pension; widow's pension; jobseeker's allowance; statutory maternity pay and statutory sick pay. Incapacity benefit is *exempt* income if paid in the first 28 weeks of incapacity *or* if it is payable for a period of incapacity which began before 13 April 1995 (i.e. the incapacity formerly entitled the individual to *invalidity benefit*).

10.5.4   INTEREST PAID TO YOU UNDER NATIONAL SAVINGS CERTIFICATES

These are different from NSB deposit accounts: see **10.5.5**. There are various National Savings Certificates and it is possible to save regularly or make lump-sum deposits.

10.5.5 NATIONAL SAVINGS BANK ACCOUNTS

Up to £70 of interest received by you each year from ordinary NSB accounts is exempt from income tax: ICTA 1988, s. 325. You and your spouse, if relevant, can each claim a £70 exemption separately or £140 in respect of interest from a joint account.

10.5.6 PROFIT-RELATED PAY

If you are a participating employee in a *profit-related pay* scheme, the lower of 20% of your earnings and £4,000 is exempt income. The £4,000 limit on relief is reducing to £2,000 for so-called profit periods beginning in 1998, and to £1,000 for those beginning in 1999. The exemption will be abolished for profit periods beginning on or after 1 January 2000.

10.5.7 THE RENT-A-ROOM SCHEME

If you rent out a room in your house, gross rental income not exceeding £4,250 in the tax year under consideration will be exempt from income tax.

Read the extract from the article on 'Rent a Room Relief' by David Williams at *Cases and Materials* (10.3.1).

10.5.8 INCOME FROM TESSAS

Any interest or bonus payable on a TESSA is exempt from income tax for the first five years of its existence, provided certain conditions are met: ICTA 1988, ss. 326A–D. The conditions are that:

(a) You are at least 18 years old when you open the TESSA.

(b) No more than £3,000 is deposited by you in the TESSA in the first 12 months after the TESSA is opened.

(c) No more than £1,800 is deposited by you in the TESSA in any of the succeeding 12-month periods.

(d) No more than £9,000 is deposited by you in the TESSA in total.

(e) The money you have deposited in the TESSA must be left there for five years. If you leave it in the account for longer than five years, you will begin to pay income tax at the 20% rate on it.

What do you think is the main disadvantage of a TESSA?

The capital deposited in the TESSA is frozen for a minimum of five years.

It should, however, be stressed that interest earned in one year, less lower rate tax on the interest for that year, can be withdrawn without jeopardising the tax-free status of the income from the TESSA: ICTA 1988, s. 326B.

Lucy has had a TESSA since 30 November 1994. In 1998/99, the *interest* earned on the capital deposited is £70. How much of that interest can she withdraw without affecting its tax-free status?

£56.00, i.e. £70 − 20/100 × £70 = £70 − £14.00 = £56.00.

You will be able to open a TESSA till 5 April 1999 under the above rules. The Individual Savings Account (ISA) will be introduced from 6 April 1999.

10.5.9   INCOME FROM PERSONAL EQUITY PLANS (PEPS)

The main advantage of a PEP is that a capital profit generated by the disposal of investments in a PEP is exempt from CGT: see **23.3.2**. However, dividends generated by shares held in the PEP and interest generated by loans made by the PEP, provided it is reinvested, are also exempt from income tax.

A PEP is a scheme under which you deposit up to £6,000 with an authorised PEP manager, that person being authorised by you to buy, sell and hold investments in mainly UK companies on your behalf. The PEP manager claims the exemptions from income tax and CGT to which you are entitled. The manager (e.g. a bank, a building society or a unit trust) claims a percentage commission of the sum invested by you in the PEP.

10.6   Value Added Tax: Deductions and Reliefs

After the previous discussion of income tax, we now turn to VAT, so *think VAT* in this section!

For a taxable person, the full right of input tax deduction is crucial. It means that where, in a VAT return period (see **4.3.4**), that person's output VAT is greater than their input VAT, it can reduce its liability for output VAT by deducting the input TAXAT from the output VAT. Equally, where that person's input VAT is greater than its output VAT in a return period, it can reclaim the excess of its input VAT over its output VAT for that period.

A taxable person has one month *after the end of the VAT return period* to submit its VAT return to Customs, otherwise interest and penalties may be payable: see **19.5**. On the VAT return, the taxable person *either* reclaims from Customs the amount by which its input VAT exceeds its output VAT, or pays to Customs the amount by which its output VAT exceeds its input VAT.

If the taxable person is a so-called *fully taxable person*, then it is entitled to claim all the input VAT which it incurred in the making of taxable supplies in the return period or, if its output VAT exceeds its input VAT, the taxable person is entitled to deduct its input VAT in full from its output VAT.

Reread 3.4.2.

Matco Ltd is a fully taxable person. In the return period from 1 January 1999 to 31 March 1999, it incurs *input VAT* of £100, which it uses to make taxable supplies, the *output VAT* on those supplies in that period being £100,000. What is its VAT liability in the return period?

£99,900, i.e. £100,000 − £100.

Datco Ltd is a fully taxable person. In the return period from 1 January 1999 to 31 March 1999, it incurs *input VAT* of £100,000, which it uses to make taxable supplies, the *output VAT* on those supplies in that period being £100. What is its VAT liability in the return period?

Nothing. It can reclaim input VAT of £99,900 from Customs.

The situation envisaged in **SAQ 128** is admittedly unusual. An unusually large acquisition by Datco in the return period (e.g. of new business premises), on which VAT was payable to the supplier, would cause this effect.

Datco Ltd is entitled to reclaim all of its input VAT in SAQ 128, but does it suffer *any* detriment in so doing?

Yes – it has to wait until the end of the return period to get the repayment of input VAT.

The way to solve this problem is for Datco Ltd to make major acquisitions on which VAT is payable as close as possible to the end of the return period.

All of this depends on the taxable person (the 'trader') being a fully-taxable person. However, the trader might also not be a fully-taxable person, since it might also make exempt supplies or non-supplies, i.e. it might be *partially exempt* for VAT purposes. The question therefore is this. How much of the trader's input VAT must be attributed to exempt supplies made by the trader and thus be irrecoverable? The answer is provided by VATA 1994, ss. 25 and 26 and VATR 1995 (SI 1995 No. 2518):

■ The trader can *recover fully* input VAT which is *directly attributable* to supplies of goods and services used by it, or to be used, in making *taxable* supplies.

■ The trader cannot recover *at all* input VAT which is *directly attributable* to supplies of goods and services used by it, or to be used, in making *exempt* supplies or non-supplies (i.e. *exempt input VAT*).

■ The trader can recover *an apportioned part* of input VAT which is attributable to taxable supplies, exempt supplies and non-supplies (i.e. *residual input VAT*). The apportioned part is found by applying the *standard method of apportionment* or another method agreed with Customs.

There is a *de minimis* rule, which says that the taxable person can treat all of its input VAT as being attributable to taxable supplies, and thus be treated as a *fully taxable person*, where its exempt input VAT does not exceed:

■ £7,500 over the year; or

■ £625 per month *on average*;

and is no more than:

■ 50% of all of the trader's input VAT.

We are concerned only with the standard method of apportionment. This is as follows:

■ First the trader attributes the residual input VAT according to the ratio of taxable supplies made by it in the return period to all supplies and non-supplies.

■ The trader then reduces that ratio to a percentage of taxable supplies to all supplies.

■ Finally, the trader multiplies the *residual input VAT* by the percentage of taxable supplies to all supplies, in order to arrive at the residual input tax recoverable by the taxable person.

You will have an opportunity of applying these rules in the End of Chapter Assessment Question.

Traders may also be entitled to a *reduction* in output VAT or a *refund* of input VAT where debts owed to them have gone bad (*'VAT bad debt relief'*).

10.7 NIC Reliefs

Finally, we turn to NICs. NIC reliefs are somewhat limited. They fall into two categories. First, an employer liable to pay secondary Class 1 NICs may be entitled to a *contributions rebate* for new employees who have been unemployed for two years or more (the *employer's contributions holiday*). Secondly, employees who are contracted-out of SERPS can have their primary Class 1 NICs reduced by the *contracted-out rebate*.

10.7.1 THE EMPLOYER'S CONTRIBUTIONS HOLIDAY

Employers are entitled to a contributions holiday in relation to certain new employees commencing their employment on or after 6 April 1996. An employer can decide to apply it to some new employees only, or to none at all. The employee will have to satisfy the following conditions before the employer can participate in the scheme, i.e. the employee must have:

■ begun to work for the employer on or after 6 April 1996; *and*

■ been employed by the employer for at least 13 weeks; *and*

■ been under state pension age when the employment began; *and*

■ agreed to participate in the scheme; *and*

■ been unemployed and receiving benefits for two years or more.

10.7.2 THE CONTRACTED-OUT REBATE

This rebate is relevant to employees. Part of your primary Class 1 NICs, as an employee, qualifies you for the State Earnings-Related Pension Scheme (SERPS). SERPS is in addition to the basic state pension, to which you are entitled by virtue of your NICs on the part of your earnings up to the LEL. The part of your NICs which entitles you to SERPS is that on your *band earnings*, i.e. the earnings band between the LEL and the UEL. As an employee, you can *contract out* of SERPS, and thereby elect to receive a pension, in addition to your basic state pension, from one of two types of private pension scheme, i.e. an *occupational pension scheme* or a *personal pension scheme*. The important point here is that, as an employee contracted-out of SERPS, the NICs you must pay on your band earnings are reduced *below* what they would have been, had you remained in SERPS: see **8.5.1**.

This reduction is referred to as the *contracted-out rebate*. Depending on whether the contracted-out scheme is an occupational pension scheme or a personal pension policy, it is paid *either* by your employer and yourself direct to the scheme, or by the DSS to the scheme at the end of the tax year under consideration.

10.8   Summary

In this chapter, we have continued the survey begun in **Chapter 9**. We have been concerned only with income tax, VAT and NICs.

In relation to income tax, the personal reliefs we have considered are either deductions from total income, at Stage Three of your income tax calculation, or deductions from total tax at Stage Five. Note *exactly* which are which. We have also considered deductions and reliefs operating outside your income tax calculation, as well as exempt income for income tax purposes.

In addition, we have considered VAT and NICs. In **10.9** below, you will have an opportunity to consider the effect of *partial exemption*, with an example. Note the limited categories of NIC reliefs.

REDUCING INCOME TAXATION (2)

10.9   End of Chapter Assessment Question

Refer to the facts concerning Amber Ltd in **2.6**, **3.6**. As stated, usually it makes only standard-rated supplies. However, by mistake, in the return period from 1 January 1999 to 31 March 1999, it makes certain supplies of financial services, i.e. exempt supplies (VATA 1994, sch. 9, Group 5). Amber Ltd's input VAT in that period is:

(a)   input VAT attributed to *taxable* supplies: £40,000;

(b)   input VAT attributed to *exempt* supplies: £12,000; and

(c)   residual input VAT: £25,000.

Amber Ltd therefore has total input VAT in that period of £77,000, i.e. £40,000 + £12,000 + £25,000. In the same period, Amber Ltd has made exempt supplies of £30,000 and taxable supplies of £100,000.

Applying the standard method, how much of Amber Ltd's residual input VAT is recoverable?

(100 marks.)

See *Cases and Materials* (**10.5**) for a specimen answer.

CHAPTER ELEVEN

REDUCING INCOME TAXATION (3)

11.1   Objectives

By the end of this chapter, you should be able to:

■   distinguish a *trading company* from an *investment company*;

■   explain the significance of *management expenses* for an investment company;

■   state the rules for making allowable deductions from *income* from land;

■   state the rules for making allowable deductions from *trading income*;

■   state the rules for making allowable deductions from *employment income*;

■   explain the concept of a *loan relationship* of a company;

■   explain the significance of *interest paid* by a company under a loan relationship in its corporation tax calculation.

11.2   Introduction

In this chapter, we continue our survey of how legislation permits the burden of income taxation to be reduced. However, we confine ourselves entirely to income tax and corporation tax. The discussion applies to both taxes, unless the contrary is clearly indicated.

With two exceptions, we are concerned with the deductions made at Stage One of the income tax or corporation tax calculation, under Schedule A, Schedule D (Cases I and II), and Schedule E. The two exceptions are the *management expenses of an investment company*, and payments under *non-trading loan relationships of a company*, both of which involve Stage Three of the corporation tax calculation. These apart, we are concerned with the calculation of income profits. Remember, there is an income profit under each of the Schedules if the making of allowable deductions from income results in a positive figure. If it gives a negative figure, there will be an *income loss*: see **2.3.2**. An examination of reliefs for income losses forms **Chapter 13**. Income receipts under the Schedules are discussed in **Chapters 14** to **17**.

11.3 Management Expenses of Investment Companies

A legislative distinction is made between *investment* income and *trading* income, which is explored in **Chapters 14** to **17**. For the present, it should be noted that, for a company, the general rule is that Schedule D, Case I income counts as *trading* income, whilst Schedule A and Schedule D, Case III income is *investment income*. Both trading and investment are *business* activities, the term *business* encompassing both of these activities. Since a company's income could consist mainly of investment income, some way of providing tax relief for its running costs is needed. This provision is made through the concept of the *management expenses* of an *investment company*.

An investment company is defined in ICTA 1988, s. 130 as:

> . . . any company whose business consists wholly or mainly in the making of investments and the principal part of whose income is derived therefrom.

Management expenses, or *expenses of management*, are the general running costs of the company, e.g. the salaries paid by the company to its employees, its administrative costs, etc. An investment company is permitted to deduct management expenses, not at Stage One of its corporation tax calculation, but at Stage Three. In other words, the company deducts them from its total profits, at the same Stage as it deducts any charges it may pay, in order to give its profits chargeable to corporation tax: see **7.4**, s. 75(1) and 75(3). Only a company whose sources of income were wholly or mainly rental income and/or interest could come within this definition. If, instead, a company's business is mainly that of trading, it cannot be within the definition, and no management expenses may be deducted by it from its total profits. Such a company can only make the allowable deductions discussed in **11.5**.

The restrictive definition of an investment company is easily explained. Since an investment company deducts management expenses, not from its income under Schedule A, and not from its income under Schedule D, Case III, but from its total profits, any wider definition of an investment company would provide such companies with a considerable tax avoidance opportunity.

11.4 Allowable Deductions from Rental Income

Rental profits are calculated under Schedule A. From 1 April 1998, the same rules apply for calculating a company's rental profits as for the rental profits of an individual.

The rules for determining the rental income from which allowable deductions are to be made are discussed in **Chapter 17**. Schedule A now relies on the same rules for *allowable deductions* as Schedule D, Case I or II. Therefore, in the absence of contrary statutory provision, the rules of Schedule D, Case I or II and generally accepted accounting principles (**1.5.3**) determine what allowable deductions can be made by a company in calculating its Schedule A profits. In addition, where the company qualifies as an *investment company*, it is entitled to deduct its management expenses from its total profits.

SAQ 130

Once a person's Schedule A profits have been calculated, what happens to the resulting figure?

It goes in Stage One of the income tax or corporation tax calculation, as the case may be.

On this basis, the rule for making allowable deductions from income under Schedule A is therefore that the expenditure must be incurred by the person receiving the Schedule A income *wholly and exclusively* for the purpose of its Schedule A business. In addition, since the rules of Schedule D, Case I and II apply, the deduction must not fall within the list of prohibited deductions for traders: see **11.5.1.3**. The recipient of Schedule A income (generally a landlord) is therefore allowed to make the following deductions from Schedule A income in the tax period under consideration, in order to give the rental profit for that period (or rental loss):

- any repairs carried out to let properties;

- any insurance premiums incurred on the let properties;

- the fees of any surveyors or architects who have charged for maintenance work, i.e. *not* improvements;

- services which the landlord is obliged to provide for its tenants, for which it receives no payment separate from the rental income;

- electricity and gas bills for heating and lighting corridors and landings incurred by the landlord.

If the landlord has had to pay input VAT on any of these items of expenditure, that VAT will only be an allowable deduction for income tax or corporation tax purposes if the landlord is not entitled to obtain credit for any of it as input VAT: see **10.6** and **17.7.1**.

Arkwright Ltd owns a number of houses in Canal Street, Coketown. All are tenanted. Its accounting period ends on 30 September in each calendar year. In the accounting period ended on 30 September 1998, the company has incurred, in relation to 2 Canal Street, insurance costs of £300, repair costs of £1,250 (including VAT) and water rates of £150. It was legally obliged to pay each of these amounts, under the terms of its standard-form rental agreement. In the 1998 accounting period, the company's rental income from all of the properties is £7,500.

What are Arkwright's rental profits, for inclusion in Stage One of its corporation tax calculation for the accounting period ending on 30 September 1998? (Arkwright Ltd is not a taxable person for VAT purposes.)

£5,800, i.e. £7,500 − £300 − £1,250 − £150.

11.5   Allowable Deductions from Trading Income

We move to Schedule D, Cases I and II now, as we consider the allowable deductions available to a person with income from a trade, profession or vocation. We consider the meaning of the expressions 'trade', 'profession' and 'vocation' in detail in **Chapter 15**. As a quick explanation, however, the term 'trade' means the exchange of goods or services, or a combination of goods and services, for reward. For historical reasons, as we shall discover, it does not generally include renting out property, even though this is a provision of services by the landlord.

In this section, we consider in turn the allowable deductions rules for individuals and companies. Where the trader is an individual, the rules are the same, whatever the capacity in which that individual seeks to make the allowable deductions from trading income. Although the rules are basically the same, recent legislation on companies' *loan relationships* means that individuals and companies need to be considered separately. This complements the point made in **9.4** that interest payments made by a company are not deductible as charges on income.

11.5.1   INDIVIDUAL TRADERS

The allowable deductions of individuals are subject to three conditions. Expenditure by an individual trader is an allowable deduction from trading income if:

■ it is incurred *wholly and exclusively* for the purpose of the trade, profession or vocation: Schedule D, Cases I and II;

■ it is an *income expense*, as opposed to a capital one; *and*

■ its deduction from Schedule D, Case I or II income is *not prohibited* by statute.

Note the vital point that it is the second of these conditions which makes the concept of capital allowances necessary: **Chapter 12**. We shall concentrate on each of the three conditions in turn, and then consider some typical items of expenditure which you might incur as a trader which should be deductible from your trading income as allowable deductions in the accounting period. It should be stressed that, for the purposes of this chapter, the term *trader* is synonymous with a professional person or a person following a vocation: Schedule D, Case II. Note, however, that there are important differences between Schedule D, Cases I and II, considered in **Chapter 15**.

If expenditure satisfies all of the three conditions, it will be an allowable deduction from trading income in calculating the trader's income profits under Schedule D, Cases I or II.

11.5.1.1   *Wholly and exclusively* for the purpose of the trade

This condition is the first head of disallowance, (a) in ICTA 1988, s. 74(1), which sets out a list of items of expenditure *not* satisfying the conditions and therefore not ranking as allowable deductions: see **11.5.1.3**. There has been a certain amount of case law on whether the wholly and exclusively test has been satisfied on the facts of a particular case, most recently *McKnight* v *Sheppard* [1996] STC 627 and *Abbott* v *IRC* [1996] STC 41. From the cases, the position seems to be as follows.

First, there must be *no dual purpose* behind the expenditure. However, it may be possible to split a payment made, so that part of it is incurred wholly and exclusively for the purpose of the trade and is therefore an allowable deduction, and the other is not. The need for only one purpose, where no such split is or can be made, was stated forcibly in *Bentleys, Stokes & Lowless* v *Beeson* [1952] 2 All ER 82, the actual decision in which has been overturned by s. 577, ICTA 1988 (see **1.5.3** and **11.5.1.3**).

Bentleys, Stokes & Lowless were a firm of solicitors, the partners of which found it convenient to discuss matters with clients over lunch, claiming an allowable deduction for the lunches, on the basis that expenditure on them had been incurred wholly and exclusively for the purposes of the trade. The Court of Appeal held that this was indeed the case and that there was no dual purpose in the expenditure. Romer LJ said:

. . . the purpose must be the *sole purpose*. The [statute] says so in clear terms. If the activity be undertaken with the object both of promoting business and also with some other purpose, for example, with the object of indulging an independent wish of entertaining a friend or stranger or of supporting a charitable or benevolent object, then the paragraph is *not* satisfied *though in the mind of the actor the business motive may predominate*. For the statute so prescribes. *Per contra*, if, in truth, the sole object is business promotion, the expenditure is not disqualified because the nature of the activity necessarily involves some other result, or the attainment or furtherance of some other objective, since the latter result or objective is necessarily inherent in the act. [*Emphases added*.]

What, do you imagine, was the crucial factor in the solicitors' firm winning this case?

The capable way in which the facts were presented to the General Commissioners: see **19.3.9**. (An ounce of *fact* is worth a ton of *law*!)

It follows that, if the Revenue can establish a dual purpose, the expenditure will not be deductible as an allowable deduction. Take *Mallalieu* v *Drummond* [1983] 2 All ER 1095: see *Cases and Materials* (**11.1.1.1**). The (now) Lady Mallalieu had a practice at the bar which necessitated her spending her time predominantly in court. The Bar Council had issued guidance on how lady barristers should dress in court. In accordance with that guidance, she wore a black dress or a black suit, tights and shoes and white shirts or blouses, not only for court, but also in chambers and for travelling to and from court. Her claim to deduct as an allowable deduction more than £500 in one tax year as the cost of replacing and laundering this clothing was disallowed by the Revenue and this disallowance was eventually upheld by the House of Lords. What was fatal to Lady Mallalieu's claim was the fact that the clothing could have been worn by her outside court, as well as in court. Lord Brightman, delivering the only full speech in the majority of the Law Lords, said that it was an inescapable conclusion that she had purchased the clothes partly with the object of meeting her personal needs, as well as partly for the purpose of appearing in court: it would have been 'impossible' for the Commissioners to have reached any other conclusion on the facts.

It should, however, be noted that *Mallalieu* v *Drummond* only dealt with expenditure relating to clothing such as suits and blouses, etc. worn by barristers. Barristers can in practice claim an allowable deduction from their Schedule D, Case II income equal to the cost of their wig and gown in the tax period it is bought by them, although this practice must be open to the technical objection that expenditure on these items is capital expenditure: see **11.5.1.2**.

Read the extracts from the speech of Lord Brightman in *Mallalieu* v *Drummond* at *Cases and Materials* (11.1.1.1). Consider *exactly* what expenditure Lady Mallalieu wanted to deduct, and *why*.

Despite constant re-affirmation by the courts that there must be only one purpose in the payment which you are claiming as an allowable deduction, it may be possible to split the purpose of the payment into a trading component and a non-trading component, an allowable deduction being given to you only for the former.

Catherine is a music-teacher. She uses her drawing-room to give piano and singing lessons. The income of her business falls under Schedule D, Case II. Although the room where she give the lessons is used by the members of her family when she is not teaching, they are not allowed into the room when *she is*.

Will she be able to deduct a proportion of the heating and lighting of the room used in the lessons from her Schedule D, Case II income?

Yes.

Refer also to **22.4.4** on the need to preserve private residence relief, for CGT purposes, on the sale of the house.

11.5.1.2   An income expense, not a capital one

The condition that, in order to qualify as an allowable deduction, expenditure must be income expenditure, rather than capital expenditure, is one of general principle. A capital expense is merely the converse of a capital *receipt*. Likewise, an income expense is merely the converse of an income receipt. Capital expenditure has the same one-off quality as a capital receipt. It simply involves you paying a sum of money, rather than receiving one.

Jim Smith, a property developer and sole trader, buys an hydraulic digger in his accounting period ending in 1998/99. It is for use in his business. In that tax year, his income under Schedule D, Case I, is £10,000. The digger cost £12,000. Does he make a trading loss in 1998/99?

No, but he may be able to claim capital allowances on machinery and plant for the expenditure: see **Chapter 12**.

In most cases, it will be easy to tell whether an expense is a revenue or a capital one and therefore whether an allowable deduction can be made.

Go back to the facts of SAQ 133. Say Catherine buys a new carpet for the living room. All other facts are the same. Is this an *income* or a *capital* expense?

A capital one: see above. However, it might just be possible to claim capital allowances: see **Chapter 12**.

In some cases, however, it may be unclear whether an expense is a capital or a revenue one, e.g. in an old case, the following happened: see *Associated Portland Cement Manufacturers* v *Kerr* [1946] 1 All ER 68. There was a cement manufacturing company, i.e. a trading company. It had two directors with great expertise in cement but who wanted to retire from the offices they held as directors of the company. The company, fearing that competitors would seek to profit from the directors' expertise after they had left, paid them to enter into restrictive covenants with the company, to the effect that they would not engage in the manufacture or sale of cement for the rest of their lives, except with the company's consent. The company paid one of them £20,000, the other £10,000.

On these facts, what do you think the company claimed to the Inland Revenue?

That it was entitled to deduct the £30,000 from its Schedule D, Case I income for the relevant accounting period.

The Revenue disallowed the claim and this disallowance was upheld. It was important that they had entered into the covenants without time limit. This being the case, the payments by the company of £20,000 and £10,000 respectively, were held to be *capital* payments. They were analytically identical to payments for permanent property owned by the company, i.e. they were payments for increasing the goodwill of the company. Note, however, that s. 313, ICTA 1988, read with FA 1988, s. 73(2) and (3), now *deems* such payments to be revenue payments, and therefore to be deductible from the trading income of the employer company. FA 1988, s. 73(2) and (3) disapplies, in relation to these particular payments, s. 74(1), ICTA 1988.

Note also the widely-cited test of whether a payment is a capital one in *British Insulated and Helsby Cables* v *Atherton* [1926] AC 205, per Viscount Cave LC: '. . . when an expenditure is made, not only once and for all, but with a view to bringing into existence an asset or an advantage for the enduring benefit of a trade . . .' (p. 213).

11.5.1.3   Deduction not prohibited by statute

Revenue expenditure which is specifically prohibited from qualifying as an allowable deduction includes the following:

(a)   Any cost which you can recover under an insurance policy or other contract under which you are indemnified against losses: ICTA 1988, s. 74(1)(l).

(b)   Most entertainment expenses: see below.

(c)   Royalty payments: ICTA 1988, s. 74(1)(p). These should be deductible by companies as *charges on income*, however: see **9.4**.

We have already encountered one type of expenditure, the deduction of which is prohibited by statute. This is entertainment expenditure, the deduction of which is prohibited by s. 577, ICTA 1988, except in limited circumstances. Section 577(10) is obviously intended to spell out one of the limited circumstances in which entertainment expenditure is an allowable deduction, but unfortunately it is virtually unintelligible, even by the standards of current tax legislation.

Section 577(10) states that the prohibition on deducting entertainment expenditure does not extend to expenditure incurred in:

> . . . the provision by any person of anything which it is his trade to provide, and which is provided by him in the ordinary course of that trade for payment or, with the object of advertising to the public generally, gratuitously.

In *Fleming* v *Associated Newspapers Ltd* [1972] 2 WLR 1273, Megarry J had originally been persuaded by a newspaper company that the £67,143 it had expended in providing hospitality to informants and contributors of copy, in a particular accounting period, was an allowable deduction in calculating its trading profits. The company's contention had been that persuading such people to provide news items was part of its trade within ICTA 1988, s. 577(10). However, the House of Lords reversed Megarry J's decision on the basis that, rather than being in the trade of providing hospitality or entertainment, the company's trade was in news and newspapers. The House of Lords reached this decision with an obvious intellectual struggle, and Lord Reid said that the legislation was ' . . . so obscure that no meaning can be given to it'. He continued (at p. 1283C):

> Draftsmen as well as Homer can nod, and Parliament is so accustomed to obscure drafting in Finance Bills that no one may have noticed the defects in this subsection.

How might the courts seek to solve any similar difficulty today?

By referring to Parliamentary materials, under the strict conditions laid down in *Pepper* v *Hart*: see **4.6**. (The figure of speech that 'Homer nodded' means a momentary slip or inattention.)

Payments which *can* qualify as allowable deductions include the following:

Employees' wages
If, as a trader, you have employees, you will have to pay them wages. They will pay tax on the wages under Schedule E, usually by your deducting the tax at source under the PAYE mechanism: see **19.3.7**. The gross amount of their wages (i.e. before the deduction of income tax at source by you) will be deductible from your trading income as an allowable deduction in calculating your trading profits. This is under the general rule that you may deduct from your Schedule D, Case I income any expenditure incurred wholly and exclusively for the purpose of the trade.

Rent paid for business premises

If, as a trader, your business premises are rented from a landlord, you will have to pay rent to that landlord. The deduction of this as an allowable deduction in calculating your income profit under Schedule D, Case I, is specifically envisaged by s. 74(1)(c). Section 74(1) allows deductions by using a negative, rather than a positive mode of speech. Thus, you are *not* allowed to deduct:

> . . . the rent of the whole or any part of any dwelling-house or domestic offices, except any such part as is used for the purposes of the trade . . . and where any such part is so used, the sum deducted shall not, unless in any particular case it appears that having regard to all the circumstances some greater sum ought to be deducted, exceed two-thirds of the rent bona fide paid for that dwelling-house or those offices.

Pre-trading expenditure

If, before you began to trade, you incurred expenditure that would have qualified as an allowable deduction after the trade had commenced, you can deduct it as an allowable deduction of the trade after the trade has started, provided the expenditure was *not* incurred by you more than seven years prior to the commencement of the trade: ICTA 1988, s. 401.

Bad debts

If you have customers who do not pay you, the non-payment will in time become a cost of the trade. For this reason, an allowable deduction is given for bad debts when they are shown to be bad: s. 74(1)(j). If, having obtained an allowable deduction for a bad debt in one tax period, the bad debt is repaid in a later one, the later payment will be trading income of the later period and be added to your other trading income.

Travelling expenses

These must, however, be incurred wholly and exclusively for the purpose of the trade, if they are to count as an allowable deduction. Thus, in *Newsom* v *Robertson* [1953] 1 Ch 7, a property law barrister worked in London when the courts were sitting and worked mostly at home, in vacation time. The Court of Appeal rejected his contention that his travelling expenses were an allowable deduction from his Schedule D, Case II income, on the basis that these expenses were not incurred wholly and exclusively for the purpose of his profession.

Irrecoverable input VAT

If you cannot recover input VAT incurred by you in full, it will be a permanent cost to your business: see **10.6**. However, irrecoverable input VAT may be deducted as an allowable deduction, unless it relates to capital expenditure in respect of which capital allowances are available: see **Chapter 12**.

Interest

Payments of interest made by you, as a trader, which do not fall within the categories of charges on income (see **9.3.2**), may none the less be allowable deductions in calculating your trading profits, provided that the payments are made wholly and exclusively for the purposes of the trade. Section 368(4), ICTA 1988 ensures that payments of interest, which can be deducted as charges on income, *cannot also* be allowable deductions in calculating trading profits.

11.5.2   COMPANY TRADERS

The trading profits of a company are calculated in the same way as the income profits of an individual. However, rather than being calculated for an accounting period ending in the tax year under consideration, they are calculated for a corporation tax accounting period. For present purposes, the only major difference is the regime governing the deductibility of interest payments made for the purpose of the trade. Individual traders, including partners, trustees and PRs, might get relief for a particular interest payment *as a charge on income* or as an *allowable deduction*. A company is treated differently, however, following the introduction of the concept of the *loan relationship* in FA 1996.

A company is in a loan relationship under s. 81, FA 1996, where it is either a debtor or a creditor in respect of a *money debt* arising from a *transaction for the lending of money*. Each component of this definition has implications beyond the scope of this book, and only the most general explanation is offered here. A transaction for the lending of money is defined in FA 1996, s. 81(2), where this is stated to include the situation where a company issues an *instrument* as security for any *money debt*. However, although the expression does *not* include a money debt owed by a customer to a seller, in respect of the supply of goods or services by the latter to the former, it *does* include any interest payable on such a debt.

In its accounting period ending on 30 November 1998, Banana Ltd, a fruit wholesaler, has been involved in two transactions:

(a)   on 1 February 1999, it obtains a bank loan of £150,000, which is secured by a charge over the company's assets; and

(b)   on 3 March 1999, it takes delivery of a consignment of apples, worth £145,000, for which it pays the supplier, Raspberry & Co., on 3 June 1999. Interest is payable on the £145,000, since payment of the price of the apples had been due on 3 November 1998.

Which of the two payments of interest involve a money debt *arising from a transaction for the lending of money*?

Both.

Thus, where a company is the debtor under a loan relationship entered into for the purpose of a trade carried on by it, any interest and expenses payable, in the accounting period under consideration, are an allowable deduction from trading income: see FA 1996, s. 82(2).

Where interest paid by an individual trader counts as an *allowable deduction*, are the rules for the deduction of the interest, in calculating trading profits, *in effect*, the same as those for a company?

Yes, although the other implications of *loan relationships* (see **11.7**) apply only to companies.

11.6 Allowable Deductions from the Income of an Office or Employment

The emphasis of our discussion now changes yet again, as we consider the deductions and reliefs available to an individual who is an employee or an office-holder, e.g. a director of a company. We look in detail at the rules for determining what must be included in your *employment income* in **Chapter 14**. In this section, we are concerned only with the rules under which allowable deductions from that income may be made, in order to calculate your *emoluments*, i.e. your income profit under Schedule E. These are contained in ICTA 1988, s. 198. We refer to *employees* and *employment income*, although the points made below apply equally to office-holders, whose income profits also fall under Schedule E.

By comparison with allowable deductions under Schedules A and D, Cases I and II, allowable deductions under Schedule E are far more restrictive. As Lord Blanesburgh said, speaking of an *older version* of ICTA 1988, s. 198, in *Ricketts* v *Colquhoun* [1926] AC 1: '. . . undoubtedly [s. 198's] most striking characteristic . . . is its jealously restricted phraseology, some of it repeated to heighten the effect'. The *seriously flawed* authority of *Ricketts* v *Colquhoun* was a case in which a barrister who practised in London, but who had been appointed Recorder of Portsmouth, unsuccessfully claimed his hotel and travelling expenses from London to Portsmouth, as an allowable deduction from his emoluments in the office of Recorder.

Income and Corporation Taxes Act 1988, s. 198, as modified by FA 1998, now provides that:

(1)   If the holder of an office or employment is obliged to incur and defray out of the emoluments of the office or employment—
(a)   qualifying travelling expenses, or
(b)   any amount (other than qualifying travelling expenses) expended wholly, exclusively and necessarily in the performance of the duties of the office or employment,
there may be deducted from the emoluments to be assessed the amount so incurred and defrayed.

How many conditions must be satisfied for an item of *non-travelling* expenditure incurred by an employee to qualify as an allowable deduction?

Three.

Therefore:

How many conditions must be satisfied for *travelling* expenditure incurred by an employee to count as an allowable deduction?

One. The expenditure must be *qualifying travelling expenses*.

It is therefore necessary to consider non-travelling expenses and travelling expenses incurred by you, the employee, separately from each other.

11.6.1   NON-TRAVELLING EXPENSES

As an employee, you must first incur the non-travelling expenses *in performing the duties of your employment*. The decision of the House of Lords in *Smith* v *Abbott* [1994] 1 All ER 673 illustrates that you will have to be able to demonstrate that the expenses were incurred in the performance of the duties, not in *preparing* to perform those duties.

In *Smith* v *Abbott*, journalists on *The Mail* and *The Mail on Sunday* had claimed as an allowable deduction the expenses which they had incurred in the purchase of other newspapers, in order to keep abreast. The House of Lords based their decision on the distinction between preparing to perform the duties and acting in the performance thereof. The reading by journalists of other newspapers fell into the former category and the buying of those other newspapers did not therefore qualify as an allowable deduction from their employment income. This approach, doubtless based on a perceived public policy need (see Lord Templeman's speech), contrasted with the approach taken by Nolan LJ (as he then was) in the Court of Appeal, where his Lordship stated that, because of the ephemeral nature of news stories, no general benefit was derived by the journalists from reading the newspapers:

> The purpose which their reading was designed to serve, and did serve, was the production of the next edition of the *Daily Mail* or the *Mail on Sunday*. In these circumstances, the reading seems to me to constitute preparation for a particular assignment.

The House of Lords was not, however, prepared to adopt that line of analysis.

ACTIVITY 19

Read the discussion of *Smith* v *Abbott* in the article by Phillip Ridgway at *Cases and Materials* (11.2.1). Note the explanation for the decision given in the article.

Secondly, you must *necessarily* incur the expenses in the performance of the duties. In other words, the expenses must not be a matter of choice on your part. It must arise from the nature of the employment. The most unfair aspect of this condition for the employee is that it is not enough that the employer requires you, the employee, to incur the expenses, for this condition to be satisfied. In *Brown* v *Bullock* [1961] 1 WLR 1095, a bank required one of its employees, a bank manager, to join a London gentlemen's club. The bank paid half of the annual subscription to the club, and the employee paid the other half. His argument was that, although the bank's contribution was an emolument of his, its effect was cancelled out by his own contribution to the subscription, since that was an allowable deduction from his employment income. The Court of Appeal rejected this argument, on the basis that joining the club was not necessary for the performance of the bank manager's duties.

The final requirement, of course, is that the expenses were *wholly and exclusively* incurred in the performance of the duties of the employment. This is the same test as we discussed above in the context of allowable deductions from trading income.

Having made all these points, it is worth noting that, in many cases, a deduction is allowed for expenses which do not satisfy these conditions. Thus, the cost of protective clothing, subscriptions to professional bodies, tools, etc. may all be covered by a specific statutory or concessionary provision, which enables an allowable deduction to be made from employment income in respect of that item, notwithstanding the conditions set out above (e.g. ICTA 1988, s. 201 – fees and subscriptions to professional bodies, learned societies, etc.).

Read the extract from the article by Cockfield and Mulholland, 'The Taxman and the Scruffy Teacher', at *Cases and Materials* (11.2.1). Consider their comments on the judicial policies at work in interpreting the legislation on employees' expenses.

11.6.2 TRAVELLING EXPENSES

In order to be deductible from your employment income, these must be *qualifying travelling expenses*: ICTA 1988, ss. 198(1)(a), 198(1A) and sch. 12A. *Qualifying travelling expenses* are amounts necessarily expended on travelling in the performance of the duties of the office or employment, or other expenses of travelling which are:

■ attributable to your necessary attendance at any place in the performance of the duties of your office or employment, *and*

■ not expenses of *ordinary commuting* or *private travel*.

Ordinary commuting is defined as travel between your home, or a place that is not a workplace in relation to your employment, and a permanent workplace: sch. 12A, para. 2(1). *Private travel* is defined as travel between your home and a place that is not a workplace in relation to your employment, or between two places neither of which is such a workplace: sch. 12A, para. 2(2).

Douglas is a lecturer employed by Stokeborough University, which has two sites. In addition to giving seminars at one site, he is also obliged to give seminars at the other. If he pays the expenses of travelling from one site to the other, will these expenses be an allowable deduction from his employment income?

Yes.

What about the cost of petrol or the bus fare incurred by him in travelling from home to work each day?

No.

Read the extract from CCH's *Benefits Bulletin*, at *Cases and Materials* (11.2.2). Reflect on the problems presented by the so-called 'triangular travel' arrangements of employees.

11.7   Interest Paid under Non-trading Loan Relationships of a Company

In **11.5.2**, we considered the effect of payments of interest under a loan relationship, where the loan is entered into for the purpose of a trade carried on by the debtor company. We need to consider the position where the debtor – the borrower company – does *not* carry on a trade but instead acts as a landlord, or holds investments, e.g. shares in other companies, and pays interest under a loan relationship for those non-trading purposes.

Briefly, the company must first ascertain whether it has made any profits under any of its loan relationships in the accounting period, from *non-trading sources*: see **16.4.2**. If the company has not made any such profits in the accounting period under consideration, the interest paid by the company on its non-trading loan relationships will obviously exceed the nil figure for profits on the loan relationships.

If this is the case, the company deducts the excess from its total profits, at Stage Three of its corporation tax calculation, to give its profits chargeable to corporation tax: see **7.4**. It does this *before* deducting any relief under ICTA 1988, ss. 392A(1) or 393A(1): FA 1996, sch. 8, para. 1(3)(b)(i), as amended by FA 1998.

What could easily happen, as a result of going through this process, in the case of a particular company?

A deficit on the company's loan relationships could easily exceed the total profits of the company, producing a loss on the company's non-trading loan relationships. The ways of relieving such a loss are discussed in **13.3.2.2**.

11.8   Summary

In relation to Schedule A income, expenditure is an allowable deduction if it is of an income nature, wholly and exclusively incurred for the purpose of the lettings business, and not specifically disallowed, e.g. by ICTA 1988, s. 577. Exactly the same conditions apply to allowable deductions from trading income. Interest is deductible according to different rules, depending on whether it is paid by an individual or a company. If paid by an *individual*, it is deductible as a charge on income if it falls into any of the categories in **9.3.2**. Outside those categories, it may none the less be deductible as an allowable deduction from rental income, or as an allowable deduction from trading income. If paid by a *company*, it is *not* deductible as a charge on income, but is an allowable deduction from trading income or, if the loan was not entered into for trading purposes, from a company's total profits. An investment company may deduct management expenses from its total profits.

The rules under which expenses can be allowable deductions from employment income depends on whether they are travelling expenses or not. If not, the expenses will be allowable deductions *only* if they were incurred wholly, exclusively and necessarily in the performance of the duties of the employment. If they are travelling expenses, they will only be allowable deductions if they are qualifying travelling expenses. To be qualifying travelling expenses, they must not be the expenses of ordinary commuting or of private travel.

11.9   End of Chapter Assessment Questions

Refer to the facts concerning Amber Ltd and Bertram, one of its directors in **2.6**, **5.6**, and **6.6**. Note these additional facts.

   (a)   Bertram is Amber Ltd's finance director. In the 1998/99 tax year, he has the following expenditure:

        (i)   £500 on bus fares from his home to Amber Ltd's premises every working day;

        (ii)   £250 on financial newspapers, which he reads to keep abreast of the financial markets; and

        (iii)   £150 on 12 issues of a specialist professional accountancy journal.

   (b)   In the accounting period to 31 December 1998, Amber Ltd has the following expenditure:

        (i)   £8,000 plus VAT on entertaining clients from Malaysia;

        (ii)   £300,000 gross wages; and

        (iii)   £80,000 plus VAT factory premises rental.

Comment on whether the items in (a) will rank as allowable deductions from Bertram's employment income, and whether the items in (b) will rank as allowable deductions from Amber Ltd's trading income.

(Word limit: 400 (100 marks).)

See *Cases and Materials* (**11.4**), for a specimen answer.

CHAPTER TWELVE

REDUCING INCOME TAXATION (4)

12.1 Objectives

By the end of this chapter, you should be able to:

■ list the *conditions* a person must satisfy to qualify for capital allowances;

■ calculate the capital allowances for expenditure on *industrial buildings* and *plant and machinery*;

■ explain the meaning of *plant* for capital allowances;

■ explain the meaning of an *industrial building or structure* for capital allowances;

■ explain the capital allowances significance of *belonging* when machinery or plant becomes a landlord's or tenant's fixture;

■ describe the income tax or corporation tax consequences of *disposing* of machinery or plant on which capital allowances have been claimed.

12.2 Introduction

This chapter is the fourth part of our survey of the ways in which tax law allows the burden of income taxation to be reduced. The chapter is solely concerned with income tax and corporation tax, the discussion being confined to capital allowances (CAs). Capital allowances are percentage deductions from income under Schedule A, or Case I or II of Schedule D, or Schedule E. They are available for both income tax and corporation tax purposes. The deductions are made in Stage One of the income tax or corporation tax calculation, i.e. in calculating a person's income profits from the source to which they relate. Capital allowances are intended to give a deduction for any capital expenditure incurred by a person on certain types of asset. The discussion in this chapter is confined to expenditure on plant and machinery and industrial buildings and structures. These are the most common types of assets the cost of which attracts CAs. Plant is basically the apparatus used by a person for carrying on its business. Machinery is what it suggests. An industrial building or structure must be one used in a manufacturing or distributive trade, although not necessarily one carried on by the owner of the building or structure. References to individuals include individuals claiming CAs in the capacities of partners, trustees or PRs.

12.3   The Need for CAs

Capital allowances are necessary because a person's capital expenditure cannot be an allowable deduction from income under the Schedules: see **11.5.1.2**. The underlying idea is therefore to enable a proportion of a person's capital expenditure to be deducted from income under a particular Schedule in a tax period. That said, not all capital expenditure is covered by CAs.

Occasionally, CAs permit the whole, or a large percentage, of a person's capital expenditure on an asset to be deducted from that person's income under a particular Schedule in a *single* tax period. Generally, however, they only permit a specified percentage of capital expenditure to be deducted over a number of tax periods. The number of tax periods varies, according to the type of asset on which expenditure has been incurred, and the percentage at which the CAs are made to that person. Most CAs permit a deduction for the *capital depreciation* of the asset, rather than for its *initial cost*. Capital allowances of the latter type are called *first year allowances* (*FYAs*); CAs of the former, more common type, are referred to as *writing-down allowances* (*WDAs*).

Which type of CAs are more valuable, FYAs or WDAs?

FYAs – relief is obtained more quickly than with WDAs.

An example may be helpful. Say you bought a new car on 1 February 1992. On 1 February 1999, you know that it has depreciated in value, during the seven years you have owned it. This is due to:

■ use;

■ obsolescence; and

■ the passage of time.

The difference between the car's original cost, i.e. your capital expenditure on it, and the amount for which you could sell it on 1 February 1999, might be illustrated graphically:

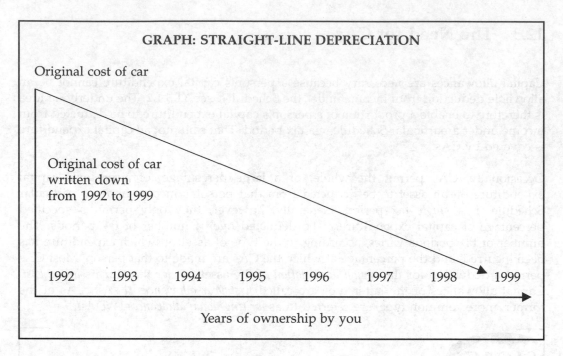

GRAPH: STRAIGHT-LINE DEPRECIATION

Original cost of car

Original cost of car
written down
from 1992 to 1999

1992   1993   1994   1995   1996   1997   1998   1999

Years of ownership by you

It should be clear from this that, instead of waiting until 1999 to find out how much the car had depreciated in value, you might have said to yourself in 1992:

Each year, I will estimate the car to have depreciated by a certain percentage of its original value. That way, I should have at least some idea of what the car is worth in 1992 or 1993 or 1994 or 1999.

When accountants prepare their clients' accounts, they perform a similar process to the one in this example. However, they observe rules of generally accepted accounting principles in doing so. The graph shows the *straight-line method* of depreciation.

However, they might use the *reducing balance* method of depreciation instead in preparing their clients' accounts. This would be closer to the operation of CAs on machinery and plant than the *straight-line* method. Either method could be used for accounting purposes, although the *reducing balance* method, at the statutory rate, is the obligatory method under CAA 1990. Capital allowances are thus another example of the divergence between tax law and GAAP: see **1.5.3**.

The reducing balance method works thus. Instead of deducting a percentage of the original cost in each year, a percentage of the original cost, *as reduced by deductions previously made*, is deducted. The reducing balance basis can therefore be illustrated as follows. Say you buy an item of machinery for £10,000 on 1 November 1998, and depreciate it each year at 25%, on the reducing balance basis.

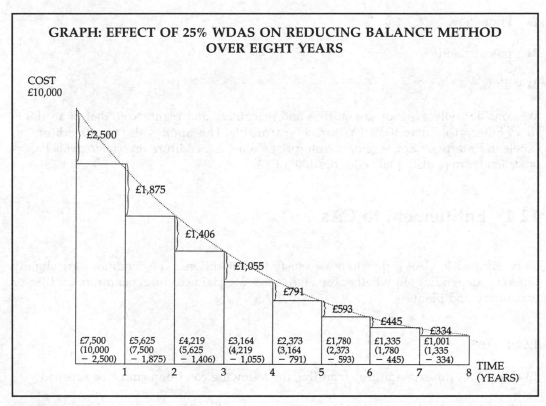

GRAPH: EFFECT OF 25% WDAS ON REDUCING BALANCE METHOD OVER EIGHT YEARS

Study this graph carefully. After eight years, how much of the original cost has been written-off?

90% – £1,001 of the original £10,000 expenditure is still unrelieved.

In the graph above, note how the 'curve' becomes shallower and shallower, as time goes by. This is a realistic method of depreciation, since it shows items losing most of their value early in their useful life.

Expenditure on 11 types of assets may qualify for CAs:

■ industrial buildings and structures (IBSs);

■ hotels;

■ plant and machinery;

■ agricultural buildings;

■ dwelling-houses let on assured tenancies (where expenditure incurred before 1 April 1992);

■ scientific research;

■ dredging;

■ mineral extraction;

- know-how;

- patents; and

- films.

We consider only expenditure on IBSs and machinery and plant. Note that, if an IBS is in an Enterprise Zone, 100% FYAs may be available. This applies also to expenditure on hotels in Enterprise Zones and, in Enterprise Zones, expenditure on *commercial buildings or structures* may also qualify for the 100% FYA.

12.4   Entitlement to CAs

To be entitled to CAs, a person must satisfy five conditions. The conditions are slightly different, depending on whether the allowances are claimed for expenditure on IBSs or machinery and plant.

12.4.1   IBSs

To claim CAs for expenditure on an IBS, the following conditions must be satisfied:

(a)   the person claiming the CAs must own the *relevant interest* in the IBS;

(b)   that person's expenditure on the IBS must be *capital expenditure*;

(c)   the capital expenditure must be *incurred* by the person claiming the CAs;

(d)   the IBS must *satisfy the statutory definition* of an IBS; *and*

(e)   the person claiming the CAs must be one of the following:

    (i)   The constructor of the building or structure in question; *or*

    (ii)   in the case of an *unused* building or structure, the purchaser from the constructor; *or*

    (iii)   In the case of a *used* building or structure, the purchaser.

The term *relevant interest* requires explanation. The relevant interest in an IBS is the interest in the building or structure to which the person who incurred the expenditure was entitled when they incurred that expenditure: CAA 1990, s. 20(1). If a person owns the relevant interest, it does not cease to be the relevant interest if a lease is created to which the interest is subject: CAA 1990, s. 20(3).

The condition that the expenditure must be *capital* expenditure necessitates special provisions for the acquisition of the relevant interest in an unused IBS from a builder. The Capital Allowances Act 1990 contains no general definition of capital expenditure. However, CAA 1990, s. 159(1) says that capital expenditure does *not* include allowable deductions (see **Chapter 11**), nor any expenditure of the purchaser which is an *income* receipt of the vendor. The latter of these exclusions once caused problems for purchasers from builders. A builder is a person carrying on the *trade* of building, so a sum paid by a purchaser to a builder is an income receipt of the builder: see **Chapter 15**. However, CAA 1990, s. 10 *deems* the purchaser's expenditure to be capital expenditure, thereby preventing that expenditure from being disqualified under CAA 1990, s. 159(1). Special provisions determine the amount of the purchaser's expenditure here: CAA 1990, s. 10(3).

In relation to condition (e)(i) above, the constructor's expenditure does *not* include the cost of the land. Where an IBS is acquired unused, the purchaser is deemed to have incurred expenditure on its construction. The amount of the capital expenditure is the smaller of the net price or the initial expenditure: CAA 1990, s. 10(1)(b).

Where a *used* IBS is acquired, the purchaser is *deemed* to have incurred expenditure: see **12.5.1.2**. The statutory definition of an IBS is discussed in **12.7**.

Freehold land is owned by Jerrybuilders Ltd. The company built a factory on the land in 1996. The factory is an IBS within CAA 1990. On 30 November 1998, the company grants a 99-year lease of the factory to Utopia Ltd. On 1 December 1998, Utopia Ltd grants a 50-year sub-lease *back to the company*. How many interests are there in the factory? Which is the relevant interest? Is CAA 1990, s. 10 applicable?

Three, i.e. the freehold, the lease and the sub-lease. The relevant interest is the freehold owned by Jerrybuilders Ltd. CAA 1990, s. 10, is not applicable – the relevant interest has not been sold.

12.4.2 MACHINERY AND PLANT

To claim CAs for expenditure on machinery or plant, the following conditions must be satisfied:

(a)   the machinery or plant must *belong* to the person claiming the CAs;

(b)   that person's expenditure on the machinery or plant must be *capital* expenditure;

(c)   that capital expenditure must be *incurred* by the person claiming the CAs;

(d)   the machinery or plant must *satisfy the relevant definitions* in case law and statute; *and*

(e)   the person claiming the CAs must be *one* of the following:

(i)   a person providing machinery or plant wholly and exclusively for the purposes of a *trade* carried on by that person; *or*

(ii)   a person providing machinery or plant wholly and exclusively for the purposes of a *profession or vocation* carried on by that person; *or*

(iii) an individual providing machinery or plant *other than a motor car* wholly, exclusively and *necessarily* for the purposes of an *office or employment* carried on by that individual; *or*

(iv)   an individual providing a *motor car* wholly and exclusively for the purposes of an *office or employment* carried on by that individual; *or*

(v)   a company providing machinery or plant for the purposes of managing the investment business carried on by that company; *or*

(vi)   an individual providing machinery or plant wholly and exclusively for the purposes of a *lettings business* carried on by that individual; *or*

(vii) a person *first letting* machinery or plant otherwise than in the course of a trade and not in the course of a Schedule A business carried on by that person.

Innocuous as it may seem, the *belonging* requirement has caused problems for fixtures, with expenditure incurred on machinery or plant in a let building: see **12.8**.

The Capital Allowances Act 1990, s. 60(1) covers expenditure on assets acquired on hire purchase. Under a hire purchase agreement, the asset acquired does not belong to the purchaser until the final sum due has been paid-off. The Capital Allowances Act 1990 provides that plant or machinery acquired on hire purchase is deemed to belong to the purchaser *as soon as* the purchaser is entitled to the benefit of the hire purchase contract: CAA 1990, s. 60(1)(a) and (3).

The definition of machinery is straightforward. The definition of plant is considered in **12.6**.

Condition (e)(vii) comes from CAA 1990, s. 61, which permits CAs to be claimed by so-called equipment lessors leasing plant and machinery otherwise than in the course of a trade. For instance, the trading profits of an insurance company would normally fall under Schedule D, Case I. If the company went into business leasing plant and machinery, it would do so *otherwise than* in the course of that trade and ICTA 1988, s. 61 could apply to its expenditure on plant and machinery.

In discussions of CAs, the term *qualifying asset* includes both machinery and plant and IBSs. *Qualifying expenditure* refers to expenditure on machinery or plant qualifying for CAs: CAA 1990, s. 25.

Julia, a sole trader, makes her accounts up to 30 November in each calendar year. On 30 September 1998, she incurs expenditure in *replacing* some machinery owned by her, and *repairing* the rest. All of the machinery is used *wholly and exclusively for the purposes* of her trade. Which of this expenditure could qualify for CAs?

Expenditure on *replacing* machinery should qualify for CAs, since it is capital expenditure. Julia will also have to demonstrate that the machinery belongs to her and that she has incurred the expenditure.

12.5   Calculation of CAs

Having decided that a person is entitled to CAs, the next step is to calculate them. This calculation varies according to three factors:

■   the *type* of qualifying asset on which the CAs are claimed;

■   whether the CAs are made as an *FYA* or as *WDAs*, or both; *and*

■   whether the CAs are made in *taxing a trade* or by *discharge or repayment of tax*.

We consider each of these three factors in turn.

12.5.1   TYPE OF QUALIFYING ASSET

The calculation of CAs differs according to whether they are claimed for expenditure on machinery or plant or IBSs.

12.5.1.1   Machinery and plant

Pooling
If a person is claiming CAs for expenditure on machinery and plant, all the expenditure on machinery and plant belonging to that person is pooled together, in order to calculate the allowances to be deducted: CAA 1990, ss. 24, 25. This creates a *pool of qualifying expenditure*. Expenditure on *short-life assets* is pooled separately from expenditure on other machinery and plant: CAA 1990, s. 38.

When a person acquires plant or machinery, its cost is added to the pool of qualifying expenditure. Likewise, when that person sells any machinery or plant, they subtract the proceeds of the sale from the balance in the pool. The amount of qualifying expenditure in the pool *at the beginning of the tax period under consideration* is the figure on which the CAs for that period are calculated.

Note also that the pool of qualifying expenditure is also reduced in each tax period by the WDA and any FYAs available in each period. The effect of this is considered fully below.

ACTIVITY 22

You are a sole trader landscape gardener, and have been in business many years. Your accounting date is 30 November in each calendar year. You bought a tractor on 1 July 1991, a digger on 3 August 1991 and a crane on 1 September 1991. The digger cost you £15,000, the tractor cost you £75,000 and the crane cost you £10,000. The balance of the pool of qualifying expenditure on 30 November 1990, was £10,000.

On 1 September 1993, you sold an old motor-mower for £2,000 and, on 22 August 1994, you sold an old hedge-trimmer for £1,000.

Calculate what goes into the pool and what is 'drained out' of the pool as a result of these acquisitions and sales. Also indicate the tax periods in which the acquisitions and sales have occurred. (*Ignore the reduction in the pool of qualifying expenditure made by WDAs/FYAs in each tax period.*)

(Assume the CYB has applied throughout: see 4.3.1.)

In the 1991/92 tax period, the cost of the digger, the tractor and the crane are added to the pool, i.e. to the opening balance. There is thus £110,000 of qualifying expenditure in the pool at the end of the 1991/92 tax period. This remains the balance till the tax period 1993/94, when the balance is reduced to £108,000, on the sale of the motor mower, i.e. £110,000 − £2,000. In the tax period 1994/95, the balance of the pool is again reduced, to £107,000, with the deduction of the sale proceeds of the hedge-trimmer from the pool as it was at the beginning of the 1994/95 tax period.

Note: (a) the tax period is the accounting period ending in the tax year under consideration; and (b) this Activity is not a complete picture, since the balance of the pool is also reduced by any FYAs given when an asset is *acquired*, and the WDAs made at the end of each tax period ((b) is explained immediately below).

The reducing balance basis
We now need to examine how pooling works in relation to determining the CAs to be deducted from income in each tax period.

Consider **Activity 22** again. WDAs for machinery and plant are deducted on a reducing balance basis, i.e. from the qualifying expenditure in the pool at the *end* of the tax period under consideration: CAA 1990, s. 24(2)(a). WDAs are deducted at 25% in each tax period. The FYA, by contrast, is deducted from the expenditure on the asset in question, with only the *balance* of that expenditure being transferred into the pool. If a WDA and an FYA are available in a tax period, both of them are deducted from the relevant income in that period.

Take the facts of **Activity 22**. In the 1991/92 tax period, the digger, the tractor and the crane were all added to the pool. The WDA on the pool was therefore £110,000 × 25%, i.e. £27,500, for deduction from Schedule D, Case I income of that period. In the 1992/93 tax period, the WDA on the pool was calculated on the balance of the pool, as reduced by the WDA given in the previous tax period, *not* on £110,000. Thus, the WDA in the 1992/93 tax period was 25% × £82,500, i.e. £20,625.

What would have been done with the £20,625?

It would have been deducted from any Schedule D, Case I income of the accounting period ending on 30 November 1992.

The pool of qualifying expenditure is merely a memorandum, and obviously does not itself form part of the income tax or corporation tax calculation.

(The above is artificial, since: (a) it assumes that your trading profits would have been calculated on the CYB in 1992/93, and (b) it assumes that CAs were 25% WDAs, with no FYAs: see **12.5.2**.)

12.5.1.2 IBSs

CAs on IBSs are calculated by considering each building separately. They are generally made as WDAs, and are calculated on a *straight-line basis*. In each tax period, the WDA is deducted by the claimant at 4% of the original cost of construction or purchase price, excluding the land: s. 3(2), CAA 1990. This means that an IBS has a so-called 'tax life' of

25 years from when it is first used. It also means that WDAs on an IBS which remains unsold in this 25-year period can be illustrated thus:

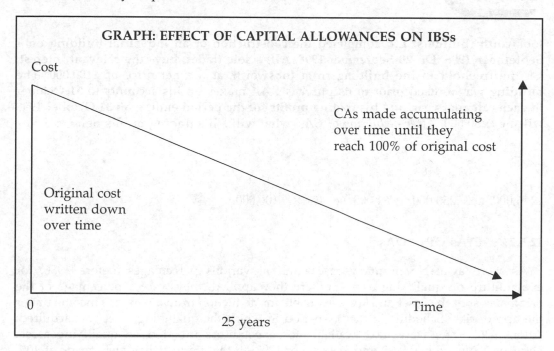

The graph would be different if the IBS were, e.g., sold during the 25-year period: see **12.9**. The residue in each tax period is called the *tax written-down value* of the IBS.

The calculation of the tax written-down value of the IBS differs according to whether it has been used when the claimant acquires it.

Used IBSs

If a person acquires the relevant interest in a used IBS, CAs are made on the expenditure, on the tax written-down value of the building, plus any *balancing charge* suffered by the seller. Balancing charges are discussed in **12.9**.

For instance, on 20 October 1998, I buy a factory from you which originally cost you £150,000 on 1 April 1997, i.e. in the 1996/97 tax year. I pay you £165,000 for the factory. Your accounting period runs from 6 April to 5 April. By 20 October 1998, you will have written down the cost of the factory to £132,000, i.e. £150,000 − £18,000 – a 4% WDA for each of three tax periods, 96/97, 97/98, 98/99. A balancing charge is made on you of £18,000, i.e. £150,000 − £132,000: see **12.9**.

The tax written-down value of the factory, plus the balancing charge imposed on you, is £132,000 + £18,000 = £150,000. I will therefore receive WDAs for the next 23 years and four months on the residue of your expenditure, namely £132,000, plus the balancing charge of £18,000. I will therefore receive WDAs on the original cost of the factory to you of £150,000. This will be 150,000/24, i.e. £6,250, in each tax period.

Unused IBSs

If a person acquires the relevant interest in an unused IBS, then the result will tend to be similar, even though the method of calculation is different.

Except where the seller of the building or structure is a builder, the rule is this. The purchaser is deemed to have incurred, on the date the price becomes payable, expenditure on the *construction* of the IBS. The amount of that deemed expenditure is the net price, or the original expenditure, if that was less: CAA 1990, s. 10(1)(b). Where the seller *is a builder*, the rule is different. The purchaser is deemed to have incurred construction expenditure equal to the *net price paid by the purchaser* for the relevant interest: CAA 1990, ss. 10(1)(b), 10(3)(a).

Jobsworth (Builders) Ltd completed the construction of an industrial building on 1 September 1996. On 20 September 1998, Alf, a sole trader, buys the relevant interest, i.e. the freehold in the building from Jobsworth, at the net price of £100,000. The building was unused prior to its purchase. Alf makes up his accounts to 31 October in each calendar year, and his trading profits for the period ending on 31 October 1998 will be £250,000. *After deduction of CAs*, what will Alf's trading profits be?

£246,000, i.e. £250,000 − £4,000, i.e. 4% × £100,000.

12.5.2   FYAs OR WDAs

FYAs were available in many cases, and at various percentages, before 1986, for expenditure on qualifying assets. Where they applied, they were a percentage of the original cost of the asset and were available for deduction from a person's income under the appropriate Schedule in the tax period in which the qualifying asset was acquired. After 1986, FYAs were next available for expenditure incurred on qualifying assets between 1 November 1992 and 31 October 1993. In that period, they were made at 40% of the cost of the qualifying asset.

FYAs were reintroduced at 50% in F (No. 2) A 1997, subject to the satisfaction of certain conditions, for expenditure incurred between 2 July 1997 and 1 July 1998. FA 1998 has extended the period to 1 July 1999, whilst reducing the FYA to 40% from 2 July 1998. In addition, although this is not discussed below, 100% FYAs are available for capital expenditure on British qualifying films costing £15 million or less.

What is the effect of a 40% FYA on machinery and plant?

It brings forward in time the benefit of the CAs, whilst leaving the remaining 60% of the cost to be relieved on the 25% reducing balance basis, as above.

12.5.2.1   FYAs

To qualify for the FYA of double the existing WDA (see **12.5.2.2**), the person claiming CAs on machinery or plant must be a small company or a small business: CAA 1990, s. 22(3C). A small business is one which would have satisfied the conditions below, had it been carried on by a company.

A small company is one which satisfies any *two* of the following conditions in the financial year in which the expenditure is incurred (CA 1985, s. 247):

■ its turnover must be not more than £11.2 million;

■ its assets must be worth no more than £5.6 million; and

■ it must have no more than 250 employees.

2.3.1 contains a definition of turnover. The FYA is 12% for the cost of long-life assets: see **12.5.2.2**.

12.5.2.2 WDAs

Whether given on a reducing balance basis, or a straight-line basis, most CAs are WDAs. With WDAs, a percentage amount is deducted from a person's income under the appropriate Schedule in successive tax periods. Since the reducing balance basis is generally used for CAs on machinery and plant, it takes eight years to write-down only 90% of the cost of plant or machinery, on the basis that WDAs are given at 25%: see **SAQ 146**. For industrial buildings, the deduction is 4%, on a straight-line basis, and it will therefore take 25 years to write-down the capital expenditure on an unused IBS: see **12.5.1.2**.

There is an exception to the 25% WDAs rate, which applies to long-life assets, i.e. to machinery or plant with a working life of 25 years or more. In such cases, WDAs are 6%, where a person incurs expenditure of more than £100,000 per year on such assets and they were acquired on or after 26 November 1996: CAA 1990, ss. 38A-38H. Introduced by the last Conservative Budget, of 26 November 1996, the main victims of these reduced WDAs were the utilities (see **1.3**), although there are important exclusions from the 6% rate which have softened the blow for them.

12.5.3   TAXING A TRADE OR DISCHARGE OR REPAYMENT OF TAX

CAs are percentage deductions from income under Schedule A, Schedule D, Cases I and II, or Schedule E whether they are made *in taxing a trade*, or by *discharge or repayment of tax*. *Discharge or repayment of tax*, which applies in relation to the qualifying assets discussed here in only limited circumstances, is more prescriptive than *taxing a trade*. It is necessary to be aware of the limited situations in which discharge or repayment of tax applies. It is in relation to the relief of income losses that the distinction between the two is most important, since an income loss can consist of or include excess CAs.

12.5.3.1 CAs made in taxing a trade

For income tax purposes, CAs made in taxing a trade are made as if they were allowable deductions under Schedule D, Cases I and II. For income tax purposes, this is clear from CAA 1990, s. 140(2):

> Allowances and charges which fall to be made for any [tax period] in taxing a trade . . . shall be given effect by treating the amount of any allowance as a trading expense of the trade in that period . . .

For corporation tax, the same point is made by CAA 1990, s. 144(2), which is identical:

> Allowances and charges which fall to be made for any accounting period in taxing a trade . . . shall be given effect by treating the amount of any allowance as a trading expense of the trade in that period . . .

(For allowable deductions see **Chapter 11**.)

For income tax, 'trade' in CAA 1990, s. 140(2) include professions, vocations, offices and employments: CAA 1990, s. 140(4). It also includes a Schedule A business, where an IBS is subject to a lease at the end of the tax period in which a WDA is made. There, the Schedule A business is deemed to be a trade set up and commenced after 5 April 1995: CAA 1990, s. 9(1A). For corporation tax, 'trade' did not previously extend to Schedule A, but it does do so following FA 1998: CAA 1990, s. 9(3) and below.

CAs are made in taxing a trade for expenditure on machinery or plant (with one exception, below) and IBSs (with one exception, below).

In its accounting period ending on 30 September 1998, Arkwright Ltd (see SAQ 131) has a WDA for *machinery and plant* of £5,000. Are CAs given to it in taxing a trade, or by discharge or repayment of tax?

In taxing a trade: CAA 1990, ss. 28A, 73, as amended by FA 1998.

12.5.3.2   CAs made by discharge or repayment of tax

For income tax purposes, CAs made by discharge or repayment of tax are deducted only from specific income relating to the type of asset in question: CAA 1990, ss. 141-143. By CAA 1990, s. 141(2):

> (a)   The amount of the allowance shall be deducted from or set off against income of [the claimant] of the specified class for that [tax period], and
> (b)   If the amount to be allowed is greater than the amount of his income of that class for that [tax period], the balance shall be deducted from or set off against his income of that class for the next [tax period], and so on for subsequent [tax periods], and tax shall be discharged or repaid accordingly.

In relation to income tax, there is only one situation relevant to us, where CAs are given by discharge or repayment of tax. This is where the person claiming CAs on machinery or plant is the person first letting machinery or plant otherwise than in the course of a trade and not in the course of a Schedule A business: ICTA 1988, s. 61, see **12.4.2**, condition (e)(vii).

In those circumstances, CAA 1990, s. 73(2) provides:

> Any allowance made by virtue of section 61(1) shall be made by way of discharge or repayment of tax, and . . . shall be available primarily against income from the letting of machinery or plant . . .

Section 73(2) applies in relation to corporation tax too. Before 1 April 1998, CAs were also made to a company by discharge or repayment of tax, rather than in taxing a trade, where IBSs were subject to a lease at the end of the tax period under consideration: CAA 1990, ss. 9(3),(7), 15(2). However, CAA 1990, s. 9 has been amended by FA 1998, to provide that such CAs are now made *in taxing a trade*, as if the Schedule A lettings business were a trade.

Refer to 12.4.2, condition (e)(vii). Is such a person entitled to CAs made by discharge or repayment of tax?

Yes.

12.6   Qualifying Assets: *Machinery* and *Plant*

There is no definition of either machinery or plant in CAA 1990. Machinery is given its ordinary meaning. The meaning of *plant* has been stretched, however, because of the higher CAs available on expenditure on it. The Capital Allowances Act 1990, sch. AA1, which applies to qualifying expenditure incurred after 29 November 1993, sets out those *buildings*, *structures* and *land* which *can* and those which *cannot* qualify as plant. The idea is to *prevent* buildings, structures and land from qualifying as plant: see **Cases and Materials (12.1)**. Schedule AA1 is designed to preserve the pre-1993 High Court case law on the meaning of plant, and to prevent its further development. It refers to 'machinery or plant', abbreviated to 'plant' below.

Some expenditure on buildings, structures or land always qualifies as expenditure on plant, despite the general ban, e.g. fire safety, safety at sports grounds and personal security, expenditure on all of which always attracts CAs, provided it falls within the relevant statutory provisions: s. 69, 70 or 71, CAA 1990. Schedule AA1 contains a general definition of a building as including not only assets actually incorporated but also ones which are normally so incorporated: sch. AA1, para. 1(2)(b). If an asset comes within this definition, it is not plant: sch. AA1, para. 1(1). A number of specific assets are within this definition, including walls, floors, ceilings, mains services and waste disposal systems: column (1), Table 1, sch. AA1. Some assets are specifically excluded from this definition of a building. These assets, even though incorporated in a building, are deemed not to be so incorporated, with the result that expenditure on these items can attract CAs on plant: column (2), Table 1. Most of the 16 items in column (2) of Table 1 are necessities in modern commercial or industrial buildings.

Read column (2) of Table 1, *Cases and Materials* (12.1).

A surprising item appears at 16, i.e. swimming pools and diving boards. It is designed to preserve *Cooke v Beach Station Caravans* [1974] 3 All ER 159. In that case, Megarry J had held that a swimming pool and a diving board were both plant, the swimming pool having an elaborate system for filtering, heating and chlorinating the water. In addition to these 16 items, there are a number of others, including cold stores and caravans for holiday lettings (sch. AA1, para. 1(3)), expenditure on which can qualify as expenditure on plant.

However, a person who can demonstrate that an asset, although incorporated in a building, is within column (2), has still not automatically made their case. The Table is to be read subject to the Notes which follow it. The effect of Note 1 is that, even if an asset incorporated in a building is deemed not to be so incorporated, it will still not qualify as plant if the principal purpose of the asset is to insulate or enclose the interior of a building, or to provide a permanent internal wall, floor or ceiling.

Schedule AA1 applies a similar methodology to structures and other works involving the *alteration* of land: sch. AA1, para. 2(1). Again, these do not generally qualify as plant. However, Table 2, column (1) particularises the term structure. Thus, if an item is within Table 2, column (1), it does not qualify, unless it is made to qualify by column (2). Column (2) lists 12 structures, expenditure on which is expenditure on plant.

Read column (2) of Table 2, *Cases and Materials* (12.1).

Table 2 is to be read subject to the Notes which follow it. Note 2 enables further items to be included in the definition of plant by excluding them from the definition of 'any other structure'. These are items such as IBSs, as defined in CAA 1990, s. 18, for which CAs are available in their own right: **12.7**. Land cannot qualify as plant under CAA 1990, sch. AA1, para. 3(1). However, the saving in para. 3(2), sch. AA1, means that CAs on plant are available for assets so installed as to become part of the land, presumably to preserve *Schofield* v *R & H Hall* (1974) 49 TC 538.

The items which continue to qualify as plant in columns (2) of the sch. AA1 Tables are intended to reflect the pre-1993 High Court case law, which is voluminous. It continues to be relevant in determining the status of assets which are either completely outside the definitions of building, structures and land or which are carved out of those definitions by columns (2) of Tables 1 and 2.

The case law draws on Lindley LJ's definition of 'plant' in *Yarmouth* v *France* (1887) 19 QBD 647, 658:

> . . . plant . . . includes whatever apparatus is used by a businessman for carrying on his business, – not his stock-in-trade which he buys or makes for sale; but all goods and chattels, fixed or moveable, live or dead, which he keeps for permanent employment in his business.

Later case law, built on this definition, leaves us with two tests. One test distinguishes between apparatus used in the business and the setting of the business: *Benson* v *Yard Arm Club* [1977] 2 All ER 366. If an asset is apparatus, it is plant. The other test says that, even if an asset is part of the setting, it may still be plant, on the basis that it performs some active function in the business: *IRC* v *Barclay Curle* [1969] 1 All ER 732. In *Wimpy International* v *Warland* [1989] STC 149, Hoffman J suggested a third test, at the same time casting doubt on the first of the tests discussed above, in particular the use of the word 'setting'. The distinction is not between setting and apparatus, he said. Rather, it is between use in the business and premises. Hoffman J's approach was upheld by the Court of Appeal in that case and acknowledged as a valuable guide by the Court of Appeal in *Gray* v *Seymours Garden Centre* [1995] BTC 320. It involved a new analysis of Lindley LJ's dictum in *Yarmouth* v *France*. Hoffman J said that it was clear from Lindley LJ's dictum that, if an asset is not used for carrying on the business, it cannot be plant. He refers to this as the *first distinction*. Secondly, if it is stock in trade, it cannot be plant either – stock in trade is used quickly and is therefore excluded from the definition of plant by Lindley LJ himself. That is the *second distinction*. That leaves as being capable of being plant an asset used for permanent employment in the business, other than premises and stock in trade. This is the *third distinction*. On this basis, in *Wimpy International Ltd* v *Warland*, Hoffman J held that tiles on walls and floors in restaurants, glass shop fronts, staircases, false ceilings, mezzanine and raised floors were not plant, since they had become part of the premises. However, he also held that light fittings, which were not an integral part of the building, were plant, since bright lights were important to Wimpy, as operators of fast-food restaurants.

As mentioned above, this approach was taken in *Gray* v *Seymours Garden Centre*. Ironically, a planteria, i.e. a plant house for maintaining plants in good condition before being sold, was held not to be plant.

ACTIVITY25

On the bases of CAA 1990, sch. AA1 and *Wimpy International Ltd* v *Warland,* consider whether any of the following are *plant*. Refer to *Cases and Materials* (12.1), where the Special Commissioner's findings in the case are extracted.

(a)   vinyl tiles fastened to a floor of a restaurant;

(b)   paintings of Italy in an Italian restaurant;

(c)   carpet tiles in an accountant's office;

(d)   carpets in a restaurant;

(e)   lift machinery; and

(f)   electrical systems provided mainly to meet the requirements of a trade.

12.7   Qualifying Assets: IBSs

The other main type of qualifying assets, for our purposes, are IBSs. Although plant is defined primarily by reference to the extensive case law discussed above, IBSs are defined exclusively by reference to s. 18(1), CAA 1990. Use for one of the following purposes will mean that a building is an IBS:

■   a mill, factory or other similar premises, which is used for the purpose of a trade; or

■   used for manufacturing materials or goods; or

■   used for subjecting materials or goods to any process, including repair; or

■   used for the storage of materials used in manufacture or in subjecting to any process.

SAQ 154

Fred is a prosperous sole trader and, as a hobby, buys vintage aircraft, which he restores. He buys a disused mill to store them in. Can he claim CAs on machinery in respect of the expenditure on the aircraft? Can he claim CAs on IBSs in respect of the expenditure on the mill?

No to both questions.

Note that an IBS does not generally include an office: CAA 1990, s. 18(4).

12.8 Plant and Machinery: *Belonging* and Fixtures

One of the five conditions which must be satisfied for a person's expenditure on machinery or plant to qualify for CAs, is the condition that the asset on which the expenditure is incurred must belong to that person: see **12.4.2**. Whether this condition has been satisfied or not is usually straightforward. However, there are two situations in which the condition produces surprising results.

12.8.1 TENANT'S FIXTURES

The first is where the machinery or plant is a tenant's fixture. This is where a person is a tenant under a lease of a building and they incur capital expenditure on machinery or plant and:

- the capital expenditure which that person has incurred is expenditure which they were obliged to incur under the terms of the lease; and

- they incurred the expenditure for the purposes of a trade carried on by them; and

- the machinery or plant is not so installed or otherwise fixed in or to a building or land so as to become part of that building or land in law.

In these circumstances, the asset on which a person has incurred the expenditure is deemed to belong to them: CAA 1990, s. 61(4). If it were not for the rule in s. 61(4), the expenditure covered by it would be incurred on an asset which belonged to the landlord, rather than to the tenant.

12.8.2 LANDLORD'S FIXTURES

The other is where the machinery or plant is a landlord's fixture. The Capital Allowances Act 1990, s. 61(4) is subject to the proviso that it does not apply where machinery or plant has become the landlord's property by being affixed to the building or land in question, i.e. a landlord's fixture. This was the problem which had arisen in *Stokes v Costain Property Investments* [1984] 1 WLR 763.

In that case, Costain's claim to CAs on machinery and plant had been disallowed by the tax inspector, on the basis that the machinery or plant in respect of which their claim had been made did not belong to them. The inspector's decision was upheld by the Court of Appeal. Costain had incurred expenditure of £465,000 on machinery and plant consisting of lifts and heating equipment. These assets had been installed by them in a building of which they had a 99-year lease. The machinery and plant installed had therefore become the landlord's fixtures.

In confirming the inspector's disallowance of the CAs claimed by Costain, Fox LJ said:

> . . . I do not think one would say that a chattel 'belongs' to X if he merely had the right to use it for five years. Nor do I think it is an apt use of language to say that landlord's fixtures 'belong' to the leaseholder. He cannot remove them from the building. He cannot dispose of them except as part of the hereditament and subject to the provisions of the lease and for the term of the lease.

In response to *Stokes v Costain Property Investments Ltd*, FA 1985 enacted a number of provisions now consolidated in CAA 1990, ss. 51ff. As a result of these provisions, as a tenant, a person can claim CAs on machinery and plant even where machinery or plant becomes a landlord's fixture once it has been installed: CAA 1990, ss. 51, 52.

SAQ 155

Loaded plc leases Handel House, an office block in London, to Briggs & Co., a firm of solicitors, who rent all five floors. In the building as a whole, Briggs & Co. install water heating systems, ventilation systems and central heating.

Will these installations be landlord's fixtures? Will the partners of Briggs & Co. be able to claim CAs on them?

Yes. They can claim CAs on machinery and plant under CAA 1990, ss. 51ff.

12.9   Consequences of Disposing of Qualifying Assets

Finally, we come to the disposal of qualifying assets. Such a disposal has consequences for the person disposing of the asset and, in the case of a sale or gift of the asset, for the person acquiring it. The consequences of disposal differ, depending on whether the qualifying asset is an IBS or plant and machinery. The consequences of *acquiring* an IBS have been discussed in **12.5.1.2**, whilst the consequences of *acquiring* plant and machinery were discussed in **12.5.1.1**.

12.9.1   DISPOSALS OF IBSs

By CAA 1990, s. 4, the following events will cause a balancing charge or, depending on the factors discussed below, a balancing allowance, on the person entitled to the relevant interest in the IBS immediately before the event occurs:

■   sale of the relevant interest in the IBS: see **12.5.1.2**;

■   termination of the relevant interest in the IBS, where it is a leasehold interest, otherwise than on the owner of the relevant interest acquiring the reversion;

■   demolition or destruction of the IBS; *and*

■   total disuse of the IBS.

On the occurrence of any of the above, there will be a *balancing charge* (CAA 1990, s. 4(4)):

> If the sale, insurance, salvage or compensation moneys exceed the residue, if any, of the expenditure immediately before the event, . . . and the amount on which it is made shall be an amount equal to the excess or, where the residue is nil, to those moneys.

The balancing charge counts as an income receipt under Schedule D, Case I. It is therefore added to any other such income at Stage One of the calculation for the period in which the event occurs. Where the IBS is subject to a lease immediately before the event occurs, the balancing charge is an income receipt under Schedule A, and is also added at Stage One: CAA 1990, s. 9 (as amended by FA 1998).

On the occurrence of any of the above, there will be a *balancing allowance* (CAA 1990, s. 4(3)):

Where there are no sale, insurance, salvage or compensation moneys, or where the residue of the expenditure immediately before the event exceeds those moneys, . . . the amount of which shall be the amount of that residue or, as the case may be, of the excess of the residue over those moneys.

Note that the person disposing of the asset will be liable to pay CGT or corporation tax on any capital profit arising on the disposal, *in addition* to a balancing charge: see **24.8**.

Refer to 12.5.1.2 and to the example in the section entitled '*Used IBSs*'. What was the amount of the balancing charge made on you there?

£18,000.

12.9.2 DISPOSALS OF PLANT AND MACHINERY

By CAA 1990, s. 24, the following events will cause a balancing charge or, depending on the factors discussed below, a balancing allowance, on the person disposing of the plant or machinery:

■ the machinery or plant ceasing to belong to the person claiming the CAs;

■ the person claiming the CAs losing possession of the machinery or plant when it is reasonable to assume that the loss is permanent;

■ the machinery or plant ceasing to exist as such, e.g. by dismantling or destruction;

■ the machinery or plant beginning to be used wholly or partly for purposes other than those of the trade; or

■ the trade being permanently discontinued, or treated as being discontinued.

On the occurrence of any of the above, there will be a *balancing charge* (CAA 1990, s. 24(5)):

For any chargeable period for which a person's qualifying expenditure is less than the disposal value which he is to bring into account, . . . and the amount on which the charge is made shall be an amount equal to the difference.

The balancing charge counts as an income receipt under Schedule D, Case I. It is therefore added to any other such income at Stage One of the calculation for the period in which the event occurs.

On the occurrence of any of the above, there will be a *balancing allowance* (CAA 1990, s. 24(2)(b)):

[F]or any chargeable period for which [the claimant of CAs] . . . has qualifying expenditure which exceeds any disposal value to be brought into account . . .
(b) if the period is the chargeable period related to the permanent discontinuance of the trade, . . . equal to the whole of the excess.

The balancing allowance is deducted in the period of discontinuance, either by discharge or repayment of tax or, more likely, in taxing a trade: **12.5.3**.

SAQ 157

Blue Ltd makes its accounts up to 30 November in each calendar year. On 30 November 1997, the opening balance of its pool of qualifying expenditure is £1,600. On 1 September 1998, it sells an item of plant and machinery for £2,000. What is the consequence of this?

An £800 balancing charge, i.e. £1,600 − 400 (i.e. 25%) − £2,000.

12.10   Summary

In practice, CAs are a very important deduction from income. Income tax and corporation tax provide for them because capital expenditure and capital depreciation cannot be allowable deductions from income. CAs are available for expenditure on a range of assets, the most important of which are IBSs and plant and machinery. The law on what constitutes plant is complex, but the most successful interpreter of the case law is Hoffman J in *Wimpy International* v *Warland*. This is now qualified by CAA 1990, sch. AA1. IBSs are statutorily defined in CAA 1990, s. 18. Strict conditions must be satisfied before CAs can be claimed, which differ according to whether the claim is in respect of expenditure on IBSs or plant and machinery. Plant and machinery CAs are calculated on a reducing-balance basis, IBS CAs on a straight-line basis. Most CAs relating to expenditure on IBSs and plant and machinery are made in taxing a trade. A disposal of a qualifying asset can give rise to a balancing charge, which is unwelcome news for the person disposing of it.

12.11   End of Chapter Assessment Question

Refer to the facts concerning Amber Ltd in **2.6** and **3.6**. Consider the following additional facts.

Amber Ltd bought two items of plant and machinery, respectively, on 1 July 1993 and on 5 December 1993, for £1,600 and £6,500. It sold two other items of plant and machinery on 1 November 1995 and 15 September 1996 for £1,900 and £3,700 respectively. The qualifying expenditure in its pool of plant and machinery at 31 December 1992 was £10,000. Deborah's car is not pooled with this plant and machinery.

Calculate the balance of the pool at the end of the accounting periods ending on 31 December 1993, 31 December 1994, 31 December 1995, 31 December 1996 and 31 December 1997.

(100 marks.)

See *Cases and Materials* (**12.3**), for a specimen answer.

CHAPTER THIRTEEN

REDUCING INCOME TAXATION (5)

13.1 Objectives

By the end of this chapter, you should be able to:

■ explain how the *rental losses* of individuals and companies can be relieved;

■ explain how the *trading losses* of individuals and companies can be relieved;

■ explain how *employment income losses* of individuals can be relieved;

■ explain how *residual income losses*, under Schedule D, Case VI, can be relieved.

13.2 Introduction

This chapter is the final part of our survey of the ways in which tax law allows the burden of income taxation to be reduced. As in **Chapter 12**, our concern is entirely with income tax and corporation tax, the discussion being confined to *income loss reliefs*. Our discussion of the income loss reliefs available to individuals includes partners, trustees and PRs.

Income losses occur when, having made the relevant allowable deductions from income under Schedules A, D (Case I or II) or E, a person is left with a *negative* amount under one or more of these Schedules and Cases for the tax period under consideration. If this happens, the figure to be entered next to the relevant Schedule and Case for the tax period is NIL, since the negative amount is an income loss. In a particular case, it could be a rental loss, or a trading loss or *even* an employment income loss. In this chapter, we discover that an income loss might also consist of, or include, deductions other than allowable deductions, e.g. excess CAs and excess charges on income, which are not fully used up in the tax period under consideration. Tax law offers a number of possibilities for making use of income losses for reducing income tax or corporation tax bills, either in the tax period of the loss, or in another one. These possibilities are known as income loss reliefs.

13.3 Rental Loss Reliefs

Prior to 1 April 1998, there were fundamental differences between the operation of rental loss reliefs for income tax purposes, and their operation for corporation tax purposes. The two have been largely harmonised by FA 1998, although significant differences remain, and the differing formats of the income tax and corporation tax calculations still justify dealing with them separately.

13.3.1   RENTAL LOSS RELIEFS FOR INDIVIDUALS

Any rental loss incurred by you is calculated for your UK lettings business as a whole, i.e. all properties let by you in the UK: ICTA 1988, s. 15(1): *Cases and Materials* (2.2). Your rental loss might therefore consist simply of an excess of allowable deductions under Schedule A. Alternatively or in addition, it might consist of an excess of CAs made under Schedule A.

If your rental loss consists of, or includes, excess CAs, you will have claimed CAs either:

■ as the owner of the relevant interest in an industrial building or structure which has been let by you (12.4.1); *or*

■ as the provider of machinery and plant treated as landlord's fixtures, wholly and exclusively for the purpose of a non-domestic lettings business carried on by you (12.4.2, 12.8).

CAs in both cases are made in taxing a trade: see 12.5.3.

Rental loss relief is given only under ICTA 1988, s. 379A. A distinction is drawn between an excess of allowable deductions, and an excess of CAs.

Where, in the tax year under consideration, you have incurred a rental loss, consisting of an excess of allowable deductions, you may only carry forward that rental loss to a future tax year. You achieve this by deducting the excess from your rental income, if any, at Stage One of your income tax calculation for the next tax year, followed by the tax year after that, the one after that, etc.: ICTA 1988, s. 379A(1). The rental loss operates as an additional allowable deduction from your rental income in those subsequent tax years.

As regards an excess of CAs, the relief is more flexible. Where excess CAs exceed the amount of any Schedule A income in the tax year under consideration:

■ they may be deducted from your total income of that tax year and the next tax year; and

■ any remaining excess may be carried forward in the same way as an excess of allowable deductions, above.

(ICTA 1988, s. 379A(3).)

It will be noted, below, that companies have the option of deducting excess amounts from other income of the accounting period under consideration. This is because individuals can deduct interest as an allowable deduction under Schedule A.

SAQ 158

Andrew owns the relevant interest in an industrial building let to Blackbird Ltd, a trading company. He owns no other tenanted properties. The Schedule A income in 1998/99 is £10,000, and the allowable deductions from it, £17,000. He is also entitled to CAs on the building in 1998/99 of £8,000. He has employment income profits of £12,000 from directorships in 1998/99. What loss reliefs are available to him?

The excess allowable deductions of £7,000 can be carried forward against future rental income in a UK lettings business carried on by him. The excess CAs of £8,000 in 1998/99 are deductible from Andrew's total income of £12,000, giving him total income for 1998/99 of £4,000.

13.3.2 RENTAL LOSS RELIEFS FOR COMPANIES

13.3.2.1 Elements of a company's rental losses

Rental loss reliefs for companies are more complex than for individuals. This is because, although your rental losses as an individual can only consist of one or both of excess allowable deductions and excess capital allowances, a company's rental losses could consist of any one or more of the following:

(a)   an excess of allowable deductions; *and/or*

(b)   an excess of CAs; *and/or*

(c)   an excess of charges on income; *and/or*

(d)   an excess of management expenses; *and/or*

(e)   an excess of deductions under the company's loan relationships.

The company will have claimed CAs either:

■   as the owner of the relevant interest in an IBS let by it (**12.4.1**); and/or

■   as the provider of machinery and plant for the purposes of managing the investment business carried on by it (**12.4.2**).

CAs are in both cases made in *taxing a trade*, since FA 1998: see **12.5.3.1**.

13.3.2.2 Effect of rental loss relief and conditions for relief

Rental losses, i.e. excess allowable deductions and/or CAs
Where, in the accounting period under consideration, a company has incurred a rental loss, the loss must be deducted from the company's total profits of that accounting period: ICTA 1988, s. 392A(1). The Finance Act 1998 now ensures that the relevant CAs are made in taxing a trade, so this rental loss includes any excess CAs.

The Income and Corporation Taxes Act 1988, s. 392A(1) requires the loss to be deducted *first* from the company's total profits of the accounting period, at Stage Three of the corporation tax calculation. Any of the loss remaining is then deducted from the company's total profits of later accounting periods, i.e. at Stage Three, for so long as the lettings business continues, and until the loss is used up: ICTA 1988, s. 392A(2). If, in any of those later accounting periods, the company has ceased to carry on its lettings business, but qualifies as an *investment company* (see **11.3**), any of the loss still remaining counts as a management expense, and continues to be deductible at Stage Three on this basis: ICTA 1988, s. 392A(3).

Excess management expenses
If the company is an investment company (see **11.3**) then, if management expenses in the accounting period under consideration exceed the company's total profits, relief for the excess management expenses is given as a deduction from total profits, i.e. at Stage Three, in the accounting period following the accounting period under consideration, then the next one, and so on: ICTA 1988, s. 75(3).

SAQ 159

Brown Ltd, an investment company, has total profits in its accounting period ending on 30 March 1999 of £2,860, but no excess CAs. Its total profits are £2,000 in the accounting period ending on 30 March 2000, and £3,500 in the accounting period ending on 30 March 2001. In the accounting period ending on 30 March 1999, it has excess management expenses of £(5,000). How will this excess be relieved?

(1) As a deduction from total profits of the accounting period ending on 30 March 1999, leaving £2,140 unrelieved;

(2) ditto, period ending on 30 March 2000, leaving £140 unrelieved; and

(3) ditto, period ending on 30 March 2001, leaving total profits of £3,360.

Excess charges on income
Where charges on income, incurred wholly and exclusively for the purpose of the company's business in the accounting period under consideration, and deducted at Stage Three of the corporation tax calculation, exceed the company's total profits, relief for the excess is given as a deduction from total profits in the accounting period following the accounting period under consideration, then the next one, and so on: ICTA 1988, s. 75(3).

SAQ 160

Continuing the example in SAQ 159, Brown Ltd has total profits of £3,360 in the accounting period ending on 30 March 2001. In that accounting period, it has charges on income incurred wholly and exclusively for the purposes of the company's business of £8,000. How is the excess relieved?

By deduction from the total profits of the accounting periods ending on 30 March 2002; 30 March 2003, etc.

Excess deductions under loan relationships

Where deductions under non-trading loan relationships exceed the company's total profits at Stage Three of the corporation tax calculation (see **11.7**), relief for the excess deductions is given as follows:

(a) as a deduction from the total profits of a company in the same corporation tax group (i.e. at Stage Three of that company's corporation tax calculation) in the same accounting period: FA 1996, sch. 8, para. 2;

(b) if the excess deductions are not fully used up in (a), as a deduction from any income profits under its loan relationships in the three accounting periods previous to the accounting period under consideration, until the excess deductions are used up. (These income profits fall under Schedule D, Case III.) Excess deductions may not, however, be carried back against income profits under loan relationships arising before 1 April 1996; and

(c) if the excess deductions are not fully used up under (a) and (b), as a deduction from total profits of the accounting period after the one under consideration, i.e. at Stage Three of the calculation. Total profits here does not include any trading profits: FA 1996, sch. 8, para. 4.

Further relief is available, if necessary, under FA 1996, s. 83(4).

13.4 Relief for Trading Losses

13.4.1 TRADING LOSSES OF INDIVIDUALS

Your trading loss for an accounting period could consist of any one or more of the following elements:

(a) excess allowable deductions under Schedule D, Case I or Case II; *and/or*

(b) excess CAs, arising as described above; *and/or*

(c) excess charges on income, i.e. annual payments (**9.3.1.2**) and interest.

If all three elements are present in an accounting period, it may be possible for you to include (b) and (c) with (a), as your trading loss for the accounting period under consideration:

■ Excess CAs can be included in your trading loss, if the CAs have been made in taxing a trade and do not fall within the rare situation in CAA 1990, s. 142: see **12.5.3.1**.

■ Excess annual payments (e.g. partnership retirement annuities, see **9.3.1.2**) can be included in your trading loss *for the purpose of carry-forward relief*, under **13.4.3.2** (individuals), where the payments were made wholly and exclusively for the purposes of the trade: see **11.5.1.1**. The *grossed-up* annual payment (see **8.4**) is then included in the trading loss for the accounting period under consideration, for the purpose of carry-forward relief only.

■ Excess interest payments, e.g. paid by you on a loan to buy machinery or plant or to acquire an interest in a partnership (see **9.3.2.1**, **9.3.2.3**) can be included in your trading loss *for the purpose of carry-forward relief* and *terminal loss relief*: see **13.4.3.3**. Such interest payments must have been laid out or expended wholly and exclusively for the purposes of the trade: ICTA 1988, s. 390.

You will have claimed CAs either:

■ as the owner of the relevant interest in an industrial building or structure (**12.4.1**); *or*

■ as the provider of machinery and/or plant wholly and exclusively for the purposes of a trade carried on by you: see **12.4.2**.

CAs are in both cases made in taxing a trade: see **12.5.3.1**. This is what enables excess CAs to be included as part of your trading loss, except in the circumstances of CAA 1990, s. 142, above.

Alf, a sole trader plumber, makes his accounts up to 30 September in each calendar year. He has spent almost 18 months convalescing, after a serious accident at work. His trading profits for the accounting period ending in 1998/99 are therefore nil. During the accounting period ending on 30 September 1998, he has paid £300 interest on a loan to buy welding equipment. Can he carry forward the £(300) to the accounting period ending on 30 September 1999 as a trading loss?

Yes, provided the conditions listed in **13.4.3.2** (individuals) are satisfied.

13.4.2 TRADING LOSSES OF COMPANIES

A company's trading loss for an accounting period could consist of any or all of the following elements:

(a) excess allowable deductions under Schedule D, Case I or Case II; *and/or*

(b) excess CAs, arising as described above; *and/or*

(c) excess charges on income, i.e. annual payments, but *not* interest.

If all three elements are present in a company's corporation tax calculation for an accounting period, it may be possible for the company to include (b) and (c) with (a), as its trading loss for the accounting period under consideration:

■ Excess CAs can be included in the company's trading loss, if the CAs have been made in taxing a trade.

■ Excess charges on income can be included in the company's trading loss *for the purpose of carry-forward relief* (companies), under **13.4.3.2**, where the payments were made wholly and exclusively for the purposes of the trade: see **11.5.1.1**. Remember that the charges on income of a company are restricted to annual payments *not* made under loan relationships and royalty payments: see **9.4**.

The company will have claimed CAs:

■ as the owner of the relevant interest in an industrial building or structure (**12.4.1**); *or*

■ as the provider of machinery and/or plant wholly and exclusively for the purposes of a trade carried on by it (see **12.4.2**); *or*

■ as the person first letting machinery or plant otherwise than in the course of a trade and not in the course of a Schedule A business carried on by the company: ICTA 1988, s. 61 (see **12.4.2**).

CAs are, in the first two cases, made in taxing a trade: see **12.5.3.1**. In the third case, they are made by discharge or repayment of tax: see **12.5.3.2**. Excess CAs can be included in a company's trading loss, provided that they are made in taxing a trade, which almost all now are.

Alf (Plumbers) Ltd makes its accounts up to 30 September in each calendar year. Its trading income for the accounting period ending on 30 September 1998 is £10,000. It has allowable deductions in that period of £5,000 and claims CAs in the same period of £12,000. Can it carry forward the £(7,000) to the accounting period ending on 30 September 1999 as a trading loss?

Yes, provided the conditions in **13.4.3.2** (companies) are satisfied.

13.4.3 CONDITIONS FOR RELIEF AND EFFECT OF RELIEF

13.4.3.1 Carry *across* of trading losses

The basic idea of *carry-across relief* is that a person is entitled to deduct any trading loss in the tax period under consideration from *total income* (Stage Three, see **7.3**) or *total profits* (Stage Three, see **7.4**), in the same tax period as that of the trading loss.

The provisions are different, depending on whether an individual or a company is being considered.

Individuals
As an individual, you may:

■ deduct a trading loss incurred by you in the accounting period ending in the current tax year from your total income of that tax year, at Stage Three of your income tax calculation: ICTA 1988, s. 380(1)(a); *or*

■ deduct a trading loss incurred by you in the accounting period ending in the current tax year from your total income of the previous tax year: ICTA 1988, s. 380(1)(b). Again, this deduction is made at Stage Three of your income tax calculation for that previous tax year; *or*

■ deduct a trading loss incurred by you in the accounting period ending in the current tax year partly from your total income of the previous tax year and *partly* from your total income of the current tax year. Each deduction is made at Stage Three of the income tax calculation for each tax year. However, relief in the current tax year must be given in priority to relief in the previous tax year: ICTA 1988, s. 380(2).

The conditions for carrying across your trading loss in this way are:

(a) you must have incurred the loss in carrying on a trade, profession, vocation or employment (see **13.5**). By ICTA 1988, s. 832(1), trade '. . . includes every trade, manufacture, adventure or concern in the nature of trade' (**Chapter 15**); *and*

(b)   you must make the claim in writing, not more than 12 months after the 31 January following the end of the tax year in which the loss was incurred by you: ICTA 1988, s. 832(1); *Grimes* v *Lethem* (1898) 3 TC 622; *and*

(c)   you must have carried on the trade in the tax year of the loss '. . . on a commercial basis and with a view to the realisation of profits' (ICTA 1988, s. 384(1), (4)).

Bert is a law lecturer employed by Stokeborough University. His salary of £24,000 per annum therefore falls under Schedule E. He also has Schedule D, Case II income of £500 per annum from a freelance lecturing business. He makes up his accounts for the freelance lecturing business to 30 March in each calendar year. His allowable deductions of £1,000, from the Schedule D, Case II, income relate exclusively to travel, subsistence and overnight accommodation for the freelance lecturing business. Will his claim to deduct the £(500) loss in the lecturing business from his total income for the 1998/99 tax year be successful?

Probably not – relatively high Schedule D, Case II allowable deductions may indicate he did not carry on the lecturing business on a commercial basis and with a view to the realisation of profits.

Since the 1991/92 tax year, you have been able to carry-across a trading loss and deduct it from any capital profits you may have. On its introduction, this relief was radical, because CGT and income tax had always been kept entirely separate from each other. The relief is given by s. 72, FA 1991, and is sometimes known as *conversion relief*, since it is regarded as converting a trading loss into a capital loss, i.e. into an allowable loss for CGT purposes: see **21.8**.

As an individual, you may therefore deduct a trading loss incurred by you in the accounting period ending in the tax year under consideration from:

■   any chargeable gains of that tax year; or

■   any chargeable gains of one following tax year; or

■   any chargeable gains of the tax year *before* the tax year under consideration.

The conditions for carrying-across your trading loss against your capital profits, i.e. chargeable gains, in this way are:

(a)   you must first have claimed relief under ICTA 1988, s. 380 (FA 1991, s. 72(1)); *and*

(b)   you must generally make the ICTA 1988, s. 380 claim and the FA 1991, s. 72 claim together. The trading loss may be deducted from your chargeable gains only if your total income for the tax year under consideration is insufficient to use up the trading loss; *and*

(c)   you must have carried on the trade in the tax year of the loss ' . . . on a commercial basis and with a view to the realisation of profits' (ICTA 1988, s. 384(1) and (4)); *and*

(d)   your trading loss must have arisen in either the same tax year as the chargeable gain or in the tax year after that in which the chargeable gain arose (ICTA 1988, s. 380(1)(a) and (b)); *and*

(e)   you must have claimed the FA 1991, s. 72 relief in writing, within the relevant time limit (FA 1991, s. 72(1); ICTA 1988, s. 380(1)); *and*

(f)   your trading loss must have been incurred in a tax year after the 1991/92 tax year (FA 1991, s. 72(9)).

The Finance Act 1991, s. 72 operates in your CGT calculation, rather than in your income tax calculation: see **21.4**.

Charles, a bookseller in Clitherton, makes his accounts up to 30 September in each calendar year. His trading loss for the accounting period ending on 30 September 1998 is £(5,000). He has no other sources of income.

Because of these losses, he sold his branch shop in nearby Accringburn on 1 August 1998. The sale of the shop gave rise to a chargeable gain, for CGT purposes, of £15,000, after his CGT annual exemption (see 22.4.1). Can he deduct the £(5,000) from the gain on the sale of the shop?

Yes, provided he satisfies the other conditions listed above.

There is a problem with carry-across relief, however. To the extent that it reduces your total income below £4,195 (1998/99), then some or all of your personal allowance is wasted. Any part of the *personal allowance* not covering total income cannot be carried forward, nor transferred to any other person.

Companies
A company may:

■   deduct a trading loss incurred by it in the accounting period under consideration from its total profits of that accounting period, at Stage Three of its corporation tax calculation: see ICTA 1988, s. 393A; *or*

■   deduct a trading loss incurred by it in the accounting period under consideration from its total profits of the previous accounting period: F (No. 2) A 1997. Again, this deduction is made at Stage Three of its corporation tax calculation for that previous accounting period; *or*

■   deduct a trading loss incurred by it in the accounting period under consideration partly from its total profits of the previous accounting period and partly from its total profits of the current accounting period. Each deduction is made at Stage Three of the corporation tax calculation for each accounting period.

The conditions for the company carrying-across its trading loss in this way are that:

(a) it must have incurred the loss in carrying on a trade: see ICTA 1988, s. 393A(1); and

(b) it must make the claim in writing, not more than two years after the end of the accounting period in which the loss was incurred by it: ICTA 1988, s. 393A(10); *and*

(c) it must have carried on the trade in the year of the loss on a commercial basis and with a view to the realisation of profits.

Refer to SAQ 162. In the accounting period ending on 30 September 1996, Alf (Plumbers) Ltd's total profits were £20,000. As stated in SAQ 162, it incurs a trading loss in the accounting period ending on 30 September 1997 of £(7,000). Can it deduct the £(7,000) from the £20,000?

Yes.

13.4.3.2   Carry *forward* of trading losses

Individuals
As an individual, you may:

■ Deduct a trading loss incurred by you in the accounting period ending in the tax year under consideration from your trading income of the subsequent accounting period. This deduction is made at Stage One of your income tax calculation for the subsequent tax year: ICTA 1988, s. 385(1).

If you receive any income in the subsequent tax year(s) from which income tax has been deducted or credited as paid (i.e. interest or dividends), this is counted as trading income for this purpose, and the loss may be deducted from this too: see ICTA 1988, s. 385(4). This will enable you to reclaim the tax deducted at source or credited as paid (see **8.4**).

■ Deduct any remaining loss from your trading income of the next subsequent accounting period, when you come to do that calculation.

The conditions for carrying forward your trading loss in this way are that:

(a) The loss has not been fully used up in the tax year under consideration.

(b) You make the claim in writing no more than five years and 10 months after the end of the tax year in which the loss was incurred by you: TMA 1970, s. 43.

(c) The trade which you are carrying on in any subsequent accounting period must be the *same trade* as that carried on by you in the accounting period of the loss. In *Gordon & Blair Ltd* v *IRC* (1962) 40 TC 358, the trade carried on by a company had changed from the previous accounting period, when it was a brewing trade, to the subsequent accounting period, when it was a bottling trade. It was held that the trading losses of brewing in the earlier accounting period could not therefore be deducted from the trading income of bottling in the later accounting period: see *Cases and Materials* (**13.1.1**).

SAQ 166

Refer to SAQ 161. It is 1 October 1998. Alf has convalesced and says that, because he is tired of plumbing, he is going to carry on a picture framer's trade instead. What should you warn him of?

If he does that, he will not be allowed to carry forward the loss of the accounting period to 30 September 1998 in the plumbing trade against any profits of framing in the accounting period to 30 October 1999.

Companies
A company may:

■ Deduct a trading loss incurred by it in the accounting period under consideration from its trading income of the subsequent accounting period. This deduction is made at Stage One of its corporation tax calculation for the subsequent accounting period: ICTA 1988, s. 393(1).

If the company receives any income in the subsequent accounting period(s) from which tax has been deducted or credited as paid (i.e. interest or dividends, see **8.4**), this is counted as trading income for this purpose and the loss may be deducted from this too: ICTA 1988, s. 393(8). This will enable the company to reclaim the tax deducted/credited as paid.

This point caused problems in the House of Lords case of *Nuclear Electric* v *Bradley* [1996] 1 WLR 529. Briefly, what had happened was that money had been set aside, although not in a separate fund, for meeting possible future liabilities, by a trading company. The House of Lords held that the income generated by the fund did not rank as trading income.

ACTIVITY 26

Read the extract from the speech of Lord Jauncey of Tullichettle in *Nuclear Electric* v *Bradley*, at *Cases and Materials* (13.1.1). Note the basis on which his Lordship concluded that the income generated by the fund was not trading income.

■   Deduct any remaining trading loss from its trading income of the next subsequent
    accounting period, when it gets round to doing that calculation.

The conditions for the company carrying forward its trading loss in this way are:

(a)   the loss has not been fully used up in the accounting period under consideration;
      and

(b)   the trade which the company is carrying on in any subsequent accounting period
      is the same trade as that carried on by it in the accounting period of the loss. The
      principle in *Gordon & Blair Ltd* v *IRC* is obviously as crucial here as it is for
      individuals: see *Cases and Materials* (13.1.1).

**Refer to 13.4.2, second item in the first list of bullet points. Imagine Blue Ltd has
excess charges on income in its accounting period ending on 30 November 1998, of
£5,000. Of this, £2,500 were payments made wholly and exclusively for the purposes
of the trade. How much of the £5,000 can be carried forward under ICTA 1988,
s. 393(1)?**

£2,500. The remainder *cannot* be carried forward under ICTA 1988, s. 393(1).

13.4.3.3   *Carry-back* of trading losses (*terminal loss relief*)

Individuals

This relief is relevant to you where a trading loss is incurred by you in the last 12 months
in which you carried on the trade. You may carry back a trading loss incurred by you in
that last 12 months, by deducting it from your trading income in the tax year the trade
terminates, and the three tax years preceding that one: ICTA 1988, s. 388. In each tax
period, the deduction is made at Stage One of the income tax calculation.

If you have received any income on which tax has been deducted or credited as paid
(e.g. interest, dividends), this will count as trading income and the loss can be deducted
from this too: ICTA 1988, s. 385(4). This will enable you to reclaim the tax deducted at
source/credited as paid.

The main condition for claiming to carry back your trading loss in this way is that the
loss has *not* been fully relieved under the other provisions discussed above in this
section.

**Refer again to Alf (SAQs 161 and 166). It is 1 October 1998. Alf wonders whether it
might be possible to close down his plumbing trade, and carry back his trading loss
in the accounting period to 30.9.98. What advice would you give him?**

Yes, provided the conditions listed above are met.

Companies
The equivalent relief to ICTA 1988, s. 388 is granted by s. 393A(2A), which provides that a company can deduct a trading loss from its total profits for a three-year period. Trading losses are deducted under s. 393A at Stage Three of the corporation tax calculation, but before charges on income are deducted.

13.4.3.4   Trading losses *in early tax periods of a trade*

As an individual, you may carry back a trading loss incurred by you in each of the three tax years in which the trade is first carried on: see ICTA 1988, s. 381. This relief is an alternative to relief under ICTA 1988, ss. 380, 385 and FA 1991, s. 72. Thus it is as relevant to an individual trader acting in the capacity of a partner, as it is to a sole trader. However, this relief is not available to a company in the early years of its trade.

Section 381 relief is given by deducting the trading loss from your total income at Stage Three of your income tax calculation in the tax year under consideration. Thus if, before setting up as a trader on your own, you were an employee, and therefore had Schedule E income profits in the tax years preceding that in which you started to trade, you would be able, in effect, to deduct the loss from that, and any other income profits you had, by claiming ICTA 1988, s. 381 relief.

The main conditions for claiming to carry back your trading loss in this way are:

(a) the loss has not been fully relieved under the other relevant provisions discussed in this section;

(b) you must make the claim within two years after the end of the tax year in which the loss was sustained by you; and

(c) even though you have made a loss, the trade must be carried on on a commercial basis with a view to profit: ICTA 1988, s. 381(4).

For the last ten years, Dougie has been an assistant solicitor in a large firm. This year he decides to set up on his own, but estimates that he will make large initial losses in his profession because of high CAs claims, and allowable deductions. What should you advise him?

Income tax relief should be available under ICTA 1988, s. 381.

13.4.3.5   Income tax relief for investments in small trading companies

As an exception to the general rule, ICTA 1988, s. 574 provides relief for certain capital losses to be given in your income tax calculation.

If you have made a loss on the disposal of shares in a *qualifying trading company* in the tax year under consideration, you may deduct the amount of the loss from:

■ your total income of that tax year; *or*

■ your total income of the previous tax year: ICTA 1988, s. 574(1)(b).

There are considerable restrictions on this relief, which are beyond the scope of this chapter.

13.4.3.6 Trading loss relief on the *incorporation of a trade*

The same rule which means that the trading losses of a company cannot be carried back against the total income of its first shareholders (see **13.4.3.4**) means that, if a sole trader, or the partners of a firm, decide to incorporate the trade carried on by them, then their losses *as individuals* cannot be carried forward and deducted *by the company* under ICTA 1988, s. 385.

The process of incorporation works briefly as follows. The assets of a trade are valued and transferred out of the ownership of individuals, into the ownership of the company, in return for the issue of new shares in the company to the transferors, i.e. the incorporators: see *Cases and Materials* (**2.3.1.2**). The Income and Corporation Taxes Act 1988, s. 386 applies where the consideration for the transfer of the business to the former proprietor or proprietors is solely or mainly the issue and allotment of shares in the company: see **2.4.1.2**. In those circumstances, they can carry forward any unused trading losses and deduct them from any income from the company as if it were their own Schedule D, Case I or Case II income.

What is this relief designed to achieve?

The removal of any disincentive to incorporation arising from the income tax position of the proprietor(s) of the unincorporated business.

13.5 Relief for Employment Income Losses of Individuals

The need for this relief is encountered rarely, for understandable reasons: see **2.3.2**. It is still provided for, however, by ICTA 1988, s. 380(1) ('. . . where . . . any person sustains a loss in any trade, profession, vocation or employment . . .'). If you sustain a loss in your employment, that loss can be dealt with as described in **13.4.3.1** (individuals). However, you will have to demonstrate clearly that the loss arose directly from the conditions of your employment. This will be easiest if, whilst being an employee, you are contractually obliged to bear losses. Interestingly, unless the *eiusdem generis* rule of statutory construction applies, s. 380 would appear to exclude losses from the holding of an *office*, since ICTA 1988, s. 380(1) refers only to employments.

Alice, a barrister, sits as a Crown Court Recorder for three weeks in each tax year. In discharging this office, her Schedule E allowable deductions (see 11.6) exceed her remuneration, and she incurs a loss. Can she claim relief under ICTA 1988, s. 380(1)?

Apparently not.

13.6 Relief for Schedule D, Case VI Losses: Individuals and Companies

The nature of Schedule D, Case VI income, explored in **Chapter 18**, means that losses under this Schedule and Case are extremely rare. The relevant rule is straightforward, however. If the allowable deductions of either an individual or a company exceed the amount of income under Schedule D, Case VI, the loss can be deducted only from other Schedule D, Case VI income of the same tax period or of future tax periods: ICTA 1988, s. 392.

13.7 Summary

Although an income loss could arise under any of Schedules A, D (Cases I, II or VI), or E, the most flexible and comprehensive loss reliefs are given for trading losses. Depending on the facts of a particular case, a *rental* loss of an individual could consist of either or both excess allowable deductions and excess CAs. A rental loss of a company could also consist of either or both of these, but it could also consist of excess charges on income and/or excess deductions under loan relationships. If the company were an investment company, then it might also have an excess of management expenses.

Excess allowable deductions and CAs of companies under Schedule A are deductible from their total profits in successive accounting periods, whilst excess charges on income and excess management expenses are deductible in the other ways described in this chapter. Excess allowable deductions and CAs of individuals under Schedule A, in one tax year, are deductible from their rental income in later tax years.

A trading loss of an individual could consist of one or more of excess allowable deductions, excess CAs and excess charges on income. The same list applies to companies, although charges on income would not include interest paid by a company. Trading losses can be carried across, by both individuals and companies, as well as carried forward. For an individual, the carry across of trading losses may involve the wastage of the personal allowance, however. Trading losses may be carried back on the termination of a trade, by both individuals and companies. They may also be carried back by individuals, but not companies, in the early tax periods of a trade. Further reliefs are given to individuals, in addition, for investments in small trading companies, and on the incorporation of a trade.

Income losses are theoretically possible under Schedule E, and Schedule D, Case VI, but rarely arise in practice.

13.8   End of Chapter Assessment Questions

Refer to the facts concerning Amber Ltd: see **2.6**, **5.6**, **6.6**, **11.9** and **12.11**. In the accounting period to 31 December 1998, it has trading income of £250,000. Assume that it has allowable deductions from its trading income of £380,000 (refer to your answer to **11.9**) in the accounting period, plus further allowable deductions of £10,000. In the accounting period ending on 31 December 1998, Amber Ltd makes gross patent royalty payments of £200, in respect of a process used by it in its trade.

Remember that, on 30 November 1998, a gross dividend of £12,000 was declared and paid: see **8.9(a)**.

(a)   Calculate the WDA available to Amber Ltd on the qualifying expenditure in its pool of plant and machinery, for the accounting period to 31 December 1998. (You will need to refer to the answer to **12.2** to do this.)

(20 marks.)

(b)   Calculate the mainstream corporation tax liability of Amber Ltd, if any.

(40 marks.)

(c)   Indicate any loss reliefs available to Amber Ltd.

(40 marks.)

See *Cases and Materials* (**13.3**) for a specimen answer.

CHAPTER FOURTEEN

INCOME RECEIPTS (1): OFFICES AND EMPLOYMENTS

14.1 Objectives

By the end of this chapter, you should be able to:

■ give the *common law* meaning of an *emolument*;

■ list *five examples* of emoluments at common law;

■ list five examples of *statutorily-deemed emoluments*;

■ explain the concept of the *cash equivalent* for the statutory code applicable to employees earning more than £8,500 per annum;

■ explain the *cash equivalent* point in *Pepper* v *Hart*;

■ calculate your income tax liability on a *termination payment* within ICTA 1988, s. 148, and in excess of the £30,000 exemption.

14.2 Introduction

We now begin a four-part survey of the *income* component in Stage One of the income tax calculation. In this chapter, we are concerned almost entirely with income tax and Schedule E, i.e. with employment income received by you in your personal capacity.

The chapter is designed solely to enable you to ascertain quickly the amount from which any allowable deductions, etc. must be made, in order to give your income profit under Schedule E: see **11.6**. There is therefore no section on VAT in this chapter (see **3.4.2**), although there is a brief NIC section, to remind you to relate the discussion in this chapter to the discussion of the NIC concept of *earnings*, or gross pay, in **Chapter 6**.

14.3 Employment Income

14.3.1 INTRODUCTION

Schedule E, Case I covers the *emoluments* of employees and office-holders resident and ordinarily resident in the UK in any tax year: ICTA 1988, s. 19: see **5.3.1.1**. An office is a post which has an existence independent of its holder for the time being: *Edwards* v *Clinch* [1980] 3 All ER 278. Directors of companies are the main examples of office-holders to concern us in this book. (Office-holders are included in references to employees, unless otherwise stated.)

'Emoluments' means the *profits* of the office or employment. ICTA 1988, s. 131 states that emoluments:

> . . . shall include all salaries, fees, wages, perquisites and profits whatsoever.

You must therefore include the emoluments of your employment in Stage One of your income tax calculation for the tax year under consideration. The test for someone who is *self-employed*, as opposed to employed, is discussed at *Cases and Materials* (14.1.1).

How is ICTA 1988, s. 131 different from Schedule A and Schedule D, Cases I and II (*Cases and Materials* (2.2))?

ICTA 1988, s. 131 is not restricted to *income* profits, e.g. by the use of 'annual'.

Section 131 includes payments *in cash* made to you, although what *benefits in kind* (i.e. goods and/or services received by you *in lieu* of cash) are so included is the subject of case law, i.e. *the common law rule*, and its *statutory modifications*. Some benefits in kind, which judges have declined to regard as emoluments, have been deemed by statute to count as such. An analysis of the common law rule and its statutory modifications does not, however, give the full picture. In addition, a *special statutory code* applies, to determine what benefits in kind count as emoluments, *for employees earning £8,500 per annum or more*, and the monetary value to be placed on those that do. There are thus *three* questions in relation to every benefit in kind:

■ does the benefit count as an emolument under the *common law* rule? *If not*

■ is the benefit *deemed* to be an *emolument* by statute? *If not*

■ does the *special statutory code* apply to the benefit?

In relation to each of these three questions, there is an important additional question, i.e. what is the value to be placed on the benefit under the applicable rule?

14.3.2   THE COMMON LAW RULE

Under the common law rule, only benefits *convertible into cash* count as emoluments. Lord Halsbury LC in *Tennant* v *Smith* [1892] AC 150 formulated the common law rule thus:

> I do not deny that if substantial things of money value were capable of being turned into money they might for that purpose represent money's worth and be therefore taxable . . . I am of opinion that the thing sought to be taxed is not income unless it can be turned into money.

Lord Watson said, in the same case, that 'profits':

> . . . in its ordinary acceptation, appears to me to denote something acquired which the acquirer becomes possessed of and can dispose of to his advantage – in other words, money – or that which can be turned to pecuniary account.

It does not therefore matter if a benefit received by an employee from his or her employer is not *in fact* converted into money. The test for whether the benefit is an emolument under the common law rule is whether it is *capable* of being converted into money. In other words, is the benefit money or money's worth?

As a reward for bringing 500 new clients into the firm in the 1998/99 tax year, Sarah's employer's, Sue, Grabbit & Runne, solicitors, pay off £20,000 of her mortgage. Will this be an emolument under the common law rule?

Yes (see also *Nicholl* v *Austin* (1935) 19 TC 531).

What figure will be included in Stage One of her income tax calculation, under Schedule E, in respect of the payment?

£20,000.

In *Tennant* v *Smith*, the employee had received from his employer the right to occupy a house, something which the employee was required to do by his contract of employment. The House of Lords held that this was *not* an emolument, since the employee could not part with possession of the house, and the right to occupy it could not therefore be turned into money by the employee. Equally importantly, however, the surrender of the right to occupy the house to the employer, by the employee, would not give rise to a cash payment to the employee. Although the actual decision has been reversed by ICTA 1988, ss. 145 and 146 (see Table B, below), the common law rule for finding an emolument holds good.

On the basis that a benefit received by an employee *can* be turned into money and is therefore an emolument under *the common law rule*, the next question is, what value is to be placed on the emolument? Case law says that it is the value of the benefit to the *employee*, i.e. its second-hand value. For instance, in *Wilkins* v *Rogerson* [1961] 1 All ER 358, the second-hand value of a free made-to-measure suit (the original 'full Monty'), which the House of Lords held to be an emolument, was only £5.

Table A summarises the common law rule. It cannot be a substitute for reading the legislation, but it should help you to identify the essential features of the law. The first column shows a specific example of an emolument under the common law rule; the second gives the source for describing it as such, although this does not necessarily represent the actual decision; the third shows who is affected; and the final column shows the figure to be included in Stage One of your income tax calculation.

TABLE A: THE COMMON LAW RULE

Item	Source	To whom applicable	Amount included in Stage One
Salaries, fees, wages, perquisites convertible into cash and profits, except certain items covered by concession/ specific provision.	ICTA 1988, s. 131: 'Tax … shall … be chargeable on … emoluments … and … "emoluments" include all salaries, fees, wages, perquisites and profits whatsoever.'	All employees and office-holders irrespective of salary-level.	'On the full amount of the emoluments … subject to such deductions only as may be authorised by the Tax Acts.'
Examples			
(1) Employer pays off employee's debt.	*Nicholl* v *Austin* (1935) 19 TC 531.	As above.	Amount of debt paid off.
(2) Reimbursement of employee's expenses where they are not allowable deductions under ICTA 1988, s. 198.	*Owen* v *Pook* [1969] 2 All ER 1.	As above.	Non-deductible 'profit' element.
(3) Termination payments if deferred remuneration, paid under compensation clauses in contracts or 'gardening leave' payments.	*Dale* v *De Soissons* [1950] 2 All ER 460; *Williams* v *Simmonds* [1981] STC 715; *Mairs* v *Haughey* [1992] STC 495.	As above.	Amount of the payment(s).
(4) Payments from third parties.	*Shilton* v *Wilmshurst* [1991] 1 AC 684.	As above.	Amount of the payment(s).
(5) Payments for past services which are inducements to continue to perform services.	Dicta in *Hochstrasser* v *Mayes* [1958] 1 All ER 369; *Shilton* v *Wilmshurst*.	As above.	Amount of the payment(s).
(6) Gifts not in appreciation of personal qualities (including tips).	*Calvert* v *Wainwright* [1947] KB 526.	As above.	Amount of the payment(s).
(7) Inducement payments, i.e. not as compensation for personal sacrifices.	*Shilton* v *Wilmshurst*; *Pritchard* v *Arundale* [1971] 3 All ER 1011; *Glantre Engineering Ltd* v *Goodhand* [1983] 1 All ER 542.	As above.	Amount of the payments(s).
(8) Compensation payments where a reward for services rather than a reward for suffering.	*Hochstrasser* v *Mayes*; *Shilton* v *Wilmshurst*.	As above.	Amount of the payment(s).
(9) Payments for entering into restrictive covenants.	ICTA 1988, s. 313; *Vaughan-Neil* v *IRC* [1979] 3 All ER 481.	As above.	Amount of the payment(s).
(10) Unearned income paid until further notice.	*O'Leary* v *McKinlay* [1991] STC 42.	As above.	Amount of the payment(s).

Shilton v *Wilmshurst* [1991] 1 AC 684 merits comment, because it explains the ambit of the requirement that the emolument must be 'from' your office or employment. Peter Shilton, the goalkeeper, transferred from Nottingham Forest to Southampton. Forest paid him £75,000, which the Revenue argued was an emolument from Peter Shilton's employment with, not Forest, but *Southampton*! So far as Southampton were concerned, Forest was a third party, but this did not affect the fact that the payment was an emolument of Peter Shilton's employment with Southampton. Lord Templeman said:

> [ICTA 1988, s. 19] is not confined to 'emoluments from the employer' but embraces all 'emoluments from employment'; the section must therefore comprehend an emolument provided by a third party, a person who is not the employer. [S. 19] is not limited to emoluments provided in the course of the employment; the section must therefore apply first to an emolument which is paid as a reward for past services and as an inducement to continue to perform services and, second, to an emolument which is paid as an inducement to enter into a contract of employment and to perform services in the future. The result is that an emolument 'from employment' means an emolument 'from being or becoming an employee'.

Alf is employed as a taxi driver and, in 1998/99, receives tips from satisfied customers totalling £10,000. Are the tips within Schedule E, Case I?

Yes (see also *Calvert* v *Wainwright* [1947] KB 526).

Also note that there must be some element of profit to the *employee*. If all that is involved is *reimbursement*, the employee has no *profit*: see *Cases and Materials* (**14.1**).

The principle in *British Transport Commission* v *Gourley* [1955] 3 All ER 796 should be noted before leaving this section. The *Gourley* principle is that damages awarded to employees for loss of earnings should be reduced to take account of any income tax the employees would pay on their wages: see **14.3.3**, Note 4 to Table B.

14.3.3 STATUTORILY-DEEMED EMOLUMENTS

We next need to consider those benefits which, although they are not emoluments under the common law rule, are *deemed* to be emoluments by statute (ICTA 1988, Part V, Chapter I). These rules apply irrespective of how much you earn. The list of such statutorily-deemed emoluments includes:

- vouchers and credit tokens, subject to exceptions: ICTA 1988, ss. 141 to 144;

- living accommodation, subject to exceptions: ICTA 1988, ss. 145 to 147;

- termination payments: ICTA 1988, s. 148; *and*

- sick pay: ICTA 1988, s. 149.

The value of the benefit received with a voucher or credit card depends on whether it is a *cash voucher* or not. In each case, a further provision may then exempt certain categories of such vouchers from counting as emoluments. A *cash voucher* is one which can be exchanged for a sum of money, not substantially less than the cost of its provision, where the sum for which it is exchangeable would have been an emolument, had it been provided directly to the employee: ICTA 1988, s. 143(3), 143(4). A *non-cash voucher* is one which can *only* be exchanged for goods and services: ICTA 1988, s. 141(7). An employee who receives a cash voucher is taken to have received its *exchange value*. An employee who receives a non-cash voucher is taken to have received an amount equal to *the cost to his or her employer* of providing the voucher: see ICTA 1988, ss. 141(1) and 142(1).

You receive a non-cash voucher in 1998/99. The cost to your employer of providing it is £400; its exchange value is £250. What amount will be included in your income tax calculation for 1998/99, at Stage One, in respect of the voucher?

£400.

There are a number of exemptions which require consideration. The provisions discussed above do not apply, for example:

> . . . in relation to a non-cash voucher to the extent that it is used by the employee to obtain the use of a car-parking space at or near his place of work: ICTA 1988, s. 141(6A).

Under current tax law, no comparable exemption is provided for vouchers to obtain the use of cycle or motor cycle parking, at or near the employee's place of work. A further exception to the rules on vouchers is granted by s. 11(6), ICTA 1988, for employees of passenger transport undertakings, i.e. undertakings whose business consists wholly or mainly in the carriage of passengers: ICTA 1988, s. 141(7). If an employee of such an undertaking is provided with a transport voucher, intended to enable the employee to obtain passenger transport services, it is exempt from being an emolument.

Table B is intended to list the statutorily-deemed emoluments. Again, it cannot be a substitute for reading the detailed legislation, but it should help you to remember the essential points. The first column shows a particular example of a statutorily-deemed emolument; the second shows the authority for it; the third shows who is affected by it; and the final column shows the figure to be included in Stage One of your income tax calculation for the tax year under consideration. References to Notes are to the numbered Notes at the end of the Table.

TABLE B: STATUTORILY-DEEMED EMOLUMENTS

Item	Authority	To whom applicable	Amount included in Stage One
(1) Living accommodation unless the employee is a 'representative occupier' within ICTA 1988, s. 145(4).	ICTA 1988, ss. 145, 146: 'where living accommodation is provided ... by reason of ... employment and is not otherwise [within Schedule E] ... he is to be treated for the purposes of Schedule E as being in receipt of emoluments'. (ICTA 1988, s. 146 applies where cost of providing accommodation exceeds £75,000.)	All employees irrespective of salary level AND All office-holders, irrespective of salary-level.	*Under ICTA 1988, s. 145*, on the value of the accommodation, i.e. the higher of gross annual value (ICTA 1988, s. 837) or rent paid by employer, less any contribution paid by employee. *Under ICTA 1988, s. 146*, on an amount equivalent to the annual additional value plus gross annual value under s. 145, less any contribution paid by employee.
(Note 1)	(Note 1)	(Note 1)	(Note 1)
(2) Vouchers and credit tokens unless for expenditure allowed under ICTA 1988, s. 198 or luncheon vouchers up to 15p per day or for car-parking facilities.	ICTA 1988, ss. 141–44.	As above.	*Non cash vouchers*: Cost to employer of providing the voucher, not its exchange value, less any reimbursement made by employee; *Credit tokens*: Cost to employer of providing goods or services; *Cash vouchers*: Exchange value (ICTA 1988, s. 143)
(Note 2)	(Note 2)	(Note 2)	(Note 2)
(3) Sick pay unless arrangements for it not entered into by employer.	ICTA 1988, s. 149(1).	As above.	Amount of sick pay, as reduced by employee's contributions to scheme.
(Note 3)	(Note 3)	(Note 3)	(Note 3)
(4) Termination payments (i.e. golden handshakes) not otherwise chargeable to tax which exceed £30,000 and which are *not* paid under an approved retirement benefits scheme nor because of death, disability or foreign service.	ICTA 1988, s. 148.	As above.	Amount exceeding £30,000.
(Note 4)	(Note 4)	(Note 4)	(Note 4)

Notes:

1. When, as an employee, you qualify as a *representative occupier* within ICTA 1988, s. 145(4), the value of the accommodation is exempted from going into your income tax calculation as Schedule E income, plus any council tax paid by the employer or reimbursed to you. Tax exempt representative accommodation is not available to a

director unless certain conditions are met: ICTA 1988, s. 145(5). For ICTA 1988, s. 146, the additional value is the excess of the cost of each property over £75,000, multiplied by the interest rate applicable at the beginning of the tax year under consideration, to find the benefit conferred by the beneficial loan under ICTA 1988, s. 160.

Read the article by Arthur Sellwood on the provision of living accommodation as an emolument: *Cases and Materials* **(14.1.2).**

2. SP 6/85 shows how the cost is calculated for both non-cash vouchers and credit tokens. ESC A2 is the concession which exempts luncheon vouchers up to 15p per day.

3. Distinguish between these payments and *statutory sick pay*, which is also not exempt: ICTA 1988, s. 150 (see **10.5.3**).

4. The Income and Corporation Taxes Act 1988, s. 148, as amended by FA 1998, relates to termination payments. It has been amended as part of the *tax law rewrite* project (see **4.6**), but s. 148(3) contains a substantial amendment: see below. The amendment applies to payments or benefits received on or after 6 April 1998. Section 148(1) says:

> Payments and other benefits not otherwise chargeable to tax which are received in connection with–
> (a)   the termination of a person's employment, or
> (b)   any change in the duties of or emoluments from a person's employment, are chargeable to tax under this section if and to the extent that their amount exceeds £30,000.

Benefits are defined as items which would have been emoluments, *had the employment continued*: ICTA 1988, s. 148(2). Section 148(3) says that any part of the payment *not* covered by the exemption is treated as received in the tax year *when the payment or benefit is actually received*. Previously, it was the one when the termination, etc. *occurred*. You can *opt* for FA 1998 treatment if your employment terminated between 6 April 1996 and 5 April 1998.

Note that a number of types of payment are *excluded* from ICTA 1988, s. 148. Most importantly, you do not get the benefit of s. 148 where the payment *is* otherwise chargeable to tax, e.g. *Dale* v *De Soissons* [1950] 2 All ER 460.

Note also the application of the *Gourley* principle to damages for loss of earnings, e.g. on wrongful dismissal: see above. If such damages are awarded to an employee, they are reduced by applying *Gourley*. If the net damages then exceed £30,000, it is necessary to estimate what income tax would be payable on the slice of the award *not* exempted by ICTA 1988, s. 148. It is necessary to reflect realistically the actual loss suffered: *Shove* v *Downs Surgical* [1984] 1 All ER 7.

Bob receives a termination payment of £100,000, *within* **ICTA 1988, s. 148, on 1 May 1999. His employment terminated on 1 April 1999. For what tax year must the £70,000** *not* **covered by the exemption be included in Stage One of his income tax calculation?**

1999/2000.

Read the extract from the article on termination payments by Paul Yerbury in *Cases and Materials* (14.1.2), remembering it was published *before* the new s. 148 was inserted by FA 1998.

14.3.4 SPECIAL STATUTORY CODE FOR EMPLOYEES WITH EMOLUMENTS OF £8,500 PER ANNUM OR MORE AND MOST DIRECTORS

Finally, we need to consider the *special statutory code* applicable to benefits received by employees earning £8,500 or more per annum. In deciding whether you earn £8,500 or more, you assume that no allowable deductions will be made under s. 198, ICTA 1988: see **11.6**.

In 1998/99, your employment income is £9,000, and you have allowable deductions under ICTA 1988, s. 198, of £1,000. Does the statutory code apply to you?

Yes.

Besides employees, the statutory code applies to a director of a company, *other than* one who does not have a material interest in the company (i.e. 5%), and *either* (a) is a full-time working director of it; *or* (b) the company is charitable or non-profit-making. However, as a director, you will still be within the code if you are *also* an employee earning £8,500 per annum or more: ICTA 1988, s. 167(5).

The details of the statutory code are contained in ICTA 1988, ss. 153–68. Where it applies, the rule is that all benefits and facilities, of whatever nature, are to be treated as emoluments of the employment, subject to a number of exemptions: ICTA 1988, s. 154. It is important to recognise that, not only is the code inapplicable to employees earning less than £8,500 per annum, it does not apply to benefits counting as emoluments under the rules discussed above, *even* though the employee earns £8,500 per annum or more. The Income and Corporation Taxes Act 1988, s. 153(1) provides that the code is only applicable to '. . . any sums which, apart from this section, are not chargeable to tax . . .'.

There are two significant differences between the special statutory code and the other rules discussed so far. First, unlike the common law rule, the special statutory code does *not* insist that a benefit must be convertible into cash before it qualifies as an emolument. Secondly, unlike for both the common law rule and statutorily-deemed emoluments, the employee is deemed to have received *not* the value of the benefit to the *employee*, i.e. its second-hand value, but the cost *to the employer* of providing the benefit, i.e. its 'cash equivalent'. The basic provision of the special statutory code is in s. 156(1), (2), ICTA 1988:

> (1) The cash equivalent of any benefit chargeable to tax under section 154 is an amount equal to the cost of the benefit, less so much (if any) of it as is made good by the employee to those providing the benefit.
>
> (2) . . . [T]he cost of a benefit is the amount of any expense incurred in or in connection with its provision, and . . . includes a proper proportion of any expense relating partly to the benefit and partly to other matters.

In certain cases, the cost to the employer is determined by specific provisions of the code, which state exactly *how* the cash equivalent is to be calculated, e.g. in relation to the private use of non-pooled cars and vans: ICTA 1988, ss. 157, 159, 159AB and sch. 6.

The provisions on non-pooled company cars should be noted. If a *non-pooled car* is made available for your private use in the tax year under consideration, you must include an amount of Schedule E income at Stage One, calculated according to the cash equivalent of the car: ICTA 1988, s. 157, sch. 6. The cash equivalent is 35% of the manufacturer's list price. This is reduced by a maximum of £5,000, if you contribute to the provision of the car, although there is a cap on the list price of £80,000. The cash equivalent is then further reduced:

■ by ⅓ if your business mileage is between 2,500 per annum and 17,999 per annum; *and*

■ by ⅔ if your business mileage is 18,000 or above per annum.

Note, however, that you must be required by the nature of your employment to use your car to this extent. In addition, the cash equivalent is reduced by ⅓ of the list price if the car is more than four years old. Also, if you make a capital contribution towards your *private use of the car*, the amount you are deemed to receive is accordingly reduced, on a pound-for-pound basis.

The Income and Corporation Taxes Act 1988 contains a scale charge for the *private use of petrol and diesel*, i.e. car fuel benefits: ICTA 1988, s. 158. The 1998/99 scales are shown below, petrol and diesel being dealt with separately.

Petrol		*Diesel*	
Engine Size	*Cash Equivalent (£)*	*Engine Size*	*Cash Equivalent (£)*
1,400cc or less	1,010	2,000cc or less	1,280
1,400cc to 2,000cc	1,280	Over 2,000cc	1,890
Over 2,000cc	1,890		

Where statute does *not* determine the cash equivalent of a benefit, it is necessary to find it by more subtle means. The leading case in this area is *Pepper* v *Hart* [1993] 1 All ER 42: see **4.6**. That case involved members of staff at Malvern College. The point at issue was the figure which they should have been entering in Stage One of their income tax calculations, representing the benefit of having their children educated at the college for only one-fifth of the cost to other pupils: see *Cases and Materials* (**4.1**). The Revenue argued that the cash equivalent of the benefit was the *average* cost of educating the children. The members of staff argued that it should be the *marginal* cost.

SAQ 179

What would the *average* cost have involved?

Including in Stage One of their income tax calculations a proportion of the costs of running the school *for the boys as a whole*.

What would the *marginal cost* have involved?

Calculating the *additional cost* of educating the sons of the staff members.

On the facts, taking the *marginal cost* meant that there was *no need* to include any amount in Stage One. By reference to Parliamentary materials, a majority of the House of Lords ruled in favour of the staff.

There remain to be considered benefits which involve the conferring of a loan by the employer on you, the employee. For instance, interest-free loans or loans at favourable rates of interest, for the purchase of season tickets for public transport. Neither type of loan would be an emolument at common law, nor would it be a statutorily-deemed emolument. However, both types of loans might well come within the provisions of the statutory code, i.e. ss. 160 and 161, ICTA 1988. Subject to certain *de minimis* limits, a loan made by your employer to you, by reason of your employment, will qualify as an emolument if is *interest-free* or made at a *low rate of interest*. The cash equivalent of the loan is the difference between the interest for the tax year, calculated at the *official rate*, and no interest; or the interest for the tax year calculated at the *official rate* and any favourable rate of interest *actually paid* by you. The *de minimis* limit means that the employee is not treated as receiving an emolument where the aggregate amount of all beneficial loans outstanding in a tax year does not exceed £5,000: ICTA 1988, s. 161(1)(a). Given the sums involved, it should therefore be possible to make such a loan to you, without your receiving an emolument under the statutory code. It is important to recognise, however that, if the loan were ever to be written-off or released by the employer, the amount of the loan released or written-off would form part of your emoluments from your employment for the tax year in which it was written-off or released.

Table C below is intended to summarise the provisions of the special statutory code. Again, the Table cannot be a substitute for reading it, but it should help in remembering its essential features. The first column shows a particular example of an emolument within the code; the second shows the authority for it; the third shows who is affected by it; and the final column shows the figure to be included in Stage One of your income tax calculation for the tax year under consideration. The references to the Notes are to the Notes at the end of the Table.

TABLE C: THE SPECIAL STATUTORY CODE

Item	Authority	To whom applicable	Amount included in Stage One
(1) Benefits provided by reason of employment. Generally, benefits are accommodation (other than living accommodation), domestic services and other benefits and facilities of whatever nature other than sick pay (ICTA 1988, s. 149) and other benefits subject to special rules.	ICTA 1988, ss. 153–68.	Any employee with emoluments of £8,500 per annum or more. Directors, irrespective of salary-level, except those with no material interest in the company who are full-time working directors or those with no material interest in the company who are part-time, if the company is non-profit-making or charitable.	Cash equivalent, i.e. cost incurred by employer in providing the benefit, less any payment made by the employee (ICTA 1988, s. 156(1)). Special rules where asset made available for use by employee/director.

Examples

Item	Authority	To whom applicable	Amount included in Stage One
(1) Cars and vans available for private use, except where pooled.	ICTA 1988, ss. 159, 159AB, 157 and sch. 6.	As above.	Cash equivalent in accordance with sch. 6.
(2) Fuel for employee's car.	ICTA 1988, s. 158.	As above.	Cash equivalent in accordance with scale in s. 158.
(3) Mobile telephones provided for private use unless obligation to reimburse employer which is in fact reimbursed by employee.	ICTA 1988, s. 159A.	As above.	Cash equivalent, i.e. £200 per phone per annum.
(4) Beneficial loan arrangements:			
(a) Loan by reason of office or employment (ICTA 1988, sch. 7, Part 1), either interest-free or at a low rate of interest.	ICTA 1988, s. 160.	As above.	Cash equivalent, i.e. difference between interest for tax year calculated at official rate and any interest actually paid by employee.
(b) Release or writing-off of loan	ICTA 1988, ss. 160(3) and 161(6).	As above.	Cash equivalent, i.e. an amount equivalent to amount released/written-off.
(Note 1)	(Note 1)	(Note 1)	(Note 1)
(5) Shares issued to an employee partly-paid.	ICTA 1988, s. 162.	As above.	Notional loan charge, based on difference between price paid and market value of shares at that time.
(6) Scholarships awarded to employee's children unless payments do not exceed 25% of fund and award does not result from employment, i.e. is fortuitous.	ICTA 1988, s. 165.	As above.	Amount of scholarship.

Item	Authority	To whom applicable	Amount included in Stage One
(7) Reimbursement of expenses/expense allowance not otherwise chargeable to tax and not an allowable deduction under s. 198. (Note 2)	ICTA 1988, s. 163. (Note 2)	As above. (Note 2)	Profit element, i.e. amounts not qualifying as allowable deductions under ICTA 1988, s. 198. (Note 2)

Notes:

1. Because of ICTA 1988, s. 160, golden handshakes should *never* be given as releases of any loan made to the employee. The £30,000 exemption cannot apply to such a release, since the release is *otherwise chargeable to tax*.

2. In practice, employers agree particular amounts with the Revenue, which are thereby deemed not to involve any profit element for the employee: see *Cases and Materials* **(14.1.1)**.

ACTIVITY 29

Read the extract from the article by Colin Masters and Susan Ball in *Cases and Materials* (14.1.3) as to what could happen if you change your company car, part-way through the tax year!

14.4   National Insurance Contributions: a Reminder

When analysing the amount to be included in Stage One of your income tax calculation under the rules of Schedule E described above, it is essential to bear in mind that many of these sums will also be *earnings*, i.e. gross pay, for NIC purposes: see **6.4**. (You might find it useful here to re-read *Cases and Materials* (**6.1**), along with **6.4**.)

14.5   Summary

Under Schedule E fall the emoluments of your employment. The common law rule as to what constitutes an emolument has been modified by statute in two ways. First, some benefits are deemed to be emoluments for all employees. Secondly, benefits which are not emoluments under these rules are emoluments if the special statutory code applies to the employee. The special statutory code applies to all employees earning £8,500 per annum or more and most directors. Under the special statutory code, an employee is deemed to receive the cash equivalent, not the second-hand value of the benefit. Many benefits in kind, notably company cars and fuel provided for private use, have a statutorily-specified cash equivalent.

14.6   End of Chapter Assessment Question

Refer back to **6.6**, and note the following additional facts. The non-pooled car provided for Deborah's general use by the company is retained by her throughout the 1998/99 tax year. It has an 1,800cc petrol engine, and she is reimbursed by Amber Ltd for the petrol used by her for private purposes. The manufacturer's list price of the car is £28,000, including the CD-player and alloy wheels with which it is fitted. In the 1998/99 tax year, her business mileage for Amber Ltd is 2,000.

Comment on the significance of these facts in terms of Deborah's income tax position in 1998/99.

(Word limit: 400 (100 marks).)

See *Cases and Materials* (**14.3**), for a specimen answer.

CHAPTER FIFTEEN

INCOME RECEIPTS (2): TRADES, PROFESSIONS AND VOCATIONS

15.1 Objectives

By the end of this chapter, you should be able to:

■ explain the terms *trade*, *profession* and *vocation*;

■ discuss the six *badges of trade*;

■ distinguish the *various* bases on which trading profits have been calculated prior to the relevant provisions of FA 1998 taking effect;

■ explain the basis on which trading profits will be calculated from 6 April 1999.

15.2 Introduction

This is the second part of our survey of the *income* component in Stage One of the income tax or corporation tax calculation. In this chapter, we are concerned entirely with income receipts falling under Schedule D, Case I or II. For this to be the case, the receipts in question must be income derived from a trade, profession or vocation. In the earlier part of the chapter, we therefore explore the implications of these three terms. We then examine how capital receipts are excluded, and consider the implications of the requirement that the receipts must be derived from the trade. The chapter is then rounded-off with a brief reminder of the VAT and NIC aspects of Schedule D, Case I or II receipts. The expression *trader* includes both individuals and companies carrying on a trade, unless otherwise indicated. Subject to the same qualification, the expression *trading income* includes income from a profession or vocation.

15.3 Income Tax and Corporation Tax: *Trades*, *Professions* and *Vocations*

15.3.1 WHAT IS A *TRADE*?

In *Ransom* v *Higgs* [1974] 3 All ER 949, Lord Wilberforce suggested the following definition:

Trade involves, normally, the exchange of goods, or of services, for reward, not of all services, since some qualify as a profession . . . or vocation [see **15.3.2**], but there must be something which the trade offers to provide by way of business. Trade, moreover, presupposes a customer (to this too there may be exceptions, but such is the norm), or, as it may be expressed, trade must be bilateral – you must trade with someone.

The legislation itself contains only an unhelpful inclusive definition (ICTA 1988, s. 832(1)):

Trade includes every trade, manufacture, adventure, or concern in the nature of trade.

It does however make clear that, besides the profits of everyday trading activities, the income profits of an adventure *in the nature of trade* must be included in Stage One of a person's income tax or corporation tax calculation.

Given the lack of an exclusive legislative definition, there is no shortage of case law on *trade* and *adventure in the nature of trade*. In addition, there are the *six badges of trade* in the 1955 *Final Report of the Royal Commission on the Taxation of Profits and Income* (1955, Cmd. 9474). The six badges of trade are derived from an analysis of the case law, and they are used to determine whether a business activity is a trade, or an adventure in the nature of trade, in a difficult case. They are as follows.

15.3.1.1   The *subject-matter* of the transaction under consideration

Sometime in the mid-1920s, Mr Andrew Rutledge, who was 'a businessman with many interests,' went to Berlin to buy a film for a cinema company of which he was a director. While he was there, he was:

. . . put into touch with a man interested in finding money for German firms, and through him he made a deal with a bankrupt firm of paper manufacturers to purchase one million rolls of toilet paper for £1,000 sterling.

On his return to the UK, Mr Rutledge sold the toilet paper at a profit of £10,895: *Rutledge v IRC* (1929) 14 TC 490. The Court of Session held that the huge profit which Mr Rutledge had made on the sale was a profit from *an adventure in the nature of trade*. Lord Sands said, icily:

The nature and quantity of the subject dealt with exclude the suggestion that it could have been disposed of otherwise than as a trade transaction. Neither the purchaser nor any purchaser from him was likely to require such a quantity for his personal use.

This case typifies the first badge of trade, i.e. that, if a person cannot obtain either investment income from property, nor personal enjoyment, its sale by that person must be an adventure in the nature of trade. (What on earth does someone do with a million rolls of toilet paper?) With real property and shareholdings, and other types of property capable of generating income, it may not be as obvious as it is with toilet paper that the property sold can neither produce income nor personal enjoyment. In these cases, the seller's chances of arguing that a sale was not an adventure in the nature of trade may be all the greater.

Land was the property sold in *Marson v Morton* [1986] 1 WLR 1343. In that case, Sir Nicolas Browne-Wilkinson V-C held that the Commissioners were correct to hold that Brian Morton and his brothers, who were all shareholders in a family potato-trading company, did *not* make a trading profit when they resold land they had originally bought in 1977 with the benefit of planning permission. The Vice-Chancellor stressed that the facts were very unusual, since the brothers did not themselves intend to develop the land. He continued:

The subject matter was land with planning permission, which is an item of property which I would have thought was neutral, namely it could have been bought for investment purposes. On the other hand, it is of course manifestly a commodity which is dealt with by way of property deals [i.e. trading transactions: see **12.4.1**]. It is not to my mind the same as whisky [*Cape Brandy Syndicate* v *IRC* [1921] 1 KB 64] or toilet paper, in relation to which profit is incapable of being realised other than by a quick sale . . . I can see no reason why . . . the mere fact that land is not income-producing should not be decisive, or even virtually decisive, on the question whether it was bought as an investment.

On this basis, it should be possible for a seller to argue, even when land is not bought to rent out, that the profit realised is not a trading profit.

If the profit does not fall under Schedule D, Case I, does it escape tax altogether?

No: see **3.3.3**, **18.4.1**.

15.3.1.2   How long the seller has owned the property sold

If a person sells property at a profit, very shortly after having bought it, this points to the profit being a trading profit, i.e. falling under Schedule D, Case I. However, it is a much less persuasive badge than might be imagined, because the facts of a specific case might indicate that, when bought, the property was intended to be held by the seller as an investment.

15.3.1.3   How often similar transactions have been repeated

It is important to realise the exact relationship between this badge and the others discussed above. A person does not need to be a trader, in order for a one-off profit to be the profit of an adventure in the nature of trade: *Rutledge* v *IRC*. Even if a transaction is not an adventure in the nature of trade, however, any profit generated by it may still fall under Schedule D, Case I, if it is *repeated* often enough: *Pickford* v *Quirke* (1927) 13 TC 251. In *Pickford* v *Quirke*, an individual was a member of a number of syndicates which bought and sold cotton mills. A syndicate would buy a company which owned a cotton mill, liquidate it, and sell its property to anyone who was willing to buy it. The members of a syndicate were not always the same, although the individual involved in *Pickford* v *Quirke* had taken part in three such transactions. The Court of Appeal held that, although each transaction *by itself* was not an adventure in the nature of trade, his participation in three transactions meant that he was carrying on a trade, and the profits on the three sales therefore fell under Schedule D, Case I. A similar decision was reached in *Leach* v *Pogson* (1962) 40 TC 585, where a person sold 30 driving school businesses.

15.3.1.4   Whether the seller has done any supplementary work on the property

If a person neither sets up an organisation to market the property sold, nor to do any work on that property, any profit made on its sale is not a Schedule D, Case I profit: *Martin* v *Lowry* [1927] AC 312, *Cape Brandy Syndicate* v *IRC* [1921] 1 KB 64, [1921] 2 KB 403. The latter was the case in which Rowlatt J famously remarked that tax statutes have to be given their ordinary meaning, there being 'no equity about a tax': see **4.6**. *Martin* v *Lowry* is a case dating from the time when aeroplanes were constructed on wooden or metal frames, across which linen was stretched and doped, in order to form the flying surfaces. Mr Martin, who did not usually buy and sell aircraft linen, bought 45 million yards of it from the relevant Government department in June 1919, i.e. the whole of the Government's surplus stock after the First World War. 'Failing to dispose of it in one bulk sale', the report says, ' . . . he rented an office in High Holborn from July, 1919, until

March, 1920, and set up a large and skilled organisation for disposing of it in smaller quantities'. He made a profit of over £1.5 million. On these facts, the House of Lords held that this profit fell under Schedule D, Case I, Mr Martin having set up a trading organisation.

Cape Brandy Syndicate v *IRC* illustrates the other point made above, that if a person does work on goods, in order to sell them, any profit will fall under Schedule D, Case I. In that case, three individuals, who were wine traders, formed a syndicate to buy 3,000 casks of one type of brandy. They blended it with another type of brandy, recasked it, and sold it to customers at a healthy profit, from July 1916 to September 1917. Neither Rowlatt J, at first instance, nor the Court of Appeal interfered with the finding of the General Commissioners, that the profit was a trading profit.

15.3.1.5 Circumstances giving rise to the transaction

The idea with the fifth badge is that, if a person is *forced* to sell property, by circumstances beyond that person's control, any profit on the sale will tend *not* to fall under Schedule D, Case I. This idea was used in *West* v *Phillips* (1958) 38 TC 203, to hold that a Stockport builder, who had made a profit on the sale of a large number of houses originally built to hold as an investment, had been *forced* to make the sale, i.e. by Government rent control, and rising rates of taxation. In the circumstances, therefore, the profit on the sale of the houses was not derived from the builder's trade and thus did not fall within Schedule D, Case I: see **15.4.1**.

SAQ 182

In 1958, the fact that the profit did not fall under Schedule D, Case I meant that it escaped taxation. For which of the cases above would that not have been the case?

Marson v *Morton*, decided after the introduction of CGT (and note ICTA 1988, s. 776 at **18.4.1**).

15.3.1.6 The seller's motive on buying the property sold

If a person buys property with the intention of making a profit on its resale, this is an indication that the profit falls under Schedule D, Case I. However, the mere fact of a person intending to make a profit on a resale does not necessarily make the profit a trading profit: *Marson* v *Morton*. There is a link between this badge and the first badge, illustrated by *Wisdom* v *Chamberlain* [1969] 1 All ER 332. In that case, said Harman LJ, Norman Wisdom wanted '. . . a nest-egg . . .' for his future, since '. . . after all a comedian's life does not go on for ever and he needs something for his declining years . . .'. Accordingly, in 1961, Norman Wisdom bought £200,000 in silver bullion, as a hedge against a devaluation in the pound sterling. He eventually made a profit of £48,000, which the Court of Appeal held to be a profit from an adventure in the nature of trade.

15.3.1.7 The six badges of trade: additional points

So much for the six badges of trade. In certain hard cases, they are not needed, because statute *deems* certain businesses to be trades, e.g. (ICTA 1988, s. 53):

All farming and market gardening in the United Kingdom shall be treated as the carrying on of a trade . . . .

Bearing in mind the flexibility of *trading loss relief* (see 13.4), what might be the tax benefit of market-gardening?

By doing it badly, you might be able to generate a trading loss, and thus a tax relief.

Unfortunately, this will not work, e.g. ICTA 1988, s. 384(1),(4) (see **13.4.3**).

15.3.2   WHAT IS A *PROFESSION* OR *VOCATION*?

In *IRC* v *Maxse* [1919] 1 KB 647, Scrutton LJ stated that the term *profession* involved:

> . . . the idea of an occupation requiring either purely intellectual skill, or of manual skill, controlled, as in painting and sculpture, or surgery, by the intellectual skill of the operator, as distinguished from an occupation which is substantially the production or sale or arrangements for the production or sale of commodities.

Like trade, the term 'profession' is not defined in the legislation. If a person's business activities fall within this description, the profits from the business fall under Schedule D, Case II, unless that person is *employed* to carry them out. Moreover, it seems that the world's oldest profession is actually a trade: *IRC* v *Aken* [1990] 1 WLR 1374.

Andrew is an assistant solicitor employed by a firm of solicitors, in which Fergus is a partner. Which of them has income falling under Schedule E, and which under Schedule D, Case II?

Andrew – Schedule E; Fergus – Schedule D, Case II.

Carrying on a profession must involve more than one transaction, and thus an element of continuity. There is no adventure in the nature of profession! One-off professional income would therefore fall under the general part of Schedule D, Case VI: see **18.3**.

For the meaning of *vocation*, we must again go beyond the legislation, to *Partridge* v *Mallandaine* (1886) 18 QBD 276, which concerned a bookmaker. There Denman J (Hawkins J concurring), in holding that the term *vocation* included the business of a bookmaker, said that a vocation was '. . . the way in which a man passes his life'. This does not, however, mean that full-time gambling is a vocation: *Graham* v *Green* [1925] 2 KB 37. In that case, Rowlatt J distinguished bookmakers from full-time gamblers, thus:

> . . . I do not think that he [the full-time gambler] could be said to organise his effort in the same way as a bookmaker organises his, for I do not think the subject matter from his point of view is susceptible of it . . . I think all you can say of that man [i.e. the full-time gambler], in the fair use of the English language, is that he is addicted to betting.

. . . But the source of a legal right is relevant to the first problem involved in the application of the rule to the particular case, namely, to identify what the compensation was paid for. If the solution to the first problem is that the compensation was paid for the failure of the trader to receive a sum of money, the second problem involved is to decide whether, if that sum of money has been received by the trader, it would have been . . . an income receipt of that trade.

Why did the Revenue claim tax under Schedule D, Case I, on the damages awarded for the loss consequential on the physical damage?

These damages represented non-receipt of Schedule D, Case I income, whereas the damages for the physical damage did not do so.

15.5   Income Tax and Corporation Tax: Methods of Calculating Trading Profits

The process of identifying trading income requires us to determine which trading income is to be included in an income or corporation tax calculation in a particular tax period. This involves some discussion of the relationship between GAAP and these taxes: **1.5.3**. In **15.5.1**, we consider the general nature of the debate which has resulted in the specific measure discussed in **15.5.2**.

15.5.1   RELATIONSHIP BETWEEN SCHEDULE D, CASE I PROFITS AND GAAP

Profits made by traders, as shown in their accounts, often do not correspond to their income profits under Schedule D, Case I: see **1.5.3**. Disparity between accounting deductions and allowable deductions (see **1.5.3**), timing differences, and the operation of CAs (see **12.3**), all contribute to this divergence. Some of the principles of GAAP are embodied in SSAPs, and some in FRSs. In addition, there are company law rules about the preparation of company accounts.

Recent cases deal with the relationship between GAAP and tax law. They also consider which principle of GAAP should be applied when they conflict on the same facts. The case on the relationship between GAAP and tax is *Gallagher* v *Jones* [1994] Ch 107, where Sir Thomas Bingham MR said:

. . . given the plain language of the legislation [i.e. that of Schedule D, Case I] I find it hard to understand how any judge-made rule could override the application of a generally accepted rule of commercial accountancy which: (a) applied to the situation in question, (b) was not one of two or more rules applicable to the situation in question and (c) was not shown to be inconsistent with the true facts or otherwise inapt to determine the true profits or losses of the business.

The case on resolving conflicts between accounting principles themselves is *Johnston* v *Britannia Airways Ltd* [1994] STC 763. This case, a decision of Knox J, turned on the question of which of two accounting principles should be applied to expenditure incurred by an airline on major overhauls of aero engines. In order for a certificate of airworthiness to be granted to an airline in respect of an aircraft, such an overhaul was required every 17,000 flying hours. Should the expenditure on the overhaul be deducted according to one accountancy principle or according to another? They produced different results! In choosing the one contended for by the airline rather than that for which the Revenue argued, Knox J applied the principle that it is for a court, taking account of professional evidence, to decide which of the two principles is to apply.

Read the extract from the article by Barry Akin in *Cases and Materials* (15.1.1), which discusses *Gallagher* v *Jones* and *Johnston* v *Britannia Airways*.

15.5.2 BASES FOR CALCULATING TRADING INCOME

Against the background of this divergence, persons carrying on a trade, profession or vocation have traditionally had great freedom in choosing the *basis* on which their trading profits are calculated. That freedom has now effectively been removed by FA 1998, for accounting periods beginning after 6 April 1999. The three traditional bases are the *earnings* basis, the *cash* basis and the *bills delivered* basis. The last two of these are referred to as the *conventional* bases.

The *bills delivered* basis implies that a trader's income for the accounting period under consideration consists of the bills sent out to its customers in that period. By the same token, the trader's expenditure is identified according to the bills received by it in that period. The trading profit (or loss) is, of course, the difference between the two. If a trader adopts the *cash* basis, however, it will take the payments *actually* received from its customers in the accounting period as its income for that period. Equally, the trader's expenditure will be identified as the sums actually paid out in that period. The trading profit (or loss) for the period is again the difference between the two. The *cash* basis does not therefore reflect accurately the effect of any credit arrangements, and the trader does not need to ascribe any value to *trading stock*, nor to *work-in-progress*.

By contrast with the conventional bases, the *earnings* basis means that the trader takes the income *earned*, rather than the bills sent out or cash received, as its income for the tax period under consideration. The trader's expenditure is identified according to the expenditure incurred, irrespective of whether the trader has actually paid the bills, and irrespective of whether its customers have paid the trader. The income profits (or loss) for the period under consideration are again, of course, the difference between these two figures.

The major difference between the earnings basis, and the conventional bases is that, with the earnings basis, the trader *does* need to ascribe a value to *trading stock* (i.e. to stock-in-trade), where the trader supplies *goods*, or to work-in-progress, where the trader supplies *services*. Work-in-progress is work which is not finished, and is therefore not yet billed at the end of the period. The fact that, under the *earnings* basis, the trader must include work-in-progress or closing stock in its trading income, simply means that income profits are included in the trader's tax calculation in an earlier tax period than would have been the case under the *conventional* bases. It also means that bad debts are deductible from income only in the tax period when they are actually shown to be bad.

With limited exceptions, FA 1998 applies the earnings basis to all Schedule D, Case I and Case II profits, for accounting periods beginning after 6 April 1999 (FA 1998, s. 42(1)):

For the purposes of Case I or II of Schedule D the profits of a trade, profession or vocation must be computed on an accounting basis which gives a true and fair view, subject to any adjustment required or authorised by law in computing profits for those purposes.

The limited exceptions include Lloyd's underwriters (for whom there are special rules of computation), and barristers (in Scotland, advocates). The exception for barristers applies for accounting periods ending within the first seven years of their beginning to practise. In this period, they may by concession apply either the cash basis or the bills delivered basis. Once a basis has been adopted, it must be applied consistently.

Read the article from *The Lawyer*, relating to what became FA 1998, s. 42(1), in *Cases and Materials* (15.1.2). Consider *why* these measures have annoyed barristers so much.

15.6   Value Added Tax: a Reminder

Remember that a trading receipt will also be the consideration for a supply for VAT purposes: see **3.4.2**. For a taxable person, that will impose an obligation to account for VAT on the trader, i.e. supplier, unless the supply is exempt or zero-rated: see **8.6**, **8.7**. If the trader is a fully taxable person, the amount of VAT (i.e. output VAT) for which it is liable to account will be reduced by the amount of any directly attributable input VAT: see **10.6**.

15.7   National Insurance Contributions: a Reminder

Remember that trading income will also count as earnings for NIC purposes. As an individual trader, you could be liable to pay both Class 2 and Class 4 NICs: see **8.5.2**, **8.5.3**.

15.8   Summary

For a person's receipts to be trading income, they must be income derived from a trade. A basic definition of a trade is the exchange of goods or services for reward. However, in a hard case, the existence of a trade must be determined by reference to the six badges of trade. The six badges of trade are: (a) the subject matter of the transaction; (b) the length of time for which the seller has owned the property sold; (c) how often similar transactions have been repeated; (d) whether the seller has done any supplementary work on the property; (e) the circumstances giving rise to the transaction; and (f) the seller's motive on buying the property sold. Sometimes, as in the cases of farming or market gardening, statute deems a business activity to be a trade. Although it is often unnecessary to distinguish between income from a trade, and income from a profession or vocation, the distinction may occasionally be important. A profession is an occupation requiring purely intellectual skill, or manual skill controlled by the intellectual skill of the operator. A vocation is the way in which you pass your life. Income receipts from a trade include damages awarded for non-receipt of trading income and, for accounting periods beginning after 6 April 1999, subject to limited exceptions, trading profits must be computed on a basis which gives a true and fair view.

15.9   End of Chapter Assessment Questions

The three partners of Brown & Co. (see **4.9**, **9.6**) have traditionally calculated their Schedule D, Case II profits on the bills delivered basis.

In their accounting period to 30 November 1998, they are awarded damages for loss of profits of £5,000 against a company of computer consultants. This sum relates to the disruption to their business caused by defective installation of a computer system in January/February 1995.

Advise them:

(a)   How FA 1998 will affect them, as to the basis on which their Schedule D, Case II profits are calculated.

(50 marks.)

(b)   Whether the £5,000 damages are a receipt falling under Schedule D, Case II.

(50 marks.)

See *Cases and Materials* (**15.3**), for a specimen answer.

CHAPTER SIXTEEN

INCOME RECEIPTS (3): SAVINGS INCOME

16.1 Objectives

By the end of this chapter, you should be able to:

■ list the types of savings income falling under *Schedule D, Case III*;

■ describe the types of interest in savings income which *beneficiaries under trusts* may have;

■ describe the types of interest in savings income which *beneficiaries of deceased individuals' estates* may have;

■ explain how income tax and corporation tax are charged on *interest of money* falling under Schedule D, Case III;

■ explain how income tax and corporation tax are charged on *annuities and other annual payments* falling under Schedule D Case III;

■ explain how income tax is charged on *dividends* under Schedule F.

16.2 Introduction

This chapter is the third of our four-part survey of the income component in Stage One of the income tax or corporation tax calculation. Neither NICs nor VAT are relevant to our discussion here: see **3.4.2**. The expression *savings income* includes the four types of income covered by Schedule D, Case III, as well as dividend income within Schedule F. The expression savings income therefore includes all forms of investment income, other than income from land. The four types of income covered by Schedule D, Case III are: interest of money; annuities and other annual payments; discounts; and income from securities payable out of the public revenue of the UK (see **1.4**). The third of these requires some explanation. Discounts come from so-called discounted securities. Instead of paying the lender interest over a period of time, discounted securities pay the lender a single lump sum when they are redeemed. They are within Case III of Schedule D if there is any possibility that the amount payable by the borrower to the lender on their redemption could count as a deep gain. A deep gain is where the gain on redemption exceeds, by a specified percentage, the amount originally lent.

The organisation of this chapter requires some explanation also. In **Chapters 14** and **15**, we have assumed that the person receiving the income in question is absolutely entitled to it (e.g. an individual's right to employment income). However, savings income requires us to think more deeply about the nature of a person's right to receive that income. This is because, in many cases, savings income is received by the beneficiaries of a trust, or of a deceased individual's estate, i.e. people whose right to receive the income may be circumscribed by a trust deed, a will or the intestacy legislation. These various types of entitlement are considered in **16.3** and, unless otherwise indicated, the comments made apply to all savings income paid by trustees, or PRs, to beneficiaries. The rest of the chapter deals separately with the receipt of each type of savings income by individuals (other than beneficiaries), companies, trustees and PRs. In so far as the last of these may make onward payments to beneficiaries, they are linked to the discussion in **16.3**.

16.3   Types of Entitlement to Savings Income

16.3.1   BENEFICIARIES OF A TRUST

As an individual, you might be the beneficiary of a trust. The trust income is perhaps most likely to consist of savings income of one kind or another. However, the trust income might equally consist of trading income, or rental income. If the trust income consists of rental income or trading income, then the points discussed below should be read in conjunction with the discussion in **Chapter 17**.

As a beneficiary, your right to trust income could be any of the following:

(a)   you might be an adult beneficiary with a *vested interest* in the income; *or*

(b)   you might be an *infant beneficiary* with a vested interest in the income; *or*

(c)   you might be an adult beneficiary with a *contingent interest* in the income; *or*

(d)   you might be an *infant beneficiary* with a contingent interest in the income.

A contingent interest is an interest which will come into effect only if an event which is not certain to occur does in fact occur. Thus, if an interest in income is dependent only on the death of an individual, it is not a contingent interest. This is because, for individuals, death is absolutely certain to occur. By contrast, if your right is, e.g. dependent on the marriage of an individual, it is a contingent interest only.

Albert wishes to put his shares in United Conglomerates plc into trust for his nephew Bertram (aged 14) for life. The trust deed provides: '. . . [M]y shareholding in United Conglomerates plc to my nephew Bertram for life, on reaching his eighteenth birthday'. Is Bertram's interest a vested or contingent one?

Contingent only. Bertram's right to the income generated by the shares will come into effect only if an event which is not certain to occur does in fact occur, i.e. Bertram reaches 18 years of age.

We need to consider each of the four types of right to the savings income of a trust in turn. The points in **16.3.1.1** to **16.3.1.3** apply to you, the beneficiary, whatever type of savings income is involved.

16.3.1.1　Adult beneficiary with a *vested* interest in the income

You, the adult beneficiary, have a vested interest in the income of the trust. The most obvious example of such an interest would be a life interest. When you have a vested interest in savings income, you must include the grossed-up amount of the income in Stage One of your income tax calculation for the tax year under consideration, even if you do not actually receive the income: *Baker* v *Archer-Shee* [1927] AC 844.

The reason why you must include the grossed-up amount is that, although the trustees will *not* have deducted tax on paying the savings income over to you, tax will have been deducted at source or credited as paid by the payer in the usual way. Thus, if you receive interest falling within Schedule D, Case III, income tax will probably have been deducted at source at 20%: ICTA 1988, s. 349(2): see **Cases and Materials** (**9.2**). Equally, if you receive dividend income falling under Schedule F, ACT will have been credited as paid on it at source: see **8.3**. Credit is given by you at Stage Six of your income tax calculation, in calculating your *sub-total tax due*. This is the same as for any other individual.

In 1998/99, you receive net dividend income of £800 from a trust in which you have a vested interest in the income. What will be included in your income tax calculation at Stage One? For what amount will you receive a credit at Stage Six?

In Stage One, Schedule F income of £1,000 (i.e. £800 × 100/80 = £1,000); in Stage Six, a £200 credit.

16.3.1.2　Infant beneficiary with a *vested* interest in the income

You, the infant beneficiary, have a vested interest in the income of the trust. The general rule is for the income to be treated as yours as it arises. Again, the most obvious example of such an interest is a life interest, although one of which you are an infant beneficiary. Thus, the grossed-up amount of the savings income must be included in Stage One of your income tax calculation for the tax year under consideration, as above, with credit being given at Stage Six.

An exception to the general rule is provided by TA 1925, s. 31. If s. 31 applies then you, the infant beneficiary, have no vested interest in the income until you reach 18. This is because s. 31, although it can be excluded from the trust instrument when it is being drafted, divests you of the interest you would have had if the general rule had applied. Thus, as Lord Greene MR said, in *Stanley* v *IRC* [1944] 1 KB 255:

> The infant does not during infancy enjoy the . . . income. It is not his in any real sense. The title to it is held in suspense to await the event, and if he dies under [18] his interest in it . . . is destroyed. He is, in fact, for all practical purposes *in precisely the same position as if his interest in [the] . . . income were contingent*. [*Emphasis added*.]

If s. 31, TA 1925 applies, the trustees will be liable to pay tax on the income profits of the trust. They will be liable to pay the *special rate applicable to trusts*: see **7.6.1**. On the basis that s. 31 applies, only if you actually receive savings income from the trustees will you, the beneficiary, be liable to pay income tax on it, as in **16.3.1.3**.

SAQ 190

Sally is 10 years old. Shares are held in trust for her for life, remainder to her cousin Jim (aged 30) absolutely. The Trustee Act 1925, s. 31 is not excluded. The trust receives net dividend income of £1,200 in 1998/99. At what rate will the trustees be liable to pay income tax on the dividend income? Will Sally be liable to pay any tax?

34%; No.

ACTIVITY 32

Read the extract from Barry McCutcheon's article on TA 1925, s. 31, at *Cases and Materials* (16.1.1). Note how, in a near-classical analysis, he distinguishes between the 'deferring' and 'accelerating' effect of s. 31.

16.3.1.3 Adult or infant beneficiary with a *contingent* interest in the income

You, the adult beneficiary, have a contingent interest in the income of the trust. The rule is, not that the income is treated as yours as it arises, but that it is included in Stage One of your income tax calculation for the tax year under consideration only if you actually receive it.

Examples of such an interest would be an interest under a discretionary trust, including an accumulation and maintenance settlement and, as discussed in **16.3.1.2**, an interest under a trust to which TA 1925, s. 31 applies: see **2.4.2.2**, **7.6.1**. The trustees will be liable to pay tax on the savings income at the special rate applicable to trusts: see **7.6.1** and below. The grossed-up amount of the savings income must therefore be included in Stage One of your income tax calculation for the tax year under consideration, if you receive it from the trustees. If you do not receive it from the trustees, you do not include it in Stage One.

Assuming that you do receive it, as a basic rate taxpayer, credit is given at Stage Six of your income tax calculation for only 11% of the gross dividend, *not 14%*, as you might have imagined. In other words, you get no credit for 3% of the tax paid by the trustees.

SAQ 191

You are a basic rate taxpayer and a beneficiary under a discretionary trust. In 1998/99, the trustees receive net dividends of £750 in total. They pay all of this dividend income over to you on 1 December 1998, in the exercise of their discretion. What amount will be included in Stage One of your income tax calculation? What credit will you receive at Stage Six?

Stage One: £937.50. Stage Six: credit of £187.50.

In addition, you can claim *repayment* from the Revenue of £103.12, i.e. the difference between tax at 34%, and tax at 23%, on £937.50. You cannot reclaim the other 3% (i.e. £28.13) paid by the trustees.

As an infant beneficiary, your position would be the same, with the additional points discussed in **16.3.1.2**.

ACTIVITY33

Read the extract from Roger Kerridge's article on the taxation of trust income, at *Cases and Materials* **(16.1.1). At the time the article was written, a consultative document had just been published on the taxation of trusts, the basic rate of income tax was 25%, and the special rate applicable to trusts was 35%.**

16.3.2   BENEFICIARIES OF A DECEASED INDIVIDUAL'S ESTATE

As an individual, you might be the beneficiary of any of a number of different types of legacy. The legacy might carry rental income, or even trading income: **Chapter 17**. It is more likely, perhaps, to carry savings income, of one kind or another.

As a beneficiary, your right to income of the estate could be any of the following:

(a)   you might be a *general* legatee; *or*

(b)   you might be a *specific* legatee; *or*

(c)   you might be an *annuitant*, albeit rarely these days; *or*

(d)   you might be a *residuary beneficiary*. If so, your interest might be one of two types:

    (i)   a *limited interest* in the residuary estate; or

    (ii)   an *absolute interest* in the residuary estate.

A limited interest in the residuary estate is an interest in income only. By contrast, an absolute interest in the residuary estate is an interest in both capital and income.

SAQ 192

The residue of Sheila's uncle Jack's estate is left to her for life, on his death on 1 October 1998. On Sheila's death, the residue is to pass to her sister Amy absolutely. Is Sheila's interest a limited interest or an absolute interest?

A limited interest.

16.3.2.1   General legatee

As a general legatee, you are entitled to a pecuniary legacy which is not charged on any particular fund. This legacy is of course capital, and you will also receive Schedule D, Case III if interest is payable to you under the will or under the intestacy rules, as the case may be. If interest is payable to you, then it will be paid to you *gross*, rather than net of tax.

You must include this gross amount in Stage One of your income tax calculation for the tax year under consideration. However, if you do not actually receive the interest from the PRs, you do not include it in Stage One at all. This is shown by *Dewar* v *IRC* [1935] 2 KB 351, where the Court of Appeal held that, since a general legatee had not actually received the interest to which he was entitled, it must not be included in his statutory income for the tax year under consideration.

Fred's uncle died on 1 September 1997, leaving Fred a legacy of £1,000. The will stipulated that his executors were to pay Fred interest on the legacy of 6% per annum, from the date of his uncle's death, to receipt of the legacy by Fred. Fred receives both legacy and interest on 1 September 1998. What amount will be included in Stage One of his income tax calculation for 1998/99?

£60.

16.3.2.2   Specific legatee

As a specific legatee, you are entitled to a specified asset from the deceased's estate and to any income generated by it from the date of the deceased's death. The specified asset might not be an income-generating asset, of course, in which case the situation imagined here does not arise. Once the asset is vested in you, the income from it, from the testator's death to your receipt of it, must be included in Stage One of your income tax calculation for each tax year in which the income arose, with credit being given at Stage Six. The figure to be included must be the grossed-up amount, if tax has been deducted at source/credited as paid.

On 1 August 1999, shares in Megabucks plc are vested in you by the executors of the will of your uncle Bob. Bob died on 12 May 1998, and the executors received a dividend declared and paid by Megabucks plc on 15 December 1998 of £800 net. What amount should be included in your income tax calculation and for which tax year?

£1,000, in Stage One, with credit being given at Stage Six. It must be included in your calculation for 1998/99.

16.3.2.3   Annuitant

As an annuitant, you are entitled to a pecuniary legacy, which is payable to you in instalments. The gross amount of each instalment is included in Stage One of your income tax calculation for the tax year in which it is received. You will have received the net amount after deduction of basic rate tax at source by the PRs, under ICTA 1988, ss. 348. Such annuities are within ICTA 1988, s. 348, since ICTA 1988, s. 347A only excludes annuities paid by PRs from being charges on income where (ICTA 1988, s. 347A(3)):

(a) the deceased would have been liable to make the payment if he had not died, and

(b) [Section 347A] would have applied to the payment if he had made it.

As the recipient of the annuity, you therefore claim the credit for the tax deducted at source at Stage Six of your income tax calculation.

16.3.2.4 Residuary beneficiary

With a limited interest in the residuary estate
As a beneficiary with a limited interest in the residuary estate, you are entitled to receive the income of the residuary estate during your lifetime. The gross amount of each payment is included in Stage One of your income tax calculation, although you will actually have received the net amount, after deduction of tax at source by the PRs. Credit is therefore given in Stage Six of your income tax calculation of the tax year under consideration.

With an absolute interest in the residuary estate
You, a beneficiary with an absolute interest in the residuary estate, are entitled to receive both income and capital. You are, of course, liable to pay income tax on the income component only. Other points apply as in the previous paragraph.

16.4 Interest of Money

16.4.1 INDIVIDUALS

The points in this section apply irrespective of whether you are an individual receiving interest in your personal capacity, or in the capacity of a partner. As an individual, they also apply when you receive the interest as the beneficiary of a trust or estate. Remember, as a beneficiary under a trust, you are liable to pay the income tax if the income accrues to you directly: see **2.4.2.2**.

Andrew and Bertram are the trustees of a life interest trust. The income of the trust consists of interest falling under Schedule D, Case III, on deposit accounts at a bank. They sign a mandate, directing that the bank pay the interest arising under the trust direct to the beneficiaries. Are the trustees liable to pay income tax on the interest or are the beneficiaries?

The beneficiaries: *Williams* v *Singer* (1920) 7 TC 387, and see **2.4.2.2**.

Remember that interest is treated as being 100% pure income profit. There are no allowable deductions to be made from it and the whole amount received, or deemed to be received, in the tax year under consideration will be included in Stage One of your income tax calculation, under Schedule D, Case III. Where income tax has been deducted at source (i.e. at the lower rate), then it is the grossed-up amount which is included in Stage One. Credit is then given for the tax deducted, at Stage Six.

The concept of interest was defined by Lord Wright in *Riches* v *Westminster Bank Ltd* [1947] 1 All ER 469:

. . . [T]he essence of interest is that it is a payment which becomes due because the creditor has not had his money at the due date. It may be regarded either as representing the profit he might have made if he had had the use of the money, or, conversely, the loss he suffered because he had not that use. The general idea is that he is entitled to compensation for the deprivation. From that point of view, it would seem immaterial whether the money was due to him under a contract, express or implied, or a statute, or whether the money was due for any other reason in law.

Marden, an individual mortgagee, receives interest under a loan secured by a charge by way of legal mortgage given by Monoservice Ltd, for £25,000. Interest is payable at a fixed rate of 9% per annum for four years. Will Marden receive the interest net or gross? What figure will be included in Stage One of his income tax calculation for each tax year?

Net. £2,250 will go in Stage One in each tax year. Credit will be given at Stage Six.

More pithily than Lord Wright, and arguably more exactly, Rowlatt J said, in *Bennett* v *Ogston* (1930) 15 TC 374:

[I]nterest is payment by time for the use of money.

Only two further points need to be remembered in the context of *individuals*:

■   If interest is paid by cheque, it is included in Stage One of your income tax calculation for the tax year in which it is credited to your bank account. This rule comes from *Parkside Leasing Ltd* v *Smith* [1985] 1 WLR 310, where Scott J explained it thus:

The receipt of a cheque does not of itself place the sum for which the cheque is made out or the proceeds of the cheque at the payee's disposal. It is not certain that the cheque will be honoured. It may be cancelled by the drawer before it is presented. It may be dishonoured by the bank on which it is drawn. The drawer may die before the cheque can be presented. The bank may fail before the cheque can be presented.

■   If a payment of interest, although due, is not actually made, it is not included in Stage One of your income tax calculation for the tax year under consideration: *Woodhouse* v *IRC* (1936) TC 673.

Note that, although the recipient of the interest in *Parkside Leasing Ltd* v *Smith* was a company, this rule has now been disapplied for interest received by companies. Note also that the second of the above points is disapplied for beneficiaries of trusts covered by *Baker* v *Archer-Shee*: see **16.3.1**.

16.4.2   COMPANIES

Companies receive interest under their non-trading loan relationships: see **11.7**. In this section, we deal with the *converse* situation, i.e. where the company is the *lender* under the loan relationship in the accounting period under consideration. As lender, the company may either be:

- the creditor as respects any money debt which arose from a transaction for the lending of money (FA 1996, s. 81(1)); *or*

- the creditor under an instrument issued as security for any money debt which arose from a transaction for the lending of money (FA 1996, s. 81(1)).

Section 81(2) defines a money debt as one which will be settled either by the payment of money, or by the transfer to the creditor by the debtor of the right to the settlement of the money debt.

The interest will, of course, go in at Stage One of the corporation tax calculation, under Schedule D, Case III. If income tax has been deducted at source, e.g. when the payer is another company (ICTA 1988, s. 349(2)), then the grossed-up amount of the interest is included at Stage One. Credit is then given for the tax deducted at source, at Stage Five of the corporation tax calculation.

Do these rules apply to a debt owed by a company to a shareholder in the form of a final dividend declared, but not paid?

No. That type of debt is not a money debt arising from a transaction for the lending of money.

16.4.3 TRUSTEES

To appreciate the position of trustees in relation to interest received by them, it is necessary to keep three points in mind, i.e.:

- trustees will be liable to pay income tax on the income profits of the trust where the beneficiaries have no immediate entitlement to the income of the trust: see **2.4.2.2**;

- on the assumption that the trustees are liable to pay the income tax, rather than the beneficiaries, the rate at which they will pay tax will be the basic rate (below), *except where* the trust is either one for which the trustees have a power to accumulate the income, or one which gives the trustee a discretion as to the distribution of the income to the beneficiaries. If the trust is of either of these two types, the trustees will be liable to pay the *special rate applicable to trusts* on the taxable income of the trust: see **7.6.1**; and

- trustees, like individuals, will most often receive interest falling under Schedule D, Case III, i.e. net of lower rate tax: ICTA 1988, s. 349(2): see *Cases and Materials* **(9.2)**.

These three points need to be considered in relation to the points made earlier in **16.3.1.1** to **16.3.1.3**. It is assumed that income tax has been deducted at source at the *lower* rate on the interest received by the trustees. This might not always be the case, of course (e.g. interest from National Savings received gross).

As a trustee, your liability to pay income tax at the basic rate on the taxable income of the trust will be satisfied, in relation to any interest you receive, by lower rate tax deducted at source by the payer. When you come to pay the interest over to the relevant beneficiary, you will give him or her a tax credit for the tax deducted by the payer of the interest *at source*. Your liability will not be satisfied in this way however if you are liable, as a trustee, to pay income tax at the special rate applicable to trusts. You will give the beneficiary a tax credit, exactly as above, but you will obviously have to pay extra tax on the interest to the Revenue, i.e. 14% of the gross amount of the interest.

You are a trustee of the JB Smith 1998 Discretionary Trust. In 1998/99, you receive interest falling under Schedule D, Case III, of £800 net. You pay the net interest over to Jack, a beneficiary. What will the tax credit received by Jack be? How much extra tax will you, the trustee, have to pay?

The tax credit will be for £200. You, the *trustee*, will have to pay extra tax of £140. This mechanism ensures that the interest will have borne tax at the special rate applicable to trusts of 34%.

16.4.4   PERSONAL REPRESENTATIVES

To appreciate the position of PRs, in relation to interest received by them, it is again necessary to remind ourselves of certain points:

■   PRs must make at least two separate income tax calculations, i.e. to calculate the total income tax due from the deceased (see **7.6.2.1**) and to calculate the total income tax due on the estate income in the administration period (see **7.6.2.2**); *and*

■   during the administration period, the PRs will be liable to pay income tax at the lower rate on interest received by them. With the exception of dividends, discussed below, PRs are liable at the basic rate on other income profits received: see **Chapter 17**. Interest is generally received by them net of lower rate tax unless, e.g. it is interest from National Savings, which is paid gross.

In the following discussion, it is assumed that tax has been deducted at source, at the lower rate, on the interest received by the PRs.

As a PR, your liability to income tax at the basic rate on the income profits of the estate will be satisfied, in relation to any interest you receive, by lower rate tax deducted at source by the payer. When you come to pay the interest over to the relevant beneficiary, you will not be liable to pay any further income tax on it (for the beneficiaries' position, see **16.3.2** above).

SAQ 199

You are an executor of the will of the late NJ Smith, who died on 6 April 1998. His will leaves a specific legacy to his nephew, Jim, consisting of loan stock in Gigantic plc. In 1998/99, you receive interest under Schedule D, Case III, of £1,200 net on the stock. You vest title to the stock in Jim on 31 March 1999. Do you, as executor, have any tax liability on the interest?

No.

16.5   Annuities and Other Annual Payments

16.5.1   INDIVIDUALS

We have considered these types of savings income before: see **Chapter 9**. That said, however, we have considered them solely from the standpoint of the individual making the payments. This was because there are only certain annual payments made by you, the individual, which can qualify as charges on income, and these are exceptions to the general rule in ICTA 1988, s. 347A. The exceptions to the general rule are: covenanted payments to charity, alimony payments made by you, provided you were ordered to make them before 16 March 1988, and payments for *bona fide commercial reasons* in connection with your trade, profession or vocation.

The implication of the *general rule* for the payer, in relation to you, the *recipient*, is that such payments do *not* form part of your statutory income, and do not therefore form part of your income tax calculation: ICTA 1988, s. 347A(1)(b). However, a partnership retirement annuity, satisfying the conditions of ICTA 1988, ss. 347A(2) and 660A(9) *would* do so, the grossed-up amount of the annual payment (i.e. at 23%) being included in Stage One of your income tax calculation, with credit being given at Stage Six for the basic rate tax deducted at source.

SAQ 200

After many years as a partner in the law firm of Sue, Grabbit & Runne, Harold retires on 1 September 1998. The partnership deed provides that, on retirement, partners are to be paid an annuity of £20,000 per annum (gross). The agreement satisfies the conditions of ICTA 1988, ss. 347A(2). How will this be dealt with in his 1998/99 income tax calculation?

The net amount of £15,400 (i.e. £20,000 − £4,600) will be received by him, but the *gross* amount will go into Stage One of his income tax calculation for the tax year 1998/99, credit for the £4,600 deducted at source being given at Stage Six.

16.5.2 COMPANIES

Annual payments received by a company, otherwise than under its loan relationships, will go into its corporation tax calculation gross, at Stage One, credit being given for the tax deducted at source at Stage Five.

Utopia Ltd receives an annuity of £10,000 net in its accounting period ending on 31 December 1998. What figure will be included in Stage One of its corporation tax calculation? What figure will be deducted from its total tax to give its sub-total tax due, at Stage Five?

At Stage One: £12,500; at Stage Five, £2,500.

16.5.3 TRUSTEES

Where the beneficiaries do *not* have an immediate entitlement to the income of the trust property, the trustees will be liable to pay income tax on the taxable income of the trust: see **2.4.2.2**, **7.6.1**. In this situation, the special rate applicable to trusts could apply. If, as a trustee, you receive an annuity or other annual payment within ICTA 1988, ss. 348 or 349, you will give the beneficiary the tax credit for the tax deducted by the payer at source. Thus, depending on the type of trust involved, you will either have no further tax to pay, and you will give the beneficiary a tax credit, as above, or you will have to pay extra tax to the Revenue (the difference between income tax at 34% and 23%, i.e. 11% of the gross amount of the annual payment).

You are a trustee of the ZB Smith 1998 Discretionary Trust. In 1998/99, you receive a patent royalty from Brown Ltd (ICTA 1988, s. 349(1)(b)), of £1,000 net. You pay the net annual payment over to Jill, a beneficiary. What will the tax credit received by Jill be? How much extra tax will you, the trustee, have to pay?

The tax credit will be for £299, i.e. £1,299 − £1,000: see **9.4**. You, the trustee, will have to pay extra tax of £142.66. (Jill will be entitled to a refund of the £142.66 if she is a basic rate taxpayer.)

Before leaving Schedule D, Case III, some further points about annual payments generally are appropriate:

- Although the annual payments falling within Schedule D, Case III are limited, it may be necessary sometimes to revisit the five conditions which must be satisfied before a payment will qualify as an annual payment. These were laid down by Jenkins LJ in *IRC v Whitworth Park Coal Co. Ltd* [1958] 2 All ER 91, and include the condition that the payment must be pure income profit, so far as the recipient of the payment is concerned.

- *Patent* royalties *can* be annual payments within Schedule D, Case III: see **9.3.1.2** and **9.4**. The payer deducts basic rate tax at source, under ICTA 1988, s. 348(2)(a) or 349(1)(b) (*Cases and Materials* (**9.1.1.1** and **9.2**)), and the receipt is dealt with in Stages One and Six of the individual's income tax calculation, or Stages One and Five of the company's corporation tax calculation, as discussed above: ICTA 1988, ss. 524 and 527.

16.6 Dividends

16.6.1 INDIVIDUALS

The position of private individuals receiving dividends has already been considered in **8.3**.

Note the following problem with the present imputation system. Companies pay ACT at 1/4 × the net dividend, or 25% of that net dividend. The tax credit satisfies the individual shareholder's basic rate income tax liability, although it is for only 20% or 1/5 × the *gross* dividend.

SAQ 203

What percentage of a company's profits are taxed twice, therefore, once in the company and again in the shareholder's hands?

11% for companies not qualifying as small companies (i.e. 31%, less 20%); 1% for small companies (i.e. 21%, less 20%).

If you are the beneficiary of a trust, in receipt of dividends, the rules discussed in **16.3.1** will determine how any dividends received by you from the trustees are dealt with in your income tax calculation.

16.6.2 COMPANIES

A company receiving dividend income does not include that income in Stage One of its corporation tax calculation: ICTA 1988, s. 208: see **7.4**. A dividend received by a company, together with the credit for the ACT paid to the Revenue by the paying company, is called franked investment income (FII).

16.6.3 TRUSTEES AND PERSONAL REPRESENTATIVES

A brief reference to **16.3** and **16.4** should help you to work out the income tax position of trustees and PRs, in relation to dividends received by them. A further point can be made, which in part refers to **2.4.2.2** and **7.6.1**.

The general rule is that the expenses of trustees in administering a trust (i.e. *administrative expenses* or *management expenses*) are not deductible in calculating the *total income tax due* from trustees. There is an *exception* to this rule, where the trustees are liable to pay the special rate applicable to trusts: see **7.6.1**. If the trustees are liable to the special rate, then so much of the trust's income profits as are applied in defraying the administrative expenses of the trust are taxed at the rate which would have applied in the absence of the special rate: ICTA 1988, ss. 686(2AA) and 689B(3). In the case of dividends and Schedule D, Case III income profits, this means the lower rate of 20%. In the case of other income profits, it of course means 23%. Administrative expenses are deducted from dividend income before other income, for the purpose of determining how much income is sheltered in this way from the special rate applicable to trusts: ICTA 1988, s. 689B(1)(b).

In the tax year 1998/99, the trustees of a discretionary trust receive net dividends of £750, plus rental profits of £1,000. They also have administration expenses of £200. How do the administration expenses affect the amount of income tax payable by the trustees?

The administration expenses are deducted first from the dividend income, which means that the £200 out of which they are paid bears tax at only 20%.

The tax on the dividends has already been credited as paid, of course. This means that £550 (i.e. £750 − £200) of the dividend income must bear tax at 34% although, because 20% tax has been credited as paid on the £550 at source, the trustees will only have to pay the difference of £96.25. The £96.25 difference is found by grossing-up the £550 at 20%, to give £687.50. Tax at 34% on this grossed-up figure, i.e. £233.75, less the tax of 20% credited as paid at source, i.e. £137.50, gives £96.25.

Study the extracts from the article by Good and Birkett in *Cases and Materials* (16.2).

Although this is beyond the scope of the present discussion, note that the changes to the taxation of dividends from 6 April 1999 (see **8.3.2**) means that the effective rate of income tax on distributed dividends will be *dramatically* increased.

16.7 Summary

Savings income is often income to which a beneficiary under a trust or a beneficiary of a deceased individual's estate is entitled. As an adult beneficiary of a trust, you could either have a vested or a contingent interest in the trust income. If your interest is contingent, then although you only pay income tax on savings income actually received by you, you do not obtain full credit for the income tax paid by the trustees in cases where the trustees are liable to pay the special rate applicable to trusts. As an infant beneficiary, your interest will be turned into a contingent one if TA 1925, s. 31 applies to the trust deed. This will place you in the same position as an adult beneficiary of a discretionary trust. As the beneficiary of a deceased individual's estate, the income tax treatment of savings income paid to you will depend on the nature of your interest under the will or intestacy. The consequences of receiving savings income depend on the person receiving it and the type of savings income involved. For instance, dividends received by an individual are treated quite differently from dividends received by a company. It is important to remember these differences, and particularly to understand the relationship between the income tax position of the trustees, and the beneficiaries to whom trust income is paid by them.

16.8   End of Chapter Assessment Questions

Refer to the facts involving Amber Ltd and its shareholders in **2.6** and **8.9**. In 1998/99, Deborah receives interest on securities held for her by Georgina and Harry, who are the trustees of Deborah's uncle Frederick's will trust. Deborah has a life interest in possession under the will trust. In 1998/99, she receives £800 net in interest from the debentures in Megabucks plc (see **8.9**). Under Charlie's will, cash gifts of £2,000 each are made to Alan, Bertram and Deborah. The will provides for them to receive interest on their cash gifts, from Charlie's death (on 28 September 1998), to the date of the receipt of the separate cheques for the gifts and the interest in March 1999.

(a) Having calculated the amounts for inclusion in Deborah's 1998/99 income tax calculation (see **8.9**), comment on the total income tax due from the trustees, on the basis that the trust has no other source of income in 1998/99.

(50 marks.)

(b) On the assumption that the cheques for £2,000 are paid over to Alan, Bertram and Deborah on 1 March 1999, together with cheques for interest of £150 each, comment on the income tax position of each of the beneficiaries in relation to the interest received.

(50 marks.)

(Word limit: 250.)

See *Cases and Materials* (**16.4**), for a specimen answer.

CHAPTER SEVENTEEN

INCOME RECEIPTS (4): INCOME FROM LAND

17.1 Objectives

By the end of this chapter, you should be able to:

- list the different types of income from land falling under Schedule A;

- describe the types of interest in Schedule A income which *beneficiaries under trusts* may have;

- describe the types of interest in Schedule A income which *beneficiaries of deceased individuals' estates* may have;

- explain how income tax and corporation tax are charged on *lease premiums* falling under Schedule A;

- outline how income tax and corporation tax are charged on *furnished holiday lettings*;

- comment on the relevance of *VAT* and of *landfill tax* to Schedule A income.

17.2 Introduction

This chapter is the final part of our survey of the income component in Stage One of the income tax or corporation tax calculation. Our concern is entirely with Schedule A, as amended by FA 1998: see *Cases and Materials* (**2.2**). Although we have so far referred to 'rental income', Schedule A income includes much more than rent, as we shall discover. To reflect this, we refer in this chapter to income from land. The organisation of the chapter follows an almost identical pattern to the last. **17.3** therefore recaps on the various types of entitlements to income from land which beneficiaries under a trust or estate may have. The rest of the chapter deals separately with the receipt of income from land by individuals (other than beneficiaries), companies, trustees and PRs, the discussion of the last two being linked of course to the discussion in **17.3**. In relation to beneficiaries, trustees and PRs, the same points apply to Schedule D, Case I or II profits as to Schedule A profits. This would be important if you were, e.g., a trustee or beneficiary of a trust carrying on a trade. However, it should be noted that what the beneficiary receives are Schedule A profits, i.e. Schedule A income, less allowable deductions. In **17.3.1.1** to **17.3.1.3** the references are therefore to Schedule A profits, rather than Schedule A income, or income from land.

17.3 Types of Entitlement to Schedule A Profits

17.3.1 BENEFICIARIES OF A TRUST

As a beneficiary, your interest in Schedule A profits could be any of the four types of interest discussed in **16.3.1**.

17.3.1.1 Adult beneficiary with a *vested* interest in Schedule A profits

When you have a vested interest in Schedule A profits arising under a new-style trust of land, you must include those Schedule A profits in Stage One of your income tax calculation, under Schedule A: *Baker* v *Archer-Shee* [1927] AC 844. You must include them *even if* you have not actually received the money from the trustees. Basic rate income tax is deducted by the trustees on paying the Schedule A profits over to you. The trustees may make a further deduction for administrative expenses: see **7.6.1**, **17.4.3**. The amount included in Stage One of your income tax calculation is therefore the grossed-up amount of the profits received, but *no account* is taken of administrative expenses in the grossing-up process. Credit is given at Stage Six of your income tax calculation for the tax deducted by the trustees. The credit is given at the basic rate of 23%.

In the tax year 1998/99, you receive Schedule A profits of £800 from a trust in which you have a vested interest in the income. You have no entitlement to any additional income profits in 1998/99. What will be included in your income tax calculation at Stage One? For what amount will you receive a credit at Stage Six?

In Stage One, Schedule A profits of £1,038.96 (i.e. £800 x 100/77 = £1,038.96); in Stage Six, a credit for £238.96. (This SAQ ignores the effect of administrative expenses: see **7.6.1**, **17.4.3**.)

17.3.1.2 Infant beneficiary with a *vested* interest in Schedule A profits

The general rule is that the income of the trust is treated as yours as it arises. Thus, the amount of the Schedule A profits, grossed-up at the basic rate, must be included in Stage One of your income tax calculation for the tax year under consideration. Credit is given at Stage Six for the tax deducted by the trustees. The points made in relation to TA 1925, s. 31, apply to Schedule A profits, just as they apply to savings income: see **16.3.1.2**.

Ben is 12 years old. A tenanted property, let on a 99-year lease, is held in trust for him for life, remainder to his cousin Bill (aged 32) absolutely. The trust has Schedule A profits from the property of £1,800 in the 1998/99 tax year. The Trustee Act 1925, s. 31 is not excluded. At what rate will the trustees be liable to income tax on the Schedule A profits?

34%: see **16.3.1.2**.

17.3.1.3 Adult or infant beneficiary with a *contingent* interest in Schedule A profits

The rule is, *not* that the Schedule A profits are treated as yours as they arise, but that they are included in Stage One of your income tax calculation only if you actually receive them. Surprisingly, they go into Stage One next to *Schedule D, Case III*, rather than as Schedule A profits. This is because such a payment is an annual payment, being capable of recurring: see **16.5**. In practice, discretionary trustees deduct income tax at 34% on making a payment to a beneficiary. As a recipient, the figure which goes into Stage One of your income tax calculation is grossed-up at 34%. Credit is then given at Stage Six of your income tax calculation for the income tax deducted at source. As a basic rate taxpayer, your receipt of dividends is taxed at 23%, rather than 20%, since your repayment claim is for 11%, rather than 14%: see **16.3.1.3**. Payments to beneficiaries by discretionary trustees (whether they represent Schedule A profits or trading profits), are different in this respect. Such payments carry a full 34% credit for the tax deducted by the trustees.

As a basic rate taxpayer, you are a beneficiary under a discretionary trust. In 1998/99, the trustees have Schedule A profits of £750. The trustees pay all of these profits over to you, in the exercise of their discretion, less income tax at 34%, i.e. £255. What amount will be included in Stage One of your income tax calculation? What credit will you receive at Stage Six?

Stage One: £750. Stage Six: £255. This exceeds your 23% tax liability (i.e. £172.50) by £82.50, which you can reclaim from the Revenue.

As an infant beneficiary, the position would be the same, with the additional points discussed in **17.3.1.2**.

17.3.2 BENEFICIARIES OF A DECEASED INDIVIDUAL'S ESTATE

As a beneficiary, the legacy you receive might well carry Schedule A income, or even trading income. We need only consider the position of the specific legatee, since a specific legatee is entitled to a specified asset from the deceased's estate, and to any income generated by it from the date of the deceased's death to receipt by the legatee. Land producing Schedule A income is a classic example of a specific legacy. Once the asset is vested in you, the beneficiary, the grossed-up amount of any Schedule A profits from it, from the testator's death to your receipt of the asset, must be included in Stage One of your income tax calculation for each tax year in which the income arose. Credit is given at Stage Six of the calculation, in the usual way.

On 1 July 1998, the freehold title to a block of tenanted retirement flats is vested in you by the executors of the will of your uncle Jim. Jim died on 12 April 1997, and the executors have received Schedule A profits of £10,000 since then.

On making the payment, they deduct basic rate tax of £2,300. What amount should be included in your income tax calculation and for which tax year?

£10,000, in Stage One, with credit at Stage Six for the £2,300 deducted by the PRs on making the payment to you.

17.4   Rents

17.4.1   INDIVIDUALS

The points in this section apply irrespective of whether you, the recipient of rent, are an individual receiving rent in your personal capacity, or in the capacity of a partner. As an individual in your personal capacity, they also apply where your right to the rent is as a beneficiary of a trust or an estate. As always, bear in mind that, as a beneficiary under a trust, you may be liable to pay income tax on the income profits of the trust, rather than the trustees, if the trust income accrues directly to you: 2.4.2.2.

Charles and Douglas are the trustees of a life interest trust with Schedule A profits. They delegate their management power under the TLA 1996, s. 9, to the beneficiary with the life interest. Are the trustees or the beneficiary liable to pay income tax on the rent?

The beneficiaries.

Although the most typical income falling under Schedule A is rent, ICTA 1988, s. 15(1) is capable of including much more: see *Cases and Materials* (2.2). Two cases indicate the scope of Schedule A, although they were decided on the basis of similar expressions in the old Schedule A. *Lowe v JW Ashmore Ltd* [1971] 1 Ch 545 involved a company which carried on the statutory trade of farming. It had income from contractors who had paid the company for the right to remove turves from the farm. Megarry J held that these payments fell within Schedule A, on the basis that they were income receipts from an equitable *profit à prendre* in gross:

> A profit in the soil, giving the right to take sand, gravel and so on, is a well-known form of profit, and so is a profit of turbary, giving the right to dig and take turf or peat for fuel . . . In this case, the right to take the turf seems to me to be aptly described as being, or being in the nature of, a *profit à prendre* in gross.

Again, in *McClure* v *Petre* [1988] 1 WLR 1386, Sir Nicolas Browne-Wilkinson V-C held that receipts of an individual landowner from a motorway contractor were outside Schedule A, as capital receipts rather than income ones. The contractor was building the M65 motorway near Blackburn, in Lancashire, and paid Captain Petre, the landowner, for a licence to dump subsoil on his land. The Vice-Chancellor said:

> [T]he payments were received by the taxpayer as consideration for a once-and-for-all disposal of a right or advantage appurtenant to the land – namely, the right or advantage of using it for dumping. Immediately before the licence was granted the value of the land itself included the value of the right to turn it to advantage by using it for dumping. After the licence that right or advantage had gone for ever in return for a lump sum.

SAQ 210

Captain Walmesley, a landowner, receives a one-off payment of £15,000 from a refuse contractor in return for a licence to dump household rubbish on his land. Does this sum fall within Schedule A?

No.

Only two further points need to be remembered in the context of individuals in their personal capacity:

- Schedule A covers all UK properties owned by the individual and refers to the income from them together as a Schedule A business.

- Rent from furnished holiday lettings is subject to different rules: see **17.6**.

Note the availability of *rent-a-room* relief, which turns rental income from lodgers into exempt income provided the conditions of FA 1992, s. 59, sch. 10 and the Income Tax (Furnished Accommodation) (Basic Amount) Order 1996 (SI 1996 No. 2953) are satisfied: see **10.5.7**. Rent-a-room relief exempts rental income up to £4,250 per annum from income tax.

ACTIVITY 35

Read the extract from the article by David Williams at *Cases and Materials* (17.1.1). (Note that the references to the 'new regime' are to the Schedule A discussed above, remodelled from 1995/96 onwards.)

17.4.2 COMPANIES

From 1 April 1998, the same Schedule A applies to companies as applies to individuals. Prior to that date, there was a separate Schedule A for each!

Bellborough Ltd owns Blackacre, and has the benefit of a charge by way of legal mortgage over Whiteacre. On 20 April 1998, it granted the Deer Valley Anglers Club the right to fish a lake on Blackacre for 20 years from that date, at an annual rental of £500. The mortgage carries interest at a fixed rate of 7% per annum. Which of these two sources of income falls under Schedule A?

The annual rental of £500 for the fishing right (the interest from the mortgage falls under Schedule D, Case III).

17.4.3   TRUSTEES

Two of the three points made in **16.4.3** apply here in exactly the same way as they applied in relation to interest received by the trustees. Unlike with interest, however, trustees will not receive Schedule A income net of tax. That said, allowable deductions will be made by them, to give them their Schedule A profit, and tax deducted by them from the balance, before it is paid over to the beneficiaries. If, as a trustee, you are liable to pay the special rate applicable to trusts, you deduct tax on making the payment to the beneficiaries at 34%, rather than 23%, and a credit is given to the beneficiary for the tax deducted: see **17.3.1.3**. No deduction from the trust's income profits is given for the trustees' administrative expenses, unless the trustees are liable to pay the special rate applicable to trusts: see **16.6.3**.

As the sole trustee of the JK Smith 1998 Interest in Possession Trust, you receive Schedule A income of £10,000 in 1998/99. There are allowable deductions of £500 and administrative expenses properly chargeable against income of £150. You pay the whole net amount over to Jack, a beneficiary. What will the net amount paid over to Jack be?

£7,050, i.e. £9,500 [i.e. £10,000 − £500], less £2,300 [tax at 23% on £10,000], *less* £150 [administrative expenses].

What amount is included in Stage One of Jack's income tax calculation?

£9,156, i.e. £7,050 x 100/77.

For how much tax will he be given credit at Stage Six of his income tax calculation?

£2,106, i.e. £9,156 x 23/100.

For how much tax does he *not* therefore receive credit at Stage Six?

£194, i.e. £2,300 – £2,106.

The answer to **SAQ 215** illustrates the effect of the administrative expenses being paid out of *taxed* income. Some relief is given for the effect of this in relation to trusts subject to the special rate applicable to trusts: see **16.6.3**.

17.4.4 PERSONAL REPRESENTATIVES

During the administration period, the PRs will be liable to pay income tax at the basic rate on rental profits. Rental income will, of course, have been received by them from the appropriate payer without deduction of tax at source.

It will therefore be up to you, as the PR, to deduct basic rate tax from rental profits received, before paying them over to the relevant beneficiary. On this basis, you will not be liable to pay any further income tax on it: see **7.6.2** (**17.3.2** above describes the beneficiaries' position).

You are an executor of the late JB Jones, whose residuary estate was ascertained on 8 April 1998. His will leaves a specific legacy to his nephew, Jack, consisting of Haydn House, a tenanted office block. In 1998/99, the estate has Schedule A profits of £150,000. You execute an assent in Jack's favour on 1 April 1999. Is any income tax due from you, the executor, on the Schedule A profits in this period? Of how much?

Yes: see **7.6.2.2**. £34,500, i.e. 23/100 × £150,000.

17.5 Lease Premiums

The provisions discussed in this section apply for both income tax and corporation tax purposes. They apply irrespective of the capacity in which a person is acting. If the provisions apply, they deem any premium received by the landlord to be an income receipt. If they do not apply, then the sum received by the landlord may be subject to CGT on the basis that it is deemed to be a chargeable gain arising on the chargeable disposal by a chargeable person of a chargeable asset: see **21.3.1**. The Income and Corporation Taxes Act 1988, s. 34(1) contains the basic charging provision. If it applies, a proportion of the premium is treated as income falling under Schedule A:

> Where the payment of any premium is required under a lease, or otherwise under the terms subject to which a lease is granted, and the duration of the lease does not exceed 50 years, the landlord shall be treated for the purposes of the Tax Acts as becoming entitled when the lease is granted to an amount by way of rent (in addition to any actual rent) equal to–
>
> $$P - \frac{(P \times Y)}{50}$$
>
> where P is the premium and Y is the number of complete periods of 12 months (other than the first) comprised in the duration of the lease.

Conveyancing and commercial solicitors are expected to know about the provision: *Cases and Materials* (**1.4.2**).

On 6 November 1998, Len grants Tom a 48-year lease of a shop, taking a premium of £50,000. The annual rent of the shop is £1,500. Assuming Len has no other Schedule A income in the 1998/99 tax year, what amount is included in Stage One of his income tax calculation for 1998/99, *excluding* the first year's rent?

£3,000, i.e. $50,000 - \dfrac{(50,000 \times 47)}{50}$

On 6 November 1998, Len grants Tom a 2-year lease of a shop, taking a premium of £50,000. The annual rent of the shop is £1,500. Assuming Len has no other Schedule A income, what amount is included in Stage One of his income tax calculation for 1998/99, *excluding* the first year's rent?

£49,000, i.e. $50,000 - \dfrac{(50,000 \times 1)}{50}$

From these examples, the following conclusions follow:

(a)   the longer the lease, the smaller the amount to be included in Stage One;

(b)   the shorter the lease, the greater the amount to be included in Stage One; *and*

(c)   with a lease for 12 months or less, the *whole* of the premium is included in Stage One.

There are detailed rules for working out how long a lease will last in ICTA 1988, s. 38. It is not possible to avoid these provisions by any of the following devices, among others:

(a) Requiring the tenant to carry out work on the property, instead of taking a premium in cash. Generally, the landlord must include in Stage One of its income or corporation tax calculation the amount by which the current value of its reversion has been increased by the works. (In some circumstances, this charge is disapplied however: ICTA 1988, s. 34(2).)

(b) Disguising the duration of the lease by options for the tenant to surrender the lease, etc., in circumstances such that the tenant is likely to do so. ICTA 1988, s. 38 takes such options into account only if they are *likely to be exercised*.

On 6 November 1998, Len grants Tom a 70-year lease of a shop, taking a premium of £80,000. The lease provides for the annual rent to be £1,500 for the first 12 years. However, in the 13th year, the rent will increase fifty-fold. The lease gives Tom the option to surrender the lease at the end of the twelfth year. Will the lease be treated as a 70-year lease or a 12-year lease?

A 12-year lease.

17.6   Furnished Holiday Lettings

The same provisions apply, whether the lettings are by an individual or by a company: ICTA 1988, ss. 503, 504. The rental profits fall under Schedule A, but are treated as though they were trading profits: ICTA 1988, s. 503(1)(a). The holiday accommodation must be publicly available for letting for at least 140 days in the tax year, and must in fact be let for 70 days: ICTA 1988, s. 504(3).

17.7   Other Relevant Taxes

17.7.1   VALUE ADDED TAX

In the case of non-domestic or non-charitable property, the landlord has an *option to tax* (i.e. to charge VAT on) the rent payable under the lease: VATA 1994, sch. 10, paras 2, 3. Certain formalities must be complied with. The effect of the election is to turn exempt supplies into supplies taxable at the standard rate. The landlord therefore has a full right of deduction for any input VAT directly attributable to rents on which VAT is charged in this way. Opportunities for VAT-avoidance to which this might give rise are severely restricted by the very complex FA 1997, s. 37.

Read the extracts from the articles by Gordon Pickering and Sinfield and Davis at *Cases and Materials* (17.2.1). These offer the briefest summary of complex legislation on the VAT *option to tax* (also known as the *election to waive exemption*).

17.7.2   LANDFILL TAX

If a person has income from licences to tip waste on land, it will need to ensure that it is the holder of a waste management licence. (Captain Petre in *McClure* v *Petre*, above, would today have been required to have such a licence.) It will be necessary for the holder of the licence to collect *landfill tax* from the other party. Landfill tax is charged on a so-called *taxable disposal*: FA 1996, s. 40. A taxable disposal is a disposal of material as waste, which is made by way of landfill, at a landfill site, on or after 1 October 1996: FA 1996, s. 40(2). It is generally chargeable at £7 for each whole tonne disposed of: FA 1996, s. 42(1)(a). Landfill tax is administered by Customs: FA 1996, s. 39(2). VAT is chargeable in addition to the landfill tax itself, where the landfill site operator (FA 1996, s. 41(2)) is a taxable person for VAT. Unlike VAT, landfill tax has no concept of 'input tax'.

17.8   Summary

Schedule A income is often income to which a beneficiary under a trust is entitled. If you are an adult beneficiary with a contingent interest in Schedule A profits, you can obtain full credit for the income tax paid by the trustees. As an infant beneficiary, your interest in the Schedule A profits will be a contingent one if TA 1925, s. 31 applies to the trust deed. Administrative expenses are payable out of Schedule A profits *after* tax, in cases where the trust is *not* subject to the special rate. This means that, where the special rate is inapplicable, administrative expenses are payable out of the taxed income profits of the trust. Some relief (see **16.6.3**) is given for administrative expenses, where the special rate applies. All of these points apply equally, where the income of the trust falls under Schedule D, Case I. In relation to Schedule A income, beware of ICTA 1988, s. 34(1), which brings premiums into a person's Schedule A income. The longer the lease, the greater the amount of the premium that will have to be included in the landlord's Schedule A income. Be able to outline the landlord's VAT option to tax the rents, in relation to commercial properties.

17.9   End of Chapter Assessment Questions

(a)   Hugh, the barrister (see **7.9**), is one of three trustees of The Smallpiece (1998) Discretionary Trust. None of the income profits of the trust has been appointed to any of its class of beneficiaries in 1998/99. For 1998/99, the trust accounts show *expenditure* totalling £2,400, made up as follows:

	£
Auditors' remuneration	750
Other administrative expenses	50
Allowable deductions under Schedule A	1,600

In 1998/99, the trust has Schedule A income of £9,200, and receives *net* dividends from its shareholding in Moneybags Ltd of £3,000.

Calculate the total income tax due from Hugh and his fellow-trustees for 1998/99.

(90 marks.)

(b)   Refer to **2.6**. Will Deborah be liable to pay income tax on the rental of £150 per month from Edwina?

(10 marks.)

See *Cases and Materials* (**17.4**), for a specimen answer.

CHAPTER EIGHTEEN

INCOME TAXATION: ANTI-AVOIDANCE ISSUES

18.1 Objectives

By the end of this chapter, you should be able to:

■ describe the *general* element of Schedule D, Case VI;

■ explain the *specific element* of Schedule D, Case VI;

■ describe the circumstances in which a *capital profit on the disposal of land* will fall under Schedule D, Case VI, because of ICTA 1988, s. 776;

■ identify the circumstances in which an individual may be deemed to receive Schedule D, Case VI income on the *transfer of assets abroad*;

■ identify the circumstances in which a *settlor* will be deemed to receive Schedule D, Case VI income;

■ state *when* a company will be a *close company*;

■ describe the *effects* of a company being a close company.

18.2 Introduction

Schedule D, Case VI is the anti-avoidance Schedule. It has a general element, covering all income profits not falling under the other Schedules and Cases. It also has a specific element, which brings particular profits within Schedule D, Case VI, simply because legislation says that those profits are within it. Case VI of Schedule D is not our only concern in this chapter, however. In **18.5**, we examine close companies, and assess the ways in which they prevent income tax avoidance through the use of 'tame' or 'pocket-book' companies. Finally, in **18.6**, we gather together a range of special rules from the Schedules and Cases, other than Schedule D, Case VI, which are designed to prevent income tax or corporation tax avoidance in ways the law deems to be unacceptable. Unless otherwise stated, the provisions discussed in this chapter apply whether individuals or companies are concerned, and irrespective of the capacity in which those persons are acting. Although there are VAT and NIC anti-avoidance provisions, considerations of space mean that only the briefest mention of them is possible. The emphasis throughout is on income tax and corporation tax.

18.3   Schedule D, Case VI: the General Element

In its general element, Schedule D, Case VI chiefly covers income profits from casual supplies of services. The Income and Corporation Taxes Act 1988, s. 18(3) refers to:

> . . . [A]ny annual profits or gains not falling under any other Case of Schedule D and not charged by virtue of Schedule A or E.

Note the now-familiar reference to annual profits or gains, denoting income profits. Note also the residual or 'sweeping-up' nature of s. 18(3), apparent from the last half-dozen words. The inference that the general element of Schedule D, Case VI covers income profits from casual supplies of services comes from *Scott* v *Ricketts* [1967] 1 WLR 828, where Lord Denning MR said that Schedule D, Case VI covers:

> . . . [A] contract for services or facilities provided, or something of that kind.

Two cases illustrate the ambit of ICTA 1988, s. 18(3). In *Earl Haig's Trustees* v *IRC* (1939) 22 TC 725, the trustees of Field Marshal Earl Haig, architect of the disastrous Somme offensive of 1916, had allowed the author Duff Cooper to make use of the Earl's diaries to write a highly sympathetic biography, published in 1936. In return, the trustees got a half-share of the royalties. The Court of Session held that the half-share did *not* fall under Schedule D, Case VI. The half-share was a profit from the *part-disposal* of the diaries by the trustees: see **21.3.3.3**. In *Jones* v *Leeming* [1930] AC 415, the Revenue argued that an individual, who was a member of a syndicate, had obtained an income profit falling under Schedule D, Case VI. The syndicate had acquired options to purchase two rubber estates in the Malay Peninsula, later selling the options at a considerable profit. The Revenue was unable to convince the General Commissioners that the profit on sale of the options was a profit from an adventure in the nature of trade. Both the Court of Appeal and the House of Lords held that the profit did not fall under Schedule D, Case VI either. In the Court of Appeal, Lawrence LJ said:

> It seems to me that in the case of an isolated transaction of purchase and re-sale of property there is really no middle course open. It is either an adventure in the nature of trade, or else it is simply a case of sale and re-sale of property.

In the House of Lords, Lord Buckmaster said: 'It is to my mind, in the circumstances, purely an affair of capital'.

SAQ 220

You are the only survivor of a shipwreck on a desert island. When you get rescued, you sell your story to a newspaper for £1 million. Will the £1 million go in Stage One of your income tax calculation under Schedule D, Case VI?

Yes.

Three final points need to be made about the general element of Schedule D, Case VI:

■   Schedule D, Case VI profits go into Stage One of a person's income tax or corporation tax calculation only if they are *actually received*: ICTA 1988, s. 69;

■   since there are no rules for allowable deductions, any expenses deductible from the receipt must be agreed on an *ad hoc basis* with the Revenue; *and*

■ if expenses exceed a receipt under Schedule D, Case VI, the loss can be deducted only from other Schedule D, Case VI income of the same tax period or of subsequent tax periods: ICTA 1988, s. 392: see **13.6**.

18.4   Schedule D, Case VI: the Specific Element

18.4.1   CERTAIN TRANSACTIONS IN LAND: ICTA 1988, SECTION 776

18.4.1.1   Effect of ICTA 1988, s. 776 applying

Where ICTA 1988, s. 776 applies, it deems a capital profit on the disposal of land to be an income one instead. That deemed income profit is a Schedule D, Case VI profit of the person making it. It is included in Stage One of the income tax or corporation tax calculation: ICTA 1988, s. 776(3). Section 776(6) states:

> For the purposes of this section, such method of computing a gain shall be adopted as is just and reasonable in the circumstances, taking into account the value of what is obtained for disposing of the land, and allowing only such expenses as are attributable to the land disposed of . . .

Whose position is strengthened by this vagueness?

The Revenue's.

Refer to 7.4. Andrew Ltd, a company with trading profits of £150,000 in its accounting period ending on 31 January 1999, realises a capital profit of £50,000, within ICTA 1988, s. 776, in that period. At what rate will the profit be taxed?

21%.

Refer to 7.3. Charles, an individual with taxable income of £55,000 in the 1998/99 tax year, realises a profit within ICTA 1988, s. 776, of £50,000. At what rate will this profit be taxed?

40%.

Two points arise in relation to capital profits realised by *trustees*, which are caught by ICTA 1988, s. 776. First, where the income of a trust does *not* accrue directly to the beneficiaries, and the trustees are *not* liable to pay the special rate applicable to trusts, it seems that they can only ever be liable to pay income tax at the *basic* rate on any profit caught by ICTA 1988, s. 776. Secondly, it seems that the special rate applicable to trusts *may not* apply to a profit caught by s. 776 which is realised by the trustees of a discretionary trust. The argument in support of this second point is that s. 686, ICTA 1988, which imposes the special rate applicable to trusts, refers to *income* as the term is used in trusts law, i.e. it does not cover *deemed* income receipts, such as those encountered in tax law. This second point may have become very significant indeed, following the introduction of the 34% CGT rate for capital profits realised by all trusts: see **21.7.1**.

18.4.1.2   Conditions for ICTA 1988, s. 776 to apply

Section 776 brings a capital profit within Schedule D, Case VI, if *all three* of the following conditions are satisfied:

(a)   a person acquires land, or any property deriving its value from land, with the sole or main object of realising a gain from disposing of the land; *or*

a person holds land as trading stock (see **15.5**); *or*

a person develops land with the sole or main object of raising a gain from disposing of the land when developed; *and*

(b)   a *capital profit* is obtained from a disposal of the land; *and*

(c)   the gain is obtained:

(i)   by the person acquiring, holding or developing the land, or by any connected person, *or*

(ii)   where any arrangement or scheme is effected as respects the land which enables a gain to be realised by any indirect method, or by any series of transactions, by any person who is a party to, or concerned in, the arrangement or scheme.

On the basis of these three conditions, consider this:

Besthouses, an elegant row of five smart town houses, is owned by the trustees of The Douglas Discretionary Trust. The trustees grant five separate leases to Edward Developers Ltd. Each lease contains covenants, under which the company is to convert each house into four elegant flats. Edward Developers will then grant 99-year leases of the flats to tenants, for premiums of £150,000 each, plus annual rentals of £12,000. For each flat, 75% of each premium will be paid to the trustees and 25% will be paid to the company. In addition, all rental payments will be divided between the trustees and the company in the proportion 40:60. Advise the trustees whether their receipt of the premiums will fall within ICTA 1988, s. 776.

(**Read the extracts from *Page* v *Lowther* [1983] STC 799 at *Cases and Materials* (18.1.1).**)

Under ICTA 1988, s. 776(11), a person can apply for a ruling in advance from the Revenue, as to whether s. 776 will apply to a particular capital profit. However, very careful consideration is needed as to whether such an application should be made. This is because applications under ICTA 1988, s. 776(11) are not considered by a specialist Revenue office. It will be difficult to reverse a ruling contrary to the one sought by the applicant.

18.4.2   TRANSFERS OF ASSETS ABROAD: ICTA 1988, SECTIONS 739 AND 740

18.4.2.1   Effect of ICTA 1988, s. 739 or s. 740 applying

The Income and Corporation Taxes Act 1988, s. 739 can apply when an individual who is ordinarily resident in the UK in the tax year under consideration, transfers an income-generating asset to a person resident outside the UK. It might naturally be asked why anyone would want to make such a transfer. The answer is that, since the transferee is not resident in the UK, it will not be liable to UK income tax on any income which does not have a UK source. Section 739 is designed to prevent you achieving this result. When you, the transferor (or the transferor's spouse), are caught by ICTA 1988, s. 739, you are deemed to have received a certain amount of Schedule D, Case VI income, which income is included in Stage One of your income tax calculation for that tax year. The main conditions which need to be satisfied before you are caught by ICTA 1988, s. 739 are summarised in **18.4.2.2**.

The Income and Corporation Taxes Act 1988, s. 740 complements s. 739 and provides that s. 739 does not apply where the transfer is covered by ICTA 1988, s. 740. Section 740 can apply to you if you are someone, other than the transferor or the transferor's spouse, who receives a benefit as a result of a transfer of assets abroad. Under ICTA 1988, s. 739, the amount of Schedule D, Case VI income deemed to have been received by you differs, according to whether you fall within subsection (2) or subsection (3) of s. 739. If s. 739(2) applies, you are deemed to have received, under Schedule D, Case VI, the whole of the transferee's income from all sources, not just from the assets transferred: *Congreve* v *IRC* [1948] 1 All ER 948; *Vestey* v *IRC* [1980] AC 1148. If s. 739(3) applies, there is included under Schedule D, Case VI of your income tax calculation only the capital sum you are entitled to receive, plus any income arising from it in the tax year of the transfer. In subsequent tax years, you are also treated as receiving any income arising from it. The conditions which must be satisfied before each of these subsections apply are summarised below.

You are UK-resident in 1998/99. On 1 May 1998, you transfer the legal title to a number of income-generating assets to trustees resident in Guernsey. The trust deed provides that the trustees are to act in accordance with your instructions in relation to the application of the capital of the trust fund, and the fund includes a deposit account of £50,000. You instruct the trustees to make an interest-free loan to your spouse, on 2 June 1997. What amounts will be included in Stage One of your income tax calculation for 1998/99, under Schedule D, Case VI?

The amount of the loan and any other amounts mentioned above.

18.4.2.2   Conditions to be satisfied for ICTA 1988, s. 739 or 740 to apply

The Income and Corporation Taxes Act 1988, s. 739(2) applies where:

- there is a transfer of assets by an individual; *and*

- as a result of the transfer, whether by itself or by associated operations, income is payable to a non-UK resident or non-UK domiciled person; *and*

- the transferor has ' . . . power to enjoy the income of a person resident or domiciled outside the UK'.

Section 739(3) applies where you, the transferor (or your spouse) receive or are entitled to receive, a capital sum. A capital sum includes any amount which is paid, or which is payable, by way of loan. Section 740 applies where:

- there is a transfer of assets by an individual; *and*

- as a result of the transfer, whether by itself or by associated operations, income is payable to a non-UK resident or non-UK domiciled person; *and*

- Someone other than the transferor/transferor's spouse ' . . . receives a benefit provided out of assets which are available for the purpose by virtue or in consequence of the transfer or of any associated operations': ICTA 1988, s. 740(1).

'Associated operations' include any operation other than death, carried out by absolutely anyone. However, it must result in income being payable as envisaged by s. 739 or 740. Whether an individual has power to enjoy income under ICTA 1988, s. 739(2) is determined by reference to the five alternative situations set out in ICTA 1988, s. 742(2). These are:

(a)   the income is dealt with in such a way as to be calculated to enure, in any form, for the benefit of the transferor: ICTA 1988, s. 742(2)(a); *or*

(b)   the receipt or accrual of the income increases the value to the transferor of assets held by the transferor or for the transferor's benefit: ICTA 1988, s. 742(2)(b); *or*

(c)   the receipt or entitlement to any benefit from the income or assets representing the income: ICTA 1988, s. 742(2)(c); *or*

(d)   membership of a class of beneficiaries who may become entitled to the income as the result of the exercise by any person of a power: ICTA 1988, s. 742(2)(d); *or*

(e)   control of the application of the income in any way, although not necessarily for the transferor's own benefit: ICTA 1988, s. 742(2)(e).

In relation to each of these, ICTA 1988, s. 742(3)(a) provides that regard shall be had to the substantial result and effect of the transfer or associated operations.

You are UK-resident in 1998/99. You transfer your shares in Megabucks plc, which are worth £1 million, to Emerald Ltd, a Jersey-resident company, 75% of the issued share capital of which is owned by you. On the basis of which of (a) to (e) above could you enjoy the income of Emerald Ltd?

Alternative (c) – you will have the right to any dividends declared and paid on the shares.

ACTIVITY38

Read the article by Philip Dearden in *Cases and Materials* (18.1.2). This discusses three recent cases on ICTA 1988, s. 739: *IRC* v *Willoughby* [1997] BTC 393, *IRC* v *Botnar* [1997] BTC 613 and *IRC* v *McGuckian* [1997] 3 All ER 817. (For *IRC* v *McGuckian*, refer also to 4.4.)

18.4.3   SETTLEMENTS OF CAPITAL: ANTI-AVOIDANCE PROVISIONS: ICTA 1988, ss. 660A, 660B, 677, 678

18.4.3.1   Effect of anti-avoidance provisions applying

The Income and Corporation Taxes 1988, s. 347A, which was introduced by FA 1988, made settlements of income ineffective in all but three cases: see **9.3.1**. Measures were also introduced in FA 1988, to make settlements of capital, which had previously been used to achieve a similar result, ineffective too.

SAQ 226

It is September *1987*. You want to put your shares in Megabucks plc into trust for your grandson, Frank, without executing a deed of covenant in his favour, i.e. without creating an *income* settlement, but in such a way as to ensure that dividends on the shares are paid to him. What is the alternative to a deed of covenant?

To transfer the shares to trustees of a trust, giving Frank an interest in possession in the shares.

The general effect of the anti-avoidance provisions is to deem the settlor to have received Schedule D, Case VI income, whilst giving the settlor a right to recover any higher rate tax from the trustees, or a right to a tax credit: ICTA 1988, s. 660C(1). The deemed Schedule D, Case VI income is included in Stage One of the settlor's income tax calculation, grossed-up where indicated below. In detail, the provisions have the following effects:

(a)   where, during the settlor's lifetime, property subject to a settlement may become payable to, or may be applied for the benefit of, the settlor or the settlor's spouse, the income of the settlement is deemed to be the settlor's income. It is included in Stage One of the settlor's income tax calculation, for the tax year in which the income arises, as Schedule D, Case VI income: ICTA 1988, s. 660A(1);

(b)   where the settlor's unmarried minor children receive income from a settlement within ICTA 1988, s. 660B, or when payments are made for their benefit from the settlement, that income is also deemed to be the settlor's income. It is again included in Stage One of the settlor's income tax calculation for the tax year in which the payment is made, as Schedule D, Case VI income: ICTA 1988, s. 660B; *and*

(c)   where capital payments are made by the trustees to the settlor or the settlor's spouse, the capital payments are deemed to be the settlor's income. The settlor is treated as receiving an amount equal to the undistributed income of the settled fund, up to a maximum of the available income up to the end of the tax year under consideration: ICTA 1988, s. 677(1). If the capital sum paid out is less than the available income, then the remainder may be deemed to be the settlor's income for the following tax years: ICTA 1988, s. 677(1).

To reflect the tax paid by the trustees, the grossed-up amount of the payment is included in Stage One of the settlor's income tax calculation for the tax year in which the capital payment is made. The grossing-up is at the special rate applicable to trusts of 34%. Full credit is given for the tax paid by the trustees at Stage Six of the settlor's income tax calculation, in the usual way.

As at 6 April 1998, the undistributed income of the Crunch (No. 1) 1993 Discretionary Trust is £50,000. The settlor, Miss Annette Crunch, asks the trustees to make her an interest-free loan of £55,000, and they do so. What amount will be included in her income tax calculation at Stage One for the tax year 1998/99, and for how much will she receive credit at Stage Six?

At Stage One, £75,758, i.e. £50,000 × 100/66; at Stage Six, credit for £25,758.

18.4.3.2 Conditions to be satisfied for the anti-avoidance provisions to apply

Property payable to, or applied for, the settlor's benefit: ICTA 1988, s. 660A
As a settlor, ICTA 1988, s. 660A will apply to you if there is any possibility that the settled property, or any *derived property* can be:

■ paid to you; *or*

■ paid to your spouse; *or*

■ applied for your benefit; *or*

■ applied for your spouse's benefit,

in any circumstances whatsoever.

Derived property is defined in ICTA 1988, s. 660A(10). It can include, among other things, income from the settled property; other property representing the proceeds of sale of the settled property; and income from the proceeds of sale of the settled property.

You are a settlor. On 1 December 1998, you transfer shares in Utopia plc to the trustees of a discretionary trust. At the time of the transfer, they are worth £100,000. On 10 December 1998, the trustees exercise a power of sale in the deed of settlement, and sell the shares for £150,000. They reinvest the proceeds of sale in shares in Megabucks plc, which declares and pays a special dividend to shareholders on 20 December 1998. In the trust deed, there is a power for the trustees to pay the income of the trust to you or your spouse. Will you, the settlor, be subject to ICTA 1988, s. 660A? If so, what will happen as regards your income tax calculation for the 1998/99 tax year?

The grossed-up amount of the dividends will be included in Stage One of your income tax calculation for the 1998/99 tax year. In addition, you will be able to recover the tax paid from the trustees if necessary: ICTA 1988, s. 660D.

Settlements on unmarried minor children: ICTA 1988, s. 660B
As a settlor, ICTA 1988, s. 660B will apply to you if income of the settlement is paid during your lifetime to or for the benefit of your unmarried child who is a minor. Section 660B can apply in a case where ICTA 1988, s. 660A does not apply. Payments cover payments in money's worth; a minor is someone under 18 years old; and a child includes a stepchild or an illegitimate child: ICTA 1988, s. 660B(6)(a) and (b).

You are a settlor. On 30 November 1998, you transfer shares in Dodgem plc to the trustees of a discretionary trust. In the trust deed, there is a power for the trustees to pay income of the trust to your children. Dodgem plc declares and pays a dividend to its shareholders on 12 December 1998, which the trustees pay over to Jack, your 17-year old son, on 14 December 1998.

What will happen as regards your income tax calculation for 1998/99?

You will be deemed to have received the grossed-up amount of the dividend, which will be included in Stage One of your income tax calculation, as Schedule D, Case VI income.

Note that there will be no Schedule D, Case VI charge if the amount paid to the minor unmarried child is £100 or less in any tax year: ICTA 1988, s. 660B(5).

Capital sums which are paid to the settlor: ICTA 1988, ss. 677 and 678
As a settlor, ICTA 1988, ss. 677 and 678 will apply to you if any capital sum is paid to you from the settlement by the trustees, directly or indirectly. A capital sum includes any loan or repayment of a loan, plus any other non-income amount not paid for full consideration in money or money's worth: ICTA 1988, s. 677(9)(a).

18.4.3.3   Conclusion on the application of the anti-avoidance provisions

The lesson to be learned from the provisions discussed above is that a capital settlement will not come within the provisions discussed above, provided that you, the settlor, have absolutely no interest whatsoever in the settled property. One obvious omission from the situations discussed above is where you, the settlor, have grandchildren. In those circumstances, a settlement of capital may avoid the provisions discussed above. The problem with a capital settlement in favour of your child is that the income profits of the trust will be subject to income tax at 34%. Even if you are a higher rate taxpayer, and are content for the income to be accumulated by the trustees, you will be saving only 6% tax, and this may not be enough to make settling capital worthwhile.

18.4.4   OTHER SPECIFIC APPLICATIONS OF SCHEDULE D, CASE VI

We have discussed a number of illustrations of the specific element of Schedule D, Case VI. There is just space to remind ourselves of two others, already discussed:

■ *ICTA 1988, ss. 757–764*: if you dispose of a material interest in an offshore fund, your capital profit is deemed to be an income one and falls under Schedule D, Case VI: see **3.3.2**.

■ *ICTA 1988, ss. 103, 104*: if you sell your trading stock at a profit after your trade has ceased, the profit falls under Schedule D, Case VI: see **5.4**.

18.5 Close Companies

18.5.1 EFFECTS OF A COMPANY BEING A CLOSE COMPANY

If a company is treated as being a close company, because it satisfies the conditions described in **18.5.2**, there are consequences both for the company itself, and for the shareholders in it.

18.5.1.1 The concept of dividends is extended to benefits: ICTA 1988, s. 418

Dividends are made to include the situation where benefits are conferred by the company on its shareholders or debenture-holders. However, if the debenture-holder or shareholder is also a director, or an employee of the company who is paid more than £8,500 per annum, then the dividend concept is not extended in this way: ICTA 1988, ss. 418ff. Imagine, therefore, that you are a shareholder or debenture-holder in a close company. You are not, however, an employee earning more than £8,500 per annum, nor a director (see **Chapter 14**). If the company provides you with any benefit:

■ you, the individual shareholder, will be deemed to have received net dividend income, for the tax year in which the benefit is received by you. This dividend income will be included in Stage One of your income tax calculation, under Schedule F, grossed-up at 20%; *and*

■ the close company will be deemed to have declared and paid a net dividend of the value of the benefit, and will therefore have to pay ACT at ¼, i.e. 20/80 x the net value.

SAQ 230

Bearing in mind the points just discussed, consider this possibility. The close company in which you are a shareholder makes an absolute gift to you of a Mercedes worth £50,000, sometime in 1998/99. What amount is included in your income tax calculation? How much ACT will the company be liable to pay?

The amount included in your income tax calculation is £62,500 (i.e. £50,000 × 100/80); the company is liable to pay ACT of £12,500.

18.5.1.2 Loans made by the company are treated as though they were dividends: ICTA 1988, s. 419

Loans made by the company to its participators, or associates of its participators, are treated in roughly the same way as if they were dividends. There is at least one important difference, however, which will be considered in a moment. The concept of a *participator* in a close company is considered in **18.5.2**. Loans to participators need to be considered in *two* stages:

(a) the making of the loan; *and*

(b) any release or writing-off of the loan.

Each of these two stages has a consequence both for the company and for the individual participator.

The making of the loan
The two consequences of the making of the loan by the company are:

■ The company is treated as if it had declared and paid a dividend, and it must pay an amount representing ACT on the loan, equal to × the loan; *and*

■ the shareholder is not entitled to any credit at Stage Six of his or her income tax calculation for the 'ACT' paid by the company.

It is important to recognise that the sum which the company must pay, and for which the shareholder receives no tax credit, is not ACT. It is merely a sum representing ACT.

On 1 March 1999, Closeco Ltd, a close company, makes an interest-free loan to Albert, a shareholder, of £10,000 repayable on 1 March 2002.

What are the tax consequences of the loan for Closeco?

It must pay ACT of £2,500 to the Revenue.

Any release or writing-off of the loan
The two consequences of any release or writing-off of the loan by the company are that:

■ the company loses permanently the 'ACT' being held by the Revenue, and no deduction can be made for that amount for tax purposes; *and*

■ the shareholder is treated as receiving Schedule F income, which must be grossed-up and included at Stage One of his or her income tax calculation for the tax year of the release or writing-off. However, no credit for the forfeited 'ACT' is made to the participator.

It is important to recognise that the sum which the company must pay, and for which the shareholder receives no tax credit, is not actually ACT. It is merely a sum representing ACT, which is subject to forfeiture by the Revenue in the circumstances outlined above.

(Refer to SAQ 231.) On 1 March 2002, Closeco releases the balance of the loan, in Albert's favour. Exactly half of the loan has been repaid by that date.

What is the income tax effect of this for Albert?

He must include £6,250 (i.e. £5,000 × 100/80) under Schedule F, in Stage One of his income tax calculation for that tax year.

18.5.1.3 The small companies rate of corporation tax may be disallowed: ICTA 1988, ss. 13A and 231(3C)

This will only happen if the company is, in addition to being a close company, a close investment-holding company ('CIC'). CICs are defined by exclusion in ICTA 1988, s. 13A. Companies which are *not* CICs include:

■ a close company which is a trading company, i.e. one which exists wholly or mainly for the purposes of trading on a commercial basis;

■ a close company which is a member of a trading group; *and*

■ a close company which carries on the business of property investment on a commercial basis.

Pugwash Ltd, a close company, owns a block of flats in Coketown. All the flats are leased to tenants, and the rents under the leases always produce a profit. Is Pugwash Ltd a CIC?

No.

18.5.2 CONDITIONS TO BE SATISFIED FOR A COMPANY TO BE A CLOSE COMPANY

A company's status as a close company is one which it attains merely by satisfying the definition of a close company in the relevant legislation. There are no formalities which have to be observed before it achieves that status! The definition of a close company appears in ICTA 1988, s. 414(1):

> For the purposes of the Tax Acts, a 'close company' is one which is under the control of five or fewer participators, or of participators who are directors . . .

The first point to note about this definition is the phrase 'For the purposes of the Tax Acts'. This phrase emphasises the fact that the concept of the close company is relevant lonly for the purposes of income tax and corporation tax: see ICTA 1988, s. 831(2). Next, note the word '*participators*'. 'Participators' is a very wide term, and it includes any person who has any ' . . . share or interest in the capital or income of the company': see ICTA 1988, s. 417(1). Although the term can include any loan creditor of the company (see ICTA 1988, s. 417(1)(b)), it does not include a banker making a loan to a company in the ordinary course of its banking business: ICTA 1988, s. 417(9).

The Eastminster Bank lends £10,000 to Closeco in the ordinary course of its banking business. The loan is secured by a charge over the assets of the company. Sid, a friend of one of Closeco's directors, also lends Closeco £10,000. Both loans are at commercial rates of interest. Which of them are participators?

Sid is a participator, but the bank is *not* one.

Next, note the word *'directors'* in the definition of a close company. For the purpose of these provisions, this term is much wider than its usual meaning, and includes ' . . . any person in accordance with whose directions or instructions the directors are accustomed to act': ICTA 1988, s. 417(5). Finally, note the word 'control'. As a participator, you will have *control* of a company if:

■ You exercise, or are able to exercise, direct or indirect control over the company's affairs, in particular if you possess, or are entitled to acquire, the greater part of the share capital or voting power of the company (the *control test*); *or*

■ You possess, or are entitled to acquire (the *apportionment test*):

EITHER

Such part of the issued share capital as would give you a right to the greater part of the company's income if in fact it were all to be distributed;

OR

The entitlement to the greater part of the assets available for distribution among the participators on a winding-up of the company, or in any other circumstances.

(ICTA 1988, s. 416(2).)

Note that the legislation provides for various companies which cannot be close companies, e.g. quoted companies, non-UK-resident companies.

Closeco, a UK-resident company, has eight shareholders, each of whom own 12.5% of its issued share capital. Is it a close company?

Yes.

Most UK-resident companies will be close companies, unless they are members of a *quoted* group of companies. If the holding company of a group is a close company, then all of its subsidiaries will usually be close companies also. However, if the holding company is not close then, except where this is because it is non-UK-resident, companies under its control will not usually be close companies either: ICTA 1988, s. 414(5). In practice, if a company is not a close company, the reason is generally that the share capital of the holding company of the group is listed on the London Stock Exchange.

18.6   Other Income Tax and Corporation Tax Anti-avoidance Provisions

There are a number of other anti-avoidance provisions throughout the income tax and corporation tax legislation.

18.6.1   THE RULE IN *SHARKEY* V *WERNHER* AND ICTA 1988, s. 770

The rule in *Sharkey* v *Wernher* [1955] 3 All ER 493 is relevant to persons whose income profits fall under Schedule D, Case I, but not to those whose income profits fall under Schedule D, Case II: *Mason* v *Innes* [1967] 2 All ER 926. The rule states that if a trader disposes of trading stock, otherwise than in the ordinary course of trade, it must add the full market value of the trading stock to its trading income for the tax period of the disposal.

You are an art dealer. A valuable painting by Romney, which you bought in 1990 for £65,000, is part of your trading stock. You give it to your nephew, as a wedding present, when it is worth £100,000. What trading profit are you deemed to have made on the transaction?

£35,000, i.e. £100,000 − £65,000. (See also **21.3.3.6**.)

In *Mason* v *Innes*, the novelist Hammond Innes assigned the copyright in his novel, *The Doomed Oasis* to his father, in consideration of natural love and affection. At the time of the assignment, the copyright was worth £15,000. The Court of Appeal held that the novelist (whose profits fell under Schedule D, Case II) was *not* to be deemed to have received £15,000 under the rule in *Sharkey* v *Wernher*. The rule did not apply to income from a profession, only to income from a *trade*: see **15.3.2**.

18.6.2 SALE OF INCOME: ICTA 1988, s. 775

If arrangements to exploit income derived from professional activity have been made and, as part of those arrangements, you put another person in a position to enjoy that income, the capital sum received is capable of falling under Schedule D, Case VI.

18.7 Value Added Tax and National Insurance Contributions: Anti-avoidance

Although there is not space for a detailed discussion here, briefly note the existence of anti-avoidance rules in VAT and NIC law. In relation to VAT, the concepts of *self-supply* and the *capital goods scheme* are good examples of anti-avoidance provisions. *Self-supply* is designed to nullify any VAT advantage to traders generated by producing certain items for use in their own business, rather than buying them elsewhere. One example of a self-supply charge is where an exempt or partially-exempt trader (see **10.6**) produces its own stationery: see VAT (Special Provisions) Order 1995 (SI 1995 No. 1268), reg. 11. The *capital goods scheme* enables Customs to 'claw-back' input VAT recovered by a taxable person on the acquisition of certain capital items used in its business (i.e. computer equipment and land and buildings), where the capital items in question subsequently cease to be used for the purpose of making taxable supplies. In addition, FA 1997, s. 37, is designed to prevent abuse of the option to tax: see **17.7.1**. In relation to NICs, there are certain provisions designed to prevent liability to NICs being avoided by paying employees in precious stones or gold bullion: SSCR 1979, reg. 19(5)(d).

18.8 Summary

There are a number of provisions designed to counter income tax and corporation tax avoidance. First, Schedule D, Case VI can itself be characterised as the anti-avoidance

Schedule. It has a general element, bringing casual earnings into the scope of each tax. It also has a specific element, which brings profits from certain specific activities within the scope of income tax or corporation tax. The main examples of these activities are certain transactions in land (ICTA 1988, s. 776), the transfer of assets abroad (ICTA 1988, ss. 739 and 740) and settlements of capital: ICTA 1988, ss. 660A, 660B, 677, 678. Secondly, there is the concept of the close company, which is designed to prevent people obtaining tax advantages through having a share in the income or capital of a company. Most UK-resident companies are close companies, unless they are members of a quoted group of companies. A company's status as a close company means that a benefit provided to a participator is treated as though it were a dividend, unless the benefit falls under Schedule E. Also, the making or writing-off of a loan to a participator will have consequences for both the participator and the company. Furthermore, if the close company is in addition a CIC, the availability of the small companies' rate may be jeopardised. Finally, there are a number of VAT and NIC anti-avoidance provisions, the existence of which should merely be noted.

18.9   End of Chapter Assessment Question

Refer to the facts involving Amber Ltd and its shareholders: see **2.6**, **8.9**. In Amber Ltd's accounting period ending on 31 December 1998, Bertram, who is short of money, proposes that Amber Ltd makes him an interest-free loan of £10,000, repayable in full on 31 December 2002. Alan and Deborah are amenable to the proposal, provided any company law requirements are complied with, although they are concerned about its tax implications.

Advise them.

(Word limit: 250 (100 marks).)

See *Cases and Materials* (**18.3**) for a specimen answer.

CHAPTER NINETEEN

INCOME TAXATION: COMPLIANCE AND APPEALS

19.1 Objectives

By the end of this chapter, you should be able to:

■ explain the functions of *tax inspectors* and *tax collectors*;

■ explain the function of the *Revenue Adjudicator*;

■ discuss the *impact of self-assessment* on individuals;

■ list the *deadlines* for the submission of tax returns to the Revenue;

■ specify the *deadlines for appealing* against assessments;

■ describe the *PAYE system*;

■ describe the procedure on an *income tax appeal*;

■ outline the rules of compliance for *corporation tax* purposes;

■ outline the rules of compliance for *VAT* purposes;

■ outline the rules of compliance for *NIC* purposes.

19.2 Introduction

In this chapter, we shall be considering the compliance and appeals aspects of income taxation. For reasons of space, only a brief discussion of these aspects of corporation tax, VAT and NICs is possible. We shall therefore concentrate on income tax, beginning with a discussion of the duties of the Revenue officials entrusted with assessing and collecting it. We shall then consider the issue of how the Revenue obtains information from you, which involves considering whether you are obliged to make a tax return at all and, if so, the date by which you must submit it. The issue of the dates for paying the tax is a separate one, and you will find the rules relating to it rather surprising. For instance, even if you appeal against the amount of tax due from you, some of that tax will have to be paid as a condition of the appeal going forward! That is not the only surprise the income tax appeals process has to offer.

19.3 Income Tax

19.3.1 TAX INSPECTORS AND TAX COLLECTORS

Income tax is '. . . under the care and management of the Commissioners of Inland Revenue (. . . "the Board") . . .': TMA 1970, s. 1(1). The Board, which is subject to HM Treasury, appoints *inspectors of taxes* and *collectors of taxes*: TMA 1970, s. 1(2). An inspector of taxes is the civil servant in charge of a tax district. The inspector receives a tax return from you, the taxpayer, and either makes an assessment, or amends the assessment you have made yourself. A collector of taxes is also a civil servant. A collector is responsible for actually obtaining the total income tax due from you. The offices of tax inspectors and tax collectors are currently being restructured, into *taxpayer district offices* and *taxpayer service offices*. In some tax districts, e.g. Nottingham 1, there is also a *taxpayer assistance office*, where you can obtain help from the Revenue in person. Under The Taxpayer's Charter, you can expect the Revenue to be fair, to help you, to provide an efficient service, to be accountable and to tell you how to complain if you are dissatisfied. Complaints can be made free of charge to the Revenue Adjudicator, and ultimately to the Ombudsman, via your Member of Parliament. In return, under the Charter, you are expected to be honest with the Revenue, to provide it with accurate information and to pay on time any tax due.

Read the article by the Revenue Adjudicator at *Cases and Materials* (19.1.1). Note *exactly* the scope of the Adjudicator's functions.

Sid, a sole trader, is aggrieved that the tax inspector dealing with his claim for loss relief is *taking a long time to reply to letters*. What should he do first?

Set out the details of his complaint for the Revenue Adjudicator.

The Revenue must treat information it receives from you in confidence. However, for certain purposes only, information may be shared between the Revenue, the Contributions Agency and Customs.

19.3.2 SELF-ASSESSMENT OF INCOME TAX LIABILITY

The essential point about self-assessment is that, if you wish, you are allowed to calculate the total income tax due from you for a tax year by yourself. It assumes that, where you are obliged to complete a tax return, you will do so. If you want the Revenue to calculate the total income tax due from you, you can still request it to do so. In this situation, you must submit your tax return four months earlier than if you choose to self-assess.

SAQ 238

Bill was dismayed when he heard about self-assessment. 'I can't do maths for peanuts', he said, 'does self-assessment mean I have no choice but to get clued-up?' Does he have a choice?

Yes. He can get the Revenue to do the calculations for him, provided he acts promptly.

Self-assessment has shifted the *cost of compliance* with income tax law from the public sector to the private sector. In consequence, tax inspectors will have more time to concentrate on any irregularities in your tax affairs.

19.3.3 TAX RETURNS AS A SOURCE OF INFORMATION

Besides being required from individuals, whatever the capacity in which they are liable to pay income tax, returns are required from the following:

■ employers, who are obliged to operate the PAYE system (see **19.3.7.1**);

■ contractors in the construction industry, in relation to their sub-contractors (see **19.3.7.2**); *and*

■ banks and other payers of interest under deduction of lower rate income tax: see **9.4**.

The *cash equivalent* of benefits provided to employees and directors subject to the special statutory code (see **14.3.4**) is recorded by employers on Form P11D. Benefits provided to other employees are recorded on Form P9D. All employees employed on the last day of the tax year under consideration must be provided with a copy of Form P9D or P11D (i.e. a Form P60) within 92 days after the end of that tax year, i.e. by the following 6 July: see Income Tax (Employments) Regulation 1993 (SI 1993 No. 744), reg. 46AA(1).

19.3.3.1 Your personal return

If you are liable to pay income tax for any tax year, you are obliged to notify the Revenue, unless you are within one of the categories of exceptions discussed below: TMA 1970, s. 7(1). Assuming you are obliged to notify the Revenue, you have a six-month period after the end of the tax year under consideration to request a return form: TMA 1970, s. 7(1). If you have any unpaid tax by the following 31 January, you will become liable to pay a maximum penalty *for failing to make the return* of the total income tax due from you for that tax year: see **19.3.8**.

SAQ 239

Carl, a sole trader, makes his accounts up to 30 June in each calendar year. Had he worked it out, the total income tax due from him would have been £5,000 for 1998/99. If the Revenue neither send him a return form, nor does he request one, what will the maximum *penalty* which can be imposed on him for that tax year? On what date will it become payable?

£5,000, payable on 31 January 1999.

You are *not* obliged to notify the Revenue where your total income (see **7.3**) consists of: (a) income from which tax has been deducted at source by your employer under PAYE; (b) income (e.g. interest) from which tax has been deducted at source by the payer, provided you are not a higher-rate taxpayer; or (c) income (e.g. dividends) on which tax has been credited as paid, subject to the same proviso: TMA 1970, s. 7(1) to 7(4). In addition, SP1/96 states that if, as an employee, you are satisfied that your Form P11D is correctly completed, you are not obliged to request a personal return form. The Pay As You Earn system ('PAYE'), discussed in **19.3.7**, means that, as someone receiving employment income only, you will not need to make a return for the tax year under consideration.

However, on the basis that you *do* need to submit a personal return, the following points should be noted:

■ penalties can be imposed on you if you fail to keep records substantiating the details shown on the return: see **19.3.8**, *Cases and Materials* (**19.1.2**); *and*

■ the return must be *signed* by you: TMA 1970, s. 8(2). 'One of the most common reasons for us having to send a return back is that the taxpayer has failed to sign and date it', said a Revenue spokesman recently.

The *deadline* for submitting your personal return depends on whether or not you have elected to *self-assess*: see **19.3.2**. Assuming that you have done so, the deadline for submitting your personal return depends on whether or not the Revenue issued you with the return form before 31 October after the end of the tax year under consideration: TMA 1970, s. 8(1).

■ If it has done so, then the deadline is 31 January following the end of the tax year under consideration; *and*

■ If it has not done so, the deadline is the last day of the period of three months, beginning with the day on which your return form was sent to you.

Darrell, a sole trader, has elected to self-assess. The Revenue sends a return form to him on 2 December 1999. What is the deadline for submitting the return to the Revenue?

2 March 2000.

If you elect *not to self-assess*, then the deadline for submission of your personal return depends on whether or not the Revenue has issued you with the return form on or before 31 July after the end of the tax year under consideration: TMA 1970, s. 9(2).

■ If it has done so, then the deadline is 30 September following the end of the tax year under consideration; *and*

■ If the Revenue has not done so, the deadline is the last day of the period of two months, beginning with the day on which your return form was sent to you.

19.3.3.2 Partners

As a partner, you must complete your return for the tax year under consideration, as if your share of the Schedule D, Case I or Case II profits accrued directly to you from carrying on a trade by yourself: see **7.5**. The obligation to submit a personal return, summarised in **19.3.3.1**, still applies to you, even though you are acting in the capacity of a partner. In addition, a *partnership return*, relating to the partnership as a whole, can be required from a specified partner, or another person selected according to particular rules: TMA 1970, s. 12AA. The deadline for submitting the *partnership return* depends on whether or not the Revenue has issued the *partnership return* form before 31 October after the end of the tax year under consideration: TMA 1970, s. 12AA(4).

■   If it has done so, then the deadline is 31 January following the end of the tax year under consideration; *and*

■   If it has not done so, the deadline is the last day of the period of three months, beginning with the day on which your return form was sent to you.

Briggs & Co., a partnership, makes its accounts up to 31 July in each calendar year. The Revenue issues a partnership return form for 1998/99, on 2 January 2000. What is the deadline for the submission of Briggs & Co.'s partnership return?

2 April 2000.

19.3.3.3   Trustees

The Revenue may issue a trust return form to any one or more of a number of trustees, for the purpose of making an assessment on trustees, settlors, or beneficiaries alike: TMA 1970, s. 8A. The Revenue cannot, however, request information which relates to income received by the trustees in a tax year ended more than three years before the issue of the notice. As a trustee liable to pay the *special rate applicable to trusts*, you must include details of all distributions of income and capital, plus details of accumulated income: see **Chapters 16** and **17**. As an individual acting in the capacity of a trustee, the obligations in **19.3.3.1**, in relation to your *personal return*, still apply.

Assuming that the trustees elect to self-assess, the deadline for submitting the trust return depends on whether or not the Revenue has issued a return form or forms to any one or more of the trustees before 31 October after the end of the tax year under consideration: TMA 1970, s. 8A(1A).

■   If it has done so, then the deadline is 31 January following the end of the tax year under consideration; *and*

■   If it has not done so, the deadline is the last day of the period of three months, beginning with the day on which the return form was sent to the trustees.

The Revenue issues a notice requesting the trustees of The Pointer 1985 Discretionary Trust to submit a trust return for 1998/99 on 25 October 1999. What is the deadline for the submission of the return?

31 January 2000.

If the trustees elect *not* to self-assess, then the deadline for submission of the trust return depends on whether or not the Revenue has issued a return form or forms to any one or more of the trustees on or before 31 July after the end of the tax year under consideration: TMA 1970, s. 9(2).

■ If it has done so, then the deadline is 30 September following the end of the tax year under consideration; *and*

■ If it has not done so, the deadline is the last day of the period of *two* months, beginning with the day on which the return form was sent to the trustees.

19.3.3.4 Personal representatives

As a PR, you must supply the Revenue with:

■ details of payments to beneficiaries;

■ the names and addresses of beneficiaries; *and*

■ notification of completion of the administration of the estate.

If requested to do so by the PRs, the Revenue will issue a tax return form before the end of the tax year in which the death occurred and confirm quickly whether they wish to ask further questions about the deceased's tax affairs.

Egbert died on 12 April 1998. You are one of the two executors of his will. It bequeaths a number of specific legacies, each carrying income. What information will the Revenue require from you?

Full details of the beneficiaries and of payments to them.

19.3.4 SOURCES OF INFORMATION OTHER THAN RETURNS

Subject to an appeal to the Commissioners within 30 days of the notice, the Revenue may by that notice call for such documents, accounts and particulars as it may reasonably require: TMA 1970, s. 19A. Certain papers belonging to a tax adviser may not be accessed by the Revenue: TMA 1970, s. 20B. This rule does not apply to accounts and accountants' working papers (also SP5/90). If tax accountants are convicted of an offence in relation to tax, or suffer penalties for assisting in the preparation of incorrect returns, they may be required to disgorge the relevant documents by a properly authorised inspector: TMA 1970, s. 20A(1). There is power for the Revenue to enter premises, by force if necessary, to search them for evidence of serious fraud. The 'appropriate judicial authority' must be satisfied that there are reasonable grounds for suspecting an offence involving serious fraud: TMA 1970, s. 20C(1).

19.3.5 ASSESSMENTS, DETERMINATIONS AND CLAIMS

19.3.5.1 Assessments and determinations

Assessments are made where persons do not self-assess. Where a person makes a self-assessment, and it is incorrect, the inspector makes an amended assessment. A *determination* is made, under self-assessment, where there is a failure to submit a return within the time limits discussed above. The Revenue must serve a notice of assessment on the person it has assessed: TMA 1970, s. 30A(3). Once served, the assessment must not be adjusted, except as a result of an appeal: TMA 1970, s. 30A(4). An assessment cannot generally be made later than five years after the 31 January next following the tax year to which it relates: TMA 1970, s. 34(1)(a).

A tax inspector makes an assessment on Wilfred, on 12 September 2012, in relation to the tax year 1998/99. Is the assessment out of time?

Yes.

This rule is subject to two important *exceptions*:

■ The time limitation does not apply where there has been *fraudulent or negligent conduct* by the individual taxpayer. In that situation, an assessment may be made up to 20 years after the 31 January next following the tax year to which it relates: TMA 1970, s. 36(1)(a).

■ PRs have the benefit of a shortened time period in relation to income of the deceased up to the deceased's death: see **7.6.2.1**. No assessment can generally be made on them beyond the period of three years beginning with 31 January next following the tax year of death (TMA 1970, s. 40), unless there has been fraudulent or negligent conduct.

Harold died on 5 September 1998. He has not committed fraudulent or negligent conduct. What is the latest date on which an assessment can be made on his PRs for income accruing to Harold during his lifetime?

31 January 2003. The tax year of death is 1998/99; the 31 January next following that tax year is 31 January 2000.

19.3.5.2 Claims for relief

Claims for relief are subject to a general time limit of five years and 10 months after the 5 April on which the tax year in relation to which they are claimed came to an end. However, some reliefs must be claimed within a *much shorter* period than this, including some income loss reliefs, e.g.:

■ *the personal reliefs* deducted at Stage Three and Stage Five of your income tax calculation must be claimed within the period of five years from 31 January next following the tax year under consideration: TMA 1970, s. 43(1); *and*

■ *carry across of trading losses* must be claimed within 12 months after the 31 January next following the end of the tax year under consideration: ICTA 1988, s. 380(1), (2).

Great care must therefore be taken, when considering reliefs, whether the relief actually needs to be claimed and, if so, the time period for claiming it. FA 1998 provides for an experimental scheme for *telephone claims* in Scotland: see FA 1998, s. 118.

19.3.6 PAYMENT OF INCOME TAX AND INTEREST ON LATE PAYMENT

19.3.6.1 Dates for payment of tax

Dates for payment of tax are determined by TMA 1970, s. 59A. When applicable, s. 59A obliges you to make *up-front* payments of income tax, i.e. *payments on account*, to the Revenue. This means making income tax payments for a tax year before that tax year has ended. However, TMA 1970, s. 59A does *not* apply to the tax year under consideration if, in the previous tax year:

- your whole income tax and NIC liability, less tax deducted at source or tax on dividends, was less than £500; *or*

- over 80% of the whole of the income tax and NICs paid by you for that tax year was deducted at source or credited as paid.

You are not therefore obliged to make payments on account for a tax year if, in the previous tax year, your payment of income tax was mainly by deduction of tax at source, or by being credited as paid at source, e.g. as for dividends (see **8.3.1**).

In the tax year 1997/98, Olive had Schedule E income of £50,000, Schedule F income of £5,000 (gross), and Schedule D, Case II income of £2,000. Will any payments of tax on account be due from her in 1998/99?

No.

However, if TMA 1970, s. 59A does apply to you, at least two equal payments on account, plus a possible third, will be required from you:

- the first will be due on the 31 January in the tax year under consideration;

- the second will be due on the 31 July immediately following the end of the tax year under consideration; and

- a possible third payment of tax will be due from you on the following 31 January. The amount of this third payment will be any difference between:

  A. The total income tax due, according to your self-assessment under TMA 1970, s. 9 for the tax year under consideration; *and*

  B. The total of any payments on account made by you in respect of that tax year, and any income tax which, in respect of that year, has been deducted at source.

(TMA 1970, s. 59B(1).)

This difference is due and payable on or before the 31 January after the tax year under consideration: TMA 1970, s. 59B(4). If the difference between A and B is a minus-figure, tax is repayable to the taxpayer on or before the same date: ICTA 1988, s. 59B(4). The level of the payments on account is based on the previous tax year. It can be reduced if you make a claim explaining fully the reason for the reduction.

SAQ 247

Sarah, a barrister, has income profits falling under Schedule D, Case II. For 1997/98, her Schedule D, Case II profits were £60,000. She is also a part-time lecturer, from which activity she received Schedule E income profits of £1,200 in that tax year. Will she be obliged to make payments on account in respect of the 1998/99 tax year?

Yes.

19.3.6.2   Interest on tax paid late

If you pay your total income tax due late, you will automatically be liable to pay interest on it. Payment can be made by cheque, or by electronic funds transfer. In the latter case, payment is treated as being made one working day after payment is received by the Revenue. In the former case, it is treated as being made on the day the Revenue receives it: TMA 1970, s. 70A. Interest is calculated from the so-called *relevant date*, to the actual date of payment. The actual date of payment is straightforward, on the basis of the two rules just described. Determining the *relevant date* is less straightforward, however, since it varies according to whether you are liable to make payments on account or not and, if you are, which of the payments on account is being made. If you *are not* liable to make payments on account, then the relevant date is 31 January following the end of the tax year under consideration. If you *are* liable to make payments on account, then the relevant dates are each of the dates for the payments on account listed above.

Interest is calculated in accordance with a specific formula, which is designed to make the interest rate on unpaid tax comparable with commercial rates of interest. Since there is no tax relief for such interest payments, the real cost of them is greater than it may at first appear.

SAQ 248

(Refer to SAQ 247.) If Sarah does not make the required payments on account, from when until when will interest run?

From each due date until the actual date of payment.

19.3.6.3   Postponement of payment of tax pending an appeal

If you are dissatisfied with an assessment or amendment to your self-assessment, you must notify the inspector within 30 days of the assessment that you intend to appeal and the amount of the tax which you consider to be excessive. If you fail to do this, you will have to pay the whole amount in exactly the same way as if there had been no appeal by you. You must either agree the amount of tax in dispute with the inspector or, failing this, have it determined by the Commissioners: TMA 1970, s. 55(5). Once there has been an agreement or a determination, the amount which is not in dispute is due and payable within 30 days after the agreement, or the Commissioners' decision as the case may be.

SAQ 249

Giles appeals against an assessment and agrees the amount of the assessment not in dispute on 1 November 1998. When will the undisputed amount be due and payable?

30 days after 1 November 1998.

19.3.7 COLLECTION OF INCOME TAX

19.3.7.1 Employees: PAYE

PAYE imposes a duty on your employer to deduct income tax from the emoluments of you, the employee, when the emoluments are paid to you. It applies to all income falling under Schedule E, including benefits in kind qualifying as *tradeable assets* and assets for which there are *trading arrangements*: ICTA 1988, ss. 203F-203L. PAYE is also applied to *cash vouchers, non-cash vouchers and credit-tokens*: see **Chapter 14**, Table B(2). It is not, however, applied to vouchers reimbursing you, the employee, for certain expenses.

ACTIVITY 40

Read *Re Selectmove* at *Cases and Materials* (19.1.3). Consider the lessons to be learnt from this case.

The PAYE system is a refined one, although it is not perfect. Each time your wages are paid to you, it aims to take account of the reliefs to which you are entitled. Codes indicate the reliefs to which you are entitled, e.g.:

L   personal relief;
H   personal relief and married couple's allowance/additional personal allowance, if you
     are a basic rate taxpayer; and
P   personal relief if you are 65 or above.

The employer is provided by the Revenue with the code number which applies to a particular employee. In addition, the employer must keep records of all deductions made from the employee's salary. Any adjustments needed at the end of the tax year, to collect more tax, can be made through the PAYE system in the next tax year.

ACTIVITY 41

Study the example payslip below, and read the extract from IR 34 at *Cases and Materials* (19.1.3). In the example, the figures have been replaced with letters. The employer's name is shown as Smith Company Ltd; the employee's name is shown as Mr K Black. Note how NICs are deducted along with income tax: see 19.6.

Smith Company Ltd Staff Payroll			Payslip No		Payroll	Employee Ref
Mr K Black			[A]		[B]	[C]
Location: Public Relations Department						
Pay and allowances	Deductions		Totals		Total Pay	
Salary [D]	Tax	[E]	Earnings to date	[F]	[G]	
	Nat Ins	[H]	Taxable pay to date	[I]	NON-TAXABLE PAY	
	Pension	[J]	Tax to date	[K]	nil	
			Pension to date	[L]		
			NICs to date	[M]		
					DEDUCTIONS	
					[N]	
					NET PAY	
					[O]	
			Date 20/9/98			
			Tax period 6			
	NICS Earnings Total:	[P]	Tax Code 376L		PAYDAY	
NI CAT D	NICsC/0	[Q]	NI No XXXXXX		20/9/98	

Consider the following points:

■ Whether Mr K Black is married or single.

■ Which is the gross Schedule E income figure for inclusion in his 1998/99 income tax calculation.

■ Why the tax period is shown as 6.

Note that, if Mr K Black calculates the total income tax due from him for 1998/99, as in **7.3**, the resulting figure will include the income tax already deducted under PAYE.

19.3.7.2 Payments to sub-contractors in the construction industry: deduction of basic rate tax

The Income and Corporation Taxes Act 1988, ss. 559-67 cover payments to sub-contractors in the construction industry. The provisions are considerably amended in FA 1998, with effect from August 1999. In specified circumstances, contractors must deduct basic rate income tax on making payments to sub-contractors, allowance being made for any direct cost of materials to any other person.

19.3.8 INCOME TAX PENALTIES

The Revenue can generally determine penalties, the penalised individual having a right of appeal to the Commissioners. The Commissioners also have jurisdiction to impose penalties themselves. When the Revenue determines a penalty, it will be due 30 days after the issue of the relevant penalty notice: TMA 1970, s. 100A(2). You have six months after the end of the tax year under consideration, in which to ask the Revenue to send you a return form, should you need to make a return: see **19.3.3.1**. Failure to do so makes you liable to pay a penalty. However, the penalty will only become due if you do not pay off the outstanding tax by the 31 January following the end of the tax year.

It is 10 October 1999. Fred, a barrister, has just finished his pupillage on 30 September 1999. Today, his clerk sent out the first fee note on his behalf. Fred has thus become liable to pay income tax in the 1999/2000 tax year. He has never received a tax return form from the Revenue, since all his income has been scholarship income: see 10.5.2. What should he do?

He should request a return form from the Revenue, to avoid any penalties.

In addition, if you fail to submit a return on time, see above, you will suffer an initial automatic penalty of £100, which will rise to £200 if the omission continues for six months after the filing date: TMA 1970, s. 93(4). If it then continues for a further six months (i.e. until a year has elapsed from the original date for submission), you could be liable to pay a penalty of anything up to the tax outstanding. On appeal against the penalty to the Commissioners, the penalty may be set aside (TMA 1970, s. 93(8)):

> . . . if it appears to them that, throughout the period of default, the taxpayer had a reasonable excuse for not delivering the return.

The penalty is confirmed if this does not appear to them to be the case. Finally, you must keep appropriate records, generally for up to six years, or suffer a penalty of up to £30,000. This requirement will generally be satisfied by taking copies of documents, and maintaining books, although the originals of, e.g. tax credits for dividends received, will be required: see **Activity 12**. There are various penalties for making negligent or fraudulent returns, as well as for failing to produce documents. In addition, you can be prosecuted, e.g. for perjury in making a false return, for falsifying accounts and for forgery.

19.3.9 APPEALS AGAINST INCOME TAX ASSESSMENTS/AMENDMENTS TO SELF-ASSESSMENTS

Once you have appealed against an assessment, you may enter into a binding agreement with the inspector for the assessment to be:

- upheld without variation; *or*

- varied in a particular manner; *or*

- discharged; *or*

- cancelled.

Each possibility is provided for by TMA 1970, s. 54(1). By s. 54(2), you can change your mind and resile from the agreement within a 30-day period. It is important to remember, however, that the inspector is under no obligation to reach an agreement with you. In the absence of such an agreement, the case goes to a hearing before either a panel of *General Commissioners*, or a single *Special Commissioner*: TMA 1970, s. 45. The full titles of these, as the case may be, are the Commissioners for the General Purposes or Special Purposes of the Income Tax. The latter are tax specialists of some distinction. The former, while generally not tax specialists, are local business people, able to bring commercial experience to bear on the cases before them. They are assisted in technical matters by a clerk, who is often a solicitor: TMA 1970, s. 3.

In theory, you have a choice as to whether to appeal to the General Commissioners or the Special Commissioners: TMA 1970, s. 46.

The procedure at the hearing is the same for both the General Commissioners and the Special Commissioners: TMA 1970, s. 48(1). It is governed by TMA 1970, s. 50(6):

> If, on an appeal, it appears to the majority of the Commissioners present at the hearing, by examination of the appellant on oath or affirmation, or by other evidence–
>
> . . .
>
> [that the appellant is overcharged by an amendment to a self-assessment or by an assessment]
>
> . . .
>
> the assessment or amounts shall be reduced accordingly, but otherwise the assessment . . . shall stand good.

SAQ 251

What strikes you about this wording, if anything?

It shows that the assessment is *presumed* to be correct unless the appellant demonstrates it to be wrong.

You, the appellant, may be represented by an accountant, a barrister or a solicitor. An inspector normally appears for the Revenue. Whilst the General Commissioners have no power to award costs in favour of one or other party, the Special Commissioners can award costs to either the appellant or the Revenue, where the other has acted *wholly unreasonably*. Any appeal from the Commissioners can only be on a question of law, not of fact: *Edwards* v *Bairstow and Harrison* [1955] 3 All ER 48. The dividing line between law and fact is notoriously difficult to draw, and it is perfectly possible for a clever advocate to disguise pure facts as a question of law. None the less, it is important to keep in mind that the higher court should not disturb the Commissioners' decision simply because it would have reached a different conclusion on the facts.

Within 30 days of the General Commissioners' decision, you must declare your written dissatisfaction with it, and require the Commissioners to 'state and sign a case for the opinion of the High Court'. The case will then go before a Chancery Division judge, from whom appeal lies to the Court of Appeal, and thence to the House of Lords. Appeal from decisions of the Special Commissioners is no longer by case stated, but by a more straightforward procedure, which merely requires the dissatisfied party to appeal on receipt of the Commissioners' written decision. The appeal would be heard by a Chancery Division judge, then by the Court of Appeal and finally by the House of Lords. There is a procedure for *leapfrogging* the Chancery Division, and going straight to the Court of Appeal.

ACTIVITY 42

Read the extract from the article by his Honour Judge Stephen Oliver QC, at *Cases and Materials* (19.1.4). Consider whether the present system of appeals is satisfactory on the basis of the criteria he suggests. (Judge Oliver is himself the presiding Special Commissioner.)

19.4   Corporation Tax

Like income tax, corporation tax is '. . . under the care and management of the Commissioners of Inland Revenue (. . . "the Board")': TMA 1970, s. 1(1). Many aspects of the compliance and appeal procedures are the same as for income tax: see **19.3**. For accounting periods which ended on or after 1 October 1993, the system of Pay and File applies. Pay and File uses self-assessment, and the company must pay any corporation tax not later than nine months after the end of the accounting period under consideration. This is the *due date* for corporation tax purposes, and interest will run from that date if the company has not paid its tax for that period. In addition, companies must complete and submit a tax return on Form CT200, which must be delivered to the Revenue within 12 months after the end of the accounting period under consideration. Audited accounts and calculations must be submitted with the return.

Failure to submit a return attracts penalties. If the company submits a return within 15 months after the end of the accounting period under consideration, the penalty is £100; within 18 months, and it is £200. Between eighteen months and two years, the penalties begin to get very serious, i.e. £200 plus 10% of tax unpaid, a percentage which rises to 20% if the return is submitted later even than 24 months.

SAQ 252

Cobalt Ltd's current accounting period ends on 30 November 1998. How long has it got to Pay and File, and how long has it got to submit its return?

It must pay its corporation tax by 31 August 1999; its return must be submitted by 30 November 1999.

For *large companies*, this system will change for accounting periods ending on or after 1 July 1999. As from that date, large companies will begin to pay corporation tax in four equal instalments every quarter. The instalments will be calculated on the basis of their anticipated corporation tax liability for the period. (For further details, refer to the article by Malcolm Gammie, at *Cases and Materials* (**8.1**).)

19.5   Value Added Tax

Under VATA 1994, sch. 1, a person *must* register for VAT if, at the end of any calendar month, the level of its taxable supplies for the previous 12-month period has exceeded £50,000. However, if that person can satisfy Customs that its taxable supplies for the next 12 months will *not* exceed £48,000, it is not obliged to register. A person *must* also register for VAT at any time if there are reasonable grounds for believing that the level of its taxable supplies in the following 30-day period will exceed £50,000. A person may register for VAT *voluntarily* if it makes taxable supplies in the course or furtherance of a business: VATA 1994, sch. 1, para. 9(a).

Why would a person wish to register voluntarily for VAT?

To be able to reclaim input VAT: see **10.6**.

VAT is generally accounted for on a quarterly basis, and Customs allocate the relevant quarterly periods on the trader's registration: see **4.3.4**. Customs send a blank form VAT 100 to the registered person towards the end of each quarterly period. It must be returned to Customs, together with the payment of the tax, not later than the end of the following month. It must be received by Customs before the end of the month after the end of each VAT quarter. Any excess of input tax over output tax, which gives rise to a repayment of VAT (see **10.6**), must be paid to the registered person within ten days of Customs receiving the return: VATA 1994, s. 83. VAT is notorious for the strength and variety of the penalties imposed for non-compliance.

Black Ltd's VAT quarters end on 31 March, 30 June, 30 September and 31 December. It is 26 January 1999. By what date must Customs have received the completed VAT return?

30 April 1999.

19.6   National Insurance Contributions

As an employed earner, the obligation to *collect* your primary Class 1 NICs is imposed on your employer, at the same time as income tax is collected under PAYE: SSCBA 1992, sch. 1, paras 3(1), 6(1): see **Activity 41**. If your employer is liable to pay Class 1A NICs (see **6.4**), then these are paid by your employer on the 19 July following the end of the tax year. Class 2 NICs are collected from self-employed earners mostly by direct debit, although quarterly billing is also possible. Class 4 NICs are collected by direct assessment, together with the total income tax due from the self-employed earner for the tax year under consideration. Contributions Agency inspectors monitor compliance, and have wide powers of enforcement. The Social Security Administration Act 1992, s. 114(1) imposes *criminal sanctions* for failure to collect NICs of Classes 1 and 4, whilst the income tax sanctions apply for non-payment or late payment of Class 2 NICs.

19.7   Summary

This chapter, which has concentrated on income tax, began with a discussion of the duties of tax inspectors and tax collectors. There was then a consideration of how the Revenue obtains its information, especially through the submission of tax returns. Although the income tax of many taxpayers is deducted at source, through PAYE, there are many more who are liable to pay it by direct assessment. For these, compliance can involve payments on account before the end of the tax year under consideration, plus interest and penalties for late payment. In relation to appeals, some of the tax bill appealed against must be paid as a condition of the appeal going forward, whilst on the appeal itself, the burden of proof on the appellant is high indeed. This completes our survey of income taxation. In **Chapter 20**, we begin our discussion of investment taxation.

19.8   End of Chapter Assessment Questions

Refer to the facts relating to Deborah: see **2.6**, **4.9(b)**, **5.6**, **8.9**, **9.6**, **14.6**, **15.9**, **16.8** and **18.9**.
Advise her:

 (a)   whether she is obliged to submit a tax return for 1998/99;

(20 marks.)

 (b)   the date by which it must be submitted; *and*

(20 marks.)

 (c)   whether there is any danger that she will have to make payments on account in
       1998/99.

(60 marks.)

(Assume that Deborah has elected to self-assess.)

(Word limit: 520.)

See *Cases and Materials* (**19.3**) for a specimen answer.

CHAPTER TWENTY

INVESTMENT TAXATION: INTRODUCTION AND SCOPE

20.1 Objectives

By the end of this chapter, you should be able to:

■ define the scope of the expression *investment taxation*;

■ relate your study of investment taxation to its *historical* and *political* context;

■ explain the scope of the term *capital profits*;

■ explain the scope of the term *capital losses*;

■ identify the two main types of *person* liable to pay investment taxation, i.e. the individual and the company;

■ identify the *capacities* in which an individual may be liable to pay investment taxation;

■ decide whether VAT is a form of investment taxation.

20.2 Introduction

At the heart of **Chapters 20** to **25** is one idea. That one idea is the taxation of a capital profit realised by a person on the sale of investment property. One definition of a sale is the transfer of property from one person to another for money. A good illustration of a capital profit realised by the sale of investment property would be a sale by me of a valuable painting, for say £100,000, which I originally acquired as an investment in 1985 for £10,000. Capital gains tax is the main form of investment taxation for individuals, and corporation tax on chargeable gains is its equivalent for companies. An important part of the discussion in this chapter is the problem of deciding when a profit attracts CGT or corporation tax on chargeable gains, and when it attracts income tax, or corporation tax on income. Another important part of the discussion is the conceptual similarity between an income loss, with which you are already familiar, and a capital loss, with which you are about to become familiar. You will need to think quite deeply about this similarity. You should appreciate generally that there are close similarities, as well as significant differences, between CGT and income tax, and their corporation tax equivalents.

20.3   Investment Taxation

20.3.1   FORMS OF INVESTMENT TAXATION

In **Chapters 20** to **25**, we shall be discussing three forms of investment taxation:

- CGT;

- corporation tax on chargeable gains; *and*

- stamp duty.

Stamp duty is a tax on some, although by no means all, legal documents. If a document which is used to give effect to a transaction falls within one of the categories of stampable documents in sch. 1 to the Stamp Act 1891, then duty is payable on that document, unless it is covered by an exemption or relief in the legislation. Two categories of stampable documents are particularly relevant to the discussion in this part of the book, i.e. *conveyances or transfers on sale* and *leases and agreements for leases*: Stamp Act 1891, sch. 1. These two categories will be discussed as the need to do so arises. For completeness, it should be mentioned that there is also *stamp duty reserve tax*, a kind of substitute stamp duty, which is chargeable on some share transactions where there is no stampable document. It is not considered further in this book. You may find the omission of VAT from the list somewhat surprising. However, for reasons which should become clear, I shall be arguing that VAT is not a form of investment taxation, at least not in the same way that it can be a form of income taxation: see **3.4.2**. That said, it is essential to be aware that a sale of investment property by a taxable person is likely to be a taxable supply for VAT purposes, and therefore subject to VAT: see *Cases and Materials* (8.3).

The expression *investment taxation* is used as a collective term for the three forms of taxation listed above. CGT, together with corporation tax on chargeable gains, will occupy most of our attention. Corporation tax on chargeable gains, which is the equivalent of CGT for companies, uses the rules of CGT, although with some important differences. References to CGT therefore include corporation tax on chargeable gains, unless indicated otherwise. Both taxes are payable by *chargeable persons* on *chargeable gains* produced by *chargeable disposals* of *chargeable assets*: see **3.3.1**. We shall be considering each of these four elements in **Chapter 21**. Only if all four are present in a particular case will there be a CGT charge.

As we mentioned in **1.4**, income tax was originally devised in reliance on the distinction between income and capital. It was thus almost inevitable for CGT to be as reliant on the concept of the capital profit, as for income tax to be reliant on the concept of an income profit. We therefore begin by revisiting the distinction between capital and income.

20.3.2   THE DISTINCTION BETWEEN CAPITAL AND INCOME

In **1.4**, we adopted an initial statement of the difference between income and capital. We then went on to contrast income profits with capital profits (i.e. investment profits), and discussed two basic tests for deciding whether a profit is an income one or a capital one.

ACTIVITY 43

Re-read **3.3.3, identifying the two tests discussed there for deciding whether a profit is an income profit or a capital profit.**

There are at least *two more tests* for answering the question of whether a particular profit is an income one or a capital one:

20.3.2.1   The analogy of the fruit and the tree

This draws on the distinction referred to in **3.3.3**, between *fixed capital* and *circulating capital*. In truth, it may not add much to that test. The tree represents the fixed capital, and the fruit represents the circulating capital. A profit on the sale of the former will be a capital one, and a profit on the sale of the latter, i.e. the fruit, will be an income one. The distinction between fixed and circulating capital was discussed by Viscount Haldane in *John Smith & Son* v *Moore* [1921] 2 AC 13.

Read the extract from Viscount Haldane's speech at *Cases and Materials* (20.1.1). Note *exactly* why the distinction between income and capital was important there (refer to 11.5.1.2).

20.3.2.2   Whether the consideration received is in the form of periodical payments

The fact that the price of property is paid in instalments may mean that the instalments count as a *stream of income* for the seller, rather than as instalments of capital: *IRC* v *Church Commissioners* [1976] 2 All ER 1037.

Read the extracts from Lord Wilberforce's speech in *IRC* v *Church Commissioners* (*Cases and Materials* (20.1.1)). Note the facts which Lord Wilberforce regarded as crucial in classifying the payments under the rentcharge as *income of the seller*.

In borderline cases, the status of a particular profit as income or capital will still be very difficult to determine. In *Strick* v *Regent Oil Co. Ltd* [1966] AC 295, Lord Upjohn said that

' . . . no part of our law of taxation presents such almost insoluble conundrums as the decision whether a receipt or outgoing is capital or income for tax purposes'.

20.4   Historical and Political Contexts

The taxation of capital profits is a sensitive political issue. Arguments about the role of CGT figured prominently in the debates conducted by the major parties before the May 1997 general election. Historically, the Labour Party has favoured investment taxation, whilst the Conservatives have opposed it. The election of the current Labour Government has heralded significant reforms to CGT. In his July 1997 Budget Speech, Chancellor Gordon Brown announced a consultation process on the taxation of capital profits, with a view to strengthening CGT, rather than abolishing it. The consultation process (to which the Government received only 171 replies) has culminated in the considerable changes to CGT law introduced by FA 1998. The basic idea of the changes is to encourage long-term investment, especially entrepreneurial investment, by taxing sales of investment property held for a long time more favourably than property held for only a short time.

Capital gains tax was introduced by a Labour Government in 1965. Its aim was to correct a perceived anomaly in tax law, which had previously existed. This was the fact that income profits, largely obtained by individual effort, were taxed, but profits arising on the sale of investment property were not. The issues raised by the point were central to Chancellor James Callaghan's Budget Speech introducing the tax: *Cases and Materials* (**3.2.1**). Although subsequent Conservative Governments have reluctantly allowed CGT to continue in existence, it is perceived by many Conservatives simply as a disincentive to investment. In his 1995 Budget Speech, Chancellor Kenneth Clarke explained the aim of Conservative policy under the last Government:

> Investment is important for prosperity. Investment depends on capital. We want to reduce taxes on capital to encourage and reward the investment that the millions of people who work for private businesses depend on. We remain committed to abolishing capital gains tax when resources allow.

He stated a similar aim in his 1996 Budget speech and, in doing so, reflected more than a political or economic ideal. The words 'when resources allow' in the quotation betray even the Conservative Chancellor's concern over the loss to the Treasury that a simple abolition of CGT would produce. This is because CGT acts as a *'book-end tax'*. It does so because, historically, the exploitation of the distinction between income and capital has been used to greater effect than any other tax avoidance device: see **3.3.2**. Abolish CGT, and many sales cease to be subject to direct taxation at all. So long as CGT is retained, it will offer the Revenue the possibility of taxing a profit that is not subject to income tax or corporation tax on income.

In 1965, Chancellor James Callaghan did not originally envisage that CGT would be a high-yield tax and this is borne out by published figures. These show that, in the 1993/94 tax year, e.g., income tax cost 2.44p per £ to collect, whilst CGT cost 5.90p per £ to collect.

Refer to 1.5.5. What would Adam Smith have had to say about CGT?

It violates the economy principle.

Although the *abolition* of CGT would appear to be off the present political agenda, it is a good idea to be aware of the outline of the cases both for, and against, its abolition.

20.5 *Capital Profits* and *Capital Losses*

These two terms share a common idea. Capital gains tax and corporation tax on chargeable gains are charged on capital profits, i.e. investment profits. *Profit* is a highly specific concept in the context of capital profits.

20.5.1 CAPITAL PROFITS

Capital profits can come from sales of a wide range of investment property, e.g. from:

- land or land and buildings;

- capital assets used in carrying on a trade;

- capital assets used in carrying on a profession or vocation; and

- shareholdings.

Note that this list corresponds closely to the sources from which income profits could come: see **2.3.1**. Note also that it is an inclusive, not an exhaustive, list. In relation to this first point, income profits can be thought of as being made from owning investment property over a period of time, whilst capital profits can be thought of as arising on the eventual sale of that property. This is a useful way of thinking about the distinction between income profits and capital profits, although it does not always provide a correct analysis. We can illustrate this by reference to builders. If you refer to **12.4.1**, where we discussed the acquisition of an industrial building from a builder, we said that a builder is a person who carries on the trade of building. Income profits of the builder are therefore derived from sales of property. Because those sales are in the course of a trade, however, profits made from them are treated as income profits, rather than as capital ones.

As to the second point, the reason why the above is not an exhaustive list is that, for CGT purposes, property is conceived of as being very wide-ranging in scope. CGT law uses the concept of the *chargeable asset*: see **21.3.4**. In fact, the term is so wide-ranging that it includes property which does not normally generate an income.

What would be examples of valuable non-income-generating property?

A valuable oil-painting, or a Ming vase.

(Even here, however, bear in mind that, for the same reason that a builder is carrying on a trade, so also is an art dealer or an antiques dealer: see **SAQ 13**.)

In relation to both CGT and corporation tax on chargeable gains, a person is taxed, not on the proceeds of sale as such, but on their capital (or investment) *profits*. For instance, say I own a valuable painting, which I bought in 1986. Capital gains tax provides, in essence, that I will be taxed on the difference between its sale proceeds and its acquisition cost, provided that the difference represents a profit, i.e. is a positive figure.

SAQ 257

I own a painting by Turner. I sell it for £150,000. It cost me £75,000 in 1986. My *capital profit* is therefore £75,000, i.e. the difference between the two. The difference is a positive figure.

On which amount will I pay CGT, £150,000 or £75,000?

£75,000.

This conclusion is, however, subject to two *major* qualifications:

■ Precise CGT rules tell me exactly how to calculate the figures for the proceeds of sale and my acquisition cost. The total acquisition cost of property is referred to as its *base cost*: see **21.4**.

Equally, I may be deemed to have received sale proceeds of the market value of the property when I dispose of it, even though I have *not* actually received such an amount: see **27.5**.

■ Subject to certain exceptions, I cannot include any revenue, i.e. income, item in my acquisition cost. That is why I *can* include the cost of *enhancing the value of the property*, but *not* the cost of repairs. Repairs are an income expense, e.g. see **11.4**.

The term *capital profit* or *investment profit* is therefore always used in tax law in the sense of the proceeds, less the deductions which you are allowed to make from those proceeds, under the relevant statutory rules. You may like to think of the base cost, in the CGT context, as being the equivalent of *allowable deductions* in the context of income tax. We shall be considering the base cost of property in **21.4**. The Taxation of Chargeable Gains Act 1992, s. 38(1) uses the language of 'allowable deductions'.

All this should be relatively straightforward, and I would like to draw your attention to three other points:

■ First, the terms *capital profits* and *investment profits* are interchangeable.

■ Secondly, say I lent you £10,000 in 1984. If I charged you interest on it, that would have fallen under Schedule D, Case III in calculating the total income tax due for every tax year since then. However, the value of the principal amount of the debt, i.e. £10,000, would have fallen *in real terms*. CGT gives me no relief for this fall in value, unless the principal amount of the debt falls within certain very tightly-restricted categories, to be considered in **24.7**.

■ Thirdly, just as I may have a pure income profit for income tax purposes, I may have a pure capital profit for CGT purposes, i.e. a 100% gain.

In relation to the third point, consider the following example. Suppose I am a dairy farmer. I decide to sell some milk quota, which I originally acquired free of charge, on its allocation to me by the Government in 1984. A milk quota is essentially a licence to produce milk up to a certain level, which dairy farmers need under directives implementing the Common Agricultural Policy of the EU. For CGT purposes, it counts as investment property, i.e. as a chargeable asset, in its own right: *Cottle* v *Coldicott* [1995] STC (SCD) 239.

Albert, a dairy farmer, sells his milk quota. How will the gain on the sale of the *milk quota* be different from any gain on the sale of other property he may own?

It will be 100% pure capital profit.

Whilst recognising that milk quota has no base cost at all, you should note that there are a number of situations where, although property does not seem to have a base cost, it *does* do so because of *special rules*. For instance, as a beneficiary of the estate of a deceased individual, the base cost of a legacy is deemed to be its open market value at the date of the deceased's death: see **27.6.2**.

Is any profit on a sale by you, the beneficiary, a pure capital profit for CGT purposes?

No. The property sold has a base cost of the market value of the property at the date of the deceased's death.

Bill inherited an antique cabinet from his grandfather, Alonzo, on the latter's death in 1993. At the date of the death, the cabinet was worth £20,000. On 1 September 1998, Bill sells the cabinet to Catherine for £60,000. On what amount will Bill be liable to pay CGT, £60,000 or £40,000?

£40,000. He is deemed to have acquired the cabinet for £20,000. (We shall return to this rule in **27.6.2**.)

20.5.2 CAPITAL LOSSES

Just as a capital profit could arise on any of the sales discussed above, so also could a capital loss. In relation to capital losses, CGT provides that, if the difference between the proceeds and the base cost of the property is a loss, i.e. a negative figure, then I am not liable to pay CGT on that sale. The same point applies for the purpose of corporation tax on chargeable gains.

SAQ 261

As in SAQ 257, I own a valuable painting by Turner. I sell it for £75,000. It cost me £150,000 in 1986. My capital or investment *loss* is therefore £(75,000), i.e. the negative difference between the two. On which amount will I pay CGT?

I will not pay CGT on the sale at all, since I have made a *capital loss*.

This conclusion is, however, subject to one *major* qualification. Precise CGT rules tell me *exactly how* to calculate the figures for my proceeds and base cost, as above. I cannot therefore 'create' capital losses without satisfying these rules. The term capital loss is therefore always used in tax law in the sense of the negative figure produced by the proceeds, less the base cost, which is calculated according to specific rules. Again, this should be fairly straightforward, although the following related points need to be made. When you make a capital loss on the sale of a chargeable asset:

■ No figure is included in the CGT (or corporation tax on chargeable gains) calculation for the tax period in which it is realised.

■ Although the negative figure, i.e. the capital loss, *may* be available for use as a deduction in the same or another tax period, such use is subject to very strict rules. In particular, with one exception, a capital loss may not be deducted from income.

You are *prevented* from making a capital loss by giving property away, or selling it at an undervalue. Where you give property away, the CGT rules deem you to have sold it for its value on the *open market at the time of the gift*: TCGA 1992, s. 17. This fundamentally important point will be discussed in detail in **27.3.2**.

SAQ 262

Refer to 13.4.3.5. What is the exception to the rule that a capital loss may not be deducted from income?

The Income and Corporation Taxes Act 1988, s. 574 (income tax relief for investments in small trading companies).

(Relief under ICTA 1988, s. 574, is subject to extremely tight restrictions.)

20.6   Persons and Capacities

20.6.1   PERSONS

20.6.1.1   Individuals

For individuals, it is the sale of investment property at a profit which is the essence of liability to pay CGT. Note, however, that even if you *give property away*, you are deemed to have received its market value: see **27.3.2**.

SAQ 263

Refer to SAQ 16. On 1 November 1998, the current tenancy terminates, and you sell the cottage. You acquired it in 1982 for £10,000, and you sell it for £100,000. What is your capital profit on the sale?

£90,000, i.e. £100,000 − £10,000.

You are liable to pay CGT on your capital profits in the tax year under consideration, provided you are *resident* or *ordinarily resident* in the UK in that tax year: see **4.5**. It is irrelevant whether the property sold is located in the UK or overseas: TCGA 1992, s. 2(1). As a foreign taxpayer, you are liable to pay CGT as discussed in **21.3.2.1**.

20.6.1.2 Companies

A company can generate a capital profit, just like an individual, by selling investment property.

SAQ 264

Refer to SAQ 19. Imagine that Alexander Ltd sells the houses previously let out to students on the termination of the tenancies. Who will receive any capital profit on the sale?

Alexander Ltd. The directors may decide to pay the profit out to the shareholders, as a dividend.

Refer to **16.6.1**. Remember that, when dividends are paid by a company to its shareholders, there is an element of double income taxation, despite the imputation system. Capital profits cause an even greater degree of double taxation, when they are retained in the company, rather than paid out as dividends to shareholders. Consider the tax position of a shareholder in Alexander Ltd, e.g. Ben: see **SAQ 20**. If Alexander Ltd sells the houses at a profit, it will pay corporation tax on chargeable gains at 21% of that profit, assuming that Alexander Ltd qualifies for the small companies rate. Additionally, as a shareholder, Ben may still be liable to pay CGT on a profitable sale of *his shares in Alexander Ltd*. Say the capital profit realised by Alexander Ltd, on the sale of the houses, is £500,000. Before tax, the value of Ben's shareholding will have increased by £125,000 (i.e. £500,000/4). Alexander Ltd will be liable to pay corporation tax at 21% on the £500,000 gain, i.e. £105,000. Of that tax,   of the cost of paying it will be borne by Ben, as one of the four shareholders, i.e. £26,250. After tax, Ben's shareholding will therefore have increased in value by £98,750 (i.e. £125,000 − £26,250).

SAQ 265

Suppose Ben sells the shares, realising a chargeable gain of £98,750, on which he pays CGT at 40%. What percentage of tax will the gain have incurred?

52.6%. CGT of 40% × £98,750 = £39,500 is paid by Ben. Corporation tax of 21%, i.e. £26,250, is paid by the company.

% at which gain taxed = $\frac{65,750}{125,000}$ × 100 = 52.6% effective rate of tax.

ACTIVITY 46

Using the above figures, try to work out why the effective rate of tax would be as high as 58.6%, in the case where Alexander Ltd did not qualify for the small companies rate (e.g. on the basis that it is a CIC: see 18.5.1.3).

UK companies (see **5.3.2.1**) are liable to pay corporation tax on chargeable gains, on any capital profits realised in an accounting period. It is irrelevant whether these capital profits have a source in the UK or overseas: ICTA 1988, ss. 6(4), 8(1): see **4.3** and **4.5**. An overseas company is liable to pay corporation tax on chargeable gains in the circumstances discussed in **21.3.2.2**.

20.6.2 CAPACITIES

You, the individual, could realise a capital profit either in your own personal capacity or in one of a number of other capacities.

20.6.2.1 Partners

The rules under which CGT is charged on the capital profits of partners involve dividing-up the investment profits of the partnership on the sale of *partnership property*.

This division may be in accordance with the *profit-sharing ratio* agreed between the partners, or it may be according to an *asset surplus entitlement*. An *asset surplus entitlement* is designed to reflect the proportions in which the partners have contributed to the capital assets of the business carried on by the partnership.

Ping, Pang and Pong are in partnership as solicitors. Under the partnership agreement, the asset surplus entitlement is in the proportions 1:2:3. The partners sell office premises, i.e. partnership property, on 20 November 1998, for £400,000. The premises were acquired by them in 1982 for £100,000. What is the partners' capital profit?

On what amount will each of them be liable to pay CGT?

£300,000, i.e. £400,000 − £100,000. This will be divided-up in the proportions 1: 2: 3, i.e.:

Ping   £50,000;
Pang   £100,000; *and*
Pong   £150,000.

There are few, if any, statutory provisions concerning the CGT position of partners and partnerships. Instead, there are three SPs: D12, 1/79 and 1/89. This dearth of regulation is surprising, since partners and partnerships can give rise to very complex CGT issues indeed.

Read quickly through the article on the CGT treatment of partners by Tim Good, at *Cases and Materials* (20.2.1.1). (Some of the material discussed there relates to the taxation of gratuitous transfers.)

20.6.2.2 Trustees

Trustees receive any capital profits generated by the sale of trust property for the beneficiaries. As a trustee, you may sell trust property if authorised to do so by the trust instrument or the general law.

Whether the trustees or the beneficiaries are liable to pay CGT on capital profits of the trust involves asking a question similar to that of whether the beneficiaries have an immediate entitlement to the income of the trust property: see **2.4.2.2**. With capital profits, however, the question is whether the property sold is *settled property* or not. If the trust property is not settled property, then it will be held by the trustees simply as *nominees* or *bare trustees*. If it is settled property, the trustees will be liable to pay any CGT on the sale of trust property. If, by contrast, it is held by the trustees simply as nominees or bare trustees, the *beneficiaries* will be liable to pay any CGT on the sale.

The question of whether property is settled property or not is answered by reference to TCGA 1992, s. 68, read with TCGA 1992, s. 60. Section 68 defines settled property as follows:

'Settled property' means any property held in trust *other than* property to which section 60 applies. [*Emphasis added.*]

Section 60(1) is set out in *Cases and Materials* (**20.2.1.2**).

Read TCGA 1992, s. 60(1) very closely indeed, especially the words in brackets.

I have asked you to read s. 60(1) very closely, because it is important to appreciate the significance of every word of it. It means, most importantly, that property may be held in trust, without being *settled property*. We develop this point in **Chapter 27**.

Property is held on trust by you and me, as trustees, for Anne for life, with remainder to Belinda absolutely. Anne is 30 and Belinda is 40. Is the property settled property for CGT purposes?

Yes. Anne and Belinda are not *jointly absolutely entitled*, as they are required to be if the property is *not* to be settled property: *Kidson* v *MacDonald* [1974] 1 All ER 849, *Booth* v *Ellard* [1980] 3 All ER 569. (A trusts lawyer, as opposed to a trusts-and-tax lawyer, would probably say that Anne and Belinda *were* jointly absolutely entitled.)

We return to the meaning of 'settled property' for CGT purposes in **27.4.1.1**.

You hold shares in Megabucks plc on trust for Charles, aged 20, absolutely. Are the shares settled property?

No. Charles can bring the trust to an end at any time, under the rule in *Saunders* v *Vautier* (1841) 49 ER 282.

20.6.2.3   Personal representatives

Any CGT liability of the PRs for the capital profits of the estate must be considered separately from the personal CGT position of the individuals acting as PRs. As a PR, if you sell property in the estate, any capital profit will basically be any positive difference between the market value of the property at the date of the deceased's death, and the proceeds of sale: TCGA 1992, s. 62(1)(a), and see **27.6.2**.

Daniel, who died on 20 May 1998, owned shares in Megabucks plc, worth £20,000 at his death. You are his executor, and you sell the shares when they are worth £30,000. On what amount will you, in your capacity as a PR, pay CGT?

£10,000, i.e. £30,000 − £20,000.

20.7   Value Added Tax: a Form of Investment Taxation?

In **Chapter 3** we concluded, somewhat controversially, that VAT could be a form of income taxation for persons who do not have a full right of input VAT deduction, and who obtain no income tax or corporation tax deduction for irrecoverable VAT: see **3.4.2**. However, VAT can only be thought of as a form of investment taxation with considerable qualification. This is because, as we shall discover in **21.4**, input VAT for which a person does not have a full right of input VAT deduction *can* generally be taken into account in calculating a capital profit. This is not true for income tax and corporation tax on income, unless the input VAT for which no right of deduction is available qualifies as an allowable deduction under Schedule D, Case I or II, or Schedule A: see **3.4.2**, **11.5.1.3**. That said, every time a taxable person sells investment property, the VAT implications will need to be considered. It is *unimportant* for VAT purposes whether the consideration for a taxable supply is a capital receipt or an income receipt of the seller, i.e. the supplier. All that matters is whether there is a *taxable supply*. The seller must charge output VAT, where necessary, on the sale of investment property. The buyer must decide whether any right of input VAT deduction is available to it. For these reasons, there is very little to be added, in **Chapters 20** to **25** in relation to VAT. The relevant rules were discussed in **Chapters 1** to **19**.

20.8   Stamp Duty as a Form of Investment Taxation

Stamp duty is almost always paid by the purchaser, rather than the seller. It therefore presents an analytical problem similar to VAT. As we shall discover in **21.4**, stamp duty *can* be taken into account in calculating a capital profit. Like non-deductible input VAT, it can only be thought of as a form of investment taxation subject to considerable qualification. That said, many sales, e.g. sales of land or shares, will need to be effected using stampable documents, so stamp duty will be a relevant concern for purchasers. Equally, many other sales will not require a stampable document.

20.9   Summary

Capital gains tax, together with corporation tax on chargeable gains, is the most important form of investment taxation. References to CGT include corporation tax on chargeable gains, unless the context indicates otherwise. Subject to the rules to be discussed in the following chapters, the seller of investment property will be liable to pay CGT on any capital profit. In addition to the permanent structure test and the fixed capital test, the analogy of the fruit and the tree, and whether the consideration received is paid periodically or not, are useful for verifying that a profit is indeed a capital profit. A capital profit is not necessarily the full amount received by the seller. Precise CGT rules provide for the calculation of the base cost of investment property. A gift of investment property is deemed to be made in return for its market value at the time. Specifically, a gift of investment property does not generate a capital loss. A capital loss occurs only where the base cost of investment property exceeds its actual or deemed sale proceeds. Individuals resident and ordinarily resident in the UK in a tax year are liable to pay CGT on all their capital profits, irrespective of where the property sold is located. UK companies are liable to pay corporation tax under a similar rule. Capital profits (and losses) on the sale of partnership property are divided between partners according to their profit-sharing ratio or asset surplus entitlement. Trustees are liable to pay CGT on sales of settled property. Where trust property is not settled property, the beneficiaries are liable to pay CGT on any capital profit realised by its sale. Capital profits on the sale by PRs of investment property in a deceased's estate are calculated on the difference between the market value of the property at the death and the proceeds of its sale.

CHAPTER TWENTY-ONE

INVESTMENT TAXATION: LIABILITY AND CALCULATION

21.1 Objectives

By the end of this chapter, you should be able to:

■ list the *elements necessary* for liability to pay CGT to arise;

■ calculate the *CGT due from you* for any tax year;

■ describe the *differences* between your CGT calculation in your personal capacity, and in the capacity of a trustee or PR;

■ explain the significance of *allowable losses* for CGT purposes;

■ calculate the *ad valorem* stamp duty payable on a conveyance or transfer on sale of *shares* or *land*.

21.2 Introduction

In **Chapter 20**, we described CGT as being charged on a capital profit realised by a person on the sale of investment property. The first part of this chapter is devoted to a detailed consideration of the four elements necessary for a CGT charge to arise. Briefly, there must be a chargeable gain realised by a chargeable person on the chargeable disposal of a chargeable asset. Significantly, we shall discover that the concept of a chargeable disposal can include transactions other than sales, most importantly gifts. The discussion of gifts begins in **Chapter 26**, although other disposals which are not sales are considered here. In the second part of the chapter, we consider the calculation of the CGT due from an individual, including an individual calculating it in the capacity of a partner, a trustee or a PR. The shape of each of the CGT calculations has undergone considerable changes as a result of FA 1998, which has, however, left untouched the calculation of the chargeable gains of a company. Changes to the calculation of the chargeable gains of companies could therefore form part of future FAs.

21.3 Liability to Pay CGT and Corporation Tax on Chargeable Gains

21.3.1 THE FOUR ELEMENTS

Not all capital profits realised on the sale of investment property attract a CGT liability. A CGT liability arises only when:

■   a chargeable person

■   makes a chargeable disposal

■   of a chargeable asset

■   and there is a gain as a result.

If, for any reason, any of the four elements is missing, there is no CGT on the capital profit. The Taxation of Chargeable Gains Act 1992, s. 15(2) provides that *every gain is a chargeable gain*, unless otherwise expressly provided. We now need to consider each of the four elements in detail.

21.3.2   A CHARGEABLE PERSON

21.3.2.1   Individuals

The general rule is as follows. You are liable to pay CGT on your chargeable gains arising anywhere in the world during a tax year, *provided that* you are either resident *or* ordinarily resident in the UK in that tax year: TCGA 1992, s. 2(1), see **4.5**. It follows that, if you are *neither* resident *nor* ordinarily resident in the UK in the tax year, then you are not liable to pay CGT on your chargeable gains, even if they arise on chargeable disposals of chargeable assets located in the UK. There are *three exceptions* to this rule. In the tax year under consideration:

(a)   If you are resident or ordinarily resident, but *not* domiciled in the UK, you are liable to pay CGT on any chargeable gains only if those gains are remitted to the UK. The Taxation of Chargeable Gains Act 1992, s. 275 contains the rules on the location of assets.

(b)   If you are *neither* resident *nor* ordinarily resident in the UK in the tax year under consideration, you are still liable to pay CGT on any chargeable gain from the disposal of a chargeable asset used in a trade, profession or vocation carried on in the UK through a branch or agency: TCGA 1992, s. 10.

(c)   If you are resident or ordinarily resident in the UK, and the chargeable gain is made on the disposal of assets located overseas which cannot be remitted to the UK because of local restrictions, you will be liable to pay CGT on that chargeable gain only if the restrictions cease: TCGA 1992, s. 279.

(a)   **Albrecht, a German lawyer, is *neither* resident *nor* ordinarily resident in the UK in 1998/99. He has a branch office in London, and sells the office premises.**

(b)   **Jan is resident, *but not domiciled*, in the UK in 1998/99. He makes a chargeable gain on the chargeable disposal of a house in Holland, leaving the sale proceeds in a bank account there.**

(c)   **Andrew, resident in the UK in 1998/99, makes a chargeable gain on the disposal of a holiday villa in Ruritania. Ruritanian exchange control legislation forbids the return of the money to the UK.**

Which of the three is liable to pay CGT on their gain for 1998/99?

Albrecht only. Exceptions mentioned above apply for (b) and (c).

21.3.2.2   Companies

A UK company (see **5.3.2.1**) is liable to pay corporation tax on its chargeable gains, wherever they arise. An overseas company is liable to pay corporation tax on chargeable gains on any chargeable gain arising from the chargeable disposal of a chargeable asset used in a trade, profession or vocation carried on in the UK through a branch or agency: TCGA 1992, s. 10.

Pierre SA, a trading company resident in France, has a branch in the UK. It sells its UK premises, realising a chargeable gain of £100,000. Is Pierre SA liable to pay CGT on the gain?

Yes.

The provisions designed to prevent manipulation of the residence rules, so as to remove the chargeable person element, are discussed in **25.3.1**.

21.3.3   MAKES A CHARGEABLE DISPOSAL

21.3.3.1   Disposals of the whole

The Taxation of Chargeable Gains Act 1992 does not define the term *disposal*. Given its ordinary meaning, a disposal includes sales, exchanges and gifts. Until **Chapter 26**, we are only concerned with sales and exchanges. The ordinary meaning of the word is extended by TCGA 1992 to include transactions other than these, however. That said, it does *not* include an *issue* of shares by a company, although it *does* include a *sale* of shares: see **2.4.1.2**. A key point is that death is *not* a disposal for CGT purposes: see **27.6.2**.

Douglas sells his valuable stamp collection to Edward for £15,000. Has he made a disposal of the collection for CGT purposes?

Yes.

There are special rules in TCGA 1992, s. 28, for determining the *time* at which an asset is disposed of:

■ Where a contract of sale is *not* a conditional one, the disposal takes place at the date of the contract, not completion. If completion never takes place, then an adjustment of tax is made: TCGA 1992, s. 28(1).

■ Where a contract of sale is a conditional one, i.e. subject to a condition precedent to liability under the contract, rather than to completion under it, the disposal takes place on satisfaction of that condition: TCGA 1992, s. 28(2).

■ Where the condition to which a contract of sale is subject is the exercise of an option, the disposal takes place when the option is exercised: TCGA 1992, s. 28(2).

■ Where there is a compulsory acquisition of land by a local authority, the disposal by the landowner takes place when the parties agree the level of compensation or, if earlier, when the local authority enters the land.

Farmer Brown agrees to sell Greenacre to Charlotte for £20,000 on 30 July 1998. Charlotte wishes to build a cottage on it, and the contract is therefore subject to a condition precedent that planning permission is obtained. The condition is satisfied on 21 October 1998. At what date will Farmer Brown be deemed to have disposed of the property?

21 October 1998.

21.3.3.2   Disposals where a capital sum is derived from an asset: TCGA 1992, s. 22(1)

If the owner of a chargeable asset derives a capital sum from it, there is deemed to be a disposal of the asset by the owner. This is unaffected by the fact that the person *paying* the capital sum may not acquire an asset: TCGA 1992, s. 22(1); see *Cases and Materials* (**21.1.1**). A problem arose in *Zim Properties* v *Proctor* [1985] STC 90. That case was concerned with whether there was a capital sum derived from an asset, where a firm of solicitors had been sued for negligence, and an out-of-court settlement had been agreed of £69,000. The question was whether the £69,000 was a *capital sum derived from an asset* within TCGA 1992, s. 22(1). Warner J held that it was. The £69,000 was derived from the plaintiff's right of action in negligence against the firm of solicitors. One implication of this is that such a sum must be grossed-up, if the plaintiff is not to be out-of-pocket. The Revenue have since indicated in ESC D33 that there will be no capital sum derived from an asset in the circumstances discussed in the ESC.

Although TCGA 1992, s. 22(1) covers every legal right which can be turned to account by the payment of a capital sum, four particular examples are given in TCGA 1992, s. 22(1). These are:

■ where a person receives a capital sum by way of compensation for damage to, or the loss, destruction or dissipation of an asset;

■ where a person receives a capital sum under an insurance policy for damage to, or loss of, an asset;

■ where a person receives a capital sum in return for the forfeiture or surrender of rights; and

■ where a person receives a capital sum as consideration for the use or exploitation of assets.

In each of these cases, the disponer (i.e. the person making the disposal) is treated as making the disposal when the capital sum is received by it: TCGA 1992, s. 22(2).

ACTIVITY 49

Read the extract from the article by Jeremy de Souza, at *Cases and Materials* (21.1.1), followed by the extract from the judgment of Rattee J in *Chaloner* v *Pellipar Investments* [1996] STC 234. Summarise the question concerning TCGA 1992, s. 22(1)(d) in the case, and Rattee J's answer to it.

In relation to the first two possibilities (TCGA 1992, s. 22(1)(a) and (b)), the disponer can elect *not* to make a disposal or part-disposal, where the asset has not been totally destroyed or lost. As a result of such an election, the disponer is permitted to postpone any CGT by deducting the compensation/insurance money from the base cost of the chargeable asset in question: TCGA 1992, s. 23, ESC D19. This election depends on one of three conditions being satisfied:

■ the asset is not a wasting asset (see **22.4.2**); *or*

■ the compensation money is either:

    (a)   wholly applied in restoring the asset; *or*

    (b)   at least 95% of the compensation money is so applied; *or*

■ the capital sum received is small in relation to the value of the asset.

SAQ 274

On 23 November 1998, Farmer Brown's barn is damaged in a storm. Its base cost is £40,000, and its open market value at the time the damage occurs is £60,000. He receives £16,000 in insurance money, which he applies in repairing the barn. What happens, in CGT terms, if he makes an election under TCGA 1992, s. 23 (i.e. for the disposal to be ignored)?

He is permitted to postpone CGT by deducting the insurance money from the base cost of the barn, the barn's base cost becoming £24,000.

Note:

    (a)   the effect of the deduction counting as part of the base cost: see **21.4**; and

    (b)   how the s. 23 election relates to the *part-disposal rules*: see **21.3.3.3**.

21.3.3.3   Part-disposals: TCGA 1992, s. 42

These occur when a chargeable person disposes of less than the whole of an asset, or less than the whole of its interest in an asset. In such circumstances, it is necessary to work out the *base cost of the part you have sold*. This is done by using the following formula (TCGA 1992, s. 42(2)):

$$\text{Base cost of whole asset} \times \frac{\text{Proceeds of part sold}}{\text{Proceeds of part sold} + \text{Market value of retained part}}$$

SAQ 275

You own the freehold title to three fields, Whiteacres, Blackacres and Greenacres, all of six acres. You acquired them together, on 1 February 1988, for £40,000. You sell Greenacres for £15,000 on 30 November 1998, when the remaining two fields are worth £50,000. What is the base cost of Greenacres?

£9,231, i.e.:

$$£40,000 \times \frac{£15,000}{£15,000 + £50,000} = £9,231$$

Note that, where the consideration received by the disponer is 20% or less of the value of the whole, you can elect to postpone a CGT charge by deducting the proceeds of sale from the base cost of the whole asset.

The formula in TCGA 1992, s. 42(2) is also relevant where a capital sum is derived from an asset under TCGA 1992, s. 22: see **21.3.3.2**. When the disponer receives compensation or insurance money, but does not use all of it to restore the asset, the disponer may be deemed to make a part disposal of the asset if the unused amount is not 'small'.

21.3.3.4   Disposals on the total loss or destruction of a chargeable asset: TCGA 1992, s. 24(1)

Say a person owns a chargeable asset, which is totally destroyed. The owner is uninsured and therefore receive no insurance money. Total loss or destruction of an asset is a disposal for CGT purposes. If the asset is tangible moveable property, you are deemed to have disposed of it for £6,000. The effect of this is to restrict your allowable loss relief for CGT purposes: below.

SAQ 276

You buy a valuable watch for £20,000, which you lose. The watch is uninsured. What will be the amount of the capital loss?

£(14,000), rather than £(20,000). You are deemed to have sold it for £6,000.

For the purposes of a deemed disposal in these circumstances buildings, and the land on which they are built, are deemed to be separate assets.

You pay £100,000 for the construction of a factory for use in your sole trade, on land that you already own. The factory burns down when uninsured. How much will the capital loss be?

£(100,000).

21.3.3.5 Disposals when chargeable assets become of negligible value: TCGA 1992, s. 24(2)

A person is deemed to make a disposal where it owns an asset which has become negligible in value. The mechanics of the disposal are that the owner is deemed to have disposed of the asset and immediately reacquired it at its market value.

What will this market value be?

Negligible.

(Negligible is interpreted by the Revenue as meaning considerably less than 5% of its value at 31 March 1982.)

Your shares in Nadir plc have ceased to be worth anything, the company having gone into insolvent liquidation on 1 January 1999. The market value of the shares on 31 March 1982 is £10,000. At what value are you deemed to have disposed of the shares?

Nil. Loss relief is discussed below.

21.3.3.6 Disposals when chargeable assets appropriated by traders to their trading stock: TCGA 1992, s. 161

Say you are a sole trader. You appropriate an asset in your stock-in-trade to your personal use. You are deemed to have received Schedule D, Case I income equal to its full market value, under the rule in *Sharkey* v *Wernher*: see **18.6.1**. The market value at that time will be the base cost of the asset for CGT purposes, on any future disposal of it. However, this might also happen the other way round. You might acquire a chargeable asset for your personal use, and *later* appropriate it to your trading stock. The appropriation counts as a disposal for CGT, and CGT is calculated on any positive difference in value between its value when you acquired the asset, and its value at the time of the appropriation. Under TCGA 1992, s. 161, however, you can elect to postpone a tax charge until you ultimately sell the asset. When you *do* sell it, you will be treated as receiving a Schedule D, Case I profit of any positive difference between its original acquisition cost and the sale proceeds. Section 161 applies to both individuals and companies. For income tax, the election must be made by 31 January after the end of the tax year in which ends the accounting period during which the appropriation was made. For corporation tax, it must be made not later than two years after the end of the relevant accounting period: TCGA 1992, s. 161(3A).

21.3.4 OF A CHARGEABLE ASSET

A chargeable asset can be any form of property, unless the asset in question is specifically declared by the legislation to be an exempt asset. TCGA 1992, s. 21 provides:

> All forms of property shall be assets for the purposes of this Act . . . including:
> (a) options, debts and incorporeal property generally, and
> (b) any currency other than sterling, and
> (c) any form of property created by the person disposing of it, or otherwise coming to be owned without being acquired.

'Incorporeal property' is property having no material body or form. It is not necessary for the asset to be capable of being bought or sold. It can still be a chargeable asset: *O'Brien* v *Benson's Hosiery (Holdings) Ltd* [1979] 3 All ER 652.

ACTIVITY 50

Read the extract from the speech of Lord Russell of Killowen in *O'Brien* v *Benson's Hosiery*, at *Cases and Materials* (21.1.2). Ask yourself why Lord Russell was persuaded that the Revenue's argument was correct.

Another illustration of the scope of the concept of the chargeable asset is *Marren* v *Ingles* [1980] 3 All ER 95. The shareholders in JL Ingles (Holdings) Ltd sold their shares to a purchaser called ICFC under an agreement which contained an earn-out provision, summarised in Lord Wilberforce's speech as follows:

> By a contract of 15 September 1970 the taxpayer, as one of several vendors, agreed to sell to . . . ICFC . . . 69 shares in JL Ingles (Holdings) Ltd. For 41 of those shares ICFC agreed to pay a cash price of £1,500 per share. For the remaining 28 shares ICFC agreed to pay an immediate cash price of £750 per share plus a sum to be paid at a future date defined as 'half the profit'. This was to be one-half of the amount by which the sale price should exceed £750. The sale price was, broadly, to represent the middle market price on the first day of dealings after a flotation of the company, if a flotation should occur. Thus, for the 28 shares in question, there was a consideration consisting of (i) an immediate ascertained cash sum and (ii) *a conditional and unquantified amount payable at an unascertained future date*. [*Emphasis added*.]

Two years after the £750 per share was originally paid, the company obtained a Stock Exchange quotation.

The House of Lords held that the concept of a chargeable asset was wide enough to include the seller's right, acquired in 1970, to receive the unquantified amount, payable at the unascertained future date. The right to this amount was a chose in action, in itself a chargeable asset separate from the £750 per share actually paid in 1970. Acquired by the seller in 1970, the chose in action was ultimately disposed of by the seller when the company obtained its Stock Exchange quotation, since a capital sum was derived from an asset at that point: TCGA 1992, s. 22. The chose in action therefore formed part of the disposal proceeds in 1970, and its value in 1970 was its base cost for its disposal on the obtaining of the quotation.

Why does *Marren* v *Ingles* present problems for sellers?

The value of the chose in action when it is acquired, may be greater than it is when the chose is disposed of. It is small comfort to sellers that they may be able to claim an allowable loss on the subsequent disposal.

Chapter 24 is devoted to a detailed discussion of the problems presented by particular types of chargeable asset, and how the CGT rules attempt to solve them.

21.3.5   AND THERE IS A GAIN AS A RESULT

When a chargeable person makes a chargeable disposal of a chargeable asset, there will be a gain if the disposal proceeds exceed the base cost of the asset. Section 15(2) provides that this gain is a chargeable gain, unless otherwise expressly provided. Provisions exempting particular gains from CGT are discussed in **21.4** and **23.3**. If the *base cost* of the asset exceeds its disposal proceeds, there will be an *allowable loss*: see **21.8**. Certain statutory provisions restrict the amount of the allowable loss in particular cases.

21.4   Calculating the *CGT due* from an Individual

21.4.1   THE STAGES IN CALCULATING THE CGT DUE

This calculation has 10 Stages. Like the income tax calculation (see **7.3**), it is done for a particular tax year, e.g. 1998/99. In what follows, X represents a number. An X appearing in round brackets is to be deducted from the number represented by the X above it.

Stage One is to identify all *chargeable disposals* made by you in the tax year under consideration: see **21.3.3**.

Stage Two is to identify the *disposal proceeds* on each chargeable disposal. These may sometimes need to be quantified (e.g. in a *Marren* v *Ingles* case), and a figure will need to be agreed with the Revenue: see **21.3.3**. In other cases, such as absolute gifts and undervalue sales, the market value of the asset disposed of will have to be substituted for the actual sale proceeds: see **27.3.2, 27.5**.

Stage Three is to calculate the *base cost* of each chargeable asset disposed of. The Taxation of Chargeable Gains Act 1992, s. 38 specifies the items of expenditure which can be included in the base cost. For instance, you are not allowed to include the *notional* cost of any work done yourself (*Oram* v *Johnson* [1980] 2 All ER 1), although the cost is *not* notional where it represents a right foregone, and is quantifiable in money: *Chaney* v *Watkis* [1986] STC 89. If you have owned the chargeable asset disposed of since before 6 April 1965, you can choose whether it should be treated as having been acquired by you on 6 April 1965 or 31 March 1982: see **21.4.2**.

Read TCGA 1992, s. 38 at *Cases and Materials* (21.2). Paying close attention to its wording, try to formulate *eight* separate categories of expenditure which s. 38 allows you to include in the base cost of an asset.

Stage Four is to calculate the *unindexed chargeable gain* or *allowable loss* on each chargeable disposal. This is done by deducting the base cost(s) calculated in *Stage Three* from the figure(s) identified in Stage Two, in relation to *each* chargeable disposal. A memorandum is kept of any allowable losses, so that they can be relieved as discussed in **21.4.5** and **21.8**. Remember that there is an *allowable loss* when the base cost of a chargeable asset exceeds its disposal proceeds.

Stage Five is to deduct the *indexation allowance* (the IA) from the unindexed chargeable gain(s) calculated in Stage Four: TCGA 1992, s. 53(1). This gives the *indexed chargeable gain* for each chargeable disposal generating a chargeable gain. The IA, now frozen at April 1998, is discussed in **21.4.3**.

Stage Six is to total up the *indexed chargeable gain(s)*, to give the *gross chargeable gains* of the tax year. This is the first stage of the calculation itself:

Gross chargeable gains   X

Stage Seven is to deduct from the gross chargeable gains of the tax year any *allowable losses* from Stage Four above, or unused from any previous tax year not earlier than 1965/66: TCGA 1992, s. 2(2). This gives the *net chargeable gains* of the tax year.

Gross chargeable gains   X
Less Allowable losses   (X)

Net chargeable gains   X

Stage Eight is to deduct from the net chargeable gains of the tax year any *taper relief* to which you are entitled, to give your *tapered chargeable gains* of that year: TCGA 1992, s. 2A. *Taper relief* is discussed in **21.4.4**. It interacts with *allowable losses* in a specific way: see **21.4.5**.

Net chargeable gains   X
Less Taper relief   (X)

Tapered chargeable gains   X

Stage Nine is to deduct from your tapered chargeable gains your annual exempt amount, to give your *gains chargeable to CGT*. Your annual exempt amount is discussed in detail at **22.4.1**. For 1998/99, it is £6,800.

Tapered chargeable gains   X
Less Annual exempt amount   (X)

Gains chargeable to CGT   X

Stage Ten is to apply whichever of the CGT rates apply, to give the CGT due from you.

Gains chargeable to CGT   X

CGT due   X

Joining all these parts together, the layout of your specimen CGT calculation is therefore:

YOUR CGT CALCULATION FOR THE TAX YEAR 1998/99

Gross chargeable gains   X
Less Allowable losses   (X)

Net chargeable gains   X
Less Taper relief   (X)

Tapered chargeable gains   X
Less Annual exempt amount   (X)

Gains chargeable to CGT   X

CGT due   X

21.4.2 REBASING

The basic rule is that only gains accruing from 31 March 1982 are chargeable. If therefore, the chargeable asset disposed of today was owned by you on 31 March 1982, it is necessary to ascertain what its 31 March 1982 valuation was. The machinery for this is fairly simple. You are deemed to have disposed of chargeable assets owned by you on 31 March 1982 for their open market value and to have immediately reacquired them on that date. However, there are two exceptions to this:

(a) if the chargeable gain or allowable loss would be smaller by using the *actual* cost of acquisition after 6 April 1965, then that cost of acquisition is used instead of the 31 March 1982 valuation; and

(b) if one calculation would produce a chargeable gain, and the other an allowable loss, then you will be taken to have suffered *neither a gain nor a loss* on the disposal of the chargeable asset.

You are a musicologist. You bought a now-valuable autograph score of an opera by Handel, for £5,000, in April 1963. On 1 September 1998, you sell the score for £150,000. In 1965, the demand for such material had risen dramatically, and the market value of the score on 6 April 1965 was £70,000. Demand had fallen again by 1982, when the score would have fetched £15,000 on the open-market.

On the sale in 1998, should you accept the 31 March 1982 valuation, or opt for the 6 April 1965 valuation?

The 6 April 1965 valuation.

21.4.3 THE INDEXATION ALLOWANCE

The IA, now frozen at 6 April 1998, is designed to ensure that the gain is a real gain, rather than merely a paper gain: see **3.3.2**. In other words, it is designed to inflate the base cost of the chargeable asset, and thus to reduce the gain to reflect the real cost of the asset. However, if you make a chargeable disposal of a chargeable asset on or after 6 April 1998, the IA is made only up to April 1998.

Revenue guidance to the Finance Act 1998 gives the following illustration of the frozen IA. Suppose you acquired a chargeable asset in June 1996 for £10,000, and you sell it in August 2003 for £30,000. Throughout that period, it is a non-business asset: see **21.4.4**. The unindexed gain, calculated as at *Stage Four*, is £20,000, i.e. £30,000 − £10,000. The IA is calculated by applying the indexation factor for the period June 1996 to April 1998 to the base cost of £10,000. The indexation factor is calculated by reference to the change in the RPI over this period. Say the indexation factor is 0.052. The IA is thus 0.052 x £10,000, i.e. £520. This is deducted from the unindexed gain, at *Stage Five*, to give the indexed chargeable gain of £19,480.

Note that the IA cannot be used to create or increase an allowable loss: TCGA 1992, s. 53(1), (2A). It can reduce a gain to nil, unlike taper relief, as to which see **21.4.4**.

21.4.4 TAPER RELIEF: FA 1998

Under TCGA 1992, s. 2(2), you deduct from the gross chargeable gains of the tax year under consideration any allowable losses: *Stage Seven*. These can be from the tax year itself (*Stage Four*) or previous tax years. This gives your net chargeable gains, from which taper relief is deducted, to give your tapered chargeable gains. Taper relief is better for chargeable disposals of *business assets* than for non-business assets: TCGA 1992, s. 2A(3). You need only have owned a *business asset* for at least *one year* to qualify for taper relief. With a *non-business asset*, you must have owned it for *three years*, to qualify for the relief.

These periods begin on 6 April 1998, or the later date on which the asset was actually acquired, and end on the date of the chargeable disposal. They are referred to as *qualifying holding periods*. Section 2A(9) provides for a *bonus year*. Where you acquired the chargeable asset before 17 March 1998, an extra year is added to the actual number of complete years which, by the date of the disposal, have elapsed since 6 April 1998.

You acquired a business asset on 1 September 1997, and you sell it on 1 July 1999. How many years taper relief will you be entitled to?

Two.

Business assets are defined in TCGA 1992, sch. A1, paras. 3 to 9. A business asset is an asset used for the purposes of a trade you carry on, or an asset used for the purposes of a trade carried on by your trading company, or an asset used for the purposes of your office or employment, where you are required to devote substantially the whole of your time to the office or employment. This is similar to the definition of chargeable business assets used for retirement relief: see **23.3.1.3**.

The rates of taper relief are governed by the following table (TCGA 1992, s. 2A(5)):

Gains on disposals of business assets		Gains on disposals of non-business assets	
Number of whole years in qualifying holding period	Percentage of gain chargeable	Number of whole years in qualifying holding period	Percentage of gain chargeable
1	92.5	–	–
2	85	–	–
3	77.5	3	95
4	70	4	90
5	62.5	5	85
6	55	6	80
7	47.5	7	75
8	40	8	70
9	32.5	9	65
10 or more	25	10 or more	60

The maximum taper relief will therefore be 10 years after 6 April 1998, or any later date of acquisition. There is thus no CGT incentive not to sell after that period has expired.

As an illustration, it is useful to return to the Revenue's illustration of the indexed chargeable gain of £19,480: see **21.4.3**. You deduct taper relief from this at *Stage Eight*. Your qualifying holding period is April 1998 to August 2003. You are entitled to the bonus year, since you acquired the chargeable asset before 17 March 1998. One extra year is therefore added to the period for which you actually held the asset after 5 April 1998, i.e. six years in total.

Refer to the table above. What percentage of the gain is chargeable?

80% (six whole years, non-business asset).

What is the tapered chargeable gain therefore?

£15,584, i.e. 80/100 × £19,480

21.4.5 ALLOWABLE LOSSES AND TAPER RELIEF

By TCGA 1992, s. 2A, allowable losses are deducted from gross chargeable gains before taper relief: *Stages Seven and Eight*. TCGA 1992, s. 2A(6) then says that allowable losses are deducted from gross chargeable gains:

> . . . in such order as results in the largest reduction under this section of the amount charged to capital gains tax under section 2.

This is, however, subject to the idea that allowable losses must be taken before tapering which, in turn, leads to complications in relation to the order in which carried forward losses and the annual exempt amount are taken.

Revenue guidance provides the following illustration. Suppose you make *three* chargeable disposals in one tax year:

(a)   Disposal of business asset held for *four years* – gross chargeable gain of £10,000.

(b)   Disposal of non-business asset held for *seven years* – gross chargeable gain of £8,000.

(c)   Disposal of chargeable asset realising an allowable loss of £5,000.

The allowable loss in (c) is deducted from the chargeable gain which qualifies for the least taper relief. In disposal (a), the tapered chargeable gain will be 70% of the gross chargeable gains, whilst in disposal (b), the tapered chargeable gain will be 75% of the gross chargeable gains. The £5,000 allowable loss is therefore deducted from the gain on disposal (b). The gain on (b) becomes £3,000 (i.e. £8,000 − £5,000). Of these, 75% of £3,000 is chargeable, i.e. £2,250, whilst 70% of £10,000 is chargeable. Your tapered chargeable gains are therefore £9,250.

For further details of allowable losses, refer to **21.8**.

21.4.6   RATES OF CGT

You may find it helpful to re-read **7.3** at this point. The rates at which the CGT due from you is calculated depend on the rates at which you are liable to pay income tax for the tax year in which the gains are realised. Although your CGT calculation is separate from your income tax calculation, TCGA 1992, s. 4 basically treats any gains chargeable to CGT as though they were additional amounts of your taxable income. Your gains chargeable to CGT might therefore be charged to CGT in a combination of rates, i.e. 20%, 23% and 40%. For this purpose, TCGA 1992, s. 4 provides rules about the order in which the three income tax bands are to be used up. Your 20% band, i.e. the first £4,300 of taxable income, is first used up by income *other than* savings income. This is followed by any *gains chargeable to CGT*, which are in turn followed by any *savings income*. Section 4 provides for a *different* order in which the basic rate band, i.e. the next £22,800 of taxable income is to be used up. The basic rate band is first used up by income other than savings income, followed by savings income, followed in turn by gains chargeable to CGT.

Three examples will illustrate these rules. First, suppose in 1998/99 that you have taxable income of £26,000, none of which is savings income. You also have gains chargeable to CGT of £2,000. Your bands of taxable income are used up as follows:

Band of taxable income	Gains chargeable to CGT	Savings income	Non-savings income
£4,300 at 20%	–	–	4,300
£22,800 at 23%	1,100	–	21,700
Excess at 40%	900	–	–

On this basis, the CGT due is £613, i.e. the total of £1,100 × 23/100, plus £900 × 40/100.

Next, suppose in 1998/99 that your taxable income is £35,000, of which £2,500 is income *other than* savings income. Again, you have gains chargeable to CGT of £2,000. This time, your bands of taxable income are used up thus:

Band of taxable income	Gains chargeable to CGT	Savings income	Non-savings income
£4,300 at 20%	1,800	–	2,500
£22,800 at 23%	–	22,800	–
Excess at 40%	200	9,700	–

On this basis, the CGT due is £440, i.e. £1,800 × 20/100 and £200 × 40/100.

Finally, suppose in 1998/99 that your taxable income is £15,000, all of which is savings income. Again, you have gains chargeable to CGT of £2,000. This time, your bands of taxable income are used up as follows:

Band of taxable income	Gains chargeable to CGT	Savings income	Non-savings income
£4,300 at 20%	2,000	2,300	–
£22,800 at 23%	–	12,700	–
Excess at 40%	–	–	–

On this basis, the CGT due is £400, i.e. £2,000 × 20/100.

21.5 Calculating the *Corporation Tax on Chargeable Gains* Liability of a Company

This is part of the corporation tax calculation in **7.4**. The net chargeable gains so calculated are included at *Stage Two* of the corporation tax calculation. The differences with the individual's calculation, in **21.4**, are that: (a) a company has no annual exempt amount; (b) the IA continues to apply for disposals after April 1998, and there is consequently no taper relief; and (c) the rate of corporation tax on chargeable gains is the rate or combination of rates at which the company is liable to pay on its profits chargeable to corporation tax. *Stages One* to *Seven* of the calculation in **21.4** are identical here, with the exception of the references to the frozen IA.

21.6 Calculating the *CGT due* from a Partner

If I am a partner in a firm, I will own property which belongs to me in my private capacity, but I may also own a share in the assets of the partnership. (A partnership asset, or partnership property, is property to which the partners of the firm are entitled *in their capacity* as partners: *Morris* v *Barrett* (1829) 3 Y & J 384.) The partnership agreement will provide for chargeable gains to be divided up either in accordance with their *profit-sharing ratio*, or in accordance with an *asset surplus entitlement*. In either case, a partner's calculation is identical to that of individuals in their personal capacity, except that the figure to be entered in *Stages Two* and *Three* will be the proportion of the whole gain on the disposal of the partnership asset to which the partner is entitled.

Calculating the CGT due from individual partners can be illustrated thus. Suppose Ping, Pang and Pong are in partnership as solicitors, as in **SAQ 266**. Their asset surplus entitlement is fixed in the proportions 1: 2: 3. Ping's base cost for the office premises is £16,667.

(Look again at SAQ 266.) Assuming that Ping makes no other chargeable disposals in 1998/99, what is his base cost on the disposal of the office premises? He has no allowable losses for use in 1998/99. (Ignore the IA.)

£16,667.

21.7   Calculating the CGT due from Trustees and PRs

21.7.1   TRUSTEES

The CGT due from trustees is generally calculated in the same way as the CGT due from individuals in their personal capacity. The following modifications apply. At *Stage Nine*, trustees can deduct from their tapered chargeable gains only half of the annual exempt amount to which individuals in their personal capacity are entitled. For 1998/99, this means that only £3,400 can be deducted. The annual exemption is divided between settlements where more than one of them have been created by the settlor, subject to a minimum exemption per settlement of £680. If the settlement is for a disabled beneficiary, the trustees have the same annual exemption as a private individual, i.e. £6,800. At *Stage Ten*, the CGT rate to be applied is *always* 34%, for chargeable disposals by trustees after 5 April 1998: TCGA 1992, s. 1AA.

21.7.2   PERSONAL REPRESENTATIVES

The CGT due from PRs is calculated in the same way as the CGT due from individuals in their personal capacity, subject to the following modifications. PRs are entitled to the same annual exempt amount as individuals in the tax year of the death, and the following tax year. In the tax year after that, they have no annual exempt amount at all. For disposals by PRs of estate assets after 5 April 1998, the rate of CGT to be applied at *Stage Ten* is 34%: TCGA 1992, s. 1AA.

21.8   Allowable Losses

Allowable losses can only be generated by the base cost of a chargeable asset exceeding its disposal proceeds on a chargeable disposal. Allowable losses arising in one tax period can be deducted from the gross chargeable gains of subsequent tax periods without time limit: TCGA 1992, s. 2(2). However, they must initially be deducted from the gross chargeable gains of the same tax period: TCGA 1992, s. 2(2)(a). There are certain other restrictions on relief for allowable losses:

- With one exception, an allowable loss in the tax period under consideration cannot be deducted from gross chargeable gains of previous tax periods. The exception is an allowable loss of a deceased individual in the tax year of the death. Such an allowable loss can be carried back and deducted from gross chargeable gains of earlier tax years: TCGA 1992, s. 62(2).

- If the allowable loss is incurred on a disposal to a connected person (see **27.5.1**), then the allowable loss can only be deducted from gross chargeable gains on disposals to that same person: TCGA 1992, s. 18(3).

- The only case in which you can deduct an allowable loss from income is where the conditions of ICTA 1988, s. 574 are satisfied (i.e. losses on investments in small trading companies: see **13.4.3.5**). You are then basically permitted to deduct the allowable loss from your total income, at Stage Three of your income tax calculation: ICTA 1988, s. 574(1).

- Since 6 April 1998, allowable losses incurred by settlors of certain trusts or recipients of capital from offshore trusts in their personal capacity cannot be deducted from chargeable gains attributed to such settlors or recipients: TCGA 1992, s. 2(4): **25.3.1.2**.

21.9   Stamp Duty

21.9.1   LIABILITY OF A STAMPABLE DOCUMENT TO STAMP DUTY

A stampable document is liable to stamp duty if it is executed in the UK or, if executed outside the UK, if it relates to anything done or to be done in the UK: SA 1891, s. 14(4).

It must be stamped not later than 30 days after it is 'first executed', if it is executed in the UK. If it is executed outside the UK, it is liable to stamp duty not later than 30 days after it was 'first received' in the UK: SA 1891, s. 15(2)(a).

21.9.2   CALCULATION OF STAMP DUTY

21.9.2.1   Conveyance or transfer on sale of land

For most conveyances or transfers on sale executed after 24 March 1998, stamp duty is banded. No *ad valorem* stamp duty is payable if the consideration in the document is £60,000 or less. If it is more than £60,000, but is not more than £250,000, it is 1%. If it is more than £250,000, but not more than £500,000, it is 2%; and if it is more than £500,000, it is 3%. The 2% rates do not apply to conveyances or transfers executed after 23 March 1998, pursuant to a contract entered into on or before 17 March 1998.

21.9.2.2   Conveyance or transfer on sale of shares

For transfers on sale of shares, stamp duty is not banded. Instead, it is chargeable at 0.5% of the consideration in the document, i.e. stock transfer form: **24.6.1.1**.

21.10   Summary

CGT, as well as corporation tax on chargeable gains, is charged on any gain realised by a chargeable disposal by a chargeable person of a chargeable asset. A chargeable person is either a UK-resident individual or a UK company. In exceptional circumstances, a non-UK-resident individual may be liable to pay CGT or corporation tax on chargeable gains. Chargeable disposals include a range of transactions, of which sales are only one. Chargeable assets include options, debts and incorporeal property generally. The calculation of the CGT due from an individual has 10 Stages. The IA has been frozen for individuals, whatever the capacity in which they make the calculation, at April 1998, although not for companies. The availability of taper relief depends on having held the asset disposed of for a qualifying holding period. Taper relief is better in relation to business assets than non-business assets. It is not available for qualifying holding periods of more than ten whole years. The calculation of the CGT from trustees and PRs is similar to that for individuals in their personal capacities, although with a number of significant differences. The most important of these differences is the 34% CGT rate that applies to chargeable disposals by trustees and PRs after 5 April 1998, across the board. The use of allowable losses is subject to a number of detailed restrictions. Conveyances or transfers on sale of land and shares are subject to *ad valorem* stamp duty, although at different rates.

21.11 End of Chapter Assessment Question

In 1990, Edward bought a derelict cottage in Worcestershire, with a view to rebuilding it and letting it to tenants. The cottage cost him £20,000 and he incurred a solicitors' fee of £400, excluding VAT.

He did part of the work of rebuilding the cottage himself, between 1992-93, estimating the market value of the work at £18,000. However, he also paid contractors to install a new roof, which cost him £12,000 plus VAT in 1994. Also in 1994, he incurred an architect's fee of £500, including VAT, for the design of an extension, planning permission for which was subsequently refused by the local authority. In addition, he incurred a solicitor's fee of £3,080, including VAT, in 1995 in relation to a boundary dispute, in which he was victorious before the Lands Tribunal. He has never got round to letting the property.

He has now decided that the cottage is more trouble than it is worth, and contracted to sell it for £100,000 on 1 November 1998. His estate agent is proposing to charge a commission of 2% of the selling-price plus advertising fees of £40 (both figures exclusive of VAT). In addition, solicitors' fees on the sale will be £850 plus VAT.

In the 1998/99 tax year, he has gross Schedule E income of £37,000. He makes no other chargeable disposals in the tax year, and he has no carried forward allowable losses.

  (a)   Explain how the CGT due from him for 1998/99 will be calculated. Do *not* attempt the calculation itself.

(Word limit: 680 (90 marks).)

  (b)   Explain whether the conveyance will need to be stamped by the purchaser and, if so, what amount of stamp duty will be chargeable.

(Word limit: 120 (10 marks).)

See *Cases and Materials* (**21.4**) for a specimen answer.

CHAPTER TWENTY-TWO

REDUCING INVESTMENT TAXATION (1)

22.1 Objectives

By the end of this chapter, you should be able to:

■ list which *assets* are exempt from CGT;

■ list which *gains* are exempt from CGT;

■ explain the *effect* of CGT private residence relief (PRR);

■ list the *conditions* for PRR;

■ identify clearly some of the main *problem areas* with PRR.

22.2 Introduction

This chapter and the next consider the ways in which the burden of CGT can be alleviated. Although the title of both chapters may seem fairly straightforward, one of the most important aspects of each one is the precise way in which the alleviation is achieved. We have constantly reiterated the rule that the liability to pay CGT arises when a gain is produced by a chargeable disposal, by a chargeable person, of a chargeable asset. A number of the provisions discussed in **Chapters 22** and **23** operate by removing one of these four elements from a particular type of transaction. Others operate, as we shall discover in **Chapter 23**, by postponing the CGT charge. In this chapter, we begin by examining the rules which make some assets exempt rather than chargeable assets. We then go on to consider the private residence relief (PRR), which operates by making the gain exempt. The discussion in this chapter is mainly concerned with CGT. It will be clear from the context when the discussion applies equally to corporation tax on chargeable gains.

22.3 Exempt Assets

A number of categories of assets are exempt assets. There is therefore no chargeable gain or allowable loss when they are disposed of. Two main categories of exempt assets are as follows:

■ Sterling, but not other currencies: TCGA 1992, s. 21(1)(b).

■ Mechanically propelled road vehicles constructed or adapted for the carriage of passengers: TCGA 1992, s. 263.

I bought a car in 1991 for £14,000. I sell it on 1 June 1998 for £4,000. Can I claim an allowable loss on the disposal?

No, because the car is not a chargeable asset.

22.4   Provisions Making Gains Exempt Gains

22.4.1   THE ANNUAL EXEMPT AMOUNT ('ANNUAL EXEMPTION')

22.4.1.1   Persons affected

The annual exempt amount, or annual exemption, is deducted from your net chargeable gains, or tapered chargeable gains, of the tax year. It is available to you, subject to different rules, whatever the capacity in which you are calculating the CGT due from you. Three important points must be made, however:

■ It is not available to companies: TCGA 1992, s. 3(1).

■ The amount of the annual exemption depends on whether you are acting in your personal capacity, or in either of the capacities of trustee or PR: see **22.4.1.2**.

■ Partners in firms are entitled to only one annual exemption per year, whether chargeable gains are made by them in their personal capacities, or as partners.

22.4.1.2   Effect of the annual exempt amount

The annual exempt amount is deducted from your net chargeable gains or tapered chargeable gains of a tax year. It is therefore deducted at *Stage Nine* of the CGT calculation: see **21.4.1**. Its deduction gives your gains chargeable to CGT. In 1998/99, the annual exempt amount is £6,800 for individuals in their personal capacity. For PRs, the annual exempt amount is the same amount as for individuals in their personal capacity for the tax year of the death, and the two subsequent tax years only: TCGA 1992, s. 3(7). For the third and fourth subsequent tax years, PRs are entitled to no annual exempt amount in their capacity as PRs: see **22.4.1.4**. For trustees, the annual exempt amount is half of the amount to which each of them is entitled in their personal capacity: TCGA 1992, sch. 1. For the tax year 1998/99, this is therefore £3,400. If, as a trustee, you are a trustee of more than one settlement set up by the same settlor, each settlement takes a proportion of £3,400. This rule is subject to a minimum exemption per settlement, in the 1998/99 tax year, of £680. These rules are subject to one exception. If the settlement is a trust for the benefit of a disabled individual, its trustees have an annual exempt amount of £6,800, i.e. as for individuals in their personal capacities. This is divided up, as above, if there is more than one such settlement.

There is an interrelation of the annual exempt amount and the points discussed in **21.4.5** (allowable losses and taper relief). Allowable losses are deducted from the gross chargeable gains of the tax year before taper relief and before the annual exempt amount:

see **21.4.1**. In the absence of special provision, this would mean that the annual exempt amount would be wasted where there were losses from previous tax years. The Taxation of Chargeable Gains Act 1992, s. 3(5) ensures that such losses are not wasted. Section 3(5) states that, where the gross chargeable gains of the current tax year, less allowable losses of the current tax year, are no more than the annual exempt amount, losses from previous years can be carried forward to subsequent tax years.

22.4.1.3 Conditions for the annual exempt amount

The only condition relevant to the annual exempt amount appears to be that the individual is otherwise liable to CGT. In other words, that the individual realises a chargeable gain or gains in the tax year under consideration, on which that individual is liable to pay CGT: **20.6.1.1**.

22.4.2   CHATTELS WHICH ARE WASTING ASSETS

22.4.2.1   Persons affected

This relief is relevant to a disposal by a person of a chattel which is also a wasting asset. The range of assets within this category will be discussed in **24.4**, although they are essentially assets with a predictable life of not more than 50 years: TCGA 1992, s. 44(1). Whether the disponer is an individual or a company is unimportant for this purpose. In the absence of the relief, disposals of such assets would be more likely to generate allowable losses than chargeable gains.

22.4.2.2   Effect of the relief for wasting assets

The relief means that no figure is entered in a CGT or corporation tax calculation in respect of a gain on the disposal of a wasting asset. By the same token, no allowable loss can be claimed by a person disposing of such an asset.

22.4.2.3   Conditions for relief for wasting assets

The relief applies if TCGA 1992, s. 45(1) applies. This provides as follows:

> Subject to the provisions of this section, no chargeable gain shall accrue on the disposal of, or of an interest in, an asset which is tangible moveable property and which is a wasting asset.

Most importantly, the other provisions of this section state, among other things, that if a person disposes of an asset (TCGA 1992, s. 45(2)):

> . . . [U]sed and used solely for the purposes of a trade, profession or vocation and if that person has claimed or could have claimed any capital allowance in respect of any expenditure attributable to the asset or interest . . .

then a gain on the disposal of the asset is a chargeable gain, since the exemption does not apply: **24.8**.

22.4.3   CHATTELS WHICH ARE *NOT* WASTING ASSETS

22.4.3.1   Persons affected

This relief is relevant to a disposal by a person of a chattel which is not a wasting asset. The capacity in which that person is disposing of the chattel is unimportant for this purpose. The definition of a chattel given in TCGA 1992, s. 262 is as 'tangible movable property'. The relief means that it would be possible, say, for you to build up a collection of water-colour paintings and, provided that the consideration on their disposal did not exceed £6,000, to avoid paying CGT on your capital profit. It is useful if you want to acquire an investment the value of which will keep pace with, or possibly exceed, the rate of inflation. It also means that the Revenue need not concern itself with relatively small chargeable gains.

22.4.3.2   Effect of the relief for chattels which are *not* wasting assets

The relief makes some or all of what would otherwise be a chargeable gain on the disposal of a chattel into an exempt gain, provided that the conditions summarised in **22.4.3.3** are satisfied. The Taxation of Chargeable Gains Act 1992, s. 262(1) says:

> . . . [A] gain accruing on a disposal of an asset which is tangible moveable property shall not be a chargeable gain if the amount or value of the consideration for the disposal does not exceed £6,000.

On 1 May 1998, Sid sells a water-colour painting by an early nineteenth century watercolourist. He makes a chargeable gain of £5,900, the proceeds of the painting's sale being £6,000. Will the £5,900 be included in *Stage Two* of his CGT calculation for 1998/99?

No.

If a person's disposal proceeds are more than £6,000, then the chargeable gain is limited to $^5/_3$ × the difference between £6,000 and the actual amount of the sale proceeds.

Assume the same facts as in SAQ 287. Imagine, however, that the sale proceeds of the water-colour are £10,000. How much of the £10,000 will be included in *Stage Two* of his CGT calculation for 1998/99?

£4,000 × $^5/_3$ = £6,667.

It is worth noting that the relief works by making exempt what would otherwise be some, or all, of a chargeable gain. It does not affect the amount of the annual exempt amount deductible at *Stage Nine* of the CGT calculation. Nor does it affect the status of the non-wasting chattel as a chargeable asset.

22.4.3.3   Conditions for relief for non-wasting chattels

The relief applies if the asset disposed of is:

■ not a wasting asset;

■   tangible moveable property; and

■   the sale proceeds are £6,000 or less.

If the sale proceeds are more than £6,000, the relief applies as summarised in **22.4.3.2**.

22.4.3.4   A problem area with non-wasting chattels

A problem associated with the relief is as follows. We have said that the status of the non-wasting chattel as a chargeable asset is unaffected by the relief. This does not mean, however, that a person is automatically entitled to claim the full amount of an allowable loss if the chattel is sold at a loss. If a person makes such a loss, they are deemed to have received sale proceeds of £6,000, where the actual amount received was less than £6,000: TCGA 1992, s. 262(3). This provision severely restricts the amount of the allowable loss which may be claimed by a person disposing of a non-wasting chattel at a loss.

On 1 June 1998, you sell an antique table for £4,500, having bought it in 1988 for £8,200. Your actual loss is therefore £(3,700). For how much will you be deemed to have sold it?

£6,000.

What is the effect on you of being deemed to have sold it for £6,000?

Your loss is restricted to £(2,200), i.e. £6,000 − £8,200.

22.4.4   PRIVATE RESIDENCE RELIEF

22.4.4.1   Persons affected

Private residence relief is relevant to a disposal by you of a dwelling-house, whether you make the disposal as an individual in your personal capacity, or in the capacity of a trustee or PR. Where you are acting in the capacity of a trustee, PRR will apply on a disposal of the house if it is the residence of someone who is entitled to occupy it under the terms of the settlement: TCGA 1992, s. 225. Although the relief can apply where an individual occupies a house held in trust, pursuant to a discretion exercised by the trustees, such an occupation may have disadvantageous IHT consequences. This is because the IHT analysis does not mirror the CGT one, IHT not providing for an equivalent relief from the IHT charge which arises when an interest in possession is created: SP 10/79, *Sansom* v *Peay* [1976] 3 All ER 375 (see **27.4.2.1, 28.4.2**). The relief will also apply to disposals by PRs, provided that both before and after the deceased's death, the residence was occupied by an individual entitled to all, or substantially all, the proceeds of its sale: ESC D5.

SAQ 291

Saul and his brother Samuel live in Samuel's house, the title to which is vested in Samuel alone. Samuel dies on 1 December 1998 and the house is left to Saul under the terms of Samuel's will. Saul continues to live in the house after Samuel's death.

If Saul decides to sell the house, will any gain be exempt from CGT?

Yes.

Private residence relief is the reason why CGT has no impact on most people. Their dwelling-house is their only chargeable asset of significant value, and any gain on its disposal is exempted by PRR.

22.4.4.2   Effect of private residence relief

Private residence relief makes some or all of what would otherwise be a chargeable gain into an exempt gain on the disposal of a chargeable asset, i.e. the dwelling-house, provided that the conditions summarised in **22.4.4.3** are satisfied. TCGA 1992, s. 223(1) provides:

> No part of a gain to which section 222 applies shall be a chargeable gain if the dwelling-house or part of a dwelling house has been the individual's only or main residence throughout the period of ownership, or throughout the period of ownership *except for all or any part of the last 36 months of that period*. [*Emphasis added*.]

The significance of the emphasised words is considered in **22.4.2.3** below. Their purpose is clearly to give you a period of grace if you do not manage to sell your old house before acquiring a new one. What is worth noting in this section is that the relief works by making exempt what would otherwise be some, or all, of a chargeable gain. It does not affect the status of the house as a chargeable asset. This means that if:

■   you are going to make a loss on the sale of the house; and

■   you have a chargeable gain or chargeable gains in the tax year under consideration, in excess of your annual exemption,

it may actually be advantageous to you to manipulate the rules so that the relief does *not* apply, thereby ensuring that there is an allowable loss on the disposal of the house. This is because of TCGA 1992, s. 16(2), the wording of which repays close examination:

> Except as otherwise expressly provided, all the provisions of this Act which distinguish gains which are chargeable gains from those which are not, or which make part of a gain a chargeable gain, and part not, shall apply also to distinguish losses which are allowable losses from those which are not, and to make part of a loss an allowable loss, and part not . . .

Because manipulating this rule would disentitle you to the relief, such an operation requires the most careful planning, if it is to have any possibility of success. (For some of the dangers, consider *Jones* v *Wilcock* [1996] STC (SCD) 389 in **22.4.4.3**.)

SAQ 292

Bill makes a loss of £(10,000) on the sale of his house, during the tax year 1998/99, in circumstances such that the relief applies. In the same tax year, he makes a chargeable gain of £20,000 on the sale of his shareholding in Megabucks plc. Can he deduct the £(10,000) loss from the £20,000 gain?

No – because PRR applies.

22.4.4.3   Conditions for private residence relief

The relief applies if the chargeable asset disposed of is either (TCGA 1992, s. 222(1)):

(a)   a dwelling-house or part of a dwelling-house which is, or has at any time in your period of ownership been, your only or main residence; or

(b)   land which you have for your own occupation and enjoyment with that residence as its garden or grounds, up to the permitted area.

The permitted area is either 0.5 of a hectare, including the site of the house itself, or such larger area as is required for the reasonable enjoyment of the house, having regard to its size and character: TCGA 1992, s. 222(3).

Note that s. 222(1) refers to the disposal of an interest in a dwelling house, etc., as well as the disposal of the house itself.

SAQ 293

You bought the freehold of your house for £70,000 in 1988. You sell it on 1 September 1998 for £100,000. Will CGT be chargeable on your gain of £30,000?

No.

Note also that you must not have acquired the dwelling-house wholly or partly for the purpose of realising a gain from its disposal: TCGA 1992, s. 224(3). This condition came into play in an unexpected way in *Jones* v *Wilcock* [1996] STC (SCD) 389. There, the owner of the house wanted to claim an allowable loss on its disposal. Logically, he therefore had to argue that the relief did not apply. He tried to argue that the relief did not apply because he had acquired the house with the aim of selling it at a profit. The Special Commissioner rejected the argument on the basis that the owner had acquired the house with the expectation or hope of making a profit, but not with the *purpose* of so doing. On this basis, no allowable loss could be claimed by the owner.

22.4.4.4   Problem areas with private residence relief

Some of the problems associated with PRR are as follows:

No dwelling-house
You might not have disposed of a dwelling-house. This problem is rarely encountered in practice, although it has sometimes arisen in the reported cases. For instance, in *Makins* v *Elson* (1976) 51 TC 437, an individual had purchased a plot of land with the benefit of outline planning permission. He intended to build a house on the land, although he

never got round to doing this. Instead, after just under three years of ownership of the land, he sold both land and caravan at a profit. Foster J held that the caravan was a dwelling-house. It was resting on bricks, and was connected to the water and electricity services, as well as to the phone network. By contrast, the caravan in *Moore v Thompson* [1986] BTC 172 was held not to qualify as a dwelling-house. It was never taken off its road-wheels, and the mains services were never connected to it. Millett J stressed that, although a caravan could be a dwelling-house, whether it was one in fact depended on a consideration of all the facts of the case.

Building disposed of not part of a dwelling-house

You might not have disposed of part of a dwelling-house. This problem arises where a house has separate accommodation, such as a bungalow or lodge in its grounds. When the bungalow in the grounds is sold separately from the main house, the problem is whether any gain on its sale is covered by the relief. Two different solutions have emerged from the case law. One is the '*entity test*', whilst the other is the '*curtilage test*'. In addition, the Revenue has itself issued guidance on the application of the 'curtilage test' in practice.

The entity test was devised by the Court of Appeal in *Batey v Wakefield* [1982] 1 All ER 61, and was applied by Vinelott J in *Williams v Merrylees* [1987] 1 WLR 1511. The curtilage test was devised by Walton J in *Markey v Saunders* [1987] 1 WLR 864, without regard to the entity test, and was endorsed by the Court of Appeal in *Lewis v Lady Rook* [1992] 1 WLR 662. The entity test requires you to identify the entity which can properly be described as the dwelling-house. Vinelott J's formulation of the test in *Williams v Merrylees* was as follows:

> What one is looking for is an entity which can be sensibly described as being a dwelling house though split up into different buildings performing different functions. In deciding whether this test is satisfied on the facts of a particular case the commissioners must look at all the circumstances, and of course the propinquity or otherwise of the buildings having regard to their scale is a very important factor to be weighed.

The curtilage test concentrates on the proximity of the building sold to the house itself. The test accepted by the Court of Appeal in *Lewis v Lady Rook* was that the building sold had to be 'appurtenant to, and within the curtilage of, the main house': [1992] 1 WLR 662, 670B, per Balcombe LJ. If it is not so appurtenant and within the curtilage, therefore, the relief does not apply.

From published Revenue guidance (see *Tax Bulletin*, August 1994, p. 148), the position seems to be as follows:

(a) if groups of buildings constitute an integral whole, they fall within a single curtilage. Thus, the separation of buildings, e.g. by a wall or fence, will mean that the buildings are not within a single curtilage;

(b) for groups of buildings to constitute an integral whole, they must be so intimately associated with each other that they are part and parcel of each other; and

(c) For buildings to be part and parcel of each other, there must be a close geographical relationship between them. Thus, the fact that buildings on an estate are within a single boundary does not mean that they are within a single curtilage.

Dwelling-house a residence but not *your* residence

The dwelling-house you are disposing of might not be *your* residence. In *Goodwin v Curtis* [1996] STC 1146, Sir John Vinelott held that occupation of a dwelling-house for a period of a month and a day was not sufficient to make a residence *your* residence. Whether a dwelling-house is your residence depends on a number of factors, including ' . . . the degree of permanence, continuity and the expectation of continuity'. His decision was recently upheld by the Court of Appeal.

Dwelling-house your residence but not your only or main residence
There are a number of reasons why a dwelling-house which is your residence might not be your only or main residence. That said, absence from the dwelling-house does not debar you from the full amount of the relief automatically. Instead, the relief may be reduced by the proportion specified in TCGA 1992. However, certain periods of absence are ignored, so that they are not regarded as removing the relief for the whole gain at all. In addition, there are special provisions dealing with lodgers. SP 14/80 states that:

> Where a lodger lives as a member of the owner's family, sharing their living accommodation and taking meals with them, no part of the accommodation is treated as having ceased to be occupied as the owner's main residence, and the exemption will not be restricted at all.

(Also Inland Revenue Leaflet CGT 4.)

Periods of absence which do not *affect the relief*
Periods of absence which do *not* affect your entitlement to relief of the whole gain are as follows:

■ The first 12 months of ownership where occupation was delayed because of building works or alterations: ESC D49.

■ The first two years of ownership, where there are good reasons for the delay in going into occupation: ESC D49 also.

■ The last three years of ownership: TCGA 1992, s. 223(1).

■ On the basis only that: (a) you have no other residence in relation to which the relief can be claimed; and (b) you reside in the dwelling-house both before and after the relevant absence:

   (a) any period or periods of absence not exceeding three years altogether; and

   (b) any period when you were employed outside the UK; and

   (c) any period or periods of absence together not exceeding four years during which, as an employee, you were prevented from residing there because of the location of your place of work.

(TCGA 1992, s. 223(3).)

You acquired your house in Nottingham on 6 April 1989. Between 6 April 1991 and 5 April 1993, you were required by your employer to work in Paris, so you let the property for that period. Between 6 April 1993 and 5 April 1994, you again lived in the house as your only residence. On 6 April 1996, you moved out of the house, to rent a property in London, having got a new job there. From 7 April 1996, you let your house in Nottingham to tenants, and on 6 April 1997, it was sold.

Will any of these periods of absence affect the relief applying in full to any gain on the disposal of your Nottingham house?

No.

Periods of absence which do affect the relief

If the period for which you have been absent from the property is not covered by any of the above, then the amount of any gain which is exempted is reduced proportionately. Thus, *the part of any gain which is exempt from CGT* is found by using the following formula:

Chargeable gain × Period for which the dwelling-house was your only or main residence	= Exempt part
Period for which the dwelling-house was owned by you	of gain

The period for which the dwelling-house was your only or main residence in the formula includes the last three years of its ownership by you. The various periods in the formula are calculated in months.

Relief when house has been let out to tenants

The application of the formula may be modified where the reason why you have been absent from the property is that it has been let to tenants at some point during its period of ownership by you. This situation is covered by TCGA 1992, s. 223(4). Under TCGA 1992, s. 223(4), where:

■ a gain arises on the disposal of a dwelling-house; *and*

■ the whole or part of it has been let as residential accommodation,

then the gain is exempt to the extent that it is not more than the lesser of:

(a) £40,000; or

(b) any amount of the gain which is exempted from CGT by the provisions discussed above.

For instance, say that you bought a house in Nottingham, on 6 April 1985, for £50,000. On 6 April 1988, you let the house to tenants for two years, having had to move to London in accordance with the requirements of your employer. On your return, on 6 April 1990, instead of moving back into the house, you began to live in another house in Nottingham, inherited from an aunt, reletting the first property until 5 April 1998, when it was sold. You made a gain of £50,000 on the sale, after deducting the IA. In these circumstances, the house would be deemed to have been your only or main residence for a total of six years, including the last three years. You would, of course, have owned it for exactly 13 years.

How much of the indexed gain would be exempt from CGT, in the absence of the lettings relief?

£50,000 × $\frac{72}{156}$ = £23,077.

What, therefore, would be your chargeable gain on the disposal of the house, in the absence of lettings relief?

£26,923 (i.e. £50,000 − £23,077).

How would this differ after lettings relief had been applied?

Find the gain attributable to the period of the letting.

How long is that period?

10 years.

10 years in months is 120 months. What do you do therefore to find the gain attributable to the letting?

Divide 120 by 156, the total period of ownership of the house, and multiply the resulting figure by the indexed gain of £50,000.

What figure does that give for the gain attributable to the period of the letting?

£38,462.

What is the letting relief therefore?

The lower of £38,462 and £40,000.

What do you do with the figure of £38,462?

Deduct it from £26,923, as above.

When you have more than one residence

If you have more than one residence, you can elect for one of them to be treated as your main residence: TCGA 1992, s. 222(5). Having more than one residence means having a *proprietary interest* in more than one residence: ESC D21. You must be very careful about the timing of the election. It cannot be made more than two years after the acquisition of the later residence or residences: *Griffin* v *Craig-Harvey* [1994] STC 54. If you omit to make the election, the Revenue may dispute *as a matter of fact* which of one or more residences is your main residence.

Land not occupied and enjoyed with the residence

You might have disposed of land which has not been occupied and enjoyed with the residence.

Refer to the two conditions for relief in 22.4.4.3. How does the phraseology of (a) differ from that of (b)?

(b) refers to the situation at the time of the disposal only, whilst (a) refers to the situation both at the time of the disposal and previously to then.

The case law demonstrates that the land disposed of might not be enjoyed with the residence in one of a number of situations as follows.

Land might be sold after the dwelling-house is sold

If you sell the land *after* the dwelling-house has been sold, you will lose the benefit of the relief. This is clear from *Varty* v *Lynes* [1976] 3 All ER 447.

Read the extracts from the judgment of Brightman J in *Varty* v *Lynes*, at *Cases and Materials* (22.1.1). Think very carefully about the reasons for his Lordship's decision.

What would have happened if the remainder of the garden had been sold before or at the same time as the sale of the house?

Any gain on its disposal would have been exempt.

Brightman J was even more specific than this, however. He said:

> On the construction advanced by the Crown it must follow, I am disposed to think, that if the taxpayer goes out of occupation of the dwelling-house a month before he sells it, the exemption will be lost in respect of the garden. That, however, is merely my impression, and I do not intend so to decide because it is not a matter for decision before me.

The Revenue have, however, confirmed in the *Tax Bulletin* referred to above, that they do not propose to advance arguments for disapplying the relief which are based on this dictum of Brightman J.

Land might be sold before the dwelling-house is sold
In this situation, any gain on its disposal should be exempt: see above.

The land you dispose of might not be for occupation and enjoyment *with* the residence. This is shown by *Wakeling v Pearce* [1995] STC (SCD) 1996. This case involved a layout of a house and garden of a type commonly come across in English villages. In that case, an individual had put up a washing line and maintained a garden in a field ('Field 528') which was separated from her residence, called Cartref, by another property not in her ownership. The gain on the disposal of Field 528 was held to have the benefit of the relief since, according to the Special Commissioner, it was not necessary for the land to be contiguous with the residence nor to adjoin it.

ACTIVITY53

Read the extracts from the judgment of Special Commissioner THK Everett in *Wakeling* v *Pearce* at *Cases and Materials* (22.1.1). Then read the article by Patrick Soares, in which he discusses both *Wakeling* v *Pearce* and the problems which can arise when the garden or grounds exceed 0.5 of a hectare.

All or part of dwelling-house not a residence
It is important to avoid using any part of the dwelling-house solely for business purposes. It could mean a proportionate reduction in the exemption: TCGA 1992, s. 224(1). This can be a particular problem for doctors and dentists using part of their house as a surgery.

22.5 Summary

Capital gains tax law provides for the CGT burden to be alleviated by, among other things, deeming certain assets to be exempt assets, and certain gains to be exempt gains. Importantly, exempt assets include sterling, although not other currencies, and mechanically propelled road vehicles constructed or adapted for the carriage of passengers. These, together with PRR, help to explain why CGT has little impact on most individuals. Part of this explanation also is the annual exempt amount which, for individuals in their personal capacity, exempts net chargeable gains or tapered gains of up to £6,800 per annum. Chattels which are not wasting assets, as well as ones that are, are taken out of the scope of CGT by provisions which exempt any gain on their disposal from CGT, although it may be more significant that these provisions thereby deny allowable losses to be realised on the disposal of such assets. Although it very often applies without problems, care should be taken with PRR. There are a number of instances where a gain on the disposal of the whole or part of a dwelling-house, or its garden or grounds, will not qualify for exemption. There are also other instances where the amount of the gain covered by the exemption will be restricted.

22.6   End of Chapter Assessment Question

Discuss the circumstances in which a gain on the disposal of the garden or grounds of a residence will *not* be an exempt gain.

(Word limit: 700 (100 marks).)

See *Cases and Materials* (22.3) for a specimen answer.

CHAPTER TWENTY-THREE

REDUCING INVESTMENT TAXATION (2)

23.1   Objectives

By the end of this chapter, you should be able to:

- explain the *effect* of retirement relief;

- list the *conditions* for retirement relief;

- identify the *problem areas* with retirement relief;

- list nine other types of disposal which produce *exempt gains* for CGT purposes;

- state the circumstances in which the *disposal of a debt* is an exempt disposal;

- explain the *effect* of roll-over relief on the replacement of business assets;

- list the *conditions* for roll-over relief on disposals of business assets;

- identify the *problem areas* with business assets roll-over relief.

23.2   Introduction

In this chapter, we stay with CGT and, where appropriate, corporation tax on chargeable gains. The emphasis shifts, however, to reliefs which are relevant to those involved in business. We begin with retirement relief, which is ultimately to be abolished from 6 April 2003. In the period until then, it is to be progressively reduced, beginning in 1999/2000. The idea is for it to be replaced by taper relief on business assets, although taper relief will be less generous than retirement relief. Retirement relief operates in largely the same way as PRR, in that it exempts the whole or part of what would otherwise be a chargeable gain. For reasons of space, other provisions exempting gains are noted only briefly by us. We then consider the provision which makes the disposal of debts an exempt disposal, before going on to discuss a number of reliefs which operate by postponing a charge to CGT. As ever, it is important to be aware of the effect of a particular relief, the conditions for it applying, and any problem areas associated with it.

23.3   Provisions making Gains Exempt Gains

23.3.1   RETIREMENT RELIEF

23.3.1.1   Persons affected

The relief is relevant to a disposal by you of your business interests fairly late in life, or through ill-health. For instance, you might be an individual carrying on a trade alone or in partnership. In each case, the relief is designed to cover any chargeable gain on your disposal of the business or your interest in the business. Retirement relief should also cover a gain on a disposal by you of your shares in what is referred to by TCGA 1992 as your personal company. The specific meaning of this term is discussed at **23.3.1.3**. In some circumstances, the relief also covers disposals of business interests by trustees of life interest trusts, on the retirement of the life tenant: TCGA 1992, s. 164(3). The availability of retirement relief is the reason why CGT is rarely paid on any gain realised by a person disposing of a family business.

23.3.1.2   Effect of retirement relief

The relief makes some or all of what would otherwise be a chargeable gain into an exempt gain, provided the conditions summarised in **22.4.3.3** are satisfied. The effect of the relief is set out in TCGA 1992, sch. 6. It varies, depending on the length of time for which you have owned the interest in the business:

(a)   If you have owned the interest for 10 years or more, then the relief does two things:

    (i)   it makes the whole of a gain up to £250,000 exempt from CGT; and

    (ii)   it makes half of any gain between £250,000 and £1 million exempt from CGT.

(b)   If you have owned the interest for less than 10 years, the relief under each of (i) and (ii) is reduced by 10% for each year during which you did not own the interest.

Bert set up a business on 1 April 1991. He sells the business on 1 April 1999, making a chargeable gain of £800,000. Retirement relief applies to the disposal. How much of the chargeable gain will be exempt from CGT?

Bert has owned the business for eight years. 20% of the chargeable gain will therefore be exempt from CGT on the gain up to £200,000 (i.e. £250,000, reduced by 20%), and on half of the gain between £200,000 and £800,000 (i.e. £1,000,000, reduced by 20%).

SAQ 306

What is the maximum chargeable gain which may be exempted by the relief, i.e. where you have owned the interest in the business for 10 years or more?

£625,000, i.e. £250,000 + £375,000.

Where you are disposing of shares in your personal company, a special formula is used to decide how much of the gain on the disposal of the shares is attributable to chargeable business assets of the company and, therefore, how much of the gain is covered by the relief. The formula is necessary because such a company will tend to own non-business assets, as well as business assets. In order to calculate how much of the gain is covered by the relief in this situation, it is necessary to divide the value of the chargeable business assets of the company, at the time of the disposal, by the value of the total chargeable assets of the company at that time, and to multiply that fraction by the total gain on the disposal of the shares. The resulting figure is the amount of the gain exempted by retirement relief. As a formula, this may be expressed as follows:

$$\text{Gain covered by retirement relief} = \frac{\text{Value of chargeable business assets}}{\text{Value of total chargeable assets}} \times \text{Total gain on disposal of shares}$$

SAQ 307

Imagine similar facts to SAQ 305, except that Bert formed a personal company, which began to trade on 1 April 1991. He is the only shareholder. He sells the company on 1 April 1999, realising a chargeable gain of £8,000 on the disposal. Retirement relief applies to the disposal in full, i.e. he is entitled to £625,000 relief. The chargeable business assets of the company are worth £16,000 at the time of the disposal. Chargeable assets of the company other than business assets are worth £32,000.

How much of the chargeable gain will be exempt from CGT?

$$\text{Gain covered by retirement relief} = \frac{£16,000}{£48,000} \times £8,000 = £2,667.$$

This means that Bert has surplus retirement relief of £647,333, and that the other £5,333 of the gain is a chargeable gain.

23.3.1.3 Conditions for retirement relief

Retirement relief applies if four conditions are satisfied:

(a)   you have owned the interest in the business for a minimum of one year; *and*

(b)   at the time of the disposal, you are either:

    (i)   50 years of age or above; or

    (ii)   under that age, but being forced to retire on grounds of ill-health; *and*

(c)   you are making a material disposal; *and*

(d)   you are disposing of chargeable business assets.

The conditions which must be satisfied for the ill-health requirement in (b)(ii) to be satisfied are contained in TCGA 1992, sch. 6, para. 3. You must satisfy the Revenue that you have retired because of ill-health and that you are likely to remain incapable of being able to perform work of the kind on which you were engaged previously.

We need to consider each of conditions (c) and (d) in some detail. Condition (c) requires you to be making a material disposal. Material disposals come in three forms, which basically correspond to the types of disposal which an individual might make, and which were indicated above:

■   a disposal by you of a business or part of a business: TCGA 1992, s. 163(2)(c) and (8);

■   a disposal by you of assets which, at the time at which you ceased to carry on the business, were used for the purposes of the business: TCGA 1992, s. 163(2)(b); and

■   a disposal by you of shares or securities in a personal company: TCGA 1992, s. 163(2)(c), (5)-(7).

Let's concentrate on the last of these for a moment. A personal company is one in which you exercise at least 5% of the voting rights. It must either be a trading company, or a company which is a member of a group of companies, the holding company of which is your personal company. In addition, you must be a full-time employee or officer of your personal company, required to devote substantially all your time to the service of the company or another company in the group, if relevant. The Revenue seem to regard working 30 hours per week as satisfying this condition.

Condition (d) requires you to be disposing of chargeable business assets. Where you are a sole trader or partner, chargeable business assets are obviously the assets which are used in the trade. Where you are disposing of shares in your personal company, the special formula discussed in **23.3.1.2** determines how much of the gain on the disposal of the shares is attributable to chargeable business assets.

The second type of disposal mentioned above is the one which has historically caused the most trouble, especially for farmers disposing of farming assets in stages. We consider this next.

23.3.1.4   Problem areas with retirement relief

Disposal not a disposal of a business or part of a business
One problem with retirement relief seems to have arisen more than any other. It arises when retirement relief is claimed on a disposal of the second type listed above, i.e. a disposal of assets which, at the time at which the business ceased, were used for the purposes of the business: TCGA 1992, s. 163(2)(b). The cases show that such a disposal has caused a particular problem for farmers. The problem is that the business must have *ceased* for there to be a material disposal of this second type. If the business continues beyond the disposal in relation to which the relief is claimed, then there is no material disposal of this second type. The only basis on which the person claiming the relief will

then succeed is to show that the disposal is of the first type instead. In other words, that what has been disposed of is a part of a business, rather than simply a business asset.

The solution adopted in the most recent cases has been for the judge to ask one simple question. That question is whether an identifiable part of the business been sold. It was asked in both *Pepper* v *Daffurn* [1993] STC 466, and *Jarmin* v *Rawlings* [1994] STC 1005. The answer in each case was a different one on the facts. In *Pepper* v *Daffurn*, Jonathan Parker J had to decide whether the sale of a covered yard by a farmer, was the disposal of a business or part of a business. He said:

> . . . [T]he question for present purposes is whether the sale of a particular business asset – in this case, the covered yard – amounted on the facts to the sale by the taxpayer of part of his farming business.

The covered yard was required for rearing cattle, but not for *grazing* them. It had been sold after a gradual change in the farmer's business, from rearing cattle to grazing cattle. The disposal of the covered yard did not therefore qualify for retirement relief.

In *Jarmin* v *Rawlings*, Knox J had to answer a slightly different question. It was whether separate disposals of assets, farmyard, milking shed and cattle, together amounted to a single disposal of part of a business, so as to qualify for the relief. Knox J held that, on the facts of the case, they did. In that case, the farmer had contracted to sell his milking parlour and yard at auction in October 1988. By the end of the following three-month period, prior to completion of the sale on 27 January 1989, he had sold almost half of his dairy herd also. The rest he transferred after completion to another farm, having ceased to have any financial interest in their milk on completion of the sale of the other assets. Even these remaining cattle had all been sold by May 1989. Knox J said:

> . . . [T]he right question . . . in my view is whether the sales of cattle were part of the same transaction as the disposal of the farmyard and milking shed.
> . . .

> In my view it is legitimate to have regard to simultaneous disposals entered into of other assets used in the business in assessing whether or not a particular disposal can be categorised as a sale of a business or part of a business. I consider therefore that the sales of cattle between contract and completion could properly be taken into account by the Commissioners.

His Lordship therefore held that the disposal was covered by the relief.

In *Wase* v *Bourke* [1996] STC 18, Anthony Grabiner QC, sitting as a deputy High Court judge, faced a very similar question, although with different facts. In that case, a farmer had sold the whole of his dairy herd in March 1988. Almost a year later, in February 1989, he sold his milk quota at a considerable profit. He ceased dairy farming on the sale of the herd in March 1988. Mr Grabiner asked himself the following question:

> Was the disposal by the taxpayer of his milk quota 'a disposal of the whole or part of a business'?

He said that, had the General Commissioners asked themselves that question, they would have concluded that the disposal of the milk quota:

> . . . was simply the disposal of an asset which had formerly been used in or was part of the dairy farming business but that it was not by itself the disposal of either the whole or part of that business. The relevant business activity consisted of the production and sale of milk.

His Lordship therefore held that the disposal of the milk quota was *not* covered by the relief. By contrast with what had happened in *Jarmin* v *Rawlings*, the disposal of the dairy herd was not a disposal simultaneous with the disposal of the quota.

The simple question of whether an identifiable part of the business has been sold has thus been the question asked in the most recent cases. It should perhaps be stated that there was an earlier test, formulated by Fox J in *McGregor* v *Adcock* [1977] 3 All ER 65, which was as follows:

> It must be a question of fact in each case whether there has been such an interference with the whole complex of activities and assets as can be said to amount to a disposal of the business or a part of the business.

In each of the above later cases, the *McGregor* v *Adcock* test of Fox J has been criticised for substituting a further test for the simple one outlined above. In the joined appeals of *Atkinson* v *Dancer* and *Mannion* v *Johnston* [1988] STC 758, the *McGregor* v *Adcock* test had been accepted as the appropriate test by counsel for the parties, and was therefore not discussed by Peter Gibson J.

Business not the business of the individual making the disposal
This problem again arises in relation to the second of the types of material disposal referred to in **23.3.1.3**. The assets you are disposing of might not be assets of a business carried on by you. This might sound a rather fanciful problem to arise. However, the way in which the problem has in fact arisen is well illustrated by the facts of *Plumbly* v *Spencer* [1997] STC 301.

Read the extracts from the judgment of Lightman J in *Plumbly* v *Spencer*, at *Cases and Materials* **(23.1.1)**. Make a careful note of the facts, and of the reasons for his decision.

Not clear when the business ceased
This problem also arises in relation to the second type of material disposal referred to above. This is because there will be no material disposal of the second type, unless the business has ceased. Whether a business had ceased was the question considered by Scott V-C in *Marriott* v *Lane* [1996] 1 WLR 1211. In that case, land owned by the claimant of the relief had been disposed of. The land had previously been let by him to a company of which he was effectively the owner. The Revenue argued that relief was not available because the business had not ceased when the land was disposed of. It appeared that, when the company had ceased trading in October 1988, there was some possibility that it would begin to do so again. It never did do so, however. Scott V-C stated the relevant test in the following terms:

> [I]f, when the claim to . . . relief is made, it is clear that the business will not in fact be recommenced, it will consequently be clear that the business has ceased to be carried on and that the date on which it ceased to be carried on was the date on which the closure of the business in fact took place.

This is obviously quite a difficult question of fact.

23.3.2 OTHER EXEMPT GAINS

Memorise the following list, if you can. Exempt from CGT are gains:

■ On disposals of qualifying corporate bonds (QCBs): TCGA 1992, s. 115.

■ On disposals of investments in a PEP.

■ On damages for personal injuries: TCGA 1992, s. 51.

■ On gambling winnings: TCGA 1992, s. 51(1), ESC D33.

■ On disposals of decorations, unless acquired by the disponer for money or money's worth: TCGA 1992, s. 268.

■ On disposals of non-UK currency for private use: TCGA 1992, s. 269.

■ On disposals of annual payments: TCGA 1992, s. 237.

■ On disposals of ordinary shares in a VCT, where the cost of acquiring the shares did not exceed £100,000 in any one year: TCGA 1992, s. 151A.

■ On disposals of ordinary shares in an EIS company: TCGA 1992, s. 150A(2).

■ On some disposals of beneficial interests under settlements: TCGA 1992, s. 76(1): see **24.9**.

23.4 Provision making *Disposals* Exempt: Debts

The main provision making a disposal exempt is that which makes the disposal of a debt into an exempt disposal. The exemption provision is to be found in TCGA 1992, s. 251.

23.4.1 PERSONS AFFECTED

The exemption does not apply to companies, whose loan relationships are governed by the rules discussed in **11.5.2** and **11.7**. It does, however, apply to disposals of debts owed to individuals, whatever the capacity in which that individual makes the disposal. We have already discussed the reason for the exemption in **20.5.1**. By way of reminder, the real value of the principal amount of a debt will fall over time. This is because of the effect of inflation. Lenders therefore compensate themselves by charging debtors interest on loans made by them. The exemption is therefore directed at preventing allowable losses, rather than at taxing chargeable gains: **22.4.4.2**.

23.4.2 EFFECT OF THE EXEMPTION FOR DEBTS

The exemption turns a chargeable disposal into an exempt disposal, provided that the conditions summarised in **23.4.3** are satisfied. The Taxation of Chargeable Gains Act 1992, s. 251(1) says that:

> Where a person incurs a debt to another, whether in sterling or in some other currency, no chargeable gain shall accrue to that (that is the original) creditor or his personal representative or legatee on a disposal of the debt . . .

A disposal of a debt by the creditor could include the following events:

■ its repayment by the borrower to the lender, i.e. the satisfaction of the debt: TCGA 1992, s. 251(2);

■   the assignment of the benefit of the debt by the lender to a third party; *and*

■   its becoming of negligible value, e.g. through the insolvency of the borrower: see **21.3.3.5**.

In each case, provided the conditions summarised in **22.5.3** are satisfied, there will be no liability to CGT on the lender. What is worth noting in this section is that the exemption does not affect the status of the debt as a chargeable asset: TCGA 1992, s. 21. Instead, it exempts the disposal of the debt in all but one case, i.e. a *debt on a security*: see **24.7**. Much effort has been expended by professional advisers in attempting to manipulate debts on a security to create allowable losses.

Why?

Because of the general exemption for disposals of debts in TCGA 1992, s. 251.

23.4.3   CONDITIONS FOR THE EXEMPTION FOR DEBTS TO APPLY

The disposal of the debt is exempt, provided:

(a)   you, the creditor, are the original creditor, or his PR or beneficiary: TCGA 1992, s. 251; and

(b)   the debt is not a debt on a security, as defined by case law, e.g. *WT Ramsay Ltd* v *IRC* [1982] AC 300; *Taylor Clarke International* v *Lewis* [1997] STC 499.

You are the assignee of the benefit of a debt which is not a debt on a security. Will any disposal of it by you be a chargeable disposal?

Yes. One of the conditions for the exemption is not satisfied, i.e. you are not the original creditor.

We return to the definition of a debt on a security in **24.7**.

23.5   Provisions Postponing a CGT Charge on Gains Chargeable to CGT

23.5.1   INTRODUCTION

The provisions we shall be discussing in this section operate by postponing the charge to CGT which would otherwise arise on a chargeable disposal by a chargeable person of a chargeable asset. Newcomers to tax law often find this idea a bizarre one. Be that as it may, the provisions fall broadly into two categories:

■ *Roll-over reliefs*: these operate by postponing any CGT payable until some later disposal or event takes place.

■ *Hold-over reliefs*: these operate by postponing any CGT payable for a specified length of time.

In each of the sections below, we shall allocate the relief under consideration to one or other of these categories. That said, however, the terminology used in TCGA 1992 itself is sometimes inconsistent, so the practical effect of a particular relief postponing CGT may not be exactly reflected in the relevant legislation. Additionally, roll-over reliefs may operate in one of three basic ways, although there are variations on each:

(a) by deeming the disposal to take place for such a consideration as produces neither a gain nor a loss for both the person who disposes of the asset and the person who acquires it (*no gain/no loss disposals*);

(b) by separating out the CGT position of the person disposing of the asset and the person acquiring it, so that:

(i) The person disposing of the asset is treated as disposing of it for an amount equal to its base cost, the base cost of a replacement asset being reduced by the amount of the gain which would otherwise have been the chargeable gain; and

(ii) the person acquiring the asset is treated as acquiring it for the actual base cost to it. Thus, the position of the person acquiring the asset is unaffected by the roll-over relief given to the person disposing of it in (i); and

(c) by deeming there to have been no disposal and assuming that the replacement asset is one and the same as the original asset.

Hold-over relief is discussed in detail in **32.3.1**. Chargeable disposals include gifts as well as sales, and hold-over relief may be available to postpone the CGT payable on a gift.

23.5.2 REPLACEMENT OF BUSINESS ASSETS: TCGA 1992, ss. 152-159

23.5.2.1 Persons affected

Replacement roll-over relief is relevant to disposals of business assets, irrespective of the capacity in which a person may be disposing of those assets. In essence, it is designed to postpone a CGT charge when a person replaces an old business asset with a new one. As an individual, you might own a business asset which is used by a company in which you are a shareholder. Equally, you might own an asset which is used by a partnership of which you are a partner. In both cases, replacement roll-over relief should be available to you on the disposal of the asset, subject to satisfying the conditions summarised in **23.5.2.3**. If the asset is used by a company in which you are a shareholder, then the company must be your personal company, however: see below. As an employee, you might own a business asset which is used by you in your employment. Again, subject to the conditions summarised in **23.5.2.3**, the relief may be available to you on the disposal of the asset. The relief is the reason why a person carrying on a trade, profession or vocation would not normally expect to have to pay CGT on merely replacing assets used in the business.

23.5.2.2 Effect of replacement roll-over relief

Where replacement asset is not a depreciating asset
Here the relief operates in the second of the ways mentioned above. It therefore separates out the CGT position of the person disposing of the original asset and the person who

acquires it. The person *disposing* of the original asset is treated as disposing of it for an amount equal to its base cost, the base cost of the replacement asset being reduced by the amount of the gain which would otherwise have been the chargeable gain. The position of the person acquiring the original asset is unaffected by the operation of the relief for the seller: TCGA 1992, s. 152(1). Section 152(1) says that the person disposing of the original asset is to be treated:

(a)   as if the consideration for the disposal of . . . the old assets were . . . of such amount as would secure that on the disposal neither a gain nor a loss accrues to him, and

(b)   as if the amount or value of the consideration for the acquisition of . . . the new assets were reduced by the excess of the amount or value of the actual consideration for the disposal of . . . the old assets over the amount of the consideration which he is treated as receiving under paragraph (a) above.

Section 152(1) means that CGT which would otherwise be due on the disposal of the original asset is postponed indefinitely. This means that it should be possible to claim replacement roll-over relief when the replacement asset is itself disposed of, and the proceeds of its sale reinvested.

On 1 November 1998, the partners of Red, Brown & Co., a firm of solicitors in London, sell their freehold office premises, realising a gain of £2 million. On the same day, they acquire replacement freehold office premises for £2.5 million.

On the assumption that replacement roll-over relief can be claimed by them, will the partners be liable to pay CGT on the disposal?

No. It will be treated as having been made for such an amount as would produce neither a gain nor a loss.

For what consideration will the partners be deemed to have acquired the replacement premises?

£500,000, i.e. £2.5 million – £2 million.

Suppose the replacement premises are themselves sold on 1 April 1999 for £2.8 million, and the partnership dissolved. What will the chargeable gain on that disposal be?

£2.3 million, i.e. £2.8 million – £500,000.

Where replacement asset is *a depreciating asset*

A depreciating asset is an asset which will be a wasting asset in ten years' time. Where the replacement asset is a depreciating asset, replacement roll-over relief works in a different way. Rather than reducing the base cost of the replacement asset, the gain is 'held-over'. This is another way of saying that the gain is held in suspense. The gain will become chargeable if any one of the following events occurs:

■ the replacement depreciating asset is itself disposed of; or

■ except because of death, the claimant stops using the asset for the purpose of its business; or

■ ten years pass following the acquisition of the replacement asset.

The gain held in suspense may be deducted from the base cost of a second replacement asset, provided that it is not also a depreciating asset.

On 1 September 1992, Black Co. Ltd sold a business asset, realising a chargeable gain of £100,000, reinvesting the proceeds of sale in a depreciating asset on the same day. On 1 September 1998, it sold the depreciating asset and replaced it with a non-depreciating asset.

How is each disposal treated if replacement roll-over relief is successfully claimed in each case?

1 September 1992 – chargeable gain on disposal of original asset, which is held in suspense, rather than being deducted from the base cost of the replacement asset; 1 September 1998 – the gain held in suspense on the disposal of the original asset is deducted from the base cost of the second replacement asset.

23.5.2.3 Conditions for replacement roll-over relief to apply

Eight main conditions must be satisfied, which are as follows:

(1) The person disposing of the original asset must be:

■ an individual carrying on a trade; or

■ an individual carrying on a profession or vocation; or

■ an individual employee; or

■ a company carrying on a trade, profession or vocation.

(TCGA 1992, s. 158(1).)

(2)   The replacement asset must be bought not more than one year before, or three years after the disposal of the original asset.

In *Watton* v *Tippett* [1996] STC 101 (*Cases and Materials* (**23.2.1**)), Sir John Vinelott rejected a claim for roll-over relief because this condition was not satisfied. An individual had acquired freehold land and buildings, the whole of which was known as Unit 1, for an unapportioned consideration. Retaining what he designated Unit 1B, he then sold part of the same freehold land and buildings, designating the part sold Unit 1A. There was a chargeable gain on the disposal of Unit 1A. He claimed roll-over relief under ss. 152–159, TCGA 1992 in relation to the disposal of Unit 1A. The learned judge held that the relief was not available in these circumstances. Unit 1B had not been acquired as Unit 1B, but as part of the whole of Unit 1. Relief could however have been available, if the land and buildings had been acquired as Units 1A and 1B.

AND

(3)   Both the original and the replacement assets must be qualifying assets. This means that they must be included under one of the Classes of assets in TCGA 1992, s. 155.

The Classes of assets are as follows:

CLASS 1

■   Head A: land and buildings used and occupied for the purposes of the trade.

■   Head B: fixed plant and machinery not forming part of a building.

CLASS 2

Ships, aircraft and hovercraft.

CLASS 3

Satellites, space stations and spacecraft.

CLASS 4

Goodwill.

CLASS 5

Milk quotas and potato quotas.

CLASS 6

Ewe and suckler cow premium quotas.

It is not necessary for the original and replacement assets to fall within the same Class.

SAQ 314

Sid, a farmer, sells land and buildings (Class 1), investing the proceeds of sale in a hovercraft (Class 2). Will roll-over relief be available on the disposal of the land and buildings?

Yes, subject to the other conditions of the relief being satisfied.

AND

(4)   In the case of land and buildings (Class 1), the original assets must be used and occupied only for the purpose of the trade, etc. of the claimant.

AND

(5)   In the case of assets other than land and buildings, the original assets must be used only for the purposes of the trade, etc. of the claimant.

In relation to conditions (4) and (5), you may own the asset which is used or occupied, as the case may be, by a company in which you are a shareholder, or a partnership of which you are a partner. In the former case, the company must be your family company, as for retirement relief.

If you are an employee, the condition is satisfied where you provide the asset for use by your employer generally: SP 5/86.

AND

(6)   The person disposing of the original asset must acquire the replacement asset with the purpose of using it in their trade, etc. and not wholly or partly for the purpose of realising a gain on its disposal: TCGA 1992, s. 152(5).

AND

(7)   The replacement assets must be taken into use on their acquisition: TCGA 1992, s. 152(1) and *Campbell, Connelly & Co. Ltd* v *Barnett* [1994] STC 50.

AND

(8)   Replacement roll-over relief must be claimed by the person disposing of the original asset within six years after the end of the tax period in which the disposal takes place: TCGA 1992, s. 152(1); TMA 1970, s. 42.

In reading the above conditions, you should also note the problem areas discussed in **23.5.2.4**.

23.5.2.4   Problem areas with replacement roll-over relief

Some of the problems associated with this relief are as follows:

Person disposing does not use and occupy the asset for the purpose of the trade, etc.
A person might be disposing of the original asset but they might not use and occupy it themselves. This problem can easily arise, for instance, where:

■   as a partner, you might be disposing of partnership property used and occupied by one of your partners; *or*

■   a company might be disposing of property used or occupied by its employees.

In any such case, the availability of the relief on the disposal of the original asset is unaffected, provided that the occupation is *representative of the owner's occupation*. The occupation will be representative, provided that one of two conditions is satisfied. These conditions are derived from a dictum of Lord Upjohn in the rating case of *Northern Ireland Valuation Commissioner* v *Fermanagh Protestant Board of Education* [1969] 1 WLR 1708, 1722. From that case, it is apparent that either:

■   it is essential for the partner or employee to occupy the property, in order for them to carry out their duties; or

■ the partnership agreement or contract of employment contains an obligation for the partner or employee to occupy the property and they are enabled to perform their duties better by so doing.

SAQ 315

Alf, his wife Bertha, and Charlie, their son, own a farm, and run the farming business in partnership. They sell a field to a property developer, and use the chargeable gain to build a house for Charlie on one of the fields retained. It is not essential for Charlie to live in the house, nor is there any provision in the partnership agreement obliging him to do so. Alf, Bertha and Charlie wish to claim replacement roll-over relief on the disposal of the field.

Will Charlie's occupation of the house be representative of its occupation by the partnership?

No: *Anderton v Lamb* [1981] STC 43, from which the above facts are adapted.

Replacement asset not used in the same trade, etc. as the original asset
The original asset might be used in one trade, but the person disposing of it might wish to use its replacement in another. This does not affect the applicability of the relief. However, where one trade is carried on in succession to another, by the person disposing of the original asset, the period between the cessation of the one, and the commencement of the other, must not be greater than three years: SP 8/81.

SAQ 316

Utopia Ltd, a trading company, carries on two separate trades, Trade 1 and Trade 2. On 1 November 1998, a building which it uses and occupies for the purpose of Trade 1 is sold by it, and the proceeds of its sale are used to acquire a replacement building, for use in Trade 2.

Does the fact that the original and replacement buildings are used in different trades make roll-over relief unavailable?

No.

Replacement asset is a wasting asset
The replacement asset might be a wasting asset. If this is the case, then the operation of the relief is modified: see **23.5.2.2**.

There is an allowable loss on the disposal of the original asset
The disposal of the original asset may not realise a chargeable gain. Instead, it may realise an allowable loss. If so, then there is obviously no need to claim the relief!

Only part of the proceeds of sale of the original asset are reinvested in the replacement asset
In some cases, the person disposing of the original asset may not use the whole of the proceeds of its sale to acquire a replacement. A typical example of this is where the cost of the replacement asset is less than the proceeds of sale of the original asset. As you might imagine, in that situation, the availability of roll-over relief is limited to the amount actually reinvested.

On 1 September 1998 Terry, a sole trader, realises a chargeable gain of £55,000 on the disposal of his shop premises. On 1 October 1998, he acquires replacement shop premises for £40,000. What gain must be included in his CGT calculation for 1998/99?

£15,000, i.e. £55,000 − £40,000. £15,000 is the amount not reinvested.

The gain is less than your annual exempt amount
This situation will not be relevant to companies, of course. As an individual (including a trustee or PR), you should not, of course, claim roll-over relief under TCGA 1992, ss. 152-159, if the gain on the disposal of the original asset is less than your annual exempt amount, taking into account any other relevant chargeable disposals.

23.5.4 INCORPORATION OF A BUSINESS: TCGA 1992, s. 162

A sole trader, or the partners of a partnership, decide to incorporate the trade carried on by them. To do so, they dispose of the business carried on by them as sole traders or partners, including its assets, in return for the issue to them of shares in the company, or part shares and part cash: **13.4.3.6**. Note that the issue of shares by the company is not a disposal by the company of a chargeable asset – it is merely the consideration for the disposal of the assets of the business.

Section 162, TCGA 1992 provides a form of roll-over relief in respect of the gain on the disposal of the business in return for shares, although *not* for any gain on a disposal in return for cash. Any chargeable gain on the disposal of the business assets is deducted from the base cost of the newly-issued shares in the company.

23.5.5 THE ENTERPRISE INVESTMENT SCHEME

In practice, this is a very important relief, although there is space to discuss it only very briefly. For income tax purposes, EIS provides a deduction from total tax (see **10.3.3**), but there are CGT benefits also. In a nutshell, EIS enables an individual or trustee who has realised a chargeable gain, to postpone liability to pay CGT by reinvesting that gain in a *qualifying investment*: TCGA 1992, sch. 5B, para. 1(1)(c). A qualifying investment is a subscription for new shares, i.e. eligible shares, in an EIS company, in relation to which the investor is entitled to income tax relief: see **10.3.3**. In addition, gains on disposals of EIS shares are exempt if they have been held for at least five years: TCGA 1992, ss. 150A(2) and 150B. This was mentioned at **23.3.2**.

23.6 Summary

A number of reliefs reduce the CGT burden by turning what would otherwise be a chargeable gain into an exempt gain. Instances are disposals of investments in a PEP, gambling winnings and disposals of shares in an EIS company. Retirement relief exempts the whole or part of a gain on the disposal of your business interests at the age of 50 or over, or through ill-health. At present, the maximum chargeable gain which could be exempted by the relief would be £625,000. In order to qualify for retirement relief, you must have owned the interest in the business for at least a year, although you get the maximum relief only if you have owned that interest for 10 years. Considerable problems have arisen with retirement relief, especially with farmers, and the first two types of disposals covered by the relief. In at least one case, that of debts, it is the disposal, rather than the gain which is exempted from CGT. Other provisions postpone liability to CGT, most importantly perhaps replacement roll-over relief for the replacement of business assets. The reliefs discussed in this chapter mean that, properly managed, a business can avoid paying CGT on profitable disposals of its capital assets. Equally, they mean that small businesspeople, and shareholders in small companies, can avoid paying CGT until they retire. Together with the provisions relating to shareholders discussed in the next chapter, they help to explain why, even for people with considerable investments, the impact of CGT is often insignificant.

23.7   End of Chapter Assessment Question

Refer to the facts concerning Amber Ltd: see **2.6**, **6.6** and **8.9**. It is 1 December 1998. The four shareholders in the company have been approached by Megabrackets plc with an offer hard to refuse. Megabrackets plc has offered to buy all of the issued share capital of Amber Ltd from each of the four shareholders. In spite of Amber Ltd's relatively poor trading performance recently, each of the four would make a profit in the region of £500,000. Alan, who will be 62 on 3 March 1999, and Bertram, who is 45 but in poor heath, are keen to accept the offer, since they would both like to retire. Deborah, 35, wishes to devote more time to her work as a partner in Brown & Co., so she is also amenable. Bertram, in his capacity as the executor of Charlie's estate, has no qualms about accepting the offer. All four shareholders acquired their shareholdings on the incorporation of Amber Ltd, on 20 April 1990.

Advise Alan, Bertram and Deborah whether any reliefs from CGT would be available to shelter the gain on the disposal of the shares, and the effect of those reliefs. (Advise Bertram in his personal capacity only.)

(Word limit: 750 (100 marks).)

See *Cases and Materials* (**23.4**) for a specimen answer.

CHAPTER TWENTY-FOUR

INVESTMENT TAXATION: PARTICULAR TYPES OF CHARGEABLE ASSET

24.1 Objectives

By the end of this chapter, you should be able to:

■ explain *why* options, wasting assets, goodwill, shares and debts on a security present problems of analysis for CGT;

■ identify those *analytical problems* for each type of chargeable asset;

■ explain the *solutions* to those analytical problems provided by the CGT rules.

24.2 Introduction

Certain categories of chargeable assets present problems of analysis for CGT. The problems vary depending on the type of chargeable asset under consideration. To illustrate the problems, as well as the solutions offered by the CGT rules, I have selected a range of assets. These are options, a number of categories of wasting assets, goodwill, shares and debts on a security. In relation to wasting assets, I have included a short section about disposals of capital allowance-bearing wasting assets. I have also included a brief reference to interests under settlements, as a type of asset. This is intended as an indication of the types of issue we shall be discussing in **Chapters 28** and **29**. I hope in the course of this chapter to distil some unifying themes from this wide-ranging discussion, and I have therefore adopted a particular approach to each asset. I would encourage you to take this approach too. For each type of asset, note exactly what problems of analysis are presented by it, and follow this up with a note of how the CGT rules attempt to solve those problems. References to CGT include references to corporation tax on chargeable gains, unless otherwise indicated.

24.3 Options

24.3.1 CGT PROBLEMS PRESENTED BY OPTIONS

An option is a chargeable asset for CGT purposes, because of TCGA 1992, s. 21(1)(a). Section 21(1)(a) says that chargeable assets include:

. . . [O]ptions, debts and incorporeal property generally . . .

Options can be of two kinds: options *to sell* and options *to purchase*. The former are sometimes referred to as *put options*. The latter are sometimes referred to as *call options*. Each raises specific problems for CGT purposes:

■ An *option to sell*, a put option, is one where you pay me a sum of money, in return for which I grant you the option of selling property to me for a specified price within a fixed period.

■ An *option to purchase*, a call option, is one where you pay me a sum of money, in return for which I grant you the option of buying property from me for a specified price within a fixed period.

With a *put option*, the main problem is that of the relationship between the price you pay me to acquire the option and the proceeds of your sale to me of the property over which the option subsists. With a *call option*, the main problem is that of the relationship between the price paid to me to acquire the option and the cost of acquiring from me the property over which the option subsists. In both cases, I am the grantor of the option. In both cases, the assumption is that the option is in fact exercised. In both cases, you might simply abandon the option, rather than exercise it.

24.3.2   SOLUTIONS PROVIDED BY THE CGT RULES

The solutions offered by CGT to these problems are in TCGA 1992, ss. 144-147. In each case, the grant of the option by me will count as a disposal by me of a chargeable asset, i.e. the option. However, rather than charging CGT on the amount received by me on this disposal, the grant of the option and its exercise are usually analysed as a single transaction. On this basis:

■ In the case of a *put option*, the consideration for the grant of the option is added to your base cost of the asset over which the option is eventually exercised.

■ In the case of a *call option*, the consideration for the grant of the option is also added to your base cost of the asset over which the option has been exercised.

I own Blackacre. On 1 February 1999, I grant you an option to purchase Blackacre for £90,000 at any time between 1 February 1999 and 1 February 2000. You pay me £1,000 for the option. On 1 April 1999, you exercise the option. How are we each dealt with for CGT purposes?

In my CGT calculation for 1998/1999, the disposal proceeds of Blackacre will be £91,000. When you come to dispose of Blackacre, your base cost will be £91,000.

You own Greenacre. On 1 February 1999, I grant you an option to sell Greenacre to me for £90,000 at any time between 1 February 1999 and 1 February 2000. You pay me £1,000 for the option. On 1 April 1999, you exercise it. How are we each dealt with for CGT purposes?

In my CGT calculation for the tax year in which I eventually make a chargeable disposal of Greenacre, my acquisition cost for Greenacre will be £89,000, i.e. £90,000 − £1,000. Your disposal proceeds of Greenacre in 1998/99 will be reduced by the cost of the option, i.e. from £90,000 to £89,000.

If, in each case, if you had abandoned the option, rather than exercised it, then you would not have been able to claim an allowable loss for the £1,000 spent by you in acquiring it. This is because an option is a wasting asset (see **24.4**), unless it falls within one of the following categories (TCGA 1992, s. 146):

■ quoted options to subscribe for company shares;

■ quoted traded options;

■ financial options; and

■ options to acquire business assets.

There is a further exception to the non-availability of allowable losses where I, the grantor, pay you, the grantee, to release my option. If I do so, then *you* will have made a disposal because *you* will have derived a capital sum from an asset: TCGA 1992, s. 22(1): **21.3.3.2**. In these circumstances, you should be able to claim an allowable loss: *Golding* v *Kaufman* [1985] STC 152.

Read the extracts from the judgment of Vinelott J in *Golding* v *Kaufman* [1985] STC 152, at *Cases and Materials* (24.1.1). Read also the article by Patrick Soares which follows it. List the conclusions which can be drawn from these sources about the CGT treatment of options.

24.4 Wasting Assets

24.4.1 CGT PROBLEMS PRESENTED BY WASTING ASSETS

Wasting assets are assets with a predictable life of 50 years or less: TCGA 1992, s. 44(1). The problem they present for CGT is that, on their disposal, they have a scrap value only. Wasting assets include:

■ all tangible moveable property with a predictable life of 50 years or less, subject to the exceptions in **22.4.3**, and not including commodities which are dealt in on a terminal market: TCGA 1992, s. 45(4);

■ options, except those listed in **24.3.2**;

■ some intellectual property rights, including patents and some copyrights; and

■ leases with 50 years or less to run.

Anyone who buys a wasting asset from me will only be able to enjoy it to some lesser extent than I did, simply because of its finite useful lifetime. The general principles of CGT seem inappropriate in this situation. A special solution is therefore required. Leases of land which have 50 years or less to run are subject to a different solution from leases of other property having 50 years or less to run: **24.4.2.2**.

24.4.2 SOLUTIONS PROVIDED BY THE CGT RULES

The CGT rules tackle the problem by sometimes turning a loss on the disposal of a wasting asset into a gain! They achieve this by reducing the base cost of the wasting asset by its scrap value, and reducing the amount left by a proportion determined by reference to the remainder of its useful life.

24.4.2.1 Wasting assets *other than* leases of land with 50 years or less to run

In order to apply the rules in TCGA 1992, I need to know what the predictable useful life of the asset in question is. I also need to know what its scrap value is at the time at which I dispose of it. If I know both of these things, then I can go through the following stages (ignoring the IA):

(a) write down the proceeds of sale of the wasting asset;

(b) deduct the scrap value of the asset from its base cost;

(c) deduct from figure found in (b) the fraction of years for which the person disposing of the asset has owned it, over its predictable useful life, multiplied by the figure in (b); and

(d) deduct the figure found in (c) from the *proceeds of sale* of the asset.

I bought a wasting asset on 1 November 1988 for £15,000. It has a predictable useful life of 20 years. On 1 November 1998, I sell it for £12,000. On 1 November 1998, its scrap value is £1,500. What will the chargeable gain on the sale be (ignoring the IA)?

	£	£
Disposal proceeds		12,000
Base cost	15,000	
Less scrap value	(1,500)	
	13,500	
Less		
10/20 × 13,500	(6,750)	
	6,750	(6,750)
Gain		5,250

24.4.2.2 Leases of land with 50 years or less to run

A lease is still a wasting asset even if there is a statutory right of extension beyond 50 years: *Lewis* v *Walters* [1992] STC 97; see *Cases and Materials* (24.2.1). If I grant a lease out of my superior estate in land, I make a part disposal of that estate for CGT purposes: **21.3.3.3**. Thus, if I charge a premium on the grant of the lease, I will realise a chargeable gain. The answer to **SAQ 320** shows how wasting assets *other than* leases of land are written-off by an equal amount each year. This is not the case with leases of land. Instead, they are written-off according to the table in TCGA 1992, sch. 7, which produces an increasingly steep curve towards the end of the lease. This is designed to reflect the fact that the value of leases can *plummet* towards the end of their term. Where the grant of a lease premium is subject to income tax or corporation tax under Schedule A (see **17.5**), that tax reduces the disposal proceeds of granting the lease for CGT purposes.

ACTIVITY56

Read the judgment of Mummery J in *Lewis* v *Walters* [1992] STC 97, at *Cases and Materials* (24.2.1).

24.5 Goodwill

24.5.1 CGT PROBLEMS PRESENTED BY GOODWILL

Goodwill is a chargeable asset, for CGT purposes, because of TCGA 1992, s. 21(1)(c). Section 21(1)(c) says that chargeable assets include:

> . . . [A]ny form of property created by the person disposing of it, or otherwise coming to be owned without being acquired.

This obviously includes goodwill built up from scratch. Goodwill, or a share in goodwill, can also be bought, e.g. by an individual becoming a partner in a firm. Goodwill creates two specific problems for partners, one for retiring partners, the other for the continuing ones:

- whether, having originally paid for a share of the goodwill, a retiring partner can claim an allowable loss if that goodwill is written-off by the continuing partners; and

■ whether, so far as the continuing partners are concerned, the writing-off of the outgoing partner's goodwill enables them to make a negligible value claim in respect of it, under TCGA 1992, s. 24(2): see **21.3.3.5**.

24.5.2 SOLUTIONS PROVIDED BY THE CGT RULES

Unfortunately, CGT currently provides no easy solution to either problem. To the first problem, the solution would appear to be that you, the retiring partner, can do so, although there would appear to be no direct authority for this proposition.

You have been a partner in Bloggs & Co., solicitors, since 1982. You retire on 1 November 1998. On becoming a partner, you paid £60,000 for a share of the firm's goodwill. The continuing partners have resolved to write-off goodwill when a partner retires, so you will receive no payment for your share. Will you be able to claim an allowable loss?

Yes, apparently.

To the second problem, however, the answer would appear to be No, although again there seems to be no direct authority. In general terms, the Revenue seem to take the view that writing-off the goodwill does not give rise to a negligible value claim because goodwill keeps its value, even though an incoming partner may not pay for it, and even though it is not shown in the partnership's balance-sheet: see *Cases and Materials* (**1.4.3**).

24.6 Shares

24.6.1 CGT PROBLEMS PRESENTED BY SHARES

Shares in a company are a very common type of chargeable asset. The analysis of transactions involving shares raises particular CGT problems, because of two features possessed by them:

■ The fact that they cannot be identified individually. As a shareholder, I cannot physically identify the shares I own at any one time, except by the share certificate or certificates which relate to them. There is nothing to prevent a share certificate being merged with another share certificate and reissued to me, for instance. This is why shares are sometimes referred to, perhaps misleadingly, as *fungible assets*. For instance, I might own a number of shares in a large public company over a period of many years and, as the years go by, I might buy some more shares in the same company, or sell some of them. Shares sold by me might be ones acquired after my original shareholding in the company, or they might be part of my original shareholding itself. The obvious question, in CGT terms, is what the base cost of the shares sold is when I am calculating any chargeable gain on their disposal.

■ The wide variety of transactions in which shares may be involved. I might simply sell some or all of my shareholding in a company, in order to realise my investment. However, other events might happen in the life of the company which, whilst not necessarily involving a sale of shares by me, the shareholder, may none the less mean that I acquire new shares or dispose of old ones. If so, then those events will have CGT implications, either in relation to the base cost of my original shareholding, or in relation to disposal proceeds on a later disposal of some, or all, of my shares.

ACTIVITY 57

Find a good dictionary, and look up the meaning of *fungible*. Consider how accurate it is to describe shares in a company as fungible assets.

Let's concentrate on the second of the features above, for a moment. Examples of such events in the life of the company might be as follows:

(a) a company in which I am a shareholder might be taken over by another company; *or*

(b) a company in which I am a shareholder might decide to alter any voting or other rights attaching to the shares owned by me; *or*

(c) a company in which I am a shareholder might issue and allot new shares to me, in respect of and in proportion to my existing shareholding.

The second and third of these events are both types of reorganisation in a company's share capital. The question will be whether any of these three events in the life of the company involves an acquisition or a chargeable disposal of shares, for the purposes of CGT.

A sale of some or all of my shares will obviously involve me in making a disposal, which means that (a) above, which will involve me selling shares for cash or kind, will do so too. Somewhat less obviously, (b) and (c) may involve acquisitions and chargeable disposals also for CGT purposes. We shall consider the detail of each of these possibilities in a moment.

Before going any further, however, I should emphasise that the events discussed above are merely illustrations of the range of transactions in which shares can be involved. The aim of the next section is to establish the exact nature of the events, or transactions, to be discussed. This type of information is important because you must be able to understand the transactional contexts in which the CGT rules operate.

24.6.1.1   Sales of shares

Share sales are simple enough in concept. They occur on widely differing scales. I might own 3,000 shares in a large company whose shares are quoted on the Stock Exchange and decide to sell some or all of them through stockbrokers.

At the other end of the scale, I might own 100% of my personal trading company and, together with the other shareholder or shareholders, might be selling my shares in the company to other individuals or to another company. Such a sale to another company was the situation you were asked to consider in **23.7**. If all the shares in a company are sold in this way, then naturally the ownership of the company will be transferred from the original shareholders to the purchasers of the shares.

In relation to shares acquired before 6 April 1965, slightly different CGT rules can apply, as we shall discover, depending on whether the shares I am selling are those of a quoted company or an unquoted company.

SAQ 322

Refer to SAQ 2. If I buy the company from you, what am I in fact buying from you?

All the issued share capital of the company.

If I am selling you the whole of my shareholding in a company, I will have to complete a stock transfer form. This is the 'proper instrument of transfer', which is required by the CA 1985, s. 183(1). It will show the transfer of the shares from me, the seller, to you, the purchaser. I will then send the form, together with my share certificate, or share certificates, to you.

You will pay the stamp duty chargeable on the stock transfer form (see **21.9.2.2**), and return both the share certificate and the stock transfer form to the company. Your name will then be registered in the register of shareholders of the company and a new share certificate will be issued to you.

If I am selling you *only some* of my shares, the procedure is the same, except that I will send the stock transfer form and either my share certificate, or sufficient share certificates to cover the shares sold, to the company. The company will then certify that I, the seller, have produced a certificate to the company which shows that I am the owner of the shares I am selling. The company will send a new certificate to me, certifying my ownership of the shares I have retained. The stock transfer form will then be sent on to you, the purchaser, for payment of the stamp duty on the transfer by you.

You will then return the share certificate to the company, so that your name can be entered on its register of members and a new certificate can be issued to you for the part of my original shareholding which I have sold to you.

I own 100% of the issued share capital of Andrew Ltd, my personal trading company. I agree to sell the whole of this shareholding to you. What is the procedure for effecting the sale?

(As above.)

24.6.1.2 Takeovers

A takeover involves the acquisition of one company's shares by another company. The company whose shares are acquired is known as the *Target*. The company acquiring the Target is naturally referred to as the *Purchaser*. The result of the transaction is that the Purchaser will own all of the shares in the Target. As a shareholder in the Target, I will therefore be disposing of my shareholding in the Target, in favour of the Purchaser company. I may receive the consideration for the sale in a number of forms:

(a)   I might be offered cash in return for my shares. If so, the effect of the transaction will be exactly the same as for the sale of shares described above, and the CGT analysis of the transaction will be the same as that described below. This will be what takes place if, e.g., I sell-up and retire from my personal trading company. I will cease to have any financial interest in the Target. *Or*

(b) I might be offered newly-issued shares in the Purchaser in return for my shares in the Target. If so, the effect of the transaction will be different from the sale of shares described above. This is because I will become a shareholder in the Purchaser, along with its existing shareholders.

Diagrammatically, the two stages of the transaction in (b) can be shown thus:

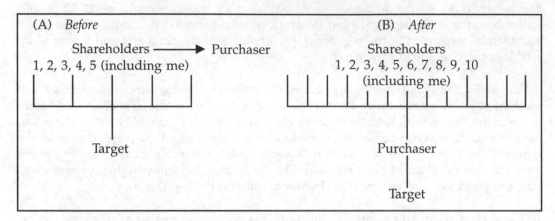

As stressed above, this is *not* the effect of the transaction if I sell my shares in the Target for cash. There, I will walk away from the Target altogether.

(A) above shows my shares being sold to the Purchaser. (B) shows me as a shareholder in the Purchaser, the Purchaser owning all the shares of the Target. In (B), I will continue to have a financial interest in the Target, by virtue of my shareholding in the Purchaser. *Or*

(c) I might be offered newly-issued loan-stock, i.e. debentures, in the Purchaser, in return for my shareholding in the Target. If so, the analysis will be similar to that in (b) above although, instead of becoming a shareholder in the Purchaser, along with its existing shareholders, I will become a loan stock-holder or debenture-holder in the Purchaser. Again, in this situation, I will continue to have a financial interest in the Target, by virtue of my holding of debentures in the Purchaser. *Or*

(d) I might be offered any combination of each of the above. If so, my shareholding or debenture-holding in the Purchaser will be proportionately reduced by the amount of cash I will have taken in addition to shares and/or stock.

In each of situations (a) to (d) above, the Purchaser's offer will be made to me, as a shareholder in the Target. However, the directors of the Target, who may be shareholders of it, as well as directors of it, may recommend me either to accept the offer or to reject it.

One further point needs to be mentioned. If the Target, the company in which I own my shares, is a large public company, the offer will be made to me by letter, as well as to all the other shareholders in it. However, if my shareholding is in a small private company, the Purchaser or its representatives will negotiate the offer with me personally, or through my professional advisers, in consultation with me. If the Target is a public company, the offer will be subject to the procedural rules of *The City Code on Takeovers and Mergers* which, although it does not have binding legal force, is strictly observed in practice. The main rules of *The City Code on Takeovers and Mergers* include the following:

(a) the Purchaser must offer to acquire the whole of the Target's shares, at such time as it holds 30% of the Target's shares;

(b) an offer by a Purchaser must be equally favourable to all of the Target's shareholders; and

(c) strict time-limits must be observed in relation to the offer.

24.6.1.3 Reorganisations of share capital

Alteration of rights attaching to shares
This may simply involve the alteration of rights attaching to shares. However, it may also involve the conversion of loans or loan-stock into shares. This will require the company to observe particular company law rules, which are not relevant to the position of the individual shareholder. The question will be whether the alteration of the rights, or the nature of the investment, i.e. as loan-stock or shares, will involve an acquisition or chargeable disposal of shares by the shareholder for CGT purposes.

Bonus issues and rights issues
If there is a *bonus issue* of shares in the company of which I am a shareholder, it means that there is a *free* distribution of shares to me. For example, I might receive two new shares free of charge for each share which I already own in the company. A rights issue is similar, except that I have to pay for the new shares which I receive. Again, the question will be whether the bonus issue or rights issue involves an acquisition or chargeable disposal of shares by the shareholder for CGT purposes.

Demergers
There could be a demerger involving the company in which I am a shareholder. For our purposes, a demerger can take one of *two* forms:

■ a direct distribution of shares in a subsidiary company to me; or

■ an indirect distribution of shares in a subsidiary company to me.

For me, as a shareholder, each of these has the effect for me set out below. It may be helpful to think of each of the first two forms as *reversing* the takeover – or merger – transaction discussed above (hence the term *demerger*).

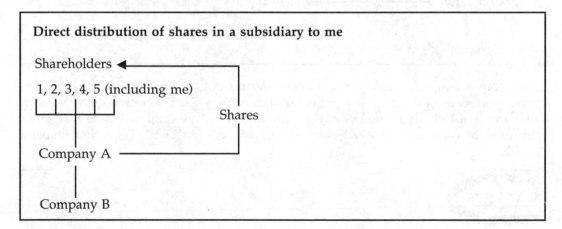

Company A distributes its shares in Company B direct to its shareholders. This is called a direct distribution because the shares in Company B pass directly from ownership by Company A to ownership by the shareholders of Company A, i.e. 1, 2, 3, 4 and 5 (including me).

What is the result of this process?

The result is that, instead of owning a holding company (Company A) and a subsidiary (Company B), the shareholders of Company A own two separate companies, Company A and Company B:

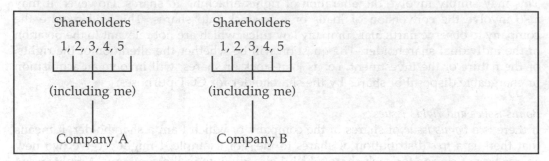

Note that no cash is involved in the transaction, and Company B is owned by A's shareholders rather than Company A.

This transaction could take a more elaborate form, where Company A has a second subsidiary, Company C. In that case, Company C could also be demerged by distributing its shares, as shown above.

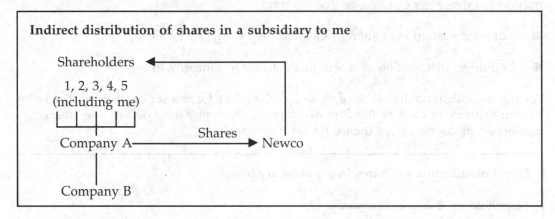

In this transaction, Company A distributes its shares in Company B to its shareholders *indirectly*, instead of directly. It is called an indirect distribution because the shares in Company B, its wholly owned subsidiary, are transferred by Company A to Newco, in return for the issue of shares by Newco to Company A's shareholders, *not* to Company A itself.

What is the result of this process?

The result is that, instead of owning a holding company (Company A) with its subsidiary (Company B), the shareholders of Company A own two companies, Company B having been moved from the ownership of Company A to the ownership of Newco:

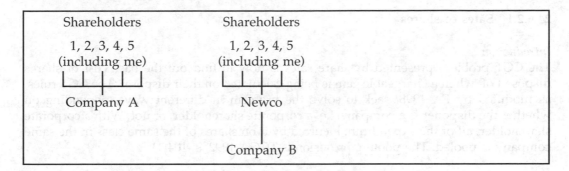

This transaction could take a more elaborate form, where Company A has a second subsidiary, Company C. In that case, Company C could be transferred to Newco 2, a second newly-formed company. Company A would transfer its shares in Company C to Newco 2, in return for the issue of shares by Newco 2 to Company A's shareholders.

The result is of this more elaborate form is that, instead of owning a holding company (Company A) with two subsidiaries (Companies B and C), the shareholders of Company A would then own three companies, Company B having been moved from the ownership of Company A to the ownership of Newco (see above) and Company C having been moved from the ownership of Company A to the ownership of Newco 2. Company A could then be wound up or dissolved.

Sinclair v *Lee* [1993] 3 All ER 926 involved an indirect distribution of shares, basically in the form shown above. *Sinclair* v *Lee* concerned trustee shareholders of life interest trusts. The question was whether, as a matter of trusts law, the newly-issued shares in Newco were received by them as an addition to the capital of the trust fund, or as an income receipt. For trustees of life interest trusts, the issue was a crucially important one. If they were an income receipt, they belonged to the life tenant. If they were a capital receipt, they belonged to the remainderman: **26.4.2**. In a much-criticised judgment, Sir Donald Nicholls V-C held that they were a *capital* receipt.

(I should acknowledge my indebtedness in this section to the article, 'Private Company Reconstructions', by R K Hutchinson, *The Tax Journal*, 10 October 1991, p. 10.)

24.6.2 SOLUTIONS PROVIDED BY THE CGT RULES

We now need to consider the CGT consequences of each of these transactions. Since this chapter is about particular types of chargeable assets, we shall be considering only the consequences for the shareholder, not for the company in which the shares are held.

For CGT purposes, there are two key issues:

■ whether any of these transactions involves an acquisition, or a chargeable disposal, of a chargeable asset; and

■ if so, what is the chargeable asset acquired or disposed of.

There is no comprehensive definition of 'shares' for CGT purposes. Section 288(1), TCGA 1992 merely defines them to include stock, as distinct from loan-stock: see above. However, it is clear that the word 'share' must be given its ordinary meaning, namely a share or a definite portion of a company's capital.

'Stock' is an older form of share, which is divisible into fractions. In TCGA 1992, the term 'securities' is often used to include shares, stock and loan-stock, and the definition used in a particular statutory provision will make it clear whether one or another of these is intended in the particular context.

24.6.2.1 Sales of shares

Introduction

The CGT problem presented by share sales is how to find out the base cost of shares disposed of, when a chargeable gain is being calculated on their disposal. The CGT rules, as modified by FA 1998, seek to solve the problem in different ways, depending on whether the disponer is a company, i.e. a corporate shareholder, or not. With a corporate shareholder, all of the expenditure incurred by it on shares of the same class in the same company is pooled. The pooling provision is TCGA 1992, s. 104(1):

> Any number of securities of the same class acquired by the same person in the same capacity shall for the purposes of this Act be regarded as indistinguishable parts of a single asset growing or diminishing on the occasions on which additional securities of the same class are acquired or some of the securities of that class are disposed of.

Note that s. 104 uses the term *securities*, which includes shares, although not QCBs: TCGA 1992, ss. 104(3), 108. Section 104(1) then states that pooling does not apply to any shares acquired by a corporate shareholder before 1 April 1982. Pooling only applies to shares acquired by an individual after 5 April 1982, and before 6 April 1998: TCGA 1992, s. 104(2)(aa). It does not therefore apply to non-corporate shareholders acquiring shares after 5 April 1998. A pool of shares to which TCGA 1992, s. 104 applies is described as a Section 104 Holding: TCGA 1992, s. 104(3).

The cost of shares acquired on or before 5 April 1982 (for non-corporate shareholders) or 31 March 1982 (for corporate shareholders) must be dealt with separately from any Section 104 Holding. The legislation sets up two categories of such expenditure:

(a) expenditure on shares acquired between 5 April 1965 and 5 April 1982 (*'the 1982 Holding'*); and

(b) expenditure on shares acquired before 6 April 1965 (*'the Pre-CGT Holding'*).

The 1982 Holding is, like the Section 104 Holding, *frozen*. However, unlike the Section 104 Holding, which can still grow and diminish so far as shares acquired by corporate shareholders are concerned, the 1982 Holding is frozen for *both* individual and corporate shareholders. The reason for the freeze is that TCGA 1992, s. 109(2)(a) says that, although expenditure on shares comprised in the 1982 Holding is regarded as expenditure on a single asset, the 1982 Holding:

> . . . cannot grow by the acquisition of additional [shares] of the same class . . .

For the purposes of a *Pre-CGT Holding*, a distinction is drawn between quoted shares and unquoted shares. The distinction is explained below.

There are therefore *five* separate sets of rules, i.e.:

■ rules for *corporate shareholders* for shares acquired and disposed of after 5 April 1982;

■ rules for *individual shareholders* for shares acquired *and* disposed of after 5 April 1998;

■ rules for *individual shareholders* for shares disposed of after 5 April 1998 and acquired before 6 April 1998;

■ rules for both *individual* and *corporate shareholders* for shares disposed of after 5 April 1998 and comprised in a *1982 Holding; and*

■ rules for both *individual* and *corporate shareholders* for shares disposed of after 5 April 1998 and comprised in a *Pre-CGT Holding*.

We now consider each of these in turn.

Corporate shareholders: shares acquired and disposed of after 5 April 1982
A corporate shareholder has a Section 104 Holding for all shares of the same class acquired by it on or after 6 April 1982. Every time the corporate shareholder acquires more shares of that class, their acquisition cost will go into the Section 104 Holding set up for all shares of that class.

What does the Section 104 Holding therefore represent?

The total base cost of all shares acquired by the corporate shareholder in a single company on or after 6 April 1982.

If the corporate shareholder disposes of all of the shares in a Section 104 Holding, their base cost will be the expenditure in that Section 104 Holding at the time of the disposal. Equally, if it disposes of only some of the shares comprised in a Section 104 Holding, the base cost of the shares disposed of will be found by using the statutory formula for part-disposals: see **21.3.3.3.** Finding the base cost of the shares in a Section 104 Holding should therefore be simple enough. What complicates matters, however, is the need to apply the IA to the base cost. This is achieved by maintaining two separate pools of expenditure. One pool is an Unindexed Pool of Expenditure. The other is an Indexed Pool of Expenditure. These two pools of expenditure can be shown in two columns as follows, with details of the number of shares acquired, within the Section 104 Holding:

Number of shares acquired	Unindexed Pool of Expenditure £	Indexed Pool of Expenditure £

Before considering an example of the pooling system for corporate shareholders, two further points should be noted.

■ If the corporate shareholder is disposing of shares in the Section 104 Holding which were acquired by it between 1 April 1982 and 1 April 1985, the opening value of the Indexed Pool of Expenditure is the value of shares owned at 1 April 1985, plus the IA which would have applied if the shares had been sold on 1 April 1985.

■ Every time the corporate shareholder acquires more shares, the IA is applied to the Indexed Pool of Expenditure. Every time shares in the Section 104 Holding are disposed of, the IA is also applied to the Indexed Pool of Expenditure.

Utopia Ltd buys 100,000 shares in Megabucks Ltd for £100,000 in July 1982. Utopia Ltd then buys 75,000 more in August 1983 for £100,000. What is the value of the Indexed Pool of Expenditure on 6 April 1985? (Assume an indexed rise decimal of 0.158 for the July 1982 acquisition, and an indexed rise decimal of 0.106 for the August 1983 acquisition.)

Number of shares acquired	Unindexed Pool of Expenditure £	Indexed Pool of Expenditure £
175,000	200,000	200,000
Plus IA:		
(a) £100,000 × 0.158		15,800
(b) £100,000 × 0.106		10,600
Value of Indexed Pool of Expenditure on 6 April 1985		226,400

If Utopia Ltd later disposes of only some of the shares comprised in the Indexed Pool of Expenditure for its *Megabucks Ltd Section 104 Holding*, any chargeable gain or allowable loss on the shares disposed of will be found as follows:

(a) calculate the unindexed base cost of the shares disposed of, by using the part-disposal formula: see **21.3.3.3**;

(b) calculate the IA applicable to the base cost in (a), by applying the part-disposal formula to the Indexed Pool of Expenditure;

(c) calculate the IA available on the disposal, by deducting (a) from (b); *and*

(d) calculate the chargeable gain by deducting the sum of (a) plus (c) from the disposal proceeds of the shares.

SAQ 328

On 1 October 1998, Utopia Ltd sells 87,500 of the 175,000 shares for £350,000. The value of the remaining 87,500 shares at that date is also £350,000.

What is the unindexed base cost of the shares disposed of? (See 21.3.3.3 for the part-disposal formula.)

$$£200,000 \times \frac{£350,000}{£700,000} = £100,000.$$

SAQ 329

What is the IA applicable to this base cost? (Assume an indexed rise decimal of 0.683.)

Pool as indexed to 1 October 1998 =

£226,400 × 0.683   = £381,031.

$$\frac{£350,000}{£700,000} \times £381,031 = £190,516.$$

What is the IA available on the disposal?

£190,516 − £100,000 = £90,516.

What is the chargeable gain on the disposal?

£350,000 − [£100,000 + £90,516] = £159,485.

One final feature of the pooling system for corporate shareholders needs to be mentioned. It applies equally to Section 104 Holdings and to 1982 Holdings. It is the set of three *matching rules* in TCGA 1992, ss. 105 and 107. These matching rules apply when shares of the same class are acquired or disposed of by the same corporate shareholder, on the same day and in the same capacity. Section 105 provides that in this situation:

(a)   all the securities so acquired shall be treated as acquired by a single transaction and all the securities so disposed of shall be treated as disposed of by a single transaction, and

(b)   all the securities so acquired shall, so far as their quantity does not exceed that of the securities so disposed of, be identified with those securities.

TCGA 1992, s. 107(3) then provides that if, 'within a period of 10 days', shares are acquired which form a Section 104 Holding or increase the size of a Section 104 Holding, and subsequently a number of shares of the same class are disposed of, the shares disposed of must be identified with those acquired in that 10-day period. Any remaining shares are identified with shares of the same class, on a *'last in, first out'* basis. This means that, if there are Section 104 Holdings and 1982 Holdings of shares in the same class, the corporate shareholder is deemed to use up the 1982 Holding *after* the Section 104 Holding.

Individual shareholders: shares acquired and *disposed of after 5 April 1998; shares disposed of after 5 April 1998 and comprised in a Section 104 Holding*
The pooling rules discussed above apply *only* to corporate shareholders. Where, as an individual shareholder, you dispose of shares after 5 April 1998, the *new matching rules* apply, irrespective of the capacity in which you make the disposal: TCGA 1992, s. 106A. Shares disposed by you after 5 April 1998 are matched thus:

(a)   *first*, with any shares of the same class acquired on the same day as the day of the disposal;

(b)   *secondly*, with any shares of the same class acquired within the period of 30 days *after* the shares disposed of;

(c) *thirdly*, with any shares of the same class acquired after 5 April 1998;

(d) *fourthly*, with any shares in a frozen Section 104 Holding;

(e) *fifthly*, when the Section 104 Holding is used up, with shares comprised in a 1982 Holding; and

(f) *sixthly*, with any Pre-CGT Holding.

An example of the new matching rules in operation is given in the Revenue's guidance to the Finance (No. 2) Bill 1998, now FA 1998. Suppose you own shares of one class in a company. You acquired them as follows:

April 1980	1,000 acquired;
July 1988	1,500 acquired;
October 1993	2,000 acquired;
December 1996	3,000 acquired;
July 1998	5,000 acquired; and
September 2001	2,000 acquired.
Total shares	14,500

In August 2002, you sell 14,000 of the 14,500 shares held by you.

Up to and including the December 1996 acquisition, the shares form part of your Section 104 Holding. The acquisitions in July 1998 and September 2001 do not form part of that holding, however. Your Section 104 Holding consists of 6,500 shares. The 1980 acquisition makes up your 1982 Holding, of 1,000 shares.

Your disposal of the 14,000 shares in 2002 is therefore matched with the following acquisitions, in the following order: 2,000 – September 2001; 5,000 – July 1998; 6,500 – your Section 104 Holding, *plus* 500 of your 1982 Holding.

Your 500 retained shares are the remainder of your 1982 Holding.

Individual and corporate shareholders: shares disposed of after 5 April 1998 and comprised in a 1982 Holding
As a shareholder, I will have a 1982 holding for all shares of the same class acquired by me between 6 April 1965 and 5 April 1982. The basic idea is the same as for Section 104 Holdings. The big difference is that the 1982 Holding is a frozen pool, whether the disponer is an individual or corporate shareholder.

Does this make matters more difficult, or easier, for disposals of shares in the 1982 Holding?

Easier. Since it cannot be added to, the IA is basically applied to their April 1982 value as for any other asset: TCGA 1992, s. 109.

Individual and corporate shareholders: shares disposed of after 5 April 1998 and comprised in a Pre-CGT Holding
It is a general CGT rule that gains accruing before 1982 are not chargeable gains. Different rules apply for quoted shares and unquoted shares, each of which is worth commenting

on briefly. With *unquoted shares*, the gain is calculated on a straight-line basis, as for any other chargeable asset. Thus, only gains accruing after 5 April 1982 are chargeable. Also, as for any other chargeable asset, you can elect to take instead the value of the shares at 6 April 1965 as their base cost. With *quoted* shares, the gain is calculated according to their market value on 6 April 1965: TCGA 1992, sch. 2, paras 1-6. However:

■ if using the original cost would produce a greater gain or loss, then that value is used; and

■ if using one value produces a gain, whilst the other produces a loss, there is deemed to be neither.

An election can be made by shareholders to have the Pre-CGT Holding treated as part of their 1982 Holding: TCGA 1992, s. 109(4). The election is open to corporate shareholders, as well as to individual shareholders.

24.6.2.2 Takeovers

You may find it helpful to reread **24.6.1.2** for the context in which the following rules operate. If I receive *cash* for my shares in the Target, then the analysis in **24.6.1.2** applies. In these circumstances, a chargeable gain on the sale is unlikely to be relieved or exempted from CGT. That said, the sale may be such that I qualify for retirement relief or EIS relief on the disposal: see **23.3.1**, **23.5.5**, **23.7**.

If I receive *newly-issued shares or loan-stock* in the Purchaser, the CGT analysis is a rather diffcrent one. Such a transaction is referred to as a *paper-for-paper exchange*. It is very common in practice. This is because TCGA 1992, ss. 135-137 can give me the benefit of roll-over relief in this situation. The effect of roll-over relief under TCGA 1992, ss. 135-137 is to deem there to have been no disposal and to assume that the replacement shares or loan-stock are one and the same asset as my original shares in the Target. It therefore operates in the third of the basic ways identified in **23.5.1**: TCGA 1992, ss. 135(3), 127-131. The conditions which must be satisfied relate to the degree of control the purchaser will exercise over the Target. In addition, the transaction must not be part of a tax-avoidance scheme, and it must be effected for *bona fide* commercial reasons.

Read TCGA 1992, s. 135 in *Cases and Materials* (24.3.1.1). List the conditions which must be satisfied for section 135 to apply to a takeover. Then read the extract from the offering circular for the recommended cash offer for East Midlands Electricity on behalf of DR Investments at *Cases and Materials* (24.3.1.1). Note any points additional to those mentioned above. Also relate the information on income tax and stamp duty back to your knowledge from elsewhere in this book.

A problem area associated with the relief is where the loan-stock in the Purchaser, which I receive in return for my shares in the Target, satisfies the definition of a QCB. The definition of a QCB (TCGA 1992, s. 117(7)) is wide enough to include most debentures issued by companies. Gains arising on the disposal of QCBs are exempt from CGT: see **23.3.2**. Exceptional relief for allowable losses on disposals of QCBs has been abolished by FA 1998.

Refer to paragraph 6(a)(ii) of the extract from the offering circular at *Cases and Materials* (24.3.1.1). Consider why the warning in 8(a)(ii) has been included.

Note that if I take a combination of cash, on the one hand, and loan-stock and/or shares in the purchaser on the other, I will make a part-disposal of the shares sold for cash and the general rules discussed in **24.6.2.1** will apply.

24.6.2.3   Reorganisations of share capital

Alteration of rights attaching to shares
One form of reorganisation of share capital is where the rights attaching to shares in a company are altered. The general rule for CGT purposes is in TCGA 1992, s. 127:

> [A] reorganisation shall not be treated as involving any disposal of the original shares or any acquisition of the new holding or any part of it, but the original shares (taken as a single asset) and the new holding (taken as a single asset) shall be treated as the same asset acquired as the original shares were acquired.

Two points should be noted, however. First, special rules apply where the reorganisation involves QCBs: TCGA 1992, s. 116. This might be the case, for instance, where loan-stock is converted into shares. Secondly, the reorganisation may give rise to a CGT charge if the *value-shifting* rules apply: see **25.3.2**.

Bonus issues and rights issues
Bonus issues are reorganisations (see previous paragraph). Section 127, TCGA 1992 therefore applies to them, so the bonus shares are treated as acquired when the original shares were acquired.

I own 10,000 shares in Megabrackets plc, all acquired in December 1991. On 23 January 1998, the company makes a bonus issue of one new share for each one held. When will they be deemed to have been acquired?

With the original shares in 1991.

I will have had to pay for *rights issue* shares taken up by me. The acquisition of rights issue shares is therefore analysed just like the acquisition of bonus issue shares, but with one big difference. The cash paid by me for the rights issue shares is added to the base cost of my original shareholding.

Demergers
Direct distribution of shares in a subsidiary to me   Where there is a direct distribution of shares, TCGA 1992, s. 192 applies to the transaction. Two consequences follow:

■ I will not be treated as receiving a capital distribution, since TCGA 1992, s. 122 is disapplied (see below); and

■ I will be treated as if my shares in Company A and my shares in Company B were shares in one company, and the distribution were a reorganisation of its share capital: see above.

This treatment depends on the company's position being governed by ICTA 1988, s. 213(3)(a). This provision relates to the corporation tax position of the company in which the demerged shares were held. It is not considered further in this book.

Are these consequences beneficial to the shareholder?

Very much so.

Indirect distribution of shares in a subsidiary to me   The treatment given to the individual shareholder in the preceding paragraph does not apply where the demerger is an *indirect demerger*. In the case of an indirect demerger, there is a risk that I, the individual shareholder, will be regarded as receiving a capital distribution: TCGA 1992, s. 122. This means that I could be regarded as making a disposal or part-disposal of the demerged shares. To avoid this, I will need to seek to rely on TCGA 1992, s. 136. Section 136 covers amalgamations and reconstructions involving the issue of securities. To rely on it successfully, it will be necessary to show that there is a *scheme of reconstruction*, which is not being effected for tax avoidance but for *bona fide* commercial reasons: TCGA 1992, ss. 136 and 137, SP5/85. Revenue clearance may be applied for under TCGA 1992, s. 138.

Read the extract from the demerger document on the rights issue by Zeneca Group plc on 12 May 1993 (*Cases and Materials* (24.3.1.2)). Note how the points mentioned above are dealt with in the information given to the ICI shareholders, plus the reference to *Sinclair* v *Lee* [1993] 3 All ER 926: 24.6.1.3.

24.7   Debts on a Security

24.7.1   CGT PROBLEMS PRESENTED BY DEBTS ON A SECURITY

Debts generally go down in value over time, which means that, as a general rule, gains on their disposal are exempt from CGT: see **23.4**.

It is none the less theoretically possible that some debts might increase in value, because of the terms on which the loans represented by them were made.

24.7.2   SOLUTIONS PROVIDED BY THE CGT RULES

To deal with this possibility, the drafters of the CGT legislation came up with the concept of the debt on a security. The disposal of a debt on a security, unlike other debts, was to be a chargeable disposal. Debts on a security are not defined as such in the legislation, although the word 'security' is defined in TCGA 1992, s. 132(3) as follows:

'[S]ecurity' includes any loan stock or similar security whether of the Government of the United Kingdom or of any other government, or of any public or local authority in the United Kingdom or elsewhere, or of any company, and whether secured or unsecured.

Although the definition of security appears to be an inclusive one, the Revenue have indicated that they regard it as being an exhaustive one.

None the less, the task of defining a debt on a security has been left to the judges. It was considered in *WT Ramsay* v *IRC* [1982] AC 300 (and [1979] STC 582, 588 (Templeman LJ)), and by Robert Walker J in *Taylor Clarke International* v *Lewis* [1997] STC 499: *Cases and Materials* (**24.4.1**).

24.8   Capital Allowance-bearing Plant and Machinery

A quick reread of **22.4.2.3** and **24.4** will remind you of the following point. A gain on the disposal of a chattel which is a wasting asset is exempt from CGT, unless the wasting chattel was used solely for the purposes of a trade, profession or vocation. If the chattel was so used, any gain is a chargeable gain. Plant and machinery, the expenditure on which has attracted CAs, are wasting assets capable of giving rise to a chargeable gain in this way. The question therefore arises of how a CA balancing charge (see **12.9.2**) interacts with the chargeable gain or allowable loss (the latter being much more likely). The answer can be stated thus:

- If there is a *chargeable gain*, CGT will be charged on that gain. *In addition*, the disponer will be treated as receiving trading income *equal to* the balancing charge arising on the disposal.

- If there is an *allowable loss*, no CGT will of course be charged. The disponer will still be treated as receiving trading income *equal to* the balancing charge on the disposal. However, the allowable loss will be reduced by the amount of the balancing charge. The allowable loss can thus be reduced to zero in an appropriate case. It *cannot*, however, be converted into a chargeable gain in this way.

24.9   Interests of Beneficiaries under Settlements – a Brief Note

Refer to **23.3.2**. Suppose I am a beneficiary under a settlement. I sell my interest, e.g. a life interest. Section 76(1), TCGA 1992 exempts from CGT a gain on such a disposal, provided the interest has never been acquired for money or money's worth, and the trustees are resident in the UK. Consideration in money or money's worth does *not* include the interest of another beneficiary under the settlement: TCGA 1992, s. 76(1). Bear these points in mind for **Chapter 28**.

24.10   Summary

You should now have a reasonably clear idea of how CGT addresses the problems of analysis presented by certain types of asset. The problem with options is that they involve two transactions, their grant and their exercise or abandonment. The grantor of a call option makes two disposals, the grant of the option and the sale of the property over which the option subsists. The grantor of a put option *disposes* of the option, but *acquires* the property over which the option subsists. Wasting assets, other than wasting chattels, present a different problem. Without special provisions, the owner would be able to claim an allowable loss on their disposal. The CGT rules therefore reduce the base cost of wasting assets by their scrap value, and reduce the amount left by a proportion determined by the remainder of its useful life. Leases of land with 50 years or less to run, as wasting assets, are treated in such a way as to reflect the steep fall in their value towards their termination date. Wasting assets carrying CAs are treated as though they were ordinary chargeable assets, but allowable losses on their disposal are reduced by balancing charges. Disposals on the writing-off of goodwill can present problems for retiring and continuing partners, which the CGT rules have failed to resolve satisfactorily. This is also true of shares which are sold for cash, share sales necessitating a comparison between disposal proceeds and base cost of fungible assets. In contrast, the rules relating to disposals of shares on paper-for-paper takeovers, on reorganisations, bonus issues and demergers are successful precisely because they avoid the need to compare disposal proceeds with base cost on the occurrence of any of these events. With disposals for cash, even the CGT solutions present problems, and these have been exacerbated by the changes effected by FA 1998. In the context of wider share ownership, promoted with zeal by the last Government, the easy solutions provided by the rules on paper-for-paper takeover, reorganisations, etc. are very important. Even Sid the shareholder is, to some extent at least, sheltered from the effects of CGT. If you are a Sid, next time an offering circular lands on your doormat, read the taxation section rather carefully!

24.11   End of Chapter Assessment Question

The source of the dividend income possessed by Hugh the barrister in 1998/99 (see **7.9**) is his shareholding in Superlucre plc. He originally bought 5,000 ordinary shares in Improvements Ltd on 31 March 1986, for £5,000. In 1986, Improvements Ltd was becoming increasingly successful, and it was taken over by Superlucre plc on 1 September 1992, on the basis of a one-for-one share exchange. On 1 April 1994, there was a one-for-one rights issue by Superlucre plc at £2 per share, which was taken up by Hugh. Finally, on 6 June 1997, Superlucre plc made a one-for-one bonus issue to all its shareholders.

Explain the CGT implications of each of these events so far as Hugh is concerned.

(Word limit: 400 (100 marks).)

See *Cases and Materials* (**24.6**) for a specimen answer.

CHAPTER TWENTY-FIVE

INVESTMENT TAXATION: ANTI-AVOIDANCE ISSUES AND COMPLIANCE

25.1 Objectives

By the end of this chapter, you should be able to:

- give *examples* of how attempts have been made to escape CGT;

- explain *how* attempts to manipulate allowable losses were met by the *Ramsay principle*;

- state the *dates for payment* of CGT and corporation tax on chargeable gains.

25.2 Introduction

In this chapter, we complete our investigation of investment taxation with a discussion of some anti-avoidance issues relating to CGT and corporation tax on chargeable gains. At the end of the chapter, we also note some brief compliance issues in relation to these taxes. CGT-avoidance has historically sought to achieve one, or both, of two main aims. First, to escape CGT altogether by attempting to remove one of the four elements on which a charge to CGT depends. This might, for instance, have taken the form of ensuring that a disposal of a chargeable asset at a gain was made by someone other than a chargeable person. If successful, this would obviously ensure that no CGT was payable on the gain realised. We shall be considering a number of instances in which such an attempt has been made. We shall also be considering how the legislature has responded to it. Secondly, attempts have been made to reduce CGT by manipulating the rules on allowable losses, reliefs and exemptions. Of these two aims, this latter has perhaps been the more notorious. This is because an ingenious manipulation of the rules on allowable losses was met by the judges with the so-called *Ramsay* principle, already encountered in **4.4**. The recent House of Lords decision in *IRC* v *McGuckian* [1997] 3 All ER 817 has provided a reminder, had the reminder been needed, that the *Ramsay* principle is of general and continuing application, and is not simply a way of dealing with CGT avoidance: *Cases and Materials* (**4.3**).

25.3   Removing One of the Four Elements Needed for a CGT Charge

25.3.1   NO CHARGEABLE PERSON

25.3.1.1   Individuals: 'going non-resident'

You may already have come across the expression 'going non-resident'. It is a shorthand expression for a person ceasing to be resident in the UK, before disposing of a chargeable asset at a profit. Going non-resident is therefore a way of removing one of the four elements necessary for a CGT charge to arise on a disposal of a chargeable asset at a gain: see **21.3**. FA 1998, together with an amended ESC D2, seeks to counter the practice in relation to departures from the UK on or after 17 March 1998. The meaning of *residence* was discussed in **4.5** and **21.3.2.1**. It should be apparent from the discussion that, even before FA 1998, 'going non-resident' was not as simple as it may at first have seemed. One reason for this is the general rule that you are resident in the UK if you are present here for any 183 days in the tax year under consideration. Moreover, even if the rule means you are not resident in the UK in the current tax year, you may still be *ordinarily resident* in the UK in that tax year: see *Cases and Materials* (**4.4.1**). None the less, it was believed that, if you were away from the UK for three complete tax years, you would be neither resident, nor ordinarily resident, in the UK.

This idea has been dispelled by TCGA 1992, s. 10A, inserted by FA 1998. Section 10A provides that you remain a chargeable person *unless* you are neither resident, nor ordinarily resident, for at least *five* complete tax years. If you are abroad for any shorter period then, even if you cease to be resident or ordinarily resident in the UK in that period, you will be treated as realising any gains or losses realised while abroad in the year of your return to the UK. ESC D2, which applies to individuals in their personal capacity, allows the tax year under consideration to be divided into a period of *residence* in the UK, and a period of *non-residence*. On 17 March 1998, it was amended to take account of the new TCGA 1992, s. 10A. The problem with ESC D2 from your perspective is that, like other ESCs, it is not possible to rely on it if you are using it for tax-avoidance purposes. ESC D2, as amended on 17 March 1998, says:

> An individual who leaves the United Kingdom and is treated on departure as not resident and not ordinarily resident here is not charged to capital gains tax on gains from disposals made after the date of departure, provided that the individual was not resident and not ordinarily resident in the United Kingdom for the whole of at least four of the seven years of assessment [i.e. tax years] in which he or she left the UK.

Note that you are treated *on departure* as not resident and not ordinarily resident in the UK if either: (a) you leave the UK for permanent residence abroad; or (b) you leave the UK to take up a full-time trade, profession or employment all the duties of which are to be performed abroad.

(To answer this question, note that TCGA 1992, s. 58 provides that disposals between husbands and wives are deemed to be made for such a consideration as produces neither a gain nor a loss: see 27.7.1.) Charles is married to Wilhelmina. He is planning to leave the UK at the end of November 1998, in order to take up permanent residence in Austria. A month before Charles's departure, Wilhelmina gives a valuable chargeable asset to him. On 1 February 1999, having left the UK, he sells it, realising a large chargeable gain. Will he be liable to pay CGT on the gain?

Yes.

Would the position be any different if, instead of leaving the UK part-way through the 1998/99 tax year, Charles had waited till 6 April 1999 before leaving for permanent residence abroad?

No.

Note *R v IRC, ex parte Fulford-Dobson* [1987] STC 344, *Cases and Materials* (**25.1.1**).

25.3.1.2 Trustees

Between 1981 and 19 March 1991, it was possible to obtain considerable CGT benefits by transferring property into a non-resident or offshore trust. You relied on the general rule that a non-resident person is not a chargeable person, as well as on the special CGT-charging system applicable to offshore trusts. Gains could therefore be realised by non-resident trustees, escaping CGT at the time of the disposal. Even though distributions of the gains and the other trust capital to UK domiciled and resident beneficiaries were taxed under the special system, it was easily manipulated. There was always the option of leaving the gains and the other trust capital in the offshore trust account anyway. The CGT benefits of setting-up a non-resident trust from the beginning, or exporting a trust by getting the UK-trustees to retire in favour of non-UK resident trustees, could therefore be great indeed. Following public consternation that CGT could be avoided so easily by cleverly-advised people, FA 1991 introduced three key anti-avoidance provisions designed to remove the CGT benefits of offshore trusts. They did not remove the CGT benefits of offshore trusts entirely, however, and the remaining CGT benefits of offshore trusts were restricted still further by FA 1998. The detail of these provisions is outside the scope of this book, although noting these points should at least give you an idea of the CGT issues raised by non-resident trusts.

25.3.2 NO CHARGEABLE DISPOSAL: VALUE-SHIFTING

Value-shifting is the term given for transferring value out of one asset into another, without making a chargeable disposal of it. In the absence of the special provisions in TCGA 1992, s. 29, such a transfer would escape CGT on the basis that one of the four essential elements in CGT liability, i.e. a chargeable disposal, was missing. The anti-avoidance rule for value-shifting is contained in TCGA 1992, s. 29(1). Value-shifting transactions are deemed to be chargeable disposals, even though no consideration is passing, provided that the person deemed to be making the chargeable disposal ' . . . could have obtained consideration, or additional consideration, for the disposal'. The remainder of TCGA 1992, s. 29 provides several specific instances. However, the concept of value-shifting can perhaps be illustrated most easily by reference to leases: TCGA 1992, s. 29(4). This provides that:

> If . . . there is any adjustment of the rights and liabilities under the lease, whether or not involving the grant of a new lease, which is as a whole favourable to the lessor, that shall be a disposal by the lessee of an interest in the property.

I sell the freehold of an industrial building to you for £10,000. You immediately lease it back to me for five years at a rental of £1,000 per annum. There is a provision in the lease for the rent to be adjusted upwards by agreement between us. Under that provision, we adjust the rent to £4,000 per annum. Will there be a deemed disposal by me under TCGA 1992, s. 29 in this situation?

Yes.

Section 29 is not confined to transactions involving leases. It also applies, e.g., to the controlling shareholder in a company so exercising that control as to cause value to pass out of his or her shares into the shares of another shareholder: see **24.6.2.3**. Value-shifting provisions directed at other problems are contained in TCGA 1992, ss. 30-34. Section 30 is designed to prevent value being passed out of a chargeable asset into an exempt asset. Sections 31–34 are designed to prevent value-shifting transactions within groups of companies.

25.4   Manipulating Allowable Losses, Reliefs and Exemptions

25.4.1   MANIPULATING ALLOWABLE LOSSES: THE *RAMSAY* PRINCIPLE

When we discussed private residence relief, we touched on the possibility that some CGT reliefs might be capable of being manipulated in such a way as to create allowable losses: see **22.4.4.3**. The response of the courts to attempts in contexts *other than* PRR led to a judicial anti-avoidance principle of general application, i.e. the *Ramsay* principle. The *Ramsay* principle takes its name from the House of Lords case *WT Ramsay Ltd* v *IRC* [1982] AC 300, which was joined with the appeal in another tax-avoidance case, *Eilbeck* v *Rawling*. In *Ramsay* v *IRC*, a company artificially tried to create an allowable loss, to deduct from its chargeable gains. (Allowable losses are discussed in **Chapter 21**.) On the advice of its tax consultants, the company:

(a)   Acquired the whole of the issued share capital of a company called Caithmead Ltd for £185,034.

(b)   Made two loans of £218,750 each to Caithmead Ltd, the first for 30 years, the second for 31 years. Both loans carried interest at 11% per annum, payable quarterly.

The loan documentation gave the company the right to decrease the interest rate on one of the loans, whilst making a corresponding increase in the interest rate on the other.

(c)   Accordingly increased the interest on the second loan to 22% per annum, interest on the first loan being decreased to zero.

(d)   Disposed of the second loan to a finance company for £391,481, producing a 'gain' of £172,731. Caithmead repaid the first loan at its par value.

(e)   Disposed of its shares in Caithmead Ltd, which were now of little value, to an outside company for £9,387.

The company provided no finance for these transactions. All the finance was provided using loans from a finance house. The company argued that the disposal of the loan at a profit in (d) was exempt from CGT: see **23.4**. Crucially, for our purposes, it also argued that it had made an *allowable loss* when it disposed of its shares in Caithmead at (e) for £9,387.

What was the amount of the allowable loss claimed by the company?

£175,647, i.e. £185,034 − £9,387.

The House of Lords decided the appeal in favour of the Revenue. Their Lordships held that they could consider the scheme as a whole, even though on its face, it was a 'genuine' one. Looking at the scheme as a whole, the company had suffered neither a gain nor a loss. This is why *Ramsay* is sometimes said to have involved a circular, or self-cancelling, scheme.

Was this surprising, given *IRC* v *Duke of Westminster* [1935] All ER Rep 259 (see 4.4, 9.3)?

Yes. *IRC* v *Duke of Westminster* suggested that, where a transaction was in *form* of one type, but in *substance* another, the courts would examine only the *form* of the transaction.

Read the extracts from Lord Wilberforce's speech in *Ramsay* v *IRC* (*Cases and Materials* (25.2)). Consider carefully the circumstances in which his Lordship considers it permissible for a court to apply the *Ramsay* principle.

To 'add insult to injury', their Lordships found that the disposal of the second loan, in (d), at a 'gain' of £172,731, was a disposal of a *debt on a security*.

Why did this 'add insult to injury' (24.7)?

It meant that the disposal of the loan was a chargeable disposal, and the gain a chargeable gain.

The *Ramsay* principle was applied in *IRC* v *Burmah Oil Co. Ltd* [1982] STC 30 and in *Furniss* v *Dawson* [1984] 1 All ER 530. It was extended in both cases to factual situations significantly different from those in *Ramsay* itself. In *IRC* v *Burmah Oil*, the *Ramsay* principle was applied to another 'genuine' transaction which attempted to create an allowable loss, *even though* there was no preconceived plan, and *even though* the money to carry out the taxations in question was not provided in the form of loans. In *Furniss* v *Dawson*, the *Ramsay* principle was held to apply to a scheme that was not a circular, or self-cancelling, one. The detail is discussed below, since it involved the manipulation of roll-over relief, rather than the manipulation of allowable losses.

ACTIVITY62

Write down the *Ramsay* principle: see 4.4, if you have forgotten the exact formulation!

25.4.2 MANIPULATING EXEMPTIONS AND RELIEFS

25.4.2.1 The annual exempt amount: 'bed and breakfasting' of shares

The new matching rules, discussed in **24.6.2.1**, have put an end to the bed and breakfasting of shares by individuals and trustees. It is worth commenting briefly on the impact of the new matching rules here. Bed and breakfasting shares involved disposing of (i.e. selling) shares at the close of trading on one day, only to buy them back at the commencement of trading the next day. It involved shareholders in little risk, and enabled chargeable gains to be realised, but sheltered by the annual exempt amount: see **22.4.1**. As a consequence of the transaction, the base cost of the shares would also increase, thus reducing the gain on a later disposal. The new matching rules (TCGA 1992, s. 106A) prevent this happening, by requiring *a disposal* of shares within a single class to be matched with *acquisitions* of shares in the same class, in the 30-day period *subsequent* to the disposal, *before* any acquisition of the shares *prior* to their disposal: see **24.6.2.1**.

25.4.2.2 Roll-over relief under TCGA 1992, ss. 135–137

The *Ramsay* principle has been applied to attempts to *postpone* tax, as well as to attempts to avoid it altogether: *Furniss* v *Dawson* [1984] 1 All ER 530. What had happened in *Furniss* v *Dawson* was as follows:

(a) Members of the Dawson family resolved to sell their shareholdings in two clothes-manufacturing companies for £152,000, to Wood Bastow Holdings Ltd.

(b) To postpone the liability to CGT on the disposal, they were advised to make use of what are now TCGA 1992, ss. 135–137: see **24.6.2.2**. The Dawsons therefore sold the shares in the two companies for £152,000 to Greenjacket Investments Ltd, a company incorporated in the Isle of Man, in return for newly-issued shares in Greenjacket.

(c) Greenjacket immediately resold the shares in the two companies to Wood Bastow for £152,000.

The transaction was intended to ensure that the CGT which would otherwise have been payable on the disposal of the shares in the manufacturing companies, was postponed. Sections 135–137, TCGA 1992 should have ensured that there was no disposal, and that the new shares owned by the Dawsons in Greenjacket were treated as the same asset as their original shares in the manufacturing companies. No chargeable gain was realised by Greenjacket, since it resold the shares for the price at which it had acquired them. The House of Lords held that the *Ramsay* principle applied to the transactions. Lord Brightman was the only one of their Lordships who reasoned through the application of the *Ramsay* principle in detail. His Lordship acknowledged that the scheme was:

> . . . a simple and honest scheme which merely seeks to defer payment of tax until the taxpayer has received into his hands the gain which he has made.

However:

> The result of correctly applying the *Ramsay* principle to the facts of this case is that there was a disposal by the Dawsons in favour of Wood Bastow in consideration of a

sum of money paid with the concurrence of the Dawsons to Greenjacket. Capital gains tax is payable accordingly.

In reaching this conclusion, it was immaterial that the parties were not contractually bound to enter into each stage:

> The day is not saved for the taxpayer because the arrangement is unsigned or contains the magic words 'this is not a binding contract'.

ACTIVITY 63

Before leaving this section, re-read *Cases and Materials* **(4.3).**

25.5 Compliance Issues for CGT and Corporation Tax on Chargeable Gains – a Brief Note

The whole of the *CGT due* from you (see **21.4.1**) must generally be paid by 31 January following the end of the tax year under consideration. However, by TMA 1970, s. 59B, the date is *instead* three months after the issue of the tax return, where the return is issued after the 31 October following the end of the tax year under consideration. This is on the basis that you are not guilty of a failure to notify liability under TMA 1970, s. 7(1): see **19.3.3.1**. There is a facility for paying CGT in *instalments*, where the consideration is receivable by you in instalments over a period in excess of 18 months. This is subject to certain formalities: TCGA 1992, s. 280. Other CGT payment provisions, in relation to transactions with an element of gift, will be discussed at **33.4.2**. Corporation tax on chargeable gains is payable as part of a company's *mainstream corporation tax* liability: see **19.4**.

25.6 Summary

In this chapter, an attempt has been made to relate the objectives listed at the beginning to areas of CGT with which you are now familiar. You should therefore have had no problem in understanding the mechanics of the legislation and cases discussed. You should aim for more than an understanding, however. You should attempt to form a view as to the legal and moral quality of the anti-avoidance issues discussed. In particular, you should decide which of the following views your own opinion coincides more closely with:

■ The statutes contain certain omissions and loopholes. All the person avoiding tax is seeking to do is to make use of those loopholes.

■ The omissions in the statutes are there as a result of Parliamentary oversight. Rather than allowing people to take advantage of these omissions, the judiciary should be ready to supply them if necessary, using the *Ramsay* principle.

Make sure that the view you have is an opinion, rather than mere bias. Ask yourself what the reasons are in favour of each of the above views. If you can, gather together as much material as possible from throughout this book in formulating your reasons.

CHAPTER TWENTY-SIX

TAXATION OF GRATUITOUS TRANSFERS: INTRODUCTION

26.1 Objectives

By the end of this chapter, you should be able to:

■ define the term *gratuitous transfer*;

■ distinguish *gifts* from *nominal transfers* and *automatic transfers*;

■ list four categories of *gift*;

■ list four categories of *nominal transfer*;

■ list three categories of *automatic transfer*;

■ list the *taxes* relevant to gratuitous transfers;

■ outline the *historical and political* context of taxing gratuitous transfers.

26.2 Introduction

So far in this book, we have discussed income taxation and investment taxation. It remains for us to examine the taxation of gratuitous transfers. If you look up the word 'gratuitous' in a dictionary, you will find that one of its uses is in referring to something which costs nothing, something which is free. A 'transfer', of course, refers to a conveyance of the ownership of property from one person to another. In discussing gratuitous transfers, therefore, we are dealing with a different type of transaction from the sale transactions which we dealt with in **Chapters 20** to **25**. In this chapter, we shall discover how gratuitous transfers can themselves be divided into gifts, nominal transfers and automatic transfers. This threefold division is what we need to consider next. The important thing is to put taxation matters out of your mind until the end of the chapter. The emphasis of the discussion in the following pages is upon the distinctions which property law draws between different types of gratuitous transfer. An understanding of these distinctions is an essential prerequisite to a proper understanding of the tax analysis that follows.

26.3 Gifts, Nominal Transfers and Automatic Transfers

The term *gratuitous transfer* comprises:

■ gifts;

■ nominal transfers; and

■ automatic transfers.

We need to consider how each one of these differs from the others.

26.3.1 GIFTS

With a gift of property, the giver intends to transfer the legal title to property to the recipient. Whether at the same time the recipient acquires the equitable entitlement to the property, depends on whether the recipient acquires the property as absolute beneficial owner, or in the capacity of trustee for another person or persons. If the recipient acquires the property in the capacity of a trustee, the ownership of the property is thereby split up. The legal title to the property is vested in the trustee, whilst the beneficiary has some kind of equitable entitlement to the property. The nature and extent of that equitable entitlement depends on the terms of the trust. However, it is the equitable entitlement which has value. The legal title is merely a 'paper' title. By contrast, if the recipient acquires the property as absolute beneficial owner, there is no splitting-up of ownership in this way. The recipient acquires the whole of the legal and equitable entitlement to the property. These two categories of gift are considered in greater detail in **26.4**. In addition, we shall be considering two further categories of gift, i.e. undervalue sales and gifts on death.

26.3.2 NOMINAL TRANSFERS

With a nominal transfer of property, the transferor also intends to transfer the legal title to property to the transferee. However, the equitable entitlement to the property is not transferred, since the transferor is acting in a fiduciary capacity, i.e. as a trustee or PR. The transferor is thus not in a position to transfer the equitable entitlement to the property. Examples of nominal transfers occur when one trustee retires in favour of a replacement trustee, or trust property is vested by trustees in a beneficiary absolutely, in accordance with the terms of the trust. Nominal transfers also occur when property comprised in the estate of a deceased individual is vested by PRs in a beneficiary, in accordance with the terms of the will or the intestacy rules: see **26.5.3**.

26.3.3 AUTOMATIC TRANSFERS

An automatic transfer may transfer the legal title alone, the equitable entitlement alone, or the legal title and the equitable entitlement together. By contrast with gifts and nominal transfers, with an automatic transfer, the transferor does not necessarily intend to transfer the legal title or equitable entitlement, or both, to the transferee. Instead, the transfer takes place under the terms of some document, or by the operation of some rule of law. That rule of law might be imposed by statutory provision or by some rule or principle of common law. An example of the automatic transfer of *a legal title alone* would be the transfer to surviving trustees of the interest of a deceased trustee in the legal title to trust property. This automatic transfer would be effected under the common law principle of *survivorship*. An example of an automatic transfer of both legal title and equitable entitlement together, under the survivorship principle, is given in **26.6.1**.

The automatic transfer of an *equitable entitlement alone* can be illustrated by interests of beneficiaries in trust property taking effect in succession. For instance, property might be held by trustees under the following trust:

   To A for life, remainder to B for life, remainder to C absolutely.

Although the trustees of such a trust will make no transfer of the legal title on the deaths of A and B, the equitable entitlement to the property will be transferred automatically to B on A's death and, in addition, to C on B's death. On C becoming absolutely entitled, the trustees will be obliged to make a nominal transfer of the legal title to the trust property to C: see **26.3.2**. Note that neither A nor B will perform any voluntary act in this situation.

The automatic transfer of legal title and equitable entitlement together, although not under the survivorship principle, is illustrated by the operation of the *intestacy rules*, i.e. when someone dies without leaving a valid will: see **26.6.3**.

On 1 November 1998, Tim and Tom, two trustees, hold shares in Megabucks plc for Benjamin for life, remainder to Barry absolutely. Benjamin and Barry are both alive at that date. If the trust continues in this form, how many times will there be an *automatic* transfer of the equitable entitlement?

Once, i.e. on Benjamin's death.

26.4   Categories of Gifts

In this section, we shall be discussing four categories of gifts: absolute gifts, gifts on trust, undervalue sales and gifts on death.

26.4.1   ABSOLUTE GIFTS

Absolute gifts are the most obvious category of gift. For instance, I might give you a valuable grandfather clock as a present. To take effect, an absolute gift must be perfect. There must be an actual transfer of the property given away, from giver to recipient. At the same time, the giver must intend to make the gift to the recipient. The result of this process is that both the legal title to, and the equitable entitlement to, the property will have been transferred by the giver to the recipient. The recipient will become the absolute beneficial owner of the property.

I hand over to you a valuable eighteenth-century pocket-watch. Have I made a gift of the watch to you?

Not necessarily. It depends on what my intention is in so doing.

26.4.2 GIFTS ON TRUST

Gifts on trust are the second category of gift. If a recipient acquires property as a trustee, the legal title to the property and its beneficial ownership are thereby split up from each other. The result is that legal title is vested in the trustees, whilst the beneficiaries have the equitable entitlement to the property.

Sam transfers 100 ordinary shares in Bigco plc to trustees Tim and Tom. At the same time, he executes a trust deed, under the terms of which they are to hold the shares for Alice for life, remainder to Ben absolutely. Whose name will appear on the share certificate?

The trustees', although their title is merely an administrative or nominal one.

Note that, as a matter of trusts law, an individual can validly declare *himself or herself* to be a trustee of property. It is not necessary for the legal title to property to be transferred to independent trustees for there to be a valid trust. Not only this, but there are certain situations, referred to as *resettlements*, where the settlor is not an individual acting in his or her personal capacity, but one acting in the capacity of a trustee. With a resettlement, a trustee is creating a new trust, under powers conferred by the original trust deed: see **26.5.1**.

26.4.3 UNDERVALUE SALES

This third category is not so obviously a gift, since it has features of both gift and sale. You may therefore wish to refer to the discussion of sales at **20.2**. In an undervalue sale, I intend to sell property to you for less than it is worth on the market. True, I have not given the property to you in the same way as I would have done if I had made an absolute gift of the property to you. However, there is an element of gift in the transaction even so. This is because I have intentionally foregone the profit on the sale which I might have made, had I sold it to a stranger in the market for its market value. Undervalue sales are an easy concept to understand. Even so, they must be carefully distinguished from bad bargains. A party to a bad bargain has no donative intent, i.e. he or she does not intend to give anything away.

I sell you a piece of antique furniture for £6,000, at a time when its market value is £600,000. It cost me £200,000 in 1985.

What is the element of gift in the transaction?

£554,000.

(The £200,000 paid by me for the furniture in 1985 will be significant for CGT, although not for other taxes: see **Chapter 30**.)

26.4.4 GIFTS ON DEATH

For many people, gifts on death are the most generous gifts they ever make! Such gifts are the fourth category of gift to be considered by us. It is important to exclude property passing by survivorship from this category, as well as property passing under the intestacy rules. Property passing by survivorship or on an intestacy passes by an automatic transfer: see **26.3.2** and **26.3.3**. A gift on death could take the form corresponding to an absolute gift, or a gift on trust: see **26.4.1** and **26.4.2**. The former is referred to as an absolute gift on death, and the latter as a gift on trust on death. A gift of personal property on death is technically known as a *devise*; a gift of real property on death is technically known as a *legacy*.

26.4.4.1 Absolute gifts on death

In the case of an absolute gift on death, the property given away is transferred from the deceased to the beneficiary in *two stages*:

■ from the deceased to the deceased's PRs; and

■ from the deceased's PRs to the beneficiaries.

The second of these stages is a nominal transfer, to be discussed in **26.5.3**. We are concerned in this section only with the first stage. In the second stage, all that needs to be transferred from the PR to the beneficiary is the 'paper title' to the legacy. Documentation to effect the transfer may not always be necessary. The title to chattels, for instance, passes by delivery: see **26.4.1**.

26.4.4.2 Gifts on trust on death

If the gift on death is a gift on trust, the legal title to the property and the equitable entitlement to it will be split up, once the deceased's debts have been paid off and all legacies paid. This will be the case, e.g., where a will provides for a number of general or specific legacies (see **16.3.2**), the residue then to be held on trusts spelt out in the will itself. The property given away is transferred from the deceased's estate to the trustees of the will trusts. These are usually the self-same individuals as the PRs, but acting in a different capacity. The transfer of the property will again take place in two stages:

■ from the deceased to the deceased's PRs; and

■ from the deceased's PRs to the trustees of the will trust.

The second of these stages is a nominal transfer, to be discussed in **26.5.4**. It is the process of creating a will trust. We are concerned in this section only with the first of these stages. In the second stage, all that needs to be passed from the PR to the trustee is the 'paper title' to the property, i.e. to the property subject to the will trust.

Timothy, a bachelor who dies aged 98 on 1 December 1998, leaves his estate to his parents, with a substitutional gift to his sister, Ethel. At Timothy's death, Ethel was 80, their parents both having predeceased them. Timothy's will appointed Edward and Edmund as his executors.

State the two stages in which his estate will be transferred to Ethel. Which is the gift on death, and which the nominal transfer?

The two stages are the transfer from Timothy to the executors, on death, and the transfer from the executors to Ethel. The first of these is the gift on death; the latter is a nominal transfer only.

In order to inherit property by virtue of a gift on death, an individual only needs to live longer than the deceased. In particularly tragic circumstances, however, it may not be possible to tell which of two or more individuals died first. These circumstances are known as *common catastrophe*. The Law of Property Act 1925, s. 184 provides a deceptively simple rule to deal with *common catastrophe*:

> In all cases where, after the commencement of this Act, two or more persons have died in circumstances rendering it uncertain which of them survived the other or others, such deaths shall (subject to any order of the court), for all purposes affecting the title to property, be presumed to have occurred in order of seniority, and accordingly the younger shall be deemed to have survived the elder.

The rule in LPA 1925, s. 184 is modified in cases of intestacy. The intestacy rules are discussed in **26.6.2**.

26.5   Categories of Nominal Transfers

26.5.1   TRANSFERS BETWEEN TRUSTEES

As mentioned above, the main category of nominal transfer is when a trustee retires in favour of a replacement trustee. The ability to retire is a point of distinction between trustees and executors: *Re Stevens* [1898] 1 Ch 162 and [1897] 1 Ch 422. If the replacement trustee is appointed by deed, then the making of a vesting declaration by the person appointing the replacement trustee is, for most types of property, sufficient to vest the legal title to the property in the replacement trustee: TA 1925, s. 40(1)(a). One type of property in relation to which such a declaration is not sufficient, however, is stocks and shares: TA 1925, s. 40(4). This is because the execution of a formal transfer of the shares from the former trustees to the replacement trustees is necessary to comply with general company law: see **24.6.1.1**.

Technical problems can arise in some cases of trust property being transferred between trustees. A notorious example is where trustees exercise a power of appointment or advancement, conferred on them by the trust deed, in favour of trustees of another trust. The trustees of the second trust may, or may not, be identical individuals to the trustees of the original trust. In *Roome* v *Edwards* [1981] 1 All ER 736, trustees exercised their power of appointment over a trust fund by transferring part of it to themselves, in their other capacity as trustees of a second trust.

In such situations, it may be a difficult question whether all that is actually taking place, when trustees exercise the power, is the appointment of replacement trustees of the trust property. If it is more than this, then the transfer will operate as a sub-trust, or re-settlement. Where a re-settlement occurs then, for a moment of time, the trustees of the second trust will become absolutely entitled to the trust property, as against the original trustees. This was explained by Brightman J in *Hoare Trustees* v *Gardner* [1978] 1 All ER 791, 810:

> The absolute entitlement of the propositus as against T, the trustee, would appear to be reasonably clear . . . as a matter of simple language. There is no particular reason to equate absolute entitlement with beneficial ownership in such cases, but rather with the ability to give a good discharge.

Whether a transfer between trustees counts as a re-settlement is crucial for CGT purposes, as we shall discover in **Chapter 28**.

ACTIVITY 64

Read the extract from the speech of Lord Wilberforce in *Roome* v *Edwards*, in *Cases and Materials* (26.1.1). Then consider the further elaboration of the points made by Lord Wilberforce in the extracts from the judgments in *Bond* v *Pickford* [1983] STC 517 and *Swires* v *Renton* [1991] STC 490, both in *Cases and Materials* (26.1.1).

26.5.2   TRANSFERS FROM TRUSTEES TO BENEFICIARIES

There will be a nominal transfer from trustees to beneficiaries when trust property is vested by trustees in a beneficiary absolutely, in accordance with the terms of the trust. This can either happen on the coming to an end of a prior interest in possession (as shown in **SAQ 346**), or on the exercise of a power of appointment by the trustees. A good example of the latter would, of course, be an appointment in favour of a beneficiary, by trustees of a discretionary trust. The actual vesting of the trust property in the beneficiaries involves the trustees executing a conveyance or transfer of the legal title to the property, where necessary, in favour of the relevant beneficiary or beneficiaries.

SAQ 346

(Refer to SAQ 343.) What will Tim and Tom do on the death of Alice, the life tenant?

They will convey the legal title to the shares to Ben, by executing a stock transfer form and sending it, together with the share certificate, to the company secretary of Bigco plc. The company secretary will amend its register of shareholders, to show that Ben is now the owner of the shares, and send the share certificate to him.

26.5.3   TRANSFERS FROM PERSONAL REPRESENTATIVES TO BENEFICIARIES

In the case of an absolute gift on death, it is important to realise that the deceased's estate is transferred first to the PRs, and then by the PRs to the beneficiaries. The second stage is the nominal transfer with which we are concerned here: see **26.4.4.1** and **26.6.3**. An interest in property which is transferred by survivorship is obviously an exception to this. In order to effect the transfer to a beneficiary, PRs execute a form of conveyance called an 'assent', in the beneficiary's favour. This vests the legal title to the property in the beneficiary. Where the property to be vested in the beneficiary is a legal estate in land, the assent does not need to be in the form of a deed. The Administration of Estates Act 1925, s. 36(1) provides that:

> An assent to the vesting of a legal estate shall be in writing, signed by the personal representative, and shall name the person in whose favour it is given and shall operate to vest in that person the legal estate to which it relates; and an assent not in writing or not in favour of a named person shall not be effectual to pass a legal estate.

26.5.4   TRANSFERS FROM PERSONAL REPRESENTATIVES TO TRUSTEES

The transfer of the legal title to estate property from the PRs to the trustees of the will trust is effected by the execution of an assent by the PRs in the trustees' favour. A technical question arises where the PRs are to act as the trustees of the will trust. There is some authority for saying that there is no need for the PRs to do anything to vest the legal title in themselves in their capacity as trustees: *Re Cockburn* [1957] Ch 438. However, it is regarded as good practice for the PRs to execute an assent vesting the legal title in the property to be subject to the trusts in themselves, but in their capacity as trustees: *Attenborough* v *Solomon* [1913] AC 76. Where the deceased died intestate, the PRs may be required to hold the deceased's estate for certain classes of beneficiaries on the so-called *statutory trusts*: see **26.6.3**. Again, it is good practice for the PRs to execute an assent vesting the legal title in the property to be subject to the statutory trusts in themselves, but in their other capacity as trustees: *Re Yerburgh* [1928] WN 208.

26.6 Categories of Automatic Transfers

26.6.1 THE SURVIVORSHIP PRINCIPLE

The survivorship principle is the principle under which the interest of one joint tenant passes to the other, or others, on the death of the first. An example of an interest in the legal title alone being transferred by survivorship was given in **26.3.3**. It is important to remember, however, that the survivorship principle can operate to transfer the interest in the equitable entitlement, as well as the legal title. The most common example of this happening is where real property is co-owned under a new-style trust of land: see **27.4**. The death of one of them will automatically transfer both the legal title and equitable entitlement to the survivor or survivors. The survivorship principle does not operate where property is held by *tenants in common*. This is why an undivided share under a tenancy in common can be the subject-matter of a gift on death, whilst an interest under a joint tenancy cannot. The survivorship principle has already operated by the time a will takes effect:

> . . . [I]n consideration of Law there is a Priority of Time in an Instant, as here the Survivor is preferred before the Devise: for Littleton saith, that the Cause is that no Devise can take Effect till after the Death of the Devisor, and by his Death all the Land presently cometh by the Law to his Companion.

So said Sir Edward Coke (1552-1634) in his famous *Commentary Upon Littleton* and, as a matter of property law, the statement remains true today. As we shall discover, it is modified for the purpose of IHT.

26.6.2 INTERESTS OF BENEFICIARIES COMING TO AN END

The situation of a beneficiary's interest coming to an end, the trust then continuing, was given as an example of an automatic transfer of an equitable title in **26.3.3**. It was illustrated by the following trust:

> To A for life, remainder to B for life, remainder to C absolutely.

It is interesting to note that the transfer of the equitable entitlement from A, to B, to C is effected automatically under the terms of the trust. In order to ensure the transfer, there is no need for A or B to do anything except to live and die. The fact that there is an automatic transfer of the equitable entitlement means that it is necessary for the relevant tax law to create certain legal fictions, which are discussed in the following chapters. In this connection, it is worth noting also that there are rules of property law designed to ensure that the interest transferred to the next beneficiary entitled under the trust is, so far as possible, just as valuable as that enjoyed by the predecessor: *Allhusen* v *Whittell* (1887) LR 4 Eq 295 and *Howe* v *Lord Dartmouth* (1802) 7 Ves 137. In the above example, whilst A is alive, the future interests of B and C are referred to as *reversionary interests*.

Both B and C could give away or sell their reversionary interests, although it would be unusual for them to be able to sell such interests at a profit: **24.8**.

26.6.3 INTESTACY RULES

If you die without leaving a valid will, then you die totally intestate. You die partially intestate if you leave a valid will which does not give away the whole of your estate. Total intestacy includes the situation where, although your will is a valid will, it does not give away any of your estate effectively. It is obviously not possible to discuss the property law aspects of intestacy in detail in this book. This section is confined to an outline of the intestacy rules applicable in England and Wales: ss. 46, 47, AEA 1925. The operation of these rules is, in some respects at least, similar to the operation of a gift on death. In the same way that a will may combine a number of legacies with the setting up of a will trust, the intestacy rules may provide for certain people to take part of the estate absolutely, and others to take part of it on trust. This depends on which categories of people survive the deceased, as we shall discover in a moment. In another respect, the operation of these rules is significantly different from a gift on death. The estate of someone who dies intestate initially vests in a judge, i.e. the President of the Family Division of the High Court. The deceased's PRs, known as administrators, must obtain their authority to deal with the deceased's estate by applying to the High Court for the grant of so-called *letters of administration*.

Once obtained, the grant relates back to the date of the death. By AEA 1925, s. 33(1), as amended:

> On the death of a person intestate as to any real or personal estate, that estate shall be held in trust by his personal representatives with the power to sell it.

It remains to consider which categories of people are entitled to share in the estate. Four different situations need to be considered.

26.6.3.1 Deceased is survived by spouse and issue: AEA 1925, s. 46(1)

In this situation, the PRs hold all of the deceased's 'personal chattels', plus a statutory legacy of £125,000 for the surviving spouse absolutely. Personal chattels are items of domestic and personal ornament and use: AEA 1925, s. 55(1)(x). If the deceased's estate, other than personal chattels, is worth less than £125,000, then the PRs hold the whole of it for the surviving spouse absolutely. As mentioned in **26.5.3**, the PRs' transfer of this property to the surviving spouse is a nominal transfer. The automatic transfer to the PRs, via the President of the Family Division, is what we are concerned with describing here. If the deceased's estate, other than personal chattels, is worth more than £125,000, then the PRs hold:

(a) one half of the residue on trust for the surviving spouse for his or her lifetime; and

(b) the other half of the residue, plus the half of the residue in (a) which is in remainder at this point, for the deceased's issue, on the so-called 'statutory trusts'.

Issue simply refers to the deceased's children, grandchildren and other lineal descendants. It is not possible to discuss the detail here of the statutory trusts: AEA 1925, s. 47. However, that part of the estate held on the statutory trusts is held for the deceased's issue equally, provided that they are alive or *en ventre sa mère* at the deceased's death. Under the statutory trusts, the issue's interest is contingent only, until they reach the age of 18, or marry below that age: for the meaning of *contingent*, refer to **16.3.1**. If a child dies under the age of 18, who is also unmarried, then that child is disregarded for the purposes of the statutory trusts.

Humphrey and Wendy own Bugthorpe Manor, which is worth £250,000, as joint tenants. On 1 November 1998, Humphrey is killed in a riding accident. He dies intestate. His estate (excluding his personal chattels) is worth £110,000. Besides Wendy, he is survived by his two children, Jack and Jill, aged seven and eight. Will the children receive anything under the intestacy rules?

No. Humphrey's interest as a joint tenant of Bugthorpe Manor passes outside the intestacy rules: see above. The whole of his estate, plus his personal chattels, will be held by his PRs for Wendy absolutely.

Assume the same facts as in SAQ 347, except that Horace and Wendy are tenants in common of Bugthorpe Manor in equal shares. Will the children receive anything under the intestacy rules in this situation?

Yes. Humphrey's half-share in Bugthorpe Manor, together with his personal chattels, will be held by his PRs for Wendy absolutely. The PRs will also hold Humphrey's estate of £110,000 for the children on the statutory trusts.

26.6.3.2 Deceased is survived by spouse, no issue but parents, brothers or sisters or their issue: AEA 1925, s. 46(1)

In this situation, the PRs hold all of the deceased's personal chattels, as above, plus a statutory legacy of £200,000 for the surviving spouse absolutely. If the deceased's estate, other than personal chattels, is worth less than £200,000, then the PRs hold the whole of it for the surviving spouse absolutely. As mentioned in **26.5.3**, the PRs' transfer of this property to the surviving spouse is a nominal transfer. The automatic transfer to the PRs, via the President of the Family Division, is what we are concerned with describing here. If the deceased's estate, other than personal chattels, is worth more than £200,000, then the PRs hold:

(a) one half of the residue for the surviving spouse absolutely; and

(b) (i) if the deceased's parents are alive, the other half of the residue for them absolutely; or

(ii) if the deceased's parents are dead, the other half of the residue is held for the deceased's brothers and sisters of the whole blood and the issue of any deceased brother and sister on the statutory trusts.

Assume the same facts as in SAQ 347, except that Humphrey and Wendy have no children, and Humphrey has predeceased his parents, who are both alive at his death. Who will receive what, on these facts?

Excluding his personal chattels, Humphrey's estate will be worth £235,000 (i.e. £125,000 + £110,000). £200,000 of this will be held by Humphrey's PRs for Wendy absolutely, and £35,000 for Humphrey's parents absolutely.

26.6.3.3   Deceased is survived by spouse but no issue, nor parents, nor brothers or sisters nor their issue: AEA 1925, s. 46(1)

In this situation, the PRs hold all of the deceased's personal chattels, as above, plus the whole of the deceased's estate for the surviving spouse absolutely. The deceased's grandparents, e.g., have no right to any property in the deceased's estate. As mentioned in **26.5.3**, the PRs' transfer of this property to the surviving spouse is a nominal transfer. The automatic transfer to the PRs, via the President of the Family Division, is what we are concerned with here.

Assume the same facts as in SAQ 349, with the modification that, not only do Humphrey and Wendy have no children, Humphrey's parents have predeceased him, and he has no brothers or sisters at his death.

Who will receive what, in this situation?

Humphrey's PRs will hold the whole of his estate, plus his personal chattels, for Wendy absolutely.

26.6.3.4   Spouse is already dead at the deceased's death: AEA 1925, s. 46(1)(i)–(vi)

In this situation, the PRs hold the deceased's estate for the classes of persons listed below. However, no individual in a class further down the list will receive anything at all, unless all of those in the preceding class have died before the deceased. Except in classes (b) and (e), the PRs will hold the deceased's estate on the statutory trusts, in cases where the beneficiaries are such that the statutory trusts apply (see above).

(a) The deceased's issue;

(b) the deceased's parents;

(c) the deceased's brothers and sisters and the issue of any deceased brother or sister;

(d) the deceased's half-brothers and half-sisters and the issue of any deceased brother or sister;

(e) the deceased's grandparents;

(f) the deceased's uncles and aunts and the issue of any deceased uncle or aunt;

(g)   the deceased's parents' half-brothers and half-sisters and the issue of any deceased half-uncle or half-aunt; or

(h)   the Crown, the Duchy of Lancaster or the Duchy of Cornwall.

In class (h), the estate is referred to as being *bona vacantia*, i.e. ownerless goods. Only if the deceased was resident in the Duchy of Lancaster or the Duchy of Cornwall, which are both geographical areas, will the PRs hold the deceased's estate for one or the other, as the case may be.

Alfred died resident in Romford, Essex, on 1 November 1998. He was 43. He left no valid will. Sadly, he had no relatives within any of the classes specified in the intestacy rules.

Who will be entitled to receive his estate?

The Crown.

26.7   Taxation of Gratuitous Transfers

In this part of the book, we shall be discussing the application of four taxes to gratuitous transfers:

■   IHT;

■   CGT;

■   VAT; and

■   stamp duty.

Of these, the most obviously relevant is IHT. However, CGT may also be chargeable on some categories of gratuitous transfer: see **27.3.2.1**. In relation to gifts, e.g., IHT and CGT interact, and may both be payable on one gift, although at different times. Indeed, the potential for the double taxation of a transaction is perhaps the strangest feature of the way in which gratuitous transfers are taxed: see **2.4.1.2**. It illustrates how problematic it is to attempt to explain CGT and IHT rules in isolation from each other. In addition, it may be necessary to consider whether any document by which a gratuitous transfer is made is liable to stamp duty and, if the transferor is a taxable person, whether they are liable to account for VAT on the transfer. You may think it surprising to find any reference at all to VAT here. However, undervalue sales can rank as supplies for VAT purposes, just like any other sale may do. So far as stamp duty and VAT are concerned, broadly similar points apply as in relation to investment taxation: see **20.7, 20.8**.

26.8   Historical and Political Contexts

We have already considered the historical and political contexts of CGT. We need briefly to do the same for IHT. At its most basic, IHT is a tax on wealth. Its origins can be traced back to death duties, which were originally a form of stamp duty imposed on wills and letters of administration introduced in 1694. As a PR, you had to pay the duty, or you could not obtain a grant of probate or letters of administration. This point may be familiar to you if you have ever attempted to trace your family history using old wills. Death duties first took a form resembling the modern IHT when estate duty was introduced by Sir William Harcourt (1827–1904), the Liberal Chancellor of the Exchequer, in 1894. Estate duty basically taxed gifts on death and automatic transfers under the intestacy rules. It produced almost £12 million in 1898, and it is claimed to have contributed the revenue needed for the British naval rearmament before the First World War.

Estate duty was replaced with capital transfer tax (CTT) in the Budget of 1974. 80 years on from Sir William Harcourt's Budget of 1894, estate duty had become horrendously complicated. Already, in 1966, Diplock LJ had made an extraordinary judicial pronouncement on estate duty in *Re Kilpatrick's Policies Trusts* [1966] Ch 730:

> As in nearly all appeals about estate duty, I reach my decision without confidence. Were I a betting man I should lay the odds on its being right at 6 to 4 (i.e. 3 to 2) on – or against. If ever a branch of law called for reform in 1966, it is the law relating to estate duty. It ought to be certain: it ought to be sensible – it is neither.

The key feature of CTT, the replacement for estate duty, was that the total value of all gifts made by an individuals in the 10-year period before death was ascertained, and CTT was charged on the total value at progressive rates. IHT, which was introduced by FA 1986, reduced the 10-year cumulation period to seven years, and exempted from IHT gifts made more than seven years before an individual's death. It also reintroduced an anti-avoidance concept which had been a feature of estate duty, the gift with a reservation: see **Chapter 32**. IHT, introduced by a Conservative Government, considerably restricted the scope of CTT, as originally framed. It is possible that IHT will itself eventually be re-extended by the current Labour Government.

Read the extracts from Madeleine Beard's book, *English Landed Society in The Twentieth Century* at *Cases and Materials* (26.2). This provides an interesting insight into the historical transition from estate duty (what the author refers to as 'death duties') to IHT.

Figures published by the Revenue on 17 March 1998 emphasise that very few pay IHT, less than 3 in 100 of all death estates in fact. The estimated number of estates subject to IHT in 1998/99 is about 17,500, and its estimated yield in the current tax year £1,900 million.

26.9   Summary

Gratuitous transfers comprise gifts, nominal transfers and automatic transfers. Gifts include absolute gifts, gifts on trust, undervalue sales and gifts on death. Gifts on death may themselves be absolute gifts or gifts on trust. Nominal transfers are made by those acting in a fiduciary capacity, e.g. trustees and PRs. They may be made between trustees, from trustees to beneficiaries, from personal representatives to beneficiaries, or from PRs to trustees. Where the same individuals who have acted as PRs go on to act as trustees of a will trust, it is best practice for them to execute an assent in their own favour as trustees. Automatic transfers take place under the terms of some document, or by the operation of some rule of law. Automatic transfers include transfers under the survivorship principle, as well as the shift in the equitable entitlement of a beneficiary under a settlement. They also include transfers on death under the intestacy rules, since these take place by operation of law, rather than by any voluntary act of the deceased whilst alive. The four taxes potentially relevant to gratuitous transfers are IHT, CGT, VAT and stamp duty. IHT is the latest stage in a centuries-old process of development from death duties, via estate duty and CTT. I have included the thumbnail sketch of English property law in this chapter, since it is apparent that students' biggest problem in relation to IHT and CGT is often that of difficulty in imagining the property law context in which the two taxes need to be considered.

CHAPTER TWENTY-SEVEN

TAXATION OF GRATUITOUS TRANSFERS: GIFTS

27.1 Objectives

By the end of this chapter, you should be able to:

■ explain the tax implications of *absolute gifts*;

■ define *settled property* for CGT purposes;

■ define a *settlement* for IHT purposes;

■ list the conditions for an *accumulation and maintenance settlement*;

■ explain the tax implications of *gifts on trust*;

■ explain the tax implications of *undervalue sales*;

■ explain the tax implications of *gifts on death*.

27.2 Introduction

In **Chapter 26**, four categories of gifts were discussed, together with four categories of nominal transfer, and three categories of automatic transfer. **Chapters 28** and **29** will discuss the tax implications of nominal transfers and automatic transfers. In this chapter, we shall discuss the taxation implications of gifts only. Each of the four categories of gifts has implications for CGT, IHT and stamp duty. In addition, VAT may be relevant to undervalue sales by taxable persons. As a matter of general company law, a company may not make absolute gifts of its assets, nor sell them at an undervalue, without the authority of 75% of its shareholders in general meeting, i.e. by special resolution. This rule does not always stop companies from attempting to do these things, however, and they have serious tax consequences.

27.3 Taxation of Absolute Gifts

27.3.1 INHERITANCE TAX AND ABSOLUTE GIFTS

27.3.1.1 Individuals

Absolute gifts may obviously be made by individuals in their personal capacity, as well as by individuals acting in the capacity of partners. Absolute gifts by partners of partnership assets are sometimes difficult to detect.

(1)   Chargeable transfers
The Inheritance Tax Act 1984 uses the concept of the *chargeable transfer*: IHTA 1984, s. 2(1).
If an absolute gift is not a chargeable transfer, then no IHT is payable. A chargeable
transfer is, according to s. 2(1), IHTA 1984:

■   a transfer of value,

■   made by an individual,

■   which is not exempt.

Thus, an absolute gift will not be a chargeable transfer if only one of these three elements
is missing in a specific case.

(2)   Transfer of value
A transfer of value is defined as any disposition, including an omission, which reduces the
value of the giver's estate: IHTA 1984, s. 3(1). By IHTA 1984, s. 3(4), transfers of value include
deemed transfers of value. However, there is a list of transactions which are not transfers of
value and, if an absolute gift falls within that list, there is no transfer of value, and therefore
no chargeable transfer. The list of transactions which are not transfers of value is as follows:

(a)   Transactions not intended to confer a gratuitous benefit: IHTA 1984, s. 10   You do not
make a transfer of value if you can show that you had no intention of conferring a
gratuitous benefit on anyone. In other words, if you can show that what appears to be
an absolute gift is in reality a *commercial transaction*. You must show that a disposition
was not intended, and was not made in a transaction intended, to confer a gratuitous
benefit on any person. You must also demonstrate one of two other things, i.e.:

(a)   that it was made in a transaction at arm's length between persons not connected
      with each other, *or*

(b)   that it was such as might be expected to be made in a transaction at arm's length
      between persons not connected with each other.

The concept of persons connected with each other is defined in IHTA 1984, s. 270, and
will be discussed in **27.5**. Suffice it to say here that, as an individual, you are connected
with your relatives, including your aunts, nephews and nieces.

**On 1 November 1998, I give my car, worth £10,000, to my daughter as a birthday
present. Will it be possible for me to show that I did not intend to confer a gratuitous
benefit on any person?**

No.

**You are a member of a Lottery syndicate, together with nine fellow employees. There
is a written agreement between you to divide up any winnings. Last Saturday, you
held the jackpot ticket and won £15 million. Will you make transfers of value when
you pay over £1,500,000 to each of the other members?**

Probably not. The written agreement should evidence satisfaction of the conditions above.

Section 10, IHTA 1984 is mainly relevant in relation to undervalue sales. We shall therefore save further discussion of it until **27.5**.

(b) Excluded property   There will be no transfer of value if the property being given away is so-called excluded property: IHTA 1984, s. 6. The most important example of excluded property for our purposes is a *reversionary interest* under a trust. However, IHTA 1984, s. 6, states that property situated outside the UK and owned by someone domiciled outside the UK is also excluded property. The concept of domicile is discussed in **4.5.5**. It is important to be clear about which reversionary interests qualify as excluded property, and which do not. It is also important to be aware of four exceptions to the rule that reversionary interests are excluded property. By IHTA 1984, s. 47, a reversionary interest is defined as:

> . . . [A] future interest under a settlement, whether it is vested or contingent . . .

For the present, read the word *settlement* as *trust*. We shall be discussing it more fully in **27.4.1.2**. The definition in s. 47, IHTA 1984 will obviously cover future interests in trust property which are fixed by the terms of the trust deed. It is doubtful, however, whether the limited rights of beneficiaries under a discretionary trust are excluded property. Beneficiaries under a discretionary trust have no clear interest in the trust property until the trustees exercise the discretion in their favour. Until the discretion is exercised, the beneficiary merely has a right to compel due administration of the trust. Remember Lord Wilberforce's words in *McPhail* v *Doulton* [1971] AC 424:

> . . . [A]s to the trustees' duty of enquiry or ascertainment, in each case the trustees ought to make such a survey of the range of [beneficiaries] as will enable them to carry out their fiduciary duty.

The limited nature of the rights of discretionary beneficiaries means that they are very unlikely to be interests in reversion for IHT purposes. The four exceptions to reversionary interests being excluded property are future interests which:

■ have at any time been acquired for a consideration in money or money's worth; *or*

■ are sold to beneficiaries with an earlier interest under the same trust; *or*

■ in the cases of leases for lives treated as settlements (see **27.4.1.2**), are reversions expectant on the termination of such leases; *or*

■ belong to the settlor or the settlor's spouse: IHTA 1984, s. 48(1)(b).

SAQ 354

Albrecht, who is domiciled in Germany, acquires a freehold house in Nottingham. Will the house be excluded property if he makes an absolute gift of it?

No.

The *situs* (i.e. location) of assets for IHT purposes is briefly determined as follows. The relevant rules are common law ones. A bank account is located at the relevant branch of the bank. The location of *registered* shares and securities is the place of their registration. Interests in land are located where the land is. Shares and debentures, the title to which passes on delivery (so-called 'bearer shares/debentures'), are located at the place where the share certificate, etc. is kept. With limited exceptions, the location of chattels is where they are kept.

Hans, a UK-resident and domiciled individual, receives 10,000 Deutschmarks, under the will of his Aunt Sophie, who has just died. The 10,000 Deutschmarks is in a bank account in Dresden. At her death, Aunt Sophie was domiciled in Germany. Is the legacy excluded property?

Yes.

(c) Waiver of dividends or remuneration   One way of making a transfer of value, if you were an employee of your own company, might be to forgo your remuneration. This would be a gift just as clearly as taking the salary and giving it away would be. By the same token, as a shareholder, you might not accept payment of dividends, with the same result. Without special provision, both of these waivers might be chargeable transfers. However, two provisions specifically state that, if certain conditions are met, such transactions will not be transfers of value and cannot therefore be chargeable transfers: IHTA 1984, ss. 14, 15. Section 14, IHTA 1984 deals with waivers of remuneration. It provides that a waiver or repayment of remuneration which would otherwise fall under Schedule E, in Stage One of your income tax calculation, is not a transfer of value. This is subject to the condition that the corresponding adjustment is made to the profits or losses of the payer. Section 15, IHTA 1984 covers waivers of dividends. It says simply:

> A person who waives any dividend on shares of a company within twelve months before any right to the dividend has accrued does not by reason of the waiver make a transfer of value.

On 1 April 1999, I sign a document waiving my entitlement to dividends payable on my shares in Utopia Ltd, up to 1 April 2000. On 1 October 1999, the company declares and pays its final dividend of £10,000 in total, for the accounting period ended on that date.

Will the waiver be a transfer of value by me?

No.

(d) Voidable transfers   Suppose I make an absolute gift of property and it is later shown that I did so under duress. Again, as in cases (a) to (c) above, the rule is that there has been no chargeable transfer: IHTA, s. 150. Any IHT which should not therefore have been paid can be reclaimed. This applies not only where duress has induced the transfer, but also to other cases where an absolute gift could be set aside because of some vitiating factor.

(3) Exemptions

If an absolute gift is not within the categories in (2), it ranks as a transfer of value. To escape liability to pay IHT, therefore, your only other chance is to show that the transfer of value is exempt. It is exempt if it is covered by the list of exemptions in Part II, IHTA

1984. If it is, then the gift is not a chargeable transfer and no IHT is payable. If it is not, then it is a chargeable transfer. The IHT exemption for transfers between spouses is discussed in outline in **27.7**. The other IHT exemptions are discussed in detail in **Chapter 32**, with IHT reliefs.

(4)   Potentially exempt transfers ('PETs')

If an absolute gift is not exempt, then it is a chargeable transfer. The next question is whether it is chargeable to IHT in the tax year in which the gift is made, or only if you, the giver, die within seven years after making the gift. This is simply another way of asking whether the absolute gift is immediately chargeable to IHT, or a potentially exempt transfer (a PET). If the gift does not satisfy the conditions for a PET in IHTA 1984, s. 3A(1), then it is immediately chargeable to IHT. If, however, the absolute gift is within the definition of a PET, IHT will be chargeable only if you, the giver, die within seven years after making the gift. There are two preliminary conditions in s. 3A(1). If the gift satisfies these conditions, then it will be a PET, provided that the recipient is either an individual or the trustee or trustees of one of three specific types of settlement.

The two preliminary conditions are that:

■   the gift was made after 18 March 1986; *and*

■   if it were not for IHTA 1984, s. 3A(1), the gift would be a chargeable transfer.

The former will obviously be satisfied if you want to make a gift today. The second merits some reflection, however. It emphasises the importance of being satisfied, before considering whether the gift is a PET, whether the gift you are making is in fact a chargeable transfer. On the assumption that these conditions are satisfied, for the gift to be a PET, the recipient must be:

■   another individual; *or*

■   the trustee or trustees of an *accumulation and maintenance settlement* or *disabled settlement*; or

■   the trustee or trustees of a settlement *with* an interest in possession.

Obviously, we need to consider the implications of these three alternatives in some detail. In this section, we consider the first one. The second and third are considered with other gifts on trust in **27.4**. An absolute gift by an individual to an individual should normally be a PET. However, the gift will be immediately chargeable, and thus not a PET, if the property given away neither becomes part of the recipient's estate, nor increases it: IHTA 1984, s. 3A(2).

I give you a valuable dining-table. Is this absolute gift a PET?

Yes.

If I pay your hotel bill, is this a PET?

Yes, see IHTA 1984, s. 3A(2)(b).

27.3.1.2 Partners

Absolute gifts by partners are governed by the same IHT rules that govern absolute gifts by any other individual. In my capacity as a partner, however, the subject matter of the gift will be my share in the partnership assets: see **21.6**. By contrast, if I am giving away non-partnership assets, then the subject-matter of the gift might be the same as for any gift made by individuals in their personal capacity. If what I am giving away is a share in partnership assets, the fact that I am making a chargeable transfer may not be obvious. There are a number of standard transactions between partners in a firm which can be analysed as absolute gifts, however.

One of them is the absolute gift which can take place when the *asset surplus sharing ratio* is changed by the partners. This simply means a change in the proportions in which we, as partners, share any profit on a sale of partnership property. The change is achieved by a variation in the terms of the partnership agreement. For instance, if you and I are in partnership, we might agree to admit a new partner to the partnership. We might give that third partner a third share in any profit we make on a sale of the capital assets of the partnership. This would give rise to a transfer of a share in the assets of the partnership from us to the third partner which might appear to be an absolute gift.

You and I are in partnership, carrying on the business of hairdressers. On 1 December 1998, we admit Claude as a partner, without his paying in any capital. On his admission to the partnership, we change the asset surplus sharing ratio from 50:50 to 40:40:20 (Claude).

Have we made an absolute gift to Claude?

It would appear so.

Comparable adjustments might be made to the asset surplus sharing ratio if I were expelled from the partnership or simply if our original agreement on the ratio were altered by mutual agreement.

The obvious question is whether any of these operations are transfers of value made by an individual or individuals, i.e. the partners, which are not exempt and thus whether they are chargeable transfers and therefore PETs. In general terms, the answer to that question is that all absolute gifts are in principle transfers of value, but that these gratuitous transfers are unlikely to be transfers of value because the transferors have no intention of conferring a gratuitous benefit on anyone: IHTA 1984, s. 10(1). Whether s. 10(1) applies, however, will depend on the particular facts of the case.

What would you and I argue, given the facts of SAQ 359, in order to demonstrate that what appeared to be an absolute gift was not a PET?

That there was no intention to confer a gratuitous benefit and that the transaction was at arms' length: IHTA 1984, s. 10(1).

27.3.1.3   Companies

It is apparent from the definition of a chargeable transfer that a company, as distinct from the individual shareholders in it, should never be able to make a chargeable transfer, even if it makes an absolute gift. For a chargeable transfer to take place, there must be a transfer of value by an *individual* which is not exempt: IHTA 1984, s. 2(1).

At an extraordinary general meeting of Utopia Ltd, its shareholders vote to make an absolute gift of the office premises owned by the company to Jack, one of their number. Will *the company* make a chargeable transfer?

No.

The gift will have corporation tax consequences, however: see **27.3.2.3**. In addition, an IHT charge could be imposed on the company under the deeming provisions to be discussed in **33.3.3**.

27.3.2   CAPITAL GAINS TAX AND ABSOLUTE GIFTS

27.3.2.1   Individuals

Absolute gifts are chargeable disposals for CGT purposes. Ponder the effect of TCGA 1992, s. 17:

> [A] person's . . . disposal of an asset shall . . . be deemed to be for a consideration equal to the market value of the asset–
>
> (a)   where he . . . disposes of the asset otherwise than by way of a bargain made at arm's length, and in particular where he . . . disposes of it by way of gift . . .

Section 17, TCGA 1992 makes a fundamentally important point. If you make an absolute gift of a chargeable asset, you will be deemed to have received its market value on the disposal. This is so, even though you have not received a penny in return. It means that the chargeable gain on the disposal is calculated by inserting the market value of the chargeable asset as your disposal proceeds in Stage Two of your CGT calculation: see **21.4**.

On 1 February 1999, Alice gives 300 of her total shareholding of 900 shares in Utopia plc to each of her three children. Her base cost for the total shareholding is £10,000. On 1 February 1999, its market value is £400,000. What are the disposal proceeds of the shareholding for inclusion in Stage Two of her CGT calculation for the 1998/99 tax year?

£390,000, i.e. £400,000 – £10,000.

When CGT was introduced, many people did not recognise the significance of what is now TCGA 1992, s. 17. One such individual was a Mr Harry Turner: *Turner* v *Follett* [1973] STC 148. In 1969, he gave his daughters 300 shares in a company called the

Hudson Bay Company Ltd, and was surprised to discover that he was deemed to have received their market value at the time he made the gift. He appeared in person before the Court of Appeal, and tried to argue that it was absurd for the legislation to deem him to have made a profit in these circumstances. In confirming the effect of what is now TCGA 1992, s. 17, Russell LJ said:

> To say that [Mr Turner's] criticisms fall on deaf ears would be impolite; but, speaking judicially, our ears cannot but be deaf to such an approach. We can do nothing but construe the Act to the best of our ability, stifling any distaste which out of court we might find ourselves sharing with the taxpayer.

Read the extract from *Turner* v *Follett*, at *Cases and Materials* (27.1), especially Mr Turner's statement. Bearing in mind that Mr Turner was not a tax specialist, consider whether his argument was a fair one.

Note the converse of the deemed market value on disposals. The corresponding acquisition is also deemed to be for the asset's market value: TCGA 1992, s. 17. It may be possible for the CGT charge to be postponed by claiming *hold-over relief*: see **32.3.1**.

27.3.2.2 Partners

Absolute gifts by partners in their personal capacity are governed by the same CGT rules that apply to absolute gifts by other individuals. However, gifts of shares in partnership assets may be made by partners in their capacity as partners. Such absolute gifts may in practice be quite difficult to detect. In **27.3.1.2**, we discussed the IHT implications of transactions between partners which may be classified as absolute gifts. We identified the standard transaction involving a change in the asset surplus sharing ratio.

Alice and Beth are in partnership. On 1 November 1998, they agree to make the asset surplus sharing ratio of the partnership 2:1, having previously shared surpluses equally, i.e. in the ratio 1:1. What has Alice acquired from Beth?

$\frac{1}{6}$ of her share in the asset surplus sharing ratio.

The question for CGT purposes is whether Beth has made a chargeable disposal in this situation and, if so, what the proceeds of that disposal are. The answer to both questions depends on whether the partnership property has previously been *revalued* in the accounts of the partnership, in such a way as to reflect its current market value:

(a) If the partnership property *has* been revalued, and no consideration has been paid by the recipient partner for the other partner's share in that property, the other partner will make a chargeable gain on a chargeable disposal of a chargeable asset when a change in the asset surplus sharing ratio is made.

However:

(b) If the partnership property has *not* been revalued, and no consideration has been paid, as in (a), the other partner will neither make a gain nor a loss on the chargeable disposal when a change in the asset surplus sharing ratios is made.

Of these, (b) could be an absolute gift. However, the market value of the part of the share disposed of will not be substituted if nothing would have been paid even if the parties had been at arm's length: SP D12, para. 7.

You and I are in partnership, sharing profits 1:1. We agree that, in future, profits should be shared 2:1 in your favour. The assets of the partnership have not been revalued. Will I be regarded as having made an absolute gift, and thus a chargeable disposal of part of my share?

No.

In cases where there *is* a CGT charge, it may be possible for it to be postponed by claiming *hold-over relief*: see **32.3.1**.

27.3.2.3   Companies

For the purposes of corporation tax on chargeable gains, an absolute gift by a company to its shareholders is a distribution by the company: ICTA 1988, s. 209(2)(f), (4). The concept of a distribution is designed to cover any method of draining profits out of a company to its shareholders. Where there is a distribution, there is currently an obligation on the company to pay ACT on the distribution: see **8.3.1**. If, as a shareholder, you accept a gift of property from the company, therefore, the company will suffer an ACT charge. In addition, you could suffer the IHT charge discussed in **33.3.3**. If a company makes an absolute gift of property to a person who is not its shareholder, then TCGA 1992, s. 17 applies. The property is deemed to have been disposed of by the company for its market value. Note that *no* hold-over relief is available to a *company*: see **32.3.1.3**.

Assume the facts of SAQ 361. Is the company obliged to pay ACT on the value of the absolute gift to Jack?

Yes.

27.3.3   STAMP DUTY AND ABSOLUTE GIFTS

Where an absolute gift needs to be made by a conveyance, the conveyance will be exempt from stamp duty if the conditions of the Stamp Duty (Exempt Instruments) Regulations 1987 (SI 1987 No. 516) are complied with. Thus, the deed of conveyance will be exempt from stamp duty if it includes a certificate signed by the giver that the conveyance is covered by the regulations. By reg. 5, the conveyance does not need to be presented for adjudication at the Inland Revenue stamp office. In the Regulations, the relevant category of exemption reads:

  L   The conveyance or transfer of property operating as a voluntary disposition inter vivos for no consideration in money or money's worth nor any consideration referred to in section 57 of the Stamp Act 1891 (conveyance in consideration of a debt etc.).

27.4 Taxation of Gifts on Trust

The concept of a gift on trust, for property law purposes, is much wider than its definition for the purposes of IHT and CGT. The consequence of this point is that an absolute gift may be regarded as a gift on trust for property law purposes, whilst not being regarded as a gift into settlement for IHT purposes or making property *settled property* for CGT purposes. We need to begin this section on the taxation of gifts on trust, therefore, with a consideration of settled property and settlements for CGT and IHT purposes. It should be noted that references to 'new-style trusts of land' are to trusts governed by the Trusts of Land and Appointment of Trustees Act 1996 (TLA 1996).

27.4.1 'SETTLED PROPERTY' AND SETTLEMENTS

27.4.1.1 Capital gains tax: settled property

Rather than defining a settlement, the CGT legislation defines settled property: TCGA 1992, s. 68. Settled property is any property held in trust, except any of the following (TCGA 1992, s. 60, *Cases and Materials* (20.2.1.2):

■ property held by a trustee on a bare trust or as a nominee for another;

■ property held '. . . for any person who would be [absolutely] entitled but for being an infant or other person under disability'; *or*

■ property held '. . . for two or more persons who are or would be jointly [absolutely] entitled'.

The common factor in each of these cases is that the beneficiary is '. . . absolutely entitled as against the trustee': TCGA 1992, s. 60(2). If the beneficiary is absolutely entitled as against the trustee, the trust property is *not* settled property. We shall return to this point in **Chapter 28**.

On 1 November 1998, Samuel gives Blackacre to Tim and Tom, who are trustees of a new-style trust of land, under which the trustees hold Blackacre on trust for Alice for life, remainder to Bertie absolutely. Is Blackacre settled property for CGT purposes?

Yes. Alice and Bertie are not jointly absolutely entitled, within TCGA 1992, s. 60: see **20.6.2.2**.

On 1 August 1998, John and Jill buy a freehold property as joint tenants under a new-style trust of land. Is the freehold property settled property for CGT purposes?

No.

27.4.1.2   Inheritance tax: settlements

The CGT legislation defines *settled property* rather than *settlement*; the IHT legislation defines *settlement*, rather than *settled property*: IHTA 1984, s. 43. For IHT purposes, a settlement is broadly any written or oral arrangement whereby:

■ property is held on trust for persons successively, or for any person subject to the fulfilment of a contingency; *or*

■ property is held on trust to accumulate the income of the property (or any part of it), or make payments out of it, at the discretion of the trustees; *or*

■ property is charged or burdened with the payment out of it of any annuity or periodical payment for a specified period.

It is interesting to note that this definition of a settlement says what a settlement is, rather than what it *is not*, which is how the CGT definition operates. Surprisingly, perhaps, a *lease for life or lives* is also a settlement for IHT purposes, unless it was granted for full consideration in money or money's worth: IHTA 1984, s. 43(3).

Assume the same facts as in SAQ 366. Is there a settlement of Blackacre for IHT purposes?

Yes. Blackacre is held for Alice and Bertie successively.

On 1 August 1998, John and Jill bought a freehold property as joint tenants, as in SAQ 367. Is the freehold property subject to a settlement for IHT purposes?

No.

27.4.2   INHERITANCE TAX AND GIFTS INTO SETTLEMENTS

The IHT consequences of a gift into a settlement depend on the classification of the settlement:

■ if the settlement is a settlement with an interest in possession, then the gift is a PET: see **27.3.1.1**.

■ If the settlement is a settlement without an interest in possession, then the gift is immediately chargeable to IHT, unless it is either an accumulation and maintenance settlement or a disabled settlement.

SAQ 370

Alfred transfers shares valued at £10,000 to the trustees of a no-interest in possession settlement which does not satisfy the definition either of a disabled settlement or an accumulation and maintenance settlement. Is the gift into a settlement a PET?

No. It is *immediately chargeable* to IHT.

The general rule, therefore, is that a transfer to trustees of a settlement not having an interest in possession is chargeable to IHT immediately. Accumulation and maintenance settlements and disabled settlements are exceptions to that rule.

27.4.2.1   Interest in possession settlements

Whether a settlement has an interest in possession depends on whether the test in *Pearson* v *IRC* [1980] 2 All ER 479 is satisfied. (This case is sometimes confusingly referred to as *Re Pilkington*). In *Pearson* v *IRC*, three sisters, Fiona, Serena and Julia, were the adult beneficiaries of a settlement. The settled fund consisted of 13,333 ordinary shares in Pilkington Brothers Ltd. Having already satisfied the relevant contingency by reaching the age of 21, each of the three sisters had an equal share absolutely in the shareholding which made up the fund. However, the settlement also gave the trustees an overriding power of appointment of the shares and any dividends generated by them, in favour of all or any one or more of the sisters. Pending exercise of this power of appointment, the settlement gave the trustees power to accumulate as much of the dividend income as they thought fit. The trustees subsequently exercised the power of appointment, by appointing the dividends generated by some of the shares in favour of Fiona for life. The question was whether, just before the power of appointment was exercised by the trustees in Fiona's favour, the sisters had an interest in possession in the shares. Edward Nugee QC, for the Crown, argued that the sisters did not have an interest in possession. The trustees' power to accumulate the income, he argued, prevented whoever was entitled to the income in default of the power being exercised, from having an interest in possession in the shares. The argument was upheld by a majority of the House of Lords.

ACTIVITY 67

Read the speech of Viscount Dilhorne in *Pearson* v *IRC*, at *Cases and Materials* (27.2.1). Note down his Lordship's test for whether a settlement has an interest in possession, and the reason why he held that there was *no* interest in possession in that case.

The settlement in *Pearson* v *IRC* may strike you as being somewhat strange. Whether or not a settlement has an interest in possession is usually a very easy question to answer.

The question is this. Does anyone have a right to the income of the settled property as it arises?

Trustees hold shares in Micro Ltd for Alice for life, remainder to Belinda absolutely. Alice is 40 years old. Does the settlement have an interest in possession?

Yes.

Read the *dissenting* speech of Lord Russell of Killowen in *Pearson* v *IRC*, at *Cases and Materials* (27.2.1). This has been praised by a number of commentators. In your opinion, is Lord Russell's analysis a better one than that of the majority of the House of Lords?

Remember that TA 1925, s. 31 could give a beneficiary a right to the income as it arises. Section 31 will apply to the settlement unless it is excluded by the deed. If it applies, a beneficiary will *automatically* get a vested interest in the income on reaching 18. This will make the settlement one with an interest in possession for IHT purposes: see **16.3.1.2**.

It is important to appreciate that, where a beneficiary has an interest in possession, that individual is *deemed* for IHT (but not CGT) purposes to be the owner of the settled property: IHTA 1984, s. 49(1).

27.4.2.2   Settlements without an interest in possession

It follows from the discussion in **27.4.2.1** that a settlement without an interest in possession is one where no beneficiary has a present right of present enjoyment of the settled property.

Terry and Theo, two trustees, hold shares in Amber plc on trust to apply the income generated by the shares (i.e. dividends) for the benefit of a defined class of beneficiaries in such proportions as, in the exercise of their discretion, they may think fit.

Are the shares in Amber plc subject to an interest in possession settlement for IHT purposes?

No.

27.4.2.3 Accumulation and maintenance settlements: IHTA 1984, s. 71

The definition of an accumulation and maintenance settlement is a detailed one. Such a settlement is basically a discretionary trust for the benefit of someone aged 25 or under. However, the conditions which a discretionary trust must satisfy before it counts as an accumulation and maintenance settlement are detailed ones. The conditions are as follows:

- on or before attaining a specified age, not over 25, one or more beneficiaries will become beneficially entitled to the settled fund, or to an interest in possession in it; *and*

- there is no interest in possession in the property subject to the settlement; *and*

- the income from the settled property is to be accumulated, to the extent that it is not applied for the maintenance, education or benefit of a beneficiary; *and*

- either one of the following conditions is satisfied:

    (a) no more than 25 years have gone by since the settlement was set up, or since the last time the settlement satisfied the three conditions set out above; or

    (b) all the individuals who are, or who have been, beneficiaries, had a common grandparent.

In relation to (b), it is sufficient if all the beneficiaries are children, widows or widowers of beneficiaries who have died before attaining the specified age, even if they do not have a common grandparent.

ACTIVITY 69

Study IHTA 1984, s. 71, summarised above, at *Cases and Materials* (27.2.1). Then consider closely the precedent accumulation and maintenance settlement which follows it. Identify how the wording of IHTA 1984, s. 71 is reflected in the wording of the precedent.

Bear in mind that the significance of an accumulation and maintenance settlement, for present purposes, is that, unlike with other discretionary settlements, a gift of property into such a trust is a PET. This is designed to ensure that the IHT effect of a gift on trust to a child, using an accumulation and maintenance settlement, is the same as an absolute gift to an adult.

27.4.2.4 Disabled settlements

The term *disabled settlement* is a shorthand way of referring to settlements which are set up for the benefit of mentally disabled individuals, and individuals receiving attendance allowance under s. 64, SSCBA 1992. Provided the conditions of IHTA 1984, s. 89 are satisfied, a gift into such a settlement is a PET for IHT purposes.

27.4.3   CAPITAL GAINS TAX AND GIFTS INTO SETTLEMENTS

As we have just discussed, it is important to distinguish between gifts into four different types of settlement for IHT purposes. Not only is such a fourfold distinction unnecessary for IHT purposes, the CGT implications of making property settled property can be stated very briefly. Whatever the type of settlement for IHT purposes, for CGT purposes the settlor will be treated as making a chargeable disposal of the property being put into the settlement, and as receiving its market value in return. The CGT effect of the gift will be the same as for an absolute gift: see **27.3.2.1**. Section 70, TCGA 1992 makes some significant additional points:

> A transfer into settlement, whether revocable, or irrevocable, is a disposal of the entire property thereby becoming settled property notwithstanding that the transferor has some interest as a beneficiary under the settlement and notwithstanding that he is a trustee, or the sole trustee, of the settlement.

I declare myself trustee of my grandfather clock, under a bare trust for you. Have I made a gift into a settlement for CGT purposes?

No: see **27.4.1.1**.

It might seem from this that a gift into settlement would necessarily be disadvantageous for CGT purposes. However, as will become clear from the discussion in **32.3.1**, in a number of situations hold-over relief will be available, which will postpone any liability to CGT.

27.4.4   STAMP DUTY AND GIFTS INTO SETTLEMENTS

Where a gift on trust needs to be made by a conveyance, the conveyance will be exempt from stamp duty if the conditions of the Stamp Duty (Exempt Instruments) Regulations 1987 (SI 1987 No. 516) are complied with. Thus, the deed of conveyance will be exempt from stamp duty if it includes a certificate signed by the settlor that the conveyance is covered by the regulations. By reg. 5, the conveyance does not need to be presented for adjudication at the stamp office. It is covered by Category L of the Regulations, being an *inter vivos* voluntary disposition. A written declaration of trusteeship by you, the settlor, is anomalously subject to stamp duty of 50p: SA 1891, sch. 1.

27.5   Taxation of Undervalue Sales

An undervalue sale by an individual may have CGT, IHT and (if you are a taxable person) VAT implications. The CGT implications arise from the provision discussed in relation to absolute gifts in **27.3.2.1**. It will be recalled that TCGA 1992, s. 17, applies to disposals of assets otherwise than by way of a bargain made at arm's length. Section 18, TCGA 1992, provides that a disposal of an asset will automatically be treated as being made otherwise than by way of a bargain made at arm's length if the parties to it are *connected*. IHT also uses the concept of connected persons in relation to undervalue sales:

see **27.3.1.1**. If a disposition was made, or might have been expected to be made, in a transaction at arm's length between persons not connected with each other, there will be no transfer of value: IHTA 1984, s. 10(1). Both CGT and IHT rely on the *same definition* of connected persons, which is what we need to consider next.

27.5.1 CONNECTED PERSONS

Section 270, IHTA 1984 adopts the definition of connected persons used for CGT purposes. This appears in TCGA 1992, s. 286. As an individual, you are therefore *automatically* connected:

- with your spouse, your spouse's relatives and their spouses;

- with a company which is controlled by you;

- as a partner, with the other partners in the firm, their spouses and their relatives;

- with the trustees of any settlement into which you transfer property; and

- as a trustee, with the settlor, any close company in which you, or any beneficiary of the settlement, is a participator.

The definitions of a *close company* and *participators* here are the same as for income tax: see **18.5.2**. In addition, one company can be connected with another company.

I sell a valuable oil painting to my son for £10,000, when it is worth £100,000. Will I have made a transfer of value for IHT purposes?

Yes.

Will I be able to rely on IHTA 1984, s. 10?

No.

27.5.2 INHERITANCE TAX AND UNDERVALUE SALES

27.5.2.1 Individuals

An undervalue sale can be a transfer of value for IHT purposes: IHTA 1984, s. 3(1). The amount of the transfer will be measured as the difference between the market value of the property, and the amount for which it is actually sold. However, there is no transfer of value if you, the seller, can demonstrate that you had no intention of conferring a gratuitous benefit on anyone: see **27.3.1.1**. It will not be possible to do this, if you are connected with the buyer: see **27.5.1**.

A bizarre illustration of these rules was given in *IRC v Spencer-Nairn* [1991] STC 60. Its bizarre nature arose from the fact that the seller did not know he was connected with the buyer, a company resident in Jersey. He therefore agreed a price of £101,350 with the buyer, on the sale of a farm. The price was fixed on the advice of the seller's financial adviser, who was also unaware that seller and buyer were connected. In the circumstances, the Revenue tried to argue that the sale was not one which might be expected to be made in a transaction at arm's length between persons not connected with each other. The Revenue accepted that the seller had no intention of conferring a gratuitous benefit on anyone. The Court of Session rejected the Revenue's argument.

Read the extract from the judgment of Lord President Hope in *IRC* v *Spencer-Nairn*, at *Cases and Materials* (27.3.1). Write down the reasons for the Lord President's decision.

27.5.2.2 Partners

The transactions discussed in **27.3.1.2** and **27.3.2.2**, involving possible transfers of value in relation to partnership assets, highlight the possibilities of similar transactions where partners might sell partnership assets at an undervalue, rather than appearing to make an absolute gift of them. As in the case of absolute gifts, the question for IHT purposes will be whether a transfer of value has been avoided on the basis that it is a commercial transaction: IHTA 1984, s. 10.

27.5.2.3 Companies

The same points apply in relation to undervalue sales by a company as in relation to absolute gifts by a company: see **27.3.1.3**.

At an extraordinary general meeting of Utopia Ltd, its shareholders vote to sell the office premises owned by the company to Jack, one of their number. The market value of the premises is £100,000, and the proposal is to sell them to Jack for £10,000. Will the company make a chargeable transfer?

No. Exactly the same points apply as in the answer to **SAQ 361**.

27.5.3 CAPITAL GAINS TAX AND UNDERVALUE SALES

Only very brief additional points need to be made here to those made for absolute gifts in **27.3.2**. All of the points made there apply equally here, since TCGA 1992, s. 17 refers to disposals otherwise than by way of a bargain made at arm's length. This obviously includes not only absolute gifts, but undervalue sales also.

Assume the facts of SAQ 361. Will the company be obliged to pay ACT on the difference between the market value of the premises and the value at which Jack will be acquiring them?

Yes: see **27.3.2.3**.

It may be possible for a giver *other than a company* to postpone the CGT charge by claiming *hold-over relief*: see **32.3.1.4**.

27.5.4   VALUE ADDED TAX AND UNDERVALUE SALES

The payment received by the seller for an undervalue sale may, if the seller is a taxable person, be the consideration for a taxable supply for VAT purposes. The consideration for the supply may be deemed to be higher than the amount actually received by the seller under VAT anti-avoidance provisions.

27.5.5   STAMP DUTY AND UNDERVALUE SALES

Any conveyance or transfer required to effect an undervalue sale is chargeable with *ad valorem* duty in the same way as one effecting a sale at market value: see **20.8**.

27.6   Taxation of Gifts on Death

Property passing by *survivorship* will be considered in **Chapter 29**, as an automatic transfer, as also will be estates passing under the intestacy rules. In this section, we discuss the IHT and CGT implications of the gifts on death which are described in **26.4.4**.

27.6.1   INHERITANCE TAX AND GIFTS ON DEATH

27.6.1.1   Individuals

It does not matter, for IHT purposes, whether the gift on death is an absolute gift on death or a gift on trust on death. This is because of the wording of IHTA 1984, s. 4(1):

> On the death of any person tax shall be charged as if, immediately before his death, he had made a transfer of value and the value transferred by it had been equal to the value of his estate immediately before his death.

The significance of the words '. . . immediately before his death . . .' will be considered in **29.3.2**. The effect of IHTA 1984, s. 4(1) is clear, however. Immediately before you die, you make a chargeable transfer of your estate for IHT purposes. Whether you are liable to pay IHT on that chargeable transfer and, if so, how much, depends on the calculations, exemptions and reliefs to be discussed in **Chapters 30 to 32**. It is not simply that there is an IHT charge on your estate immediately before you die. All PETs made by you in the seven years prior to your death, and all transfers on which IHT was immediately chargeable in the same period become liable to IHT at the IHT death rate. The calculations are described in **Chapter 30**. Excluded property does not form part of your estate at death (see **27.3.1.1**), although property in which you reserved a benefit *does* form part of your estate at death: see **33.3.1**. Simple as the rule in s. 4 appears to be, however, it gives rise to at least two quite tricky points:

(1)   Commorientes
By itself, the solution provided to the problem of common catastrophe in LPA 1925, s. 184 could produce problems for IHT: see **26.4.4**. Suppose Anne is younger than Ben. Each makes a will leaving the whole of their estate to the other. Tragically, they are both killed in circumstances where it is uncertain who died first. Under LPA 1925, s. 184, Anne's will never takes effect, because Ben is deemed to have died first. Anne's estate, as increased by Ben's, is thus transferred automatically to her statutory next-of-kin under the intestacy rules. Section 4(2), IHTA 1984 prevents two successive IHT charges, by

providing that both ' . . . shall be assumed to have died at the same instant'. The result is that the elder's estate is transferred twice, but there is only one chargeable transfer for IHT purposes.

Alec is 45, and Bertha, his wife, is 40. Each have made wills, under which Alec leaves the whole of his estate to Bertha, and Bertha leaves the whole of her estate to their son, Charles, aged 23. All three are domiciled in the UK. On 1 November 1998, Alec and Bertha both die in a flying accident. In what order will Alec and Bertha be deemed to have died, according to LPA 1925, s. 184, and who receives what?

Alec first, then Bertha. Charles receives the total of both estates.

How many chargeable transfers take place, bearing in mind that transfers between spouses are generally exempt from IHT (see 27.7)?

None.

The need for IHTA 1984, s. 4(2) does not arise where the will contains a survivorship clause: see below.

(2)   The need for survivorship clauses in wills
If you have ever studied a will, you may have wondered why it provides for beneficiaries to inherit property, only if the beneficiary survives the testator by a specified period. Such provisions are called *survivorship clauses*. For instance, clause 8 of the will precedent, at *Cases and Materials* (**30.2.2**), is a survivorship clause. Without a survivorship clause, in the event that a beneficiary died as soon as he or she had inherited property under the deceased testator's will, there would be two chargeable transfers. The first would be on the testator's death. The second would be on the beneficiary's death. In order to avoid this, IHTA 1984, s. 92(1) provides that, where there is a survivorship clause not exceeding six months in a will:

> . . . this Act shall apply as if the dispositions taking effect at the end of the period or, if [the beneficiary] does not survive until then, on his death . . . had had effect from the beginning of the period.

It is essential to remember that the period of the clause must be not more than six months. If the period is longer than six months, the clause will create a settlement, the beneficiary of which will receive the settled property only after the passage of the time specified in the clause.

27.6.1.2   Partners

As a partner in a firm, you are subject to the same rules on your death, in relation to your share of the partnership assets, as those discussed above for any other individual. In addition, *business property relief* is likely to be available to you: see **32.5.2**.

27.6.2 CAPITAL GAINS TAX AND GIFTS ON DEATH

When you die, you do not make a chargeable disposal of your estate: TCGA 1992, s. 62(1)(b). Think about this for a moment, because it is a profoundly important point. Far more important than its place at the end of this chapter may suggest! Instead, there is an acquisition of your estate by your PRs: TCGA 1992, s. 62(1)(a). That acquisition is at the market value of your estate at your death: TCGA 1992, s. 62(1)(a). We referred to this point in **20.5.1**. Any rise in value with which assets in your estate are pregnant at the date of your death is therefore eliminated by the death. This elimination of gains is often referred to as the *tax-free uplift*. Keep the acquisition of your estate by the PRs at its market value firmly in mind. It is crucial to your understanding of the next two chapters. It produces a tension between the desire for high valuation, for CGT purposes, and a low valuation for IHT purposes.

27.7 Gifts between Spouses

27.7.1 CAPITAL GAINS TAX

An absolute gift from one spouse to the other, or an undervalue sale by one spouse to the other, is treated for CGT purposes as being made for such a consideration as produces neither a gain nor a loss: TCGA 1992, s. 58. Section 58 in fact applies to all disposals between spouses.

27.7.2 INHERITANCE TAX

A gift by one spouse in favour of the other, including a gift on death, is completely exempt from IHT, except in one case, where the exempt amount is limited to £55,000: IHTA 1984, s. 18. This one case is where the spouse in whose favour the gift is made is not domiciled in the UK: see **4.5.5**. This limitation on the IHT relief is a profoundly important point, often forgotten.

27.8 Summary

For individuals, absolute gifts have both IHT and CGT consequences. In relation to IHT, an absolute gift made in your personal capacity will usually be a PET, when made to another individual. In the capacity of a partner, where a change is made in the asset surplus sharing ratio, it will usually be possible to argue that there is no chargeable transfer of a share in the partnership assets, since you have no intention of conferring a gratuitous benefit on anyone. Subject to a point to be made in **Chapter 33**, absolute gifts by companies fall outside the scope of IHT, having corporation tax consequences instead. In relation to CGT, absolute gifts of chargeable assets are deemed to have been made for their market value, a rule which applies in relation to both individuals and companies. As to the latter, questions of ACT on distributions need to be considered too. CGT will be an important consideration for partners who change the asset surplus sharing ratio of the firm, without having revalued the assets in the firm's accounts. The IHT consequences of a gift on trust depend on whether the settlement has an interest in possession or not. A settlement has an interest in possession if anyone has a right to the income of the settled property as it arises. Gifts on trust are always PETs, except where the settlement has no interest in possession and does not fall within certain categories of privileged settlements. Thus, a gift into an accumulation and maintenance settlement is a PET, but a gift into a straightforward discretionary trust is chargeable immediately to IHT. Regardless of the capacity in which they act, undervalue sales made by individuals are transfers of value for IHT purposes, unless it can be demonstrated that there is no intention to confer a gratuitous benefit. For CGT purposes, undervalue sales are treated in a very similar way to absolute gifts. IHT is charged on gifts on death, but death is not a disposal for CGT purposes. Gratuitous transfers between spouses are usually exempt from IHT. For CGT purposes, disposals between spouses are deemed to be made on a no gain and no loss basis.

27.9   End of Chapter Assessment Questions

(a)   In a single sentence for each point, comment on the IHT and CGT implications of each of the following events:

1 April 1993	Alexandra gave £2,999 to Belinda in cash.
28 February 1994	Alexandra transferred her shareholding of 10,000 £1 ordinary shares in Megabucks plc, then worth £250,000, to the trustees of a discretionary trust. The shares were all acquired by her on 30 November 1985.
23 June 1995	Alexandra gave £56,000 of loan stock to her son Charles. The loan stock was a QCB for CGT purposes.
1 April 1999	Alexandra died.

Ignore any exemptions and reliefs, and assume that Alexandra is a chargeable person for CGT purposes. In relation to the CGT aspects of this question, you will need to refer to material from earlier in the book.

(Word limit: 250 (50 marks).)

(b)   Turn to *Cases and Materials* (27.2.1), and read IHTA 1984, s. 71. Also read **7.6.1** and **18.4.3**. Comment briefly on the income tax, CGT and IHT implications of the following clauses in an accumulation and maintenance settlement:

> The Trustees shall stand possessed of the Trust Fund and the income from it upon trust for such of the Principal Beneficiaries as shall either attain the age of 35 years before or upon the Ultimate Date or shall be living under that age upon the Ultimate Date and if more than one in equal shares.
> . . .
>
> "the Principal Beneficiaries" means:
>
> (a)   the two present grandchildren of the Settlor [the deed gives their names]
> . . .
>
> "The Ultimate Date" means the date on which shall expire the period of 80 years commencing with the date of this deed (which date shall be the perpetuity period applicable to this settlement and to the dispositions made by it).

(Word limit: 250 (50 marks).)

See *Cases and Materials* (27.5) for a specimen answer.

CHAPTER TWENTY-EIGHT

TAXATION OF GRATUITOUS TRANSFERS: NOMINAL TRANSFERS

28.1 Objectives

By the end of this chapter, you should be able to:

■ explain the tax implications of transfers *between trustees*;

■ explain the tax implications of transfers from *trustees* to *beneficiaries*;

■ explain the tax implications of transfers from *PRs* to beneficiaries;

■ explain the tax implications of transfers from PRs to *trustees*.

28.2 Introduction

In **Chapter 27**, we discussed the tax implications of four categories of gift. In this chapter, we need to consider the tax implications of nominal transfers. We shall be following the categorisation in **26.5**, our discussion covering the CGT, IHT and stamp duty implications of the transfers described there. Before beginning to work through this chapter, you may wish to reread **26.5**, to ensure you know exactly the types of gratuitous transfer with which we are concerned. One point which should emerge very clearly from this chapter is that the transfer of settled property from trustees to beneficiaries can, in CGT terms, be a very expensive operation indeed. This is especially true when a settlement comes to an end. Another point which should become clear is that CGT concentrates on dealings by the trustees with the legal title to the settled property. The IHT rules, by contrast, concentrate almost exclusively on the changes in the equitable entitlement to the settled property. Finally, be alert for the concept of someone becoming absolutely entitled to the settled property as against the trustee: see **26.5.1**. This is a deeply significant concept for CGT purposes.

28.3 Transfers between Trustees

28.3.1 CAPITAL GAINS TAX IMPLICATIONS

The retirement of a trustee in favour of a replacement trustee has no effect for CGT purposes. This is because of TCGA 1992, s. 69(1), which provides:

[T]he trustees of the settlement shall for the purposes of this Act be treated as being a single and continuing body of persons (distinct from the persons who may from time to time be the trustees) . . .

There is an exception to this rule. This is the CGT *export charge* which applies when trustees 'go non-resident', i.e. retire in favour of replacement trustees who are not resident in the UK. In addition, it is important to note the effect of a *re-settlement* of settled property.

Turn back to 26.5.1, and reread the material you read for Activity 64. Note carefully the circumstances in which there will be a re-settlement of settled property.

When a re-settlement occurs, the trustees of the second settlement become absolutely entitled to the settled property as against the trustees of the first settlement. This, as we have already mentioned, is a crucial point for CGT purposes. The point is crucial because of TCGA 1992, s. 71(1). Section 71(1) is a pretty sinister provision. In the context of re-settlements, it is very sinister indeed, since it creates a trap for unwary trustees. Section 71(1) says this:

> On the occasion when a person becomes absolutely entitled to any settled property as against the trustee all the assets forming part of the settled property to which he becomes so entitled shall be deemed to have been disposed of by the trustee, and immediately reacquired by him in his capacity as a trustee within section 60(1), for a consideration equal to their market value.

In *Bond* v *Pickford* [1983] STC 517, the Court of Appeal considered the application of s. 71(1) to the following facts. In 1972, trustees exercised the power given to them by a deed of settlement, made more than ten years previously, to 'allocate' part of the settled property for the benefit of the settlor's grandchildren. The settled property consisted of a shareholding in a company called Haslemere Estates Ltd. The so-called deed of allocation provided for the trustees of the 1961 settlement to appoint and declare some of the shares to themselves, although in their capacity as trustees of a second settlement under which the grandchildren would become entitled to both the income and capital of the allocated shares at the age of 22. The Revenue argued that what had taken place was a re-settlement, and that s. 71(1) therefore applied to the exercise of the power of appointment. The Court of Appeal rejected the Revenue's argument. Slade LJ said:

> . . . [T]here is in my opinion a crucial distinction to be drawn between (a) powers to alter the presently operative trusts of a settlement which expressly or by necessary implication authorise the trustees to remove assets altogether from the original settlement (without rendering any person absolutely beneficially entitled to them); and (b) powers of this nature which do not confer on the trustees such authority.

> I will refer to these two different types of powers as 'powers in the wider form' and 'powers in the narrower form'. The distinction between them is in my opinion of great importance and is reflected in the relevant decisions.

Slade LJ concluded that the exercise of a power in the wider form might amount to a re-settlement, although it did not necessarily do so. By contrast, the exercise of a power in the narrower form could *never* amount to a resettlement.

Read SP 7/84, reproduced at *Cases and Materials* (28.1.1). This was issued by the Revenue in response to *Bond* v *Pickford*. Consider whether it represents a close reflection of the distinction drawn by Slade LJ in that case (extracted at *Cases and Materials* (26.1.1).

If you were a trustee of a settlement, contemplating the exercise of a dispositive power, what would you try to demonstrate?

That the power was a power in the *narrower* form.

If the power in question were one in the *wider* form, would that necessarily be the end of the discussion?

No. In certain cases, the exercise of a power in the wider form does *not* amount to a resettlement.

28.3.2 INHERITANCE TAX IMPLICATIONS

Matching the position for CGT, although for different reasons, the transfer on the retirement of a trustee and the appointment of a replacement trustee has no effect for IHT purposes. As we shall discover in **Chapter 29**, IHT tends to ignore transfers by the trustees, and to concentrate instead on the beneficiaries. Just as for CGT purposes, however, it is important to note the effect of a re-settlement for IHT. By contrast with CGT, IHT takes a ruthlessly simplistic approach, unless the holder of the interest in possession remains the same. It would appear that, if you are a trustee and you exercise dispositive powers over the settled property, *any* such exercise will be a resettlement. This point seems to be borne out by *Minden Trust (Cayman) Ltd* v *IRC* [1985] STC 758, although that was a decision on the effect of superseded legislation.

If this is the law, how does the IHT position differ from the CGT one?

There can only be a re-settlement for CGT purposes if the power exercised by the trustees is in the *wider form*, and not even then in every case.

28.3.3   STAMP DUTY IMPLICATIONS

No stamp duty is chargeable on a document effecting the transfer of settled property on the retirement and replacement of a trustee, provided that there is compliance with the conditions of Category A in the Stamp Duty (Exempt Instruments) Regulations 1987 (SI 1987 No. 516).

On 1 November 1998, Arthur retires as one of the trustees of the Ira Smoothy (1984) Discretionary Trust. The settled property consists of 100,000 shares in United Conglomerates plc. In his place, Bert is appointed. Will the stock transfer form, re-registering the shares, be subject to stamp duty?

No.

Even if there has been a re-settlement, the stock transfer form will still be exempt from stamp duty, although the relevant category of exemption will be category L in the Regulations.

28.4   Transfers from Trustees to Beneficiaries

28.4.1   CAPITAL GAINS TAX IMPLICATIONS

When a beneficiary becomes absolutely entitled to any settled property, as against the trustees, TCGA 1992, s. 71(1) applies: see **28.3.1**. Under s. 71(1), the trustees are deemed to have disposed of the settled property at its market value, and immediately re-acquired it at that base cost. Whether there is a CGT charge at this point depends on two factors. The first is whether or not the reason for the beneficiary becoming absolutely entitled to the settled property is the death of some individual entitled to a life interest. This obviously depends on the terms of the settlement, a point which is illustrated below. The second is whether the settlor originally claimed hold-over relief from CGT when the settled property was originally transferred to the trustees of the settlement.

28.4.1.1   Beneficiary absolutely entitled on death of a life tenant

(1)   Hold-over relief originally claimed by settlor
Imagine the situation where a beneficiary becomes absolutely entitled to settled property on the death of the life tenant. If the settlor originally claimed hold-over relief, on transferring property into the settlement, there *will* be a CGT charge on the trustees, on the beneficiary becoming absolutely entitled. This is because of the combined effect of TCGA 1992, ss. 71, 73 and 74. As discussed above, s. 71 imposes a CGT charge where a person becomes absolutely entitled as against the trustee. Section 73(1), although it imposes no CGT charge on the death of the life tenant, deems the death to be a disposal by the trustees for CGT purposes. This deeming will be discussed in detail, in the context of automatic transfers, in **29.4.1**. The key point for present purposes is the effect of s. 74 on s. 73, in the situation where the death of a life tenant gives another beneficiary an absolute entitlement to the settled property. In that situation, s. 74(2) provides that:

> [Section 73(1)] shall not apply to the disposal of the [settled property] by the trustee, but any chargeable gain accruing to the trustee on the disposal shall be restricted to the amount of the held-over gain (or corresponding part of it) on the disposal of the asset to him.

On 1 November 1994, Stan settled 1,000 ordinary shares on Ann for life, remainder to Brian absolutely, in circumstances such that hold-over relief was available. He duly claimed hold-over relief under TCGA 1992, s. 165. Ann died on 31 October 1998. Will the trustees be liable to pay CGT on Ann's death?

Yes.

(2)   Hold-over relief not originally claimed by settlor
Here, a beneficiary becomes absolutely entitled to settled property on the death of the life tenant, but the settlor did *not* claim hold-over relief on transferring property into the settlement. In this situation, there will *not* be a CGT charge on the trustees. This is because TCGA 1992, s. 74, does not apply where the death of the life tenant gives another beneficiary an absolute entitlement to the settled property, but hold-over relief was not originally claimed by the settlor.

On 1 November 1994, Simon settled his 1,000 ordinary shares on Abner for life, remainder to Barak absolutely, in circumstances such that hold-over relief was not available. On transferring the shares into settlement, Simon did *not* claim hold-over relief under TCGA 1992, s. 165. Abner died on 31 October 1998. Will the trustees be liable to pay CGT on Abner's death?

No.

28.4.1.2   Beneficiary absolutely entitled *otherwise than* on death of a life tenant

A beneficiary could become absolutely entitled to settled property *otherwise than* on the death of a life tenant in a range of situations. A good example would be a beneficiary becoming absolutely entitled to settled property on having reached such an age as to satisfy the age contingency in an accumulation and maintenance settlement: see **27.4.2.3**. Another example would be the appointment of the whole or part of the settled fund by the trustees of a discretionary trust. Under s. 71(1), the trustees are deemed to have disposed of the settled property at its market value, and immediately reacquired it at that base cost. This may give rise to a chargeable gain. Section 60, TCGA 1992, is highly significant in this context. It deems the base cost of the settled property transferred to the beneficiary to be the amount for which the trustees are deemed to have disposed and reacquired the settled property. Thus, when the beneficiary disposes of the property in the future, its base cost for CGT purposes will be that amount: see **21.4**. Section 60 has this effect because the trustees' deemed reacquisition of the settled property at its market value is deemed to be the act of the beneficiary absolutely entitled to the settled property.

On 1 November 1993, the trustees of an accumulation and maintenance settlement transferred the settled fund to Alice, on her reaching the specified age of 23. At that date, the market value of the shares was £250,000. On 12 November 1998, Alice sells the company shareholding which made up the settled fund for £500,000. What is her chargeable gain?

£250,000. Section 60 deems the base cost of the shares to have been £250,000.

Turning back to the trustees, it should be remembered that the deemed disposal and reacquisition by the trustees may produce a CGT loss. The question naturally arises as to whether the trustees or the beneficiary in whom the property is vested can treat this as an *allowable loss*: see **21.8**. Briefly, the answer is Yes. If the trustees have realised chargeable gains in the tax year in which the beneficiary becomes absolutely entitled, but before the beneficiary becomes so entitled, the trustees may deduct the loss from those gains. If the trustees have no such gains, then the loss can be claimed by the beneficiary in whom the settled property is vested: TCGA 1992, s. 71(2).

28.4.2 INHERITANCE TAX IMPLICATIONS

We have already mentioned that IHT tends to ignore transfers by the trustees, and to focus instead on the beneficiaries. One manifestation of this is the fundamental distinction which IHT makes between interest in possession settlements, and settlements without an interest in possession: see **27.4.2**. We shall return to this fundamental distinction in **29.4.2**, but the points in **28.4.2.1** below are relevant only to settlements *with* an interest in possession. The IHT implications of the termination of the life interest when someone becomes absolutely entitled to the settled property are the same as when the life interest terminates and the settlement continues. This latter situation is discussed in detail in **28.4.2.2**.

28.4.2.1 Beneficiary absolutely entitled on death of a life tenant

The life tenant is treated as owning the whole of the settled property. The value of the settled property is therefore included in the life tenant's estate on his or her death. The actual vesting of the settled property in the beneficiary who is absolutely entitled is ignored by the IHT rules.

28.4.2.2 Beneficiary absolutely entitled *otherwise than* on death of a life tenant

An example of a situation in which a beneficiary could become absolutely entitled in this way, is in relation to a particular type of interest in possession settlement. This is one where the person originally entitled in remainder becomes absolutely entitled to the trust property because the life tenant has ceased to satisfy some condition for holding his or her life interest. Such settlements used to be encountered very frequently indeed, although they are probably less common today. In such circumstances, the life tenant is treated as making a PET to the person entitled in remainder, the value transferred by which is the value of the settled property at the date of the PET.

In 1935, under his marriage settlement, Cedric became entitled to Blackacre for life, or until he remarried. On his death, or in the event of such a remarriage, it was to pass to Algernon, his cousin. Algernon was five in 1935, and is still in good health. Cedric's wife died in 1956. Late in life, Cedric has just remarried. Will Cedric be treated as making a PET on remarriage?

Yes.

Other examples of beneficiaries becoming absolutely entitled in this way would be in relation to discretionary settlements and accumulation and maintenance settlements. Under discretionary settlements, and in the exercise of their discretion, trustees may appoint all or part of the settled property to one or more of the class of beneficiaries. Section 65(1)(a), IHTA 1984 imposes an immediate charge to IHT *on the trustees* in this event. The calculation of the amount of IHT charged will be discussed in **31.4.2**.

In relation to accumulation and maintenance settlements, IHT provides for favourable treatment when a beneficiary becomes beneficially entitled to an interest in the settled fund. As mentioned in **28.4.1.2**, this could happen on a beneficiary satisfying the age contingency specified in an accumulation and maintenance settlement. The special IHT rules on accumulation and maintenance settlements mean that no IHT is chargeable in this event: IHTA 1984, s. 71(4). Section 71(4) also ensures that no IHT is charged when the beneficiary attains an interest in possession under TA 1925, s. 31: see **27.4.2.1**. It is important to note, however, that IHTA 1984, s. 71(3) can apply to remove this exemption, basically where the conditions for an accumulation and maintenance settlement cease to be satisfied: see *Cases and Materials* (**27.2.1**).

28.4.3 STAMP DUTY IMPLICATIONS

Provided that there is compliance with the conditions of the Stamp Duty (Exempt Instruments) Regulations 1987 (SI 1987 No. 516), no stamp duty is chargeable on a document effecting the transfer of settled property from trustee to beneficiary. The relevant category of exemption is category F.

28.5 Transfers from Personal Representatives to Beneficiaries

The Taxation of Chargeable Gains Act 1992 refers to all beneficiaries of an estate as *legatees*. The mechanics of the nominal transfer of the deceased's property from the PRs to the legatee are identical, whether the legatee receives the property by will or under the intestacy rules. The definition of legatee in TCGA 1992, s. 64(2) and (3) makes no distinction between someone receiving personal or real property, nor between wills and intestacies. All are legatees for CGT purposes. In the case of a will, the nominal transfer is the second stage discussed in **26.4.4.1** and **26.4.4.2**. In the case of an intestacy, it is the second stage referred to in **26.6.2**.

28.5.1 CAPITAL GAINS TAX IMPLICATIONS

The PRs of a deceased individual acquire the deceased's property at its market value at the date of the deceased's death: see **27.6.2**. When the PRs make the nominal transfer of the property from themselves to the beneficiary, they are deemed to do so for such a consideration as produces neither a gain nor a loss. Section 62(4) states:

> On a person acquiring any asset as legatee . . .
> (a)   no chargeable gain shall accrue to the personal representatives, and
> (b)   the legatee shall be treated as if the personal representatives' acquisition of the asset had been his acquisition of it.

Each of s. 62(4)(a) and (b) lays down rules. They have two distinct, and important, ramifications:

■ the costs of making the nominal transfer of the property to the legatee may be added to the base cost of the legacy for the purposes of calculating the chargeable gain on any subsequent disposal of it by the legatee; and

■ the status of the transferor as a PR, rather than a trustee, must be absolutely clear for s. 62(4) to apply. Any doubt on this point will arise only in the situation where PRs become, or are in the process of becoming, trustees: see **26.4.4.2**. Where the will does not set up will trusts, the issue does not arise. It is discussed in some detail below.

SAQ 388

On 1 November 1993, Thomas died. His will bequeathed his shareholding in Bigco plc, worth £100,000 at that date, to Barry, his nephew. Thomas's executors incurred costs of £700 in transferring the shares to him. On 15 November 1998, Barry sells the shares for £600,000. What is his chargeable gain on the sale of the shares?

£499,300, i.e. £600,000 − £700 − £100,000.

The second of the ramifications referred to above is important because, if the transferor makes the nominal transfer in the capacity of a trustee, rather than in the capacity of a PR, the sinister s. 71, TCGA 1992 applies: see **28.4**. This of course means that there could be a CGT charge on the trustee, rather than a disposal to the transferee for a no gain/no loss consideration within s. 62(4). The question of whether the transferor is a PR or a trustee must arise relatively rarely. That said, there has been some discussion of the question in two cases, *Cochrane's Executors* v *IRC* [1974] STC 335, where a solution was not strictly necessary to the decision in the case, and *IRC* v *Matthews* [1984] STC 386, where a solution was necessary, but which was not a decision on CGT. In both cases, which were decisions of the Inner House of the Court of Session, the question had arisen because the wording of the Scottish wills under consideration had appointed individuals as the testator's 'executors and trustees'. In *IRC* v *Matthews*, the Inner House held that the transfer had been made by PRs, rather than by trustees.

ACTIVITY73

Read the extract from the judgment of Lord Cameron in *IRC* v *Matthews*, at *Cases and Materials* (28.2.1). Summarise what Lord Cameron regards as the essence of the difference between PRs and trustees. (Refer also to *Cases and Materials* (2.3.2.2).)

28.5.2   INHERITANCE TAX IMPLICATIONS

Consistent with the IHT points made so far, the vesting of estate property in a legatee by PRs does not in itself have IHT consequences. For similar reasons to those applying to trustees, IHT tends to ignore transfers by the PRs, and to concentrate instead on the chargeable transfer by the deceased.

28.5.3   STAMP DUTY IMPLICATIONS

No stamp duty is chargeable on a document effecting the transfer of estate property from PR to legatee, provided that there is compliance with the conditions of the Stamp Duty (Exempt Instruments) Regulations 1987 (SI 1987 No. 516). In addition, an assent in writing by a PR, under s. 36, AEA 1925 is specifically exempted from stamp duty. Any one of a number of categories of exemption may be relevant, depending on the circumstances. Category B applies to:

The conveyance or transfer of property the subject of a specific devise or legacy to the beneficiary named in the will (or his nominee).

Note that Category B relates to specific legacies: see **16.3.2.2**. General legacies (see **16.3.2.1**) are dealt with by Category D of the Regulations, which relates to the '. . . appropriation of property . . . in satisfaction of a general legacy of money'.

'Appropriation' refers to the process of transferring part of the deceased's estate to a legatee in satisfaction of a general legacy: AEA 1925, s. 41. Any document required to vest the legal title in the legatee is exempt from stamp duty under Category D.

Under the will of Simon Finger, who collected antique watches and clocks for a hobby, Ben Hand, his nephew, is to receive a general legacy of £1,500. In satisfaction of the legacy, a clock worth £1,500 is appropriated to Ben. Will stamp duty be relevant to the vesting of the title to the clock in Ben?

No. Title to the clock will pass by delivery: see **26.4.1**, **26.4.4**.

Category E of the Regulations exempts the following from stamp duty:

The conveyance or transfer of property which forms part of the residuary estate of a testator to a beneficiary (or his nominee) entitled solely by virtue of his entitlement under the will.

Other categories deal with the equivalent transfers on an intestacy, Category C and Category D.

28.6   Transfers from Personal Representatives to Trustees

28.6.1   CAPITAL GAINS TAX IMPLICATIONS

The definition of legatee in TCGA 1992, s. 64(2), includes individuals receiving estate property in their capacity as trustees, as well as in their personal capacity:

In this Act, unless the context otherwise requires, 'legatee' includes any person taking under a testamentary disposition . . . whether he takes beneficially or as a trustee . . .

The rules discussed in **28.5** should therefore apply to any assent transferring property from the deceased's PRs to the trustees of the will trust: see **26.4.4.2**, **26.5.4**.

28.6.2   INHERITANCE TAX IMPLICATIONS

The vesting of estate property in a trustee by PRs does not in itself have IHT consequences. For similar reasons to those applying to legatees, IHT tends to ignore transfers by the PRs, and to concentrate instead on the chargeable transfer by the deceased immediately before his or her death.

28.6.3   STAMP DUTY IMPLICATIONS

An assent or conveyance by the PRs in favour of trustees is covered by the exemptions already discussed in **28.5.3**.

28.7 Summary

It should be clear from the discussion in this chapter that none of the four categories of nominal transfer should prove expensive in stamp duty terms. A CGT liability can arise on a re-settlement by trustees, and when trustees transfer settled property to beneficiaries who are absolutely entitled to it. Transfers from PRs to legatees and to trustees of will trusts, however, should generally give rise to no CGT liability, since they are deemed to be for such a consideration as produces neither a gain nor a loss. Re-settlements can produce an IHT liability, as well as a CGT liability. Since IHT concentrates on the equitable entitlements to the property comprised in a settlement, the vesting of settled property in beneficiaries who are absolutely entitled to it does not of itself produce an IHT liability. However, where the person originally entitled in remainder becomes absolutely entitled to the trust property simply because the life tenant has ceased to satisfy a condition for holding his or her life interest, there will be a PET by the life tenant in favour of the remainderman. Finally, where, in the exercise of their discretion, trustees of a discretionary trust appoint trust property to one or more of the class of beneficiaries, there will be an immediate charge to IHT on the trustees. There is an exemption from this charge in relation to accumulation and maintenance settlements. In **Chapter 29**, we complete our survey of the tax implications of gratuitous transfers by discussing the taxation implications of the three categories of automatic transfer.

28.8   End of Chapter Assessment Questions

Reread **21.8** and **24.9**. Then analyse *both* the CGT and IHT implications of each of the following:

(a)   Terry dies on 1 November 1998, aged 102. On 20 May 1998, he sold 2,000 ordinary shares in Umberto Ltd, at a loss of £10,000. He has no chargeable gains in the tax year of his death, but his chargeable gains for 1997/98 were £15,000.

(20 marks.)

(b)   It is 1 December 1998. Tom and Theo are the trustees of a settlement constituted by Damon's will, under which his two grandchildren, Beatrix and Ben, are to receive the settled fund in equal shares absolutely, on attaining the age of 18. Ben is 16 and Beatrix is 17. Both beneficiaries are rather immature for their ages. The settled fund consists of 100,000 ordinary shares in Utopia plc, worth £500,000 in total, as at 1 December 1998. The will trust contains a power for the trustees, in their discretion, to remove the whole or part of the settled fund from the will trust, and to transfer it to the trustees of another settlement. They are contemplating whether to transfer 90% of the settled fund to an identical settlement, with an age contingency of 25.

(60 marks.)

(c)   Alison is the remainderman under a life interest trust set up by her uncle Jake in 1980. The life tenant is 21 and in excellent health. Either:

(i)   Alison sells her interest to her schoolfriend, Brenda, for £10,000; or

(ii)   the life tenant is killed in a mountaineering accident.

(20 marks.)

See *Cases and Materials* (**28.4**) for a specimen answer.

CHAPTER TWENTY-NINE

TAXATION OF GRATUITOUS TRANSFERS: AUTOMATIC TRANSFERS

29.1 Objectives

By the end of this chapter, you should be able to:

■ describe the tax implications of an interest in property being transferred *by survivorship*;

■ explain the tax implications of the interests of beneficiaries under a settlement coming to an end, *the settlement then continuing*;

■ describe the special IHT provisions which apply to settlements *without an interest in possession*;

■ describe the tax implications of property being transferred under the *intestacy rules*.

29.2 Introduction

This chapter forms the final part of our examination of the tax implications of gratuitous transfers. **Chapters 30** and **31** are devoted to calculating CGT, IHT and stamp duty liability when it arises, and **Chapter 32** is devoted to ways of reducing that liability. In this chapter, we shall be discussing the tax implications of the three types of automatic transfer identified in **26.6**. The shortest part of the discussion relates to transfers under the intestacy rules, which also appears last. This needs to be worked through in conjunction with **28.5**, since that section dealt with the tax aspects of the onward vesting of estate property by PRs in the legatees. This process of vesting involves nominal transfers by the PRs in the legatees' favour. The main thrust of the discussion concerns the implications of interests under settlements coming to an end. However, the situation envisaged in this chapter is different from that discussed in **28.4**. The reason for the difference is that, in **28.4**, the consequence of the beneficiary's interest coming to an end was the absolute entitlement of another beneficiary to the settled fund. That means the end of the settlement. In **29.4**, the alternative possibility is assumed, i.e. that the settlement is continuing.

29.3   The Survivorship Principle

29.3.1   CAPITAL GAINS TAX IMPLICATIONS

When you die, your PRs acquire your estate at its market value. The Taxation of Chargeable Gains Act 1992 extends this rule to the acquisition by a surviving joint tenant of your interest under a joint tenancy: TCGA 1992, s. 62(1)(a), (10). Such an interest passes to the survivor automatically. The survivor acquires your interest under the joint tenancy at its market value: TCGA 1992, s. 62(1)(a). This rule operates successfully because TCGA 1992, s. 62, defines your estate as all the assets of which you were competent to dispose before your death. It would have been possible for you to sever the joint tenancy, and thus turn it into a tenancy in common, even though you did not actually do so. Property subject to a joint tenancy, such as a jointly owned home, is *not* settled property for CGT purposes: see **27.4.1.2**. Where the legal title to settled property is transferred to any surviving *trustees* under the survivorship principle, there is no CGT effect: see **28.3.1**.

29.3.2   INHERITANCE TAX IMPLICATIONS

In **27.6.1.1**, it was mentioned that we would be considering in this chapter the significance of the words '. . . immediately before his death' in IHTA 1984, s. 4(1). You might thus find it helpful to reread that section at this point. I imagine you can now guess the significance of these words. They are designed to ensure that any interest of a joint tenant, which passes to the survivor or survivors under the survivorship principle, forms part of the deceased's estate on death. Without these words, an interest under a joint tenancy would not do so: see **26.6.1**. Surprisingly, perhaps, the interest of the deceased under the joint tenancy is not necessarily taken to be half of the value of the whole. We shall be discussing this further in **31.3**. The spouse exemption will be relevant in many cases of survivorship: see **27.7**.

Read IHTA 1984, s. 4, at *Cases and Materials* **(29.1.1)**. Relate s. 4(2) back to the points discussed at 27.6.1.1 (commorientes).

29.4   Interests of Beneficiaries Coming to an End

29.4.1   CAPITAL GAINS TAX IMPLICATIONS

Capital gains tax has to deal with automatic transfers of the equitable entitlement to settled property in a highly artificial way. The tax has somehow to solve two problems, i.e.:

■   Since, as a matter of property law, the equitable entitlement is transferred by the automatic transfer of the equitable entitlement, the transfer is made by *neither* the trustees, *nor* the beneficiaries.

■   CGT rules on settled property emphasise dealings with the legal title, although it is the equitable entitlement which is being transferred when the interest of a beneficiary comes to an end.

These two problems are solved by the simple rule in TCGA 1992, s. 72. Section 72(1) says this (note especially s. 72(1)(b)):

On the termination, on the death of the person entitled to it, of an interest in possession in all or any part of settled property—

(a)   The whole or a corresponding part of each of the assets forming part of the settled property and not ceasing at that time to be settled property shall be deemed for the purposes of this Act at that time to be disposed of and immediately reacquired by the trustee for a consideration equal to the whole or a corresponding part of the market value of the asset; but

(b)   no chargeable gain shall accrue on that disposal.

It is thus clear that s. 72(1) is not to apply to the situation where s. 71(1) applies. The effect of s. 72 is therefore the same as the *CGT-free uplift* on the death of an individual who does not hold a life interest under a settlement. The exception to this corresponds to the exception discussed in **28.4.1.1**, i.e. there will be a CGT charge if the settlor originally claimed hold-over relief on transferring the settled fund into trust.

Theo and Tom are the trustees of a new-style trust of Blackacre. They were appointed, and the legal estate transferred into their names, on 1 July 1998. Under the trust deed, Blackacre is to be held for Ben for life, remainder to Bill for life, remainder to Boris on attaining 21. At the time the trust is set up, Ben is 20, Bill is 18, and Boris is 7.

On 1 September 1998, Ben is killed in an air accident. Tragically, Bill dies of a tropical disease, whilst exploring the jungles of South America on 4 February 1999. What are the CGT consequences of Ben's death and Bill's death (assume that the settlor did not claim hold-over relief on transferring Blackacre into trust)?

Each will give a CGT-free uplift, in the case of Bill's death, because the trust must continue in existence until Boris attains the age of 21.

29.4.2   INHERITANCE TAX IMPLICATIONS

29.4.2.1   Introduction

The IHT treatment of settlements differs considerably, in mechanical terms, depending on whether the settlement is one with an interest in possession or not. That is why it is so important to ensure that a settlement has been correctly identified, as one or the other, before seeking to apply the rules discussed below. Having made that point, it is striking that the stated purpose of the two sets of rules is to try to balance the IHT treatment of settlements with an interest in possession, with that for those without an interest in possession. What the rules discussed in **29.4.2.3** are seeking to achieve, therefore, is comparability with those in section **29.4.2.2**. This is a good justification for dealing with the two sets of rules together here, even though the interest of a beneficiary under a trust without an interest in possession cannot strictly be said to come to an end over the life of the trust. In addition, accumulation and maintenance settlements, though they are settlements without an interest in possession, must be considered separately from other settlements lacking an interest in possession.

29.4.2.2   Interest in possession settlements

Just as artificial in their own way as the CGT rules, are the IHT rules. However, because IHT emphasises changes in the equitable entitlement, rather than transfers of the legal title, the IHT rules are fundamentally different from the CGT ones. The basic rule is contained in IHTA 1984, s. 49(1):

> A person beneficially entitled to an interest in possession in settled property shall be treated for the purposes of this Act as beneficially entitled to the property in which the interest subsists.

This means that, if you are a life tenant, you are treated as owning the whole capital of the settled property. If you are one of two or more life tenants, the settled property is apportioned between all of you: IHTA 1984, s. 50(1). Think about this. It is a logical corollary of the general rule that reversionary interests are excluded property: see **27.3.1.1(b)**.

(Refer to SAQ 390 for the facts.) Whilst Ben is alive, what is he treated as owning for IHT purposes?

Blackacre itself.

It follows from this rule that, as a life tenant, the value of your life interest will be included in your estate on your death. This IHT rule is artificial in the extreme. For property law purposes, Ben would be treated as being merely entitled to any income he could raise from Blackacre during his lifetime. That said, this particular rule has always been a feature of IHT and – before that – CTT and estate duty. It contributed to the decline of the strict settlement at the end of the nineteenth century, since it made the holding of successive interests in land extremely expensive in estate duty terms: see **26.8**. Remember that a lease for life or lives is a settlement for IHT purposes, unless it was granted for full consideration in money or money's worth: IHTA 1984, s. 43(3). Such a lease is a settlement with an interest in possession. The tenant is therefore deemed to own the whole of the property subject to the lease. However, the landlord is treated as having retained the difference between the full consideration in money or money's worth and what, if anything, the tenant actually pays: IHTA 1984, ss. 50(6), 170.

29.4.2.3   Settlements without an interest in possession

It has been said that the interest of a beneficiary under a trust without an interest in possession cannot strictly be said to come to an end. That is because the interests of the beneficiaries are not measured out according to their lifetimes. In principle, such a settlement will never die, and there may be beneficiaries who might never receive anything from it. In the absence of fixed beneficiaries, the IHT rules must therefore *deem* the *settled property itself* to be subject to IHT. This is exactly what they do. Furthermore, to ensure comparability with interest in possession settlements, the rate of IHT charged on the settled property is lower than it would be on the death of a life tenant under an interest in possession settlement: see **Chapter 31**.

The most common type of trust lacking an interest in possession, is the discretionary trust. Commentaries on the IHT treatment of settlements without an interest in possession sometimes refer to discretionary trusts as if they were coterminous with settlements lacking an interest in possession. This is not necessarily so, however. Remember that settlements lacking an interest in possession cover a much wider range of settlements than discretionary ones. Any trust where none of the beneficiaries has a right to the income of the trust property as it arises, i.e. where there is no *present right to present enjoyment*, will be governed by these rules, rather than those in **29.3.2.2**: see **27.4.2.1**.

On 1 January 1998, Tim and Tom were appointed the trustees of a new-style trust of Blackacre. Under the trust deed, Blackacre is to be held for Boris, on his attaining 32. At the time the trust was set up, Boris was 14. Is the settlement one with an interest in possession? (Assume that the trust deed *excludes* TA 1925, s. 31.)

No: see **27.4.2.1**.

The IHT rules deem the settled property itself to be subject to IHT by subjecting so-called *relevant property* to a 10-yearly IHT charge. Relevant property is defined in IHTA 1984, s. 58(1) as, subject to certain exceptions:

> . . . [S]ettled property in which no qualifying interest in possession subsists . . .

Taken out of the definition of *relevant property* is property held for charitable purposes only and property held in accumulation and maintenance settlements: see **29.3.2.4**. Each of the 10-yearly anniversaries is measured from the date on which the settlement commenced: IHTA 1984, s. 61(1).

Assume the same facts as in SAQ 392. On what date will the first 10-yearly IHT charge be imposed?

1 January 2008.

By IHTA 1984, s. 64, the 10-yearly charge operates thus:

> Where immediately before a ten-year anniversary all or any part of the property comprised in a settlement is relevant property, tax shall be charged . . . on the value of the property or part at that time.

According to SP 8/86, income only becomes relevant property when it has been *accumulated*. During the time it is unaccumulated, it is not relevant property for IHT purposes. Accumulation is effected *either* by a resolution of the trustees or, possibly, after the expiration of a reasonable time after the income arose. Considerable doubt is, however, thrown on the latter proposition by *Re Locker* [1977] 1 WLR 1323. In that case, Goulding J allowed trustees to distribute – in 1977(!) – income that had arisen on settled property from 3 December 1965 to 5 April 1968:

> A tardy distribution at the discretion of the trustees is, after all, nearer to prompt distribution at the discretion of the trustees . . . than tardy distribution by the trustees at the discretion of someone else.

29.4.2.4 Accumulation and maintenance settlements

The general IHT rules applying to settlements lacking an interest in possession are modified by IHTA 1984, s. 71, where the settlement is an accumulation and maintenance settlement: see **27.4.2.3**. Most importantly, the 10-yearly charge is inapplicable to accumulation and maintenance settlements. As we have already noted, there is no IHT charge when the settled property is transferred from the trustees to a beneficiary, so long as the settlement satisfies the definition of an accumulation and maintenance settlement at that point.

29.4.2.5 Disabled settlements

These are treated rather differently from accumulation and maintenance settlements. Like accumulation and maintenance settlements, there is no 10-yearly charge, although this is because the beneficiary is *deemed* to have an interest in possession in this type of settlement: IHTA 1984, s. 89(2). In this respect, the beneficiary is treated in the same way as the life tenant of a settlement with an interest in possession.

29.4.3 STAMP DUTY IMPLICATIONS

None of the automatic transfers mentioned above involves the use of a document liable to stamp duty. This is because in none of these situations is the legal title to the settled property transferred.

29.5 Intestacy Rules

We are concerned here with the automatic transfer from the deceased to the deceased's PRs. The transfer of estate property from the PRs to the beneficiaries has been discussed in **28.5**.

29.5.1 CAPITAL GAINS TAX IMPLICATIONS

The CGT position is identical to the CGT position on a gift on death. There is no disposal by the deceased, although the PRs acquire property in the deceased's estate at its market value at the date of the death: TCGA 1992, s. 62(1). If the PRs need to sell assets in the estate, such a sale is governed by the rules discussed in **21.7.2**.

29.5.2 INHERITANCE TAX IMPLICATIONS

The automatic transfer under the intestacy rules, from the deceased to the deceased's PRs, is a chargeable transfer. The IHT position is exactly the same as for a gift on death: see **27.6.1.1**. In the event that the deceased's estate, other than personal chattels, is worth more than £125,000, the half of the estate which is held for a surviving spouse is held subject to the normal IHT rules for interest in possession settlements: see **29.4.2.2**. The half of the residue held on the statutory trusts is subject to the special rules for accumulation and maintenance settlements, since the statutory trusts are clearly of that type: see **27.4.2.3**, **29.4.2.4**.

29.6 Summary

Where an interest in jointly-held property passes by survivorship, the survivor acquires it at its market value for CGT purposes. For IHT purposes, the value of your joint tenancy interest is part of the chargeable transfer made on your death, because of the rule that you are treated as making a transfer of value immediately before your death. Where the interest of a beneficiary under a settlement comes to an end on the death, but the settlement continues, there is a tax-free uplift to match the general CGT position on death. Section 74, TCGA 1992 achieves this by deeming the settled property to be disposed of and immediately reacquired by the trustee, for a consideration equal to the market value of the fund. For IHT purposes, the interest of a beneficiary which comes to an end on death forms part of the beneficiary's estate. The beneficiary is treated as owning the whole capital of the settled property. Since such a rule cannot operate where settlement lacks an interest in possession, the property in such settlements is subject to a 10-yearly charge, which is designed to mimic the effect of the death of successive life tenants under a settlement which *does* have an interest in possession. The 10-yearly charge does not however apply to accumulation and maintenance settlements, or to disabled settlements, IHTA 1984, s. 89(2) deeming the latter to have an interest in possession. The automatic transfer of a deceased individual's estate to PRs on an intestacy (via the President of the Family Division) has the same IHT and CGT consequences as does a testate death.

29.7   End of Chapter Assessment Question

Comment on the IHT and CGT implications of the following, ignoring the availability of hold-over relief. It is 1 September 1998. Sugden transfers 100,000 ordinary shares in Olympic plc to Terence and Tara, who are the trustees of the Sugden 1998 Interest in Possession Settlement. Under the terms of the settlement, the shares are to be held for Bella for life, remainder to Charlotte for life, remainder to Douglas absolutely. Bella is 28, Charlotte is 30, and Douglas is 27. Charlotte sells her interest to her cousin Frank for £60,000, its open-market value, on 20 November 1998. On 1 December 1998, Bella is drowned in a fishing accident, dying intestate. Besides being the life tenant of the Sugden 1998 Interest in Possession Settlement, Bella was the co-owner of Makepiece Hall, under a joint tenancy, with Bill, her husband. At her death, Makepiece Hall was worth £550,000, and the shares in Olympic plc, £100,000.

(Word limit: 350 (100 marks).)

See *Cases and Materials* (**29.3**) for a specimen answer.

CHAPTER THIRTY

TAXATION OF GRATUITOUS TRANSFERS: CALCULATIONS (1)

30.1   Objectives

By the end of this chapter, you should be able to:

■ list the gratuitous transfers which require *liability to IHT* to be calculated;

■ identify which of these transfers also require the calculation of a *chargeable gain* or *base cost* for CGT purposes;

■ divide your list into *lifetime transfers* chargeable immediately, *transfers on death* and *transfers in connection with settlements*;

■ calculate the *IHT liability on a lifetime transfer* chargeable immediately;

■ calculate the *IHT liability on a transfer on death*.

30.2   Introduction

The discussion in **Chapters 27** to **29** has identified the situations in which either, or possibly both, CGT and IHT charges can arise on a gratuitous transfer. Naturally, we now need to examine how the IHT liability is calculated in each situation. Where chargeable gains arise on a gratuitous transfer, they are calculated in the five *Stages* discussed in **21.4.1**, and included in the disponer's gross chargeable gains, whether an individual or a company, for the tax period under consideration. It will therefore be necessary to refer to **21.4.1**, and the sections which follow it, when calculating the chargeable gain on a gratuitous transfer. It is important to appreciate one difference between CGT and corporation tax on chargeable gains – both of which require chargeable gains to be included in the disponer's CGT calculation for the whole tax period – and IHT, which simply requires IHT to be paid in respect of each chargeable transfer. We shall return to this difference when we consider the rules for paying IHT in **33.4.1.3**. Bear in mind that, both in this chapter and in **Chapter 31**, we do not consider the detailed effect of IHT exemptions and reliefs on the calculations. Instead, we discuss them in detail in **Chapter 32**, and we shall discover there that some of them can significantly reduce, or even totally exempt, a liability to IHT. In this chapter, the effect of the annual exemption will also be ignored, which is why each of the SAQs asks you to assume that the IHT annual exemptions have been used up. The annual exemptions will, of course, be discussed in detail in **Chapter 32**.

30.3   Calculating the IHT Liability on Lifetime Transfers

Lifetime transfers include all chargeable transfers by an individual which fail the test for a PET, and on which IHT is therefore chargeable immediately. (You may wish to turn back to the test for a PET, at **27.3.1.1**, before reading any further.) The IHT calculation for a lifetime transfer differs, depending on whether the giver assumes the burden of the IHT, or whether that burden is shifted by the giver to the recipient. This is because IHT works by taxing the reduction in value of the giver's estate caused by a transfer of value: see **27.3.1.1(2)**. If the IHT burden is assumed by the giver, the value transferred by the chargeable transfer is greater than it would have been, had that not been the case. Such a gift is often referred to as a *net gift*. IHT must therefore be calculated on the burden of the IHT assumed by the giver, as well as on the net value transferred. This requires a *grossing-up calculation*, conceptually similar to the one used for income tax purposes: see **8.4**. Calculating IHT on a lifetime transfer is fairly simple where the burden of the IHT has been shifted to the *recipient*, as opposed to being assumed by the giver. Where the recipient has the burden of the IHT, grossing-up is unnecessary.

IHT is a progressive tax, although in a rather limited sense. Progressiveness in a tax basically means that the richer you are, the greater the average rate of the tax you pay. Fundamental to this progressive quality is the so-called *cumulation principle*. Irrespective of whether or not the IHT burden is assumed by the giver, the cumulation principle governs the IHT calculation. It is discussed in detail in **30.3.1.2**. Together with the so-called *nil rate band* it ensures that, in some sense at least, IHT is a progressive tax.

30.3.1   TRANSFERS WHERE THE GIVER ASSUMES THE IHT BURDEN

30.3.1.1   Where the gift is the first chargeable transfer by the giver in seven years

Here:

■   you make a gift, without having made any other chargeable transfers in the period of seven years ending with the date of the gift: IHTA 1984, s. 7(1)(a) (*Cases and Materials* (**30.1.1**)); and

■   you assume the burden of any IHT which may be chargeable.

The calculation of the IHT liability on such a gift consists of four stages. It is essential for you to know the correct order in which they unfold.

Stage One is to identify the net value transferred. Stage One of your IHT calculation is thus:

	£
Net value transferred	X

On 1 November 1998, Gerard transfers 2,000 ordinary shares in Amber plc, worth **£250,000**, to the trustees of a discretionary settlement. The deed of transfer provides for the IHT burden to be assumed by the settlor. Gerard has already used up his IHT annual exemptions. What is the net value transferred by the gift?

£250,000.

Stage Two is to gross-up the net value transferred, in order to find the *gross value transferred*. One way of doing this is by adding together the amount of the so-called *nil rate band*, i.e. £223,000, and $^5/_4$ (or 1.25) of each £1 of the net value transferred in excess of £223,000. Another way of doing it is by adding together the *net value transferred*, and the figure produced by the following formula:

$$E \times 100/100 - T \times T\% = G,$$

where E is the amount of the net value transferred which exceeds the nil rate band, T is the relevant rate of IHT and G is the IHT on the *gross value transferred*. Which of these two formulae you use is a matter of choice. Throughout this chapter, the assumption will be made that the nil rate band has always been £223,000. In reality, it has progressively increased over the years (in 1997/98, it was £215,000).

Stage Two of your IHT calculation is thus:

	£
Net value transferred	X
Gross value transferred	X

SAQ 395

Continuing the example in SAQ 394, what is the gross value transferred?

Gross value transferred = [£223,000 + $^5/_4$(£250,000 – £223,000)];
Therefore:
Gross value transferred = [£223,000 + $^5/_4$(£27,000)];
Therefore:
Gross value transferred = [£223,000 + £33,750]; and
Therefore:
Gross value transferred = £256,750.

Alternatively, using the second formula: £27,000 × 100/80 × 20/100 = £6,750 + £250,000 = £256,750.

Stage Three is to deduct the nil rate band from the gross value transferred, to give the amount on which IHT is calculated. *Stage Three* of your IHT calculation is thus:

	£
Gross value transferred	X
Less nil rate band	(X)
Amount on which IHT is calculated	X

SAQ 396

Continuing the example in SAQ 395, what is the amount on which IHT is calculated?

	£
Gross value transferred	256,750
Less nil rate band	223,000
Amount on which IHT is calculated	33,750

Stage Four is to calculate the IHT at 20% on this figure: IHTA 1984, s. 7(2). *Stage Four* of your IHT calculation is thus:

	£
Amount on which IHT is calculated	X
IHT at 20%	X

SAQ 397

Continuing the example in SAQ 396, what is the IHT payable by Gerard?

	£
Amount on which IHT is calculated	33,750
IHT at 20%	6,750

This means that the total cost of the gift to Gerard is £256,750, i.e. £250,000 + £6,750. The trustees receive shares in Amber plc worth £250,000.

That is the end of the calculation. Joining the stages together, you get the following:

	£
Net value transferred	X
Gross value transferred	X
Less nil rate band	(X)
Amount on which IHT is calculated	X
IHT at 20%	X

30.3.1.2   Where the gift is *not* the first chargeable transfer by the giver in seven years

Here:

■ you make a gift, having made other chargeable transfers in the period of seven years ending with the date of the gift: IHTA 1984, s. 7(1)(a) (*Cases and Materials* (**30.1.1.1**)); and

■ you assume the burden of any IHT which may be chargeable.

The calculation of the IHT liability on such a gift (a *new gift*) has *five* Stages. Again, it is essential for you to know the correct order in which they unfold.

Stage One is to ascertain your *gross cumulative total* of previous chargeable transfers. Thus the first stage of your IHT calculation is:

	£
Gross cumulative total	X

Your gross cumulative total goes at the beginning of the IHT calculation because of the *cumulation principle*: IHTA 1984, s. 7(1). The cumulation principle means that the rate of IHT on the value transferred by a chargeable transfer is determined by your gross cumulative total of such transfers in the seven-year period referred to above. You *measure back* from the date of the new gift, in order to work out whether any earlier chargeable transfers have been made.

Read IHTA 1984, s. 7(1)(b), at *Cases and Materials* (**30.1.1**). **Think deeply about this subsection, since it contains the cumulation principle.**

If you turn back to **27.3.1.1(4)**, you will recall that a PET is a chargeable transfer, although one which is initially *exempt* from IHT. For the purposes of s. 7(1) and the cumulation principle, the expression *chargeable transfer* does not therefore include PETs, unless they become chargeable on the death of the giver: see **30.4.2**. The existence of the cumulation principle means that it is essential for you to keep records of *all* chargeable transfers made by you, not simply those made within a seven-year period.

On 1 November 1998, Tom transfers 1,000 ordinary shares in Bigco plc, worth £240,000, to the trustees of a discretionary settlement. The settlement deed provides for the IHT burden to be assumed by the settlor. Tom has none of his IHT annual exemptions left. On 1 November 1996, he made a chargeable transfer of £300,000 and, on 1 November 1989, he made a chargeable transfer of £100,000. What is Tom's gross cumulative total at the time of the new gift?

£300,000.

Stage Two is to calculate, in a separate calculation from this one, the IHT on your gross cumulative total. As above, for lifetime transfers, IHT is charged at 20% of the amount by which your gross cumulative total exceeds the nil rate band. The IHT on the gross cumulative total is then deducted, also at *Stage Two*, from the gross cumulative total, in order to give you your *old net cumulative total*.

	£
Gross cumulative total	X
Less IHT on gross cumulative total	(X)
Old net cumulative total	X

Continuing the example in SAQ 398, what is Tom's *old net cumulative total* at the time of the new gift?

	£
Gross cumulative total	300,000
Less IHT on gross cumulative total (i.e. £77,000 × 20/100)	(15,400)
Old net cumulative total	284,600

Stage Three is to *add* to the *old net cumulative total* the net amount of the new gift, in order to give the *new net cumulative total*.

	£
Old net cumulative total	X
Plus Net amount of the new gift	X
New net cumulative total	X

Continuing the example in SAQ 399, what is Tom's *new net cumulative total* as a result of the new gift?

	£
Old net cumulative total	284,600
Plus Net amount of the new gift	240,000
New net cumulative total	524,600

Stage Four is to calculate the IHT, again in a separate calculation from this one, on your *new net cumulative total*. As above, IHT is charged at 20% of the amount by which the new net cumulative total exceeds the nil rate band: see above.

The IHT on your gross cumulative total from Stage Two is then deducted, still at *Stage Four*, from the IHT on your new net cumulative total, to find the IHT on the new gift.

	£
IHT on new net cumulative total	X
Less IHT on gross cumulative total	(X)
IHT on new gift	X

Continuing the example in SAQ 400, what is the IHT on the new net cumulative total?

	£
IHT on new net cumulative total (i.e. £301,600 × 20/100)	60,320
Less IHT on gross cumulative total	15,400
IHT on new gift	<u>44,920</u>

Stage Five is necessary because you, the giver, are assuming the burden of the IHT: see **30.3.1.1**. Stage Five is to calculate the IHT on the total of the IHT on the new gift – *Stage Four* – and the net amount of the new gift itself. This will give the *IHT on the gross value transferred by the new gift* (grossing-up formulae above).

IHT on new gift	<u>X</u>

IHT on the gross value transferred by the new gift:

E × 100/100 − T × T%	<u>X</u>

Continuing the example in SAQ 401, what is the IHT on the gross value transferred by the new gift?

	£
IHT on new gift	<u>44,920</u>

IHT on the gross value transferred by the new gift:

£61,920[*] × 100/80 × 20%	<u>15,480</u>

[*] i.e. £240,000 + £44,920 = £284,920 − £223,000.

This means that your new gross cumulative total is the total of the new net cumulative total (from *Stage Three*) and the IHT on it (from *Stage Four*). In the example in **SAQs 398** to **402**, the new gross cumulative total is therefore £584,920, i.e. £524,600 + £60,320.

It also means that the total cost of the gift to Tom, in that example, is £300,400, i.e. £240,000 + £44,920 + £15,480. The trustees receive £240,000 on trust for the beneficiaries of the settlement.

You might also find it useful to know that, where all of the value transferred exceeds the nil rate band, in the way that the new gift does here, IHT is actually being charged on that excess at 25% — £15,480 is 25% of £61,920, for instance.

That is the end of the calculation. Joining the stages together, you get the following:

	£
Gross cumulative total	X
Less IHT on gross cumulative total	(X)
Old net cumulative total	X
Plus Net amount of the new gift	X
New net cumulative total	X
IHT on new net cumulative total	X
Less IHT on gross cumulative total	(X)
IHT on new gift	X

IHT on the gross value transferred by the new gift:

E × 100/T × T%	X

30.3.2   TRANSFERS WHERE THE IHT BURDEN IS SHIFTED TO THE RECIPIENT

Where the IHT burden on a lifetime transfer is shifted to the recipient, the calculation of IHT is straightforward, by comparison with the calculations shown above. This is because no grossing-up is necessary here. Such gifts are referred to as *gross gifts* for IHT purposes.

30.3.2.1   Where the gift is the first chargeable transfer by the giver in seven years

Here:

■ you make a gift, without having made any other chargeable transfers in the period of seven years ending with the date of the gift: IHTA 1984, s. 7(1)(a); and

■ the burden of any IHT which may be chargeable is shifted to the recipient.

The calculation of the IHT liability on such a gift only has two stages.

Stage One is to calculate the amount by which the value transferred exceeds the nil rate band, taking into account any earlier chargeable transfers within the nil rate band. *Stage One* of your IHT calculation is thus:

	£
Excess over nil rate band	X

On 1 October 1998, Edward transfers Handel House, a tenanted office block worth £500,000, to the trustees of a discretionary settlement. The conveyance provides for the IHT burden to be assumed by the trustees. Edward has not made any earlier chargeable transfers within the nil rate band, although he has no IHT annual exemption left. What is the amount by which the gift exceeds the nil rate band?

£277,000, i.e. £500,000 − £223,000.

Stage Two is to calculate IHT at 20% of the excess of the value transferred over the nil rate band. The second stage of your IHT calculation is thus:

	£
Excess over nil rate band	X
IHT at 20%	X

Continuing the example in SAQ 403, what is the IHT payable by the trustees?

	£
Excess over nil rate band	277,000
IHT at 20%	55,400

This means that the total cost of the gift to Edward is £500,000. The trustees receive Handel House and will be liable to pay IHT of £55,400 (i.e. 20/100 × £277,000).

That is the end of the calculation. Note that, where the recipients are the trustees of a discretionary settlement, the IHT burden shifted to them will eat into the trust fund, meaning that the IHT liability will be felt by the beneficiaries of the discretionary settlement.

30.3.2.2   Where the gift is *not* the first chargeable transfer by the giver in seven years

Here:

■ you make a gift, having made other chargeable transfers in the period of seven years ending with the date of the gift: IHTA 1984, s. 7(1)(a); and

■ the burden of any IHT which may be chargeable is shifted to the recipient.

The calculation of the IHT liability on the new gift breaks up into four Stages, although they are different ones from those in the last section. As ever, it is essential for you to know the correct order in which they unfold.

Stage One is to ascertain your *gross cumulative total* of previous chargeable transfers. The first stage of your IHT calculation is thus:

	£
Gross cumulative total	X

This may have been calculated following an earlier gift where other chargeable transfers had been made before this new gift: see **30.3.1.2**. To illustrate this, **SAQ 405** continues the example which ended in **SAQ 402**.

On 1 December 1998, Tom transfers 100 ordinary shares in Smallco Ltd, worth £60,000, to the trustees of a second discretionary settlement. The settlement deed provides for the IHT burden to be assumed by the trustees, i.e. the recipients. What is Tom's gross cumulative total prior to the new gift?

£584,920 (see the text after **SAQ 402**).

Stage Two is to add to the gross cumulative total the value transferred by the new gift, to produce the new gross cumulative total.

	£
Gross cumulative total	X
Plus value transferred by new gift	X
New gross cumulative total	X

Continuing the example in SAQ 405, what is Tom's *new gross cumulative total*?

	£
Gross cumulative total	584,920
Plus value transferred by new gift	60,000
New gross cumulative total	644,920

Stage Three is, in a separate calculation from this one, to calculate:

(a) the IHT on the new gross cumulative total; and

(b) the IHT on the gross cumulative total with which you began the calculation in this section, now the 'old' gross cumulative total.

Continuing the example in SAQ 406, what is: (a) the IHT on Tom's new gross cumulative total?; and (b) the IHT on his 'old' gross cumulative total?

IHT on (a), his new gross cumulative total, is 20/100 × £421,920 (i.e. £644,920 − £223,000). IHT on his new gross cumulative total is therefore £84,384.
IHT on (b), his 'old' gross cumulative total, is 20/100 × £361,920 (i.e. £584,920 − £223,000). IHT on his 'old' gross cumulative total is therefore £72,384.

Stage Four is to deduct (b) from (a), to give the IHT on the new gift.

	£
IHT on new gross cumulative total	X
Less IHT on 'old' gross cumulative total	(X)
IHT on new gift	X

Continuing the example in SAQ 407, what is the IHT on the new gift?

	£
IHT on new gross cumulative total	84,384
Less IHT on 'old' gross cumulative total	72,384
IHT on new gift	12,000

That is the end of the calculation. Joining the stages together, you get the following:

	£
Gross cumulative total	X
Plus value transferred by new gift	X
New gross cumulative total	X
IHT on new gross cumulative total	X
Less IHT on 'old' gross cumulative total	(X)
IHT on new gift	X

30.4   Calculating the IHT Liability on Transfers on Death

30.4.1   INTRODUCTION

The calculation of the IHT liability on a transfer on death, whether by will or under the intestacy rules, ought to be a fairly straightforward process. Your PRs will add together:

A.   Your *gross cumulative total* of chargeable lifetime transfers

   and

B.   The *value of your estate* immediately before your death.

If the total of A and B exceeds the nil rate band on your death, then IHT is charged on that excess at 40%. As indicated in **30.4**, the nil rate band is £223,000 for 1998/99.

Evadne dies on 20 April 1998. The value of her estate immediately before her death is £200,000. The gross cumulative total of her chargeable lifetime transfers is £400,000. What is the IHT liability on her estate at her death?

£150,800, i.e. £600,000 − £223,000 × 40/100.

The PRs will then need to adjust this figure, to take account of any IHT already paid at 20% during Evadne's lifetime, and any PETs which have become chargeable on her death. In fact, depending on the circumstances, the task of PRs could be complicated by one or more of four factors:

■ *PETs becoming chargeable*. If you die less than seven years after having made a PET, then the PET becomes a chargeable transfer on your death: see **27.3.1.1**. This has two consequences for your PRs when they are calculating the IHT liability on your death:

   (a) The PET must, as a result of your death, be included in the gross cumulative total for your lifetime: see **30.4**. Since the PET which has become chargeable will have altered that gross cumulative total, your PRs will also need to re-calculate the IHT payable on any lifetime transfers on which IHT was paid.

   (b) In addition, IHT on the PET must be calculated using the death rate of 40%, rather than the lifetime rate of 20%. Your PRs will need to take account of your gross cumulative total before the transfer on your death.

■ *Lifetime transfers*. If you made lifetime transfers, on which IHT was paid, within seven years before your death, your PRs will need to recalculate the IHT on those transfers.

■ *Problems over who is to bear the burden of the IHT*. Wills should always provide either for the burden of any IHT to be assumed by the deceased's estate, or for it to be shifted to the legatee receiving a particular legacy or devise. Problems will therefore arise for the PRs if this issue has not been dealt with properly in the wording of the will.

■ *Problems where a transfer on death is partly subject to IHT and partly exempt*. As we shall discover, IHT is a *testamentary expense*, which means that it is generally paid out of the residue of the deceased's estate: AEA 1925, s. 34 and sch. 1, Part II. There is no problem where, under the terms of the will, legacies are expressed to be subject to IHT, so that IHT on them is borne by the legatees. Conversely, there is no problem where all the legacies are *free of tax*, so that the whole burden of the IHT is thrown onto the residue, and thus borne by the residue. Problems can, however, arise in the frequent situation where the gift of the residue is exempt from IHT, because of some statutory exemption, but the will also contains an IHT-free legacy.

The first two factors concern the PRs and the Revenue. The second two are issues which concern the PRs' nominal transfer of the estate property to the legatees: see **26.5.3**, **26.5.4**. The discussion in this section concludes with the general procedure for calculating the IHT on the value transferred by a transfer on death: see **30.4.5**.

Remember that transfers on death include gifts on death (see **27.6.1.1**), automatic transfers of interests in property held under joint tenancies (see **29.3.2**), automatic transfers of the interests of life tenants under settlements (see **29.4.2.2**) and automatic transfers of property under the intestacy rules: see **29.5.2**.

30.4.2 PETS BECOMING CHARGEABLE AND IHT ON LIFETIME TRANSFERS

30.4.2.1 PETs becoming chargeable

A PET becomes a chargeable transfer on your death, if you die less than seven years after having made the PET: see **27.3.1.1**. On death, any such PETs must be included in your gross cumulative total for your lifetime. Your PRs will therefore need to calculate the IHT payable on any PET, using the death rate of 40% and bearing in mind that any PETs which have become chargeable, as a result of your death, form part of your gross cumulative total. Note that *taper relief* may be available to mitigate the impact of the recalculation. As we shall discover, where it applies, taper relief operates to reduce the amount of IHT on the PET which has become chargeable. Its effect is ignored in this section, although it is discussed in **32.4.2**.

Stage One is to ascertain which PETs were made by the deceased in the seven-year period prior to death.

In July 1995, Simon made an absolute gift of Blackacre to his son, Peter. Simon dies on 11 December 1998.

Did Simon make a PET when he gave Blackacre to Peter?

Yes.

Stage Two is to work out the deceased's gross cumulative total immediately before the first PET was made. This total will include lifetime transfers chargeable immediately. However, it will *not* include other PETs made in the period of seven years ending with the first PET.

Stage Three is to ascertain the value of the property transferred by the PET, if necessary both at the date of the PET itself and at the date of the deceased's death. As a general rule, the value transferred is taken to be the value of the property transferred by the PET at the date of the PET. Where the value of the property has gone down, it is possible to take *instead* the value of the property transferred by the PET at the date of death, for the purposes of *calculating IHT* on death: IHTA 1984, s. 131. For *cumulation purposes*, the value of the property transferred by the PET is taken to be its value at the date of the PET.

Continuing the example in SAQ 410, Simon's PRs suspect that, by the date of Simon's death, the value of Blackacre has gone down. What should they do?

Obtain a valuation of Blackacre as at the date of the death.

IHTA 1984, s. 131(2) reads as follows:

> If—
>   (a) the market value of the transferred property at the time of the chargeable transfer [i.e. PET] exceeds its market value on the relevant date [i.e. date of death], and
>   (b) a claim is made by a person liable to pay the whole or part of the tax or, as the case may be, additional tax,

the tax or, as the case may be, the additional tax shall be calculated as if the value transferred were reduced by the amount of the excess.

If s. 131 applies therefore, you calculate the IHT on the PET which has become chargeable by reference to the reduced value of the property at the date of death. Tangible moveable property which is a wasting asset does not have the benefit of s. 131 and, where the property transferred by the PET was a lease with an unexpired term of less than 50 years, special rules apply.

Continuing the example in SAQ 411, suppose the valuation shows that, at the date of the gift, Blackacre was worth £500,000, whilst at the date of Simon's death, it was worth £300,000. What is the value of Blackacre for IHT purposes?

£300,000.

Stage Four is to deduct however much of the nil rate band was still available when the PET was made from the value transferred by the PET which the death has made chargeable, to give the amount on which IHT is to be calculated at 40%.

Continuing the example in SAQ 412, what will be the amount on which IHT is calculated?

£77,000, i.e. £300,000 − £223,000.

Stage Five is to calculate the IHT at 40% on the PET made chargeable by the death.

Continuing the example in SAQ 413, what will be the IHT payable on Blackacre on the death?

£34,000, i.e. 40/100 × £85,000.

30.4.2.2   IHT on immediately chargeable lifetime transfers

If you die less than seven years after having made a transfer immediately chargeable to IHT, then that transfer is subject to IHT at 40%: see **27.3.1.1, 27.6.1.1**. Your PRs will therefore need to re-calculate your IHT liability on the lifetime transfers, using the death rate of 40%, and taking into account the 20% IHT which will already have been paid. Note that taper relief may be available to mitigate the effect of this recalculation: see **32.4.2**. Where taper relief applies, it works by reducing the amount of IHT recalculated in this way. Its effect is ignored in this section, although it is discussed in **32.4.2**. The same general rule applies as in relation to PETs, i.e. that the value transferred is taken to be the value of the property transferred by the lifetime transfer at the date of the lifetime transfer. The same exception to the rule also applies, in the event that the value of the property has gone down: IHTA 1984, s. 131. To keep the discussion as succinct as possible, such a reduction in value is not built into the following description of the calculation. If necessary, reference should be made to the discussion in **30.4.2.1**.

Stage One is to ascertain which lifetime transfers immediately chargeable to IHT were made by the deceased in the seven-year period before death.

On 1 June 1995, Bart made a gift on trust of Whiteacre, then worth £800,000, to the trustees of the Bart 1994 Discretionary Settlement. The settlement deed provided that the IHT was to be paid out of the settled fund. Bart dies on 12 January 1999, having made no other PETs or chargeable transfers. How would the settlement of Whiteacre have been treated for IHT purposes?

As a transfer chargeable immediately to IHT.

Stage Two is to ascertain the IHT at 20% on the lifetime transfer, taking into account the nil rate band (assumed to be £223,000 throughout).

Continuing the example in SAQ 415, what would have been the IHT on the lifetime transfer of Whiteacre to the trustees?

£115,400, i.e. 20/100 × £577,000. Grossing-up does not apply, since the trustees bear the IHT.

Stage Three is to ascertain the IHT at 40% on the lifetime transfer, which the death has made chargeable at the higher rate, again taking into account the nil rate band.

Continuing the example in SAQ 416, what is the IHT at 40% on the lifetime transfer?

£230,800, i.e. 40/100 × £577,000.

Stage Four is to deduct the figure found in *Stage Two* from the figure found in *Stage Three*.

SAQ 418

Continuing the example in SAQ 417, what will be the additional IHT payable on the lifetime transfer of Whiteacre, on the death of Bart?

£115,400, i.e. £230,800 − £115,400.

30.4.2.3 Mixture of IHT on lifetime transfers and PETs becoming chargeable

It is, of course, possible that you might die having made a mixture of PETs and transfers immediately chargeable to IHT. Your PRs will therefore need to calculate the IHT for the first time on the PETs, as well as to recalculate your IHT liability on the lifetime transfers. Again, taper relief may be available to mitigate the effect of the calculation and recalculation. Where taper relief applies, it operates to reduce the amount of IHT as calculated and recalculated in this way. As elsewhere in this section, its effect is ignored here. It is discussed in 32.4.2. We consider first the calculation where the PET is made *before* the transfer immediately chargeable to IHT. You should, however, be aware of the existence of the so-called *PET trap*. This is the term for the effect which can be produced where a PET is made *after* a transfer immediately chargeable to IHT, and more IHT is payable than would have been payable if the PET had not been made in the first place! The PET trap is discussed briefly below.

(1) PET made before a transfer immediately chargeable to IHT
Stage One is to ascertain which PETs and which lifetime transfers immediately chargeable to IHT were made by the deceased in the seven-year period before death.

SAQ 419

On 1 June 1994, Boris made an absolute gift of his second home, Greenacre, to his son Norris. At the time of the gift, it was worth £400,000. Four years later, on 1 June 1998, Boris transferred £500,000 in cash to the close company owned by his family, Borisco Ltd, subject to the company bearing the IHT on the transfer. Boris dies on 12 March 1999, having made no other chargeable transfers or PETs. Which of the lifetime transfers was a PET when it was made, and which was a transfer chargeable immediately to IHT?

The gift to Norris was a PET. The gift to Borisco Ltd was a transfer chargeable immediately to IHT.

Stage Two is to calculate the IHT at 20% on the transfer chargeable immediately to IHT, taking into account the nil rate band. The earlier PET is ignored at this stage.

SAQ 420

Continuing the example in SAQ 419, what would have been the IHT on the transfer of the cash sum of £500,000 to Borisco Ltd?

£55,400, i.e. 20/100 × £277,000. Grossing-up does not apply, since the trustees bear the IHT.

Stage Three is to calculate the IHT at 40% on the PET which has become chargeable because of the deceased's death, again taking into account any available part of the nil rate band.

Continuing the example in SAQ 420, what will be the IHT at 40% on the now-chargeable PET?

£70,800, i.e. 40/100 × £177,000.

Stage Four is to ascertain the gross cumulative total of the deceased at the date of the transfer chargeable immediately to IHT, on the basis that the earlier PET has become a chargeable transfer on the deceased's death.

Continuing the example in SAQ 421, what was the deceased's gross cumulative total at the date of the transfer to Borisco Ltd?

£400,000, i.e. the PET now chargeable.

Stage Five is to calculate IHT at 40% on the value transferred by the transfer chargeable immediately to IHT.

Continuing the example in SAQ 422, what is the IHT at 40% on the gift of the cash to Borisco Ltd?

£200,000, i.e. 40/100 × £500,000.

Stage Six is to deduct the IHT on the lifetime transfer, calculated at Stage Two, from the IHT at 40%, calculated at Stage Five, in order to give the extra IHT on the transfer chargeable immediately to IHT, as a result of the death.

Continuing the example in SAQ 423, what is the extra IHT payable on the gift of the cash to Borisco Ltd, as a result of the death?

£144,600, i.e. £200,000 – £55,400.

(2) The PET trap
As mentioned, this is the term for the effect which may be produced where you make a PET less than seven years *after* an immediately chargeable lifetime transfer, and your

death occurs less than seven years after the PET. The result is that more IHT may eventually be payable than would have been, had the PET never been made! The reason for this is that, when a PET is made after an earlier chargeable transfer, it will cause the earlier transfer to be cumulated. Had the PET not been made, then by the deceased's death the initial chargeable transfer would have dropped out of the cumulation process.

30.4.3   PROBLEMS OVER WHO IS TO BEAR THE BURDEN OF THE IHT

30.4.3.1   IHT problem presented by the question of who is to bear the burden of the IHT

Say I am a PR. I am about to make a nominal transfer of a legacy to a legatee. The question I have to ask myself is whether the transfer should be made to the legatee on the basis that the legatee bears the burden of the IHT, or whether the deceased's estate should bear the IHT on it. In the latter case, the IHT on the legacy will come out of the residue: AEA 1925, s. 34 and Part II. Either way, there has to be a correct answer to the question, since I must recoup the IHT which I had to pay when the letters of administration, or probate, were granted to me. Where the will has been well-drafted, the answer to the question is an easy one. Although the general rule is that a legacy is free of IHT unless the will provides to the contrary, a well-drafted will should state whether a particular legacy is to be 'free of tax' or not. If a legacy is not free of tax, then it will bear its own burden of IHT. In that case, as a PR, I can if necessary recover the IHT from the legatee: IHTA 1984, s. 211(3). The problem arises from the limitations to the general rule that the IHT on a legacy which is 'free of tax' is paid out of the residue of the deceased's estate, rather than by the legatee. One of the limitations on the general rule is IHTA 1984, s. 41:

> Notwithstanding the terms of any disposition—
>   (a)   none of the tax on the value transferred shall fall on any specific gift if or to the extent that the transfer is exempt with respect to the gift, and
>   (b)   none of the tax attributable to the value of the property comprised in residue shall fall on any gift of a share of residue if or to the extent that the transfer is exempt with respect to the gift.

In other words, a will cannot validly provide for the burden of IHT to be borne by any part of the residue which is exempted from IHT by the provisions of the IHT legislation. An example of one such exemption is the exemption for transfers between spouses in IHTA 1984, s. 18: see **27.7.2**. However, other exemptions include, e.g., gifts to charities. If I am an executor, what should I do in the difficult situation where the wording of a will seems to infringe s. 41? Where the estate is large enough to merit it, and the legatees are in disagreement, an application to court might be necessary to resolve the doubt.

30.4.3.2   Some sort of solution provided by the case law

One case which caused doubts of this kind was *Re Benham* [1995] STC 210. There, the executor sought guidance on the burden of IHT in relation to the following provision in a will. A testatrix had left the residue of her estate, after the payment of funeral and testamentary expenses and debts, on trust:

> . . . [T]o pay the same to those beneficiaries as are living at my death and who are listed in List A and List B hereunder written in such proportions as will bring about the result that the aforesaid beneficiaries named in List A shall receive 3.2 times as much as the aforesaid beneficiaries named in List B and in each case for their own absolute and beneficial use and disposal.

List A contained a number of non-charitable beneficiaries, plus one charity. List B contained more than one charity, plus several non-charitable beneficiaries. The non-charitable beneficiaries in both lists argued that their shares should be grossed up, so that the residuary estate would bear the burden of the IHT, rather than themselves. If the shares of the non-charitable beneficiaries were not grossed up, they argued, then the non-charitable beneficiaries in both lists would receive less than the charitable ones. This was plainly not the testatrix's intention.

RMK Gray QC, sitting as a deputy High Court judge, held that the non-charitable beneficiaries should receive grossed-up shares. He summed up his reasoning in a single sentence:

> I agree with Sir Patrick Sinclair and Mr Caddick [i.e. counsel for the non-charitable beneficiaries] that the plain intention of the testatrix is that at the end of the day each beneficiary, whether charitable or non-charitable, should receive the same as the other beneficiaries in the relevant list.

Note that the *principle* of grossing up is the same in relation to both lifetime transfers and transfers on death: see **30.4.4.2**.

Read the extract from *Re Benham*, at *Cases and Materials* (30.2.1), then the article on *Re Benham* by Nick Caddick, counsel for some of the non-charitable beneficiaries, which follows it. Consider what conclusions should be drawn as to how a will should be drafted to avoid the *Re Benham* problem.

I understand that, on a subsequent application in chambers, *Re Benham* was treated as being confined in its application to the particular formula under consideration.

30.4.4   PROBLEMS WHERE A TRANSFER ON DEATH IS ONLY PARTLY SUBJECT TO IHT

30.4.4.1   IHT problem when transfer on death only partly subject to IHT

I am a PR again, but this time under a different will. I am confronted with another conundrum. The deceased's will states that a particular legacy is to be 'free of tax'. The problem is that the gift of the residue is exempt, because of a provision in the IHT legislation. What should I do? Far from being an arcane point, this arises out of a fairly common situation. It arises, say, where there is an absolute gift on death 'free of tax' by the testator to his son, the residue being left to the testator's UK-domiciled wife: see **27.7**.

30.4.4.2   The solution provided by the IHT rules: IHTA 1984, ss. 36–42

Unsurprisingly perhaps, the gift 'free of tax' must be grossed-up by me, the PR. The net sum is then transferred by the PR to the legatee, and the IHT found by grossing-up is deducted from the residue.

I am an executor of the will of Samuel, deceased. Samuel was very wealthy, and left a large estate. He also had an IHT gross cumulative total at his death which was far in excess of the nil rate band. His will makes an absolute gift of his shareholding in General Amalgamations plc *free of tax* to his son, Saul. The shares are valued at £500,000. The residue of his estate, worth £1.5 million, is left to his wife, Bathsheba, who is UK-domiciled.

How much must I deduct from the residue for IHT purposes, before making the nominal transfer of the residue to Bathsheba?

£333,333, i.e. £500,000 × 100/60 × 40%.

How much will Bathsheba receive?

£1,166,667, i.e. £1.5 million − £333,333.

30.4.5 CALCULATING THE IHT LIABILITY ON THE TRANSFER ON DEATH

As noted above, your PRs will add together your *gross cumulative total* of chargeable transfers, *and* the *value of your estate immediately before your death*. The rules for valuing your estate will be discussed in **31.3**. What we need to do now, however, is to join together the discussion in **30.3** and **30.4**. On your death, your PRs will therefore go through the following calculation.

Stage One will be to ascertain the gross cumulative total of your lifetime transfers. This will of course include transfers chargeable immediately to IHT, as well as PETs which have become chargeable as a result of your death.

Continuing the example in SAQs 415 to 418, let us add the detail that the value of Bart's estate on his death is £1.3 million. In addition, his will leaves £750,000 to his son, Alan free of tax, and the residue, after payment of funeral expenses, testamentary expenses and debts, to his niece, Alice. All other facts remain the same. What is Bart's gross cumulative total at his death?

£800,000.

Stage Two is to ascertain the total value transferred by the deemed transfer of value on the death: see **31.3**. For present purposes, note that this includes life interests in property, as well as property treated as being *subject to a reservation*: see **33.3.1**.

Continuing the example in SAQ 427, what is the total value transferred on Bart's death?

£1.3 million.

Stage Three is to add together the figures produced in *Stages One* and *Two*, to find the amount on which IHT at death will be calculated by the PRs.

Continuing the example in SAQ 428, on what amount will IHT be calculated on Bart's death?

£2,100,000, i.e. £800,000 + £1.3 million.

Stage Four is to calculate the IHT at 40% on the excess over the nil rate band, *giving credit for any IHT already paid*.

Continuing the example in SAQ 429, and giving credit for any IHT already paid, what will be the IHT payable on Bart's death?

£635,400, i.e. £2,100,000 − £223,000 = £1,877,000 × 40/100 = £750,800, less IHT already paid of £115,400 (see **SAQ 416**).

Stage Five, which is only necessary when the IHT is to be borne by the beneficiaries rather than by the estate as a testamentary expense, is to calculate the *estate rate*. This is the amount of IHT to be borne by each legacy subject to IHT. To calculate the *estate rate*, the IHT calculated at *Stage Four* is divided by the total value transferred on the death (*Stage Two*), and multiplied by 100. The result is a percentage rate. The estate rate will automatically be 40% if the deceased had used up the whole of the nil rate band during his or her lifetime.

Study the 'Precedent for a Modern Will' by Withers & Co., solicitors, at *Cases and Materials* (30.2.2). Take a blank sheet of paper and note as many of the points as you can discussed in Chapters 26 to 30, which are dealt with in the article.

30.5 Summary

I am reluctant to add anything else, even by way of conclusion, to a chapter which is already perhaps overlong. That said, it is important to add just a few words of summary, as well as to indicate where we are going from here. The key point about the calculation of IHT liabilities is the cumulation principle. In essence, it is highly logical, although it presents difficulties of application where a death comes at the end of a seven-year period in which the deceased has made PETs, and possibly also transfers chargeable immediately to IHT. You should be able to understand from the material in this chapter, not only *why* IHT is a cumulative tax, but also *how* these difficulties of application are resolved in practice. That said, there are important glosses on what we have said so far. Exemptions and reliefs play their part in the IHT calculation, and they are discussed by us in **Chapter 32**. Separate IHT calculations apply to transfers in connection with settlements from those discussed in this chapter in relation to lifetime transfers, and transfers on death. The calculations applying to transfers in connection with settlements are discussed in the next chapter. In addition, for the purposes of the calculations discussed in this chapter, it will in practice be necessary to determine the value of the property in the giver's estate, both in relation to lifetime transfers and to transfers on death. The valuation rules therefore form the first part of the next chapter, whilst the rest of that chapter is devoted to a discussion of the IHT calculations in relation to transfers in connection with settlements.

30.6   End of Chapter Assessment Question

On 1 September 1988, Angus transferred a cash fund of £258,000 to the trustees of the 1993 Angus Discretionary Trust. On 1 October 1994, he made an absolute gift of his holiday home, worth £150,000, to his daughter Beth. On 1 February 1997, he gave an old master oil painting to his son Chris, at that time worth £264,000. On 31 March 1998, Angus dies, leaving an estate on his death worth £900,000. At his death, he has made no other gifts.

Describe how the IHT liability on his death will be calculated. Ignore the calculation of the estate rate, as well as Angus's annual exemptions. Assume the nil rate band has been £223,000 throughout.

(Word limit: 500 (100 marks).)

See *Cases and Materials* (30.4) for a specimen answer.

CHAPTER THIRTY-ONE

TAXATION OF GRATUITOUS TRANSFERS: CALCULATIONS (2)

31.1   Objectives

By the end of this chapter, you should be able to:

■ describe the IHT valuation rules for *lifetime transfers*;

■ describe the IHT valuation rules for *transfers on death*;

■ calculate the IHT liability of the trustees of a settlement without an interest in possession on the *10-yearly charge*;

■ calculate the IHT liability of the trustees of a settlement without an interest in possession on an *appointment of the settled property*.

31.2   Introduction

In this chapter, we complete our examination of the calculation of IHT liabilities. The first part is concerned with the IHT rules for valuing property in a person's estate. The second part is devoted to the rules for calculating the 10-yearly IHT charge where a settlement has no interest in possession. If you quickly turn back to **29.4.2.3**, you will remember why a special discussion is necessary for settlements without an interest in possession. First, however, the valuation rules. In the context of your tax law course, these rules could be important for a certain type of question, i.e. where you are required to calculate, or to describe how you would calculate, the value of property transferred. The rules are important because IHT operates by taxing the reduction in value of the giver's estate caused by a transfer of value: see **27.3.1.1**. This is why a number of these rules have a whiff of the anti-avoidance provision about them.

31.3   The Valuation Rules

Inheritance tax taxes the reduction in value of the transferor's estate caused by a transfer of value. The rules by which the property in your estate is to be valued are therefore very important. 'Property', says IHTA 1984, s. 272, 'includes rights and interests of any description'. Your estate is the aggregate of all the property to which you are beneficially entitled: IHTA 1984, s. 5(1). There is an important difference between lifetime transfers and transfers on death in this respect, since your estate for the purposes of a *transfer on death* does not include 'excluded property'. The scope of the term 'excluded property' is discussed in **27.3.1.1**. An interest in property passing under the survivorship principle also forms part of your estate for the purposes of a transfer on death by virtue of the rule in IHTA 1984, s. 4(1): see **27.6.1**, **29.3.2**. If property is subject to a liability, e.g. a mortgage, the liability will reduce the value of the property only if it was incurred for money or money's worth, or imposed by law: IHTA 1984, s. 5(5).

Since your estate only comprises property to which you are *beneficially* entitled, it does not include property the title to which you hold in a fiduciary capacity. Thus, if you had a capacity as a trustee or PR, your estate would not include the trust or estate property, except in one situation covered by IHTA 1984, s. 5(2). This is where, usually as a trustee, you have a general power of appointment over the property you hold in your fiduciary capacity. A *general* power of appointment, as opposed to a *special* power of appointment, allows you to appoint the property to yourself.

31.3.1 LIFETIME TRANSFERS

The general IHT valuation rule is in IHTA 1984, s. 160:

> Except as otherwise provided by this Act, the value at any time of any property shall for the purposes of this Act be the price which the property might reasonably be expected to fetch if sold in the open market at that time; but that price shall not be assumed to be reduced on the ground that the whole property is to be placed on the market at one and the same time.

Certain situations have given rise to special rules, where the general rule would produce a fiscally undesirable result. For instance, there are special rules for valuing life assurance policies, in the event that the benefit of them is transferred during the lifetime of the assured: IHTA 1984, s. 167. Other special rules, designed to deal with particular situations, are as follows.

31.3.1.1 Where property has no true open market value

This might be the case if there are restrictions on the sale of the property. The most obvious example of property subject to such restrictions would be that of shares in a private company. Since the shareholders will generally wish to keep the ownership of the company in the hands of a fairly small group of people, the articles of association will impose restrictions on the transfer of the shares: see **2.4.1.2**. In this situation, one cannot sensibly speak about an 'open market' in the shares. Or so you might have thought.

The principle to be applied in this situation is designated the *Crossman* principle. The *Crossman* principle comes from *IRC* v *Crossman* [1936] 1 All ER 762. It states that the value of shares subject to restrictions on transfer is to be taken to be, in the words of Viscount Hailsham LC:

> . . . estimated at the price which they would fetch if sold in the open market on the terms that the purchaser should be entitled to be registered as holder of the shares and should take and hold them subject to the articles of association, including the articles relating to alienation and transfer.

The *Crossman* principle has since been applied, e.g., in *Alexander* v *IRC* [1991] STC 112, and in *Baird's Executors* v *IRC* [1991] 1 EGLR 201: see *Cases and Materials* (**31.1.1**). In *Baird's Executors* v *IRC*, the *Crossman* principle was also held to apply for valuing an agricultural tenancy which the tenant farmer was forbidden from assigning.

The valuation of shareholdings in private companies is a specialised business, particularly where a shareholding has been transferred on death: below. It is understood that the Revenue uses the *net asset value* of a company as its *starting-point*, where a majority shareholding or an otherwise substantial shareholding is under consideration. If the shareholding is a substantial minority one, then there is a discount on this of between 10 and 15%.

Read the extract from Barlow, King and King, *Wills, Administration and Taxation*, at *Cases and Materials* (31.1.1). Consider whether the valuation of unquoted shareholdings is a highly theoretical or highly pragmatic process.

Less cunning is called for in valuing shareholdings in *quoted* companies. Quoted companies are those whose shares are quoted on a recognised stock exchange: IHTA 1984, s. 272. In relation to quoted companies, shares are valued as the lower of their *mid-price valuation* and their *quarter-up* valuation on the relevant day. The relevant day is either the day on which the deceased died or, if the death was in the night, the last or next trading day before or after the death. The *mid-price valuation* works like this. You take the figure which is mid-way between the highest and the lowest prices at which the shares were sold on the relevant day. The *quarter-up valuation* works by taking the lesser of the two prices given in the Stock Exchange *Daily Official List* for the relevant day. You then add to the lesser figure ¼ of the difference between the lesser and greater figure.

The valuation for a single ordinary 25p share in British Telecommunications plc from the London Stock Exchange *Daily Official List* for Thursday, 2 April 1998 was:

p663–668

On a separate sheet of paper work out the mid-price valuation of a single BT ordinary share on 2 April 1998, followed by the quarter-up valuation of that share. Then calculate what the IHT valuation for 100 such shares would be, for an individual dying on 2 April 1998.

31.3.1.2   The property might be 'related' to other property

Two or more items of property in a set might be worth less if sold separately than they would have been worth if sold together. If such items of property qualify as *related property*, within IHTA 1984, s. 161, they can each be valued at an appropriate proportion *of their total value*. The main situation where property in one person's estate will be treated as *related* to property in another person's estate is in relation to the estates of married couples. This particular variation on the open market rule is very much on the boundary of valuation and anti-avoidance: see **Chapter 33**.

David and Michal, a married couple, are equal shareholders in their private trading company. They each own 40% of the issued share capital, whilst the remaining 20% is owned by their son, Jonathan. Individually, David and Michal's shareholdings are worth £250,000. The total value of their combined 80% shareholding, however, is £1.5 million. How will each of their shareholdings be valued for IHT purposes?

By taking half of their *total value*, i.e. £750,000, rather than half their value individually, i.e. £250,000.

31.3.1.3   One co-owner might still be entitled to live in the property if the share of the other was sold

This situation will arise where, say, there are two co-owners of real property, holding as tenants in common, and one of them transfers his or her interest under the new-style trust of land to a third party: see **27.4**. The valuation of the interest transferred will need to take account of the fact that the third party would have to live in the property, or share it in some other way, with the remaining co-owner. That is why the valuation of the share of one co-owner may not be the full 50%: *Wight* v *IRC* [1984] RVR 163.

31.3.2   TRANSFERS ON DEATH

All of the points discussed in **31.3.1** apply equally to the valuation of property transferred on death. As mentioned above, liabilities can be deducted from the value of an individual's estate only if they were incurred for money or money's worth, or imposed by law: IHTA 1984, s. 5(5). The Finance Act 1986, s. 103 contains provisions designed to prevent givers reducing the value transferred on the deemed transfer on death by borrowing back from the recipients.

A few other points also need to be made:

31.3.2.1   Relationship between IHT valuation and PRs' CGT acquisition cost

The IHT valuation of property in the deceased's estate, determined either on the basis of IHTA 1984, s. 160, or according to one of the exceptions mentioned above, will usually form the base cost of that property for CGT purposes: see **27.6.2**.

31.3.2.2   The dangers of *lotting*

The Revenue may seek to *lot together* interests in property, on the basis that they are worth more lotted together than they would have been separately. In *IRC* v *Gray* [1994] STC 360, also known as *Lady Fox's Executors* v *IRC*, that was the argument put forward by the Revenue on the following facts. The Revenue won the argument, even though what was lotted together was very strange property indeed!

In life, Lady Fox had been one of three partners, who had together farmed freehold land owned by her. The land was let to the partnership under tenancy agreements made between herself, as landlord, on the one hand, and the two other partners plus herself, as the third partner, on the other. Under the partnership agreement, she was entitled to 92.5% of the profits, but she was also to bear most of any losses made. The Revenue argued that her interest in the partnership should be 'lotted' with her interest as landlord, even though the total was not what might be called a natural unit of property. Needless to say, the property thus 'lotted' had a much greater value than it did in its component elements. The Revenue's argument was rejected by the Lands Tribunal, but accepted by the Court of Appeal.

ACTIVITY 80

Read the extract from the judgment of Hoffmann LJ in *IRC* v *Gray*, at *Cases and Materials* (31.1.2). Then read the extract which follows it from the article by Jeremy de Souza. Note any arguments you can think of in favour of the decision in *IRC* v *Gray*, and any arguments you can think of against it.

31.3.2.3 Substituting actual sale proceeds for values worked out on death

There is provision for the situation where, when PRs sell property for less than the value at which it was valued for IHT purposes, the sale proceeds can be *substituted for* that valuation. There is a procedure for doing this, which involves the PRs in making an election. The possible substitution only applies in two situations. First, where *quoted shares or securities* are sold by the PRs not more than 12 months after the death (IHTA 1984, s. 178) and, secondly, where *land* is sold by the PRs not more than four years after the death: IHTA 1984, s. 190. If you are a PR and you are selling property of either type within the time relevant time period, you will have to make sure that the sale does not take place too late for the relief to apply: *Jones (Ball's Administrators)* v *IRC* [1997] STC 358.

31.3.2.4 Reasonable funeral expenses

These can be deducted from the value transferred immediately before death: IHTA 1984, s. 172. SP 7/87 says:

> The [Revenue] take the view that the term 'funeral expenses' in IHTA 1984, s. 172 allows a deduction from the value of a deceased's estate for the cost of a tombstone or gravestone.

31.4 Calculating IHT on transfers in connection with settlements

We need to move our attention away from lifetime transfers and death transfers, and to complete our study of IHT calculations by considering the calculations necessary for transfers in connection with settlements. That said, the valuation rules discussed above apply here also. Before reading any further, you will find it helpful to reread **28.4.2.2**, and **29.4.2.3**. In **28.4.2.2** we discussed the appointment of settled property to beneficiaries, in the context of a settlement lacking an interest in possession. In **29.4.2.3** we discussed the 10-yearly IHT charge on settlements lacking an interest in possession. This section is only about settlements lacking an interest in possession. **31.4.1** describes the calculation of the 10-yearly charge. **31.4.2** describes the IHT on the appointment of settled property. These calculations are *not* applicable to an accumulation and maintenance settlement, so long as it continues to satisfy the conditions in **27.4.2.3**. Exit charges can, however, arise even in relation to an accumulation and maintenance settlement, where any of four specified events occurs: IHTA 1984, ss. 70(6), 71(3) and 71(5). In addition, the rules in **29.4.2.3** apply once the 25-year period has expired.

31.4.1 CALCULATING THE 10-YEARLY CHARGE

Refer to the discussion of the 10-yearly charge in **29.4.2.3**, concentrating on the discussion of IHTA 1984, s. 64. In this book, we are only concerned with settlements made on or after 27 March 1974. The stages described below are designed to achieve the following result. Immediately before each 10-yearly anniversary of the settlement's creation, there is a notional (i.e. imaginary) chargeable transfer of the *relevant property* comprised in the settlement at that time. It is as though the settlement *has itself made a chargeable transfer of the relevant property*, as a person with a notional gross cumulative total consisting of the items specified in IHTA 1984: see **30.3.1.2**. Inheritance tax is then calculated on the notional chargeable transfer at a so-called *effective rate*, and charged at $^3/_{10} \times$ that rate: IHTA 1984, s. 66(1). The result is a very artificial imitation of the pattern of IHT charges on the automatic transfers which occur over the life of a settlement which *does* have an interest in possession: see **29.4.2**.

There are five Stages to the calculation. As always, you must know the correct order in which they unfold.

Stage One is to add together two possible amounts, in order to find the *notional gross cumulative total*. These two possible amounts are:

(a)   the settlor's total values transferred by chargeable transfers in the period of seven years ending with *the date the settled property was first transferred into the settlement*. Any other chargeable transfers on the same day as the day the settled property was first transferred into the settlement are ignored; *and*

(b)   the total of the amounts which have been subject to so-called *exit charges* in the *ten* years ending with the tenth anniversary of the settlement's creation: see **31.4.2**.

Thus, as the trustee of a settlement lacking an interest in possession, the first stage in calculating your 10-yearly IHT charge would be:

	£
Total values transferred by settlor	X
Plus Amounts subject to exit charges	X
Notional gross cumulative total	X

SAQ 432

Imagine it is 1 November 1998. Sally transferred her shareholding of 2,000 ordinary shares in Utopia plc, a quoted company, to the trustees of the Sally 1988 Discretionary Settlement on 1 November 1988. There is still, on 1 November 1998, no interest in possession in any part of the settled fund (see 27.4.2). At the time of the 1988 transfer, the shareholding was worth £400,000. As the only property comprised in the settlement, the shareholding is worth £900,000 on 1 November 1998. There has been no occasion of charge to IHT since 1988: see 29.4.2.3. On 1 July 1984, Sally made a transfer immediately chargeable to IHT of £60,000, which was a gross gift: see 30.3.2.

What is Sally's notional gross cumulative total on 1 November 1998?

	£
Total values transferred by settlor	60,000
Plus Amounts subject to exit charges	NIL
Notional gross cumulative total	60,000

Stage Two is to add together three possible amounts, in order to find the *amount of the notional chargeable transfer*. These three possible amounts are:

(a)   the value of relevant property in the settlement on the date of the 10-year anniversary in question; *and*

(b)   the value of any property in the settlement which is not relevant property. The value of any such non-relevant property is taken to be its value when it was first put into settlement; *and*

(c)   the value of the settled property in any *related settlement*. The value of any such property is again taken to be its value when it was first put into settlement. A *related settlement* is one with the same settlor, and which began on the same day: IHTA 1984, s. 62.

Non-relevant property would be any part of the settled property in which an interest in possession has arisen.

Thus, the second stage of your 10-yearly IHT charge calculation would be:

	£
Value of relevant property in settlement	X
Plus: Value of non-relevant property in settlement	X
Plus: Value of property in any related settlement	X
Amount of the notional chargeable transfer	X

Continuing the example in SAQ 432. What is the amount of the notional chargeable transfer on 1 November 1998?

	£
Value of relevant property in settlement	900,000
Plus: Value of non-relevant property in settlement	NIL
Plus: Value of property in any related settlement	NIL
Amount of the notional chargeable transfer	900,000

Stage Three is to calculate the IHT at 20% which an individual would have had to pay, if they had the cumulative total calculated in *Stage One* and made a chargeable transfer of the amount of the notional chargeable transfer calculated in *Stage Two*.

To do this, you add together the figure produced in each of *Stage One* and *Stage Two*. You then calculate IHT at 20% on the resulting figure, taking into account whatever is left of the settlor's nil rate band of £223,000.

Thus, the third stage of your 10-yearly IHT charge calculation would be:

	£
Notional gross cumulative total	X
Plus: Amount of notional chargeable transfer	X
IHT at 20%	X

Continuing the example in SAQ 433. What is the IHT at 20% on the total of *Stages One* and *Two*?

	£
Notional gross cumulative total	60,000
Plus: Amount of notional chargeable transfer	900,000
Total	960,000
IHT at 20% [i.e. 20/100 × (£960,000 − £223,000)]	147,400

Stage Four is to calculate the *effective rate* of IHT.

To do this, you state the IHT calculated in *Stage Three* as a percentage of the amount of the notional chargeable transfer. Thus, the fourth stage of your 10-yearly IHT charge calculation would be:

$$\text{Effective rate of IHT} = \frac{\text{IHT at 20\%}}{\text{Amount of notional chargeable transfer}} \times 100 = \underline{X\%}$$

SAQ 435

Continuing the example in SAQ 434, what is the effective rate of IHT?

$$\text{Effective rate of IHT} = \frac{147,400}{900,000} \times 100 = 16.38\%$$

Stage Five is to calculate the rate of the 10-yearly charge by calculating 30% (or $^3/_{10}$) of the effective rate of IHT. The IHT payable is the resultant percentage of the relevant property. Thus, the fifth stage of your 10-yearly IHT charge calculation would be:

Rate of 10-yearly charge = 30% × Effective rate of IHT = X%
IHT payable   = X% × Value of relevant property

SAQ 436

Continuing the example in SAQ 435, what is the IHT payable?

Rate of 10-yearly charge = 30% ×   16.38 = 4.91%
IHT payable   = 4.91% × £900,000 = £44,190

This is the end of the calculation. Joining the stages together, you get the following:

	£
Total values transferred by settlor	X
Plus Amounts subject to an exit charge	X
Imaginary gross cumulative total	X
Value of relevant property in settlement	X
Plus: Value of non-relevant property in settlement	X
Plus: Value of property in any related settlement	X

Amount of the notional chargeable transfer   X

Imaginary gross cumulative total   X
Plus: Amount of notional chargeable transfer   X

IHT at 20%   X

Effective rate of IHT $= \dfrac{\text{IHT at 20\%}}{\text{Amount of notional chargeable transfer}} \times 100 = $ X%

Rate of 10-yearly charge $= 30\% \times$ Effective rate of IHT $=$ X%
IHT payable $=$ X% $\times$ Value of relevant property

Note that the IHT payable could be reduced, possibly even to nil, by *business property relief* or *agricultural property relief*: see **32.6.1**.

31.4.2 CALCULATING AN IHT CHARGE ON APPOINTMENT OF SETTLED PROPERTY

There is a 10-yearly IHT charge, calculated as above, on each 10-yearly anniversary of the creation of the settlement. However, as described in **28.4.2.2**, it may also be necessary for trustees to calculate their IHT liability when they appoint settled property to one or more of the class of beneficiaries. Remember that, so long as a settlement satisfies the definition of an *accumulation and maintenance settlement*, it should suffer no IHT on the appointment of settled property to beneficiaries: see **28.4.2.2**.

31.4.2.1 Before the first 10-yearly charge

The Stages described below are designed to calculate the so-called *exit charge* when all or part of the settled property is appointed by the trustees to a beneficiary or beneficiaries, *before* the first 10-yearly IHT charge. The calculation is different if the appointment is made *between* 10-yearly charges. In the same way as for the 10-yearly charge, IHT is calculated at a so-called *effective rate* on a notional chargeable transfer. It is then charged at $^3/_{10} \times$ the effective rate, on the reduction in the value of the settled fund caused by the nominal transfer in favour of the beneficiary: see **28.4.2.2**. There are seven stages to the calculation. As ever, you must know the correct order in which they unfold.

Stage One is to find the settlor's total values transferred by chargeable transfers in the period of seven years ending with the date the settled property was *first transferred* into the settlement. Any other chargeable transfers on the same day as the day the settled property was first transferred into the settlement are ignored. Thus, the first stage of your IHT calculation on the appointment of settled property before the first 10-yearly charge would be:

	£
Total values transferred by settlor	X
Notional gross cumulative total	X

SAQ 437

Imagine different facts from those in SAQ 432. Suppose Sally transferred her shareholding of 2,000 ordinary shares in Utopia plc to the trustees of the Sally 1996 Discretionary Settlement, on 30 September 1996. On 30 September 1998, an interest in possession in part of the settled fund is created, the trustees making a nominal transfer of 1,000 of the shares to one of the class of beneficiaries. The beneficiary is to assume the burden of the IHT. At the time of the 1996 transfer, the shareholding was worth £400,000. 1,000 of the shares are worth £450,000 on 30 September 1998. On 1 July 1994, Sally made a transfer immediately chargeable to IHT of £60,000, which was a gross gift. What is the notional gross cumulative total on 30 September 1998?

	£
Total values transferred by settlor	60,000
Notional gross cumulative total	60,000

Stage Two is to add together three possible amounts, in order to find the *amount of the notional chargeable transfer*. These three possible amounts are:

(a) the value of relevant property in the settlement when property was first transferred to the trustees of the settlement; *and*

(b) the value of any property added to the settlement since property was first transferred to the trustees of the settlement. The value of any such added property is taken to be its value when it was added to the settled fund;

(c) the value of the settled property in any *related settlement*. The value of any such property is again taken to be its value when it was first put into settlement: see **31.4.1**.

The value of any property in a related settlement is taken to be its value when the related settlement was set up: IHTA 1984, s. 68(5). Thus, the second stage of your IHT calculation on the appointment of settled property before the first 10-yearly charge would be:

	£
Value of relevant property in settlement	X
Plus: Value of property added to the settlement	X
Plus: Value of property in any related settlement	X
Amount of the notional chargeable transfer	X

SAQ 438

Continuing the example in SAQ 437. What is the amount of the notional transfer on 1 November 1998?

	£
Value of relevant property in settlement	400,000
Plus: Value of non-relevant property in settlement	NIL
Plus: Value of property in any related settlement	NIL
Amount of notional chargeable transfer	400,000

Stage Three is to calculate the IHT at 20% which an individual would have had to pay, if they had the cumulative total calculated in *Stage One* and made a chargeable transfer of the amount of the notional chargeable transfer calculated in *Stage Two*. To do this, you add together the figure produced in each of *Stage One* and *Stage Two*. You then calculate IHT at 20% on the resulting figure, *taking into account the nil rate band of £223,000*. Thus, the third stage of your IHT calculation on the appointment of settled property before the first 10-yearly charge would be:

	£
Notional gross cumulative total	X
Plus: Amount of notional chargeable transfer	X
IHT at 20%	X

SAQ 439

Continuing the example in SAQ 438, what is the IHT at 20% on the total of *Stages One* and *Two*?

	£
Notional gross cumulative total	60,000
Plus: Amount of notional chargeable transfer	400,000
Total	460,000
IHT at 20% [*i.e.* 20/100 × (£460,000 − £223,000)]	47,400

Stage Four is to calculate the *average rate* of IHT. To do this, you state the IHT calculated in *Stage Three* as a percentage of the amount of the notional chargeable transfer. Thus, the fourth stage of your IHT calculation on the appointment of settled property before the first 10-yearly charge would be:

$$\text{Average rate of IHT} = \frac{\text{IHT at 20\%}}{\text{Amount of notional chargeable transfer}} \times 100 = \underline{X}\%$$

SAQ 440

Continuing the example in SAQ 439, what is the average rate of IHT?

Average rate of IHT $= \dfrac{47,400}{400,000} \times 100 = 11.85\%$

Stage Five is to calculate the *settlement rate* on the appointment of the property, by calculating 30% of the average rate of IHT. Thus, the fifth stage of your calculation would be:

Settlement rate $= 30\% \times$ Average rate of IHT $= X\%$

Continuing the example in SAQ 440, what is the settlement rate?

Settlement rate $= 30\% \times 11.85\% = 3.56\%$

Stage Six is to calculate the *effective rate* of IHT. This is done by taking a proportion of the settlement rate. That proportion of the settlement rate is $^1/_{40}$ of the settlement rate calculated in *Stage Five* for each *complete* period of three months (i.e. for each quarter) that has elapsed from the date the settlement was created, to the date of the nominal transfer (i.e. the appointment) in favour of the beneficiary. The sixth stage of your calculation would therefore be:

Effective rate $= 3.56\% \times \dfrac{\text{Number of quarters from creation to charge}}{40}$

Continuing the example in SAQ 441, what is the effective rate of IHT?

Effective rate $= 3.56\% \times \,^8/_{40}$
$\qquad\qquad = 0.007\%$

Stage Seven is to calculate the IHT payable, by multiplying the effective rate in Stage Six by the reduction in the value of the settled fund caused by the nominal transfer in favour of the beneficiary, i.e. by the appointment in the beneficiary's favour. The seventh stage of your calculation would therefore be:

IHT payable $= 0.007\% \times$ Reduction in value of settled fund caused by transfer

Continuing the example in SAQ 442, what is the IHT payable?

IHT payable $= 0.007\% \times £450,000$
$\qquad\qquad = £31.50.$

This is the end of the calculation. Joining the seven Stages together, you get the following:

	£
Total values transferred by settlor	X
Notional gross cumulative total	X
Value of relevant property in settlement	X
Plus: Value of property added to the settlement	X
Plus: Value of property in any related settlement	X
Amount of the notional chargeable transfer	X
Notional gross cumulative total	X
Plus: Amount of notional chargeable transfer	X
IHT at 20%	X

$$\text{Average rate of IHT} = \frac{\text{IHT at 20\%}}{\text{Amount of notional chargeable transfer}} \times 100 = X\%$$

Settlement rate = X% × Average rate of IHT = X%

$$\text{Effective rate} = X\% \times \frac{\text{Number of quarters from creation to charge}}{40}$$

IHT payable = X% × Reduction in value of settled fund caused by transfer

As in **31.4.1**, the IHT payable could be reduced, possibly even to nil, if *business property relief* or *agricultural property relief* is available: see **32.6.2**.

31.4.2.2 Between 10-yearly charges

Finally, we need to consider the stages involved in calculating the exit charge when all or part of the settled property is appointed by the trustees to a beneficiary or beneficiaries, *after* the first 10-yearly IHT charge. In fact, this calculation would take the same format on any charge between 10-yearly charges, after the first 10-yearly charge. The percentage at which IHT is charged is a fraction of the resultant percentage calculated in *Stage Five* of the calculation of the 10-yearly charge: see **31.4.1**, *Stage Five*. By IHTA 1984, s. 69, that fraction is $^1/_{40}$ for each complete period of three months from the date of the last 10-yearly charge to the date of the nominal transfer to the beneficiaries *after* the 10-yearly charge. The IHT payable is that fraction, multiplied by the reduction in the value of the settled fund caused by the nominal transfer in favour of the beneficiary. If the appointment is made within the first three months after the 10-yearly charge, there is no exit charge.

 SAQ 444

Eighteen months, i.e. six quarters, after the 10-yearly charge calculated in SAQs 432 to 436, shares worth £100,000 are appointed by the trustees of the Sally 1988 Discretionary Settlement to one of the beneficiaries of the settlement. The beneficiary assumes the burden of the IHT.

What is the IHT payable on the appointment?

£736.50, i.e. £100,000 × 4.91% × 6/40.

As in **31.4.1** and **31.4.2.1**, the IHT payable could be reduced, possibly even to nil, if *business property relief* or *agricultural property relief* is available: see **32.6.2**.

31.5 Summary

As a general rule, the value of property for IHT purposes is the price which it might reasonably be expected to fetch if sold in the open market. Property includes rights and interests of any description, and your estate is the aggregate of all the property to which you are beneficially entitled. Excluded property, e.g. reversionary interests, is so called because it does not form part of your estate for the purposes of a transfer on death. Interests under joint tenancies do form part of your estate, however. Liabilities reduce the value of your estate if imposed by law or incurred for money or money's worth. Special rules apply where property has no true open market value, where it is related to other property, and where it is co-owned. For transfers on death, the Revenue may 'lot' certain types of property, occasionally the actual sale proceeds may be substituted by the PRs for the values worked out at death, and reasonable funeral expenses may be deducted from the value transferred. There are two separate calculations for transfers in connection with settlements, i.e. the calculation of the 10-yearly charge, and the calculation of IHT on the appointment of settled property. The latter differs according to whether the appointment is made before the first 10-yearly charge, or after it.

31.6　End of Chapter Assessment Question

Alice, who died aged 75 on 20 June 1998, had been a successful novelist. At her death, she had a bank account containing royalties of £78,000, for the period from 6 April 1997 to 20 June 1998. She co-owned her freehold house and grounds in Warwickshire, with her husband Arthur, under a joint tenancy. Her executors have valued the house and grounds together at £700,000.

Alice owned a portfolio of shares in quoted companies, i.e. 1,000 ordinary £1 shares in Megabrackets plc, and 2,500 ordinary £1 shares in Utopia plc. On 20 June 1998, the London Stock Exchange quotation for the Megabrackets shares was 220p-280p per share, and the Utopia shares 650p-680p per share. Alice's personal effects were worth £15,000. Alice was the life tenant under a settlement set up by her uncle George in 1950. The value of the whole capital of the settled fund, consisting of debentures, was £10,000 at Alice's death. Net interest was due to her from the trustees of the settlement, as at 20 June 1998, of £800. Funeral expenses, including a tombstone costing £1,500, were £5,000. Other liabilities were:

(a) *General household bills*: outstanding water rates, an electricity bill, outstanding council tax and a gas bill totalling £1,000.

(b) *Outstanding tax*: income tax due from her for 1997/98, and from 5 April 1998 to 20 June 1998, is estimated by her PRs at £16,000.

Under her will, Alice bequeathed legacies of £5,000 to each of three nephews, her personal effects and shares in Utopia plc to her husband, Arthur, and the residue to her son Alan, 40, absolutely.

Calculate the IHT liability, if any, on Alice's death, on the assumption that she made no lifetime transfers. Do not calculate the estate rate. (You may need to refer to **30.5.5**, to get started.)

(100 marks.)

See *Cases and Materials* (**31.3**) for a specimen answer.

CHAPTER THIRTY-TWO

REDUCING THE TAXATION OF GRATUITOUS TRANSFERS

32.1 Objectives

By the end of this chapter, you should be able to:

■ for CGT hold-over relief, state *which persons are affected* by the relief;

■ state what the *effect* of CGT hold-over relief is;

■ list the *conditions* to be satisfied for CGT hold-over relief to be available;

■ identify some *problem areas* with CGT hold-over relief;

■ for each exemption or relief from IHT, state *which persons are affected* by the exemption or relief in question;

■ state what the *effect* of the IHT exemption or relief in question is;

■ list the *conditions* for qualifying for the IHT exemption or relief in question;

■ identify possible *problem areas* with the IHT exemption or relief in question.

32.2 Introduction

For the first part of this chapter, we return to CGT, having devoted our attention almost entirely to IHT, since the end of **Chapter 29**. By way of introduction to **32.3**, you may wish to skim-read **Chapter 27**. If you do this, you will remind yourself of a very important point. That point is that, if you make a gift of a chargeable asset, you will be deemed to have received its market value in return. Without more, that rule would be a major deterrent to giving away property of considerable value. As it is, however, hold-over relief from CGT enables the deemed gain to be postponed, and the CGT exemptions and reliefs in **Chapters 22** and **23** apply where appropriate. In this chapter, we discuss CGT hold-over relief, and IHT exemptions and reliefs for the first time. The latter operate in different ways. As you consider each one, note very carefully how it is designed to work. For instance, one might make what would otherwise be a chargeable transfer into an exempt transfer. Others might reduce the amount of IHT payable on the transfer. It all depends on how the exemption or relief is designed to work. It is usual to refer to provisions which turn chargeable transfers into exempt transfers as *exemptions*, whilst referring to provisions which reduce the amount of IHT payable as *reliefs*. In addition, some provisions apply to lifetime transfers or transfers on death only, whilst others apply to both. For this reason, the threefold subdivision of gratuitous transfers into lifetime transfers, transfers on death and transfers in connection with settlements has been retained for this chapter.

32.3   Lifetime Transfers

32.3.1   CAPITAL GAINS TAX HOLD-OVER RELIEF

32.3.1.1   Persons affected

Hold-over relief is relevant to a gift by you of any chargeable asset, where the gift does not rank as a PET for IHT purposes: see **26.5.1.4**. It is also relevant to a gift by you of business assets. If what you are giving away is not a business asset, then hold-over relief will be relevant only where you are making a gift on trust to the trustees of a discretionary trust. It is generally relevant, however, when you sell property at an undervalue: see **27.5.3**. Hold-over relief is not relevant to a gift by a company. Given the deterrent effect of corporation tax on chargeable gains, in relation to gifts by companies, this is not surprising: see **27.3.2.3**.

32.3.1.2   Effect of hold-over relief on gifts

(1)   Gifts immediately chargeable to IHT: TCGA 1992, s. 260
Hold-over relief on gifts immediately chargeable to IHT works by postponing the CGT which would otherwise be payable on the disposal: see **23.5.1**. The postponement is effected by TCGA 1992, s. 260(3). This states that:

> Where this subsection applies in relation to a disposal—
>   (a)   the amount of any chargeable gain which, apart from this section, would accrue to the transferor on the disposal, and
>   (b)   the amount of the consideration for which, apart from this section, the transferee would be regarded for the purposes of capital gains tax as having acquired the asset in question,
> shall each be reduced by an amount equal to the held-over gain on the disposal.

Section 260(3) means that CGT which would otherwise be due on the gift of the asset is indefinitely postponed.

SAQ 445

Sam owns all of the shares in his personal trading company. He transfers them to the trustees of a discretionary trust when they are worth £800,000. His base cost for the shares is £200,000. What will be the effect of an election being made under TCGA 1992, s. 260?

Sam's chargeable gain will be reduced by the amount of the held-over gain, to £200,000, i.e. £800,000 – £600,000. The trustees' base cost will also be reduced by the amount of the held-over gain, to £200,000.

Will IHT be immediately chargeable on the gift in SAQ 445?

Yes: see **27.4.2**.

The IHT paid by Sam can be added to the base cost of the shares when the trustees come to dispose of the shares, and their CGT liability needs to be calculated. This is subject to certain restrictions, e.g. it does not have the benefit of the IA.

(2) Gifts of business assets: TCGA 1992, s. 165
Hold-over relief on gifts of business assets works by postponing the CGT which would otherwise be payable on the disposal: see **23.5.1**. The postponement is effected by TCGA 1992, s. 165(4). This states that:

> Where a claim for relief is made under this section in respect of a disposal—
> (a) the amount of any chargeable gain which, apart from this section, would accrue to the transferor on the disposal, and
> (b) the amount of the consideration for which apart from this section, the transferee would be regarded for the purposes of capital gains tax as having acquired the asset or, as the case may be, the shares or securities,
> shall each be reduced by an amount equal to the held-over gain on the disposal.

Section 165(4) means that CGT which would otherwise be due on the gift of the business asset or shares is indefinitely postponed. If the recipient of the asset or shares later themselves give them away, hold-over relief under s. 165 can in turn be claimed by them.

You own all of the shares in your personal trading company. You give them to me when they are worth £300,000. Your base cost for the shares is £100,000. What will be the effect of us jointly making an election under TCGA 1992, s. 165?

Your chargeable gain will be reduced by the amount of the held-over gain, to £100,000, i.e. £300,000 − £200,000. My base cost will also be reduced by the amount of the held-over gain, to £100,000.

Will IHT be immediately chargeable on the gift in SAQ 447?

No I, the recipient, am an individual: see **27.3.1.1**.

That said, if you die within seven years of making the gift, then the IHT paid by you can be added to the base cost of the shares when I come to dispose of them, and my CGT liability needs to be calculated. This is subject to certain restrictions. This IHT does not, as above, have the benefit of the IA.

(3)   Undervalue sales and hold-over relief
Some brief comments are required on the effect of hold-over relief and undervalue sales. We remarked at the end of **27.5.3** that the CGT charge on an undervalue sale can be postponed by claiming hold-over relief. Hold-over relief creates an interesting situation where what is actually paid by the recipient is more than the giver's, i.e. the undervalue seller's, base cost. Take an example. I intentionally sell business assets to my brother Andrew for £17,500, knowing that they are really worth £26,000. The shares have a base cost of £12,500. Assume that hold-over relief applies to the disposal, and ignore the IA. Andrew has paid me £17,500 for the shares. Their base cost is £5,000 less than he has paid me. This means that, even though I am making an undervalue sale, *the sale proceeds exceed my base cost*. In this situation, I cannot hold-over the whole of the deemed profit. Instead, I am restricted to holding-over the *difference* between the open-market value and the amount I was actually paid.

How much would that be in this example?

£8,500. The balance of £5,000 will be a chargeable gain and subject to CGT unless, e.g., the annual exempt amount covers it.

32.3.1.3   Conditions for hold-over relief on gifts

(1)   Gifts immediately chargeable to IHT: TCGA 1992, s. 260
Hold-over relief on gifts immediately chargeable to IHT applies if the following four conditions are satisfied:

(a)   you, the person disposing of the asset, are either an individual or a trustee: TCGA 1992, s. 260(1)(a); *and*

(b)   the recipient of the asset, is either an individual or a trustee: TCGA 1992, s. 260(1)(b); *and*

(c)   the gift is a chargeable transfer for IHT purposes; *and*

(d)   a claim for relief is made by the recipient, as well as you, unless the recipient is a trustee: TCGA, s. 260(1)(c).

The claim must be made, in the prescribed form, not later than five years after 31 January in the tax year after the end of the tax year in which the gift is made: TMA 1970, s. 43.

I am planning to make a gift of freehold office premises to a company in which I am the only shareholder. A chargeable gain of £100,000 would arise under TCGA 1992, s. 17 on the disposal. Is relief under TCGA 1992, s. 260 available?

No (the recipient is a company).

I make a gift to you of an old master oil painting, which has an open market value of £250,000. Is relief under TCGA 1992, s. 260 available?

No. However, the gift counts as a *PET for IHT purposes.*

(2)   Gifts of business assets: TCGA 1992, s. 165
Hold-over relief on gifts of business assets applies if the following three conditions are satisfied:

(a)   you, the giver of the asset, are either an individual or a trustee deemed to be making a disposal on the coming to an end of a settlement: see **28.4.1.1**; *and*

(b)   the asset given away is a business asset, as defined in TCGA 1992, s. 165(2); *and*

(c)   a claim for relief is made by the recipient, as well as by you, unless the recipient is a trustee: TCGA 1992, s. 165(1)(b).

The claim must be made, in the prescribed form, not later than five years after 31 January after the tax year in which the gift is made: TMA 1970, s. 43.

Note that, unlike with TCGA 1992, s. 260, it does not matter whether the recipient is an individual or a company. The definition of a business asset in TCGA 1992, s. 165(2) could include assets which would not qualify as business assets for roll-over relief purposes. Section 165(2) is drafted so as to include any business asset used for the purpose of a trade, profession or vocation carried on by you or your personal company. However, it would also cover your shareholding in a trading company, or a holding company of a trading group, provided that the company in question were an unlisted company, or your personal company. The definition of personal company is the same as for retirement relief: see **23.3.1.3**.

If you, the giver, are a trustee deemed to be disposing of the business asset on the coming to an end of a settlement, three conditions set out above are modified somewhat. Basically, the business of which the asset being given away is a business asset must be carried on by the trustees, or by a beneficiary with an interest in possession in the settled property. If shares are being given away, the company must be unlisted, or the trustees must be able to exercise 25% of the votes at a general meeting of the company.

I am planning to make a gift of a business asset, to a company in which I am the only shareholder. A chargeable gain of £100,000 would arise under TCGA 1992, s. 17 on the disposal. Is relief under TCGA 1992, s. 165 available?

Yes. It does not matter that the recipient is a company.

32.3.1.4   Problem areas with hold-over relief on gifts

(1)   Gifts immediately chargeable to IHT: TCGA 1992, s. 260
The gift might be made in favour of a company. In this situation, relief under TCGA 1992, s. 165 should be available in any event.

(2)   *Gifts of business assets: TCGA 1992, s. 165*

(a)   *You may also be entitled to claim retirement relief*   As the giver, you might satisfy the conditions for retirement relief (see **23.3.1**), as well as those for hold-over relief under TCGA 1992, s. 165. The question naturally arises of how the two reliefs relate to each other. The answer is surprisingly straightforward. As explained in **23.3.1.2**, retirement relief makes some or all of what would otherwise be a chargeable gain into an exempt gain, up to a possible £625,000 of gain. Hold-over relief under TCGA 1992, s. 165 can therefore be claimed in combination with retirement relief. Retirement relief first reduces the chargeable gain. The gain as reduced by retirement relief is then held over under TCGA 1992, s. 165.

I am entitled to retirement relief of £250,000. I give you my shareholding in my personal company, which gives rise to a chargeable gain of £500,000. How much of the gain can be held over, provided we make the joint election required by TCGA 1992, s. 165(1)?

£250,000, i.e. £500,000 − £250,000.

(b)   *The relationship with the annual exempt amount*   As the giver, you might have an unused annual exempt amount (i.e. annual exemption) when you give the business asset away: see **22.4.1**. The question obviously arises of how the annual exemption and hold-over relief under TCGA 1992, s. 165 relate to each other. The annual exemption is deducted from your tapered chargeable gains, at *Stage Nine* of your CGT calculation for the tax year: see **21.4.1**, **22.4.1.2**. Hold-over relief reduces the chargeable gain by the amount of the gain held-over: see **27.4.2.2**. The problem is that there is no chargeable gain to be reduced by the annual exemption. It therefore follows that, as giver, you should not seek to claim hold-over relief under TCGA 1992, s. 165, if your chargeable gain does not exceed the annual exemption. It may even be a good idea not to claim the relief if your chargeable gain only slightly exceeds your annual exemption.

Read the article by Sylvia Elwes, at *Cases and Materials* (32.1.1), and the extract from the judgment of Knox J in *Begg-MacBrearty* v *Stilwell* [1996] 4 All ER 205. Identify the problem raised by the case, and how his Lordship solved it.

32.3.2   INHERITANCE TAX EXEMPTIONS AND RELIEFS

Four exemptions applying to lifetime transfers are considered below. Section 11, IHTA 1984 also exempts various lifetime transfers made for the maintenance of a former spouse, or children of the transferor, although such dispositions made for maintenance are not considered further below.

32.3.2.1   The annual exemption

(1)   *Persons affected*

The annual exemption is available on lifetime transfers made by individuals, including individuals acting in the capacity of partners: IHTA 1984, s.19. It is also available in relation to transfers made in connection with settlements, on the basis discussed in **32.6.1**.

(2) Effect of the annual exemption

The annual exemption exempts from IHT the first £3,000 of transfers of value made in the tax year under consideration: see **4.3.1**. If you make transfers of value in the tax year under consideration which are under £3,000, then s. 19(2) applies. This provides that:

> [T]he amount by which they fall short shall, in relation to the next following [tax] year, be added to the £3,000.

If, however, your transfers of value in that tax year exceed £3,000, then the £3,000 can be deducted from these greater amounts: IHTA 1984, s. 19(3). In this situation, the annual exemption is deducted from transfers made earlier in the tax year under consideration *before* it is deducted from those made later in that tax year. In this context, the relationship between your annual exemption and any PETs made by you is worth a brief discussion. A PET is initially treated as being exempt from IHT. Section 3A, IHTA 1984, which provides for the concept of the PET, is drafted to make transfers *which would otherwise be chargeable transfers* into PETs. A transfer which is wholly covered by the annual exemption would not otherwise be a chargeable transfer, so it cannot logically be a PET. On the other hand, a transfer which is not wholly covered by the annual exemption must be a PET, although only in so far as it exceeds the annual exemption.

(3) Conditions for the annual exemption

For the annual exemption to come into play, it is simply necessary for a transfer of value, or transfers of value, to be made by the transferor.

In 1998/99, I make a gift of £2,500 to my son. Will this be a PET?

No.

In 1998/99, I make another gift to my son, this time of £3,500. Will this be a PET?

No.

32.3.2.2 Small gifts made to any one person

(1) Persons affected

The small gifts exemption is available on lifetime transfers made by individuals, including individuals acting in the capacity of partners: IHTA 1984, s. 20. Unlike the annual exemption, it is not available in relation to transfers made in connection with settlements: see **32.6.1**.

(2) Effect of the small gifts exemption

The small gifts exemption means that you can make an absolute gift of £250 to any one individual in any tax year without the gift eating into your annual exemption.

(3) Conditions for the small gifts exemption

There are a number of conditions which must be satisfied for the small gifts exemption to apply:

(a)   The transfer to which it is sought to apply the exemption must be an absolute gift. The exemption does not apply to a gift into a settlement: see **27.4.1.2**.

(b)   The exemption only applies to absolute gifts of £250 or less.

(4)   Problem area with the small gifts exemption
It is not clear whether the annual exemption (see **32.3.2.1**) can be combined by one individual with the small gifts exemption, in order for one individual to make a gift of £3,250 to another individual, as well as further £250 gifts to any number of other individuals. Some commentators say it can, others not.

ACTIVITY82

Read the extract from the article by David Feldman at *Cases and Materials* **(32.1.2.1) on this topic.**

32.3.2.3   Payments which are normal expenditure out of income

(1)   Persons affected
People who make certain payments out of their income, which are part of their normal expenditure out of that income, make exempt transfers for IHT purposes: IHTA 1984, s. 21. The exemption is available on lifetime transfers made by individuals, including those made by individuals acting in the capacity of partners, but not in relation to transfers made in connection with settlements: see **32.6.1**.

(2)   Effect of the normal expenditure out of income exemption
The exemption under IHTA 1984, s. 21 means that you can make payments which comply with the conditions in the following paragraph, without them eating into your annual exemption.

(3)   Conditions for the exemption to apply
There are a number of conditions which must be satisfied for the exemption to apply:

(a)   the transfer of value must be made as part of your normal expenditure;

(b)   taking one year with another, it must be made out of your income; and

(c)   you must be left with sufficient income to maintain your usual standard of living, after allowing for all transfers of value forming part of your normal expenditure.

In addition, because IHTA 1984 speaks of *expenditure*, it seems plain that only transfers of value involving cash can come within s. 21. The term income has its general tax law meaning: see **3.3, 20.3.2**.

(4)   Problem areas with the normal expenditure out of income exception
Until *Bennett* v *IRC* [1995] STC 54 and, more recently the Special Commissioners' decision of *Nadin* v *IRC* [1997] STC (SCD) 107, it was very unclear what the phrase *normal expenditure* might mean. Some of the doubt has been removed by *Bennett* v *IRC*, but unanswered questions persist. Mrs Bennett was an elderly widow, and she was also the life tenant under an interest in possession trust created by her husband's will. The settled property had historically produced a fairly modest income, roughly about £300 gross per annum. However, in 1987, some of the settled property was sold and reinvested, and the income from the settled property increased dramatically in consequence. Mrs Bennett was a lady whose own needs were modest. She therefore instructed the trustees to continue to pay her £300 per annum, and to pay any surplus income from the settled property to her three sons equally. Before Mrs Bennett's untimely death, less than two

years later, each of the three sons had received large distributions of £9,300 and £60,000. On the basis that a life tenant is treated as owning the whole capital of the settled fund (see **29.4.2.2**), the Revenue contended that the distributions received by the sons were PETs made by Mrs Bennett, as life tenant, which had become chargeable as a result of her death. The sons argued that the payments were instead within IHTA 1984, s. 21. Eventually the issue came before Lightman J for resolution. Surprisingly, perhaps, he held that the payments *were* covered by IHTA 1984, s. 21.

ACTIVITY 83

Read the extract from Lightman J's judgment in *Bennett* v *IRC*, at *Cases and Materials* (**32.1.2.2**). Consider how fortunate Mrs Bennett's estate was.

32.3.2.4 Gifts made in consideration of the recipients' marriage

(1) Persons affected
Parents, grandparents, great-grandparents, even other people, who make either absolute gifts to, or gifts into settlement for the benefit of, donees who are getting married are exempt transfers: IHTA 1984, s. 22. The exemption is available for lifetime transfers made by individuals, as well as being available in relation to transfers made in connection with settlements: see **32.6.1**.

(2) Effect of the exemption
The exemption under IHTA 1984, s. 22 means that you can make payments which comply with the conditions in the following paragraph, without them eating into your annual exemption. Depending on who you are, transfers of value of different amounts are exempt:

■ If you are a parent, a transfer of value of up to £5,000 is exempt.

■ If you are a grandparent or great-grandparent, a transfer of value of up to £2,500 is exempt.

■ If you are not within either category, then up to £1,000 is exempt.

(3) Conditions for the exemption to apply
There are a number of conditions which must be satisfied in order for the exemption to apply:

(a) the gift must take place at the same time as the marriage, or before it, but can only take place afterwards if it is in satisfaction of a prior legal obligation; and

(b) the gift must be made in contemplation of a particular marriage.

SAQ 456

In contemplation of the wedding of their son Jim, and their daughter Alice, each of four parents makes gifts of £5,000 to the couple. How much *in total* can Jim and Alice receive, before the parents eat into their annual exemptions?

£20,000, i.e. £5,000 × 4.

32.4   Transfers on Death

In relation to transfers on death, we are concerned only with IHT exemptions and reliefs.

32.4.1   QUICK SUCCESSION RELIEF

32.4.1.1   Persons affected

Section 141, IHTA 1984 provides relief from IHT where you die less than five years after a chargeable transfer has been made to you. The chargeable transfer might have been made to you by a lifetime transfer, or it might have been made to you by a transfer on death. This is unimportant. It is also unimportant whether you still own the property transferred to you within that five-year period at the time of your death. The relief is also available in relation to transfers in connection with settlements: see **32.6.1**.

32.4.1.2   Effect of quick succession relief

The relief works by reducing the IHT payable on your death, by a certain percentage of any IHT paid on the earlier chargeable transfer. That percentage is 20% for every year which has elapsed between the earlier chargeable transfer, and the transfer on your death. Thus, if you die less than one year after the earlier chargeable transfer to you, the IHT payable on your death is reduced by 100%. Equally, if you die between four and five years after the earlier chargeable transfer, the IHT payable on your death is reduced by 20%.

Lord Blank dies on 1 March 1999. He was left a legacy under the will of his uncle, Cedric, who died on 2 May 1998. Under Cedric's will, the burden of the IHT on the legacy, which was worked out by Cedric's executors at £10,000, was to be borne by Cedric's estate. At what percentage will quick succession relief be available?

100% (i.e. of the IHT attributable to the increase in Lord Blank's estate).

32.4.1.3   Conditions for quick succession relief applying

There are basically only two conditions to be satisfied if some percentage of relief is to be claimed. The first is that a chargeable transfer was made to you less than five years before your death. The second is that some IHT was paid on that transfer.

Horace dies on 1 March 1999, aged 98. His wife Wendy died on 2 September 1994, aged 83, leaving him the whole of her very considerable estate of £1 million. Will quick succession relief be available on Horace's death?

Yes, but it will be 20% x nil, provided that Horace was domiciled in the UK at the time of Wendy's death.

32.4.2   TAPER RELIEF

32.4.2.1   Persons affected

Any individual who dies seven years or less after a PET or a transfer chargeable immediately to IHT.

32.4.2.2   Effect of taper relief

Taper relief applies by reducing the IHT payable on your death. If it applies, there will be an extra stage in each of the calculations discussed in **30.4.2.1** to **30.4.2.3**. In each case, the IHT calculated as payable on the transfer on death will be reduced by a specified percentage. The percentage is 20% for every year between the PET or transfer chargeable immediately to IHT and the transfer on death. At its highest, taper relief is available at 80%, where the earlier transfer was made three but not more than four years before the death. At its lowest, it is available at 20%, where the transfer was made between six and seven years before the death.

32.4.2.3   Conditions for taper relief

You must have made a PET which has become chargeable to IHT, or a transfer immediately chargeable to IHT, more than three but not more than seven years before your death.

32.4.3   WOODLANDS

Under IHTA 1984, ss. 125-130, IHT relief is available for any part of the value transferred by the transfer on your death, which is attributable to property which does not rank as agricultural property, but on which trees are growing.

32.4.4   DEATH ON ACTIVE SERVICE

By IHTA 1984, s. 154, an IHT relief is available for those killed on active service against an enemy. Interestingly, the relief operates by disapplying the IHT charge on the deemed chargeable transfer on death in the circumstances envisaged by s. 154. If, as a soldier, I made a *donatio mortis causa* in your favour, it would in principle be covered by this relief. An ordinary lifetime transfer would not be, however.

32.4.5   VARIATIONS AND DISCLAIMERS

32.4.5.1   Persons affected

When people die, especially if they die intestate, the transfer of their property on death may be highly unsatisfactory from the perspective of their surviving relatives. Some of the survivors may therefore wish to *disclaim* the share they are entitled to receive under the will or on the intestacy, in favour of another surviving relative, or into a settlement. In doing so, they will simply decline to accept the property they were due to receive. Even if they have actually received the property however, they may wish to *vary* the provision under which they received it, by giving it to another survivor. Without special provisions, such disclaimers and variations would be PETs by the varying or disclaiming relatives, or possibly even transfers immediately chargeable to IHT, where their interests are disclaimed in favour of discretionary trusts. To the IHT charge on the transfer on death would be added a possible second charge on the relatives' variation or disclaimer. Section 142, IHTA 1984, is designed to prevent the second charge from arising. Where the value transferred by the chargeable transfer on death is great enough to attract IHT, therefore, the relief provided by s. 142 can affect the legatees under the will or intestacy, as well as the PRs of the deceased individual.

Variations and disclaimers could also be chargeable disposals for CGT purposes, so a complementary relief is afforded by TCGA 1992, s. 62(6). For reasons of space, this is not discussed elsewhere in this book. In addition, the instrument by which the variation or disclaimer is effected is exempted from stamp duty by category M of the Stamp Duty (Exempt Instruments) Regulations 1987 (SI 1987 No. 516): see **28.3.3**. Again, this is not discussed elsewhere in the book. Both CGT and stamp duty exemptions have a certain logic, when you bear in mind that death is not a disposal for CGT purposes, and that a will is exempt from stamp duty.

32.4.5.2 Effect of variations and disclaimers

According to IHTA 1984, where there is a variation or disclaimer under s. 142(1):

> . . . [T]his Act shall apply as if the variation had been effected by the deceased or, as the case may be, the disclaimed benefit had never been conferred.

Inheritance tax is therefore charged as if the variation or disclaimer were originally effected by the deceased's will.

32.4.5.3 Conditions for variations and disclaimers

There are *five* conditions which must be satisfied, for IHTA 1984, s. 142, to apply:

- By IHTA 1984, s. 142(2), the people electing to *vary* the will or intestacy rules must send a written notice of the election to the Revenue, within six months after the date of the instrument effecting the variation.

  The PRs must generally be included in the notice, in the event that the variation results in extra IHT being payable on the transfer on death. However, the PRs do not need to be included in this way, where there are insufficient assets in the estate to pay the additional IHT.

- By s. 142(1), all of the people who benefit, or would benefit, under the variation or disclaimer, must execute the written instrument by which the variation or disclaimer is effected.

- Also by s. 142(1), the variation or disclaimer must take place within *two years* after the deceased's death.

- The variation or disclaimer must not be made for a consideration in money or money's worth: IHTA 1984, s. 142(3).

- The property subject to the variation or disclaimer must not be either:

  (a) An interest under a settlement with an interest in possession: see **27.4.2.1**.

  (b) Property in which the deceased is treated as having reserved a benefit: see **Chapter 33**.

  (IHTA 1984, s. 142(5).)

ACTIVITY 84

Read the note by Barry McCutcheon (*Cases and Materials* (32.2.1)) of five conditions which do *not* need to be satisfied in relation to a deed of variation (!)

32.4.5.4   Problems with variations and disclaimers

One of the decided cases indicates that a problem is likely to arise with IHTA 1984, s. 142, in practice. As a person involved in making a variation or disclaimer, you should note that you only get one chance to get it right. In *Russell* v *IRC* [1988] 2 All ER 405, Knox J upheld the Revenue's argument that it was not possible to rely on IHTA 1984, s. 142, where what had been attempted was a variation of another variation.

Read the extract from Knox J's judgment in *Russell* v *IRC*, at *Cases and Materials* (32.2.1). List the main reasons for the judge's decision. Note why the attempt had been made to vary a variation.

32.5   Lifetime Transfers and Transfers on Death

Bearing in mind that we have discussed CGT hold-over relief, and that death is not a disposal for CGT purposes, it is only necessary for us now to consider three exemptions and reliefs from IHT, which apply both to lifetime transfers and transfers on death.

32.5.1   TRANSFERS BETWEEN SPOUSES

We have already referred to the IHT exemption for transfers between spouses: see **27.7.2**. It is only necessary here to reiterate the point that, if the recipient spouse is not domiciled in the UK, a transfer of value is exempted from IHT only up to £55,000: IHTA 1984, s. 18(2). The application of the spouse exemption to transfers in connection with settlements is discussed in **32.6**.

32.5.2   BUSINESS PROPERTY RELIEF

32.5.2.1   Persons affected

Business property relief (BPR) is relevant to transfers of business property, irrespective of the capacity in which a person may be transferring that property. In essence, it is designed to minimise or eliminate any IHT charge when a person makes a gratuitous transfer of a business. The definition of *relevant business property* used in the legislation is such as to cover most interests in family businesses. It means that a family business can usually be transferred from father to son without any IHT charge. The rationale for the relief is to prevent family businesses from being destroyed by crippling tax charges when they are transferred from one generation to another. More interestingly, the relief applies to remove the IHT charge on transfers in connection with settlements. Provided the settled property is *relevant business property*, as discussed in **32.5.2.3**, a number of consequences follow. In the case of interest in possession settlements, the automatic transfer of the equitable entitlement to the property, on the death of a life tenant, is exempted from IHT by the relief: see **29.4.2.2**. This is particularly valuable, when you consider that the life tenant is treated as owning the whole capital of the settled property. Even for settlements lacking an interest in possession, however, the relief is available to mitigate both the 10-yearly charge and charges on the appointment of settled property: see **31.4.1**, **31.4.2**.

32.5.2.2   Effect of business property relief

Business property relief operates by reducing the value transferred on a transfer of value, where that value is attributable to so-called *relevant business property*. The definition of *relevant business property* is considered in **32.5.2.3**. Section 110(a), IHTA 1984 makes it clear that the percentage reduction is to be applied to the net value of the business, and s. 110(b) states that:

> [T]he net value of a business is the value of the assets used in the business (including goodwill) reduced by the aggregate amount of any liabilities incurred for the purposes of the business.

Depending on which type of relevant business property is involved, the percentage reduction could be 50%, or it could be 100%: IHTA 1984, s. 104(1). It is 50% for the relevant business property in categories (b) and (d) in **32.5.2.3**. It is 100% for the relevant business property in the other two categories. Where only part of the value transferred consists of relevant business property, then BPR can apply to that part: IHTA 1984, s. 104(1). Business property relief takes precedence over other IHT exemptions and reliefs capable of applying to the transfer. The annual exemption, e.g., would still be available for the transferor to use on another chargeable lifetime transfer.

SAQ 459

On 1 April 1998, Sid transfers his shareholding of 100,000 ordinary shares in Bolts and Screws Ltd, an unquoted company, to the trustees of a discretionary trust. The shares are relevant business property within IHTA 1984, s. 105(1)(b): see 32.5.2.3. The gross value of the shareholding on 1 April 1998 is £1,500,000, and liabilities incurred for the purpose of the business are £300,000. What is the value transferred for the purposes of BPR?

£1,200,000.

32.5.2.3   Conditions for business property relief to apply

A number of conditions must be satisfied in order for BPR to apply:

(a) The property transferred must be *relevant business property*, as defined in IHTA 1984, s. 105. The definition of the term is considered below.

(b) The property must not be property of a business which consists ' . . . wholly or mainly of . . . dealing in securities, stocks or shares, land or buildings or making or holding investments': IHTA 1984, s. 105(3).

(c) At the time of the transfer, the property must generally have been owned by the transferor for at least two years. If it has not been owned for this period, it is not relevant business property: IHTA 1984, s. 106.

   That said, a business incorporation, a replacement of property or a transfer of property on the *death* of a spouse, to another, does not interrupt the two-year period: IHTA 1984, s. 108.

(d) The property transferred must *not* be an excepted asset: IHTA 1984, s. 112. Excepted assets are basically those which are not used wholly or mainly for the purpose of the business.

(e) No contract for the sale of the property must be in place, as a general rule, at the time of the transfer: IHTA 1984, s. 113. If such a contract is in place, then the property is generally not relevant business property.

   An exception to (e) is where the sale is to a company to which the business is being transferred, and the consideration for the transfer is wholly or mainly the issue of shares in that company.

SAQ 460

On 2 April 1998, Sam transfers her shareholding of 100,000 ordinary shares in Landlords Ltd, an unquoted company, to the trustees of a discretionary trust. Landlords Ltd owns industrial properties, which are let to tenants. It collects the rents from the properties, but does not carry out any management duties. Is her shareholding in Landlords Ltd relevant business property?

No (see also **Activity 86**).

Some further comments are appropriate on the conditions listed above. Most importantly, we need to consider the definition of *relevant business property*. Section 105, IHTA 1984 currently provides for four categories of relevant business property. The property being transferred must fall into one or other of these categories, in order to qualify for the relief. The categories are as follows:

(a)   If you are a sole trader or partner, property which consists of the business, or an interest in the business. Thus, if you are a sole trader or a partner, your business or your partnership share should be relevant business property: IHTA 1984, s. 105(1)(a).

(b)   If you are a shareholder in a quoted company, the shares are relevant business property if, at the time of the transfer, they gave you *control* of the company: IHTA 1984, s. 105(1)(cc). Control is (IHTA 1984, s. 269(1)):

> . . . control of powers of voting on all questions affecting the company as a whole which if exercised would yield a majority of the votes capable of being exercised on them.

(See also **2.4.1.2**.)

(c)   If you are a shareholder in an unquoted company, then your shareholding is relevant business property if, at the time of the transfer, it gave you control, as above, of the company: IHTA 1984, s. 105(1)(b). The Finance Act 1996 extended this category of relevant business property to any unquoted shareholding in a company: IHTA 1984, s. 105(1)(bb).

(d)   If, as a shareholder or partner, you are the owner of land or buildings, machinery or plant which are used wholly or mainly for the business of the partnership or company, that property is relevant business property. In the case of a company, you must again have control of it, as defined above: IHTA 1984, s. 105(1)(d).

In addition, note that the condition in s. 105(3) (see above) basically means that the business must generally qualify as a trade, other than that of share-dealing, rather than being simply an investment business: see **15.3.2**.

ACTIVITY 86

Read the summaries of *Brown's Executors* v *IRC* [1996] STC (SCD) 277, and *Powell and Another* v *IRC* [1997] Simon's Weekly Tax Intelligence 657 at *Cases and Materials* **(32.3.1)**. Consider what conclusions can be drawn from these decisions of Special Commissioner THK Everett about the nature of the business which must be carried on.

32.5.3　AGRICULTURAL PROPERTY RELIEF

32.5.3.1　Persons affected

Agricultural property relief (APR) is relevant to transfers of agricultural property, irrespective of the capacity in which a person may be transferring that property. In essence, it is designed to eliminate or reduce any IHT charge when a person makes a gratuitous transfer of *agricultural property*. It can therefore be thought of as a farming counterpart to BPR. The relief means that a farm can usually be transferred from father to son without any IHT charge. The rationale for the relief is the same as for BPR, i.e. to prevent farmers from being crippled by IHT charges when farms are transferred from one generation to another. More interestingly, the relief applies to remove the IHT charge on transfers in connection with settlements. Provided the settled property is agricultural property, as discussed below, a number of consequences follow. In the case of interest in possession settlements, the automatic transfer of the equitable entitlement to agricultural property, on the death of a life tenant, is exempted from IHT by APR: see **29.4.2.2**. Again, for settlements without an interest in possession, APR can mitigate both the 10-yearly charge and charges on the appointment of settled property, provided that the trustees themselves farm the land: see **31.4.1**, **31.4.2**.

32.5.3.2　Effect of agricultural property relief

Agricultural property relief operates by reducing the so-called *agricultural value* transferred on a transfer of value of agricultural property. The definition of the term *agricultural property* is considered in **32.5.3.3**. The percentage reduction is to be applied to the *net* agricultural value, and IHTA 1984, s. 115(3) defines the *agricultural value* as:

> [T]he value which would be the value of the property if the property were subject to a perpetual covenant prohibiting its use otherwise than as agricultural property.

The level of the percentage reduction depends on whether your interest, as transferor, carries the right to vacant possession within the following 12 months: IHTA 1984, s. 116. Generally, it is 50% of the agricultural value, where your interest does not carry the right to vacant possession within that period. It is 100% of the agricultural value, where your interest *does* carry the right to vacant possession within that period. Where your interest does *not* carry the right to vacant possession in that period, 100% relief may exceptionally be given if your tenant succeeded to the tenancy after 31 August 1995. In addition, ESC F17 extends IHTA 1984, s. 116 to two further situations. First, where the right to vacant possession arises *only in the following 24 months*. Secondly, where the reversion will be 'lotted' with the tenant's interest, as in *IRC* v *Gray*: see **31.3.2.2**. Agricultural property relief takes precedence over other IHT exemptions and reliefs capable of applying to the transfer. Most importantly, it takes precedence over BPR: IHTA 1984, s. 114(1).

On 1 February 1999, Farmer Giles transfers agricultural property within IHTA 1984, s. 115(2): see 32.5.3.3. The gross value of the property on 1 February 1999 is £1,800,000, and the liabilities to which the property is subject are £800,000. What is the value transferred for the purposes of APR?

£1,000,000.

32.5.3.3　Conditions for agricultural property relief to apply

A number of conditions must be satisfied in order for APR to apply:

(a) The property transferred must be *agricultural property* within IHTA 1984, s. 115(2). The definition of agricultural property is considered below.

(b) At the time of the transfer, the property must either have been:

   (i) *occupied* by the transferor for the purposes of agriculture for the period of two years, ending with the date of the transfer; *or*

   (ii) *owned* by the transferor for the period of seven years, ending with the date of the transfer, and occupied by the transferor or another for the purposes of agriculture, throughout that period.

   That said, a transfer of property on the *death* of one spouse, to the survivor, does not interrupt the time periods running.

(c) No contract for the sale of the property must be in place, as a general rule, at the time of the transfer.

(d) Excess principle value must be excluded, i.e. value because of potential for development: IHTA 1984, s. 115(3).

On 2 April 1999, Sam transfers agricultural property worth £1 million to her son. It has been *occupied* by her for the purposes of agriculture for eighteen months, ending with the date of the transfer. Will the transfer qualify for the relief?

No.

By IHTA 1984, s. 115(2), agricultural property is defined as:

[A]gricultural land or pasture and includes woodland and any building used in connection with the intensive rearing of livestock or fish if the woodland or building is occupied with agricultural land or pasture and the occupation is ancillary to that of the agricultural land or pasture; and also includes such cottages, farm buildings and farmhouses, together with the land occupied with them, as are of a character appropriate to the property.

Milk quotas have already been considered in relation to CGT: see **20.5.1**. Agricultural property which is dairy pasture with the benefit of a milk quota will include the quota itself.

32.6 Transfers in Connection with Settlements

Before concluding this chapter, it is necessary to spend a few moments considering the operation of the exemptions and reliefs discussed above, for transfers in connection with settlements. It is fair to say that most IHT exemptions and reliefs are available in relation to settlements with an interest in possession. By contrast, the range of exemptions and reliefs available when the settlement does not have an interest in possession is very limited.

32.6.1 SETTLEMENTS WITH AN INTEREST IN POSSESSION

The position can briefly be summarised as follows:

32.6.1.1   The IHT annual exemption

A quick reference to **28.4.2.2** will remind you of the position where a beneficiary under an interest in possession settlement becomes absolutely entitled to the settled property *otherwise than* on the death of the life tenant. The life tenant is treated as making a PET for IHT purposes. By IHTA 1984, s. 57(3), the life tenant can elect for the annual exemption to apply to the PET so that, if the life tenant dies within the subsequent seven-year period, the annual exemption can be used to relieve the IHT charge on the transfer on death.

32.6.1.2   The small gifts exemption

Unlike the annual exemption, this is not available in relation to transfers in connection with settlements.

32.6.1.3   Normal expenditure out of income

Like the small gifts exemption, this exemption is not available in relation to transfers in connection with settlements.

32.6.1.4   Gifts made in consideration of the recipients' marriage

This exemption is available in relation to a beneficiary under an interest in possession settlement becoming absolutely entitled to the settled property *otherwise than* on the death of the life tenant. By IHTA 1984, s. 57(3), the life tenant can elect for this exemption to apply to the PET so that, if the life tenant dies within the subsequent seven-year period, the exemption can be used to relieve the IHT charge on the transfer on death, as above.

32.6.1.5   Quick succession relief

The relief applies, not only to the termination of a life interest on the death of the life tenant, but also where the life tenant makes a lifetime transfer of their life interest: IHTA 1984, s. 141.

32.6.1.6   Spouse exemption

The exemption applies where a life interest comes to an end, and the next person entitled to the settled property is the life tenant's spouse: see **29.4.2.2**.

32.6.1.7   Business property relief

As a life tenant, you will be entitled to claim BPR, subject to the conditions in **32.5.2.3**.

32.6.1.8   Agricultural property relief

As a life tenant, you will be entitled to claim APR, subject to the conditions in **32.5.3.3**.

32.6.2   SETTLEMENTS WITHOUT AN INTEREST IN POSSESSION

As mentioned in **32.5** gratuitous transfers of settled property where there is no interest in possession have the benefit of relatively few exemptions and reliefs. Of the exemptions and reliefs listed in **32.6.1**, only BPR and APR are relevant. So far as *BPR* is concerned, provided the settled property is *relevant business property*, the relief is available to mitigate both the 10-yearly charge and charges on the appointment of settled property: see **31.4.1**, **31.4.2**. In relation to *APR*, the relief is available to mitigate both the 10-yearly charge, and charges on the appointment of settled property, provided that the trustees themselves farm the land.

32.7 Summary

We end this chapter by reiterating the profoundly important CGT point emphasised in **32.2**. If you make a gift of a chargeable asset, you will be deemed to have received its market value in return. The hold-over election, whether claimed under TCGA 1992, s. 165 or 260, creates the fiction that the giver has sold the asset in question for an amount equal to its base cost. Equally, the recipient is treated as having acquired the asset at the giver's base cost. In a nutshell, hold-over relief means that the giver makes no gain and no loss, and therefore pays no CGT on the gift. The operation of this relief has to be considered in tandem with the IHT implications of a lifetime transfer. You will have noted the different ways in which IHT exemptions and reliefs operate. This is just as important for lifetime transfers as for transfers on death. As you reread each one, note very carefully how it is designed to work. Note also which provisions apply to lifetime transfers or transfers on death only, and which apply to both. In **Chapter 33**, we complete our study of the taxation of gratuitous transfers by a fairly brief examination of areas of IHT to which we have so far referred only in passing. Those areas are compliance issues and anti-avoidance issues.

32.8   End of Chapter Assessment Questions

Sidney owns 40,000 of the 50,000 ordinary £2 shares in Sidney's Greens Ltd, the company which carries on his family's trade as greengrocers. Sidney has owned his shares since the company was incorporated in 1960. Each share is worth £25. On 1 June 1998, he transfers 60,000 of the shares to Terence and Tom, the trustees of The Sidney 1998 Discretionary Settlement. The settlement deed provides that any IHT is to be borne by the settled property. The gift results in the value of Sidney's retained shares falling to £12 each. On 1 October 1998, Sidney transfers the freehold greengrocer's shop, which is owned by him personally, although used in the business, to his son Sam. The shop is valued at £150,000. Immediately prior to the transfer into the settlement, Sidney had a gross cumulative lifetime total, for IHT purposes, of £300,000. He has made no other transfers, apart from these.

(a) Comment on the IHT and CGT implications of the transfers on 1 June 1998, and 1 October 1998.

(40 marks.)

(b) Calculate the IHT liability, if any, on each transfer on the alternative bases that (a) the IHT is paid by Sidney, and (b) the IHT is borne by the settled property; and

(20 marks.)

(c) Comment on how any additional IHT would be calculated if Sidney died on 1 September 2002, assuming that the shop was transferred on 1 October 1998. Mention any relevant relief.

(40 marks.)

(Word limit: 450.)

See *Cases and Materials* (**32.5**) for a specimen answer.

CHAPTER THIRTY-THREE

TAXATION OF GRATUITOUS TRANSFERS: ANTI-AVOIDANCE ISSUES AND COMPLIANCE

33.1 Objectives

By the end of this chapter, you should be able to:

■ list three IHT anti-avoidance measures;

■ briefly state the rules of compliance for IHT purposes.

33.2 Introduction

Whilst reading the last few chapters, some rather obvious questions might have occurred to you. For instance, how does the Revenue know whether a gift has been made by one individual to another? What would make the Revenue start searching for gifts? The second part of this chapter seeks to answer these questions. It also discusses related points about who is actually responsible for paying IHT, and how the Revenue can go about making sure that they get paid. So far, these are points that we have only touched on. To round matters off, we have a fairly brief discussion of some comparable compliance issues for CGT and IHT purposes. To start with, however, we need to give some consideration to a selection of specific IHT anti-avoidance provisions. The selection includes the most well-known anti-avoidance provisions. That said, always keep in mind that the *Ramsay* principle extends to IHT: see **4.4**. Also, remember that a number of the valuation rules discussed in **31.3** have a whiff of the anti-avoidance provision about them. Bear in mind also that the Government has announced its intention to introduce a general statutory anti-avoidance measure.

33.3 Anti-avoidance Issues

33.3.1 TRYING TO HAVE YOUR CAKE AND EAT IT TOO: GIFTS WITH A RESERVATION

Without special rules, the concept of the PET would provide a splendid IHT-avoidance device. I could give property to you free of IHT by transferring the legal title to it to you whilst continuing to use it for my own benefit. Provided, obviously, that I lived for seven years after making the gift. The *gifts with reservation* rules are designed to frustrate this device. The Finance Act 1986, s. 102(1) applies if you give property away and:

(a)   possession and enjoyment of the property is not bona fide assumed by the [recipient] at or before the beginning of the relevant period; or

(b)   at any time in the relevant period the property is not enjoyed to the entire exclusion, or virtually to the entire exclusion, of the [giver] and of any benefit to him by contract or otherwise.

The relevant period is then defined as the period of seven years before the death of you, the giver. The consequences of a gift falling within this provision are twofold:

■   If, immediately before your death, the property given away is still within s. 102(1), it is treated as property to which you are beneficially entitled immediately before your death: FA 1986, s. 102(3). A quick reread of **31.3.2** should bring home the significance of this to you.

■   If, at some time in the seven-year period, the property given away ceases to fall within the section, you are treated as making a PET at that time: FA 1986, s. 102(4).

Until recently, it was argued that FA 1986, s. 102 could be avoided by what was known as *horizontal severance*, or *horizontal separation*. Instead of giving property away and reserving a benefit, the idea was to *retain* the benefit by not giving it away to begin with! The inspiration for the idea came from a dictum of Lord Simonds in *St Aubyn* v *A-G* [1951] 2 All ER 473:

In the simplest analysis, if A gives to B all his estates in Wiltshire except Blackacre, he does not except Blackacre out of what he has given: he just does not give Blackacre.

The argument was put to the test in *Ingram* v *IRC* [1997] STC 1234. It was rejected by the Court of Appeal, having been accepted by Ferris J at first instance. The argument may be accepted again, however, since then the case has been appealed to the House of Lords, although at the time of writing this appeal has not yet been heard. The giver, Lady Ingram, died in 1989. Almost two years prior to her death, on 29 March 1987, she had made a gift of property on trust to her nominee, i.e. a bare trustee. On 30 March 1987, the nominee had granted Lady Ingram a 20-year lease of the property rent-free, in accordance with Lady Ingram's instructions. Then, on 31 March 1987, he had transferred the property subject to the lease to trustees. The trustees thereupon executed settlement declarations, the beneficiaries of which did *not* include Lady Ingram. Ferris J held that the nominee's grant of the lease to Lady Ingram was totally ineffective. However, the trustees were still bound by an equitable interest in Lady Ingram's favour, which was:

. . . equivalent to that which she thought she had acquired . . . and that interest arose simultaneously with the establishment of the settlement.

On this basis, all Lady Ingram had given away in the first place was the property subject to the lease. Ferris J therefore held that FA 1986, s. 102 did not apply to it.

The Court of Appeal (Millett LJ dissenting) disagreed with Ferris J's conclusion that all Lady Ingram had given away in the first place was the property subject to the lease. In the words of Nourse LJ:

The principal right and interest which Lady Ingram would have had against the trustees was a right to possession of the property. That right mirrored the trustees' obligation to afford her possession. That obligation, just like an obligation to grant her a lease had there been one, was one to which the trustees only became subject when the freehold interest was vested in them. Thus the correlative right or interest in Lady Ingram, just like her interest under a lease had there been one, was . . . a smaller right or interest comprised in the gift itself and part of it.

The Court of Appeal therefore held that Lady Ingram was still beneficially entitled to the property on her death.

ACTIVITY 87

Consider critically the extracts from the *dissenting* judgment of Millett LJ in *Ingram* v *IRC*, at *Cases and Materials* (33.1.1). Make a note of any points which suggest to you that Millett LJ's *technical* analysis may be preferable to that of Nourse LJ.

33.3.2 ASSOCIATED OPERATIONS: ATTEMPTING TO REDUCE THE VALUE TRANSFERRED

In the absence of the special statutory provision in IHTA 1984, s. 268, transferors might be tempted to try something like this. Since IHT is designed to tax the value transferred by a chargeable transfer, how about reducing the value of the property transferred, before making a gratuitous transfer to the recipient? A good example of this type of thing is provided by *IRC* v *Macpherson* [1988] 2 All ER 753: see *Cases and Materials* (33.1.2). In that case, the trustees of a discretionary trust entered into an agreement with an individual who had a connection with one of the beneficiaries. The effect of the agreement was to reduce the value of the settled property, some valuable paintings, by giving them over to the custody of that individual for 14 years. The day after the agreement, the trustees exercised a power of appointment in favour of the individual's son, creating a particular type of life interest in the paintings: see **28.3.2**. The Revenue argued that the two transactions should be viewed together, as *associated operations*. The trustees naturally disagreed, and argued that the initial agreement was protected from an IHT charge by what is now IHTA 1984, s. 10: see **27.3.1.1**. The House of Lords held that IHTA 1984, s. 10 did not apply, and that the two operations *were* associated operations within IHTA 1984, s. 268. Section 268, IHTA 1984 provides that *associated operations* are any two or more operations of any kind, either affecting the same or related property, or income generated by it, or directly or indirectly related to each other. Operations include omissions – they do not need to be carried out by the same person, and it does not matter whether they take place at the same time or not.

ACTIVITY 88

Read the extract from *IRC* v *Macpherson*, at *Cases and Materials* (33.1.2). Note *exactly* what the effect of holding that the two operations were associated *was*. Note also any limits imposed by Lord Jauncey on the scope of s. 268.

When you actually study s. 268, you can tell that it is designed to pick up not only gratuitous transfers which reduce the value transferred, but also those which are designed to reduce the IHT payable. The sheer scope of the section is apparent from the almost impenetrable wording of the *associated operations* definition in s. 268(1) as:

(a)   operations which affect the same property . . .

(b)   any two operations of which one is effected with reference to the other, or with a view to enabling the other to be effected or facilitating its being effected, and any further operation having a like relation to any of those two, and so on,

whether those operations are effected by the same person or different persons, and whether or not they are simultaneous; and 'operation' includes an omission.

Given this convoluted wording, it is surprising that comparatively few reported cases have discussed s. 268. *IRC* v *Macpherson* is one of them. This may suggest that s. 268 actually works in practice, and that it could provide a model for the proposed general anti-avoidance provision mentioned above. Put a wet towel round your head, and read s. 268 very carefully.

33.3.3   CLOSE COMPANIES

We have already encountered close companies, although in the context of income taxation. In fact, you may wish at this stage to skim-read **18.5**, to remind yourself, and to refer briefly to **27.3.1.3** for the context of what follows. Close companies crop up in the context of gratuitous transfers for a particular reason. The reason is that companies are persons, but they are not individuals. In the absence of a special deeming provision, which is actually contained in IHTA 1984, s. 94, it might therefore have been possible for a participator (see **18.5.2**) to put value into a company, and to make further gratuitous transfers of that value through the company, thereby avoiding an IHT charge. In these circumstances, the company makes a transfer of value, which is then apportioned by s. 94 among its participators, in proportion to their rights or interests in the company. Crucially, such deemed transfers of value by the participators cannot be PETs. They are instead transfers chargeable *immediately* to IHT.

Section 98, IHTA 1984 prevents the fulfilment of a similar objective by a participator altering the rights attaching to his or her shareholding in a close company. For instance, I might vote to amend the company's articles of association, by converting my shareholding of ordinary shares into fixed preference shares, carrying a right to dividends, but carrying no voting rights. This situation is likely to be within s. 98 as a *deemed disposition* by me, the participator. The word *disposition* is discussed in **27.3.1.1**. As such, the disposition will again be a transfer chargeable immediately to IHT, rather than a PET. There is a certain overlap with the value-shifting provisions discussed in **25.3.2**.

The issued share capital of Utopia Ltd is £200,000. It is divided up into 200,000 ordinary shares of £1 each. On 1 April 1999, each share is worth £5. There are two shareholders, i.e. participators in Utopia Ltd, the brothers Jack and Jim, each holding 50% of the issued share capital. On 2 April 1999, Jack and Jim vote in favour of a special resolution, by which Jim's shares are converted into preference shares. These preference shares give Jim the right to their nominal value, if the company is wound up, to dividends, but carry no voting rights. Jim's shares fall in value to £2 each.

What is Jim's IHT position?

He is treated as making a transfer chargeable immediately to IHT, equal to the reduction in the value of his estate.

33.4 Compliance

33.4.1 INHERITANCE TAX

33.4.1.1 Liability to pay inheritance tax

If you turn back to **30.4.3.1**, you will recall that we have already considered the question of how the deceased's PRs, in the case of a transfer on death, deal with the question of who is to bear the burden of the IHT. In this section, we need to take a step back, and consider the PRs liability to pay the IHT in the first place. We also need to consider the question of liability to pay IHT in relation to lifetime transfers, and transfers in connection with settlements. These matters, and others, are dealt with in IHTA 1984, ss. 199–214.

(1) Lifetime transfers
There are four categories of people liable to pay the IHT on a lifetime transfer. The first is the obvious one, i.e. transferors and their spouses: IHTA 1984, ss. 199, 203. If this fails, liability is with the transferee, or indeed anyone else for whom the transfer has meant an increase in the value of their estate. Thirdly, it is any person in whom the property is vested or who has an interest in possession in it. Finally, if the property ends up as settled property in a discretionary settlement, any beneficiary who receives income or capital from the settlement.

(2) Transfers on death
There are four categories of people liable to pay the IHT on a transfer on death. The first are the deceased's PRs, except where the property is settled property. They are liable to pay the IHT in respect of all property owned by the deceased at his or her death. Section 204, IHTA 1984 makes it clear that, although the liability to pay the IHT is the personal liability of the trustees, that liability is limited. It is limited to the value of property which was actually received by them, or might have been received by them, but for their neglect or default: IHTA 1984, s. 204(1). Where the property transferred on death is settled property, e.g. where the deceased was a life tenant under a settlement with an interest in possession, liability for IHT is with the trustees of the settlement. The third and fourth categories are as for lifetime transfers.

(3) Transfers in connection with settlements
Again, there are four categories of people who may be liable for IHT on transfers in connection with settlements. Naturally enough, the first persons are the trustees of the settlement. If they are unable to pay, however, the next people are any of those people who are beneficially entitled to an interest in possession in the settled property. If they are unable to pay, then the next people liable for the IHT are any persons for whose benefit settled property or income from settled property has been applied. Finally, in certain circumstances, the settlor can be made liable for the IHT.

On 1 August 1994, the trustees of the settlement discussed in SAQs 432 to 436 lose the settled property by investing badly and thus committing a massive breach of trust. The IHT payable of £44,730 is still unpaid at the moment of the breach. Who is liable to pay the £44,730 in their place?

On the facts, no-one, unless income from the settled property has been applied for the benefit of any of the class of beneficiaries.

33.4.1.2   Transfers on death: duty to deliver an account

This obligation is imposed on PRs by IHTA 1984, s. 216, in the event that the *gross* value of the deceased's estate at death exceeds £180,000. An estate whose gross value does not exceed £180,000 is an *excepted estate*. The duty to deliver an account is a duty to deliver to the Revenue an account of all the property to which deceased individuals were beneficially entitled, or over which they had a general power of appointment, immediately before their death: IHTA 1984, s. 216(3) (see **31.3**). The PRs must compile the account to the best of their knowledge and belief. The account must be delivered to the Revenue not later than 12 months after the end of the month in which the deceased's died. It takes a common form, i.e. on Form 200 or Form 202.

Read the extract from *Re Clore (No. 3)* [1985] 2 All ER 819, at *Cases and Materials* (33.2.1). Imagine that you are someone's PR. Note down what you *must* do, and what you *will not need to do*, in delivering an account 'to the best of your knowledge and belief'.

33.4.1.3   Payment of inheritance tax: lifetime transfers and transfers on death

Payment of IHT is dealt with in IHTA 1984, ss. 226–236. If you refer to back to our discussion of charges on income for income tax purposes, you will see that the interest payable on a *loan* to pay IHT is deductible by PRs as a charge on income: see **9.3.2.4**. It is often necessary for PRs to do this, since they cannot obtain their grant of representation (i.e. probate, letters of administration, etc.), without paying the IHT first. Note the types of property on which PRs are permitted to pay IHT in *instalments*, and the *circumstances* in which IHT can be so paid: IHTA 1984, ss. 227, 228. Where IHT is attributable to land, or an unquoted controlling shareholding, or an unquoted non-controlling shareholding where payment of IHT all at once would cause *undue hardship*, or to certain other shareholdings, IHT can be paid by PRs in 10 annual instalments, instead of on the grant of probate. The first of these instalments will be due six months after the end of the month in which the deceased's death occurred. For lifetime transfers which are immediately chargeable to IHT, and transfers in relation to settlements, IHT must generally be paid not more than six months after the end of the month in which the chargeable transfer took place. However, if such a transfer was made after 5 April and before 1 October in any year, it may be paid at any time up to the end of April in the following year.

33.4.1.4   Revenue charge for unpaid IHT

You might remember from land law that the Revenue can impose a charge on land to recover the payment of unpaid IHT. This charge is imposed automatically by IHTA 1984,

s. 237 on settled property, where IHT is unpaid, as well as property transferred by the chargeable transfer. Since this is the case, you could become liable to pay the IHT which is the subject of the charge merely by owning the property. Purchasers of property are therefore protected by the need for the Revenue to register the charge, in the case of unregistered land, as a land charge of Class D(i): Land Charges Act 1972, s. 2(5)(i). Failure by the Revenue to register the charge as a land charge, where the land is unregistered, means that it is void as against a *purchaser*. For these purposes, the word *purchaser* is given the special meaning in IHTA 1984, s. 272:

'purchaser' means a purchaser in good faith for consideration in money or money's worth other than a nominal consideration and includes a lessee, mortgagee or other person who for such consideration acquires an interest in the property in question . . .

Where the land is registered land, a comparable result follows.

Blackacre, a freehold unregistered property owned by Vince, is subject to a Revenue charge to secure unpaid IHT of £50,000. The Revenue have not registered the charge as a Class D(i) land charge. On 1 April 1999, in order to defeat the unregistered charge, Vince sells the land to his daughter Debbie, for £1.50. Will Debbie be bound by the charge?

Yes, if she is found to have acted in bad faith. (Difficult to prove, but likely here.)

33.4.1.5 Determinations and appeals

Having made a determination of IHT liability, the Revenue serve it on the person liable to pay the IHT: above. That person then has 30 days from service to appeal in writing to the Special Commissioners: IHTA 1984, s. 222(1). In certain cases, specified in IHTA 1984, s. 222, the appeal may be to the High Court (see s. 222(3)), thus *leapfrogging* the Special Commissioners. In cases which involve the valuation of land, the appeal may be to the Lands Tribunal: see IHTA 1984, s. 222(4), (4A) and (4B). (For instance, *IRC v Gray* [1994] STC 360 was an appeal from the Lands Tribunal: see **31.3.2.2**.)

33.4.2 CAPITAL GAINS TAX

If CGT is payable on a gift which is not of property referred to below, then the time limit for paying it is usually the 31 January falling 10 months after the end of the tax year in which the disposal took place: TMA 1970, s. 59B(1)-(4). Other types of gratuitous transfers are dealt with as follows (TCGA 1992, s. 281):

■ Where there is a gift of land, or a shareholding which gave the person making the disposal control of the company, or certain minority shareholdings, CGT can be paid in 10 equal annual instalments. It must not have been possible to claim hold-over relief on the gift for this instalment option to apply, however: see **32.3.1**.

■ Where there is a nominal transfer of the legal title to settled property *otherwise than* on the death of the life tenant, CGT can be paid in 10 equal annual instalments: see **28.4.1.2**.

■ Where there is a nominal transfer of the legal title to settled property on the death of the life tenant, CGT can also be paid by 10 equal annual instalments. This will be the case where hold-over relief was originally claimed by the settlor: see **28.4.1.1**.

Where the instalment facility is available, the instalments begin on the 31 January when the whole amount would otherwise have been payable. If you, as the person making the disposal, want to pay CGT by instalments, you must give notice of this fact to the Revenue. The instalment facility would not appear to be available in relation to undervalue sales. In a somewhat curious reflection of the IHT position, if the person making the disposal fails to pay the CGT, then the Revenue can seek payment from the recipient of the property: TCGA 1992, s. 282.

Refer to SAQ 386. Will Alice be able to pay the CGT by instalments?

Yes.

33.4.3 VALUE ADDED TAX

We concluded in **27.5.4** that VAT will be relevant to undervalue sales by taxable persons. Such sales will be supplies and, if they are taxable supplies, the supplier will have to account for the VAT. The compliance requirements are exactly the same as for VAT in the context of income taxation: see **8.6**, **19.5**.

33.5   Summary

Anti-avoidance provisions combat three ways in which it has been sought to avoid IHT. The first is that of making a gift, in order to take advantage of the PET rules, whilst reserving a benefit in the property given away. At present, this will not work, both because of FA 1986, s. 102, and because *horizontal severance* has been held by the Court of Appeal in *Ingram* v *IRC* not to side-step the rules on reserving a benefit. A second way in which IHT-avoidance has been attempted is through so-called *depreciatory transactions*, as in *IRC* v *Macpherson*, although these have been held to fall foul of the associated operations rule in IHTA 1984, s. 268. Finally, close companies cannot be used to avoid IHT, because of the *apportionment rule* in IHTA 1984, s. 94. In relation to each of these attempts at IHT-avoidance, I have attempted to relate the anti-avoidance provisions to the areas of IHT law with which you should now be very familiar. As with our similar discussion for investment taxation (see **Chapter 25**), you should try to form some view as to the moral quality of the anti-avoidance legislation discussed. Do not forget that *Ramsay* is of general application, except possibly in relation to VAT, and that a general statutory anti-avoidance provision is promised. Finally, try to remember the compliance rules for both IHT and CGT. They are often forgotten, but they tell you a great deal about how each tax works in the context of gratuitous transfers.

BIBLIOGRAPHY

The author would like to acknowledge his indebtedness to the following publications in the preparation of this text.

J.S. Barlow, L.C. King and A.G. King, *Wills, Administration and Taxation*, 7th ed, 1997, London: Sweet & Maxwell

Butterworths, *Finance (No 2) Bill Handbook*, 1998, London: Butterworths

CCH Editions Ltd, *British Master Tax Guide 1997-98*, Bicester: CCH Editions Ltd

CCH Editions Ltd, *CCH's Capital Allowances 1996-97*, 3rd ed, Bicester: CCH Editions Ltd

CCH Editions Ltd, *Tax Statutes and Statutory Instruments, vols. 1A, 1B and 2* (A. Park QC and R. White, eds), 2nd ed, 1997, Bicester: CCH Editions Ltd

Davies, *Principles of Tax Law* (G. Morse, D. Williams and D. Salter, eds), 3rd ed, 1996, London: Sweet & Maxwell

S. Dencher, *Personal Trading Losses*, 2nd ed, 1996, Bicester: CCH Editions Ltd

Easson, *Cases and Materials on Revenue Law* (D. Salter and J. Kerr, eds), 2nd ed, 1990, London, Sweet & Maxwell

P. Farmer and R. Lyal, *EC Tax Law*, 1994, Oxford: Clarendon Press

K. Gray, *Elements of Land Law*, 2nd ed, 1993, London: Butterworths

M.Z. Hepker, *A Modern Approach to Tax Law*, 2nd ed, 1975, London: Heinemann

R. Jenkins, *Gladstone*, 1995, London: Macmillan

A. King and J. Barlow, *Solicitors and Their Business Clients*, 5th ed, 1990, London: Blackstone Press Ltd

A. Melville, *Taxation – Finance Act 1997* (and supplement), 3rd ed, 1997, London: Pitman Publishing

R. Reilly, *Pitt the Younger*, 1978, London: Cassell

A. Shipwright and E. Keeling, *Textbook on Revenue Law*, 1997, London: Blackstone Press Ltd

P.C. Soares, *Non-Resident Trusts*, 4th ed, 1993, London: Longman Group UK Ltd

P. Todd, *Textbook on Trusts*, 3rd ed, 1996, London: Blackstone Press Ltd

Tolley's *Accounting Principles for Tax Purposes* (M. Cochrane, ed), 2nd ed, 1996, Croydon: Tolley Publishing Company Ltd

Tolley's *Tax Cases 1992* (A. Dolton and G. Saunders, eds), 16th ed, 1992, Croydon: Tolley Publishing Company Ltd

C. Whitehouse, *Revenue Law Principles and Practice*, 15th ed, 1997, London: Butterworths

D.E. Williams, *Capital Gains Tax And The Private Residence*, 2nd ed, 1993, Bicester: CCH Editions Ltd

INDEX

Capital gains tax (CGT), inheritance tax (IHT), national insurance contributions (NICs), value added tax (VAT) are abbreviated in subheadings, but spelt out in full in main headings.